P9-CDV-333

DI

Encyclopedia of
Constitutional Amendments, Proposed Amendments, and Amending Issues,

1789–1995

Encyclopedia of
Constitutional
Amendments,
Proposed
Amendments,
and Amending
Issues,

1789–1995

John R. Vile

ABC-CLIO

Tennessee Tech Library
Cookeville, TN WITHDRAWN

Copyright © 1996 by John R. Vile

All rights reserved. No part of this publication may be reproduced, stored in a retrieval system, or transmitted, in any form or by any means, electronic, mechanical, photocopying, recording, or otherwise, except for the inclusion of brief quotations in a review, without prior permission in writing from the publisher.

Library of Congress Cataloging-in-Publication Data

Vile, John R.
     Encyclopedia of constitutional amendments, proposed amendments, and amending issues, 1789–1995 / John R. Vile.
          p.   cm.
     Includes bibliographical references and index.
     ISBN 0-87436-783-2 (alk. paper)
          1. United States—Constitution—Amendments.
     KF4557.V555   1996
     342.73'03—dc20
     [347.3023]   96-19540

02 01 00 99 98 97 96   10 9 8 7 6 5 4 3 2 1

ABC-CLIO, Inc.
130 Cremona Drive, P.O. Box 1911
Santa Barbara, California 93116-1911

This book is printed on acid-free paper ∞
Manufactured in the United States of America

This book is dedicated to three great teachers, scholars, and gentlemen:

Henry J. Abraham
Alpheus T. Mason
Walter F. Murphy

❖ CONTENTS ❖

Preface, ix

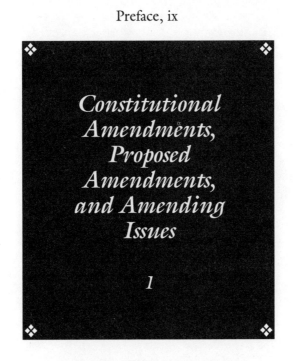

Constitutional Amendments, Proposed Amendments, and Amending Issues

1

Appendix A. The Constitution of the United States, 351

Appendix B. Dates Amendments Were Proposed and Ratified, 361

Appendix C. Number of Amendments by Decade, 362

Appendix D. Most Popular Amending Proposals by Year & Key Events and Publications Related to Constitutional Amendments, 363

Bibliography, 381

List of Cases, 407

Index, 411

❖ PREFACE ❖

Previous Works on the Subject

In 1896, Professor Herman Ames, soon to be a historian at the University of Pennsylvania, published the first book to deal with the central subject of this encyclopedia. His work, which began as a Ph.D. dissertation, covered the constitutional amendments that had been proposed in Congress during the nation's first 100 years (Ames 1896). The American Historical Association awarded this book its first prestigious Justin Winsor Prize, and the volume's continuing relevance was recognized with its republication in 1970. In addition to describing the subjects of proposed amendments in his text, Ames included a list of the topics of the 1,736 amendments proposed in the nation's first century. He also included a comprehensive index and bibliography. One hundred years later, his book is still readable and useful.

In 1929, M. A. Musmanno, then a Pennsylvania lawyer and later a judge, analyzed the 1,370 amendments that had been proposed since Ames wrote his book (Musmanno 1929). In part because Musmanno's volume was published as a government document and in part because it is less comprehensive than Ames's, it is less well known but is still a valuable resource.

Although literally hundreds of articles, essays, and books have subsequently addressed the subject of amendments and proposed amendments, no author has sought to survey the field in the same comprehensive manner as did Ames and Mus-

manno. Once between the time that Ames and Musmanno wrote (Tansill 1926) and several times afterward, lists of amendments proposed in Congress during designated periods have been published (*Proposed Amendments* 1957, 1963, 1969; Davis 1985; Harris 1992). Michael Stokes Paulsen (1993) recently compiled a more complete and accurate list than was hitherto available of state petitions to Congress for constitutional conventions (also see Van Sickle and Boughey 1990). These lists and analyses, as well as more recent entries that are now available on the Internet, form the starting point and vital foundation of my study.

From the time that Musmanno wrote, the number of proposed amendments has grown from just over 3,000 to about 10,900 (*see* Number of Proposed Amendments). I was therefore flattered and challenged, as well as a bit intimidated, when Henry Rasof, an editor at ABC-CLIO, called me about the prospect of compiling a book to cover all these proposals. No one realizes better than I how difficult it is to be an expert on every subject discussed in this volume, as well as the impossibility of covering everything of importance in essays short enough to be of value for a general reader or high school or college student. My knowledge of the limitations of this work is balanced by a realization—verified in my own research by the number of times I relied on Ames and Musmanno—of how useful it is to have a book that provides a starting point for an analysis of individual proposals and issues. I am particularly pleased that this book is being released in the year marking the hundredth anniversary of the publication of Ames's classic and hope that my own volume is a worthy successor.

Current Interest in the Amending Process

Interest in various scholarly topics waxes and wanes over time, and interest in the amending process has clearly increased over the past decade. In addition to my own multiplying works on the subject, the last 10 years have witnessed numerous other scholarly treatments of amendments and constitutional change.

Bruce Ackerman's (1992) theory of constitutional moments has received the most attention, but many other authors have also addressed the topic. Akil Reed Amar (1988) advanced the challenging thesis that it is possible to amend the Constitution outside of Article V channels, and Walter Murphy (1980) revived interest in the idea that there may be certain implicit limits on the subject of constitutional amendments (also see Suber 1990). Donald Lutz (1994) examined a number of challenging hypotheses about constitutional change in an influential article in the *American Political Science Review* that also compares the U.S. system with that in other nations. In addition to writing several scholarly articles and leading a number of panels at meetings of the American Political Science Association on the subject of constitutional change, Sanford Levinson (1995) recently compiled a book of essays presenting theoretical views of leading scholars on the subject. William Harris II devoted considerable attention to the amending process in another recent book (1993), and Stephen Griffin's (1996) new book on constitutional interpretation gives significant attention to the subject of constitutional change.

The putative ratification of the Twenty-seventh Amendment in 1993, as well as the earlier attempt to extend the ratification deadline of the proposed equal rights amendment, has spawned a great deal of commentary on the amending procedure. Much of it has taken its point of departure from an earlier essay by Walter Dellinger (1983) that asks whether such issues should be considered political questions and a response by Laurence Tribe (1983). There is also some renewed interest in the still-unused Article V constitutional convention mechanism. Russell Caplan's book on the subject (1988) complements legislation that Orrin Hatch sponsored to deal with such unresolved convention issues (see Vile 1993c, 466–83).

The Republican electoral victories of 1994 and the Contract with America have focused considerable attention on specific amending proposals, such as the balanced budget amendment, term limits, flag desecration, prayer in schools, and the item veto. What is therefore so interesting about most current academic works (including some of my own) is that they focus primarily on the *theory* of constitutional amendments and constitutional change.

Bernstein and Agel's (1993) survey of amendments is a notable exception. Although adhering to generally high scholarly standards, this book succeeds in reaching a popular audience in a fashion that earlier works—most notably the judicious treatment of amendments by Alan P. Grimes (1978), in which he concentrated on congressional debates over amendments—never quite managed. In any case, Bernstein and Agel's work is something of an exception, and their primary focus is necessarily on amendments that have been adopted rather than those that have merely been proposed.

Although their short discussion of proposed amendments is lively (Bernstein with Agel 1993, 169–98), it may unintentionally leave many readers with the impression that most proposed amendments have been trivial or ridiculous. If this impression were true, one might well question the value of this book. On such matters, each reader must ultimately make an individual judgment, but I believe that the study of proposed amendments is far from a trivial pursuit. Undoubtedly, there are proposed amendments (just as there are proposed laws) that are naive or ridiculous—proposals, for example, to outlaw war, to give the president authority over the air force, or to take citizenship away from all nonwhites. Wise or unwise, however, most proposed amendments have dealt with fairly serious subjects, and the purposes behind amendments that were not adopted have often been accomplished in other ways.

It appears that it is a rare issue indeed that has not been introduced as an amendment. The study of such proposals thus provides a unique window onto American history and politics. The fact that the goals of proposed amendments are often achieved by other means testifies to the dynamics of the U.S. federal system.

As someone who studied political theory before concentrating on U.S. constitutional law, I am probably as fascinated with the theoretical arguments about constitutional amendments as any other scholar. At the same time, I think that it is important to keep such scholarship anchored in actual practice. I see this book as an effort to do this. I have written this book so that it addresses topics of interest to those with theoretical inclinations while keeping in mind that the ultimate subject of the amending process is amendments.

Subjects Covered in This Book

Amendments and
Proposed Amendments

Altogether, there are more than 400 entries in this book. The large majority deal with the 27 amendments that have been ratified and with the approximately 10,900 others

that have been proposed. Why, then, are there not 10,900 entries? The reason is that the number 10,900 records the approximate number of amendments that have been individually introduced and not the number of subjects that have been addressed. For example, there have been almost 1,000 proposals for the equal rights amendment, but these can be discussed in a single essay. Similarly, there are hundreds of proposals dealing with reform of the electoral college, abortion, prayer in schools, balanced budgets, and so on. In most cases, I have grouped the discussion of proposals relating to a single topic into one essay rather than composing separate entries for each proposal.

A quick perusal of the Ames and Musmanno volumes demonstrates that no two authors are likely to divide the thousands of proposals in the same manner. Moreover, I cannot guarantee that I have covered all topics. In most cases, I had to work from the titles of amendments rather than from the actual texts, and in some cases, these titles turned out to be inaccurate or deceptive. Sometimes, I found it impossible to ascertain the content of a proposal, or I had to make educated guesses about what motivated a particular amendment or which proposals to group in the same essay.

From the second session of the Seventy-fourth Congress to the present, the Legislative Reference Service (1936–1996) of the Library of Congress has compiled an annual listing of all proposed laws and amendments and their sponsors. These compilations were extremely helpful, but they are surely far from foolproof. Sometimes the *Congressional Record* was an aid, but this record was often silent about the motivation or meaning of a proposed amendment. I called the staffs of members of Congress who had proposed obscure amendments, but often such members had long since retired, and an educated guess was the best that I could do. In any case, the heart of this book consists of descriptions of the 27 amendments that have been proposed and ratified and the hundreds of other topics that have been proposed as subjects of amendments.

Major Constitutional Reforms
Introduced outside Congress

Given the breadth of current musings about the amending process, a book limited to a description of amendments and proposed amendments did not seem adequate to meet the needs of a modern researcher. I therefore included a number of related types of entries.

One class of entry moves outside Congress to consider major reform proposals to rewrite the Constitution. This was the subject of my own first book (Vile 1991c). Historian Steven Boyd (1992) also addressed this topic in a book compiling the texts of proposed alternative constitutions. My own continuing research revealed that even when these results were combined, our books did not identify all such proposals. So although I included in this book descriptions of the new proposals I discovered, I am sure that there are others out there. Still, the more than 50 such proposals that are known make a fascinating supplement to discussions of more piecemeal reforms. They also highlight the fact that a new constitution is a potentially viable option to more piecemeal change.

I listed these proposed constitutions under the names of the individuals who proposed them. I also provided at least a brief biographical sketch of each such individual for whom biographical information was available.

Influential Individuals

I listed two other types of entries under individual names. One type discusses individuals who have had an important impact on how we think about the amending process. Although I have argued elsewhere that American thinkers have been influenced on

the subject by previous writers (Vile 1992, 1–21), I limited my focus in this book to Americans, including such individuals as William Penn, Thomas Jefferson, John C. Calhoun, Sidney George Fisher, and Woodrow Wilson.

In a similar vein, I included entries on individuals such as James Madison, John Bingham, Susan B. Anthony, Elizabeth Cady Stanton, Everett Dirksen, and Gregory Watson, who were especially influential in formulating or pressing for the adoption of various amendments. Here, I exercised what I hope was judicious judgment. Where it was appropriate, I mentioned the names and parties of individuals who supported amendments within the entries on proposed amendments. I found a Congressional Quarterly (1985) volume that is now out of print to be particularly useful in identifying the political parties of such individuals.

I reserved separate entries for a select number of individuals, including those listed above, whose roles in providing for an individual amendment or set of amendments were extraordinary. I included more entries on the Nineteenth Amendment, which provided for women's suffrage, than on others. I did so because this movement was clearly a grassroots effort and because the amendment was advocated so long before it was finally adopted. Support for this amendment thus spanned more than a generation of active supporters.

In this book, I omitted American reformers who were not specifically concerned with constitutional amendments. Researchers interested in such individuals will find Alden Whitman's volume on the subject (1985) to be especially helpful.

Influential Organizations

I included some entries on organizations that were influential in the adoption of amendments—especially the drive for national alcoholic prohibition, which culminated in the Eighteenth Amendment. I quickly realized, however, that literally hundreds of organizations have labored for or against one or another amendment and that there was no feasible way to discuss all of them here. Readers who are interested in such groups should find Clement Vose's magisterial discussion in *Constitutional Change* (1972) useful. Books focusing on the Eighteenth, Nineteenth, and Twenty-first Amendments often describe such groups and their influences in much greater detail than I do here.

Supreme Court Decisions

Another group of entries in this book consists of Supreme Court decisions. These particularly interest me, because I now teach American constitutional law. Moreover, as I completed entries on proposed amendments for this book, I was frequently struck by the continual interplay between Supreme Court decisions and constitutional amendments. Quite often, Court decisions have served as catalysts for amending proposals. When I was aware of such connections, I included them in individual entries on proposed amendments. When warranted, I wrote separate essays on such decisions.

I found the information in the *Oxford Companion to the Supreme Court of the United States* (Hall 1992) helpful in identifying the day that Supreme Court decisions were handed down. I also frequently consulted that volume when I needed short summaries of court decisions or information on issues of law and historical developments. High school students might also find the companion volume useful (Patrick 1994).

In addition to Supreme Court decisions that have prompted amending proposals, there is another set of important decisions—namely, those dealing with specific amending issues. Although the Supreme Court declared in *Coleman v. Miller* (1939) that issues surrounding the amending process were political questions for Congress to resolve, it had settled a number of

important amending issues in prior cases. Moreover, several subsequent court decisions have called into question the continuing legitimacy of the *Coleman* precedent. I included summaries of such relevant cases.

Unresolved Issues

In addition to the types of entries listed above, I included essays on key amending issues. These include discussions of the constitutional convention mechanism, whether there are implicit limits on the amending process, whether states can rescind ratification of pending amendments, whether governors and presidents have a role in the process, whether there are time limits on such ratifications, and so on.

Miscellaneous

From time to time, I included related entries in this book that seemed useful but did not really fit into any of the above categories. It seemed appropriate, for example, to include an entry on constitutional commissions, even though this is primarily a mechanism for state constitutional change. Similarly, I included notes on the officers that have been designated to certify amendments, and essays on such miscellaneous topics as the Articles of Confederation, the Confederate constitution, the Contract with America, and critical elections.

The Form of This Book

Ames (1896) and Musmanno (1929) discussed proposed amendments in narrative form. Others simply listed the subjects of amendments with their respective resolution numbers, who proposed them, and the dates on which they did so. After 200 years and several such compilations, it would undoubtedly be useful to have a list of such proposals in a single document, but such information would largely duplicate information that is already available. Thus, I chose instead to organize this book as an encyclopedia of separate entries, each consisting of an essay on an amendment, a proposed amendment, or one of the related themes mentioned above. I chose this format so that the information would be accessible to high school students, college students, and general readers, as well as to advanced researchers.

Although such an approach arguably sacrifices some continuity, I attempted to preserve continuity in three ways. First, I grouped multiple entries together under such headings as Congress, the Judiciary, the Presidency, Slavery, States, and Taxation. Second, individual entries are extensively cross-referenced. Third, I included fairly generous references that students and scholars can consult for further information. Individuals interested more generally in the amending process should find the bibliography and index especially useful. Because I make so many references to the Constitution and its amendments, the text of these is also included in an appendix.

The Author's View of Constitutional Change

In previous books, I have taken positions on most contemporary amending issues. It is my belief that we do not need major constitutional reforms at present and that we should generally be wary of the unintended consequences that such reforms might generate. But I see this volume as a book of analysis rather than advocacy. I tried to write essays on the individual proposals, especially those that are still viable, so that both supporters and opponents of such measures could read these essays and believe that their views have been presented fairly.

In the course of examining so many proposals, I discovered some that I initially thought were worthwhile. In many cases, however, I concluded either that the original constitutional wording was wiser or that proposed changes would require a greater expenditure of effort than was warranted. Moreover, the experience with national alcoholic prohibition serves as a caution:

those changes that I would like to see brought about—for example, a federal budget that is kept in relative balance or an end to virtual abortion on demand during the first two trimesters of pregnancy—may prove not to be susceptible to easy constitutional solutions. Many proposed amendments seem ridiculous not so much because their goals are silly or ignoble but because certain objectives are simply not amenable to solution by constitutional fiat.

As to existing amendments, I will continue to ponder the meaning of some of the broad provisions in the Ninth, Tenth, and Fourteenth Amendments, and I doubt that anyone will ever have a complete view of what these amendments were intended to mean and should mean in a modern context. I would be hard-pressed, however, if I were to be entrusted with the task of clarifying such amendments with language that was more precise yet as capable of protecting and expanding existing rights as the current provisions have proved to be.

I can say that the only amendment that I wish were not a part of the Constitution is the Twenty-second Amendment. Rather than an outright repeal of this amendment, however, I favor restricting a president to three—rather than two—full terms. Thus I would hope that most presidents elected to a second term would voluntarily continue the two-term tradition established prior to Franklin Roosevelt, yet future presidents would not be regarded as lame ducks in their second terms.

Scholars have observed that it is possible to approach the Constitution as an instrument or a symbol (Corwin 1981). I have been persuaded by James Madison's reasoning in *Federalist* No. 49 that it is often better to forgo minor constitutional changes than to overtinker with the document and thus undermine respect for it (Hamilton, Madison, and Jay 1961, 314–17). Symbolically, the Constitution gains value if it is not amended overmuch.

I believe, however, that this argument can easily be carried too far. Governments are dynamic, and constitutions will change over time. Although he has focused on this theme, Bruce Ackerman is certainly not the first to recognize that, under our system, such changes often do not alter the constitutional text. Instead, they are inaugurated by judicial interpretations, by presidential orders, by congressional interpretations, and by the development of what the British would call customs and usages (Vile 1994a).

During his debate with Stephen Douglas, Abraham Lincoln, who was otherwise strongly committed to the rule of law, opposed the Supreme Court's decision in *Scott v. Sandford* (1857). In so doing, he recognized that the Supreme Court had to have the power to resolve disputes among parties appearing before it, but he further observed that if the Supreme Court could decide each issue with finality the first time it came up, then "the people will have ceased to be their own rulers, having, to that extent, practically resigned their government into the hands of that eminent tribunal" (Murphy, Fleming, and Barber 1995, 317).

In a similar fashion, I believe that it is a mistake to argue that the judiciary and other branches of government have the right to bring about drastic changes in our understanding of the Constitution but that the written document that serves as the fundamental basis for such interpretations must somehow remain untouched. Moreover, I believe that there are occasions when the precision of an amendment is preferable to a more ambiguous ruling that is so frequently tied to the specific facts of an individual case.

Thus, I think that Old Glory will always remain a cherished symbol for most Americans, even if it never receives constitutional protection against desecration. However, those who advocate such protection would ultimately do less damage to the Constitu-

tion by adopting an amendment providing for such an explicit exception to the First Amendment than if they were to ask the justices to carve out such an exception with no explicit constitutional language to guide them. On other occasions too, I believe that there would be a distinct advantage in having popular wishes incorporated into the text, which is available for inspection by all, rather than being developed in convoluted case law and in ambiguous understandings and practices that are so often the primary province of academic experts.

Those who fear that any diminution of the Bill of Rights (or other sections of the Constitution) will lead to an avalanche of proposals are, I believe, too fearful. Moreover, if changes in constitutional understandings were actually incorporated into the text, they could serve both as tools of public instruction and as firm bases for judicial decisions. Such arguments, it should be recalled, were the primary reasons for incorporating a bill of rights into the Constitution in the first place.

Acknowledgments

It is impossible to write a book of this length and breadth without accumulating a number of scholarly debts, and I have mustered my share. I owe special thanks to Henry Rasof of ABC-CLIO for initially contacting me about this project and subsequently providing useful suggestions and editorial help and to Susan McRory, Susan Ficca, Jennifer Job, and Linda Lotz for their work in turning the manuscript into a book.

At the outset of this project, four individuals read the suggested entries and made helpful suggestions: Professors Barbara Perry of Sweet Briar College, Donna Cliders of Denison University, and Mark Byrnes and Thomas Van Dervort of Middle Tennessee State University (MTSU). At some point in my writing of this book, I called upon most members of the Political

Science and History Departments at MTSU for help, including Francine Sanders, Jack Turner, Anne Sloan, David Carleton, Everett Cunningham, and Lisa Langenbach in the Political Science Department and Janice Leone (who was especially helpful in alerting me to individuals who were influential in the adoption of the Nineteenth Amendment), Bob Hunt, David Rowe, Thad Smith, Fred Rolater, Nancy Rupprecht, Andrew Guilliford, and Lewright Sikes in the History Department. Sarah Peveler, a graduate student at MTSU, and Professor Richard V. Pierard, from the History Department at Indiana State University, also provided useful information on the Christian amendment. Gary Freedom at McNeese State University directed me to sources on cultural and linguistic rights; I also received great encouragement from Henry J. Abraham at the University of Virginia and several helpful bibliographical references from Brannon P. Denning, a Memphis attorney who shares my interest in the amending process and related issues and who will soon have some of his own views in print.

I have been blessed to teach on a campus that has an especially helpful and friendly library staff. I owe special thanks to Betty McFall and Amy Carr in the MTSU interlibrary loan department, who cheerfully and efficiently handled numerous requests for materials from other libraries. Also, Peggy Colflesh in the Periodicals Department kept me informed as each new issue of the *Index to Legal Periodicals* arrived, and Rhonda Armstrong proved helpful in tracking down citations.

On a related note, I am especially grateful to David Huckabee of the Legislative Reference Service at the Library of Congress. Convinced of the value of my project and apparently sympathetic to my own lack of computer savvy, he twice provided written copies of the proposed amendments that are now available via the Internet.

Student aides at MTSU did much of the "grunt work" of this project. Initially, they helped compile 12 long boxes of note cards on which we recorded and labeled the nearly 11,000 proposed amendments that were listed in existing books and reports—a task with which my wife and daughters also helped. MTSU student aides subsequently helped by running library errands and by writing and compiling the cards that served as the basis for the entries and bibliography for this book. Aides who helped on this project included Kathy Aslinger, Felicia Emery Rasori, Pamela Russell-Short, Clint Petty, Megan Kingree, Jaime Sparks, Robert Fletcher, Jason Reid, and Stephanie Corbin. I am especially indebted to my aide Jenny Picklesimer. In addition to doing more than her share of work transferring amending proposals to note cards, she proved to be an adept and competent proofreader. My secretary, Clare Christian, also helped coordinate the work of student aides on these and related projects.

Middle Tennessee State University has proved to be a very supportive community in which to work. I appreciate my cooperative colleagues and students, and especially the encouragement I received from students in my constitutional law classes and on the mock trial teams I help coach. I owe special thanks to Dr. John McDaniel, dean of the College of Liberal Arts, and to the Faculty Research Committee at MTSU. Both provided release time for me to work on this project and encouraged my research efforts.

I also owe special thanks to my wife, Linda, and to my twin daughters, Virginia and Rebekah, for allowing me to forgo income from summer teaching to speed this project along. More generally, my family made daily sacrifices for a husband and father who sometimes appeared to be more concerned with his scholarship than with their needs. I appreciate their sacrifices and sincerely hope that they can take pride in this volume.

Finally, I relied extensively on the work of previous scholars, especially those who compiled lists and analyses of prior amendments. Despite all my debts, the responsibility for this book is ultimately mine. Any errors in fact or judgment that have crept in must be laid at my own door.

Dedication

I dedicate this book to three professors—two alive and one deceased—who have had a particularly profound influence on my life and who have ably communicated their enthusiasm for the study of the U.S. Constitution without always convincing me that their own constitutional interpretations were correct. Although I was then engaged primarily in the study of political theory, when I was in graduate school at the University of Virginia, I was privileged to take classes with Henry J. Abraham. I subsequently participated in a Project '87 seminar that he led, which was sponsored by the Lilly Foundation and the American Political Science Association. Likewise, I participated in summer seminars sponsored by the National Endowment for the Humanities and directed, respectively, by Alpheus Mason (who has since passed away) and Walter Murphy, both of Princeton University. Like Mr. Abraham, these men exemplify the combination of great teaching, sound scholarship, and gentlemanliness that I so admire and strive to emulate.

A

❖ *ABINGTON V. SCHEMPP* ❖
(1963)

This 8-to-1 Supreme Court decision stimulated a number of proposed amendments to restore prayer and Bible reading in public schools. The decision covered both *Abington v. Schempp*, involving a Unitarian family in Pennsylvania, and another case in Baltimore involving an atheistic mother and son (*Murray v. Curlett*). *Abington* extended the Supreme Court's controversial opinion of the previous year in *Engel v. Vitale*, which had invalidated the recitation of a state-composed prayer in public schools. *Abington* held that, even in the absence of comments, student-led Bible reading and recitation of the Lord's Prayer during school time and under the supervision of public school teachers violated the establishment clause of the First Amendment, as applied to the states through the due process clause of the Fourteenth Amendment.

Justice Tom C. Clark's majority opinion focused on the "wholesome 'neutrality'" that the state was obligated to follow in regard to religion (*Abington* 1963, 222). Denying that his decision was antireligious or secularistic, Clark said that religion must depend for its support on the home, church, and individual conscience (*Abington* 1963, 226). Clark found that the practices in question were devotional rather than simply discussions of historical or literary material or nonsectarian attempts to foster morality. He

therefore ruled that they lacked an overriding "secular legislative purpose" and that they had as their "primary effect" the promotion of religion (*Abington* 1963, 222).

Justice William Brennan's extensive concurring opinion is notable for its insistence that establishment clause concerns need to be related to modern historical and educational developments rather than to any narrow view of the framers' original intent. He also denied that the failure to adopt the Blaine amendment—itself stimulated in part by judicial decisions (see *The Bible in the Public Schools* 1967)—precluded application of the establishment clause to the states. In addition, Brennan discussed previous unsuccessful attempts to adopt the Christian amendment, recognizing God in the Constitution (*Abington* 1963, 256–58).

Justice Potter Stewart's dissenting opinion extended his earlier dissent in *Engel* by focusing on his paramount concern with religious freedom. Stewart argued that since students were permitted to absent themselves from the devotional practices and since there had been no direct showing of coercion, such practices represented acceptable accommodations of the exercise of the majority's religious beliefs.

Abington indicated that, despite intense criticism and pressure for an amendment to overturn *Engel*, the Court was not going to back away from its earlier opinion. Still, early studies indicated that many public schools ignored the decision. One school superintendent responded to a survey by saying: "I am of the opinion that 99% of the people in the United States feel as I do about the Supreme Court's decision—that it was an outrage, and that Congress should have it amended. The remaining 1% do not belong in this free world" (Birkby 1973, 117).

Abington arguably increased pressure for an amendment to permit prayer in schools and for other state and congressional legislation to accommodate majority religious practices. Although a 6-to-3 majority of the Court in *Wallace v. Jaffree* (1985) struck down a state law providing for a moment of silence, it appeared to do so primarily because the law was written to favor prayer over alternative meditative activities. In *Lee v. Weisman* (1992), however, the Supreme Court extended its ruling in *Abington* to outlaw prayers led by members of the clergy at high school graduations.

See also Blaine Amendment; Christian Amendment; *Engel v. Vitale;* First Amendment; Prayer in Public Schools.

For Further Reading:
   Smith, Rodney K. 1987. *Public Prayer and the Constitution: A Case Study in Constitutional Interpretation.* Wilmington, DE: Scholarly Resources.

❖ ABOLITIONISTS ❖

The ratification of the Thirteenth Amendment followed more than 30 years of agitation by abolitionists. The transition from widely held antislavery sentiments to pressure for immediate abolition occurred in the 1820s. It coincided both with the elimination of slavery in the British empire and with American religious revivals led by Charles G. Finney and others (Pease and Pease 1965, xxx–xxxii).

William Lloyd Garrison, editor of the *Liberator*, was probably the best-known abolitionist and advocate of "immediatism" (Pease and Pease 1965, xxix). Garrison founded the New England Anti-Slavery So-

ciety. Like the individuals who supported such groups (among them Harriet Beecher Stowe, author of *Uncle Tom's Cabin*), these organizations usually proved better able to denounce slavery than to propose practical plans for its elimination. Like other reform groups, the abolitionists were torn by debates. Controversial issues included how to eliminate slavery, whether violence like that carried out by John Brown was appropriate, whether established religions were friends or foes, how to tie together the rights of blacks and women (many of whom were active in the abolitionist and temperance movements and who, after being disappointed by the Fourteenth and Fifteenth Amendments, lobbied for the Nineteenth Amendment), what role blacks should play in the movement, and what attitude to take toward the U.S. Constitution (Pease and Pease 1965, xlvii–lv).

Some abolitionists. such as Boston's Robert Rantoul, thought that the Constitution was an antislavery document. Some, such as ex-slave Frederick Douglass, argued that the document should be narrowly construed. Others, such as John Quincy Adams, wanted a constitutional amendment. William Lloyd Garrison saw the Constitution as a slave document (Pease and Pease 1965, lvii–lxii). Ultimately, the doctrine of natural rights, grounded in the language of the Declaration of Independence, appears to have been the strongest argument against slavery (see Douglass's Fourth of July Oration in Storing 1970, 28–38).

Abolitionists helped form the National Liberty Party in 1840, the Free-Soil Party later in the decade, and the Republican Party in 1854. The Republicans nominated Abraham Lincoln in 1860, and his election led to the Civil War. Even those abolitionists who had previously resisted political action supported Lincoln during the war and became strong advocates of the Emancipation Proclamation, of the Thirteenth and Fourteenth Amendments, and of the

Union, whose utility many of them had doubted (Pease and Pease 1965, lxxxi).

See also Brown, John; Declaration of Independence; Thirteenth Amendment.

For Further Reading:

Dillon, Merton L. 1974. *The Abolitionists: The Growth of a Dissenting Minority.* De Kalb: Northern Illinois University Press.

ten Broek, Jacobus. 1951. *The Antislavery Origins of the Fourteenth Amendment.* Berkeley: University of California Press.

Wiecek, William M. 1977. *The Sources of Antislavery Constitutionalism in America, 1760–1848.* Ithaca, NY: Cornell University Press.

❖ ABORTION ❖

See Right to Life.

❖ ACKERMAN, BRUCE (1943–) ❖

Currently Sterling Professor of Law and Political Science at Yale University, Ackerman has written a number of articles and the first of a projected three-volume set of books designed to explicate processes of change in the United States. Ackerman argues that the United States is a "dualist democracy" in which periods of ordinary democratic politics are interrupted by periods of intense constitutional lawmaking often designed to remove certain matters of fundamental rights from the reach of ordinary politics. Ackerman is particularly interested in those major regime changes that have occurred outside of the normal politics of ordinary Article V amending processes.

Ackerman argues that there have been three major changes in American history— that inaugurated by the Constitutional Convention of 1787, that brought about by the Civil War, and that which resulted from the New Deal. None of these "constitutional moments" has strictly followed the Article V scenario. Moreover, constitutional interpretation often involves the creative synthesis of insights from different constitutional moments.

Typically, successful periods of "higher lawmaking" involve four phases: a signaling phase, a proposal, mobilized popular deliberation, and a period of legal codification by the Supreme Court (Ackerman 1991, 266–67). If any of these phases is short-circuited—as, for example, in Reagan's unsuccessful nomination of Robert Bork to the U.S. Supreme Court—there may be a failed constitutional moment.

Widely critiqued and reviewed, Ackerman's work directs attention to the importance of extraconstitutional changes and to the fact that some such changes are more important than others.

In addition, Ackerman has proposed adding a referendum provision to the Constitution. Under Ackerman's proposal, presidents would be able to propose amendments in their second term. Such proposals would become law if approved by two-thirds of both houses of Congress and subsequently approved by three-fifths of the voters in each of the two succeeding presidential election (Ackerman 1991, 54–55).

For Further Reading:

Ackerman, Bruce. 1996. *We the People: Transformations.* Cambridge, MA: Harvard University Press.

———. 1989. "Constitutional Politics/Constitutional Law." *Yale Law Journal* 99 (December): 453–547.

———. 1988. "Transformative Appointments." *Harvard Law Review* 101:1164–84.

———. 1984. "The Storrs Lectures: Discovering the Constitution." *Yale Law Journal* 93:1013–72.

———. 1979. "Unconstitutional Convention." *New Republic* 180 (3 March): 8–9.

Vile, John R. 1993. *Contemporary Questions Surrounding the Constitutional Amending Process.* Westport, CT: Praeger.

Weiser, Philip J. 1993. "Ackerman's Proposal for Popular Constitutional Lawmaking: Can It Realize His Aspirations for Dualist Democracy?" *New York University Law Review* 68 (October): 907–59.

❖ ADAMS, FREDERICK UPHAM ❖

An inventor and engineer before becoming labor editor of the *Chicago Tribune,* Adams published a utopian novel, *President John Smith* (1896), that sold more than 750,000 copies. After copious initial chapters analyzing American politics and business cycles, the novel told the story of a one-time federal judge who ran for president as a Populist. After being cheated out of the presidency when he fell one vote short of a majority in the electoral college, the judge called a convention that met in Omaha and wrote a new constitution under which he served as first president. This constitution was based on majority rule and socialism and reflected populist themes that would continue into the Progressive Era.

Smith's proposed constitution, submitted in his novel to popular approval by the people, contained eight articles. The first provided for a president selected by direct popular vote and subject to recall. The plan made no provisions for a vice president; if the president died, he was to be temporarily succeeded by the secretary of state until a special election could be called.

Article II provided for a cabinet of 12 officers—including a superintendent of education—popularly elected and also subject to recall. The Senate was eliminated, with the cabinet taking over some of its functions—ratifying treaties, for example, by a two-thirds vote.

A unicameral Congress of 200 members was described in Article III. Fifty members could submit legislation directly to the people for approval by referendum. All major legislation was to be so approved.

The Supreme Court, outlined in Article IV, would have five members appointed by the president, approved by the people, and subject to retirement by the people's majority vote. Although it would exercise judicial review of state and local laws, the Court would have no power to declare laws adopted by the people to be unconstitutional. Instead, it would be required to give advisory opinions to Congress on ways to make its legislation acceptable.

Article V dealt with currency matters (valuing the dollar on "the average productivity of one hour's work"), and Articles VI and VII provided for the use of the government's power of eminent domain to take over unoccupied land and to socialize basic industries.

Article VIII provided for constitutional repeal, revision, and amendment by majority vote. The constitution contained no bill of rights or definition of citizenship such as that in the Fourteenth Amendment.

At the conclusion of his novel, Adams asked readers to consider forming a "Majority Rule Club" in their vicinity. Adams also advocated his ideas in a socialist magazine that he renamed the *New Times.* Boyd (1992, 96) reports that Adams appears to have abandoned his plans for a new constitution by the turn of the century.

See also Progressive Era.

❖ ADAMSON V. CALIFORNIA (1947) ❖

Justice Stanley Reed delivered a 5-to-4 ruling for the U.S. Supreme Court in *Adamson v. California* that had broad implications for the interpretation of the Bill of Rights and the Fourteenth Amendment. In *Adamson,* the Court reaffirmed an earlier decision in *Twining v. New Jersey* (1908) by deciding that the Fifth Amendment guarantee against self-incrimination did not apply to the states through the due process clause of the Fourteenth Amendment. States were thus free to permit comment on a defendant's failure to testify in his own defense.

Reed thus reaffirmed the doctrine of selective incorporation, which Justice Benjamin Cardozo had articulated in *Palko v.*

Connecticut (1937). By this doctrine, the Court did not apply the entire Bill of Rights to the states via the due process clause but only those guarantees that were most fundamental. Similarly, in his concurring opinion in *Adamson*, Justice Felix Frankfurter defended the view that the due process clause was not intended to serve as shorthand for the Bill of Rights and "neither comprehends the specific provisions by which the founders deemed it appropriate to restrict the federal government nor is confined to them" (*Adamson* 1947, 66).

In a dissenting opinion joined by Justice William O. Douglas, Justice Hugo Black argued that John Bingham and other sponsors (whose views Black analyzed in a 32-page appendix) had designed the first section of the Fourteenth Amendment to overturn the Supreme Court's decision in *Barron v. Baltimore* (1833) and apply the Bill of Rights to the states. Although advocating such total incorporation, which the Court had rejected in the *Slaughterhouse* cases (1873) and subsequent decisions, Black favored limiting the due process clause to specific guarantees in the Bill of Rights, thus avoiding the "natural-law–due-process formula" (*Adamson* 1947, 90) that Black identified with prior judicial abuses.

Although substantively agreeing with Black, Justices Frank Murphy and Wiley Rutledge argued for "total incorporation plus" (Abraham and Perry 1994, 86), or the view that although the due process clause intended to apply the protections of the Bill of Rights to the states, it might also include additional rights.

Since *Adamson*, the Court has, by a process of selective incorporation, approached Black's goal by applying all but five guarantees in the Bill of Rights to the states. In *Griffin v. California* (1965), the Court specifically applied the self-incrimination provision it had rejected in *Adamson*.

See also Incorporation.

ADMINISTRATOR OF THE ❖ GENERAL SERVICES ❖ ADMINISTRATION

From 1951 to 1984, Congress designated this individual to certify the ratification of constitutional amendments. Prior to this time, the secretary of state performed this function. Since 1984, Congress has entrusted this duty to the archivist of the Library of Congress (Bernstein with Agel 1993, 246–47).

See also Archivist of the Library of Congress; Secretary of State.

❖ AFFIRMATIVE ACTION ❖

Although not specifically mentioning race, the Constitution of 1787 permitted slavery and even counted slaves as three-fifths of a person for purposes of representation in the House of Representatives and direct taxation. In *Scott v. Sandford* (1857), Chief Justice Roger Taney declared that blacks were not and could not be American citizens. This decision was overturned by the Fourteenth Amendment, which, in Section 1, assured citizenship to "all persons born or naturalized in the United States and subject to the jurisdiction thereof" and guaranteed basic "privileges and immunities," "due process," and "equal protection" to all such citizens. Section 5 further gave Congress power to enforce these provisions.

Initially giving the amendment a narrow reading in such decisions as the *Slaughterhouse* cases (1873), the *Civil Rights* cases (1883), and *Plessy v. Ferguson* (1896), the Supreme Court reversed course in *Brown v. Board of Education* (1954) and outlawed discriminatory Jim Crow laws. Congress followed with legislation such as the Civil Rights Act of 1964, which used federal commerce powers to outlaw discrimination in places of public accommodation and in hiring.

Questions soon arose as to whether the government could now use racial classifications that had once discriminated against minorities to improve minority representation and compensate for the effects of past discrimination. Generally, liberals approved of such affirmative action plans as effective means of enforcing the Fourteenth Amendment, whereas conservatives opposed them as impositions of "reverse discrimination." The Supreme Court has faced this issue in a large number of cases. In the *Bakke* case (1978), the Supreme Court, by a narrow 5-to-4 vote, ruled against strict racial quotas for medical school admissions but decided that some consideration of race was appropriate in university admissions. Representative James Collins (R) of Texas introduced an amendment in 1978 that would have prohibited "denial of equal opportunity because of quotas or ratios based on race, color, national origin, religion, or sex" (H.J. Res. 1035). Senator Orrin Hatch (R) of Utah subsequently introduced amendments against affirmative action in 1980 and 1981. The Senate held hearings on the subject in 1981.

U.S. circuit court opinions in 1995 and 1996 have invalidated the use of race in awarding scholarships at the University of Maryland and in setting admission standards at the University of Texas. These decisions have called into question the continuing use of affirmative action programs and could furnish the opportunity for the U.S. Supreme Court to reconsider this issue (Jaschik and Lederman 1996).

For Further Reading:

Affirmative Action and Equal Protection. 1981. Hearings before the Senate Subcommittee on the Constitution of the Committee on the Judiciary, 97th Cong., 1st sess., on S.J. 41, 4 May, 11, 18 June, and 16 July. Washington, DC: U.S. Government Printing Office.

Eastland, Terry. 1996. *Ending Affirmative Action: The Case for Colorblind Justice.* New York: Basic Books.

Fiscus, Ron. 1992. *The Constitutional Logic of Affirmative Action*. Durham, NC: Duke University Press.

Jaschik, Scott, and Douglas Lederman. 1996. "Appeals Court Bars Racial Preference in College Admissions." *Chronicle of Higher Education* 43 (29 March): A26–A27.

❖ AGAR, HERBERT (1897–1980) ❖

Herbert Agar was an author, historian, and editor for the *Louisville Courier-Journal.* He also wrote a book during World War II in which he called for national spiritual and political renewal in order to save civilization. He presented his ideas for governmental reform in a chapter entitled "Can We Make Government Accountable and Understandable?" (Vile 1991c, 87–89).

There, as elsewhere in his book, Agar drew a distinction between two types of government. One was a "multiple-agency system" of government like that of the United States, "which seeks to partition and separate the powers of government and to distribute them among various agencies, so that authority will always be subject to checks." The other was a system like that in Great Britain, which "concentrates power in the executive, and sets up a representative body whose sole task is to watch and criticize the executive" (Agar 1942, 83–84). Although Agar's initial critique of the U.S. government appeared to indicate that he favored a parliamentary system of concentrated responsibility, he noted that he was not suggesting "that the Parliamentary form of government is necessarily to be preferred," but rather that it "has much to teach us about the solution of the problem" (Agar 1942, 257).

As one who spent much of his life in England, Agar drew several lessons from the British system. He believed that the executive should be responsible for formulating the budget, with the legislature serving as critic rather than having the authority to add to it. More generally, Agar believed that it was the responsibility of the executive to prepare all needed measures and the function of Congress to act on them, "rejecting them, refining them, proposing alternatives, or accepting them as they are" (Agar 1942, 261).

Agar argued that the American founders intended for the federal system to be closer to this accountability model than it turned out to be in practice. Agar tied the system's failure to achieve this accountability to the Washington administration. He cited the first Senate's unwillingness to serve as a type of privy council in formulating treaties and Congress's refusal to allow Alexander Hamilton to appear on the House floor and "establish direct relations between the heads of Cabinet departments and Congress" (Agar 1942, 265). Agar noted, "if the administration were allowed to bring its bills upon the floor of Congress and there to defend them, the executive could create policy and the Congress, unable to retreat into the darkness itself, would see to it that there was nothing hidden or obscure or unexplained about the measures proposed" (Agar 1942, 277).

Because Agar believed that the American founders had actually intended to have a more accountable system than the one that developed, he held out the possibility that reform might be achieved by "constitutional reinterpretation" rather than by amendment. He indicated, however, that "if the task cannot be done by reinterpretation, it will have to be done by revision, even if that involves a constitutional convention" (Agar 1942, 278).

❖ AGRICULTURE ❖

Although the U.S. Constitution was written at a time when the nation was chiefly agricultural, the document makes no specific mention of the subject. Undoubtedly, many of the founders anticipated that any agricultural regulations that were needed would be enacted by the states. Although the Supreme Court sometimes struck down such regulations under its interpretation of the due process clause of the Fourteenth Amendment, most nineteenth-century agricultural regulation was exercised at the state level (prices charged by grain elevator operators and railroads were frequent subjects of state concern).

Democratic Texas Senator Morris Sheppard, however, proposed an amendment in 1916 and 1917 giving Congress power to purchase, improve, and sell land and make loans for the purpose of promoting farm ownership (S.J. Res. 127; S.J. Res. 76). Similarly, New York's Republican Representative Fiorello La Guardia proposed an amendment in 1917 (probably related to the U.S. war effort) allowing Congress to regulate "production, conservation, and distribution of foodstuffs and fuel" (H.J. Res. 107). World War I resulted in the War Time Prohibition Act, which went into effect in 1919, more than six months prior to the Eighteenth Amendment (C. May 1989, 66).

The Great Depression accented the interdependency between agriculture and other aspects of the economy, and a number of Franklin Roosevelt's New Deal programs were directed toward or included agricultural regulation. Most notable were the National Industrial Recovery Act and the Agricultural Adjustment Act. Initially, the Supreme Court struck down both laws. In *Schechter Poultry Corporation v. United States* (1935), often called the "Sick Chicken" case, the Court declared that the first law, which permitted industries to set codes of fair competition to be approved by the president, was unconstitutional. The Court believed that the law permitted excessive delegation of congressional powers. In *U.S. v. Butler* (1936), the Court decided that the processing tax on agricultural commodities sanctioned by the Agricultural

Adjustment Act invaded state police powers protected by the Tenth Amendment (Kershen 1992, 22). The latter decision especially appears to have sparked a number of proposed amendments giving Congress the power to legislate for agriculture. Democrat Samuel Dickstein of New York proposed one such amendment the day after the decision, and another dozen or so proposals were introduced within the next two years. Some proposals referred only to agriculture, whereas others included regulation of commerce, industry, and labor.

Subsequent Supreme Court decisions in *Mulford v. Smith* (1939) and *Wickard v. Filburn* (1942) upheld a revised Agricultural Adjustment Act under a broad reading of the commerce clause. In the latter case, the Court even recognized congressional authority over crops that were grown for home consumption. With the Supreme Court's broad reading of the commerce clause, less restrictive interpretations of state police powers, and greater judicial deference to governmental regulations in the area of economic policies, congressional proposals for amendments to increase federal powers over agriculture have ceased.

❖ AIR FORCE ❖

Article II, Section 2 of the U.S. Constitution designates the president as "Commander in Chief of the Army and Navy of the United States," as well as of state militias when called to national service. The Air Force was separated from the other two services in 1947. The following January, Republican Representative Claude Bakewill of Missouri introduced an amendment (H.J. Res. 298) designating the president commander in chief of this branch as well. Failure to adopt the amendment does not appear to have lessened presidential powers in this area.

❖ ALCOHOLIC PROHIBITION ❖

See Eighteenth Amendment.

❖ ALIENS ❖

Article I, Section 8 of the U.S. Constitution entrusts Congress with the power to provide a "uniform Rule of Naturalization." Section 1 of the Fourteenth Amendment further extends citizenship to all persons born in the United States or naturalized. Although the United States is a nation of immigrants, disputes about the status of noncitizens, or aliens, date at least as far back as the Alien Acts of 1798. Federalists adopted the Alien Acts, along with the Sedition Acts, partly because they believed that immigrants (especially those from France and Ireland) were more supportive of the Republican stance against the British than of Federalist Anglophile policies (Urofsky 1988, 171). Since that time, amendments have been introduced both to restrict and to expand the rights of such individuals.

Laws Restricting Aliens

Most proposals would affect states where aliens reside rather than aliens themselves. Such proposals, especially prominent in the 1930s and 1940s, would exclude aliens from the population count used to apportion representatives in the House (for example, H.J. Res. 263, 1930). Section 2 of the Fourteenth Amendment currently provides that such apportionment be based on "the whole number of persons in each State, excluding Indians not taxed." Excluding aliens from the count would thus reduce representation for states with large immigrant populations, such as California, Florida, and Texas.

Subject to restrictions against discrimination such as those found in the Fifteenth, Nineteenth, Twenty-fourth, and Twenty-sixth Amendments (each of which protects citizens only), states set their own qualifications for voting and officeholding. Thus, there have also been a number of proposals, most prominent from the 1890s to about 1921, that would prevent states from extending either or both privileges to aliens. Many advocates of such restrictions were connected to the Progressive movement and hoped that such restrictions would remove a source of support for corrupt political machines (Welch et al. 1993, 171). This was clearly an objective that could be reached by state law; today, all states include citizenship as a requirement for voting and holding office.

Additional proposals relating to the rights of aliens have sought to allow states to regulate their employment or, as in a proposal introduced by Democratic Representative Thomas Wilson of Mississippi in 1927, to prohibit citizens born overseas from serving as representatives (H.J. Res. 103). Such a proposal would effectively extend the ban on officeholding that now applies, under Article II, Section 1 of the Constitution, only to the presidency.

Laws Protecting Aliens

A New York representative introduced three proposals from 1917 to 1919 that would have prevented states from passing discriminatory laws against aliens. An earlier proposal in 1913 would have granted Congress the "exclusive power to legislate on questions affecting rights and privileges of aliens resident in [the] United States" (H.J. Res. 88). All these proposals appear to have been directed primarily at laws passed by California that discriminated against immigrant Japanese. Laws such as those restricting landholding by Japanese or separating Asian children from those of Anglo-Saxon stock in schools sometimes conflicted with U.S. treaties and embarrassed U.S. foreign policy at a time when Japan was becoming a major world power (Daniels 1968, 31–45).

See also Fourteenth Amendment.

❖ AMAR, AKIL REED (1958–) ❖

Amar is currently a professor of law at Yale University and has written articles analyzing a number of constitutional amendments. Amar argues that the procedures in Article V of the U.S. Constitution are not the exclusive legal mechanisms for amending the Constitution. He believes either that a majority of voters could petition Congress to call a constitutional convention or that Congress could submit amendments to a popular vote or referendum (Amar 1988, 1994).

Amar bases his argument on the extralegal fashion in which the current Constitution was adopted, on ideas of popular sovereignty current at the nation's founding, and on such constitutional provisions as the Preamble and the First, Ninth, and Tenth Amendments. Amar's argument may also receive some support from experience with amending mechanisms at the state level, although there is one prominent example of such an experiment going awry (*Luther v. Borden* [1849]). If accepted, Amar's view would negate the need for a number of proposed procedural changes in the amending process. Dow (1990), Vile (1990–1991), and Monaghan (1996) have questioned the constitutional support for Amar's views.

For Further Reading:

Amar, Akil R. 1992. "The Bill of Rights as a Constitution." *Yale Law Journal* 100 (Winter): 1131–1210.

❖ AMENDING PROCESS ❖

See Article V of the U.S. Constitution.

❖ AMENDING PROCESS, PROPOSALS FOR CHANGING ❖

Article V of the U.S. Constitution delineates an amending process. It requires that amendments be proposed by two-thirds majorities of both houses of Congress or by a special convention called by two-thirds of the states. Such proposals then require ratification by three-fourths of the states. About 150 proposals, many redundant, have been introduced in Congress to alter this procedure.

Proposals for Popular Initiative or Referendum

A common proposal appears to have first surfaced around the time of the outbreak of the Civil War as a means of averting conflict by incorporating various slavery compromises into the Constitution. It would provide for some kind of popular initiative or referendum on amendments. Such proposals, which embody a form of direct democracy, were especially common during the Progressive Era, at the beginning of which there was a great deal of scholarly criticism of the amending process for being too "rigid" (Vile 1992, 135–56). Common variants (for example, S.J. Res. 22, 1919) provided that amendments would be initiated by 500,000 or more voters and ratified by a majority of voters in either a majority of the states or in three-fourths thereof. Similarly, Wisconsin's Republican Senator Robert La Follette proposed in 1912 and 1913 that amendments become effective after being proposed by 10 states or a majority of Congress and being ratified by a majority vote of citizens in a majority of the states (Musmanno 1929, 194). In 1923, Senator James W. Wadsworth of New York and Representative Finis J. Garrett of Tennessee proposed a "back to the people" amendment that would allow states to require a popular vote to affirm or overturn a state legislature's ratification of an amendment (Vose 1972, 246). A year earlier, in *Hawke v. Smith* (Nos. 1 and 2), the Court had invalidated such a provision in the Ohio state constitution.

Akil Reed Amar, a contemporary Yale law professor, has argued that the mechanisms in Article V are not exclusive and that citizens already have the right to propose or ratify amendments by popular majorities (Amar 1988). Similarly, Bruce Ackerman has proposed an alteration to Article V whereby a president could propose an amendment in his second term that could be ratified by a three-fifths vote in the next two elections (Ackerman 1991, 54–55).

Proposed Changes in Ratification Procedures

Three sets of changes have been proposed that would alter current ratification procedures. One would limit the power of lame-duck legislatures by requiring that one or both houses of a state legislature ratifying an amendment must have been elected after the amendment was proposed. The House of Representatives actually added such a requirement to the Twentieth Amendment, but it was dropped in conference committee (Grimes 1978, 108). In a related vein, some proposals (for example, H.J. Res. 242, 1919) have attempted to ensure that a certain majority is present when such state ratification votes are taken.

A second set of proposals has attempted to set a time limit, usually five to eight years, during which states must ratify amendments. Currently, the Constitution sets no such limits, and although the Supreme Court decided in *Dillon v. Gloss* (1921) that amendments should be ratified relatively contemporaneously, in *Coleman v. Miller* (1939), the Court suggested that such decisions might be "political questions." In 1992, the archivist of the Library of Congress and a vote in Congress certified the validity of the Twenty-seventh Amendment, even though it was not ratified until more than 200 years after being proposed.

A third set of proposals would tackle another unresolved issue by explicitly providing for state rescission of amendments prior to ratification by the necessary three-fourths majority (Musmanno 1929, 206).

Proposals Offered by the Council of State Governments

A meeting of the Council of State Governments in December 1962 resulted in a number of state petitions to Congress for amendments to liberalize the amending process. The council was clearly shaken by the Supreme Court decision in *Baker v. Carr* (1962) and its implications for judicial review of state legislative apportionment. It proposed eliminating the convention mechanism and allowing three-fourths of the states to ratify identical texts of amendments proposed by two-thirds of the states. A similar amendment was proposed again in 1990 (Tolchin 1990, A12); more recently, some state advocates have proposed allowing three-fourths of the states to propose an amendment that would become valid in two years unless two-thirds majorities of both houses rejected it ("Conference of the States" 1995). In two additional proposals offered by the Council of State Governments and severely criticized at the time by scholars (for example, Swindler 1963 and C. Black 1963), the council proposed amendments allowing states to apportion themselves without judicial oversight and setting up a Court of the Union with the power to overturn Supreme Court decisions (Vile 1991c, 98–99).

Although the proposals by the Council of State Governments prompted scholarly attention, a number of similar proposals had been introduced in Congress during the previous decade. They would have enabled states to ratify amendments that had been proposed by two-thirds majorities in both houses of the legislatures of twelve states and transmitted to the U.S. secretary of state and the secretary of state within each state.

Other Proposals

One of the earliest proposed changes affecting the amending process was introduced in 1826 and would have limited the introduction of such proposals to every ten years (H.J. Res. 232, 325); by way of comparison, a proposal introduced by New York's Progressive (and later Republican) Walter Chandler in 1916 (H.J. Res. 315) would have provided for constitutional conventions to meet every 30 years to propose amendments. This embodied an idea advocated by Thomas Jefferson, who thought that a new Constitution should be considered each generation. Other proposals have called for making ratification by state conventions (an alternative ratification method specified in Article V and used to ratify the Twenty-first Amendment) the exclusive method of state ratification. Still other members of Congress have proposed making the amending process easier by reducing the required two-thirds majorities in Congress to one-half or three-fifths, by permitting less than two-thirds of the states to call a convention to propose amendments, or by reducing the necessary ratification majority of the states from three-fourths to two-thirds (Musmanno 1929, 192–93). By contrast, an amendment offered by Rhode Island when it ratified the Constitution in 1790 would have required the consent of 11 or more of the original 13 states for any amendments proposed after 1793 (Ames 1896, 292). Consistent with concerns about the antidemocratic impact of judicial review that were expressed in the Progressive Era, Democrat James Doolittle of Kansas introduced a proposal in February 1914 that would have automatically submitted amendments dealing with U.S. laws invalidated by judicial review to states for their acceptance (H.J. Res. 221).

See also Ackerman, Bruce; Amar, Akil Reed; Corwin Amendment; Council of State Governments; Crittenden Compromise; Initiative and Referendum.

For Further Reading:

Levinson, Sanford. 1996. "The Political Implications of Amending Clauses." *Constitutional Commentary* 13 (Spring): 107–23.

❖ AMENDMENT ❖

The dictionary defines amendment as "1. a change for the better; improvement. 2. a correction of errors, faults, etc. 3. *a*) a revision or addition proposed or made in a bill, law, constitution, etc. *b*) the process of making such changes" (*Webster's New World Dictionary of the American Language* 1970). It has been described as "an extraordinarily rich word" (Levinson 1990a, 25), and scholars have made periodic attempts to distinguish "constitutional amendment" from "constitutional interpretation" or "revision" and to delineate what kinds of changes require amendments and which can be effected through other means. Historical practice appears to demonstrate that such lines, if they exist at all, are relatively fluid (Vile 1994a, 73–76). Some advocates of substantive limits on amendments base their arguments in part on the idea that the term *amendment* implicitly mandates the adoption of changes consistent with the principles and character of the document being amended.

❖ AMES, HERMAN (1865–1935) ❖

Ames was a historian at the University of Pennsylvania who compiled the first comprehensive list and analysis of proposed amendments to the Constitution. Altogether, Ames compiled 1,736 proposals—many with multiple parts—that had been offered in the first 100 years under the Constitution. The central part of Ames's book, which was honored in 1897 by the American Historical Association, was a narrative analysis of proposed amendments according to subject. An appendix listed the date, subject, and other relevant information about proposed amendments (Ames 1896, 306–422).

In discussing the history of U.S. constitutional amendments, Ames divided the amendments proposed in the first 100 years into four periods: 1789–1803, 1804–1860, 1860–1870, and 1870–1889. He associated the first period with "the perfection of details," the second with "general alterations," the third with "slavery and reconstruction," and the fourth with "general emendations" (Ames 1896, 19). Acknowledging that many proposals had failed because they "were suggested as cures for temporary evils, . . . were trivial or impracticable, [or] . . . found a place in that unwritten constitution which has grown up side by side with the written document," Ames identified "insurmountable constitutional obstacles" as the central barriers to amendments (Ames 1896, 301). Although suggesting—like other critics from the Progressive Era (Vile 1992, 140–41)—that "the majorities required are too large," Ames did not specify what majorities he would regard as ideal (Ames 1896, 304).

❖ ANTHONY, SUSAN BROWNELL ❖ (1820–1906)

Susan B. Anthony was a schoolteacher who was initially interested in the temperance and antislavery movements. She subsequently devoted her efforts to women's suffrage and has been called "the greatest individual in the American suffrage movement" (Kraditor 1981, 12).

Like her close friend Elizabeth Cady Stanton, Anthony opposed ratification of the Fourteenth and Fifteenth Amendments when they failed to extend to women the rights accorded to African American men. Anthony and Stanton subsequently established women's suffrage as an "independent feminist movement" (Dubois 1978, 202) and founded the National Woman Suffrage Association in 1869. The same year, women who had supported the Fourteenth and Fifteenth Amendments founded the rival American Woman Suffrage Association.

From 1868 to 1870, Anthony edited *The Revolution*, and in 1872 she was tried and convicted in New York State for voting (*U.S. v. Anthony*). The amendment that eventually became the Nineteenth Amendment was first introduced in Congress in 1878 (Kraditor 1981, 206) and is often called the Susan B. Anthony amendment, but it was not proposed by the necessary majorities in Congress until 1919, and the states ratified it in 1920. In the interim, the two leading suffrage organizations had merged into the National American Woman Suffrage Association (NAWSA), with Stanton serving as its first president from 1890 to 1892 and Anthony serving from 1892 to 1900, at which time Carrie Catt became president.

See also Nineteenth Amendment; Stanton, Elizabeth Cady.

❖ ANTIEAU, CHESTER (1913–) ❖

In 1995, Chester Antieau, a professor emeritus of constitutional law at Georgetown University, published a book designed to offer changes in the Constitution as the nation approaches the year 2000. The book is divided into three parts. The first identifies rights that the Supreme Court already implicitly recognizes that should be recognized explicitly. The second discusses existing constitutional provisions that need amendment. The third discusses additional rights that should be included in the Constitution. In defending his proposals, Antieau makes constant reference to earlier legal theorists and philosophers; to previous historical documents and events; to treaties, international human rights declarations, and conventions; and to provisions in the constitutions of a variety of foreign nations and the 50 states.

The four rights that courts implicitly recognize and that Antieau believes should be added to the Constitution are freedom of association, freedom of enterprise, freedom of movement, and the right of privacy. Antieau does not address the difficulties that judicial enforcement of economic rights led to during the New Deal. He does note, however, that the right of privacy could be in conflict with the right to life, but he does not indicate how he would resolve this issue.

Antieau proposes a number of changes to existing constitutional provisions. He wants to expand the guarantees in the Eighth Amendment specifically to protect "the inherent dignity of the human person," to outlaw torture, and to stipulate a right to bail (Antieau 1995, 37). He advocates changing the grounds for impeachment to "serious misconduct to the harm of the nation" (Antieau 1995, 56) and advocates establishing special nonlegislative tribunals to try such impeachments. Antieau wants to modify the Seventh Amendment to eliminate jury trials in civil cases. He further advocates allowing the president to exercise a line-item veto, eliminating the pocket veto, and allowing Congress to override presidential vetoes by less than a two-thirds majority. Antieau wants to allow the Supreme Court to issue advisory opinions and to withdraw federal diversity jurisdiction from the federal courts. He favors state-appointed counsel for indigents in civil as well as criminal cases, giving particular attention to cases of child custody. Antieau would allow naturalized citizens to be eligible for the presidency and favors the introduction of constitutional amendments by popular initiative. He also wants the First Amendment to recognize the right of both the public and the press to have access to information.

Many of the rights that Antieau would add to the Constitution are social and economic rights like those contained in other twentieth-century constitutions, including the right to an education, the right to a healthy environment, and the right to adequate social services, such as housing, health care, employment, food, clothing, and social security. He emphasizes the importance of a number of interrelated rights of movement, including the rights of asylum, departure, emigration, voluntary expatriation, and entry and return and the freedom from exile and deportation. Miscellaneous proposals would establish the people's right to recall members of Congress, the right to conscientious objection to military service, and the right not to be executed.

Although Antieau presents an interesting array of proposals, his overall scheme is fairly piecemeal. He does not discuss in any depth the degree to which the listing of social and economic rights would provide cures for such ills. He also does not discuss at any length the impact that new constitutional guarantees might have on the power of the judiciary and on the current scheme of separation of powers.

❖ ANTI-FEDERALISTS ❖

Even before the Constitution was written, there were individuals such as Virginia's Patrick Henry who feared the new national government. They were concerned that it would result in undue consolidation of the states, accent aristocratic tendencies, and jeopardize individual liberties. After the Constitution was proposed for ratification by the states, these forces opposed to a new government became known as Anti-Federalists. They led a vigorous opposition both in public debates and in the ratifying conventions for the new Constitution, noting that it was not being adopted according to the forms specified under the Articles of Confederation. The Anti-Federalists were hindered in their debate by the superior organization of the Federalists, who were pushing for the Constitution, and by the general consensus that the existing Articles were inadequate.

The two most important outcomes of the Federalist–Anti-Federalist debate were ar-

guably the writing of a series of 85 essays, known as *The Federalist Papers,* in defense of the new Constitution and the adoption of the first 10 amendments to the Constitution, known as the Bill of Rights. Although the Constitutional Convention had barely touched on this issue, the lack of a bill of rights quickly became an important Anti-Federalist rallying point. Federalists initially responded by arguing in somewhat contradictory fashion that the Constitution already protected important rights (prohibitions against bills of attainder and ex post facto laws, for example) and that additional rights were unnecessary or inappropriate. Anti-Federalists indicated that they would press the states to either propose a second convention or ratify the new Constitution conditionally. Key Federalists, among them James Madison, indicated that they would support a bill of rights once the new Constitution was adopted. This promise—kept by James Madison, who sponsored the Bill of Rights during the First Congress—undoubtedly aided, and may have been essential to, ratification of the document. Initially applying only to the national government and not to the states, the Bill of Rights had little direct impact on governmental operations until the judicial incorporation of the Bill of Rights into the due process clause of the Fourteenth Amendment, which largely occurred in the twentieth century.

At the state ratifying convention, a number of Anti-Federalists argued that the amending process in Article V of the U.S. Constitution would be too difficult (Vile 1992, 32–33). The weakness of this argument was that the new process requiring proposal by two-thirds of both houses of Congress and ratification by three-fourths of the states appeared considerably easier than the process under the Articles of Confederation. This process had required unanimous state consent to amendments proposed in Congress.

See also Bill of Rights; Federalists.

For Further Reading:

Gillespie, Michael L., and Michael Lienesch, eds. 1989. *Ratifying the Constitution.* Lawrence: University Press of Kansas, 1989.

Hamilton, Alexander, James Madison, and John Jay. 1961. *The Federalist Papers.* New York: New American Library.

Kenyon, Cecelia, ed. 1985. *The Antifederalists.* Boston: Northeastern University Press.

Lash, Kurt T. 1994. "Rejecting Conventional Wisdom: Federalist Ambivalence in the Framing and Implementation of Article V." *American Journal of Legal History* 38 (April): 197–231.

Main, Jackson T. 1961. *The Antifederalists: Critics of the Constitution, 1781–1788.* Chicago: Quadrangle Books.

Storing, Herbert, ed. 1981. *The Complete Anti-Federalist.* 7 vols. Chicago: University of Chicago Press.

❖ ANTIPOLYGAMY LAWS ❖

See Marriage, Divorce, and Parenting.

❖ ANTI-SALOON LEAGUE ❖

One of the organizations that led the push for adoption of the Eighteenth Amendment and national alcoholic prohibition was the Anti-Saloon League, founded in the 1890s. The league existed in tension with the Anti-Prohibition Party, which had been established in 1869 and in many ways had been modeled on the antislavery campaign that had resulted in the Civil War and the eventual adoption of the Thirteenth Amendment. Whereas the Prohibition Party ran its own candidates, the Anti-Saloon League adopted a "balance-of-power policy" (Blocker 1976, 162) that enabled it to ally itself with whatever party was willing to adopt its stance as part of its platform. The Prohibition Party was, for a time at least, tempted by an alliance with the Populist Party and its broad agenda of social reform. By contrast, the Anti-Saloon League "posited the existence of a unified con-

stituency closely associated with the churches, the major political parties, and the free enterprise system" (Blocker 1976, 207). The saloon was often viewed as a center of foreign—and Catholic—influence and machine politics (Grimes 1978, 84). By focusing on this institution, the league was especially successful in appealing to middle- and upper-class white Protestant progressives.

The failure of Prohibition and the adoption of the Twenty-first Amendment led to problems for the league. By 1948, it had split into the National Temperance League and the Temperance Education Foundation (Blocker 1976, 235). The Prohibition Party continues to field candidates but is a minor force in current American politics.

See also Eighteenth Amendment.

For Further Reading:

Kerr, K. Austin. 1985. *Organized for Prohibition: A New History of the Anti-Saloon League.* New Haven, CT: Yale University Press.

❖ ARCHIVIST OF THE LIBRARY OF CONGRESS ❖

The archivist is the individual currently responsible for certifying constitutional amendments. The secretary of state performed this function by custom through 1818 and by statute until 1951. Congress then transferred the duty to the administrator of general services, who published the *Federal Register.* Congress transferred both functions to the archivist in 1984 (Bernstein with Agel 1993, 246; 1 U.S. Code 106[b] [1984]).

On 18 May 1992, after 40 states had ratified it, archivist Don Wilson certified ratification of the Twenty-seventh Amendment and had it published the next day in the *Federal Register.* This was controversial because of the long time that had elapsed between the amendment's proposal in 1789 and its putative ratification in 1992. Senators Robert Byrd and Charles Grassley criticized Wilson for not submitting the issue to Congress, as the secretary of state had done with the controversial Fourteenth Amendment. It is not clear, however, that an amendment must be certified or published before it becomes part of the Constitution. Moreover, although Congress subsequently voted to confirm Wilson's judgment (Bernstein with Agel 1993, 246–47), this too was probably legally unnecessary (Dellinger 1983, 402).

❖ ARTICLE V OF THE ❖ U.S. CONSTITUTION

This is the article that delineates the constitutional amending process. It provides two ways for amendments to be proposed and two ways for them to be ratified. To date, all amendments have been proposed by a two-thirds vote of both houses of Congress, but two-thirds of the states may also petition Congress to call a convention to propose such amendments. Moreover, calls that fall short of a mandate may still serve to exert pressure on Congress to act—as they did, for example, in pressuring Congress to propose the Seventeenth Amendment, which provided for direct election of senators. All but one of the existing 27 amendments have been ratified by the legislatures in three-fourths of the states, but Congress may stipulate that ratification be effected by special conventions called in each of the states. This latter procedure was specified by the delegates to the Constitutional Convention of 1787 with respect to the Constitution itself and by Congress in the case of the Twenty-first Amendment, repealing national alcoholic prohibition.

Limits
Article V delineates two substantive limits on the amending process. One, dealing with slave importation, is no longer relevant. The second prohibits states from being denied their equal vote in the U.S. Senate without their consent. Although a number of Supreme Court decisions have rejected the notion that there are additional limits on the amending process, some contemporary scholars (W. Murphy 1980, for example) believe that the issue is still viable. The argument was raised by those who questioned the legitimacy of amendments proposed in the wake of *Texas v. Johnson* (1989) and *U.S. v. Eichman* (1990) to prohibit flag desecration.

Origins
Article V is important because it offers a peaceful alternative to the kind of revolution that the colonists were forced to proclaim in the Declaration of Independence. Although philosophers had been discussing the need for constitutional change for centuries, formal amending mechanisms were necessitated by the development of written constitutions and thus originated in colonial charters first granted by William Penn. Such mechanisms also appeared in most of the state constitutions written during the American Revolutionary War period. Early state constitutions provided for amendment by legislative action, by state conventions, or through a council of censors (Vile 1992, 25). The Articles of Confederation provided for amendments to be approved by Congress and ratified by unanimous consent of the state legislatures. The unanimity requirement made this provision ineffective and served to caution the framers of the U.S. Constitution about devising an amending process that was too difficult.

The Constitutional Convention
Delegates to the Constitutional Convention of 1787 generally agreed that a formal amending process was needed. The Virginia plan proposed that congressional consent to such amendments should not be required,

and the first formal proposal that emerged at the convention specified that Congress should call a convention to propose amendments at the request of two-thirds of the states (Farrand 1966, 2:159). George Mason expressed concern that this mechanism might be used to subvert the states, Alexander Hamilton thought that Congress should be able to propose amendments on its own, and James Madison argued that the convention mechanism was too vague. Therefore, a new proposal was offered: two-thirds majorities in Congress would propose amendments when Congress so chose or when it was petitioned by two-thirds of the state legislatures. The clause entrenching the slave importation agreement was added at this time (Farrand 1966, 2:559). Two days before the Constitution was signed, the proposed amending provision was altered so that Congress could propose amendments or states could petition Congress to call a convention to propose amendments. The convention mechanism was designed to circumvent Congress. If Congress refused to propose amendments, a convention could do so. The convention adopted this alteration after George Mason expressed fears that amendments would be impossible if Congress proved to be unresponsive (Farrand 1966, 2:559–60). The clause protecting state representation in the Senate was also added then.

Principles of Article V

Article V embodies a number of distinct concerns and principles. Consistent with the desire that the Constitution be paramount to ordinary legislation, the process is intended to be difficult but not impossible (Ginsberg 1989–1990; Vile 1993a, 101–5). There is no constitutional provision, such as that which Thomas Jefferson advocated, for automatic constitutional revision or review at periodic intervals. Consistent with federalism, the article allows states to initiate, and requires that they rat-

ify, amendments. Consistent with the desire for deliberation, the process involves at least two stages and requires supermajorities for each one. Consistent with suspicions of entrenched power and an emphasis on popular sovereignty, Article V offers a pathway around a recalcitrant Congress.

The History of Article V

Although scholars have praised the amending process throughout most of U.S. history (scholars writing around the Civil War and the Progressive Era sometimes being exceptions), the process has arguably proved more difficult in practice than was anticipated (Berry 1987). This difficulty is particularly evident when the federal process is compared with counterparts at the state level or with processes in most foreign countries (Lutz 1994) or when the history of the amending process is examined (Grimes 1978; Bernstein with Agel, 1993). The primary obstacle has been the difficulty of proposing amendments by the requisite majority of both houses of Congress. Although more than 10,000 such proposals have been introduced in Congress—many redundant and centering around a few major issues—only 33 have been reported to the states for ratification by the necessary majorities. Of these proposals, 27 have been ratified.

Many of these amendments fall into distinct clusters. The first 10 amendments, the Bill of Rights, were ratified in 1791 and were the result of Anti-Federalist criticisms of the new Constitution. The Thirteenth, Fourteenth, and Fifteenth Amendments were ratified in the five-year period after the Civil War. Four amendments were ratified during the Progressive Era. Many amendments have helped make the U.S. system of government considerably more democratic than it was when it was established. Expansions of the franchise—for example, in the Fifteenth, Nineteenth, and Twenty-sixth Amendments—have been especially important. Proposals for new or substantially altered constitutions have rarely stirred more than passing interest (see Boyd 1992; Vile 1991c).

Alternative Means of Change

The difficulty of the amending process has encouraged other means of change (Lutz 1994). Judicial interpretations of the Constitution have contributed to its flexibility, but congressional practices and presidential initiatives have also proved important (Vile 1994a). An unwritten constitution has, in effect, grown up around and supplemented the words of the written document. Although written constitutional provisions have the capacity to trump conflicting customs and usages, changes can often be effected to fill in constitutional gaps and silences. On at least four occasions (the Eleventh, the Thirteenth and Fourteenth, the Sixteenth, and the Twenty-sixth Amendments), amendments have been adopted to overturn Supreme Court decisions. The Supreme Court, in turn, interprets such amendments. At times, it may construe such provisions more restrictively or more expansively than their authors intended.

Unresolved Issues

In early American history, the Supreme Court resolved some important issues. In *Hollingsworth v. Virginia* (1798), for example, it decided that the president's signature was not needed for a constitutional amendment. In *Dillon v. Gloss* (1921), it ruled that ratification of amendments should reflect a contemporary consensus. In *Coleman v. Miller* (1939), however, the Court decided that such issues were political questions to be resolved by the elected branches of government. Many such issues remain unresolved. A number of them center on the still unused convention mechanism (Caplan 1988). Other unresolved questions involve whether states have the power to rescind ratification of amendments prior to the time

a three-fourths majority is mustered, whether states should be permitted to ratify amendments they have previously rejected, and how long states have to ratify amendments. This last issue was prominent in the case of the Twenty-seventh Amendment, which was putatively ratified more than 200 years after it was originally proposed by Congress. Additional issues involve what conditions Congress can place on proposed amendments and whether Congress can extend a previously specified ratification date, as it did in the case of the failed equal rights amendment (Vile 1992, 45–54).

A number of procedural changes in the constitutional amending process have been proposed to clarify these questions or to make the amending process easier. Akil Amar (1988) suggested that Article V mechanisms may not be the exclusive means by which formal constitutional changes can be effected. He believes that such changes might also be effected by popular initiative or ratified by referendum.

For Further Reading:

Vile, John R. 1993. *The Theory and Practice of Constitutional Change in America: A Collection of Original Source Materials.* New York: Peter Lang.

❖ ARTICLES OF CONFEDERATION ❖

The government that immediately preceded the one that the Constitution of 1787 established was a league of friendship among the states called the Articles of Confederation. Pennsylvania's John Dickinson was largely responsible for writing the document, but the Continental Congress, which approved it in 1777, modified his handiwork. Requiring unanimous state approval, the Articles did not go into effect until Maryland, which had been holding out until the larger states renounced their claims to western lands, ratified in 1781.

Formed at a time when states were extremely jealous of their powers and suspicious of strong executive power, such as that which George III had exercised, the Articles embodied the principle of state sovereignty. Article II provided that "each state retains its sovereignty, freedom, and independence, and every Power, Jurisdiction and right, which is not by this confederation expressly delegated to the United States, in Congress assembled" (Solberg 1958, 42). Whereas the current U.S. Constitution is based on the division of power among three branches, the unicameral legislative branch—in which each state has an equal vote—dominated the Articles. This branch, however, was not entrusted with power over interstate commerce, and on key matters, the consent of nine or more state was required. Members of the Confederation Congress were elected by the state legislatures, and they further depended on the states for raising revenue and mustering armies.

Article XIII provided for an amending process. Congress would vote on amendments, which were then to be approved by all thirteen state legislatures. This process ultimately proved too wooden, and despite several attempts, including two that fell but a single state shy of adoption (Bernstein with Agel 1993, 12), no amendments survived the gauntlet of unanimous state ratification.

Although the government under the Articles provided a useful transition from British to American rule and was responsible for such achievements as the Northwest Ordinance of 1787, contemporaries came to agree that it did not provide for an adequate central authority. Accordingly, when the Constitutional Convention of 1787 met, the delegates decided to start with a new plan rather than attempt to revise the existing document. Ignoring the provision of Article XIII, the delegates specified that the new document would go into effect when ratified by nine of the states. The convention delegates further provided that the new document would be ratified not by the existing state legislatures, which would lose power to the new Congress, but by special conventions called within the states. So technically, at least, the new system was adopted illegally (Kay 1987; Ackerman and Katyal 1995). Article V of the U.S. Constitution continued the two-step process for amendment, providing that two-thirds of both houses would propose amendments that three-fourths of the states would have to ratify.

For Further Reading:
Jensen, Merrill. 1966. *The Articles of Confederation*. Madison: University of Wisconsin Press.

❖ ASSOCIATION, FREEDOM OF ❖

Although the Constitution does not specifically delineate a right of association, the Supreme Court has recognized it. For example, it declared in a unanimous decision written by John Marshall Harlan II in *National Association for the Advancement of Colored People v. Alabama ex rel. Patterson* (1958, 460) that freedom of association was essential to "effective advocacy" and "an inseparable aspect of the 'liberty' assured by the Due Process Clause of the Fourteenth Amendment, which embraces freedom of speech." The Court accordingly voided an Alabama law requiring that the state chapter of the NAACP disclose the list of its members, who might then be subject to reprisals.

Ironically, when two Florida congressmen (Republican Charles Bennett and Democrat Donald Matthews) introduced amendments designed to preserve freedom of association in 1963 (H.J. Res. 728 and 775), their objective was to insulate the areas of private business, housing, and education from the effects of the Supreme

Court's decision in *Brown v. Board of Education*, which had mandated racial desegregation. Such an amendment, which appears to have had little chance of success, would have permitted states to segregate students by race and sex in public schools, subject to the "separate but equal" standard originally established in *Plessy v. Ferguson* but repudiated in *Brown* (*Congressional Record*, 16909–10, 19449 [1963]).

B

❖ BACON, SELDEN ❖

Bacon was the spokesman for a group of New York lawyers in the late 1920s and early 1930s. He argued in a pamphlet and a follow-up article that the Tenth Amendment implied limits on the amending process in addition to those explicitly stated in Article V (see Vile 1992, 169–70). Bacon contended that Roger Sherman had inserted the words "to the United States" in the Tenth Amendment specifically to limit Article V— the amending process being such a power "not delegated to the United States" but given to the states or their people. By this addition, Sherman hoped to close the potential loophole that the delegates to the Constitutional Convention of 1787 had created whereby Article V might strip people of their liberties (S. Bacon 1930, 780).

According to Bacon's interpretation, matters that the Tenth Amendment reserved to the people could be effected only through the use of the convention method of ratification. Bacon cited the Eighteenth Amendment, which provided for national alcoholic prohibition, as an amendment requiring such popular ratification (1930, 793). He argued that its effects on personal liberty were significantly different from previous amendments that the Supreme Court had recently upheld against similar challenges. Although Henry Taft (1930) attempted to refute his arguments, Bacon echoed them before the Supreme Court in *United States v. Sprague* (1931). Although

the Court rejected Bacon's arguments, such arguments continue to interest both modern proponents of substantive limits on the amending process and those who favor ratification of amendments by referendum.

See also Constitutional Amendments, Limits on.

❖ *BAKER V. CARR* (1962) ❖

Baker v. Carr was the 6 to 2 decision in which Justice William Brennan declared for the Supreme Court that matters of state legislative apportionment were not political questions unfit for judicial resolution but were justiciable under the equal protection clause of the Fourteenth Amendment. The decision remanded for consideration a Tennessee scheme of state legislative apportionment that favored rural counties and had not been altered since 1901, and it appeared to overturn an earlier plurality opinion in an Illinois case, *Colegrove v. Green* (1946). It also prepared the way for the Court to apply a one-person, one-vote standard for apportionment in both houses of a state legislature in *Reynolds v. Sims* (1964).

Focusing on a state matter rather than on a dispute among the three branches of the national government, *Baker v. Carr* does not appear to have overturned the Court's decision in *Luther v. Borden* (1849), which was that the question of whether a state government is republican is a political question. *Baker* also seems to have left standing the decision in *Coleman v. Miller* (1939), entrusting decisions about the ratification of amendments to the elected branches (discussed in *Baker* 1962, 214–15).

In *Baker*, Brennan identified six factors involved in political questions:

[1.] a textually demonstrable constitutional commitment of the issue to a coordinate political department; [2.] or a lack of judicially discoverable and manageable standards for resolving it; [3.] or the impossibility of deciding without an initial policy determination of a kind clearly for nonjudicial discretion; [4.] or the impossibility of a court's undertaking independent resolution without expressing lack of the respect due coordinate branches of government; [5.] or an unusual need for unquestioning adherence to a political decision already made; [6.] or the potentiality of embarrassment from multifarious pronouncements by various departments on one question. (*Baker* 1962, 217)

Brennan noted that the citizens of Tennessee had no initiative and that the state amending process made it difficult for the people to initiate changes in the apportionment process (*Baker* 1962, 193–94). Justices Douglas and Clark wrote concurring opinions, and Justices Frankfurter and Harlan authored vigorous dissents questioning the wisdom of judicial intervention in this complex area and suggesting that the framers of the equal protection clause had not intended for it to apply to such controversies.

Baker and follow-up opinions stimulated calls for amendments in Congress and increased public opposition to the Warren Court. In a move led by Illinois Senator Everett Dirksen, the states fell but a single vote short of mustering the necessary two-thirds majority needed to force Congress to call a special constitutional convention on the subject. The decision also generated controversial proposals for amendments by the Council of State Governments. Scholars have both praised (Ely 1980) and criticized the Court for its apportionment decisions (Elliott 1974).

See also Political Questions; *Reynolds v. Sims;* States, Legislative Apportionment.

For Further Reading:

Irons, Peter, and Stephanie Guitton, eds. 1993. *May It Please the Court.* New York: New Press.

Lee, Calvin B. T. 1967. *One Man One Vote: WMCA and the Struggle for Equal Representation.* New York: Charles Scribner's Sons.

❖ BALANCED BUDGET AMENDMENT ❖

Among the powers the Constitution grants to Congress in Article I, Section 8 is the power "to borrow Money on the credit of the United States." As early as 1798, Thomas Jefferson advocated an amendment to withdraw such authorization. Somewhat ironically, however, when he subsequently became president, he proved willing to borrow the $15 million for the Louisiana Purchase (Savage 1988, 106–7). His Republican successor, James Madison, borrowed to finance the War of 1812.

Governmental debt was not uncommon in the eighteenth and nineteenth centuries, especially during wartime. From a modern perspective, in which debt seems almost routine, it seems unusual to discover that amendments were offered in the 1820s and 1830s for spending federal surpluses. Later in the nineteenth century, the Fourteenth Amendment indicated that the United States would honor its own, but not Confederate, debt.

In the 1870s and 1880s, amendments were introduced to limit the national debt, but the last several decades have been the most active period for such proposed amendments. Hundreds of proposals have been introduced during this time. One commentator noted that, in this respect, "the balanced budget amendment has shown itself to be the constitutional equivalent of the Energizer bunny" (Kyvig 1995, 99). In 1969, the National Taxpayers Union was formed to support the balanced budget amendment. Although generally associated with conservatives, this group has also mustered some support among liberals, including Illinois Democratic Senator Paul Simon.

At one time or another, as many as 32 of the needed 34 states have petitioned Congress to call a convention to address the balanced budget amendment. Moreover, on several occasions, a balanced budget amendment has been voted on in Congress. The proposal was especially popular during the Reagan and Bush years, and as an item in the Republican Contract with America, the amendment has recently gained renewed attention.

In August 1982, the Senate voted 69 to 31 for a balanced budget amendment, but it stalled in the House of Representatives. In 1986, a balanced budget amendment fell a single vote short of the needed majority in the Senate. In 1990, it was seven votes shy of the needed majority in the House, and in 1992, it fell only nine votes short (Kyvig 1995, 114, 118–19). After the Republican gains in the 1994 congressional elections, a balanced budget amendment passed the House of Representatives, but it subsequently came up a single vote shy of adoption in the Senate. One of the amendment's supporters, Republican Senate Majority Leader Robert Dole of Kansas, ultimately cast his vote against the amendment. This parliamentary maneuver allowed him to reintroduce the measure in 1996, just before he retired to run for president. On 6 June 1996 the amendment fell two votes short of the needed majority.

Although the idea of a balanced budget appears relatively simple on the surface, its supporters are motivated by different objectives, and these are sometimes in tension. Like earlier supporters of an amendment to limit the percentage of income that could be collected through the income tax that was sanctioned in the Sixteenth Amendment, many supporters see the balanced budget mechanism primarily as a means of curtailing the increased activities and expenditures of the federal government since the New Deal. Others anticipate that such an amendment would require the government to increase taxes to pay for current programs.

Differences in objectives and approaches are reflected in the variety of amendments that have been introduced in Congress on the subject. These have included proposals to limit governmental expenditures to a fixed percentage of the gross national product, to require Congress to stay in session until it proposed a balanced budget, to prevent expenditures from exceeding revenues except in cases of war or emergency, to require every appropriation measure to be accompanied by a revenue-raising measure, to require the approval of an extraordinary majority of Congress to raise taxes, to require the approval of an extraordinary majority of Congress to raise the ceiling on the debt, to mandate increased taxes in certain deficit situations, to begin paying back the national debt, and to provide for a taxpayer's bill of rights. Some such proposals have been tied to prohibitions against unfunded federal mandates or to proposals for a presidential line-item veto.

Economists vigorously debate the desirability or undesirability of a balanced federal budget. Critics of unbalanced budgets, and of a debt that is now in the trillions of dollars, believe that such budgets contribute to inflationary pressures, lead to higher interest rates, and generally transfer burdens from the current generation to generations yet unborn. Defenders argue that the links between budget deficits and inflation and higher interest rates are problematic and point out that future generations often benefit from current expenditures (contrast J. Davidson 1992 and McIntyre 1992; also see Moore and Penner 1980 and Fink and High 1987). Moreover, the widely accepted economic theory developed by John Maynard Keynes suggests that governmental deficits can help stimulate the economy during times of recession and that balanced budgets can actually prolong such recessions. In the last 30 years or so, however, the federal government has usually run deficits even in years of prosperity—the last surplus was in 1969. This suggests to some proponents of a balanced budget amendment that the political pressures on members of Congress to reap rewards for current constituents, the price of which is deferred to future taxpayers, may need a constitutional counterweight such as a balanced budget amendment. Critics of the deficit also point to the increasing percentage of the budget that is needed to service such debt and the wealthier members of society who will profit from such payments.

Ironically, Presidents Reagan and Bush advocated balanced budget amendments at the very time their own administrations (aided, to be sure, by Democratic Congresses) engaged in massive deficit spending. Historically, deficits have often been connected in the popular mind to various forms of governmental corruption or to providing special privileges for the wealthy. Going all the way back to the conflict between Thomas Jefferson (who generally advocated fiscal austerity) and Alexander Hamilton (who argued that the public debt could be a public blessing), the debate over budget deficits has often been phrased in highly moralistic terms suggestive of conflicts between good and evil and not simply between rival economic views (Savage 1988). The analogy between governmental budgets and individual budgets is also frequently evoked, but the analogy often proves inconclusive because many households do, in fact, engage in deficit financing on a fairly consistent basis, especially on items such as houses or cars. Moreover, this analogy suggests that the federal government should distinguish between expenditures for immediate consumption and those on behalf of capital investments, which it does not do now.

Two questions that dog the balanced budget amendment are those of appropriateness and enforceability. To the extent that the amendment appears to sanction one, possibly transient, economic theory over another, some argue that it has no place in a Constitution intended to endure over time ("Balanced Budget Amendment" 1983). Other questions center on who would have standing to sue under such an amendment, how the amendment would be enforced, and, particularly, what role the courts would play in its enforcement (see J. Bowen 1994). At least since 1937, U.S. courts have generally taken a hands-off approach to economic affairs, and such an amendment might, wisely or unwisely, inject courts back into such controversies. Moreover, legislation designed to achieve balanced budgets—most notably the Balanced Budget and Emergency Deficit Control Act of 1985, better known as the Gramm-Rudman-Hollings law—has proved relatively unsuccessful in ending deficits. To some, this suggests that stronger medicine is needed; others fear that an amendment might prove similarly unenforceable and that it would ultimately bring disrespect on the Constitution. Certainly, amendments that call for government to project future budgets may enable Congress to engage in some creative predictions.

At this writing, it is difficult to predict whether a balanced budget amendment will be adopted and, if so, how it will be phrased. Certainly, however, the issue shows no sign of going away in the near future.

❖ BALDWIN, LELAND ❖
(1897–1981)

Baldwin was a retired professor of history from the University of Pittsburgh who proposed a new Constitution in a 1972 book entitled *Reframing the Constitution: An Imperative for Modern America*. Identifying the existing system of federalism, separation of powers, and a weak party system as some of the problems in the current government, Baldwin described his plan as "a modified version of the Cabinet or Parliamentary form" (Baldwin 1972, 96).

Baldwin's plan called for the creation of a unicameral Congress. It would consist of 200 elected members as well as up to 15 congressmen-pro-forma to serve as a type of shadow cabinet and enough appointed congressmen-at-large to give the majority party a 55 percent voting majority of the membership. The Constitution would entrust Congress with more explicit powers (the administration of some of which could, however, be delegated to the states), and members would be elected to five-year terms, subject to prior dissolution.

The president, similar to a prime minister, would preside over Congress and be its executive arm. Like members of Congress, the president would serve for a five-year term, subject to a vote of no confidence. The vice presidency would be eliminated; Congress would elect a successor in case of presidential death or disability.

The courts would be headed by a new body designated as the Senate and consisting of 50 law senators (two from each of the 15 new states described below) and others elected by population) and 50 senators-at-large. Senators would be appointed for life but would be required to retire at age 70. The chief justice, who would be selected by the Senate, would preside over that body and would live in the White House and serve as head of state. The entire Senate would vote on matters of constitutional in-

terpretation. The Senate could suspend the writ of habeas corpus and exercise similar power in times of emergency. It could also dissolve Congress, conduct investigations, and impose reforms on state governments. In cases of conflict between the president and Congress, the chief justice and two-thirds of the Senate could dissolve Congress.

Baldwin provided mechanisms to recognize political parties and for the nomination and selection of the elected branches. He also provides for significant state reorganization. Existing states would be divided into 15 new states. Alaska would be given the option of becoming a commonwealth or joining a group of northwestern states. Each state would draw up a new constitution consolidating existing governments and providing for a unicameral legislature and an appointive Senate.

The Bill of Rights would be modified, in accord with the twentieth-century incorporation process, to apply to both the states and the national government. Baldwin would broaden protections against discrimination to cover "sex, race, color, religion, or birth out of wedlock." He would explicitly vest Congress with power over gun ownership, thus modifying the current Second Amendment.

Baldwin also wanted to liberalize the constitutional amending process. Two-thirds majorities of the Senate or the Congress would be empowered to propose amendments, subject to ratification by either three-fourths of the state legislatures or a majority of the electorate. Alternatively, one-half of the states could propose amendments. Baldwin also specified mechanisms for calling a new constitutional convention.

For Further Reading:
Boyd, Steven R., ed. 1992. *Alternative Constitutions for the United States: A Documentary History.* Westport, CT: Greenwood Press.

Vile, John R. 1991. *Rewriting the United States Constitution: An Examination of Proposals from Reconstruction to the Present.* New York: Praeger.

❖ BANKING ❖

The U.S. Constitution neither specifically mentions banking nor authorizes Congress to establish corporations. Congressional authority to establish a national bank was a major issue in the administration of George Washington and contributed to the emerging split between the Federalist and Republican Parties. Secretary of the Treasury Alexander Hamilton, who would soon be a leading Federalist, favored broad federal powers and emphasized the development of commerce and industry; he accordingly argued that the bank was constitutional. Secretary of State Thomas Jefferson, who would soon lead the Republican Party, was wary of broad federal powers and emphasized agricultural development; he accordingly argued that the bank was unconstitutional. Washington sided with Hamilton, and Congress created a bank with a 20-year charter. Although this charter lapsed, Congress reestablished the bank in 1816.

Maryland challenged the constitutionality of this bank and attempted to tax its branch in Baltimore. In *McCulloch v. Maryland* (1819), Chief Justice John Marshall decided that the national government had the right to establish the bank under the doctrine of implied powers. He also voided Maryland's tax on the bank. This decision did not, however, prevent Andrew Jackson (who associated banks with eastern monied interests) from vetoing a bank bill that was introduced during his administration.

Three amendments proposed in Congress in 1793 and 1794 would have prohibited bankers from being eligible for Congress. Amendments proposed in 1813 and 1814 would have specifically authorized a bank. A spate of proposals made immediately after *McCulloch* and reflecting resolutions voted on in a number of state legislatures would have prohibited branches of the national bank outside the District of Columbia.

At least three proposals from 1837 to 1840, apparently stimulated by the panic of 1837, would have prohibited the issuance of state bank notes. Oklahoma Democratic Senator Thomas Gore introduced a proposal in 1933, probably in response to the Great Depression, that would have required states to get congressional consent before chartering banks (S.J. Res. 18).

See also *McCulloch v. Maryland.*

For Further Reading:

Jefferson, Thomas. 1791. "Opinion of the Constitutionality of a National Bank." In *Documents of American Constitutional & Legal History*, ed. Melvin I. Urofsky. New York: Alfred A. Knopf, 1989, 132–46.

❖ BANKRUPTCY ❖

Although the Constitution grants Congress power in Article I, Section 8 to make "uniform Laws on the subject of Bankruptcies throughout the United States," a lasting system of national legislation was not established until 1898 (Coleman 1992, 61). A proposal introduced in 1822 would have allowed states to adopt legislation in the interim (Ames 1896, 265). With some reservations, this was basically what the Supreme Court agreed to in a 4 to 3 decision in *Ogden v. Saunders* (1827), in which Chief Justice John Marshall, author of an earlier case on state insolvency laws in *Sturges v. Crowinshield* (1819), dissented.

For Further Reading:

Coleman, Peter J. 1974. *Debtors and Creditors in America: Insolvency, Imprisonment for Debt, and Bankruptcy, 1607–1900.* Madison: State Historical Society of Wisconsin.

❖ *BARRON V. BALTIMORE* (1833) ❖

In this 7-to-0 decision authored by Chief Justice John Marshall, the Court decided that the first 10 amendments to the Constitution, known as the Bill of Rights, applied only to the national government and not to the states. In this case, Baltimore had diverted streams that subsequently filled a wharf owned by Barron and rendered it useless. Citing the takings clause of the Fifth Amendment, Barron argued that he had been illegally deprived of his property without just compensation. In response, Marshall argued that the Constitution had been designed to limit the national government rather than the state governments. He pointed out that provisions of the Constitution that did limit the states (those found in Article I, Section 10, for example) concerned matters relevant to the national government and had been explicitly applied to the states. Marshall further noted that if individuals had desired alterations in their own state constitutions, they would have called conventions rather than use "the unwieldy and cumbrous machinery of procuring a recommendation from two-thirds of Congress and the assent of three-fourths of their sister states" (*Barron* 1833, 250).

Although Marshall did not say so, when James Madison had introduced his initial version of the Bill of Rights, Madison had favored an amendment limiting the states, but his proposal had failed for lack of congressional support. The Fourteenth Amendment, which was ratified in 1868, provided protections against state deprivations of privileges and immunities, due process rights, and equal protection for U.S. citizens. Some supporters of the amendment, including John Bingham, knew about *Barron v. Baltimore* and apparently hoped that the Fourteenth Amendment would overturn it. Although Justice John Marshall Harlan agreed, the rest of the Supreme Court initially rejected this interpretation. In the twentieth century, although never officially embracing the doctrine of total incorporation that Harlan and later Justice Hugo Black advocated, the Court has gradually used the due process clause of that amendment (in a process generally referred to as se-

lective incorporation) to apply almost all the guarantees found in the Bill of Rights to the states as well as to the national government.

See also Incorporation.

For Further Reading:

Schwartz, Bernard. 1992. *The Great Rights of Mankind: A History of the American Bill of Rights.* Madison, WI: Madison House.

❖ BEASLEY, ROBERT ❖

Robert Beasley proposed a new U.S. Constitution in a pamphlet published in 1864 in both English and Spanish and titled *A Plan To Stop the Present and Prevent Future Wars.* His plan, which actually preceded his proposed constitution, called for all persons to vote on whether to continue the Civil War, with nonvoters to be penalized by a $1,000 fine. If the vote was affirmative, all would then be placed in the army and "compelled to assist in prosecuting the war" (Beasley 1864, 3). The Constitution, constantly referred to as being for "the sovereign States of North and South America," followed.

Under this scheme, the House of Representatives would be composed of two representatives from each state and the Senate of one from each. The Senate would have to vote on charges of impeachment by three-fifths rather than two-thirds, and members of Congress would receive $5 for each day of service plus expenses. Perhaps in response to Lincoln's forceful actions in prosecuting the war, only Congress would have the power to suspend the writ of habeas corpus.

The president and vice president would not be permitted to serve for consecutive terms. Each voter would write the name of his preferred candidate for president on a ballot, with the Senate deciding tie votes. The president would receive a yearly salary of $40,000. His power to pardon would be restricted in cases of "lying, larceny, and impeachment" (Beasley 1864, 13). He could also be removed from office for "conviction of lying, larceny or other high crimes and misdemeanors" (Beasley 1864, 14).

Most of the provisions of the Bill of Rights would be incorporated. Government officers convicted of stealing were to be fined, with proceeds to go toward the construction of a national cemetery. Those stealing over $10,000 were to be "hung with a rope by the neck until dead" and denied burial in this cemetery (Beasley 1864, 16).

States were to be prohibited from interfering in the domestic affairs of other states and would be expelled from the Union for 50 years for so doing. States could secede and keep government property within their boundaries. Beasley would further provide for the purchase of "white servants" from Europe to become citizens after 15 years (Beasley 1864, 18). Slaveholders would be able to take their slaves into the territories (thus affirming the 1857 decision in *Scott v. Sandford*), with states subsequently deciding whether to have slavery according to the principle of popular sovereignty. The national government could call on each state for a quota of troops; if the quota were not met, "all the males and half the females in his State" would be drafted (Beasley 1864, 20). Neither slavery nor polygamy would exclude a state from the Union. In language similar to that later used in the Fourteenth Amendment, voting in federal elections and officeholding were to be limited to "white male citizens of the age of twenty-one years and upwards" (Beasley 1864, 20).

Beasley would have officially adopted the Monroe Doctrine and authorized Congress to carry it out. Adjacent islands could be admitted into the Union after 1900, but states in Europe, Asia, and Africa would have to wait until after 2000. States would have the power to prohibit their citizens from interfering in the "domestic concerns" of their neighbors or "lying to their own or their neighbor's dumb brutes [presumably slaves], or unnecessarily abusing them in

any way" (Beasley 1864, 21).

Beasley identified himself as one of the "sovereign people" of Rio Vista, California, who doubted that he was "a servant of God" (Beasley 1864, 3) and proposed four scriptures "as admonitions to all people" (Beasley 1864, 21). These dealt with the subjection of wives to husbands, instructions for familial relations, master-slave relations, and the proper allocation of responsibilities between Caesar and God.

Secret political parties were to be outlawed, and political parties could not nominate individuals for office. Amendments were to be ratified by five-sixths (rather than three-fourths) of the states, and ratification by conventions in five states would be sufficient to inaugurate the new government.

In an addendum, Beasley asserted, in apparent reference to slaves, that "whatsoever God has made inferior, man cannot make equal or superior" (1864, 23). He further proposed a census for after the war and laws "that will give every one a chance to have a husband or a wife," and he suggested that the seat of government should be "within one or two hundred miles of the 'Isthmus of Panama'" (Beasley 1864, 24).

A number of subsequent writers picked up on Beasley's idea for a referendum on war. His pro-slavery constitution was otherwise overtaken by events, and it appears to have quickly faded from public view.

❖ BECKER, THEODORE L. ❖
(1932–)

In 1976, when he was a professor of law and political science at the University of Hawaii, Becker offered a series of proposed constitutional reforms in a textbook entitled *American Government: Past—Present—Future*. He referred to his plan as a type of "eutopia," that is, a "good" or "desirable" place, as opposed to a "utopia," which literally means "no place" (Becker 1976, 432).

In an attempt to increase governmental responsiveness and accountability, Becker favors a national presidential primary (NPP). However, his ultimate aim is to institute a presidential election tournament (PET), whereby candidates would emerge (as in organized athletic contests) first from the states, then from one of four regions, then from either the East or the West, and finally from the contest between those two champions, with campaign costs funded by the government. Becker would also institute a vote of no confidence as a means of executive recall and suggests that voting should be a compulsory, perhaps even a paid, activity; citizens would, however, be given a no-preference option (Becker 1976, 459).

Becker favors a unicameral rather than bicameral Congress. He would also establish an "executive Committee, Council, or Cabinet" to run its affairs (Becker 1976, 467). He anticipates a legislature of from 500 to 1,000 people in which at least half of the representatives would be selected at random. He also favors a national initiative and referendum and anticipates that such a mechanism might be effected by home cable television or computer hookups.

Becker would like to see presidents run for office on a ticket that includes members of their cabinet. The president would, in turn, have to get 60 percent approval of Congress to fire a cabinet member (Becker 1976, 474). Greater administrative oversight would be provided by Congress and by ombudsmen, who would form a "countergovernment" (Becker 1976, 509).

Becker also anticipates numerous reforms of the judicial and criminal justice systems. He favors either setting up a national appeals court to ease the Supreme Court's workload or appointing 18 Court justices who would work on nine-judge panels. Judges would serve for 12 to 15 years rather than life and would retire at age 70. As in Congress, a good portion of the judges would be chosen by lottery, albeit from members of the bar, with all judges undergoing at least six months' training at a judicial academy. Members of the lay public would preside in many trials, the state's peremptory challenges for jurors would be eliminated, jury pools would be widened, and jury pay would be increased.

Becker favors the repeal of all so-called victimless crime laws, such as those prohibiting consensual sex, gambling, drug use, and the like.

In 1992, Becker—then at Auburn University—was working with Barry Krusch, author of *The 21st Century Constitution* (1992), to develop a national network of individuals interested in a second constitutional convention. As a class project, Becker had previously organized a simulated constitutional convention in Hawaii.

❖ BIBLE READING IN SCHOOLS ❖

See *Abington v. Schempp; Engel v. Vitale;* Prayer in Public Schools.

❖ BILL OF RESPONSIBILITIES ❖

Although individual rights and responsibilities are arguably correlative, the Constitution currently provides protection for the former without specifying the latter. At least two proponents of a new constitution, Rexford Tugwell and Jeremy Miller, have advocated a listing of such responsibilities in their proposed documents. More generally, some commentators have argued that American laws should devote more attention to citizen duties than they currently do (Glendon 1991, 76–108).

❖ BILL OF RIGHTS ❖

Collectively, the first 10 amendments to the U.S. Constitution are designated the Bill of

Rights. These amendments are among the most venerated in the entire document. Curiously, the subject of such a bill received little attention at the Constitutional Convention of 1787, although some debate was stirred near the end of the convention when George Mason of Virginia, who had authored his state's pathbreaking declaration of rights in 1776, proposed a motion for such a bill. Similarly, Virginia's Richard Henry Lee tried unsuccessfully to get the Congress under the Articles of Confederation to add a bill of rights before sending the Constitution to the states for approval (Schwartz 1992, 105).

The Federalist–Anti-Federalist Controversy

The absence of such a bill quickly became one of the rallying points for Anti-Federalists opposed to the new Constitution. Federalist proponents of the document initially argued that such a bill was unnecessary and could even prove dangerous in the event that key rights were omitted. Leading proponents of the Constitution subsequently realized that adding a bill of rights would be far less likely to jeopardize the new document than would the prospect of a second convention, which many Anti-Federalists were advocating.

James Madison, who would guide the Bill of Rights through the First Congress, also appears to have been influenced both by the wishes of his Virginia constituents, from whom he was seeking a seat in the new Congress, and by correspondence with Thomas Jefferson, who was then serving as a minister to France. Ironically, although Jefferson would later criticize the exercise of judicial review, he argued in his letters to Madison that, with a bill of rights in place, judges would be in a better position to guard civil liberties (Mason and Baker 1985, 276–94).

Actions by Congress

In the process of ratifying the U.S. Constitution, eight states submitted more than 100 substantive amendment proposals (Schwartz 1992, 157). Many in Congress wanted to postpone consideration of a bill of rights until the new Constitution had been more thoroughly tested, but congressional debates indicate that Madison especially believed that such a bill was essential to gaining the confidence of those who had opposed ratification of the document (Vile 1993c, 137–60).

Madison formulated a list of nine amendments with 42 separate rights for congressional consideration (Lutz 1992, 55); most of Madison's proposals dealt with individual political rights rather than guarantees for state sovereignty, which some Anti-Federalists had sought. In the course of debate and deliberation, Congress deleted four of Madison's proposed amendments. They would have provided a declaration of the people's right to alter the government, applied guarantees of freedom of conscience and the press to the states (thus anticipating the later incorporation controversy), limited certain appeals to the Supreme Court, and explicitly mentioned the doctrine of separation of powers (Schwartz 1992, 169). All 12 amendments that subsequently emerged from House and Senate action (including action by a Committee of Eleven, which included Madison, in the House and conference reports in both houses) were based on Madison's original draft, with changes related "to form rather than substance" (Schwartz 1992, 169). Madison was not successful in incorporating proposals into the constitutional text; instead, the Congress followed Roger Sherman's suggestion that the Bill of Rights be appended to the end of the document. The House voted to accept the Bill of Rights on 24 September 1789, with the Senate concurring the following day (Schwartz 1992, 186).

Donald Lutz has divided commentators on the Bill of Rights into four groups: those who view it as the product of a few creative minds, those who see it as the embodiment of ideas in the Magna Carta and other English precedents, those who view it as distillations of amendments that were offered in state conventions that ratified the Constitution; and those who see it as a summary of rights found within state constitutions of the founding period (Lutz 1992, 50–51). Although each point of view has some evidence to support it, Lutz emphasizes the latter view, demonstrating that 26 of the rights on Madison's original list were found in the state constitutions, 9 were found in 5 of 7 contemporary constitutions, 4 were found in 6, and 13 were found in all 7 existing state documents (Lutz 1992, 67; also see Conley and Kaminski 1992); many of these rights, in turn, had their origin in colonial charters (Lutz 1992, 68–69). Whereas the first eight amendments contain provisions protecting individual rights (with special attention to the rights of political participation and rights for those accused of criminal behavior), the Ninth and Tenth Amendments are directed toward different concerns and are thus sometimes excluded from discussions of the first eight amendments. Unlike many twentieth-century bills of rights, the U.S. version does not attempt to guarantee economic rights.

State Ratification

Of the 12 amendments proposed by Congress, one—dealing with congressional representation and originally listed as the first amendment—fell a single state shy of ratification and thus remains a dead letter (Amar 1992, 1137–45). The other, originally the second amendment, putatively became the Twenty-seventh Amendment, with a belated ratification in 1992. Apparently, the first 10 amendments became part of the Constitution with their ratification by Virginia in late 1791. Secretary of State Thomas Jefferson notified the state governors of this ratification on 1 March 1792 (Schwartz 1992, 186). In 1939, the sesquicentennial of the adoption of the U.S. Constitution, Connecticut and Georgia added their ratifications in a symbolic display that illustrates the Bill of Rights' grip on the popular mind (Schwartz 1992, 191).

The Incorporation Controversy

For all the attention that this part of the Constitution receives, the Bill of Rights was not the source of frequent judicial decision making in the first 100 years of the republic. In large part, this was because the courts interpreted the Bill of Rights as a limitation only on the actions of the national government and not on the states, where most early legislating took place. The wording of what became the First Amendment—beginning with "Congress shall make no law"—appeared to confirm that the Bill of Rights applied only to actions of the national government. This view was confirmed by Chief Justice John Marshall in *Barron v. Baltimore* (1833), where he cited the debates over the Bill of Rights as proof.

Among the supporters of the Fourteenth Amendment, which was ratified in 1868, at least some advocates—among them Congressman John Bingham, who was largely responsible for authoring the first section—appear to have been motivated by a desire to overturn *Barron v. Baltimore*. Initially, the Court rejected this incorporation doctrine in the *Slaughterhouse* cases (1873) and other contemporary decisions. In the early twentieth century, however, the Supreme Court adopted the view of selective incorporation, under which courts applied individual guarantees to the states via the due process clause of the Fourteenth Amendment on a piecemeal basis. Over time, all but five provisions were so applied to the states, with the Warren Court proving particularly active in this area (Hall 1991, 8). The result is that the Bill of Rights has had considerably more influence in the twentieth century than in the nineteenth.

The Bill of Rights Today

Periodically, scholars have expressed fear that a constitutional convention might revise the

Constitution in a way that would weaken the Bill of Rights. A review of proposals that have been offered, however, suggests that although there is sometimes stronger support for the concept of a bill of rights than for the individual guarantees listed, few proposed amendments would have directly challenged the rights specifically listed in the first 10 amendments. Many such proposals—those attempting to perpetuate slavery, for example—would today be regarded largely as historical curiosities (Vile 1991b). A number of important amendments, including the three adopted after the Civil War as well as proposals from the Progressive Era, have significantly expanded individual rights and provided for greater democracy (Grimes 1978).

Some scholars argued against proposed amendments to prevent flag desecration on the basis that such an amendment would have constituted the first narrowing of the Bill of Rights in the nation's history. Some of these scholars also argued that there are implicit limits on the amending process that would prevent its use for such purposes.

Whereas the Warren Court generally made liberal rulings on the Bill of Rights, the Burger and Rehnquist Courts have been more cautious about expanding such rights and have, in many cases, narrowed but not abandoned earlier rulings. As a consequence, some liberal scholars now argue that those seeking expanded protections for individual rights should look increasingly to their own state constitutions and their state bills of rights for protection, with the federal Bill of Rights serving more as a floor than a ceiling.

See also Anti-Federalists; *Barron v. Baltimore;* Federalists; Fourteenth Amendment; Incorporation; Madison, James.

For Further Reading:

Alderman, Ellen, and Caroline Kennedy. 1991. *In Our Defense: The Bill of Rights in Action.* New York: William Morrow.

"The Bill of Rights." 1991. Bicentennial issue of *Life* (Fall).

Bodenhamer, David J., and James W. Ely Jr., eds. 1993. *The Bill of Rights in Modern America After 200 Years.* Bloomington: Indiana University Press.

Bryant, Irving. 1965. *The Bill of Rights: Its Origin and Meaning.* Indianapolis, IN: Bobbs-Merrill.

Kurland, Philip B., and Ralph Lerner. 1987. *The Founders' Constitution.* Vol. 5. Chicago: University of Chicago Press.

Peck, Robert S. 1992. *The Bill of Rights and the Politics of Interpretation.* St. Paul, MN: West.

Schwartz, Bernard, ed. 1980. *The Roots of the Bill of Rights.* 5 vols. New York: Chelsea House.

Stone, Geoffrey R., Richard A. Epstein, and Cass R. Sunstein, eds. 1992. *The Bill of Rights in the Modern State.* Chicago: University of Chicago Press.

❖ BINGHAM, JOHN A. ❖ (1815–1900)

John Bingham was a lawyer and Republican congressman from Ohio from 1854 to 1873. He was once described by Justice Hugo Black as "the [James] Madison of the first section of the Fourteenth Amendment" (*Adamson* 1947, 74). Bingham, who served on the congressional Joint Committee of Fifteen on Reconstruction, drafted all of Section 1 of the Fourteenth Amendment except for the first sentence, which defines citizenship (Thaddeus Stevens appears to have been most responsible for the other sections of the amendment).

There is continuing dispute about Justice Black's argument that Bingham specifically intended for the privileges and immunities clause and the due process clause of the Fourteenth Amendment to overturn the Court's decision in *Barron v. Baltimore* (1833) and apply all of the Bill of Rights to the states (a process usually referred to as incorporation). There is no doubt that Bingham, who had been a strong foe of slavery and a defender of the principle of equality announced in the Declaration of Independence, was a strong advocate for the rights of African Americans, whom he hoped to protect through this amendment.

Sometimes called "the Cicero of the House" (Beauregard 1989, 97), Bingham was a special judge advocate who led the successful prosecution of the Lincoln assassins, a leader in the unsuccessful impeachment trial of President Andrew Johnson, chairman of the House Judiciary Committee from 1869 to 1873, and a minister plenipotentiary to Japan from 1873 to 1885.

See also Incorporation.

❖ BIRTHRIGHT CITIZENSHIP ❖ AMENDMENT

More than a dozen members of the U.S. House of Representatives have supported an amendment first introduced by California Representative Elton Gallegly in October 1991 and designed to deny citizenship to persons born in the United States whose mothers are not legal residents. If adopted, this amendment, which has received public support from California Republican Governor Pete Wilson, would modify the first clause of the Fourteenth Amendment, which specifies that "all persons born or naturalized in the United States, and subject to the jurisdiction thereof, are citizens of the United States and of the State wherein they reside." The Fourteenth Amendment originally was adopted to overturn the unpopular decision in *Scott v. Sandford* (1857), wherein Chief Justice Roger Taney and a majority of the Supreme Court had declared that blacks were not and could not be citizens of the United States whether they were born here or not.

On the surface, Gallegly's amendment resembles proposals that were introduced earlier in the century by members of Congress from the West Coast and designed to limit citizenship to persons born in the United States of parents who were eligible for citizenship. The primary purpose of these earlier proposals appears to have been to restrict property ownership by children born to legal Japanese immigrants living in the United States. At the time, the parents of such children were ineligible for citizenship and were prevented from owning property in the state of California (Musmanno 1929, 180–81).

By contrast, Gallegly's proposal is aimed at the problem of providing government services to illegal immigrants at a time when the nation is facing a rising tide of immigrants. Like earlier Japanese immigrants, most modern immigrants are from non-European nations. Although the topic is hotly debated, it appears that legal immigrants generally pay their own way, but illegal immigrants often cost governments more in spending on social programs than the immigrants contribute in taxes (Welch et al. 1993, 9). The costs of such illegal immigration tend to fall disproportionately on states such as Florida, Texas, and California, which have large immigrant populations.

To the extent that illegal immigrants come to the United States in the expectation that their children born here will become citizens, the birthright citizenship amendment might serve to deter immigration by such aliens and any problems they might bring with them. Those who oppose this amendment fear any erosion of the Fourteenth Amendment. They also note that the proposed amendment would treat illegal alien fathers and mothers differently and would penalize children for the status of their parents, over which they have no control (see "Birthright Citizenship Amendment" 1994). In *Plyler v. Doe* (1982), the Supreme Court used such an analysis to strike down a Texas law that allowed the public schools to exclude children of illegal aliens. Although the principle may be valid, the Supreme Court might be reluctant to apply such analysis to void an amendment.

For Further Reading:

Schuck, Peter H., and Rogers M. Smith. 1985. *Citizenship without Consent: Illegal Aliens in the American Polity*. New Haven, CT: Yale University Press.

❖ BLACK, HUGO LAFAYETTE ❖ (1886–1971)

President Franklin D. Roosevelt appointed Hugo Black, then a second-term senator from Alabama who had supported both the New Deal and FDR's court-packing plan, to the Supreme Court in 1937. Black served there for 34 years, including the entire tenure of the Warren Court. Many of his decisions significantly influenced thinking about the meaning of key constitutional amendments and the role of the Court in interpreting the Constitution.

In *Coleman v. Miller* (1939), Black wrote a concurring opinion stating that procedural questions surrounding the amending process were "political questions" for Congress to resolve.

In *Adamson v. California* (1939), Black articulated the view, repeated in numerous subsequent cases, that John Bingham and other authors of the first section of the Fourteenth Amendment intended for it to incorporate all the provisions of the Bill of Rights and make them applicable to the states. Black saw these and other guarantees as both a floor and a ceiling (Yarbrough 1988, 264); although judges were obliged to apply all the provisions of the Bill of Rights to the states, they should wait for the people to amend the Constitution via Article V before going any further.

In a number of cases, Black accused his brethren of short-circuiting this democratic process by reading their own views into the document. In *Griswold v. Connecticut* (1965), saying that Article V was "good for our Fathers" and "good enough for me" (522), Black rejected the Court's expansive

reading of privacy rights in striking down a state birth-control law. In *Harper v. Virginia Board of Elections* (1966), Black also dissented from a Supreme Court decision invalidating a state poll tax on the basis of a judicial reading of the equal protection clause of the Fourteenth Amendment that was unsupported by an act of Congress: "when a 'political theory' embodied in the Constitution becomes outdated . . . a majority of the Supreme Court are not only without constitutional power but are far less qualified to choose a new constitutional political theory than the people of this country proceeding in the manner provided by Article V" (*Harper* 1966, 678).

Similarly, in *Katz v. United States* (1967), Black dissented from the Court's decision using the Fourth Amendment to forbid warrantless electronic searches. Black said that it was not the Court's function to "'keep the Constitution up to date' or 'to bring it into harmony with the times'"; the Court was not intended to be "a continuously functioning constitutional convention" (*Katz* 1967, 373).

Black was also known for his view, articulated in *New York Times Co. v. United States* and elsewhere, that the freedom of speech guaranteed in the First Amendment was absolute. In his view, however, this amendment did not extend full protection to symbolic speech (see Black's dissent in *Tinker v. Des Moines* 1969). On another First Amendment issue, Black was a strong advocate of separation of church and state, and he authored the Court's decision in *Engel v. Vitale* (1962) outlawing prayer in public schools and prompting numerous calls for a constitutional amendment.

In *Oregon v. Mitchell* (1970), Black helped precipitate passage of the Twenty-sixth Amendment by ruling that a provision in the 1970 Voting Rights Act Amendments of 1970 lowering the minimum voting age to 18 would apply to federal but not to state elections.

For Further Reading:

Black, Hugo L. 1969. *A Constitutional Faith.* New York: Alfred A. Knopf.

Dunne, Gerald T. 1977. *Hugo Black and the Judicial Revolution.* New York: Simon & Schuster.

Freyer, Tony. 1990. *Hugo L. Black and the Dilemma of American Liberalism.* Glenville, IL: Scott, Foresman.

Newman, Roger K. 1994. *Hugo Black: A Biography.* New York: Pantheon Books.

❖ BLACK PANTHERS ❖

One of the most bizarre attempts to rewrite the Constitution occurred from 5–7 September 1970, when about 6,000 members of the radical Black Panther Party met at Temple University in Philadelphia in a "Revolutionary People's Convention" (Vile 1991c, 102–4). David Hilliard, the party chief of staff, stated the convention's hope of composing a "constitution that will guarantee and deliver to every American citizen the inviolable human rights to life, liberty and the pursuit of happiness" ("Panthers Plan New Convention" 1971, 503). Clearly, however, the Panthers intended to move beyond these fairly conventional-sounding aims.

The party's founder and minister of defense, Huey Newton, had recently been released from prison, where he had been serving time for the murder of a police officer. The convention thus served as what one author somewhat facetiously described as "the first real opportunity for the East Coasters to get a look at Huey, [and] find out if he really was God" (Pearson 1994, 226). Most such observers apparently were unimpressed with Newton's speaking abilities. Moreover, no new Constitution emerged from the Panthers' deliberations, and a subsequent gathering at Howard University in November 1970 was a failure.

Convention discussions centered on a number of subjects, ranging from socialism to women's liberation to human rights (Moore 1970, 1298). A contemporary magazine identified the primary proposals as:

•Abolishment of present political boundaries; creation of independent, self-governing communities from which political power would flow upward.

•A rotating police force of volunteers, under community control, with community councils, instead of courts, to deal with criminals.

•A national defense force of volunteers, trained in guerilla warfare.

•Free housing, health care, education and daycare centers for children.

•U.S. support of the Communist Vietcong in South Vietnam and the Communist Pathet Lao in Cambodia, return of Taiwan to Red China; "liberation" of Palestine from "Zionist colonialism." ("Rising Clamor for Black Separatism" 1970, 82)

With such a radical agenda, it is hardly surprising that the Panthers' convention had little success. The convention gives some insight, however, into the political turmoil of the era. It is fascinating because, however theatrical the convention was, it shows a radical group attempting to mimic traditional political means of effecting change.

❖ BLAINE AMENDMENT ❖

Modern controversies over prayer and Bible reading in schools date back more than a century, to the time when an unofficial Protestant establishment was increasingly challenged by Catholics, Jews, and others. These religious minorities objected both to Protestant religious exercises in public schools (readings, for example, from the King James Bible) and to the unavailability of government funding for nonpublic schools.

In 1875, President Ulysses S. Grant delivered a speech advocating an amendment requiring states to fund a system of free public schools and preventing any public funds from being allocated to parochial schools. Representative and former House Speaker James G. Blaine of Maine subsequently introduced an amendment applying the establishment and free exercise clauses of the First Amendment directly to the states and prohibiting public support of parochial schools (H.R. 1, 1875). Blaine, then seeking the Republican nomination for president, appears to have been motivated largely by political concerns (Green 1992, 40–51).

Some modern scholars cite debates over this amendment as evidence that contemporaries did not believe that the Fourteenth Amendment had intended to incorporate the provisions of the Bill of Rights and apply them to the states (A. Meyer 1951; F. O'Brien 1965). Steven Green (1992) has argued, however, that these debates are inconclusive on this point and that participants were more concerned about contemporary religious controversies.

Blaine's proposal stimulated considerable debate, including a proposed amendment by Democratic Congressman William O'Brien of Maryland in 1876 forbidding all religious tests and prohibiting ministers from holding public office. Democrats in the House Judiciary Committee accepted Blaine's proposal but weakened it by including a provision that "this article shall not vest, enlarge, or diminish legislative power in the Congress," thus making it declaratory only (Green 1992, 58). This amended version passed the House by a vote of 180 to 7. The Senate deleted the Democratic addition to the amendment. This body, however, added a clause providing that the proposed amendment "shall not be construed to prohibit the reading of the Bible in any school or institution" (cited by Green 1992, 60). This provision was added in apparent reaction to a series of decisions by school boards prohibiting religious instruction and Bible reading in public schools. One such decision had been upheld by the Ohio State Supreme Court in 1872 (Green 1992, 46–47). The Senate vote of 28 to 16 fell four votes shy of the majority needed to send it on to the states (Green 1992, 67), but a number of states adopted versions of the Blaine amendment (E. Larson 1993).

Variations of the Blaine amendment continued to be introduced in Congress throughout the nineteenth and early twentieth centuries; one scholar cited 19 proposals in addition to Blaine's (F. O'Brien 1965, 210). Such proposals were supported by a group called the National League for the Protection of American Institutions (A. Meyer 1951, 944–45). An amendment introduced by Senator Henry Blair of New Hampshire in 1888, although intended to exclude public school teachings of doctrines "peculiar to any sect," would nonetheless have required states to educate children "in virtue, morality, and the principles of the Christian religion" (F. O'Brien 1965, 196). Proposals intended to permit religious exercises in school were stimulated anew by Supreme Court decisions in *Engel v. Vitale* (1962) and *Abington v. Schempp* (1963) relating to prayer and Bible reading in public schools. Recent discussion of a religious equality amendment has been stimulated by the opinion that religious believers have suffered discrimination and that their free exercise rights have not been fully protected.

See also Prayer in Public Schools; Religious Equality Amendment.

For Further Reading:
Klinkhammer, Marie C. 1965. "The Blaine Amendment of 1875." *Catholic Historical Review* 21:15–49.

O'Brien, F. William. 1963. "The Blaine Amendment, 1875–1876." *University of Detroit Law Journal* 41 (December): 137–205.

❖ BRICKER AMENDMENT ❖

In the 1950s, Senator John Bricker, a conservative Republican senator from Ohio, spearheaded a drive for a constitutional amendment related to treaties and executive agreements. A substitute for this amendment came only one vote shy of being proposed by the necessary two-thirds majority in the Senate in 1954. Following its first introduction in 1951, more than 65 proposals like Bricker's were offered over the next 10 years. By 1954, the issue was described as "a major question of national policy" (Schubert 1954, 258), and proponents of the amendment continued offering amending resolutions into the 1980s.

Support for such amendments can be traced to a number of factors. A Supreme Court decision in *Missouri v. Holland* (1920) had suggested that Congress could exercise powers under the authority of treaties that it did not have under the Constitution. *United States v. Pink* (1942) appeared to magnify further executive powers under executive agreements. Some individuals expressed concern that the United Nations and a series of conventions it had drawn up might be used to undermine state sovereignty, afford fewer protections than Americans were accustomed to under the Bill of Rights, or interfere with purely domestic concerns. Such fears were, in turn, heightened by a California District Court opinion in *Fugii v. California* (1950) that overruled a portion of the state's Alien Land Law on the basis of a provision in the UN Charter (Tananbaum 1988, 5).

Supporters of an amendment emphasized different concerns. With a view toward *Missouri v. Holland*, Bricker's original proposal called for repeal of the supremacy clause in Article VI of the Constitution and substitution of a phrase more clearly indicating that treaties had to be made "in pursuance" of the Constitution and not simply under its authority. Bricker's original proposal would also have limited the reach of treaties and executive agreements with regard to individual rights, the form of government, and matters lacking in "mutuality of interest" or those within the U.S. "domestic jurisdiction." In addition, it called for publication of executive agreements and for their termination within six months of the end of a president's term (Tananbaum 1988, 221).

The American Bar Association supported an alternative proposal directed more toward the protection of states' rights. It provided that "a treaty shall become effective as internal law of the United States only through legislation by Congress which it could enact under its delegated powers in the absence of such treaty" (Tananbaum 1988, 222). The proposal by Georgia Senator Walter George that the Senate came close to proposing provided both that "a provision of a treaty or other international agreement which conflicts with this Constitution shall not be of any force or effect" and that agreements other than treaties "shall become effective as internal law in the United States only by an act of Congress" (Tananbaum 1988, 225).

President Eisenhower worked largely behind the scenes against such proposals, which he considered unnecessary and thought might tie his hands in foreign negotiations. Supreme Court decisions in *Rice v. Sioux City Memorial Park* (1955) and *Reid v. Covert* (1957) also allayed some of the concerns that had been raised in earlier cases. In the *Reid* case, Justice Hugo Black stated that "no agreement with a foreign nation can confer power . . . which is free from the restraints of the Constitution (1957, 16).

One scholar on the subject believes that the Bricker controversy alerted Eisenhower to the need to consult Congress on foreign policy matters. This scholar also believes that the controversy was a factor in delaying U.S. ratification of the UN Genocide Convention until 1986 (Tananbaum 1988, 218–19).

See also *Missouri v. Holland*.

❖ BROWN, JOHN (1800–1859) ❖

John Brown was the fervent abolitionist who led a bloody attack on pro-slavery settlers in Pottawatomie, Kansas, in May 1856 and on the arsenal at Harpers Ferry, Virginia (now West Virginia), in October 1859. Although he had hoped to encourage a slave revolt by the latter action, he was unsuccessful in this endeavor, a number of his sons were killed in the raid, and he was subsequently hanged.

Brown and 45 followers held a constitutional convention on 8 May 1858 in Chatham, Ontario. There they voted on a provisional constitution Brown had composed consisting of a preamble and 48 articles. It was designed to create an initial government for the free state that Brown hoped his attack on Harpers Ferry would create (Oates 1970, 243).

The unicameral Congress was to be composed of 5 to 10 members serving three-year terms and elected by the persons "connected with the organization" (Fogleson and Rubenstein 1969, 48). The president, vice president, and five members of the Supreme Court were to be selected in similar fashion, with the executive also serving a three-year term, and all subject to impeachment and removal. Members of the three branches were to choose the commander in chief for a three-year term, with a treasurer, secretary of state, secretary of war, and secretary of the treasury chosen in a similar manner. The Constitution addressed recruiting for government posts and for the army and dealing with court-martials, the treatment of prisoners and neutrals, deserters, and captured property.

All persons in the organization were responsible for laboring "for the common good," with prohibitions on "profane swearing, filthy conversation, indecent behavior, or indecent exposure of the person, or intoxication or quarreling" and "unlawful intercourse of the sexes" (Fogleson and Rubenstein 1969, 57). The Constitution also called for respecting "the marriage relation" (Brown's own two marriages had resulted in 20 children) and for setting aside Sunday for rest and for "moral and religious instruction and improvement, relief of the suffering, instruction of the young and ignorant, and the encouragement of personal cleanliness" (Fogleson and Rubenstein 1969, 57–58).

Article 46 of the Constitution proclaimed its intention to "amend and repeal" rather than dissolve the Union. It further specified that "our flag shall be the same that our fathers fought under in the Revolution" (Fogleson and Rubenstein 1969, 59).

Those who had signed the document elected Brown as commander in chief, but the office of president was left vacant after two black nominees both declined to serve (Oates 1970, 246).

For Further Reading:
Renehan, Edward J., Jr. 1995. *The Secret Six: The True Tale of the Men Who Conspired with John Brown.* New York: Crown.

❖ BROWN V. BOARD OF EDUCATION (1954) ❖

There are few, if any, twentieth-century cases that better demonstrate the ability of the Supreme Court to alter understandings of the Constitution—and thus provide a substitute for constitutional amendment—than this case. Here the Court overturned the doctrine of separate but equal that had been sanctioned in *Plessy v. Ferguson* (1896) and declared that segregation would have no place in U.S. public education. This opinion, in turn, sparked both support and opposition, including numerous attempts to trim the power of the Court in succeeding decades.

In delivering the unanimous opinion for the Court, Chief Justice Earl Warren recognized that the intention of those who wrote the Fourteenth Amendment could not be fully ascertained. Instead, he chose to focus on the importance of education in the modern context. Relying in part on contemporary psychological studies, Warren argued that racial segregation generated feelings of inferiority that adversely affected the motivation of minority students to learn (*Brown* 1954, 494).

A companion case, *Bolling v. Sharpe* (1954), extended the prohibition on segregation to the District of Columbia under authority of the Fifth Amendment, which, unlike the Fourteenth Amendment, applied to the national rather than the state governments. In the following year, the Court issued *Brown v. Board of Education II*, in which it declared that local school authorities, subject to the supervision of U.S. district courts, were responsible for seeing that desegregation was implemented "with all deliberate speed" (1955, 301).

Subsequent decisions involving race have led to proposed amendments dealing with affirmative action policies, state control of schools, and school busing.

See also Fourteenth Amendment; *Plessy v. Ferguson.*

For Further Reading:

Kluger, Richard. 1975. *Simple Justice: The History of Brown v. Board of Education and Black America's Struggle for Equality.* 2 vols. New York: Alfred A. Knopf.

McConnell, Michael W. 1995. "Originalism and the Desegregation Decisions." *Virginia Law Review* 81 (May): 947–1140.

Wilkinson, J. Harvie, III. 1979. *From* Brown *to* Bakke: *The Supreme Court and School Integration: 1954–1978.* New York: Oxford University Press.

❖ BUSING ❖

See School Busing.

C

❖ CABINET ❖

The president's cabinet consists of those individuals who head the major executive departments. They may also give the president advice, although most modern presidents rely more on their personal staffs for the latter function. The cabinet has grown from its original three officers—the secretary of state, secretary of treasury, and attorney general—to 14 individuals, with the latest addition of the secretary of veterans' affairs occurring in 1989. Cabinet officers are appointed by the president with the advice and consent of the Senate.

In April 1818, Democratic Representative William Lewis of Virginia introduced an amendment containing provisions whereby Congress would appoint members of the cabinet and the judiciary, with members of Congress apparently to be excluded from consideration as executive officers. Similarly, Whig Representative Joseph Underwood of Kentucky introduced a proposal in 1842 directed toward depriving the president of the power to select certain cabinet officers.

Article I, Section 6 of the U.S. Constitution prevents members of Congress from simultaneously serving as executive officers, and practice dictates that cabinet officers do not appear on the floor of Congress to answer questions. In the 1890s, Gamaliel Bradford argued for a bill introduced by Democratic Representative George H. Pendleton of Ohio to allow the former—since the practice is not forbidden by the Constitution, it would not require an amendment (G. Bradford 1891, 1893; Cobb 1922). At about the same time, Republican Representatives William Barrett and Ernest Roberts of Massachusetts introduced amendments to enable members of Congress to serve as cabinet officers, an idea that Supreme Court Justice and Harvard law professor Joseph Story had previously advocated (Story 1833, 2:333–37). Curiously, Woodrow Wilson, who had been an early advocate of parliamentary-oriented reforms, nixed an idea proposed by outgoing President William Howard Taft that would have granted cabinet officers nonvoting seats in Congress (Sundquist 1986, 51).

Allowing cabinet officers to hold dual memberships in the cabinet and in Congress would weaken separation of powers and move the United States closer to a parliamentary system of government, in which cabinet members are regularly selected from the legislature. The parliamentary model has been a favorite of those seeking wholesale reform of the U.S. Constitution (Vile 1991c, 157–58) but has also been subject to intense criticism (see Sargentich 1993). Although enabling members of Congress to serve on the cabinet might improve executive liaison with Congress, the pressures on an individual responsible for heading an executive agency and representing constituents from a district or state would be immense.

See also Parliamentary System.

❖ CALHOUN, JOHN C. ❖
(1782–1850)

Along with Henry Clay and Daniel Webster, John C. Calhoun was one of the congressional giants of the nineteenth century. Calhoun served as a member of the South Carolina legislature (1808–1809), member of the House of Representatives (1811–1817), secretary of war (1817–1825), vice president (1825–1832), secretary of state (1844–1845), and senator from South Carolina (1832–1844, 1845–1850).

In addition to defending slavery as a positive good, Calhoun was among the South's strongest advocates of the doctrines of nullification and secession, which eventually led to disunion and civil war. In Calhoun's *Disquisition on Government*, he outlined his theory of concurrent majorities, which, in contrast to a system built simply on numerical majorities, was intended to provide each major interest or portion of the community with "a concurrent voice in making and executing the laws or a veto on their execution" (1953, 20). Calhoun's central concern was protection of regional interests, particularly slavery. But others have noted that the principle could be extended to others, indeed, even to racial minorities (Kuic 1983).

In his *Discourse on the Constitution and Government of the United States*, Calhoun lavishly praised the constitutional amending process, calling it the *"vis medicatrix* of the system" (1852–1856, 295) and describing it (somewhat counter to James Madison's description in *The Federalist Papers*) as a purely federal mechanism that embodied Calhoun's own view of concurrent majorities. Calhoun also gave the amending process a critical role in his theory of nullification, which would have entrusted states with the power to challenge federal legislation. On occasions when a state questioned the legitimacy of federal power, Calhoun called upon the majority exercising such disputed power to validate its view by adopting a constitutional amendment. Even here, however, Calhoun appeared to reserve the states' right to challenge amendments that exceeded implicit limits on the constitutional amending process (Vile 1992, 86).

During the nullification crisis of the 1820s and early 1830s, in which Calhoun opposed higher federal tariffs and challenged President Andrew Jackson's assertion of federal authority, Calhoun advocated calling a constitutional convention to resolve the controversy. It would appear that he anticipated a body whose power "was much broader than that actually set forth in the exact language of the amending article" (Pullen 1948, 45).

Late in life, Calhoun came to fear that the amending process might be used, as it later would be in the Thirteenth Amendment, to abolish the institution of slavery, which he had defended. Accordingly, in his *Discourse*, Calhoun advocated creating a dual executive representing the North and the South, with each executive required to approve acts of congressional legislation before they became law (1852–1856, 392). Ironically, the very amending supermajorities that Calhoun praised were an obstacle to such a proposal.

A series of proposals introduced by Ohio's Democratic Representative Clement Vallandigham in February 1861 and apparently designed to forestall war appear to share features of Calhoun's thinking. One part of this proposal would have divided the nation into four sections, and another would have required a majority from all sections if a vote was so demanded by one-third or more of the senators.

For Further Reading:

Coit, Margaret L. 1961. *John C. Calhoun: American Portrait.* Boston: Houghton Mifflin.

Niven, John. 1988. *John C. Calhoun and the Price of Union: A Biography.* Baton Rouge: Louisiana State University Press.

❖ CAMPAIGN CONTRIBUTIONS AND EXPENDITURES ❖

Members of Congress introduced a number of amendments calling for congressional regulation of campaign contributions and expenditures in the 1920s. A proposal introduced by Democrat Thomas Rubey of Missouri in 1926 demonstrates the difficulty of overly specific regulation in this ever-changing area. It would have excluded from office senators who had knowingly authorized the expenditure of more than $10,000 or representatives who had authorized more than $5,000 for their nomination and election (H.J. Res. 279).

A number of laws regulating campaign contributions and expenditures have subsequently been introduced in Congress in the 1970s, 1980s, and 1990s. Such laws typically call for limits on contributions or campaign expenditures or disclosures of contributions made by individuals or political action committees. The Supreme Court examined provisions of the Federal Election Campaign Act of 1971 (subsequently amended in 1974) in *Buckley v. Valeo* (1976). In this case, the Court upheld congressionally imposed requirements for disclosure of campaign contributions as well as limits on the amount of money that an individual could contribute to another's campaign. The Court, however, struck down limits on the moneys that individuals such as Ross Perot and Steve Forbes could contribute to their own campaigns as well as congressionally imposed limits on overall spending. The Court did accept limits on the spending of presidential candidates who had voluntarily accepted such campaign limits in exchange for public funding. The Court ruled that other limits on personal expenditures or campaign spending interfered with free speech rights guaranteed under the First Amendment.

The 1980s and 1990s brought a number of new proposals for constitutional amendments permitting either state or congressional regulation in this area. Some such proposals seem directly aimed at *Buckley v. Valeo*. Thus a House Joint Resolution (No. 11) introduced in 1991 specified that campaign expenditures are not to be considered a form of protected speech under the First Amendment.

There is frequent criticism of the rising costs of political campaigns, the need for officeholders to engage in constant fund-raising, and the possibility that officeholders are improperly influenced by campaign contributions. Still, previous legislation in this area has often spawned loopholes and proved ineffective. Moreover, expenditure limits might give further advantage to incumbents, who already have significant advantages when running for reelection. Major reforms appear unlikely in the absence of a major scandal or catastrophe or firm control of the government by a party committed to such reform (Sorauf 1988, 382–88).

For Further Reading:

Alexander, Herbert E. 1992. *Financing Politics: Money, Elections and Political Reform*, 4th ed. Washington, DC: Congressional Quarterly Press.

Limitations of Expenditures in Elections. 18 February 1990. Printed Hearings. Senate.

Regulation of Contributions and Expenditures in Elections. 17 March 1988. Printed Hearings.

❖ CAPITAL PUNISHMENT ❖

The issue of governmentally imposed death penalties is a highly emotional one. Individual attitudes are likely to be shaped by fundamental moral values, by assessments of the deterrent value of such punishments, and by judgments as to whether the death penalty impacts certain groups in a discriminatory fashion.

The Fifth and Fourteenth Amendments specify that no person shall be "deprived of life, liberty, or property, without due process of law." Taken together with the Fifth Amendment requirement of a grand jury in cases of "capital" crimes, such evidence is fairly conclusive that the American founders did not intend to outlaw the death penalty. Still, like other punishments, the death penalty is subject to the provision in the Eighth Amendment against "cruel and unusual punishments." Moreover, some scholars believe that the Eighth Amendment ought to be interpreted in light of evolving moral standards that, throughout most of the world, have led to the abolition of the death penalty (see 1963 opinion of Justice Goldberg in D. O'Brien 1995, 1106–9). Still, despite massive efforts to overturn the death penalty (Epstein and Klobylka 1992), prior to 1968, the Supreme Court had never invalidated a death penalty on such grounds (White 1991, 4).

The first proposed constitutional change in the death penalty appears to have been in 1901, when Pennsylvania Republican Congressman Henry Cassel proposed the penalty for destruction of U.S. property; he also proposed deportation or lifetime imprisonment for members of anarchical societies. In the 1940s, Democratic Representative Walter Huber proposed abolishing the death penalty for all crimes other than treason. New York Representative Adam Clayton Powell proposed abolition of the death penalty in 1961, and his proposal was followed later in the decade by a number of others.

By far the largest number of amendments proposed in relation to capital punishment have called for permitting states to impose this penalty. Some proposals have also called for a federal death penalty in cases of treason or air piracy. Most proposals in favor of the death penalty appear to have been prompted by the Supreme Court's decision in *Furman v. Georgia* (1972). In that case, the Court decided that the death penalty, as then administered, was too arbitrary and hence unconstitutional. States rushed to adopt new laws.

By the time the Court rendered its next significant decision on the death penalty in *Gregg v. Georgia* (1976), 35 states had passed death penalty laws, and Congress had adopted such a penalty for cases of air piracy. In *Gregg,* the Court upheld the validity of the death penalty in cases in which there was a bifurcated trial that separated the decision on guilt or innocence from the decision on a penalty and when aggravating and mitigating circumstances were considered. In a companion case, *Woodson v. North Carolina*, the Court reversed a mandatory death penalty for first-degree murder cases.

The death penalty appears to be enjoying increased popular support, and it has figured prominently in a number of recent political campaigns (White 1991, 24). The Court continues to hear cases involving the degree of discretion to be awarded to juries in death penalty cases and the number of appeals that defendants may file in such cases. Few justices appear inclined to accept the views advocated by former Justices Thurgood Marshall, William Brennan, and Harry Blackmun that such a penalty is necessarily in violation of the cruel and unusual punishment clause.

In recent years, Representative Henry Gonzalez, a Mexican American Democrat representing the San Antonio, Texas, area (Barone and Ujifusa 1993, 1257–59), has reintroduced amendments designed to abolish the death penalty. The chances of such an amendment being adopted in the near future appear to be quite dim.

See also Eighth Amendment.

For Further Reading:
Meltsner, Michael. 1974. *Cruel and Unusual: The Supreme Court and Capital Punishment.* New York: William Morrow.

❖ CASCOT SYSTEM FOR SOCIAL ❖ CONTROL OF TECHNOLOGY

In 1970, P. G. Marduke (otherwise unidentified) published a hand-typed brochure entitled *The CASCOT System for Social Control of Technology*. Marduke's premise was that although many individuals feared technology, it could actually be a potent force for change at a time when the world was in crisis and greater democratic participation was desirable. Marduke devoted separate chapters to different areas of concern.

Marduke proposed that the political system be changed from a "system of 'power politics' to a system of 'people politics'" (Marduke 1970, 37). One specific proposal was the initiation of a system of Touch-Tone voting whereby citizens could vote on pending legislation. Marduke also advocated abolishing the Senate, with its malapportionment, and granting public officials "a life time salary" while prohibiting all other income and investment (Marduke 1970, 43). Marduke proposed conducting nominations by telephone computer system, requiring that the media give candidates opportunity to talk to the public, and limiting campaign spending to a fixed amount of money. Marduke also favored the elimination of independent regulatory agencies and an expansion of the congressional representative's role as ombudsman. Marduke would replace the presidency with an elected National Council of five officials, each heading an agency (international affairs, environment, commerce, public welfare, and administration) consisting of five persons, each, in turn, responsible for a single technical area.

Considering the existing economic system to be seriously flawed, Marduke proposed a number of far-reaching changes also based on the application of modern technology, including replacing the system of currency with electronic transactions, recording all capital assets over $25 in value,

imposing limits on individual net worth as well as a minimum below which no one should be permitted to fall, and redistributing wealth according to public vote. The system would also be designed to provide "whatever amount of credit the people wanted" (Marduke 1970, 70–71).

In the area of health care, Marduke favored establishing parallel public and private health systems. In defense matters, Marduke advocated hiring a network of foreign agents pledged to stop their nations from "the first use of atomic, biochemical or other mass-murder weaponry" (Marduke 1970, 94). The ultimate goal was a "cosmopolitan system where people, not nations or institutions, are the essential ingredients" (Marduke 1970, 95). In a chapter on international relations, Marduke thus proposed opening the doors "to any and every other nation that cares to enter the system" (Marduke 1970, 98). This would involve the sharing of economic resources as well as political ideals and would begin with pressure exerted by refusing to import goods from foreign nations.

In analyzing sex and morals, Marduke worked from the premise that "sex is fun" (Marduke 1970, 105) and argued that technological advances made traditional prohibitions against premarital sex outdated. Marduke favored the establishment of a fairly permissive "code for what is legally and morally prohibited," as well as a nonbinding code for "what is socially encouraged and discouraged" (Marduke 1970, 110). The latter would involve polling the public on attitudes about "dating, drinking and drugs; fashion, fads and fornication" (Marduke 1970, 111). Marduke further suggested a "random-sample-censorship" for media productions (Marduke 1970, 112) and the establishment of social centers to distribute drugs to addicts.

In order to deal with environmental problems, Marduke advocated the creation of mass-transit systems. Marduke also advocated banning all chemicals "applied to soil or vegetation for any purpose" (Marduke 1970, 126), creating sewage treatment plants in every city, ending offshore oil drilling, declaring minerals to be the property of all people, and making birth control available on a voluntary basis, with the possibility of a compulsory system if this did not work.

Marduke wanted to replace the existing welfare system with social centers for mass feeding and care. Marduke also advocated the establishment of more extensive consumer education and examinations for people in the repair business. Marduke favored extensive educational reform. Education would be divided into four levels, with the first levels oriented toward practical training and consumer education.

Marduke criticized the legal system for preoccupation with money and favored devising a legal system with three levels consisting of a public arbitrator, three-person investigatory boards, and an appeals investigatory board. Criminal sanctions would be designed not to punish but to motivate better behavior or to isolate the criminal from society.

Clearly, Marduke's proposals called for extensive change involving not only the Constitution but the entire social structure. Accordingly, Marduke recognized that "the most difficult problem will be to keep the change on an evolutionary, rather than a revolutionary scale" (Marduke 1970, 163). Marduke hoped to run CASCOT candidates in the 1972 elections. Senatorial candidates would be pledged to abolish that institution. Marduke also favored modifying the amending process sometime before 1980 so that a majority of the House could propose amendments to be approved by popular majorities. That change would be followed by "the chain of amendments necessary to establish the popular voting system and the economic system and the form of government that can effectively deal with

the world's crisis" (Marduke 1970, 170). Despite such hopes, Marduke's proposals appear to have had little impact.

❖ CATT, CARRIE LANE CHAPMAN ❖ (1859–1947)

Carrie Lane Chapman Catt was a former teacher and school superintendent who survived the deaths of two husbands and was a major force in the second generation of leadership in the movement for women's suffrage. This movement culminated in the ratification of the Nineteenth Amendment.

In 1889, Catt was elected secretary of the Iowa Woman Suffrage Association; in 1895, she was chair of the National Organization Committee of the National American Woman Suffrage Association (NAWSA); and in 1900, she succeeded Susan B. Anthony as president of that organization, serving until 1904. She also served as president from 1915 to 1920, when the Nineteenth Amendment (also called the Susan B. Anthony amendment) was ratified. Catt was a strong organizer with a determined "faith in God's eternal law for the evolution of the race" (quoted in Fowler 1986, 57). Before her reelection as NAWSA president, Catt was active in the International Woman Suffrage Alliance as well as in the New York State Woman Suffrage Party. Catt's decision as NAWSA president "to concentrate on a constitutional amendment rather than proceeding state by state" (Fowler 1986, 30)— as many southern suffragette advocates who favored states' rights wanted (see Wheeler 1993)—is often credited with resulting in the ratification of the Anthony amendment.

After adoption of the Nineteenth Amendment, Catt continued to be active in a number of concerns, including the League of Women Voters, which she founded in 1920, and several organizations devoted to world peace. Catt also helped organize the Woman's Centennial Congress of 1940.

See also Anthony, Susan Brownell; Nineteenth Amendment.

❖ CHANDLER V. WISE (1939) ❖

Chandler v. Wise was a companion case to *Coleman v. Miller* (1939). Taxpayers, citizens, and voters had challenged Kentucky's ratification of the child labor amendment. They argued that it should be voided because of its prior rejection by the legislature and a majority of other states and because it had not been ratified within a reasonable time, a requirement seemingly mandated in *Dillon v. Gloss* (1921). They sought a court order requiring that the state governor, who had certified and forwarded the amendment before becoming aware of the suit, notify the secretary of state that Kentucky's ratification was invalid.

The Court rejected this request by a 7-to-2 decision written by Chief Justice Hughes, with Justices Black and Douglas concurring and Justices McReynolds and Butler dissenting. Consistent with the decision in *Coleman v. Miller,* the majority decided that "after the Governor of Kentucky had forwarded the certification of the ratification of the amendment to the Secretary of State of the United States there was no longer a controversy susceptible of judicial determination" (Chandler 1939, 477–78).

See also *Coleman v. Miller;* Child Labor Amendment.

❖ CHILD LABOR AMENDMENT ❖

Throughout history, children have engaged in labor. Industrialization and the accompanying rise of manufacturing and mining, however, created situations in which children often worked long hours in hazardous and unhealthy circumstances without parental supervision and protection and in circumstances that precluded adequate time

for them to receive an education. By 1900, "one child in six between the age of ten and fifteen was gainfully employed, and there were more than 1,750,000 child laborers in America" (S. Wood 1968, 3). Many of the reform organizations associated with the Progressive movement coalesced around opposition to child labor; the most effective organization, the National Child Labor Committee (NCLC), was established in April 1904.

Initially, this committee and other organizations focused on reform at the state level, but despite successes in many states, the resulting legislation was not uniform and was especially weak in the South. There, children were frequently employed in the textile industry, and weaker regulations depressed adult wages and gave southern manufacturers a labor advantage. By 1912, the NCLC had concluded that national legislation was needed. A number of Supreme Court decisions, among them *Champion v. Ames* (a 1903 case upholding congressional powers to regulate interstate transportation of lottery tickets), suggested that such powers were within congressional authority. There was at least one proposal introduced in Congress in 1914 to proceed instead by constitutional amendment.

In 1916, Congress passed the Keating-Owen bill, attempting to discourage child labor by prohibiting for 30 days the interstate transportation of goods made by companies employing children under the age of 14 or violating standards set for the employment of children between ages 14 and 16. President Woodrow Wilson reconsidered his earlier constitutional reservations and encouraged the passage of and signed this bill, which has been described as "the crowning achievement of progressivism" (S. Wood 1968, 78).

Progressive hopes were dashed in *Hammer v. Dagenhart* (1918) when the Supreme Court declared in a 5-to-4 decision written by Justice William Rufus Day that the Keating Owen bill violated the Fifth and Fourteenth Amendments. With reasoning called into serious question by Justice Oliver Wendell Holmes's vigorous dissenting opinion, Day attempted to distinguish between the congressional regulation of items that were in themselves harmful and the regulation of those that were not. The Court also viewed the law as an unconstitutional regulation of manufacturing rather than a legitimate exercise of commerce power. The decision has been called "a breach—not a temporary breach—in constitutional interpretation that signaled return, for almost a generation, to conservative jurisprudence" (S. Wood 1968, 182).

Although several congressmen proposed a constitutional amendment to reverse this decision, a majority settled instead on an amendment to the Revenue Act of 1919 that leveled a 10 percent tax on goods produced by child labor. In an 8-to-1 decision written by Chief Justice Taft (*Bailey v. Drexel Furniture Company* [1922]), the Court subsequently struck down that law too, arguing that the provisions were designed as a penalty rather than a tax and that they unfairly impinged on state police powers in violation of federal principles, especially the Tenth Amendment.

In response, Congress proposed the child labor amendment in 1924 by a vote of 197 to 69 in the House and 61 to 23 in the Senate. Omitting references to women, which some proposals had included, it read as follows:

Section 1. The Congress shall have power to limit, regulate, and prohibit the labor of persons under 18 years of age.

Section 2. The power of the several States is unimpaired by this article except that the operation of state laws shall be suspended to the extent necessary to give effect to legislation en-

acted by this Congress. (Grimes 1978, 102)

By 1924, however, Progressive sentiment was waning, and there was widespread disappointment with the Eighteenth Amendment's attempt to enact national alcoholic prohibition; the proposed child labor amendment also faced strong opposition. In what one scholar identified as "an instructive, almost eerie, parallel with the ERA [equal right amendment]" (Mansbridge 1986, 31), this waning commitment to reform was combined with concerns as diverse as states' rights, parental control over children, the rights of private religious schools, and communist influence. Such fears were fanned by opposition groups such as the American Bar Association, the Sentinels of the Republic, a publication known as *Woman Patriot,* which had previously opposed women's suffrage, the *Southern Textile Bulletin* edited by David Clark, and southern industrial leaders (Trattner 1970, 170–74).

As 1925 ended, only four states had ratified and 19 had rejected the proposed amendment (Grimes 1978, 103). The tide seemed to turn with the coming of the New Deal. A number of states that had previously rejected the amendment now reversed themselves, an action that was challenged in the courts. In *Coleman v. Miller* (1939) the Supreme Court ruled that the validity of such appeals, as well as the issue of whether they had come within a reasonable time, were "political questions" for Congress to resolve. Eventually, 28 states ratified the amendment.

In the meantime, child labor provisions were incorporated in regulations adopted through the National Industrial Recovery Act, a law subsequently invalidated in the 1935 decision in *Schechter Poultry Corp. v. United States* (Trattner 1970, 190–200). Child labor provisions were subsequently added to the Fair Labor Standards Act of

1938 and were upheld in *United States v. Darby* (1941), when the Supreme Court explicitly overturned *Hammer v. Dagenhart* and declared that it would no longer be bound by earlier restrictive interpretations of the Fifth and Tenth Amendments. As an amendment issue, child labor has subsequently been moot.

For Further Reading:

Davidson, Elizabeth H. 1939. *Child Labor Legislation in the Southern Textile States.* Chapel Hill: University of North Carolina Press.

Freedman, Russell. 1994. *Lewis Hine and the Crusade against Child Labor.* New York: Clarion Books.

Report on the Condition of Women and Child Wage Earners. 1910–1913. U.S. Department of Labor. 19 vols. Washington, DC: U.S. Government Printing Office.

❖ CHISHOLM V. GEORGIA (1793) ❖

One of the most important cases of the pre-Marshall Court, this was also the first decision overturned by an amendment, in this case the Eleventh. At issue was whether a citizen of another state—here, the executor of the estate of a Charleston, South Carolina, merchant from whom Georgia had purchased supplies in 1777 but whom it had not paid—could sue a state without its consent. Asserting state sovereignty, Georgia refused even to argue its case.

The decision was a seriatim decision in which all the justices (Blair, Wilson, Cushing, and Jay) except Iredell agreed. The majority decided that, under the general principles and structures of the Constitution and the specific language of Article III (which extended judicial power to controversies "between a State and Citizens of another State"), a state was subject, both as a defendant and as a plaintiff, to federal judicial jurisdiction. Justice Wilson's opinion was an especially far-reaching discussion of how the U.S. Constitution recognized the

people, rather than rulers or governments, as sovereign. However, the Court's ruling contradicted explicit assurances that Federalists had given to Anti-Federalists during debates over the ratification of the Constitution (Mason and Stevenson 1993, 157).

Although not dealing directly with the constitutionality of a federal law, this case clearly anticipated the exercise of judicial review prior to John Marshall's decision in *Marbury v. Madison* (1803). Justice Iredell thus noted that an act of Congress exceeding constitutional authority would be void "because it would be inconsistent with the Constitution, which is a fundamental law paramount to all others, which we are not only bound to consult but sworn to observe" (1793, 433).

Justice Cushing seemed to anticipate, if not invite, an amendment when he noted that "if the Constitution is found inconvenient in practice in this or any other particular, it is well that a regular mode is pointed out for amendment" (1793, 468).

See also Eleventh Amendment.

For Further Reading:

Mathis, Doyle. 1967. "Chisholm v. Georgia: Background and Settlement." *Journal of American History* 54:19–29.

❖ CHRISTIAN AMENDMENT ❖

Unless one counts the reference to "the Year of our Lord one thousand seven hundred and eighty seven" that is sometimes appended to Article VII of the U.S. Constitution, the document contains no direct reference to God. The Reformed Presbyterian Church, whose roots were in the Scottish Covenant tradition, considered the absence of such a reference to, and acknowledgment of, God to be a fatal flaw. Members of this denomination accordingly refused to participate in voting or holding office. Some members participated in the War of 1812, however, and a group of "New Side" Reformers (who believed that they should support the government under the Constitution) eventually split from the "Old Side" Reformers in 1833. The Reformed Presbyterian Church remained a small denomination, and it does not appear to have significantly influenced public opinion in the nation's early years.

As the controversy over slavery developed and intensified, however, many abolitionists also began to denounce the Constitution as a flawed document. Although abolitionists typically regarded the Constitution's acquiescence in slavery rather than its failure to acknowledge God as its fatal weakness, the two critiques often merged. Reformed Presbyterians viewed the Constitution's acquiescence in slavery as a logical consequence of its failure to acknowledge the Almighty.

Ironically, when the Confederate states drafted their constitution, they rewrote their preamble specifically to invoke "the favor and guidance of Almighty God" (DeRosa 1991, 135). For their part, in 1859, the Reformed Presbyterians had passed their first resolution specifically calling on the Union to acknowledge God. Typical of many subsequent proposals, their amendment called for:

1. An express acknowledgment of the being and authority of God. 2. An acknowledgment of submission to the authority of Christ. 3. That it should recognize the paramount obligation of God's law, contained in the Scriptures of the Old and New Testaments. 4. That it may be rendered, in all its principles and provisions, clearly and unmistakably adverse to the existence of any form of slavery within the national limits. (Jacoby 1984, 55–56)

In February 1863, a convention composed of members of a number of religious denominations met in Xenia, Ohio. It supported a proposal by Presbyterian layman John Alexander for a constitutional amendment to acknowledge "the rulership of Jesus Christ and the supremacy of the divine law" (Borden 1979, 159). The National Association To Secure the Religious Amendment of the Constitution subsequently chose Alexander as its first president. The *Christian Statesman* was the official journal of this organization, which was later renamed the National Reform Association. One of the association's most prominent members was Judge William Strong, who later served on the High Court from 1870 to 1880.

The National Reform Association held conventions, presented petitions, published and distributed literature, and otherwise pressed for an amendment. The association received a diplomatic but noncommittal reply when it met with President Lincoln in February 1864. The association's mission appears to have been aided both by the soul-searching that the Civil War occasioned and by Lincoln's use of religious concepts in explaining and justifying the war.

The movement for a Christian amendment had its greatest prominence in the period from 1872 to 1875. One historian noted that during this time there were "a striking number of conflicts which raised fears that the historic Protestant basis of American society and government was being lost" (Jacoby 1984, 290). The period was also notable for support for the Blaine amendment, which would have prohibited state aid to parochial schools, often administered by and associated with Roman Catholics.

In 1876, proponents of the Christian amendment presented petitions with over 35,000 signatures to the House of Representatives. In that same year, the National Reform Association succeeded in keeping the Centennial Exposition from opening on Sunday. By then, however, the association faced increasing opposition from individuals who feared that an amendment recognizing God or Jesus might undermine the liberty of non-Christians and nonbelievers that was guaranteed by the establishment clause of the First Amendment. The association also appears to have somewhat diluted its own effectiveness by endorsing other causes with Christian backing, including the rising temperance movement that eventually resulted in the adoption of the Eighteenth Amendment.

Since 1947, there have been more than 55 proposals in Congress for variations of the Christian amendment. Sponsors have included Republican congressman, and later independent candidate for president in 1980, John Anderson. Modern proposals may have been stimulated in part by contemporary Supreme Court decisions relative to prayer and Bible reading in the public schools, but there have been far more calls for amendments specifically designed to reverse these decisions than to recognize God in the Constitution.

The National Reform Association dissolved in 1945, but the National Association of Evangelicals (NAE) subsequently took up its cause. The NAE supported an amendment under which "this nation devoutly recognizes the authority and law of Jesus Christ, Savior and Ruler of all nations, through whom are bestowed the blessings of Almighty God" (Borden 1979, 167). The NAE now supports a version of the religious equality amendment that mentions God but is chiefly concerned with guaranteeing religious liberty.

See also Blaine Amendment.

For Further Reading:

Handy, Robert T. 1971. *A Christian America: Protestant Hopes and Historical Realities.* New York: Oxford University Press.

Kramnick, Isaac, and R. Laurence Moore. 1996. *The Godless Constitution: The Case against Religious Correctness.* New York: W. W. Norton.

Morton, Robert K. 1933. *God in the Constitution.* Nashville, TN: Cokesbury Press.

❖ CITIZENS, TEACHING OF DEROGATORY MATERIAL TO ❖

In 1943 and 1945, Democratic Representative Horace Voorhis of California introduced amendments that would prohibit the teaching of derogatory materials to citizens of the United States. Voorhis had been a member of the Dies Committee on Un-American Activities, but his appointment had come after he expressed opposition to what he considered to be improper investigatory and accusatory tactics that the committee was utilizing (Voorhis 1947, 207–31). Moreover, both on the committee and throughout his service in Congress, his was generally a liberal voice. Voorhis lost the election of 1946 to Richard Nixon, who campaigned against Voorhis's alleged liberalism.

❖ CITIZENSHIP, DEFINITION OF ❖

Although the Constitution of 1787 refers to citizens in a number of places (in specifying qualifications for officeholders, for example), nowhere does it specifically define such citizenship. This omission enabled Chief Justice Roger Taney to argue in *Scott v. Sandford* (1857) that blacks were not and could not be citizens and thus had no right to appear in U.S. courts.

Democratic Representative Thomas Florence of Pennsylvania (1861) and Whig Senator Garrett Davis of Kentucky (1864) were subsequently unsuccessful in trying to have Taney's understanding explicitly written into the Constitution. Instead, the first sentence of the Fourteenth Amendment overturned *Scott* and extended citizenship to "all persons born or naturalized in the United States and subject to the jurisdiction thereof."

In *United States v. Wong Kim Ark* (1898), the Supreme Court decided that citizenship extended to children born in the United States to parents who were Chinese citizens. Only children born to diplomatic personnel in the United States, children born to foreigners during hostile occupations, or Indians subject to tribal governance were considered exempt from U.S. jurisdiction and citizenship. Citizenship has subsequently been referred to as a qualification for voting in the Fifteenth, Nineteenth, Twenty-fourth, and Twenty-sixth Amendments, although state laws rather than provisions of the U.S. Constitution currently bar aliens from the franchise. Advocates of the birthright citizenship amendment would deny citizenship to persons born in the United States of mothers who were not legal aliens.

Justice Harry Blackmun's decision in *Roe v. Wade* (1973) voiding most state abortion regulations rested in part on the view that *citizenship* as used in the Fourteenth Amendment and elsewhere in the Constitution refers only to postnatal life. This decision has prompted numerous calls for a right to life amendment.

A number of proposed amendments related to qualifications for the presidency have sought to repeal the provision in Article II, Section 1 of the U.S. Constitution that limits the presidency to "natural born" citizens.

See also Birthright Citizenship Amendment; Fourteenth Amendment.

❖ CITIZENSHIP, DUAL ❖

In September 1942, in conjunction with a bill to limit anticipated immigration from Europe following the end of World War II, Republican Senator Rufus Holman of Oregon, chair of an ad hoc Committee on Defense (Irons 1983, 51), introduced a resolution that was intended to grant Congress the power to prohibit dual citizenship (S.J. Res. 163). In his speech before the Senate (see 98 *Congressional Record* 7193–94 [1942]), Holman referred specifically to

Japanese Americans, some of whom held joint citizenship in the United States and Japan. Such dual citizenship arose from the fact that, in addition to the principle of *jus soli* (law of the soil), Japan applied the doctrine of *jus sanguinis* (law of the blood). This latter principle allowed people born abroad of Japanese nationals to maintain joint citizenship—citizenship that could, however, be renounced and did not apply to Japanese born in the United States after 1925 (see Justice Murphy's dissenting opinion, *Korematsu* [1944], n.4, 237).

Such dual citizenship contributed to suspicions that Japanese Americans constituted a disloyal "fifth column." Such fears were used in *Hirabayashi v. United States* (1943) and *Korematsu v. United States* (1944) to justify curfews for Japanese Americans and their exclusion from certain areas of the West Coast. This exclusion was accompanied by an executive order detaining some 112,000 Japanese American citizens in camps during World War II.

For Further Reading:

Irons, Peter, ed. 1989. *Justice Delayed: The Record of the Japanese Internment Cases*. Middletown, CT: Wesleyan University Press.

Smith, Page. 1995. *Democracy on Trial: The Japanese American Evacuation and Relocation in World War II*. New York: Simon & Schuster.

❖ CITIZENSHIP, LOSS OF ❖

The Constitution provided no definition of national citizenship prior to the Fourteenth Amendment. This did not stop Congress from proposing an amendment in 1810 that would have provided that a person would "cease to be a citizen" upon accepting, without congressional approval, "any title of nobility or honour . . . from any emperor, king, prince, or foreign power" (Anastaplo 1989, 298–99). The origins of this amendment relative to titles of nobility are obscure, and it fell a single state shy of ratification. If it had been adopted, it would have provided a sanction for a similar provision already in Article I, Section 9 of the Constitution.

In *Trop v. Dulles* (1958), the Supreme Court struck down as "cruel and unusual punishment" the application of a law providing for forfeiture of citizenship to a native-born American who had deserted during a time of war. On the same day, however, in *Perez v. Brownell* (1958), the Supreme Court, in a 5-to-4 vote, upheld a provision of the Nationality Act of 1940 whereby Congress provided that individuals voting in foreign elections would forfeit their citizenship. The Court saw this as a reasonable exercise of power under congressional authority to regulate foreign affairs.

In *Afroyim v. Rusk* (1967), the Court reversed itself in another 5-to-4 decision and ruled that the Fourteenth Amendment protected against loss of citizenship except by voluntary renunciation. Several members of Congress subsequently proposed amendments from 1967 through 1969 that would have given Congress authority to provide by law for loss of nationality and citizenship.

See also Titles of Nobility.

For Further Reading:
Gordon, Charles. 1982. "The Power of Congress To Terminate United States Citizenship." *Connecticut Law Review* 4 (Spring): 611–32.

CITIZENSHIP,
❖ OFFICEHOLDING RIGHTS ❖

New York's state ratifying convention proposed a resolution, never introduced in Congress, that would have excluded nonnative-born citizens not only from the presidency and vice presidency but also from Congress (Ames 1896, 74). Northeastern Federalists reintroduced this idea during debates over the Alien and Sedition Acts (Kuroda 1994, 109), at which time many

immigrants were more sympathetic to the Democratic Republican Party. Federalists introduced similar proposals during the War of 1812.

See also Presidency, Qualifications for.

❖ CIVIL RIGHTS CASES ❖

The Supreme Court's 8-to-1 decision in the *Civil Rights* cases (1883) was one of its most important nineteenth-century decisions with respect to the interpretation of the Thirteenth and Fourteenth Amendments. At issue was the constitutionality of the Civil Rights Act of 1875, a law that attempted to guarantee equal access to public accommodations without respect to race.

In his opinion for the Court, Justice Joseph P. Bradley struck down this law on the basis that Section 1 of the Fourteenth Amendment, providing that "no state shall" deny specified individual rights, did not give Congress the power to interfere with actions of private individuals that had the same effect. As he summarized the purposes of the amendment: "It does not authorize Congress to create a code of municipal law for the regulation of private rights; but to provide modes of redress against the operation of state laws, and the action of state officers executive or judicial, when these are subversive of the fundamental rights specified in the Amendment." Bradley further denied that discrimination by private individuals constituted a "badge of servitude" prohibited by the Thirteenth Amendment.

In his dissenting opinion, Justice John Marshall Harlan accused the Court of giving "too narrow and artificial" a reading to the Thirteenth and Fourteenth Amendments. He pointed out that Congress had, in the Civil Rights Act of 1866, exercised similar power under authority of the Thirteenth Amendment. He argued that places of public accommodation ceased to be merely private but were clothed with a public interest.

Moreover, rather than reading the Thirteenth and Fourteenth Amendments simply as negative prohibitions, Harlan argued (with particular emphasis on the definition of citizenship in Section 1 of the Fourteenth Amendment and the enforcement provisions of both amendments) that they were intended to be positive grants of power to government to protect individual rights. Not only did Harlan's arguments lose in this case, but in *Plessy v. Ferguson* (1896), the Supreme Court subsequently upheld state-sanctioned racial discrimination.

The Court's distinction between state action and private action has never been repudiated. Largely as a consequence, when Congress adopted the Civil Rights Act of 1964 outlawing discrimination in places of public accommodation, it relied primarily on its power to regulate commerce between the states. The Supreme Court upheld its authority under this provision in *Heart of Atlanta Motel v. United States* (1964) and *Katzenbach v. McClung* (1964).

See also Fourteenth Amendment.

❖ CIVIL SERVICE REFORM ❖

Although the Constitution mentions a number of appointed offices (members of the cabinet and the courts, for example), nowhere does it detail requirements for lesser officeholders. The so-called spoils system allowed an incoming administration to dismiss such appointed officials and replace them with its own supporters. Such a system was especially associated with the administration of President Andrew Jackson and helped both to keep government fairly responsive to public opinion and to undercut earlier notions that an office was a form of property.

The growth of government during the Civil War led to increasing concern about the corruption and incompetence that sometimes accompanied a system of personal appointment. Several proposed amendments calling for civil service reform were introduced in the 1870s, but legislative action eventually proved effective with the passage of the Pendleton Act in 1883. This act created a system whereby candidates for government jobs qualified by fulfilling objective criteria of employment and taking competitive examinations. Reaction to the assassination of President James Garfield by a disappointed office seeker helped generate support for this act (Rosenbloom 1971, 80).

Initially covering about 10 percent of the federal civilian workforce, today the civil service system applies to about 90 percent. In 1935, an amendment was proposed to establish the civil service merit principle more firmly in the federal government (H.J. Res. 378), but the prior history of civil service reform suggests that if this reform is desirable, it can be accomplished through regular legislative action.

For Further Reading:
Van Riper, Paul P. 1958. *History of the United States Civil Service*. Evanston, IL: Row, Peterson.

❖ CLAIMS AGAINST THE UNITED STATES ❖

Despite the doctrine of sovereign immunity (whereby a sovereign cannot be sued), Congress designates certain classes of cases that can be brought against the government. Since 1855, most of these cases have been heard by the U.S. Court of Claims, which was redesignated in 1982 as the U.S. Claims Court. This court relieves Congress of passing special bills to deal with such matters (Abraham 1993, 150).

After the Civil War, there were 16 proposed amendments to limit claims resulting from the war, most of which sought to deny claims by those who had been disloyal to the Union. One such proposal received a favorable vote of 145 to 61 in the House of Representatives in 1878 but was not voted on in the Senate. Several proposals would have provided a time limit within which war claims could be filed (Ames 1896, 248). On three occasions between 1905 and 1907, Republican Representative Joseph Keifer of Ohio introduced amending resolutions that would have enlarged the power of the Court of Claims and limited Congress to appropriating money for claims settled by this or other authorized commissions (Musmanno 1929, 151–52).

As of 1982, appeals from the U.S. Court of Claims are heard by the U.S. Court of Appeals for the Federal Circuit. It is considered a legislative court created under Article I of the Constitution rather than an Article III constitutional tribunal; judgments of this court are still subject to review by the Supreme Court.

❖ CLARK, WALTER (1846–1924) ❖

Walter Clark, then chief justice of the North Carolina Supreme Court, presented a speech later published as part of his papers (1906), in which he advocated a number of constitutional changes. These proposals reflected his perspective as a progressive Democrat who believed that the Constitution had been a conservative reaction to a more democratic beginning symbolized by the Declaration of Independence (for critique see Smith 1906). Almost all of Clark's proposals, at least one of which he thought would require a constitutional convention, were aimed at increasing the power of the people and reducing the power of plutocrats who he believed exerted control through their selection of federal judges and senators.

Two of Clark's proposals were eventually achieved by constitutional amendments. One, effected by the Seventeenth Amendment, called for direct election of the Sen-

ate. Another, later effected by the Twentieth Amendment, was to change the inaugurate dates to reduce the lame duck sessions of Congress.

None of Clark's other proposals have yet been adopted. One such proposal—made without reference to the Article V entrenchment clause which appears to make such a change impossible absent state consent—called for eliminating the equality of state representation in the Senate and granting each state one senator for each million inhabitants or fraction thereof over three-quarters of a million. Another proposal called for replacing the current electoral college system with a proportional plan wherein state votes would be divided among candidates according to the proportion of the popular votes each candidate received. Clark's primary objective in making such a change was to take away the advantage of pivotal states and the advantage enjoyed by candidates who came from such large states. Clark also favored changing the term of the president to six years and making him ineligible for reelection. In addition, Clark advocated removing postmasters from presidential patronage and providing that they would be elected from their districts.

As a judge, however, Clark devoted his greatest attention to the federal judiciary. In his speech, he advocated the election of judges to fixed terms—elsewhere he also suggested popular recall, congressional overrides of judicial decisions, abolition of judicial review, or alterations of judicial jurisdiction (Vile 1991, 60 n.9). Clark did not believe that the framers of the Constitution had intended to vest judges with the power of judicial review, that is, the power to declare laws to be unconstitutional. He believed such power had been abused in a number of ways. He cited the Supreme Court decision invalidating the income tax (later overturned by the Sixteenth Amendment), the Court's opinion in *Lochner v. New York* (1905) invalidating a New York wage regulation of bakers, and other judicial interferences with state autonomy. In what might otherwise appear to be a surprising recommendation coming from a progressive spokesman, Clark suggested: "Nothing can save us from the centripetal force but the speedy repeal of the fourteenth amendment, or a recasting of its language in terms that no future count can misinterpret it" (Clark 1906, 565). As a way of eliminating those judges who were then serving life terms, Clark suggested that Congress could abolish all judgeships below the Supreme Court and then have new ones elected. He also suggested that Congress could curb the jurisdiction of the Supreme Court (1906, 568).

However radical such proposals might appear, they were consistent with Clark's continuing belief that "the remedy for the halting, halfway popular government which we have is more democracy" (1906, 572).

COERCIVE USE
❖ OF FEDERAL FUNDS ❖

When the national government provides billions of dollars a year in aid to the states, the ability to condition this aid on certain state behaviors can, at least in theory, result in a significant measure of federal control. From 1943 to 1993, six states (Pennsylvania, Nevada, Oklahoma, Tennessee, Arizona, and South Dakota) have petitioned Congress to call for a convention limiting federal coercion through this funding mechanism.

Although some studies suggest that federal conditions on the use of funds more frequently lead to intergovernmental bargaining than to the direct cutoff of funds (O'Toole 1985, 202–3), states sometimes comply with federal policies rather than risk the loss of aid. Thus, just over half of the states accepted small bonuses that the national government offered to states regulat-

ing billboards on interstate highways, but the threat to withhold 10 percent of state constructive funds brought the rest into line (O'Toole 1985, 213). The national government enacted similar laws to get states to reduce speed limits at the time of the Arab oil embargo and to get states to raise the legal drinking age from 18 to 21.

In *U.S. v. Butler* (1936), the Supreme Court, while striking down the Agricultural Adjustment Act on Tenth Amendment grounds, ruled that congressional power to tax and spend under Article I, Section 8 was, as Alexander Hamilton had previously argued, an independent power that could be used to advance the general welfare.

In *South Dakota v. Dole* (1987), the Court, in a 7-to-2 decision, upheld a law withholding 5 percent of a state's federal funds for road construction when the state sold alcohol to individuals under 21. In so ruling, the Court established four conditions: (1) the exercise of taxing and spending power must be in pursuit of the general welfare, with the Court indicating a general willingness to defer to congressional judgments; (2) Congress must clearly state its intentions; (3) conditions must be related to a federal interest (identified in this case as safe interstate travel); and (4) the behavior rewarded must not violate another constitutional provision (207–8). In this same case, the Court rejected arguments that the federal conditions were in possible violation of state control of alcohol guaranteed in the Twenty-first Amendment.

❖ COLEMAN, CHARLES H. ❖
(1900–?)

One of the most modest attempts to rewrite the Constitution was offered by Dr. Charles Coleman in a 1938 publication of the National Council for the Social Studies. Divided into nine articles, Coleman's proposal was actually somewhat shorter than the existing U.S. Constitution. Coleman suggested that such a change would not require a convention but could be adopted by Congress as an amendment after a joint committee held hearings on the subject.

Article One of the new constitution dealt with citizenship, basically drawing from the Fourteenth, Fifteenth, and Nineteenth Amendments. Article Two dealt with the legislative branch. Innovations would have included giving the president power to determine the conditions under which appropriate moneys were spent, four-year terms for the House and eight-year terms for the Senate, and a prohibition (similar to that later ratified in the Twenty-seventh Amendment) on salary increases during a term of office. Congress would have been given a number of new enumerated powers, including the power "to regulate corporations," "to regulate the conditions of labor," "to promote the conservation of natural resources," and "to encourage agriculture" (Coleman 1938, 24–25). Treaties would be approved by a majority of both houses rather than by a two-thirds vote of the Senate.

Article Three described the executive department. The electoral college would be retained, but individual electors would be eliminated. Also, the vice presidency would be eliminated. Article Four, the judicial article, contained few innovations other than prohibiting individuals convicted of treason from serving in public office. Similarly, Article Five basically repeated provisions relative to relations among the states that are currently found in Article IV of the Constitution.

Article Six dealt with prohibitions on the national government, on the states, and on both. Secession was specifically forbidden to the states. The due process clause and equal protection clause, albeit not the entire Bill of Rights, applied to both sets of government.

Article Seven specified that amendments could be ratified by two-thirds of the states, as long as such states contained at least three-fourths of the population. Article

Eight contained the supremacy clause, and Article Nine provided that the new constitution would go into effect when ratified by conventions in 36 states. Coleman's plan appears to have had little contemporary impact (Vile 1991c, 79).

❖ *COLEMAN V. MILLER* (1939) ❖

This decision involved a suit brought by Kansas legislators questioning the constitutionality of the state's putative ratification of the child labor amendment. At issue was whether the lieutenant governor had the right to cast the deciding vote in the state senate. Litigants also argued that the proposed amendment had lost its validity because state legislatures in Kansas and other states had previously rejected it and because the 13-year gap between the amendment's proposal and ratification was unreasonable.

Chief Justice Charles Evans Hughes's opinion for the Court accepted the right of state senators to bring their suit on the basis that the issues they raised were federal rather than state matters. As to the role of the lieutenant governor, the Court pronounced itself "equally divided" (*Coleman* 1939, 447), thus leaving in place the ruling by the Kansas Supreme Court validating his role. Although he did not repudiate language in *Dillon v. Gloss* to the effect that amendments should be ratified within a reasonable time, Hughes decided that the effect of prior rejection and the lapse of time between proposal and ratification were "political questions" for Congress to resolve. Hughes's decision has been criticized for relying on the anomalous precedent set by congressional promulgation of the disputed Fourteenth Amendment (Dellinger 1983, 389–405).

Four justices, led by Hugo Black, would have stated the political questions doctrine even more broadly. Justice Butler's dissent relied on *Dillon v. Gloss* (1921) to declare that Kansas's ratification was invalid because it was not contemporary with the amendment's proposal.

Coleman has never been overturned and may have been partly confirmed when Congress voted to accept the long-delayed ratification of the Twenty-seventh Amendment in 1992. Continuing scholarly criticisms of *Coleman*, as well as judicial modifications of the political questions doctrine and a district court decision in *Idaho v. Freeman* (1981), however, cast some doubt on *Coleman*'s continuing validity.

See also *Idaho v. Freeman;* Political Questions.

For Further Reading:
"Sawing a Justice in Half." 1939. *Yale Law Journal* 48:1455–58.

❖ COLONIAL CHARTERS ❖

Although many American states wrote their first constitutions during the Revolutionary War period, most had previously attempted to defend their liberties on the basis of colonial charters that had been issued to them, usually by the king. A scholar who has examined such charters identified eight elements that most had in common:

> the identification of a grantor; the creation of identification of a grantee; a statement of the reason for the grant; a statement of what was being granted; the license or exclusive use given by the grant; a statement of how the grant was to be administered; specific restrictions or limits on the grant; and the reciprocal duties owed the grantor by the grantee. (Lutz 1988, 35)

In the period preceding the outbreak of the Revolutionary War, the fact that most such grants were made directly by or under the authority of the English king enabled the colonists to deny Parliament's claim to legislate for them. The colonists claimed that their rights as English citizens derived from their loyalty to the king rather than from any acceptance of parliamentary authority (Reid 1993). The general structure of the colonial charters was later reflected in the organization of state constitutions as well as in that of the U.S. Constitution itself.

Charters granted by William Penn in 1682 to 1683 to Pennsylvania appear to have been the first to provide explicitly for an amending process. Such changes required extraordinary majorities—namely, a six-sevenths majority of the Assembly. This and a number of subsequent charters also presaged future entrenchment clauses, such as that in Article V, which guarantees that no state shall be deprived of its equal representation in the Senate without its consent. Early charters also reflected concerns for rights, such as those later protected in the U.S. Bill of Rights. In the charter granted to Delaware in 1701, William Penn thus provided, "That the First Article of this Charter relating to Liberty of Conscience, and every Part and Clause therein, according to the true Intent and Meaning thereof, shall be kept and remain, without any Alteration, inviolably for ever" (Thorpe 1909, 560–61).

Whereas early charters were viewed primarily as grants from the king to his people, later constitutions more clearly resembled compacts, or covenants (with especially deep roots in the Calvinist religious tradition), made collectively by the people by virtue of their own authority (Lutz 1988, 37–38). This foundation in popular sovereignty, in turn, provides the theoretical foundation for the people's right to alter their constitution.

See also Penn, William.

For Further Reading:
Covenant, Polity, and Constitutionalism. 1980. Special issue of *Publius: The Journal of Federalism* (Fall).

❖ COMMITTEE ON THE CONSTITUTIONAL SYSTEM ❖

The bicentennial of the U.S. Constitution provided a time for reflection about American constitutionalism and the prospect of constitutional change (Vile 1991c, 125). A nonpartisan Committee on the Constitutional System, which had already served as a sounding board for changes (Robinson 1985), issued a report in January 1987 that received considerable attention. The committee, consisting of a number of prominent politicians and scholars, was co-chaired by Senator Nancy Landon Kassebaum of Kansas; C. Douglas Dillon, a former secretary of the treasury; and Lloyd N. Cutler, former counsel to President Carter and later to President Clinton.

Noting signs of strain in the system the framers had created, the committee traced such phenomena as divided government, lack of cohesion, lack of accountability, and the inability to replace failed or deadlocked governments to the separation of powers and to a number of developments that had undercut the power of political parties. The committee majority agreed on three proposals to strengthen such parties: to allow party officeholders to serve as uncommitted delegates to national nominating conventions, to require all states to provide an optional straight-ticket voting mechanism, and to permit public funding of political campaigns. It also recommended three proposals to improve legislative-executive collaboration: to change congressional terms so that members of the House of Representatives would serve for four years and members of the Senate for eight, to allow members of Congress to serve in the cabinet, and to allow majorities of both houses of Congress to approve treaties. The committee also favored a constitutional amendment allowing Congress to set limits on campaign spending.

The committee offered a number of other proposals, which did not have majority support of its members, for consideration. These included encouraging the president to appear before Congress, allowing the minority party to form a "shadow cabinet," requiring straight-ticket voting, scheduling elections for Congress after the president and vice president were selected, calling for new elections when the government was deadlocked, and convening conventions every 10 years to make recommendations on how to better divide state and federal responsibilities.

Although committee reforms fell far short of the wide-ranging changes that some might have hoped for, it stirred considerable debate and diverse criticism. Thus, political scientist Jeanne Hahn (1987) argued that committee reforms would further entrench the status quo and put more power in the hands of elites. Political scientist James Ceaser critiqued those elements of the plan that imitated the parliamentary model. Defending separation of powers, he blamed most modern political problems on "reformism, collectivism, whiggism [congressional dominance of government], and judicial activism" (Ceaser 1986, 187). The widespread veneration for the Constitution that the bicentennial celebrations reinforced probably worked against changes at that time (Vile 1991c, 162).

❖ COMMUNISM ❖

On 7 July 1965, Mississippi sent petitions to Congress to call conventions to propose three amendments. One was directed at overturning Supreme Court decisions—most notably *Reynolds v. Sims* (1964), which had applied the "one person one vote" standard—dealing with apportionment of state legislatures. A second—most likely a continuing reaction to the Supreme Court's desegregation decision in *Brown v. Board of Education* (1954) and subsequent cases—called for giving states exclusive control over public education. The third proposed an amendment designed to control communism.

Mississippi pointed to "the existence of the world Communist conspiracy and the fact that the Communist Party, U.S.A., operates as an arm of such conspiracy in seeking to bring about the overthrow of the Government of the United States by force and violence." The state further observed that "the Supreme Court of the United States through its various decisions has circumscribed, limited, or invalidated such congressional enactments" (*Congressional Record*, 7 July 1965, 15770). Mississippi accordingly asked for an amendment designed to invest Congress with the power to control communism. Among provisions to be legalized were those preventing the dissemination of communist propaganda in the United States and the expulsion of noncitizens engaged in disseminating such propaganda.

The concern with Supreme Court decisions relating to communism appears to have been more prevalent in the late 1950s than in the period that Mississippi offered its amendment. In a number of decisions from 1955 to 1957, the Supreme Court overturned convictions of American communists, and in *Watkins v. United States* (1957) it overturned a citation for contempt against a labor leader who had refused to answer certain questions before the House Un-American Activities Committee (HUAC) about possible communist associates. These decisions prompted the unsuccessful Jenner bill, in which Congress attempted to restrict judicial jurisdiction over such cases (W. Murphy 1962). In a number of subsequent decisions, *Barenblatt v. United States* (1959) being the most prominent, the Court appeared to retreat from its earlier rulings (Belknap 1992, 172). In *Barenblatt*, the Court refused to use the First Amendment to extend exemptions for

witnesses testifying before congressional committees.

❖ CONCURRENT POWERS ❖

Because the United States has a federal system, some powers are exercised exclusively, or predominantly, by the state or national governments. A larger number of powers—for example, taxation—are shared; these are called concurrent powers. Section 2 of the Eighteenth Amendment, which imposed national alcoholic prohibition, entrusted Congress and the states with "concurrent power to enforce this article." The national government interpreted this clause expansively in the *National Prohibition* cases (1920), even upholding provisions of the Volstead Act that outlawed beer and wine.

Perhaps with such contemporary construction of the Eighteenth Amendment in mind, New York Democratic Representative Frank Oliver (H.J. Res. 42, 5 December 1927) proposed construing "concurrent power" so as to prevent an act of Congress from invalidating an act adopted by a state. Although the Twenty-first Amendment repealed the Eighteenth, the national government and the states share an increasing number of powers. An expert on federalism has argued that contemporary federalism thus more closely resembles a "marble cake" arrangement than a "layer cake" scheme (Grodzins 1966).

❖ CONFEDERATE DEBT ❖

During discussions of the Fourteenth Amendment, members of Congress expressed fears that the former rebels might one day gain office with the intention of either repudiating federal debts that had been used to wage the war or assuming the debts that the Southern states had made to prosecute the conflict. Several proposals were introduced to prevent either contingency (Flack 1908, 133–36). Section 4 of the Fourteenth Amendment subsequently both guaranteed "the validity of the public debt of the United States . . . including debts incurred for payment of pensions and bounties for services in suppressing insurrection or rebellion" and repudiated either federal or state payment of "any debt or obligation incurred in aid of insurrection or rebellion against the United States, or any claim for the loss or emancipation of any slave."

See also Fourteenth Amendment.

❖ CONFEDERATE STATES OF AMERICA, CONSTITUTION OF ❖

The constitution that bears the greatest similarity to that of the United States was the one the Confederate States of America adopted. Written by a Committee of Twelve and debated by a convention held in Montgomery, Alabama, in March 1861 (C. R. Lee 1963), the document replaced a similar provisional constitution adopted the previous month. The new constitution was subsequently approved by the Confederate Congress and by the Southern states; approval by five states was necessary for the document to go into effect. Reflecting the philosophy of John C. Calhoun and other Southern constitutionalists (DeRosa 1991, 18–37), the Confederate constitution was built on the doctrine of state sovereignty. It also included a number of provisions designed to control federal spending on special interests.

Although the Confederate constitution followed the outline of the U.S. Constitution, several provisions were different. The preamble included an acknowledgment of God. The constitution explicitly referred to slaves rather than using euphemisms. It permitted two-thirds majorities of state legislatures to impeach judicial or other federal officials acting within a state. In imitation of parliamentary systems, it permitted Congress to grant a seat on the floor of Congress for members of the cabinet to discuss measures but did not, like the provisional constitution, allow members of Congress to hold other offices. The permanent constitution gave the president an item veto of appropriations bills and prohibited congressional appropriations for internal improvements other than aids to navigation and harbor improvements. Although slave importation was prohibited, the right to property in the form of slaves was explicitly affirmed. Appropriations required a two-thirds vote of both houses of Congress, with a provision that all appropriations bills "shall specify in federal currency the exact amount of each appropriation, and the purposes for which it is made." Bills were limited to a single subject.

The president and vice president were to serve single six-year terms and were chosen by an electoral college rather than, as under the provisional constitution, by Congress. The constitution granted the chief executive explicit power to remove department heads at his pleasure and others for specified grievances. Although the constitutional arrangement of the courts was not significantly altered, the Confederate states, perhaps remembering the consolidating effect of U.S. Supreme Court decisions, never got around to establishing their own equivalent.

The constitution did not explicitly prohibit membership by free states, but it did require a vote of two-thirds of both houses to admit new states. The constitution also explicitly granted the government the right to acquire new territory where the right to own slaves was protected.

The provisional Confederate constitution had permitted amendments by a two-thirds vote in Congress (Urofsky 1988, 400). The permanent constitution provided no method for Congress to propose amendments but allowed three states to request Congress to summon a convention to propose amendments. These required ratification by two-thirds of the states. No such amendments were adopted during the Confederate states' brief life.

The Confederate constitution provided a number of innovations for the consideration of future reformers (see, for example, Schouler 1908). The circumstances surrounding the constitution's adoption also contributed to fears of a runaway revolutionary convention (Jameson 1887, 257).

For Further Reading:
Davis, William C. 1995. *"A Government of Our Own": The Making of the Confederacy.* New York: Free Press.

❖ CONFESSIONS ❖

One of the most prominent symbols of the activist Warren Court was its decision in *Miranda v. Arizona* (1966). In this case, the Court decided by a 5-to-4 vote that it would no longer accept confessions in cases of custodial police interrogation unless suspects had been informed of their rights, including notification of their right to remain silent, the fact that any statements could be used against them, their right to an attorney, and the fact that an attorney would be provided if they were too poor to afford one.

This decision was in many ways a logical follow-up to a number of earlier Supreme Court rulings. It was based on the Court's reading of the self-incrimination clause of the Fifth Amendment as applied to the states via the due process clause of the Fourteenth Amendment. *Miranda* prompted "a firestorm of criticism" by those concerned that the decision would hamstring law enforcement (Bodenhamer 1992, 121). Within a month, North Carolina Democratic Senator Sam Ervin (a constitutional expert who would later chair the Senate Watergate Committee) introduced an amendment to permit the use of "volun-

tary" confessions and withdraw the jurisdiction of federal courts to "reverse, modify, or set aside" determinations by trial courts that such confessions were voluntary (*Congressional Record*, 22 July 1966, 16721). Several other such amendments were introduced from 1966 to 1968, including at least one that would have permitted police to question individuals outside the presence of counsel (H.J. Res. 1260, 1966).

Senator Ervin also attempted to limit federal judicial review of state criminal convictions through writs of habeas corpus that could be introduced in any federal court. Ervin proposed that appeals to federal courts should be limited to instances in which such cases had received a final judgment from "the highest court of that State having jurisdiction to review such judgment" (*Congressional Record*, 22 July 1966, 16721).

Although Ervin's amendment was not adopted, disputes continue over both the use of confessions and the appropriate extent of federal habeas corpus review. The Court under Warren Burger and William Rehnquist has allowed a limited number of exceptions to the *Miranda* rules (*New York v. Quarles* [1984], for example, accepted a "public safety" exception), but most observers have concluded that the *Miranda* warnings did not have the significant negative impact on confessions that many had anticipated (Bodenhamer 1992, 123). Lower courts have also tightened up the number of habeas corpus reviews they will accept. Thus, in *Stone v. Powell* (1976), the Court decided not to accept federal habeas corpus review of Fourth Amendment claims that had already been given a full hearing in state courts. Federal habeas corpus review continues to be controversial, especially in cases involving the death penalty. Habeas corpus review is now granted in about half of such cases, often significantly delaying executions (Hoffman and Stuntz 1994, 119).

❖ CONGRESS, AGE OF MEMBERS ❖

As a means of securing a minimal level of maturity, the framers of Article I, Sections 2 and 3 of the U.S. Constitution set age minimums of 25 and 30 for members of the House of Representatives and the Senate, respectively. These articles did not establish any maximum or mandatory retirement age.

In 1971, the Twenty-sixth Amendment was ratified. It lowered the national voting age to 18—most states having previously set the age at 21. Perhaps stimulated by this change, the rest of the decade witnessed numerous amending proposals to lower the minimum age for members of Congress. The most commonly advocated proposal, most frequently associated with Democratic Representative Robert Drinan of Massachusetts, called for lowering the minimum age of members of the House to 22 years and senators to 27 years.

The 1970s also saw the introduction of a number of proposals to set a mandatory retirement age for members of Congress. Proposed retirement ages ranged from 65 to 75. Some of these proposals would also have altered the length of congressional terms, set a maximum age for judges, or set limits on the total number of terms or consecutive terms that members of Congress could serve. With no such limits in place, South Carolina's Republican Senator Strom Thurmond (a Dixiecrat candidate for president in 1948) assumed chairmanship of the Senate Judiciary Committee after the congressional elections in 1994 at the age of 92, although, after complaints, he subsequently gave in to committee members' desire for greater autonomy (Hook and Cassata 1995, 466). In 1996, at age 93, Thurmond began a campaign for reelection to a six-year term in the Senate. If adopted, congressional term limits might tend to reduce the age of members of Congress.

❖ CONGRESS, ATTENDANCE OF MEMBERS ❖

The Constitution makes no provision for the attendance of members of Congress, and some have been known to be absent frequently. For example, Adam Clayton Powell, the flamboyant Harlem representative whose expulsion from the House was voided by the Supreme Court in *Powell v. McCormack* (1969), was present for only 30 percent of all roll-call votes in the 82d Congress and only 54 percent when he became chair of the House Education and Labor Committee (Weeks 1971, 4–5)

Amendments were introduced throughout the 1970s to declare the seats of House and Senate members vacant for excessive absences. One of the earliest, introduced by Maine's Republican Senator Margaret Chase Smith, would have declared a vacancy whenever members failed to be present for a total of 200 or at least 60 percent of roll-call votes (S.J. Res. 192, 1972). Some later proposals would have raised this minimum to 70 percent. By the end of the 1970s, some proposals included exemptions for absences due to hospitalization necessitated by illness or accidents.

❖ CONGRESS, COMMERCE POWERS ❖

No provision of the Constitution has been more frequently or effectively used as a basis for the expansion of national powers than the commerce clause. Indeed, between 1789 and 1950, it was the most frequently litigated provision in the Constitution (Steamer 1992, 167). Found in Article I, Section 8 among the powers of Congress, this provision—which was lacking in the Articles of Confederation—grants Congress power "to regulate Commerce with foreign Nations, and among the several States, and with the Indian Tribes." Without this, or an equivalent, provision, it is likely that the expansion of federal powers in the twentieth century would have required adoption of a number of amendments.

Early in U.S. history, Chief Justice John Marshall, most notably in *Gibbons v. Ogden* (1824), gave an expansive reading to the commerce clause, using congressional powers to strike down conflicting state regulation—in the *Gibbons* case, a grant of a steamboat monopoly by the state of New York. The question of whether federal power prohibited all state commercial regulations was more difficult. In *Cooley v. Board of Wardens* (1852), the Court adopted the doctrine of "selective exclusiveness," under which it decided whether a particular area of commerce was one that required a single uniform national rule or whether it was one, like the Philadelphia pilotage regulation upheld in *Cooley*, in which some state variation was permissible.

As the United States industrialized, the national government began to turn to the commerce clause for authority to regulate activities not otherwise delineated in the Constitution. The Court found itself picking and choosing among those activities it was willing to allow Congress to regulate. The Court's belief in laissez-faire economics, and its development of the doctrine of substantive due process, often led it to hedge congressional commerce powers through various limiting doctrines. Thus, in *U.S. v. E. C. Knight Company* (1895), the Court held that Congress could not prevent the acquisition of a near-monopoly in the sugar-refining industry; it reasoned that manufacturing and production were distinct from subsequent commerce and that monopoly was a local rather than a national matter. From the 1890s through 1937, the Court also distinguished between the regulation of goods that were harmful and those that were not (see, for example, the decision in *Hammer v. Dagenhart* [1918] invalidating a national child labor law), the control

of goods that had a "direct" effect and those that had only an "indirect" effect on commerce, and the regulation of goods that were within the "stream of commerce" and those that were not.

From the 1920s through the 1930s, a number of amendments were introduced to give Congress more explicit authority over areas such as the regulation of coal, oil, and gas; agriculture; minimum wages; child labor; hours of labor; and other such matters that Congress might otherwise have regulated under its commerce powers. President Franklin Roosevelt effectively resurrected the commerce clause with his New Deal programs, but many went down to defeat, prompting his Court-packing plan.

Although Congress rejected Roosevelt's plan, the Court subsequently reversed course in 1937 and began reading the commerce clause quite expansively. By 1964, the Court in *Heart of Atlanta Motel v. United States* and *Katzenbach v. McClung* upheld the public accommodations section of the Civil Rights Act of 1964 under authority of the commerce clause. Although the Court read one implicit restriction into federal commerce powers in *National League of Cities v. Usery* (1976) when it limited the scope of federal wage regulations as applied to state employees, it subsequently reversed course in *Garcia v. San Antonio Metropolitan Transit Authority* (1985), renewing some calls for strengthening the Tenth Amendment or otherwise strengthening states' rights.

In 1995, in *U.S. v. Lopez*, the Supreme Court's 5-to-4 decision written by Chief Justice William Rehnquist struck down the federal Gun-Free School Zones Act, which prohibited possession of a gun within 1,000 feet of a school, as exceeding federal powers under the commerce clause. Citing *United States v. Darby Lumber Company* (1941), Rehnquist wrote that "the scope of the interstate commerce power 'must be considered in light of our dual system of government and may not be extended so as to embrace effects upon interstate commerce so indirect and remote that to embrace them, in view of our complex society, would effectively obliterate the distinction between what is national and what is local and to create a completely centralized government'" (4345). The full implication of this decision on the exercise of other federal powers is not yet clear.

For Further Reading:

Benson, Paul R., Jr. 1970. *The Supreme Court and the Commerce Clause, 1937–1970.* New York: Denellen.

Frankfurter, Felix. 1964. *The Commerce Clause under Marshall, Taney and Waite.* Chicago: Quadrangle Books.

Maltz, Earl. 1995. "The Impact of the Constitutional Revolution of 1937 on the Dormant Commerce Clause—A Case Study in the Decline of State Autonomy." *Harvard Journal of Law and Public Policy* 19 (Fall): 121–45.

❖ CONGRESS, COMMITTEE ❖ COMPOSITION

Although the role of congressional committees is not specified in the U.S. Constitution, it is difficult to imagine Congress operating without them. Committees allow members to develop their expertise by specializing in areas of particular interest to them.

Committee assignments are made by leaders within each party, with the majority party appointing committee chairs. Seniority is an important but not exclusive factor in such determinations. The majority party may attempt to enhance its control by assigning a greater proportion of its members to key committees. House Republicans complained about such policies in the 1980s and early 1990s, when Democrats held a majority, but Republicans were unsuccessful when they challenged such rules in court (Davidson and Oleszek 1994,

211). A number of amendments were also introduced. One introduced on 1 July 1992 proposed that membership on congressional committees be apportioned either equally or according to the proportion of members each party held in the House (H.J. Res. 522).

❖ CONGRESS, DISTRICT ❖ REPRESENTATION

Article I, Section 2 of the U.S. Constitution requires that members of the House of Representatives be inhabitants of the states that elect them, but it does not require that they live in their districts. Indeed, although the Constitution apportions representatives according to a state's population, nowhere does it require that such representatives be selected by districts.

In the nation's early history, a number of states selected representatives through use of a general ticket (Ames 1896, 56). This situation led to 34 resolutions from 1820 through 1826 proposing that the Constitution be amended to require election of representatives by districts. In 1819, 1820, and 1822, these resolutions passed the Senate but were not voted on in the House. In 1842, Congress passed a law accomplishing the same objective, and petitions for such an amendment subsequently ceased (Ames 1896, 56–57).

The single-member district system of representation is generally believed to contribute to the maintenance of a two-party system. To win any seats in the House of Representatives, a political party's candidate must get a plurality of the votes in one or more districts. By contrast, in systems that use a scheme of proportional representation, minor parties may be rewarded with some seats even if they do not capture a plurality of any single district (for a general analysis of electoral systems, see Sartori 1994, 27–79). Most American party reformers have aimed to strengthen political parties (American Political Science Association 1950; however, see also Krusch 1992, 98, who would prohibit members of Congress from being party members). There thus appears to be little current sentiment for altering the method of selecting House members by district.

One of the reasons that the Court in *Colegrove v. Green* (1946) rejected the opportunity to reapportion Illinois congressional districts was the fear that a judicial remedy might require statewide elections. Subsequent decisions accepting justiciability over such questions and mandating approximate equality of districts, most notably *Baker v. Carr* (1962) and *Wesberry v. Sanders* (1964), have worked within the existing single-member district scheme.

❖ CONGRESS, EMERGENCY ❖ FUNCTIONING

World War II ended in 1945 after the United States dropped atomic bombs that wiped out the Japanese cities of Hiroshima and Nagasaki. Shortly thereafter, a protracted cold war developed between the United States and the Soviet Union. In 1949, Russia exploded its first atomic bomb, and hydrogen bombs followed in the next decade. By the 1960s, both powers had enough weapons to destroy each other, and although this precarious balance of terror may actually have served to deter world war, it also raised popular fears of a war-induced apocalypse.

In such an atmosphere, it is not surprising that concerns arose about the possibility that a war might cripple the government. From 1948 through 1971, there were at least 20 amendments introduced to provide a government for the United States in case of a disaster. The most common proposal allowed for state governors, acting under authority of a presidential proclamation, to make temporary appointments whenever the number of vacancies in the House of Representatives exceeded 145. A proposal introduced by Tennessee Democratic Senator Estes Kefauver on the subject in 1960 was not successful but became the catalyst for an amendment to repeal the poll tax (Bernstein with Agel 1993, 137).

Despite a number of close calls, most notably the Cuban missile crisis of 1962, the nation has not yet faced a disaster involving massive numbers of congressional vacancies. Questions continue to remain about how the nation would function, and how powers would be allocated, if it were ever faced with such a catastrophe. In 1992, there were revelations of a bunker at the Greenbriar Hotel in White Sulphur Springs, West Virginia, that had been built in the 1950s and designed to house members of Congress in such an emergency. Shelters had been built elsewhere for other members of the government ("Congressional Bomb Shelter Revealed" 1992, 681). Other contingencies for governmental operations after a nuclear war make for fascinating, if somewhat macabre, reading (Zuckerman 1984).

❖ CONGRESS, FILIBUSTERS ❖ IN SENATE

One of the Senate's most hallowed folkways is the filibuster, which has been in use since 1841. This procedure permits individuals to delay or stop action on a pending bill by monopolizing floor debates in the hope that its sponsors will eventually concede. The first limits were imposed on this mechanism in 1917 after Woodrow Wilson called a group of antiwar progressives opposed to his plans to arm merchant ships "a little group of willful men [who] have rendered the government of the United States helpless and contemptible" (Gettlinger 1994, 3198). In 1975, the Senate modified an earlier rule and permitted a cloture vote by three-fifths of the entire membership rather than the previously required two-thirds of those present and voting (S. Smith 1989, 342). Such cloture votes are still quite difficult to achieve, however, and with some other changes in the way filibusters are conducted, their number has actually increased, with one-half of the total occurring since 1975 (Gettlinger 1994, 3198).

At least three proposed amendments would have altered filibuster procedures. Two proposals introduced in 1916 by West Virginia Democratic Senator William Chilton were designed to cut off debate, one after 10 days and the other after 20 hours. In 1969, Democratic Senator Mike Mansfield of Montana offered a proposal preventing the Senate from limiting or closing debate by less than three-fifths of those present and voting (S.J. Res. 36). Although filibusters are often associated in the popular mind with racist senators opposed to progressive civil rights legislation, the mechanism allows for delay by any senator with strong views. Now, as in 1929 (see Musmanno 1929, 21), the filibuster seems to be a particularly unlikely candidate for amendment.

❖ CONGRESS, IMMUNITY OF MEMBERS OF ❖

In an attempt to insulate them from political reprisals and to ensure free and open debate, Article I, Section 6 of the U.S. Constitution specifies that members of Congress "shall in all Cases, except Treason, Felony and Breach of the Peace, be privileged from Arrest during their Attendance at the Session of their respective Houses." It further provides that "for any Speech or Debate in either House, they shall not be questioned in any other Place." At least seven proposals have been introduced from 1917 to 1983 to alter one or both of these provisions.

The congressional privilege against arrest is not as broad as it may appear, since the Supreme Court has held that it applies only to civil arrests, which are no longer carried out (R. Baker 1992, 175). The Court's interpretation appears to call into question the need for an amendment introduced in 1983 allowing members going to or returning from Congress to be arrested for traffic violations (H.J. Res. 318)

The most common proposals for alterations have focused on the speech and debate clause and have been directed toward preventing members of Congress from using the congressional platform for libeling individuals. Generally, the Court has interpreted the speech and debate clause liberally. It has thus extended protection beyond the floor of Congress to remarks members make before committees. Moreover, in *Gravel v. United States* (1972) the Court extended some collateral protection to congressional aides, who were described as congressional alter egos.

In *Hutchinson v. Proxmire* (1979), however, a case involving Wisconsin Democratic Senator William Proxmire's much-publicized "Golden Fleece" Awards, the Court ruled that members of Congress could be sued if statements in their press releases were libelous. Similarly, in *United States v. Brewster* (1972), the Court held that the speech and debate clause did not provide a defense for a member of Congress convicted of taking a bribe. Also, in *Gravel v. United States* (1972), the Court said that congressional immunity did not extend to contracts that members of Congress made with book companies. It further decided that a grand jury could inquire into how members of Congress got classified information. In that case, Alaska Democratic Senator Mike Gravel had obtained a copy of the Pentagon Papers and read them into the record of a subcommittee he chaired. Two days after he had done so, California Republican Representative Charles Gubser introduced an amendment (H.J. Res. 754) providing that members of Congress could be prosecuted for disclosing classified information.

For Further Reading:

Betts, James T. 1967. "The Scope of Immunity for Legislators and Their Employees." *Yale Law Journal* 77 (December): 366–89.

❖ CONGRESS, LEGISLATIVE VETO OF ❖

The doctrine of separation of powers suggests that Congress makes the laws, the president enforces them, and the courts interpret them. The reality is considerably more complex. Sometimes because of inadequate drafting, sometimes because of the complexity of the subject, and sometimes because Congress has made a conscious attempt to avoid or defer controversial decisions, administrative agencies issue numerous rules designed to implement congressional laws. Congress is understandably concerned that such rules do not usurp its own legislative functions. After numerous reports of agency abuse and incompetence, "criticism of agency rulemaking . . . reached a shrill pitch in the 1970s" (L. Fisher 1991, 142). Although several laws and amendments were introduced in Congress to grant itself a veto over all agency regulations, such attempts failed.

Congress increasingly turned to the so-called legislative veto mechanism, whereby one or both houses granted wide rule-making power to a particular agency while reserving the power to veto administrative decisions that Congress did not approve. Although the mechanism had been used for about 50 years and arguably made Congress somewhat more willing to delegate power to administrative agencies than it otherwise would have been, most presidents were on record as challenging the constitutionality of this mechanism. In *Immigration and Naturalization Service v. Chadha* (1983), a case involving congressional revocation of a decision by the INS to grant permanent-resident status to an East Indian from Kenya who held a British passport, the Supreme Court outlawed such vetoes. It declared that they were contrary to the presentment clause, which allows the president the chance to veto all legislation, and, in the immediate case, to the bicameralism requirement specifying that all legislation pass both houses of Congress (Craig 1988). Within days, an amendment was introduced (H.J. Res. 313) to reinstate the legislative veto mechanism. Although such an amendment was not adopted, Congress appears to have developed a number of informal mechanisms, often at the congressional committee level, by which it still maintains oversight of legislative rule making (L. Fisher 1993, 286–88).

❖ CONGRESS, MEMBERS' ELIGIBILITY FOR OTHER OFFICES ❖

Article I, Section 6 of the U.S. Constitution prohibits a member of Congress from being appointed "to any civil Office under the Authority of the United States, which shall have been created, or the Emoluments whereof shall have been encreased [*sic*] during such time." Throughout the nineteenth century, there were over 30 attempts to extend this ban to exclude appointment to any civil office, sometimes making exceptions for appointments to the judiciary and sometimes extending the ban for two years after a member of Congress left office (Ames 1896, 30–33). One such proposal was offered by Andrew Jackson. He may have been influenced by the "corrupt bargain" he alleged had been struck when, after the four-way election of 1824 involving Jackson, Henry Clay, William Crawford, and John Quincy Adams, Clay shifted his support to Adams and was subsequently rewarded by the newly elected Adams with an appointment as secretary of state (Van Deusen 1937, 179–95). At least four amending proposals introduced from 1929 to 1945 have sought a ban similar to that advocated in the nineteenth century.

Controversies have sometimes been raised when members of Congress have been suggested for, or appointed to, judicial posts or cabinet offices for which salaries have been increased during their tenure. As a remedy, Congress generally adopts legislation reducing the pay for the appointee to that in effect at the beginning of the appointee's term. Thus, when President Clinton appointed Texas Senator Lloyd Bentsen as secretary of treasury, Congress passed a law reducing "'the compensation and other emoluments attached to the office of Secretary of the Treasury' to those in effect on January 1, 1989" (Paulsen 1994, 909). Although acknowledging that such legislation meets "the rationale" behind the emoluments clause, a law professor recently argued that it actually violates the constitutional "rule" itself (Paulsen 1994, 911). This suggests either that current practices should be altered or that an amendment should be adopted to bring the Constitution in line with current practice.

❖ CONGRESS, OVERRIDING ❖ JUDICIAL DECISIONS

Of all the powers exercised by the courts, none has been either more important or more controversial than the power of judicial review. This allows courts to strike down state and federal laws or executive orders that they find to be unconstitutional. Not explicitly stated in the Constitution, the power is arguably an important ancillary to the doctrines of separation of powers and the supremacy of a written constitution. Chief Justice John Marshall first exercised and justified this power to strike down a

federal law in *Marbury v. Madison* (1803), a decision that continues to be at the center of scholarly debate (Alfange 1994).

The Court did not exercise its power to strike down another federal law until the notorious decision in *Scott v. Sandford* (1857). By the end of the nineteenth century, however, the Court was increasingly using its power to strike down state and federal legislation, especially in the realm of economic regulation. Shortly after President Franklin D. Roosevelt threatened to "pack" the Court in 1937, it executed a historic turnabout (see *West Coast Hotel v. Parrish*) and has subsequently given only minimal scrutiny to most economic legislation. Consistent with reasoning expressed by Justice Harlan Fiske Stone in footnote 4 of the *Carolene Products* case the next year, however, the Court has increasingly exercised its power of judicial review over legislation thought to violate guarantees in the Bill of Rights or the Fourteenth Amendment.

This power is controversial, partly because it is not stated in the Constitution. It also stirs controversy because, since judges are neither elected by nor directly accountable to the people, the exercise of judicial power can serve to thwart democratic wishes. Its exercise thus presents what Alexander Bickel has called "the counter-majoritarian difficulty" (1982, 16).

Many proposals have been made with the intention of reining in judicial review. From just before the Court's turnaround in 1937 through the 1980s, at least 25 proposals have been advanced that would have allowed Congress to overturn such decisions. Although other majorities have been suggested, the most common proposal would allow Congress to override court decisions by a two-thirds vote. If adopted, this would give Congress power over judicial decisions equivalent to that which it now exercises over presidential vetoes.

Congress already has the power to override decisions of the Court that are based simply on statutory interpretation. In such cases, which are relatively frequent, Congress can simply adopt new laws to clarify its intentions (Eskridge 1991; Paschal 1991). Currently, if Congress wishes to override a constitutional interpretation of the courts, it must proceed by constitutional amendment. Congress so acted in the case of the Eleventh, Fourteenth, Sixteenth, and Twenty-sixth Amendments. An amendment granting Congress power to make such reversals by a two-thirds vote, without subsequent consent of three-fourths of the states, could significantly impact the operation of the current amending process. The impact of a more recent proposal encouraging Congress to draft amendments to overturn specific decisions from seven months to a year after the Supreme Court's yearly term is more difficult to measure (T. Baker 1995b).

❖ CONGRESS, PRIVATE BILLS ❖

Most laws that Congress passes are public laws that are phrased in general terms and refer to broad classes of individuals. Indeed, the French philosopher Jean-Jacques Rousseau argued that just laws were necessarily general, always considering "the subjects as a body and actions by their genera or species, never one man in particular or one unique individual action" (Rousseau 1978, 190). Despite such admonitions, Congress sometimes adopts private laws to provide relief for a single individual. From 1989 to 1991, such laws accounted for only 2.4 percent of the total, but the number was as high as 90 percent from 1905 to 1907 (*Congressional Quarterly* 1991, 359–60), during which time such bills were often the target of the presidential veto power.

Approximately 20 proposals were introduced from 1876 to 1909 to prohibit or limit private bills, but the number of private bills has been reduced both by the adoption of legislation and by the establishment of

courts to hear claims that used to occupy congressional attention. Moreover, members of Congress who have introduced private bills or promised to introduce private bills for personal gain—as in the Abscam investigation—have been successfully prosecuted (*Congressional Quarterly* 1991, 166–67). No amendments related to private bills have been introduced in recent years.

For Further Reading:
Morehead, Joe. 1985. "Private Bills and Private Laws: A Guide to the Legislative Process." *Serials Librarian* 9 (Spring): 115–25.

❖ CONGRESS, QUORUM ❖

Article I, Section 5 of the Constitution specifies that a majority of each House of Congress constitutes a quorum, or the number of members required to do business. The House can evade this provision by working as a Committee of the Whole, in which case only 100 members must be present (Kravitz 1993, 215). Either house may also operate with less than a quorum as long as no member objects.

In 1883, Democratic Representative Joseph Wheeler of Alabama introduced an amending resolution to reduce the quorum to one-third of the members of each house (Ames 1896, 39). In 1947 and 1949, Republican Representative Charles Plumley of Vermont introduced resolutions that would accept an individual's quorum call only when one-fifth of the members present called for one.

❖ CONGRESS, RECALL OF MEMBERS ❖

Although the Constitution provides for the impeachment and conviction of officials guilty of criminal misconduct, it does not provide for the recall of individuals on grounds of incompetence or unrepresentativeness. There have been a number of proposed amendments to recall members of Congress, a practice that was permitted under Article V of the Articles of Confederation (Solberg 1958, 43).

The first such proposals focused on senators and came from Virginia representatives from 1803 to 1810. Such proposals, which seem to have reflected concerns over states' rights rather than popular democracy, would have allowed the state legislatures to recall and replace senators. Such proposals may have reflected a view—prominent at the time of the American Revolution—that such legislators were subject to instruction by their constituents, in this case, the state legislatures (G. Wood 1969, 188ff.). Interestingly, at least three senators, including future president John Tyler, resigned in the nineteenth century when they were unable to follow the wishes of the state legislatures that had selected them (Ames 1896, 65). Similarly, John Quincy Adams resigned his seat after the Massachusetts legislature elected his successor nine months early (Leish 1968, 1:178).

The recall, like the initiative and referendum, was popular with reformers in the Progressive Era. Most twentieth-century proposals would permit voters to recall both senators and members of the House. A 1987 Gallup poll indicated that 67 percent of the people favored such a mechanism (Cronin 1989, 132). Advocates believe that such a mechanism would promote democracy and accountability. Opponents fear that it might undermine representative government.

See also Initiative and Referendum.

❖ CONGRESS, ❖ REPRESENTATION IN

One of the most difficult issues the delegates to the Constitutional Convention faced was the issue of representation. Advocates of the Virginia plan wanted states to be represented in both house of Congress according to population. Advocates of the New Jersey plan wanted to preserve the system under the Articles of Confederation whereby states would be represented equally. In the Connecticut, or Great, Compromise, delegates agreed that representation in the House would be by population and that states would be equally represented in the Senate. The only stated substantive limit on the amending process that is in force provides that no state shall be deprived of such representation without its consent. This provision did not deter two members of Congress from introducing resolutions in 1882 and 1892 to increase the number of senators for more populous states.

The Constitutional Convention was also torn by debates between the slave and free states. The former wanted slaves to count for purposes of congressional representation but not for taxation, whereas the free states had opposite interests. In one of the least defensible parts of the Constitution, the delegates settled on a three-fifths formula, which they incorporated into Article I, Section 2. Under this formula, "three-fifths of such other persons [slaves]" were to count for purposes of taxation and representation (Vile 1993a, 27–28). When the Thirteenth Amendment prohibited slavery, the Southern states—dominated by Democrats who had fought against the Union—actually stood to gain representation. When Section 2 of the Fourteenth Amendment subsequently obliterated the three-fifths clause by providing that representation would now be based on "the whole number of persons in each State, excluding Indians not taxed," it also provided a mechanism whereby representation would be reduced for those states that restricted the vote other than to males under the age of 21 or those who were guilty of crimes or of participation in rebellion. These provisions followed numerous resolutions for amendments that had been introduced in Congress. In part because it was difficult to ascertain how many people were actually being deprived of the franchise, this provision was never actually put into effect (Congressional Quarterly 1991, 742).

A number of reforms relating to representation have been proposed in the twentieth century. The 1920s witnessed several proposals to require reapportionment after each decennial census. The topic was then of particular concern, because this was the only time in U.S. history that Congress, faced for the first time with an apparent majority of urban residents, failed to reapportion after such a census (Congressional Quarterly 1991, 742–43). Several subsequent proposals would have limited the number of senators from new states.

There have been several proposed amendments that would base representation on the number of U.S. citizens and legal resident aliens within each state rather than on a state's total population, which the Census Bureau now tries to record. There was a proposal for reapportioning representation in the House after each presidential election, based on the number of voters in such elections. Another proposal (perhaps goaded by the large number of lawyers who are elected to Congress) called for apportioning representatives according to vocation. Others proposed increasing the number of members of the Senate.

The Constitution guarantees that each state will have at least one member in the House of Representatives, and law now caps House membership at 435. This has inevitably meant that, however influential Supreme Court decisions such as *Wesberry v. Sanders* (1964) have been in mandating numerical equality among districts in the same state, interstate numerical equality of districts has been impossible to attain. Thus, in 1980, Nevada and Maine both had two seats, although the former had a population of 787,000 and the latter a population of 1,125,000. By contrast, South Dakota, with a population of 690,000 got only one seat (Butler and Cain 1992, 18). Throughout American history, a number of different mechanisms have been used to ascertain representatives for states with a fraction over or under what they would receive simply on the basis of population (Butler and Cain 1992, 19). The method now used is known as the method of equal proportions and was developed in 1921 by Edward V. Huntington of Harvard and adopted by Congress in 1941. After assigning each state a seat, "'priority numbers' for states to receive second seats, third seats, and so on are calculated by dividing the state's population by the square root of n(n-1) where 'n' is the number of seats for that state. The priority numbers are then lined up in order and the seats given to the states with priority numbers until 435 are awarded" (Congressional Quarterly 1991, 745). This method of apportionment was upheld in *U.S. Department of Commerce v. Montana* (1992), in which Montana protested its loss of a House seat that reduced its representation to one member. Such situations have led to a number of calls to give each state at least two representatives.

See also Congress, Size of.

❖ CONGRESS, SIZE OF ❖

Article I, Section 2 of the U.S. Constitution specifies that the membership of the House of Representatives "shall not exceed one for every thirty Thousand [people]," and Article I, Section 3 guarantees that each state will have at least two senators. The first of 12 amendments proposed by Congress in 1789 (10 of which were ratified as the Bill of Rights) would have provided that when membership in the House reached 100, there would be at least one representative for every 40,000 persons. It also would have mandated that when House membership reached 200, it should not fall below this number, nor should there be more than one representative for every 50,000 persons—requirements that, at some population stage, may well have been contradictory (Amar 1992, 1143). Unlike an accompanying provision that was putatively ratified as the Twenty-seventh Amendment in 1992, the congressional representation amendment was not ratified and is today irrelevant.

There were 65 members in the first House. After the 1800 census, the number grew to 106, and by 1900, it reached 391. This led to concerns that the size of the House might become too unwieldy. Beginning with a proposal introduced by Anti-Democrat–States' Rights Senator James Barbour of Virginia in 1821, there were just over a dozen proposed amendments to cap the size of the House (the proposed size gradually increasing) until 1911, when the number of House members was set by law at 435 (Congressional Quarterly 1991, 741–42).

Since 1911, there have been a few proposals to raise the number of House members to 450, 480, or 500, as well as a number of proposals to reduce such membership to 300, 350, or 400. There have also been some proposals to increase the size of the Senate by equally increasing the number of senators for all states or by increasing the number of senators apportioned to the more populous states. Unless all states approved the latter amendment, it would be in apparent violation of an entrenchment provision now in Article V.

See also Constitutional Amendments, Limits on.

❖
CONGRESS, SPECIAL ELECTIONS
❖

In Great Britain, which is typical of other parliamentary systems, the prime minister and members of Parliament are elected to five-year terms, but the prime minister may call an early election when the minister believes that an election will bolster party support. The prime minister may also call a new election after receiving a vote of no confidence in Parliament (Rasmussen and Moses 1995, 82). There is no such provision in the U.S. Constitution, and, if called, such an election would be counter to the fixed terms of office provided therein.

Numerous individuals who favor incorporation of one or more parliamentary features into the U.S. government have called for Congress or the president to be able to call such special elections. At least two amendments have been introduced in Congress to this effect, one by Populist Senator William Peffer of Kansas in 1895 and another by Republican Representative Charles Potter of Michigan in 1951. The former was directed specifically at issues of finance and foreign relations. The latter resolution would have required Congress to hold a national election if requested to do so by a two-thirds vote of its members.

See also Parliamentary System.

❖ **CONGRESS, TERM LENGTHS** ❖

The Constitution sets the terms of members of the House of Representatives at two years and the terms of senators at six years. The terms of House members were designed to keep them especially close and accountable to the people; by contrast, the terms of senators were designed to give them greater independence (Vile 1993a, 27, 31).

Because all members of the House are elected every two years, there is a chance for a large turnover in presidential election years, and the president's party almost always loses seats in so-called off-year, or midterm, House elections that occur between presidential contests. By contrast, only one-third of senators run for election in presidential election years, and swings in nonpresidential election years tend to be less dramatic than those in the House.

A recent study lists just over 200 proposals that sought to alter House terms and just over 50 more that would have both altered such terms and limited the number of terms that an individual could serve (S. Richardson 1991, 72–80, 87–90). Proposals have ranged from those calling for yearly election of House members to those calling for terms of three, four, or six years. Similarly, from 1789 to 1991, 13 proposals were introduced to lower the terms of senators to three or four years or to raise them to eight years; another four would also have limited the number of terms (S. Richardson 1991, 91, 100). Some versions of the four- and eight-year terms have been designed so that such terms would be more closely tied to presidential fortunes and thus encourage greater party discipline and coherence.

By far the most common proposal in regard to congressional term lengths has been to raise the terms of members of the House of Representatives to four years. This would arguably give members greater independence and allow them to devote more time to legislating and less to fund-raising. Critics argue that such terms would also mean that House members would not stay in close touch with their constituents.

At least one proposal introduced in 1989 to increase House terms to four years would also have required House members running for the Senate to vacate their seats (H.J. Res. 203). Proposals for raising the length of congressional terms have sometimes been made in conjunction with proposals for a recall mechanism; as described above, they are often also tied to proposals for congressional term limits. It is possible that members of the House who are otherwise reluctant to propose term limits might be more willing to do so in exchange for longer terms, but at present, there seems to be much more pressure for the former change than for the latter.

See also Congress, Term Limits.

❖ CONGRESS, TERM LIMITS ❖

In 1951, the states ratified the Twenty-second Amendment, limiting the service of presidents to two full terms. Ever since, proposals have periodically been introduced to limit the terms that members of Congress can serve. Between 1789 and 1991, 141 such proposals were introduced (S. Richardson 1991, 45), and most have been introduced from the 1950s onward. Frequently, such proposals have been tied to proposals to alter the length of terms of members of Congress, but from the 1970s to the present, the focus appears to have shifted from congressional term lengths to term limits (S. Richardson 1991, 39).

Neither idea, however, is new. The Articles of Confederation limited delegates to serving three one-year terms out of a possible six, and in the early history of the Constitution, Anti-Federalists pressed the idea of limiting the number of terms that members of the Senate could serve (Kesler 1990, 21). In recent years, however, the idea appears to have gained momentum. A number of presidents have expressed their support of the idea; Republican presidential candidates supported the idea in 1988 and 1992; in 1990, a lobby group called Americans To Limit Congressional Terms (ALCT) was formed to press for such an amendment; and it was incorporated into the Republican Contract with America (S. Richardson 1991, 53). The House of Representatives voted 227 to 204 in March 1995 for a proposal to limit service by members of the House and Senate to 12 years. By larger margins, it rejected proposals to limit service in the House to six years, to apply term limits retroactively, and to allow states to impose their own stricter limits. Although term-limit proposals had stronger support among Republicans than among Democrats, Republicans were far from united. Illinois Republican Representative Henry Hyde thus voted against such limits, saying, "I just can't be an accessory to the dumbing-down of democracy" (Babson 1995, 918).

In large part, the movement for term limits, like the putative ratification of the Twenty-seventh Amendment, is tied to popular frustration with Congress. This has occurred with the increased professionalization of a body that now seems far removed from the idea of "citizen legislators" that the founders originally contemplated. Ironically, reelection rates for members of Congress have been quite high. People appear to like their own representatives while disliking the institution as a whole (Prinz 1992, 150). This may stem in part from members' focus on constituent service rather than on more controversial political issues. Members also gain name recognition and access to the media through their service and have privileges, such as franking (free use of the mails), that are unavailable to other officeholders.

Advocates of term limits believe that they would help overcome such advantages and bring in "new blood" and new ideas—some amending proposals have been designated as the Citizen Representative Reform Act New Blood Provision. Increased turnover would also decrease the role that seniority plays in congressional assignments and might encourage members to devote more time to issues. Opponents argue that voters already have the power to impose term limits by refusing to reelect their representatives and argue that additional limitations are contrary to the spirit of democracy. Some also fear that term limits would weaken Congress as an institution and give greater power to unelected bureaucrats, many of whom would be able to serve longer than congressional representatives (S. Richardson 1991, 39–41; also compare Frenzel 1992 with Mann 1992).

One obvious obstacle to term limits is the fact that those who have achieved leadership positions in Congress (where seniority plays an important, albeit not dispositive, role) can hardly expect to favor a measure that would undercut their own power. It is possible that outside pressure for such an amendment could be exerted by state petitions to call an Article V constitutional convention on the subject, but to date, states have preferred to attempt to limit congressional terms through state laws and referendums (S. Richardson 1989). After considerable academic debate (see, for example, Whitaker 1992), the Supreme Court recently declared in *U.S. Term Limits v. Thornton* (1995) that the requirements for members of Congress listed in the Constitution are exclusive and that such state attempts were therefore unconstitutional.

Another obstacle to terms limits is that proponents have not been united on precisely what limits are appropriate. Supporters of limits for the Senate have typically advocated from one to three terms. Proposals relative to the House of Representatives have varied from three to ten terms; some proposals also advocate increasing House terms from two to four years, with a two- or three-term limit.

Proposals for term limits have frequently been combined with proposals for altering congressional terms, especially in the House of Representatives. Some proposals have sought to limit the total number of terms an individual can serve, whereas others have focused on the total number of consecutive terms or the total number of years an individual can serve within a given time period (for example, 10 out of 12 years). Some proponents of term limits have attempted to limit the total number of years that an individual can serve as president, vice president, a member of the cabinet, or a member of Congress—a proposal that could drastically affect the pool of candidates for these offices. Some proposals have also sought to limit the number of years that individuals can serve as ambassadors, judges, and justices. Obviously, each proposal has a potentially different effect on how U.S. government operates, and it is possible that some of the effects have not been fully anticipated.

Some advocates of term limits are now pressing for a constitutional convention. Others are pushing for a national referendum on the subject in the 1996 elections.

See also *U.S. Term Limits v. Thornton.*

For Further Reading:

Cloud, David S. 1996. "Term Limits Stall in Senate; GOP Blames Democrats." *Congressional Quarterly* 54 (27 April): 1153–.

❖ CONGRESS, VACANCIES IN ❖

The Seventeenth Amendment provides that state governors may make appointments to fill vacancies in the U.S. Senate until the next general election. Because the Constitution makes no such provision for the House of Representatives, vacancies there continue to be governed by the provision in Article I, Section 2 that specifies that "when vacancies happen in the Representation from any State, the Executive Authority thereof shall issue Writs of Elections to fill such Vacancies." Thus, such vacancies can be filled only by special election (Clem 1989, 66). When there is less than a year left in a member's term, states may simply leave a House seat vacant until the next term.

Within a decade after ratification of the Seventeenth Amendment, a New Jersey representative proposed that state governors be permitted to make temporary appointments until House vacancies could be filled by election. This proposal came long before later concerns generated by nuclear weapons and reflected in more than a score of proposals to provide for the emergency functioning of Congress.

❖ CONSTITUTIONAL AMENDMENTS, LIMITS ON ❖

Article V of the Constitution establishes the formal procedures by which the document may be amended and specifies two explicit limits (sometimes called entrenchment clauses) on the content of amendments. One such provision that has since expired was introduced on 10 September 1787 at the Constitutional Convention by South Carolina's John Rutledge and was designed to guard a compromise between the North and the South regarding slavery. It prohibited any changes in Article I, Section 9 of the Constitution, which allowed for the importation of slaves until 1808 (Farrand 1966, 2:559).

The other provision, introduced at the convention on 15 September by Pennsylvania's Gouverneur Morris and presumably in effect as long as the Constitution stands, provides "that no State, without its Consent, shall be deprived of its equal Suffrage in the Senate" (Farrand 1966, 2:631). This was designed to protect the Connecticut, or Great, Compromise introduced by Connecticut's Roger Sherman at the Constitutional Convention. It was formulated as a way of mediating the desires of the small states, which favored equal state representation, and those of the large states, which wanted representation to be based on population. This compromise provided that representation in the House of Representatives would be based on population and that representation in the upper house would be apportioned equally among the states, each of which would have two senators. The convention had rejected an earlier proposal by Sherman that, in addition to guaranteeing equal state suffrage, would have prevented each state from being affected "in its internal police" without its consent (Farrand 1966, 2:630).

Just before the Civil War, several amendments, including the Corwin amendment, were proposed that would have permanently frozen the institution of slavery within the Constitution in an attempt to reassure the South and avert war. Abraham Lincoln indicated that he did not oppose such a compromise, but it was not adopted. Ironically, if ratified, this, rather than the amendment abolishing involuntary servitude, would have become the Thirteenth Amendment.

From the time of John C. Calhoun to the present, politicians and scholars have speculated as to whether there are any additional unstated limits on the substance of amendments to the Constitution. Conservative spokesmen such as Selden Bacon and William Marbury challenged the validity of the Fifteenth, Eighteenth, and Nineteenth Amendments on the grounds that they exceeded such implicit restraints. The Court ignored or rejected such arguments in *Myers v. Anderson* (1915), the *National Prohibition* cases (1920), *United States v. Sprague* (1931), and *Leser v. Garnett* (1922).

A number of contemporary scholars, most notably Walter Murphy, have argued that the Constitution embodies certain fundamental values, such as the protection of human dignity, that implicitly limit any conflicting changes. Such scholars have therefore hypothesized that there are a number of conceivable amendments that would be unconstitutional. Similarly, Eric Isaacson (1992) and Jeff Rosen (1991) argued that the proposed amendment designed to prohibit flag burning would be unconstitutional and would be subject to judicial invalidation. Vile (1985) has argued that the explicit prohibitions in Article V were intended to be exclusive and that acceptance of other implicit limits would unduly elevate judicial powers.

See also Bacon, Selden; Corwin Amendment; Marbury, William; Murphy, Walter F.

For Further Reading:
Linder, Douglas. 1981. "What in the Constitution Cannot Be Amended?" *Arizona Law Review* 23:717–31.

Wright, R. George. 1991. "Could a Constitutional Amendment Be Unconstitutional?" *Loyola University of Chicago Law Review* 22: 741–64.

❖ CONSTITUTIONAL ❖ COMMISSIONS

One of the mechanisms of state constitutional revision that has not been used at the national level is the constitutional commission. Although the legislative or executive branch sometimes creates such commissions individually, they generally have the support of both branches. Such commissions may propose constitutional reforms for legislative consideration and approval, or they may prepare amendments for a constitutional convention (Rich 1960, 89). Often such commissions attract high-caliber individuals, but their work is usually at the mercy of the state legislatures. Because such commissions lack "the strong legal position and the dynamic character and drama of a convention," a student of the commission has concluded that such commissions are "no substitute" for such conventions (Rich 1960, 99).

As the bicentennial of the Declaration of Independence approached, political scientist Conley Dillon (1974) proposed the establishment of a national constitutional commission to recommend needed changes. The Constitution mentions no such mechanism, but there appears to be no legal obstacle to the creation of such a body, as long as it is only advisory.

See also States, Constitutional Revision.

❖ CONSTITUTIONAL ❖ CONVENTION OF 1787

The U.S. Constitution was written at a convention that met in Philadelphia from May through September 1787 (C. Bowen 1966; W. Peters 1987; Rossiter 1987; Van Doren

1948). The idea of a convention emerged from an earlier meeting by representatives of five states to discuss commercial matters, known as the Annapolis Convention. Congress subsequently authorized a convention "for the sole and express purpose of revising the Articles of Confederation and reporting to Congress and the several legislatures such alterations and provisions as shall . . . render the federal constitution adequate to the exigencies of Government and the preservation of the Union" (Solberg 1958, 64). Altogether, 55 delegates from 12 states (Rhode Island did not send any delegates) attended the convention, which elected George Washington as chairman and quickly began to focus on alternatives to the Articles of Confederation rather than attempting merely to amend that document. Many states were spurred to send delegates by Shay's Rebellion, a taxpayer revolt centered in Massachusetts in the winter of 1787–1788 that convinced many men of property that civil order was endangered.

Much of the deliberation at the Constitutional Convention centered on conflicts between the large states, whose interests were initially represented in the Virginia plan, and the small states, whose interests were reflected somewhat later in the New Jersey plan (Vile 1993a, 15–16). These plans and other proposals and controversies also reflected tension between advocates of expanded national powers and those who wished to retain many of the states' prerogatives under the Articles of Confederation. Compromises were also necessary to reconcile the conflicting interests of the slave and free states.

Most convention delegates, all of whom had lived through the Revolutionary War, appear to have agreed that a constitutional amending process was a necessary alternative to revolution. Thus, Virginia's George Mason reflected that "the plan now to be formed will certainly be defective, as the Confederation has been found on trial to be. Amendments therefore will be necessary, and it will be better to provide for them, in an easy, regular and Constitutional way than to trust to chance and violence" (Farrand 1966, 1:203).

The Virginia plan's initial provision for an amending process was more a statement of intent than a viable mechanism, but it did specify that congressional assent should not be required for amendments. At the end of July, a five-member Committee of Detail proposed a scheme under which Congress would call a convention upon receiving petitions from two-thirds of the states (Farrand 1966, 2:159). Delegates debated these proposals during the last week of the convention, beginning on 10 September. Elbridge Gerry of Massachusetts feared that the proposal did not protect minority state interests; Alexander Hamilton of New York thought that Congress should have a role in initiating amendments; and Virginia's James Madison was concerned about the vagueness of the convention mechanism (Vile 1992, 29). The response was a proposal introduced by Madison and seconded by Hamilton, allowing two-thirds majorities of Congress or two-thirds of the states to propose amendments, which would be ratified by three-fourths of the states. After an objection by South Carolina's John Rutledge, a provision was added prohibiting the importation of slaves for 20 years.

The amending issue reemerged on 15 September, with Virginia's George Mason now objecting that the amending mechanism was too much under the control of Congress. This objection resulted in the provision allowing two-thirds of the states to propose a convention for amending the Constitution. One of Pennsylvania's representatives, Gouverneur Morris, apparently shared earlier concerns raised by Connecticut's Roger Sherman; Morris successfully introduced a provision that states could not, without their consent, be deprived of their equal representation in the Senate.

When the delegates to the Constitutional Convention reported their work, it was clear that they had exceeded their mandate to revise the Articles of Confederation. Moreover, new Article VII specified that the Constitution would be ratified by conventions rather than by state legislatures. The success of this ratification is attributable to the better organization of the supporters of the Constitution, the Federalists; to the fact that they were advocating a positive remedy to ills that were generally recognized; and to the strength of their arguments. To date, the formal amending process that the convention developed remains unchanged; it has been used to adopt 27 amendments.

❖ CONSTITUTIONAL ❖ CONVENTIONS

The U.S. Constitution was drawn up by the delegates meeting at the Constitutional Convention of 1787. This convention delineated two convention mechanisms in Article V, the amending article. One provided that amendments could, at congressional specification, be ratified by conventions in three-fourths of the states; to date, this mechanism has been used only in the case of the Twenty-first Amendment repealing national alcoholic prohibition.

A second convention mechanism outlined in Article V permitted two-thirds of the state legislatures to petition Congress to call a convention "for proposing Amendments." Although states have submitted hundreds of petitions for such a convention, to date, the necessary two-thirds of the states have not applied for either a general convention or a convention on a single specified topic (but see Van Sickle and Boughey 1990). In part because no Article V convention has ever been called, a host of unanswered questions continue to surround this process.

No question has dominated the discussion of the convention mechanism more than two interrelated issues: whether a convention must be general or whether it can be restricted to a single topic; and if such a convention is not limited, whether it might become a "runaway" body (Vile 1993b, 55–73). Those who believe that a convention cannot be limited believe that any other kind of convention would not be free to propose amendments in the manner that Article V appears to contemplate. Thus, they conclude that any state applications for a convention that are predicated on such limitations are invalid. As one such scholar argued, "Applications asking for something other than what is meant by Article V are nullities, and thirty-four times zero is zero" (C. Black 1979, 628). This position is bolstered by the fact that most nineteenth-century petitions for conventions appeared to contemplate a general convention rather than one limited to a specific topic.

Walter Dellinger has further argued against a limited convention on the basis that such conventions would allow states "to propose and ratify amendments that enhance their power at the expense of the national government" (Dellinger 1979, 1630), something that he believes is contrary to the intentions of those who wrote the Constitution. Dellinger argues: "States were empowered under Article V to *ratify* amendments; the power to *propose* amendments was lodged in two national bodies, Congress and a convention. The proceedings suggest that the framers did not want to permit enactment of amendments by a process of state proposal followed by state ratification without the substantive involvement of a national forum" (1979, 1630).

By contrast, a number of scholars have argued that an Article V convention could be limited. William Van Alstyne argues: "a generous construction of what suffices to present a valid application by a state for consideration of a particular subject or of a particular amendment in convention, is far more responsive to the anticipated use of Article V than a demanding construction that all but eliminates its use in response to specific, limited state dissatisfactions" (1978, 1303). Similarly, Grover Rees III (1986) argues that the convention mechanism was designed to facilitate state amendments, and an interpretation that would force the states to risk all or nothing would not meet such an objective. Reflecting some reservations, the author of a book on the subject concluded that "a national convention is in all likelihood constitutionally limited to proposing amendments described in the state applications that generated the call" (Caplan 1988, 157). From a somewhat different angle, two other authors have concluded that there are various "political" safeguards, including the requirement that any proposed amendments be ratified by three-fourths of the state legislatures, that make a runaway convention unlikely (Weber and Perry 1989, 105–25).

Legislation proposed by Senators Sam Ervin and Orrin Hatch dealing with constitutional conventions has been predicated on the idea that states do have the authority to call limited conventions. Such legislation has also attempted to address a variety of other questions, including the length of time that petitions calling for a convention are valid, and whether states have the power to rescind them; how states would be represented at a convention; whether a convention would vote by a simple majority or whether it would have to muster a two-thirds vote; and—related to whether conventions may be limited—whether Congress could refuse to submit amendments to the states for ratification, or whether courts might invalidate proposed amendments that appeared to exceed a limited convention call. It is possible that many of these issues will not be resolved until an Article V convention actually convenes.

Conventions are common at the state level, where they are frequently used to revise constitutions or propose new ones. The lessons of such conventions are not, however, necessarily applicable at the national level (F. Heller 1982).

See also Constitutional Convention of 1787.

❖ CONSTITUTIONAL ❖ INTERPRETATION

The United States prides itself on a written Constitution that is unchangeable by ordinary acts of legislation. Still, it is clear that far more changes have been effected in constitutional understandings through interpretations, especially by the judicial branch, than by constitutional amendment. Few areas have been more frequent or controversial subjects of inquiry in recent years than questions of constitutional interpretation. Some controversies center on the terminology, and others center on the hermeneutical, or interpretive, principles that should guide members of the judiciary or others who are called upon to apply the Constitution.

Terminologically, debate sometimes centers on a distinction between judicial activism and judicial restraint (Halpern and Lamb 1982; Wolfe 1991); at other times, it centers on a distinction between interpretivism and noninterpretivism (J. H. Ely 1980). Neither set of terms is altogether luminous.

When critics accuse judges of being too "activist," they may well respond that they are simply enforcing the Constitution as they see it. Moreover, a judge might arguably exercise "restraint" by failing to heed constitutional mandates. This caveat noted, judicial activism is a term frequently used to describe a judge who reaches out to deliver opinions in uncharted waters and gives little or no deference to past precedents or to legislative judgments. Such an advocate may argue that judicial activism is necessitated by the failure of the other two branches (A. Miller 1982). An advocate of judicial restraint, by contrast, would give issues maximum time to develop and would typically be respectful and deferential toward both precedents and determinations of constitutionality by other branches of the government. When the Warren Court was frequently criticized for being overly activist and, indeed, for judicially amending the Constitution, Justices Felix Frankfurter and John Marshall Harlan often counseled against getting unduly involved in "political questions" or unnecessarily overturning prior judicial or legislative judgments.

Another dimension in constitutional interpretation centers on the dichotomy between interpretivism and noninterpretivism. Interpretivists attempt to limit their decisions to those that they can justify from within the confines of the constitutional text, refusing to give judicial solutions to questions that, in their opinion, the Constitution does not address. Frequently, interpretivists advocate the idea of "original intent." Although there are numerous versions of this principle, all ultimately attempt to answer questions of interpretation whenever possible by asking what the authors or ratifiers of a particular phrase in the Constitution understood or intended for it to mean. Noninterpretivists, by contrast, are likely to look beyond the text to considerations of policy, democracy, or justice, or with a view toward keeping the Constitution up to date. During the Reagan administration, there was a serious public debate on this subject between Attorney General Edwin Meese, an advocate of original intent, and Justice William Brennan, who thought that this interpretive principle was too narrow (see Rakove 1990). This debate also figured prominently in the confirmation hearings of Robert Bork, who, like Meese, was a strong advocate of original intent (Bork 1990; for a critique of original intent, see Levy 1988).

Knowing that an individual is an advocate of judicial activism or restraint, or that such an individual is an interpretivist or a noninterpretivist, does not always allow one to predict how this individual will decide a given case. This is because everyone has supplementary notions about how much weight to give to words and how to interpret them, about what the historical record of given clauses means, about constitutional structures and relationships, about the need to defer to past precedents (the principle of *stare decisis*), and the like (see Bickel 1986; Bobbitt 1992; L. Goldstein 1991; Tribe and Dorf 1991).

The difficulty of the constitutional amending process undoubtedly prods the judiciary to be more creative than it might be if the process were easier. Overly creative interpretations might, in turn, make authors of amendments nervous about including broad or vague language in constitutional additions.

For Further Reading:

Murphy, Walter F., James E. Fleming, and Sotirios A. Barber. 1995. *American Constitutional Interpretation,* 2d ed. Westbury, NY: Foundation Press.

❖ CONTRACT WITH AMERICA ❖

In an attempt to derive a mandate from the 1994 midterm congressional elections, Republican candidates for the House of Representatives, led by Georgia Representative and soon-to-be Speaker of the House Newt Gingrich, drew up a Contract with America that outlined an ambitious program of legislative and constitutional reform (Wilcox 1995, 69–71; Gillespie and Schellhas 1994). Modeling their agenda on Franklin Roosevelt's broad program of an earlier day, the Republicans hoped to adopt many of these reforms within the first 100 days if they proved successful in the general election. Proposals included adoption of a balanced budget amendment, a legislatively mandated line-item presidential veto (rather than a constitutional amendment), and an amendment to provide for congressional term limits. Although not in the contract, Republicans also promised prompt consideration of an amendment to restore prayer in public schools. One critic subsequently noted that Congress faced a "glut of amendments" (Ornstein 1994, 5), and another referred to "amendment fever" (Sullivan 1995).

Although the 1994 election brought Republican control of the House of Representatives for the first time since 1952 (as well as control of the Senate), there are those who dispute that the Contract with America was responsible for this victory (Wilcox 1995, 211), and there is continuing speculation as to whether 1994 marked a critical election. Moreover, once in power, Republicans realized that bold legislative initiatives often face considerable opposition and that constitutional amendments are particularly difficult to enact. Although getting the balanced budget amendment through the House in the first 100 days, Republicans were one vote short in the Senate. In the House itself, Republicans split over the appropriate length of time for limited congressional terms and whether the limit should apply to the total number of years or the number of consecutive years in office. The year after the Contract with America, the Christian Coalition proposed a Contract with the American Family (Reed 1995). Among other proposals, it advocated a Religious Equality Amendment. However, it focused on legislation rather than on an amendment as a way of limiting abortion. Many of the issues raised by the two contracts await the outcome of the 1996 presidential election and subsequent elections.

See also Balanced Budget Amendment; Congress, Term Limits; Prayer in Public Schools; Presidency, Veto Power of.

For Further Reading:

Ornstein, Norman J., and Amy L. Schenkenberg. "The 1995 Congress: The First Hundred Days and Beyond." *Political Science Quarterly* 110 (Summer 1995): 183–206.

Redinger, Paul. 1996. "The Faltering Revolution." *ABA Journal* 82 (February): 56–59.

❖ CONTRACTS CLAUSE ❖

Article I, Section 10 of the U.S. Constitution provides that "no State shall . . . pass any Law impairing the Obligations of Contracts." This was a much-litigated clause in early American history (B. Wright 1938) that was strictly construed to restrict state regulatory powers (in, for example, the cases of *Fletcher v. Peck* [1810] and *Dartmouth College v. Woodward* [1819]). The clause has been interpreted far more liberally in the twentieth century (for example, *Home Building and Loan Association v. Blaisdell* [1934]).

From 1884 to 1889, a time during which the Supreme Court was beginning to rely increasingly on the idea of substantive due process rather than on the contracts clause to protect property rights, a Maryland representative introduced several proposals to circumvent the contracts clause. His amendment would have voided any promises a state may have made to a corporation exempting it from taxes.

Perhaps because it was thought that the multiplicity of interests at the national level would serve as adequate protection, there is no provision comparable to the contracts clause limiting the national government (Rossum and Tarr 1991, 286). In 1871, New York Democratic Representative Clarkson Potter offered an amendment prohibiting Congress from chartering corporations or impairing the obligation of contracts. Similarly, in 1982, Republican Representative Robert Walker of Pennsylvania offered two resolutions prohibiting Congress from adopting any laws to abridge the right of citizens to enter into contracts, except when this was necessary to preserve vital and pressing governmental interests (H.J. Res. 466).

❖ CORPORATIONS ❖

The U.S. Constitution does not specifically mention corporations, but in cases such as *Dartmouth College v. Woodward* (1819), the Supreme Court recognized such entities as artificial persons with legal rights. As artificial persons, the rights of corporations grew with the adoption of the Fourteenth Amendment after Roscoe Conkling argued in *San Mateo Co. v. Southern Pacific R.R.* (1883) that one of the intentions of the joint congressional committee on which he had served to draft the amendment was to protect such corporations—an argument later disputed by Howard Jay Graham (Mason and Stephenson 1993, 274). The number and sizes of corporations grew tremendously after the Civil War, leading to concerns that states might be dwarfed by corporate power. Initially, most regulation of corporations took place under state law. The Securities Act of 1933 and the Securities Exchange Act of 1934 subsequently introduced increased federal regulation of corporations, but much regulation continues at the state level (R. Hamilton 1987, 8–9).

Four proposals were offered in the 1880s to enable states to tax corporations, even if such states had provided tax exemptions when granting corporate charters. Another proposal would have prohibited state grants or loans to such corporations. Several other amendments were introduced at the turn of the century, most by New Jersey Democratic Representative Allan McDermott, to give Congress control over corporations. During this time, the Supreme Court, in cases such as *Lochner v. New York* (1905), used the due process clauses of the Fifth and

Fourteenth Amendments as bulwarks for laissez-faire economics, and arguments about the potentially broad scope of federal power (Goodnow 1911) were not immediately accepted. During this same time, many states were eliminating statutory restrictions to induce corporations to incorporate within their states (R. Hamilton 1987, 6–7).

With modern latitudinarian constructions of congressional power under the commerce and taxing clauses, increased federal control of corporations does not appear to need further constitutional authorization.

❖ CORWIN AMENDMENT ❖

From the election of President Abraham Lincoln in November 1860 through the session of the lame-duck Congress that met from December 1860 to March 1861, a number of proposals were introduced to preserve the Union and avert war. These included a series of proposals known as the Crittenden Compromise. Also, the Washington Peace Convention met in February 1861 to accomplish the same end. The Corwin amendment was the only compromise actually approved by the requisite majorities in Congress and is one of six amendments not subsequently ratified by the requisite number of states.

In December 1860, outgoing President Buchanan proposed an "explanatory amendment" (J. Richardson 1908, 5:638) that was actually a series of three proposals. It would give "express recognition of the right of property in slaves in the States where it now exists or may hereafter exist," recognize the right to own slaves within the territories (thus legitimizing the 1857 decision in *Scott v. Sandford* that the incoming Republican president had opposed), and recognize slave owners' right to have escaped slaves returned to them (J. Richardson 1908, 5:638).

The House of Representatives subsequently created a committee of 33 (one representative from each state), with Republican Thomas Corwin of Ohio as chairman, to address this issue. The Senate created a committee of 13, chaired by Democrat Lazarus Powell of Kentucky, with a similar aim (R. Lee 1961, 7–8). The so-called Corwin amendment actually appears to have originated in the latter committee and was apparently the product of New York Republican William Seward (soon to be Lincoln's secretary of state), who had access to the new president. The amendment was introduced in the House committee by Massachusetts Republican Charles Francis Adams, son of former president John Quincy Adams and a confidant of Seward's (R. Lee 1961, 17). In the final form proposed by Representative Corwin, the amendment provided for an entrenchment clause that would guarantee the existence of slavery within its contemporary limits: "No amendment shall ever be made to the Constitution which will authorize or give to Congress power to abolish or interfere, within any State, with the domestic institutions thereof, including that of persons held to labor or service by the laws of the said State" (R. Lee 1961, 22).

On the first try, on 28 February 1861, the House fell short of the necessary majority, voting 123 to 71 for the measure. The next vote, held the following day, was 133 to 65. The Senate proposed the amendment by a vote of 24 to 12 on 3 March 1861 (R. Lee 1961, 23–24). In a highly unusual move, outgoing President Buchanan signed the amendment (Bernstein with Agel 1993, 91).

In his first inaugural address, President Lincoln (who was willing to permit slavery in the South but adamantly opposed to its expansion in the territories, as the Crittenden Compromise would have allowed) indicated his support for the amendment. He said, "Holding such a provision to now be implied constitutional law, I have no objection to its being made express and irrevocable" (J. Richardson 1908, 6:11). One of his central concerns, shared by other congressional supporters of the amendment, appears to have been to keep border states, in which slavery was permitted, within the Union.

Ohio ratified the Corwin amendment in May 1861; Maryland and Illinois followed in January and February 1862. By then, however, it was clear that the compromise had not been enough to keep the South in the Union. The Thirteenth Amendment, which would be ratified after the war, did not protect the institution of slavery but abolished it. The Corwin amendment continues to raise questions about whether there are any unstated substantive limits on what can be added to the Constitution (Brandon 1995).

See also Crittenden Compromise; Peace Convention.

For Further Reading:
Keogh, Stephen. 1987. "Formal & Informal Constitutional Lawmaking in the United States in the Winter of 1860–1861." *Journal of Legal History* 8 (December): 275–99.

❖ COST-OF-LIVING ADJUSTMENTS ❖

Automatic cost-of-living adjustments (COLAs) became popular during the inflationary 1960s and 1970s, and they were added to the Old Age and Survivors Insurance Program in 1972 (Watson 1985, 628). Although they help protect workers and pensioners against inflation, COLAs also contribute to increased prices. Democratic Representative Bill Burlison of Missouri offered a proposal on 13 June 1977 (H.J. Res. 514) to prohibit automatic increases in the prices of goods or services under any law, contract, or other authority.

❖ COUNCIL OF CENSORS ❖

At the time the U.S. Constitution was written, those states that had amending procedures used one of three means—legislative action, conventions, or a council of censors (Traynor 1927, 61–62). Pennsylvania and Vermont employed the latter mechanism. Thus, the Pennsylvania state constitution of 1776 called for a council consisting of two persons from each of the state's cities and counties to meet every seventh year "to enquire whether the constitution has been preserved inviolate in every part; and whether the legislative and executive branches of government have performed their duty as guardian of the people" (Meador 1898, 265). The council would also check into other matters of government and have the authority—the only such power specified in the constitution—to call a convention to propose constitutional amendments.

The Pennsylvania Council of Censors met as scheduled in 1783, but its deliberations were torn by partisan controversy (*Records of the Council of Censors, 1783–1784*). A majority recommended establishing a bicameral rather than a unicameral legislature. It also proposed substituting a governor with veto power for the existing president and council, providing independence for state judges, and eliminating the council of censors mechanism (Meador 1898, 288). Since two-thirds of the council did not agree, however, no convention was called to accomplish these purposes.

The second Pennsylvania Council of Censors was scheduled to meet in 1790, but the year before, the legislature called for a constitutional convention. It proposed a constitution that incorporated most of the suggestions made by the earlier council. The new constitution, which was subsequently adopted, omitted the council of censors mechanism. A commentator noted that the citizens had "become wearied with so unwieldy a piece of political machinery"

(Meador 1898, 298). The provision remained in the Vermont constitution until 1869 (Meador 1898, 266).

When, in *Federalist* No. 50, James Madison opposed plans for periodic appeals to the people for constitutional change, he cited the experience of Pennsylvania. He observed that its council had been split into violent factions, consisting in part of individuals who had served in the very government they were called upon to assess. He concluded that "this censorial body, therefore, proves at the same time, by its researches, the existence of the disease, and by its example, the inefficacy of the remedy" (Hamilton, Madison, and Jay 1961, 320).

❖ COUNCIL OF STATE GOVERNMENTS ❖

In *Baker v. Carr* (1962), the Supreme Court declared that it would no longer consider issues of state legislative apportionment to be "political questions." This decision stirred considerable controversy, including a drive for a constitutional convention led by Republican Senator Everett Dirksen of Illinois. The Council of State Governments issued one of the strongest responses when the General Assembly of States, which it sponsored, proposed three amendments at its December 1962 meeting (Committee on Federal State Relations 1963; for further discussion, see Vile 1991c, 97–100).

The first proposal would have made the amending process easier by allowing two-thirds of the state legislatures to propose amendments by submitting identical texts of such amendments to Congress; this proposal would also have eliminated the convention method of ratifying amendments. The second proposal, clearly aimed at *Baker v. Carr*, would have declared that "no provision of this Constitution, or any amendment thereto, shall restrict or limit any state in the apportionment of representation in its legislature (Committee 1963, 9). Much along the lines of the Eleventh Amendment, this proposal also would have restricted judicial jurisdiction over this issue. The third proposal would have created a Court of the Union consisting of the chief justice from each state. This court, whose decisions would be final, would hear petitions from state legislatures concerning issues alleged to be reserved to the states.

The scholarly reaction to these proposals was quite negative. William Swindler (1963) of the College of William and Mary saw these proposals as an attempt to return to a government like that under the Articles of Confederation. Focusing on the proposed reform of the amending process, Yale's Charles Black called the amendments "A Threatened Disaster" (1963); Princeton's Alpheus Mason called the amendments the "'Dis-Union' Amendments" (1964, 199). The title of a popular magazine article summarized such sentiments when it proclaimed, "Seventeen States Vote To Destroy Democracy as We Know It" (Morgan 1963).

Although the proposals by the Council of State Governments failed, and the issue of state legislative apportionment no longer appears to be of great concern, issues of federalism continue to stir controversy. By 1990, largely prompted by decisions in *Garcia v. San Antonio Metropolitan Transit Authority* (1985) and *South Carolina v. Baker* (1988), 15 states had adopted resolutions proposing amendments to redress the balance between the state and national governments (Tolchin 1990, A12). More recently, the Council of State Governments has sponsored the move for a Conference of the States.

❖ COURT OF THE UNION ❖

See Council of State Governments.

❖ COURT-PACKING PLAN ❖

Proposed constitutional amendments often represent dissatisfaction with judicial decisions, but amendments are certainly not the only way that such dissatisfaction can be expressed. One of the most dramatic confrontations between the presidency and the judiciary took place with the introduction of President Franklin D. Roosevelt's so-called court-packing plan. He announced this plan in a fireside address in February 1937.

Almost from the time he assumed the presidency, Roosevelt realized that the Supreme Court had the power to scuttle many of his New Deal programs. On 27 May 1935, or Black Monday as it came to be called, the Court delivered three unanimous opinions that struck at various New Deal programs. In *Louisville Joint Stock Land Bank v. Radford*, it invalidated a bill providing mortgage relief to farmers; in *Humphrey's Executor v. United States*, it ruled that the president could not remove members of independent regulatory agencies; and in *Schechter Poultry Corporation v. United States*, it invalidated the National Industrial Recovery Act. The next year, the Court continued its attack on the New Deal, albeit by much closer votes, by invalidating the Agricultural Adjustment Act, the National Bituminous Coal Act, and a New York minimum-wage law.

Although Roosevelt was increasingly concerned about the Court's ability to stymie the New Deal, he bided his time through the 1936 election, hoping to keep the focus on other issues. After winning this election in a record landslide, Roosevelt and his aides directed significant attention to the Court issue, exploring a number of options before finally settling on the court-packing plan.

One of the most obvious paths that Roosevelt could have taken would have been to propose one or more constitutional amendments to reverse judicial decisions or to curb judicial decision making. There was no shortage of proposals, some of which dated back to the Progressive Era. These included plans to expand congressional powers under the general welfare clause, to require more than a simple majority of the Supreme Court to declare legislation unconstitutional, to require that judges retire at age 70, and to allow the attorney general to seek early rulings on the constitutionality of congressional legislation and then permit the next session of Congress to override adverse decisions (Kyvig 1989, 471–73).

Such proposals encountered a number of obstacles. These included the difficulty of deciding on satisfactory language that would grant Congress the necessary power without entrusting it with dangerous authority; the anticipated difficulty of ratification and the time that even a successful ratification might take; the fear that the courts could ultimately restrictively interpret any new amendments; and the fact that if Roosevelt supported an amendment to expand federal powers, "it might seem tantamount to conceding that he had been wrong and the Supreme Court right in their dispute over the constitutionality of New Deal measures" (Leuchtenburg 1995, 111). Roosevelt appears to have been especially influenced by the example of the child labor amendment, which had been proposed by Congress but stymied in the state legislatures. Roosevelt was especially concerned that the Liberty League would be able to muster effective opposition to any proposed amendments at the state level (Kyvig 1989).

Working with Attorney General Homer Cummings (who, in turn, appears to have been influenced by Princeton political science professor Edwin S. Corwin), Roosevelt came up with a plan. Ironically, the central plank of this plan had been supported by one of the sitting conservative justices, James McReynolds, when he had served as Woodrow Wilson's attorney general (Leuchtenburg 1995, 120). This plan would have allowed the president to add an additional Supreme Court justice, up to 15 justices, for any justice with 10 years or more of service who did not retire at age 70. It also provided for additions to lower courts and for expediting judicial work.

Roosevelt justified his plan as a means of helping the aging justices (often contemporaneously referred to as "the nine old men") keep up with their work, but the political implications of the plan were too apparent to hide. In a March fireside chat, Roosevelt compared the three branches of the federal government to three horses, one of which was pulling in the wrong direction (R. Jackson 1941, 340–51). The Senate Judiciary Committee subsequently issued a report that was quite critical of the president's plan, but it was probably the unexpected death of Roosevelt's Senate floor leader, Joe Robinson, that doomed it.

Within two months of the proposal of the court-packing plan, however, the Court issued a decision in *West Coast Hotel Co. v. Parrish*. That decision, and one coming two weeks later in *National Labor Relations Board v. Jones & Laughlin Steel Corporation*, appeared to mark a judicial shift, contemporaneously dubbed the "shift in time that saved nine." Justice Owen Roberts, always a swing vote, had deserted the conservative "Four Horsemen" on the Court, and thereafter, the Supreme Court upheld fairly expansive federal powers. Scholars still dispute whether the court-packing plan led to this shift, but it appeared to many that Roosevelt lost his court-packing battle but won the war for the soul of the Court.

Scholars continue to debate the consequence of Roosevelt's strategy. The changes inaugurated by the Court's shift certainly seem as consequential as many that had previously been made by constitutional amendments. Bruce Ackerman argues that this shift marks one of three major "constitutional moments" in U.S. history. David Kyvig believes that Roosevelt may have overestimated the difficulty of the amending process and appears to lament the lack of a "specific constitutional sanction" for the New Deal (1989, 481).

❖ COURTS ❖

See Judiciary.

❖ CRAM, RALPH (1863–1942) ❖

Ralph Cram offered one of the most iconoclastic schemes of constitutional reform to be proposed in the twentieth century (Vile 1992, 75–78) in a book entitled *The End of Democracy* (1937). Cram was a noted architect whose works, often patterned on medieval structures, included the Cathedral Church of St. John the Divine in New York City (Shand-Tucci 1975).

As the title of his book indicates, Cram was a critic of modern or what he called "Low Democracy." In its place, he proposed substituting a "High Democracy" or an "Aristocratic Republic" (Cram 1937, 19), which is what he believed the American framers had intended. Indeed, by extending democracy and increasing governmental powers, the Fourteenth through Nineteenth Amendments had elevated the masses over individuals of character who could exercise true leadership. The result was "quite a new world where quantitative have taken the place of qualitative values and the tabloid type of man controls all things" (Cram 1937, 93). In such a situation, the solid middle class on which democracy should be based had become "the Forgotten Class" (Cram 1937, 94).

To restore this middle class, existing "*political* organization" needed to be replaced by a new "*functional* organization, representation and control" (Cram 1937, 120). Cram advocated a corporate state, which he described as "the substitution for professional politicians chosen on a partizan [*sic*] or territorial basis, of non-political, non-partizen [*sic*] delegates or representatives made up of voluntary associations of the functional factors in society" (Cram 1937, 122). Elsewhere, Cram described a quaint scheme whereby individuals were associated in largely autonomous units of 500 families, each with their own farms, gardens, town halls, and professional personnel (Cram 1935, 201–22).

Concentrating more directly on the national government in *The End of Democracy*, Cram critiqued universal suffrage. Recognizing that it would now be difficult to abolish, he advocated restrictions for those convicted of crimes and for those applying for naturalization.

Cram favored rearranging Congress along functional representative lines. Although elsewhere in his book he criticized parliamentary systems, he borrowed a number of their features. He proposed that the president and Congress work together on a legislative budget. He would repeal the Seventeenth Amendment so as to provide for a Senate known as "a body of men of high character, noble intelligence and wide vision; men of mature judgment, of scholarly attainments and of knowledge of the world" (Cram 1937, 166). Cram thought that such a body could best be chosen partly by appointment and partly by indirect election, some appointments being made by the major secular and religious interests in society. Members would serve from 10 years to life. All laws would originate in the House of Representatives, a body that would apparently remain largely unchanged.

Cram, who admired Franklin Roosevelt, also liked the strong presidency that had developed in the United States. He would further strengthen this institution by providing that the president would be chosen for life, quite possibly by members of the House from among those in the Senate. Personally preferring that the president be designated as king, Cram settled on "His Highness the Regent of the Republic of the United States" (Cram 1937, 187). As head of state, the regent would appoint a prime minister, who would choose a cabinet. Like William Yandell Elliott, with whom he was familiar, Cram believed that the head of state should be able to dissolve the House of Representatives; unlike Elliott, Cram thought that the regent should appoint a new prime minister if the vote went against him.

Again drawing from Elliott, Cram thought that the Court should not be able to invalidate federal laws except by an extraordinary majority. Cram favored unanimity. Like Elliott, he also believed that the Supreme Court should issue advisory opinions.

Continuing to draw from Elliott, Cram further advocated dividing the nation into five or six provinces or commonwealths and decentralizing administration. He wanted to create an order of nonhereditary knighthood, with recipients being designated as "Sir" as a means of recognizing the natural aristocracy. He also advocated expansion of the civil service and the creation of a "Civilian West Point" (Cram 1937, 218). Suspicious of the existing exercise of such freedoms as those of speech and the press, Cram nonetheless recognized that the evils of state licensing might prove worse than current abuses. The key here, as elsewhere, was "the placing of men of character, capacity, and intelligence in all positions, social, economic, political" (Cram 1937, 237).

For Further Reading:

Shand-Tucci, Douglass. 1995. *Boston Bohemia, 1881–1900: Ralph Adams Cram: Life and Architecture.* Vol. I. Amherst: University of Massachusetts Press.

❖ CRITICAL ELECTIONS ❖

The amending process is often likened to a "safety valve" that provides an alternative to revolution, but elections perform a similar function on a more regularized basis. Just as some amendments—for example, the Fourteenth—are more far-reaching than others, so too are some elections. Political scientists refer to these as critical, or realigning, elections.

There appear to have been at least five critical elections in the United States. They occurred in 1800, 1828, 1860, 1896, and 1932 (Burnham 1970, 1). Such elections are associated with "short-lived but very intense disruptions of traditional patterns of voting behavior"; they exhibit high intensity on the part of voters, are often associated with the rise or demise of minor parties, and tend to occur with fairly "uniform periodicity" (Burnham 1970, 6–10).

Amendments, like realigning elections, often have a generational dimension (Strickland 1989, 48–50). At least a few amendments appear to have resulted from realigning elections. The Twelfth Amendment remedied a flaw in the electoral college that was evident in the election of 1800. The Civil War amendments (Thirteen through Fifteen) were made possible by Republican gains in 1860 and 1864. Although the election of 1896 kept Republicans in control, a number of Progressive Era amendments reflected reform elements from that election. The election of 1932 manifested itself chiefly in changed judicial interpretations rather than in amendments, but it is recognized by some as a key "constitutional moment," equivalent to others affirmed by constitutional amendments (Ackerman 1991).

Because U.S. political parties have weakened in recent years, it has been difficult to establish whether there has been another realigning election; the 1994 midterm congressional elections have been the subject of special attention (Burnham 1995; Wilcox 1995). With a view toward recent ambiguity, a number of political scientists refer to a "dealigning" process (Rohde 1994), and other observers caution that apparent re-alignments are sometimes fairly transitory (Berke 1995, E-3). Whatever the status of such elections, they serve as a reminder that political changes often occur in clusters (Silva 1970), and majorities that are successful in mustering support for one amendment often develop sufficient momentum to initiate others as well.

❖ CRITTENDEN COMPROMISE ❖

The period between the election and the inauguration of Abraham Lincoln was marked by a series of attempts to introduce compromises that would keep the Southern states from seceding. Among the most prominent, albeit ultimately unsuccessful, attempts was a series of unamendable amendments offered by Kentucky Unionist Senator John J. Crittenden and first introduced in the Senate on 18 December 1861. Crittenden's proposals, if accepted, would have marked the first attempt to settle the slavery issue by amendment rather than by ordinary acts of legislation (Kirwan 1962, 374). This was a logical approach, since the Southern movement for secession was stimulated in part by fears, raised much earlier by John C. Calhoun and accentuated by Lincoln's election and the growth of the free states, that the amending process could one day be used to abolish slavery throughout the nation.

Altogether, Crittenden proposed seven amendments. Tennessee Senator (later president) Andrew Johnson also introduced a series of amendments designed in part to split the presidency, vice presidency, and membership of the Supreme Court between the North and the South (Dumond 1973, 159). Crittenden's proposals would have (1) restricted and extended the Missouri Compromise line to California, prohibiting slavery north and permitting it south of the line, with new states making their own choices as to whether they would be slave or free; (2) prohibited Congress from abolishing slavery on federal property within slave states; (3) prohibited Congress from abolishing slavery in the District of Columbia as long as it existed in Maryland or Virginia, and even if it did not, abolition would require consent of District residents and compensation; (4) prohibited Congress from interfering with interstate slave transit; (5) provided compensation for owners of fugitive slaves rescued by mobs; and (6) prohibited future amendments altering the three-fifths clause or the fugitive slave clause or interfering with slavery in the South (Kirwan 1962, 375). Crittenden's compromise also called on Congress to pass resolutions recognizing that (1) the fugitive slave laws were constitutional and should be enforced, (2) conflicting state laws should be repealed, (3) provisions of fugitive slave laws offensive to Northerners should be repealed, and (4) laws prohibiting the foreign slave trade should be strengthened (Kirwan 1962, 375–76).

Debates about these proposals occupied much of the lame-duck session of Congress. The Peace Convention meeting in February 1861 submitted proposals to Congress much like Crittenden's.

The Crittenden Compromise has been called "a Southern plan in search of Northern support" (Keogh 1987, 283). Outgoing President Buchanan endorsed the plan. It failed because most Republicans, including incoming President Lincoln, balked at the provisions relating to slavery in the territories and decided instead to support the Corwin amendment, which merely guaranteed that the national government would not interfere with slavery in those states where it already existed. The version of the Crittenden Compromise that was submitted by the Peace Convention was voted down in the Senate on 4 March 1861 by a vote of 7 to 28 (Keogh 1987, 292).

One of the most fascinating aspects of the

Crittenden Compromise was that Crittenden hoped to break the congressional logjam of opposition by having the people vote on the plan in a national plebiscite, or referendum. Crittenden recognized that such a vote would be extraconstitutional and hence nonbinding, but the Senate refused to send it to the people (Keogh 1987, 288).

See also Corwin Amendment.

❖ CROLY, HERBERT (1870–1930) ❖

Herbert Croly published *The Promise of American Life* in 1909 (1965) and went on to become editor of the *New Republic* from 1914 to 1928. Typical of intellectuals in the Progressive Era, Croly critiqued the amending process in *Progressive Democracy* (1914).

Arguing that the constitutional amending process was overly rigid, Croly agreed with Professor Munroe Smith in stating "that the first article of any sincerely intended progressive program must be the amendment of the amending clause of the Constitution" (Croly 1914, 230). Croly suggested that constitutional changes should be made by a majority of voters, with provisions for due "deliberation" and "territorial distribution of the prevailing majority" (Croly 1914, 231). Croly specifically commended Senator Robert La Follette's plan, whereby amendments could be proposed by a majority of both houses of Congress or one-fourth of the states and subsequently ratified by a majority of voters in a majority of states.

Croly perceived that the rigidity of the amending process had contributed to the role that the Supreme Court had assumed in interpreting and adapting the Constitution. Believing that the Court was beginning to defer more readily to legislative bodies, Croly argued that the power of the people was superior to both. The amending process had converted the democracy of the

Constitution into "a golden hoard." Croly intended to open this treasure directly to the people (Croly 1914, 237).

❖ CULTURAL AND LINGUISTIC RIGHTS ❖

At a time when there have been increasing calls for an amendment making English the official language of the United States, Representative Jimmy Hayes and Senator John Breaux, both Democrats from Louisiana (although Hayes has subsequently switched parties), have introduced a different amendment. Designated the cultural rights amendment (Baron 1990, 24), it would enable people "to preserve, foster, and protect their historic, linguistic, and cultural origins" and see that no one is denied equal protection of the law for exercising such a right (H.J. Res. 408, 1989).

These proposals reflect Louisiana's recent interest in reviving and preserving its unique Acadian heritage, including its French language (J. Taylor 1976, 177–78). The 1921 Louisiana state constitution contained a compulsory English provision, and teachers of the day, from both French and English backgrounds, often humiliated children who continued to speak French in school (Estaville 1990, 116; Brasseau 1989, 11–12).

❖ CURRENCY ❖

Article I, Section 8 of the U.S. Constitution invests Congress with power "to coin Money, [and] regulate the value thereof." A controversial exercise of this power occurred during the Civil War when the government issued paper bills, known as "greenbacks," and subsequently passed a law, the Legal Tender Act of 1862, requiring that such currency be accepted in payment for debts. When initially challenged in *Hepburn v. Griswold* (1870), the Supreme

Court held by a 4 to 3 vote that this law—at least as applied to preexisting contracts—violated both the due process clause of the Fifth Amendment and the contracts clause (J. W. Ely 1992, 84). The day the opinion was issued, President Grant appointed two new justices, and when the case was reargued the next year, the Court reversed itself in *Knox v. Lee* in a 5-to-4 vote, again split along partisan lines (Ely 1992, 84).

Several contemporary amending proposals, some undoubtedly motivated by these developments, would have made gold and silver the exclusive legal tender or would have limited the issuance of paper currency. Some proposals introduced in 1892 provided for issuing paper money in the amount of $20 per person and equalizing its value with that of gold and silver (Musmanno 1929, 110).

In *Norman v. Baltimore & Ohio Railroad Co., Nortz v. United States,* and *Perry v. United States* (the *Gold Clause* cases of 1935), the Supreme Court endorsed broad congressional powers over currency. In these cases, it decided that the government could annul requirements in private contracts calling for payment in gold.

❖ CUSTOMS AND USAGES ❖

Although the text of the Constitution can be changed only by constitutional amendment, its interpretation can be altered in a variety of ways, the most common of which is judicial interpretation. Other customs and usages, however, may also develop as the legislative and executive branches make moves that serve as precedents for future actions. Conceptually, then, the "written" Constitution is surrounded by a larger "unwritten" constitution, more familiar in nations such as Great Britain that are not regarded as having a written constitution (Tiedeman 1890; W. Harris 1993; Vile 1994a).

The most authoritative, albeit dated, dis-cussion of U.S. customs and usages is found in a book published by Herbert Horwill, a scholar from Great Britain, in 1925. In describing the "Law of the Constitution," Horwill referred to the Constitution and its amendments, as well as to the "Statute Law" and "Common Law" surrounding it. He described other conventions that grew up around the Constitution as "customs and usages."

Among the customs that Horwill identified were conventions that had democratized the electoral college, the precedent whereby a vice president who takes over for a president who has died takes his title rather than merely serving as an "acting president," the two-term presidential limit (in force when Horwill wrote, broken by Franklin D. Roosevelt, and later reestablished by the Twenty-second Amendment), the role of the president's cabinet, various customs regarding the appearance of cabinet officers before Congress, the appointment and removal powers, and the custom whereby a member of Congress is expected to be a resident of his district. Horwill noted that customs and usages may change or may be incorporated into the Constitution. Thus, prior to the adoption of the Seventeenth Amendment, many state legislatures had already agreed to accept the popular choice for U.S. senators (Horwill 1925, 203–5). Similarly, Woodrow Wilson changed a custom that had been in force since Thomas Jefferson when he decided to read a presidential message before Congress (Horwill 1925, 199).

Describing a similar phenomenon, a recent British author noted the existence of certain "abeyances" in government. He describes such abeyances as contrasting with more determinable conventions and as representing "a form of tacit and instinctive agreement to condone, and even cultivate, constitutional ambiguity as an acceptable strategy for resolving conflict" (Foley 1989, xi).

Like the idea of customs and usages, the concept of abeyances serves as a reminder that, even in a nation that professes adherence to a written constitution, the text needs to be interpreted in light of practices, both written and unwritten, that surround it. Reformers who fail to give attention to such surroundings are likely to misunderstand the operation of government, propose amendments that are not needed, or be frustrated by the effects of their own proposals.

For Further Reading:

Wilson, James G. 1992. "American Constitutional Conventions: The Judicially Unenforceable Rules That Combine with Judicial Doctrine and Public Opinion To Regulate Political Behavior." *Buffalo Law Review* 40 (Fall): 645–738.

D

❖

❖ DECLARATION OF ❖ INDEPENDENCE

One of the foremost documents in American history is the one that explained the reasons that the colonies were declaring their independence from Great Britain. The Second Continental Congress delegated the task of writing this document to a committee of five men consisting of Thomas Jefferson, John Adams, Benjamin Franklin, Roger Sherman, and Robert Livingston. Jefferson did the initial drafting, and the document was subsequently debated and revised by Congress as a whole. Congress voted to accept the document on 4 July 1776, and it was signed over the next several months.

The Declaration of Independence was firmly based on a philosophy of natural rights. According to this philosophy, men are created equal and are equally entitled to the right to "life, liberty, and the pursuit of happiness." Governments are instituted to secure such rights. Accordingly, "whenever any form of government becomes destructive of these ends, it is the right of the people to alter or abolish it, and to institute new government, laying its foundation on such principles, and organizing its powers in such form, as to them shall seem most likely to effect their safety and happiness."

After arguing that humans were generally more inclined to suffer deprivation of rights than to alter their form of government, Jefferson argued that when faced with attempts to set up a despotism, the people have both the "right" and the "duty" to "throw off such government, and to provide new guards for their future security." Much of the remainder of the Declaration focuses on specific grievances the colonists had against the English king.

The Constitution arguably gave life to many of the principles embodied in the Declaration of Independence. The eventual ratification of the equal protection clause of the Fourteenth Amendment was an especially important step toward governmental protection of equal rights to liberty. The constitutional amending process provides a viable "safety valve" against the necessity for revolution.

In his original draft of the Bill of Rights, James Madison had proposed adding a prefix to the Constitution specifying "that all power is derived from the people, who have a right to reform or change their government whenever it is found inadequate" (Schwartz 1992, 166). In a similar vein, in July 1976, the bicentennial of the Declaration, Representative Robert Michel, a Republican from Illinois, introduced an amendment (H.J. Res. 1016) to incorporate certain principles of the Declaration of Independence into the preamble of the U.S. Constitution.

See also Jefferson, Thomas.

For Further Reading:

Adler, Mortimer J. 1987. *We Hold These Truths: Understanding the Ideas and the Ideals of the Constitution.* New York: Macmillan.

Becker, Carl L. 1970. *The Declaration of Independence: A Study in the History of Political Ideas*. New York: Vintage Books.

Gerber, Scott D. 1995. *To Secure These Rights: The Declaration of Independence and Constitutional Interpretation*. New York: New York University Press.

Vile, John R. 1993. *A Companion to the United States Constitution and Its Amendments*. Westport, CT: Praeger.

Wills, Garry. 1978. *Inventing America: Jefferson's Declaration of Independence*. New York: Doubleday.

❖ DEFAMATION ❖

The First Amendment to the Constitution prohibits the national government from abridging freedom of speech. This protection has been extended via the due process clause of the Fourteenth Amendment to the states as well. The Supreme Court has ruled, however, that some forms of expression do not constitute free speech. These include "fighting words," obscenity, and libel. Libel refers to written communication that "is injurious to the reputation of another" (*Black's Law Dictionary* 1969, 824). Defamation is libel in spoken rather than written form.

Up to 1964, laws against libel were handled by the states. In *New York Times v. Sullivan* (1964), however, it became clear that such laws could be used to stifle criticism of public officials, in this case an Alabama police commissioner taking action against civil rights protesters. Accordingly, the Supreme Court ruled that, in proving libel, public officials have a substantial burden of proof. They have to show that libelous statements made about them were made with "actual malice," that is, with knowledge that they were false or with "reckless disregard" to their truth or falsity. Subsequent rulings have extended this standard to other public figures who are not officials, but not to private individuals who are merely caught up in public controversy (*Getz v. Robert Welch, Inc.* [1964]).

Although some individuals favor further liberalization of libel laws, others fear that current laws allow too much leeway to those who would abuse free speech. In April 1982, Democratic Representative Bill Burlison of Missouri introduced an amendment that would provide that nothing in the First Amendment "shall prevent the recovery by any person, including any person deemed newsworthy, of damages in a civil action, or the imposition of criminal penalties, in cases involving defamation of such persons" (H.J. Res. 1285).

For Further Reading:

Lewis, Anthony. 1991. *Make No Law: The Sullivan Case and the First Amendment*. New York: Random House.

❖ DILLON, CONLEY (1906–1987) ❖

Political scientist Conley Dillon offered a number of proposals to revise the Constitution about the time of the bicentennial of the Declaration of Independence and the Constitution (Vile 1991c, 25–27). His proposals were closely tied to a resolution by the American Society for Public Administration (ASPA) (C. Dillon 1974). It proposed the establishment of a Permanent Commission for Constitutional Review consisting of 15 members appointed by the president, the president pro tempore of the Senate, and the Speaker of the House of Representatives (C. Dillon 1977, 14).

Following the ASPA report, Dillon suggested nine areas of study for the commission: (1) "the constitutional basis of our federal structure"; (2) the "selection, removal, and succession" of the president and vice president, as well as "executive branch accountability" and the possibility of "a modified parliamentary system"; (3) "the method of selecting and removing members of Congress, their terms of office, and the[ir] organization and procedures"; (4)

the selection and removal of judges; (5) the "distribution and sharing" of powers among the three branches; (6) the "constitutional status and role" of political parties; (7) the "scope of individual and group freedoms and rights"; (8) the organization of a constitutional convention; and (9) ways to deal with loss of confidence in government (C. Dillon 1977, 22).

Dillon also discussed other plans for constitutional change, including plans by Rexford Tugwell, the Reuss Resolution, and the proposal by James L. Sundquist to allow Congress to remove the president, dissolve itself, and call a new election. Dillon acknowledged that "a realistic assessment, however, does not promise action on constitutional review in the near future" (C. Dillon 1977, 22).

❖ DILLON V. GLOSS (1921) ❖

This case arose from a habeas corpus petition filed by a petitioner who had been convicted of transporting alcohol in violation of the National Prohibition Act (also known as the Volstead Act), adopted pursuant to the Eighteenth Amendment. The petitioner questioned the legitimacy of the seven-year time limit for ratification that had been incorporated into that amendment. He also claimed that the amendment, which contained a one-year implementation delay, had not been in effect when he was arrested because his arrest had been less than a year from the time the secretary of state had certified the amendment.

Noting that Article V of the Constitution did not specify a ratification time period, Justice Willis Van Devanter observed for a unanimous Court that, without such an understanding, four amendments would still be pending. Analyzing Article V, he concluded that since it treated proposal and ratification not "as unrelated acts, but as succeeding steps in a single endeavor, the

natural inference" was that "they are not to be widely separated in time" (*Dillon* 1921, 374–75). He further concluded:

[A]s ratification is but the expression of the approbation of the people and is to be effective when had in three fourths of the states, there is a fair implication that it must be sufficiently contemporaneous in that number of states to reflect the will of the people in all sections at relatively the same period, which, of course, ratification scattered through a long series of years would not do. (*Dillon* 1921, 375)

Although the Constitution did not specify how long the ratification period should be, Van Devanter concluded that the seven-year span that Congress had established in the case of the Eighteenth Amendment was reasonable. Van Devanter further decided that the Eighteenth Amendment became effective when ratified by the requisite number of states and not when such ratification was certified 13 days later by the secretary of state.

The current status of *Dillon v. Gloss* is not clear. In *Coleman v. Miller* (1939), the Supreme Court ruled that the question of contemporaneousness was a "political question" for Congress to decide. Moreover, although *Dillon* suggested that it would be "quite untenable" (375) to consider an amendment proposed in 1789 without a specified time limit to be pending, Congress did exactly this when it voted in 1992 to accept ratification of the Twenty-seventh Amendment.

See also *Coleman v. Miller.*

❖ DIRKSEN, EVERETT MCKINLEY ❖ (1896–1969)

Everett McKinley Dirksen of Illinois served in the U.S. House of Representatives from

1933 to 1949 and in the Senate from 1951 to 1969. In his Senate years, he was the minority leader during the heyday of President Johnson's Great Society years and the activism of the Warren Court. Dirksen often led the opposition to both. He is remembered for his deep, gravelly voice and for advocating making the marigold the national flower (Penney 1968, 91–92).

When first elected to the House, Dirksen was one of the few Republicans who ran on a platform of repeal of the Eighteenth Amendment (Kyvig 1979, 168). He was subsequently a leading advocate of two proposed amendments. One would have overturned the Supreme Court's decision in *Engel v. Vitale* (1962) and permitted "voluntary participation by students and others in prayer." The other was designed to overturn *Baker v. Carr* (1962) and *Reynolds v. Sims* (1964) by allowing states to apportion at least one house of their state legislatures other than by population. After the apportionment amendment failed to pass in the Senate by a vote of 57 to 39, Dirksen formed a Committee for Government of the People (CGP) to promote the calling of a national constitutional convention on the subject (Schapsmeier and Schapsmeier 1985, 180). This movement apparently came but a single state shy of the necessary two-thirds majority before faltering (*Proposals for a Constitutional Convention* 1979, 2).

For Further Reading:

Bonfield, Arthur E. 1968. "The Dirksen Amendment and the Article V Convention Process." *Michigan Law Review* 66 (March): 949–1000.

Dirksen, Everett M. 1968. "The Supreme Court and the People." *Michigan Law Review* 66 (March): 837–74.

❖ **DISTRICT OF COLUMBIA,**
REPRESENTATION FOR ❖

Article I, Section 8 of the Constitution entrusts Congress with the power to legislate on behalf of the nation's capital. During the time of the Articles of Confederation, Congress was threatened in Philadelphia by militiamen who wanted to collect back pay, and the experience persuaded the framers that the national government should control its own immediate surroundings (Report to the Attorney General 1987, 52–55). The early capital moved from New York to Philadelphia to the current site. The selection of a spot ceded by Virginia and Maryland was one of the first examples of "logrolling." Southerners interested in the site got their wish in exchange for their support for Alexander Hamilton's plan to pay off Revolutionary War debts in full (Bernstein with Agel 1993, 144–45).

In 1802, Congress provided for a charter that allowed for a mayor and a city council, a plan that continued until 1871. At that time, it was replaced by a territorial government. After a scandal, Congress took control in 1874 and governed the District through congressional committees until 1966. At this time, President Lyndon Johnson used an executive order to appoint a mayor—later elected by the District (Schrag 1985, 10–12). In 1971, Congress granted the District a nonvoting member in the House of Representatives, and Democrat Walter Fauntroy was elected to this post.

As early as 1825, Augustus Woodward had proposed that the District be given representation in Congress. More than 150 such proposals were introduced from the 1880s through 1978 (Report 1987, 11). The Twenty-third Amendment, ratified in 1961, granted the District representation in the electoral college, but it still had no voting members in Congress. After a 289-to-127 vote in the House on 1 March 1978, followed on 22 August by a 67-to-32 vote in the Senate, a proposal was sent to the states to remedy this long-standing issue (Bernstein with Agel 1993, 146).

The amendment consisted of four parts. The first provided that "for purposes of representation in the Congress, election of the President and Vice President, and article V of this Constitution, the District constituting the seat of government of the United States shall be treated as though it were a State." Section 2 somewhat ambiguously provided that "the exercise of the rights and powers conferred under this section shall be by the people of the District constituting the seat of government, as shall be provided by the Congress." Section 3 would have repealed the now redundant, and possibly contradictory, Twenty-third Amendment, and Section 4 provided for a seven-year ratification deadline.

The District of Columbia subsequently held a convention to write a constitution for the state of New Columbia (Schrag 1985). This convention proved to be overly optimistic, and by the 1985 deadline, only 16 states had ratified. A key problem with the amendment was political—the District of Columbia was predominantly African American and Democratic, thus offering little to the Republican Party (Vose 1979; Horn 1990). Beyond that, some believed that the amendment violated the one remaining limit on Article V in that, by granting an entity that was not a true state representation in the Senate, it would deprive the others of their equal representation therein and would thus require unanimity. Others were uncomfortable with the notion of treating an entity, still somewhat under congressional control, "as though it were a state."

Some have sought to add the District as a state through ordinary legislation, but given the District's constitutional status, there are doubts about the constitutionality of such a move (but see Raven-Hansen 1975). Another possibility is retrocession—giving the District, perhaps exclusive of federal enclaves, back to Maryland; Virginia's portion has already been so retroceded. Yet another possibility is to allow District residents to vote in Maryland elections, but it is by no means clear that Maryland would favor this move, which might also require repeal of the Twenty-third Amendment.

The District thus remains something of a constitutional anomaly. Although it remains the center of free government, its inhabitants are denied direct representation in the Congress that meets there.

For Further Reading:
Best, Judith. 1984. *National Representation for the District of Columbia*. Frederick, MD: University Publications of America.

Bowling, Kenneth R. 1991. *The Creation of Washington, D.C.: The Idea and Location of the American Capital*. Fairfax, VA: George Mason University Press.

Hatch, Orrin G. 1979. "Should the Capital Vote in Congress? A Critical Analysis of the Proposed D.C. Representation Amendment." *Fordham Urban Law Journal* 7: 479–539.

❖ DIVIDED GOVERNMENT ❖

Few issues have done more to generate concern among proponents of a parliamentary system alternative to U.S. government than the issue of divided government. Such a divided government occurs when one party captures the presidency and another captures one or both houses of Congress. This situation is made possible by a system of separation of powers. In parliamentary systems, a scheme of fused powers guarantees that the prime minister, who is chosen by parliament, heads the majority party or coalition. In the United States, by contrast, the president and Congress have different electoral bases. Thus, in the 44 years from 1946 to 1990, control was divided between Democrats and Republicans for 26 years (Mayhew 1991, 1).

Critics of separation of powers contend that this system leads to needless controversy and to legislative gridlock. Defenders argue that divided government often reflects a popular unwillingness to invest either party with control over both branches and that such a division helps guard liberty and deter precipitous legislation. The author of a recent study who investigated the progress of lawmaking and the success of congressional investigations since the end of World War II concluded that, "surprisingly, it does not seem to make all that much difference whether party control of American government happens to be unified or divided" (Mayhew 1991, 198). Another author critiquing the parliamentary model of fused powers has argued that legislative-executive party conflict can be healthy (Sargentich 1993, 707).

See also Parliamentary System.

❖ DODD, WALTER F. (1880–1960) ❖

One of the most important books on the process of amending state constitutions was written by Walter F. Dodd. Dodd, a professor at Johns Hopkins University, published his book on state amendments in 1910. Although many of the specifics of this work are obviously outdated, Dodd's book is still surprisingly relevant, especially in explaining the development and early use of the constitutional convention mechanism and its relation to the state legislature.

Dodd noted that the development of this mechanism followed three steps: establishing "the distinction between the constitution and ordinary legislation"; developing the convention as a body distinct from the legislature; and submitting the constitution "to a vote of the people, after it has been framed by a constitutional convention" (Dodd 1910, 22). Of these steps, he viewed the first as fundamental and the others as "but the elaboration of machinery to carry out more clearly the distinction between constitutions and ordinary legislation" (Dodd 1910, 22).

In his classic work on constitutional conventions, Judge John Jameson (1887) argued that the constitutional convention mechanism was necessarily subject to legislative control. Dodd argued that, in at-

tempting to cut one would-be sovereign down to size, Jameson had elevated another. Believing that "the process of piecemeal amendment of state constitutions is absolutely under the control of the state legislatures except in the states which have adopted the popular initiative," he argued that constitutional conventions were in a somewhat different category: "The calling of constitutional conventions is also to a large extent subject to legislative control, but the convention method of altering constitutions is the one more independent of the regular legislatures. . . . The convention loses a large part of its usefulness as an organ of the state if it be treated as strictly subject to control by the regular legislative body" (Dodd 1910, 79).

On another issue, Dodd authored an article supporting the decision in the *National Prohibition* cases (1920), which struck down arguments that the Eighteenth Amendment was unconstitutional. Dodd noted that an understanding that permitted the courts to void amendments "would introduce into American constitutional practice a highly undesirable type of judicial control" (Dodd 1921, 334).

See also Jameson, John A.

❖ *DODGE V. WOOLSEY* (1856) ❖

This case involved a suit by a bank stockholder contesting a new tax that Ohio had laid on a bank. This tax violated a prior act under the previous state constitution limiting such taxes on newly chartered banks to 6 percent.

In declaring that the new tax violated the contract clause, Justice James Wayne declared that the U.S. Constitution was supreme "over the people of the United States aggregately and in their separate sovereignties, because they have excluded themselves from any direct or immediate agency in making amendments to it, and have directed that amendments shall be made representatively for them" (1856, 348) through the Article V amending process. An author has recently cited this decision in attempting to refute Akil Reed Amar's contention that popular majorities have authority to amend the Constitution outside of Article V provisions (Monaghan 1996, 128).

DOLBEARE, KENNETH (1930–), ❖ and ❖ JANETTE HUBBELL (1948–)

These two authors, self-described as "an eastern iconoclast who teaches politics at a small college and a southwestern populist who left elementary school teaching to launch a successful small business," recently published a book set in the year 2012 (1996, xiv). *USA 2012: After the Middle-Class Revolution* centers around a college student who reviews with his parents the developments that led to a successful middle-class revolution based on the concept of "economic nationalism" (xiii).

This program was instituted as a result of economic deterioration and a sense of middle-class outrage that resulted in the adoption of a new Declaration of Independence on 4 July 2000. Whereas the document of 1776 was directed against the British, the new Declaration aims at the two-party system, at large corporations and banks (who come in for particularly intensive criticism by the authors), at the media, at special interests, and at the bureaucracy (22–23). The authors also reflect concern about the effect of free-trade policies, especially the GATT (General Agreement on Tariffs and Trade) and NAFTA (North American Free Trade Agreement) treaties, on workers.

The book describes how, after extensive debate and discussion, the people decided to adopt four amendments to restore the United States to its prior prosperity. Most important is the first of those amendments

providing for quarterly popular referendums on major issues of public policy. Neither the president nor the Congress could veto such referendums (118–19). This referendum mechanism allowed for a more direct democracy than is currently practiced and helped convert members of Congress into delegates of the people rather than independent decision-makers.

The second proposed amendment would limit campaign contributions to $100 for any individual or group and mandate that television and radio stations make free time available to candidates. Elections would be shortened, with campaigning prohibited from 60 days prior to a primary election or 90 days prior to a general election.

The third amendment would provide for proportional representation, both within the electoral college and within Congress. The intention of this amendment, which would also lift existing restrictions on third parties, was to encourage a multiparty system. This amendment would also lift voting registration requirements, extend voting to a two-day weekend, and allow voters to cast their ballots for "None of the Above" (NOTA).

The fourth amendment would be aimed at the judicial system and would attempt to balance considerations of individual rights against public concerns. It would specifically mandate consideration of "comparative liability and contributory negligence," would allow judges to review jury awards, and would attempt to reduce litigation (134).

The authors aim their book at an undergraduate audience. Although the authors believe it is important that the changes they propose be adopted by amendments, they offer their proposals as "discussion drafts" rather than as final products.

❖ DOMESTIC VIOLENCE, PROTECTION AGAINST ❖

Article IV, Section 4 of the Constitution authorizes the United States to protect states against domestic violence when so petitioned by a state. In *Luther v. Borden* (1849), the Supreme Court upheld a congressional law vesting the power to respond to such requests in the president.

Perhaps reacting to a speech in which outgoing President James Buchanan noted that Southern women retire at night "to apprehensions of civil insurrections" (J. Richardson 1908, 637), Democratic Representative Thomas Florence of Pennsylvania introduced a series of proposals in 1861 that were designed to save the Union by recognizing that slavery was a matter of state option. He also provided, however, that the government had an obligation to come to a state's aid in suppressing slave insurrections (Ames 1896, 171). In 1870, motivated by a far different concern, Republican Senator Charles Drake of Missouri introduced another resolution that would have entitled the national government to intervene in cases of Ku Klux Klan violence even when not requested to do so by state governments (Ames 1896, 172).

❖ DOUBLE JEOPARDY ❖

The Fifth Amendment provides that no person shall "be subject for the same offense to be twice put in jeopardy of life or limb." Initially, this doctrine applied only to the national government; for a long time, the Supreme Court rejected its application to the states. In *Palko v. Connecticut* (1937), for example, the Court decided that this was not one of the rights implicit in a scheme of ordered liberty. The Court did not reverse course until *Benton v. Maryland* (1968), the last of the contemporary incorporation cases (Abraham and Perry 1994, 81–83).

In 1958, South Carolina Senator Strom Thurmond introduced a resolution to amend the Constitution so that when an individual appealed a criminal conviction and was granted a new trial, that individual

"may be convicted of any crime of which he could have been convicted upon his former trial for such offense." In *Trono v. United States* (1905), the Supreme Court had established a similar rule, but it reversed course in *Green v. United States* (1957). In that case, an individual who successfully appealed a conviction for arson and second-degree murder was subsequently retried and convicted of first-degree murder. The Supreme Court voided this conviction, ruling that when an individual files a criminal appeal, conviction of a lesser offense bars subsequent prosecution of a greater offense (Sigler 1969, 71–72).

❖ DUELING ❖

In the eighteenth and nineteenth centuries, gentlemen—especially in the South—sometimes resolved matters of personal honor by engaging in duels. These were closely bounded by recognized social norms (Stowe 1987, 5–49; Wyatt-Brown 1948, 350–61). It was in such a duel that Aaron Burr killed Alexander Hamilton. Andrew Jackson also engaged in such duels.

In 1828, the year Jackson was elected president, an amendment was introduced to prohibit dueling. In February 1838, William Graves, a Whig congressman from Kentucky, killed Jonathan Cilley, a Democratic congressman from Maine, in such a duel. Graves was censured, but the House rejected a committee report calling for his expulsion (Seitz 1929, 278). Similarly, two resolutions that would have excluded individuals who participated in such duels from holding office came to naught. Over time, state laws and public sentiment combined to eliminate this vestige of feudal aristocracy.

❖ DUTIES ❖

See Tariffs; Taxation, Export.

❖ *DYER V. BLAIR* (1975) ❖

John Paul Stevens, who subsequently became a U.S. Supreme Court justice, wrote this U.S. district court decision. The case involved Illinois' ratification of the equal rights amendment. Members of the legislature had sued Robert Blair, Speaker of the Illinois House of Representatives, for declaring state ratification of the amendment dead after it failed to achieve the three-fifths vote that the legislature and the state constitution had mandated for such amendments (Vile 1993b, 28–30).

Despite the Supreme Court's decision in *Coleman v. Miller* (1939), Stevens declared that this particular amending issue was not a "political question." Citing *Powell v. McCormack* (1969), Stevens argued that, however difficult, this case involved "no more than an interpretation of the Constitution" (*Dyer* 1975, 1301). As to the requisite vote for ratification, Stevens concluded that although Article V of the Constitution does not re-quire an extraordinary majority by ratifying state legislatures, it also does not prohibit states from adopting such a majority.

Citing *Hawke v. Smith, No. 1* (1920) and the *National Prohibition* cases (1920), which had decided that a state could not require ratification of amendments by popular referendum, Stevens struck down a provision in the Illinois state constitution that required the election of a new legislature before a vote was taken on a constitutional amendment. Stevens further ruled that since states were performing a federal function when they ratified amendments, any language in a state's constitution regarding a supermajority requirement would be "precatory" (*Dyer* 1975, 1308) or recommendatory only.

This case suggests that caution is in order in interpreting earlier cases, such as *Coleman v. Miller* (1939), that seemed to withdraw the courts from consideration of key amending issues.

See also *Coleman v. Miller.*

E

❖ EDUCATION, ESTABLISHMENT OF A NATIONAL UNIVERSITY ❖

Each of the first six presidents is on record as favoring a national university to train public servants, but some, including Thomas Jefferson, had reservations about congressional authority to establish such an institution (Ambrose 1966, 11, 17). James Madison, Charles Pinckney, and James Wilson suggested a measure at the Constitutional Convention of 1787 that would have entrusted such power to Congress, but it was not adopted (Eidelberg 1968, 27). As president, both Thomas Jefferson and James Monroe proposed in annual messages that such an amendment be adopted, and one was introduced in Congress in 1825 (Ames 1896, 274–75).

Although Jefferson had argued as a member of Washington's cabinet that Congress had no authority to establish a military academy, he supported the establishment of West Point during his presidency (Ambrose 1966, 18–19). This and other military academies are the only universities currently operated by the national government. Other U.S. universities, including the University of Virginia, which Jefferson founded after leaving the presidency, are either state or privately funded and operated.

❖ EIGHTEENTH AMENDMENT ❖

The Eighteenth Amendment providing for national alcoholic prohibition is distinctive for two reasons: it represents the only successful attempt to incorporate sumptuary legislation into the Constitution, and it is the only amendment to have been repealed. The first Prohibition amendment to be introduced in Congress was offered by Republican Representative Henry Blair of New Hampshire in 1876, with amendments being introduced sporadically thereafter until 1913. This was the year that the Anti-Saloon League decided to focus its energy on a national amendment. After this decision, dozens of proposals were introduced until the amendment was adopted in 1919.

Some of the American founders, most notably Dr. Benjamin Rush, expressed concern over the health effects of alcohol, and both politicians (including Abraham Lincoln, who signed an abstinence pledge) and religious reformers subsequently encouraged temperance. Maine established statewide Prohibition in 1851 (Grimes 1978, 83), but the primary waves of Prohibition at the state level occurred in 1864–1865, in the 1880s, and beginning in 1907. It was during the last of these waves that the focus of reform moved from the state to the national level. By 1917, 23 states had Prohibition laws, although only 13 were completely dry (U.S. Senate 1985).

Scholars continue to debate the weight to assign to various motivations behind Prohibition. Clearly, some supporters (especially those in the influential Women's Christian Temperance Union) were motivated by religious beliefs, some by medical evidence of the detrimental effects of alcohol use, and some by the belief in moral reform and progress so characteristic of the Progressive Era, during which a constitutional amendment was finally adopted (Timberlake 1970).

More negative cultural forces undoubtedly played a part as well. Many people viewed the saloon as "a political brothel in which corrupt liaisons were formed between foreign-born voters and political bosses" (Grimes 1978, 84), and the Anti-Saloon League became a major focus for Prohibition. Reformers were disproportionately rural white Protestants of northern European ethnic stock, and such reformers sometimes saw Prohibition as a means of controlling or reforming Catholics, immigrants, African Americans, Indians, and poor whites. With the advent of World War I, some reformers also found that Prohibition and anti-German sentiment went well together, since Germans were frequently associated with breweries.

Many advocates of temperance opposed the idea of Prohibition as unwarranted state interference in personal decision making and saw national Prohibition as an improper interference with states' rights. Opponents pointed to the injustice of shutting down what had previously been legitimate businesses. Opponents also pointed out that, under the amending process, it was possible for a minority of the people to adopt an amendment that the majority did not support.

Proponents nonetheless insisted on the evils of alcohol. A preface to an amending resolution introduced in Congress in 1914 explained their views:

Exact scientific research has demonstrated that alcohol is a narcotic poison, destructive and degenerating to the human organism, and that its distribution as a beverage or contained in foods lays a staggering economic burden upon the shoulders of the people,

lowers to an appalling degree the average standard of character of our citizenship, thereby undermining public morals and the foundations of free institutions; produces widespread crime, pauperism, and insanity; inflicts disease and untimely death upon hundreds of thousands of citizens and blights with degeneracy their children unborn, threatening the future integrity and the very life of the Nation. (U.S. Senate 1985, 50)

As early as 1890, Congress adopted the Wilson Act, subjecting imported liquor to state regulation. But in *Leisy v. Hardin* (1890), the Court said that such alcohol was not subject to state regulation as long as it remained in its "original package" (Musmanno 1929, 228–29). The Webb-Kenyon Act of 1913 further strengthened federal control over interstate shipment of alcohol, but proponents of Prohibition obviously wanted more.

In 1914, the House of Representatives defeated a Prohibition amendment, but support for such an amendment increased as war loomed. In 1917, Congress adopted the Lever Food Control Act restricting the importation of alcohol and prohibiting the use of foodstuffs in its production. That same year, Democratic Texas Senator Morris Sheppard reintroduced a Prohibition amendment that the House and the Senate subsequently adopted in December.

As amended, the proposal had a number of unique features. The first paragraph provided for a one-year transitional period, probably in the hope of allaying concerns about putting people out of work. Although it prohibited "the manufacture, sale, or transportation of intoxicating liquors within, the importation thereof into, or the exportation thereof for beverage purposes," the amendment left open the possible use of alcohol for medicinal and other purposes; moreover, the amendment did not explicitly outlaw the purchase of alcohol. The second paragraph of the amendment rather ambiguously provided that the state and national governments would have "concurrent power" to enforce the amendment. The third paragraph was the first to contain a seven-year ratification deadline. A somewhat shorter deadline was initially proposed by Republican Senator (later president) Warren G. Harding in the unrealized hope that the provision might undermine the amendment. The amendment was adopted despite arguments by Idaho's Republican Senator William Borah that the deadline provision was unconstitutional (Grimes 1978, 87).

The amendment was ratified in just over a year, and in 1919, Congress overrode President Woodrow Wilson's veto to adopt the Volstead Act. It defined as intoxicating any beverage—including beer and wine—that contained more than 0.5 percent alcohol.

In *Hawke v. Smith* (1920), the Court ruled that a state could not require approval of this or other amendments by referendum, thus arguably creating the impression in the public mind that the amendment did not have majority support. That decision might also have paved the way for the decision to have the Twenty-first Amendment adopted through state conventions rather than by state legislatures. In the *National Prohibition* cases (1920) and again in *Sprague v. United States* (1931), the Supreme Court rejected arguments that the Eighteenth Amendment exceeded implicit limitations alleged to inhere in Article V. The *National Prohibition* cases also defined concurrent powers to allow the state and national governments to enforce their own provisions and upheld the definition of alcohol in the Volstead Act.

The Prohibition movement and the Eighteenth Amendment appear to have reduced but not eliminated alcohol consumption (Kyvig 1985, 13). Although it sanctioned increased governmental power over individuals, Prohibition was widely flaunted, and the Eighteenth Amendment is generally believed to have contributed to the rise of organized crime by providing it with a profitable source of illegal revenue. In 1932, the Eighteenth Amendment was repealed by the Twenty-first Amendment.

See also Anti-Saloon League; Twenty-first Amendment; Women's Christian Temperance Union.

❖ EIGHTH AMENDMENT ❖

The Eighth Amendment was proposed by the First Congress and ratified in 1791 as part of the Bill of Rights. It provides that "excessive bail shall not be required, nor excessive fines imposed, nor cruel and unusual punishments inflicted." The prohibition against excessive fines has roots in the English Magna Carta, whereas the provisions against excessive bails and cruel and unusual punishments originated in the Massachusetts Body of Liberties and the Virginia Declaration of Rights (Lutz 1992, 53). Both the Virginia and the North Carolina ratifying conventions called for amendments against cruel and unusual punishments, and James Madison linked this guarantee to the provisions against excessive bail and fines when he presented his proposal for a bill of rights before Congress.

Debates in Congress were limited but prescient. William Smith of South Carolina thought that the words "cruel and usual" were "too indefinite" (Kurland and Lerner 1987, 5:377). Samuel Livermore of New Hampshire positively noted that "the clause seems to express a great deal of humanity," but went on to doubt its necessity and raise some questions: "What is meant by the terms excessive bail? Who are to be the judges? What is understood by excessive fines? It lies with the courts to determine. No cruel and unusual punishment is to be inflicted; it is sometimes necessary to hang a man, villains often deserve whipping, and perhaps having their ears cut off; but are we in future to be prevented from inflicting these punishments because they are cruel?" Acknowledging that the legislature should adopt as limited a punishment as proved useful, Livermore said, "we ought not to be restrained from making necessary laws by any declaration of this kind" (Kurland and Lerner 1987, 5:377). Despite his objections, the provision passed overwhelmingly.

Generally, the courts have granted legislatures flexibility in deciding whether fines or bail is excessive. Most contemporary controversy about the Eighth Amendment has centered on the provision prohibiting "cruel and unusual punishments." In *Furman v. Georgia* (1972), the Supreme Court declared that the death penalty as then administered was unconstitutional, but subsequent cases have allowed for such punishment when juries consider aggravating and mitigating circumstances and when trials are bifurcated so that the determination of guilt or innocence is separated from the fixing of a penalty. Numerous amendments have been proposed that would either permit or outlaw capital punishment.

For Further Reading:
Hoffmann, Joseph L. 1993. "The 'Cruel and Unusual Punishment' Clause: A Limit on the Power to Punish or Constitutional Rhetoric?" In *The Bill of Rights in Modern America*, ed. David J. Bodenhamer and James W. Ely Jr. Bloomington: Indiana University Press.

❖ EISELEN, MALCOLM R. ❖ (1902–1965)

Historian Malcolm Eiselen used the sesquicentennial of the U.S. Constitution to argue for a second constitutional convention (Vile 1991c, 74–75). Altogether, he suggested about a dozen changes that should be contemplated, including abolishing the electoral college, changing the president's tenure of office, clarifying the power of judicial review, considering the federal initiative and referendum, allowing cabinet members to be seated in Congress, nominating presidents more democratically, clarifying issues of presidential disability, making the process of constitutional amendment easier (see Eiselen 1941), abandoning the requirement that treaties be ratified by two-thirds majorities, redistributing powers between state and national governments, and providing mechanisms to avoid "national bankruptcy and financial chaos" (Eiselen 1937, 29–33). Eiselen was particularly concerned about federal spending and suggested longer terms for the president and members of Congress and adoption of the item veto and the executive budget as possible remedies (Eiselen 1937, 32).

Eiselen proposed that members of the convention should be a mixture of elected and appointed delegates, with the American Bar Association, the American Political Science Association, and the American Economic Association among the groups making appointments (Eiselen 1937, 34). Eiselen cautioned that delegates should avoid the temptation to create a document too lengthy or detailed. He recognized that, like the document of 1787, any new constitution would have to embody compromises making it acceptable to the people.

❖ ELECTIONS, DATES OF ❖

Article II, Section 1 of the Constitution provides that Congress shall determine a uniform day for choosing presidential electors, but for a time, it merely specified that such elections should be made 34 days prior to the first Wednesday in December (Ames 1896, 114). Until Congress acted in 1845 to set the Tuesday after the first Monday in November for such elections, it received a number of petitions for an amendment setting a uniform date or allowing for more than one day during which elections would be held. Two proposals offered in 1888 to prevent state elections on the same day as federal contests were apparently motivated by concerns that political parties were trading votes for the two sets of offices (Ames 1896, 111).

❖ ELECTIONS, DISPUTED ❖

Article I, Section 5 specifies that "each House shall be the Judge of the Elections, Returns, and Qualifications of its own members." Deciding who to seat in closely contested elections can become a highly partisan decision.

Prompted by the contested election of five New Jersey representatives, States' Rights Democratic Representative Richard Habersham of Georgia introduced an amendment in 1840 to specify the kinds of evidence Congress could consult in deciding which individuals to seat (Ames 1896, 57). To date, Congress still has no specific constitutional guidelines to follow. When the 104th Congress convened in January 1995, Congress seated four members whose seats were contested, pending further investigation (MacPherson 1995, 28).

❖ ELECTIONS, PRIMARY ❖

In *Newberry v. United States* (1921), the Supreme Court ruled that Article I, Section 4 did not give Congress power to regulate party primaries. Shortly thereafter, Oklahoma Republican Representative Manuel Herrick introduced an amendment extending federal election laws to primaries as well as to general elections.

Subsequently, in *U.S. v. Classic* (1941), the Court allowed regulation of state primaries when such primaries were tied to the process of choosing candidates for federal office. In later outlawing the all-white primary in *Smith v. Allwright* (1944), the Court specifically overturned the *Newberry* decision.

❖ ELECTORAL COLLEGE ❖ REFORM

No amendment effort has been more consistent than that for reform of the electoral college. More than 850 proposals have been offered in Congress, making this topic second in overall numbers only to the equal rights amendment. Two reforms of the electoral college have been adopted, the Twelfth Amendment and the Twenty-third Amendment. The first now requires that electors differentiate between their votes for president and vice president (thus eliminating the possibility of a tie, which occurred in the election of 1800). The second provides that the District of Columbia will have representation equivalent to that of the smallest state—currently, three votes.

Operation

The electoral college system is a complicated scheme formulated at the Constitutional Convention of 1787. Under this system, each state is awarded a number of votes equivalent to its representation in the House and the Senate. States then select electors, who meet in the state's capital. Since the Twelfth Amendment, each elector casts one vote for president and another for vice president, at least one such vote going to an out-of-state candidate. Such votes are then reported to Washington, D.C., and opened in a joint session of Congress.

If no candidate receives a majority of the electoral college—currently 238 votes—the election for the president goes to the House of Representatives and that of the vice president to the Senate. The House chooses from among the top three candidates, with each state's delegation getting a single vote. Similarly, the Senate chooses between the top two candidates for vice president. Typically, the electoral college exaggerates the votes of the winner, thus providing the appearance of greater support for an incoming president and arguably making fraud within one or two states less likely to affect the outcome than if all votes were counted (for a more complete discussion of the operation of the electoral system, see Berns 1992).

Foundation and Development

When the Constitutional Convention first considered presidential elections, it contemplated that Congress would choose the president. Members feared, however, that this method would undercut the system of separation of powers and presidential independence. Similarly, a system of direct election would have been difficult to implement at a time when transportation and communications were slow. Moreover, such a system would have effectively stripped the small states of any real influence in presidential selection. The system adopted, by contrast, had the advantage of incorporating the agreement that already lay at the base of the Connecticut, or Great, Compromise (Hardaway 1994, 82). That is, the smallest states would get at least three votes, since each state was guaranteed at least one member in the House of Representatives and two senators.

Most of the operation of the electoral college has developed by usage rather than by constitutional mandate. Thus, all states now choose their electors by popular vote, but this is not mandated either in the Constitution or by the Twelfth Amendment. Similarly, all but two states (Maine and Nebraska) now use a winner-take-all system, but this has also developed by custom. There is some dispute as to whether electors were or were not originally expected to exercise independent judgment, but with a few flukes (so-called faithless electors), most follow the pledges that the parties now require of them.

Criticism

The use of the electoral college system raises the possibility that the winner of the electoral vote may not be the winner of the popular vote; to many, this departure from direct democracy is unjustifiable. The only election in which such a result clearly happened was the election of 1888, in which Benjamin Harrison amassed 230 electoral votes to Grover Cleveland's 168, even though Cleveland had received about 100,000 more popular votes.

Some critics would also include the elections of 1824, 1876, and 1960. In the election of 1824, Andrew Jackson received more popular votes than John Quincy Adams, who was selected by the House of Representatives as the winner. However, there were four candidates, and in the initial voting, none gained a majority of either the electoral or the popular vote. Similarly, there is evidence that Samuel Tilden may have captured more votes in the election of 1876 than his opponent Rutherford B. Hayes. Hayes, however, was declared the eventual winner after an electoral commission, appointed by the House of Representatives to resolve disputed electoral votes in three states, voted along party lines to give all these votes to Hayes. Corruption was so rampant on both sides in this contest that it is not clear that the electoral college system should be held responsible for the outcome (Hardaway 1994, 128–37). The dispute over who won the popular vote in the election of 1960, in which John F. Kennedy received the greater number of electoral votes, centers on whether he should have been credited with the votes cast for unpledged delegates in Alabama.

In addition to being criticized for being undemocratic, the electoral college has been criticized along a number of other lines. It has been argued that the system gives an advantage to particular types of states or minority groups that may hold the balance of power. The winner-take-all feature of the system certainly encourages candidates to go for majorities in the most populous states, whereas the three votes cast by the smallest states are more than they would be entitled to judged purely by population. The winner-take-all feature of the current system has also been criticized for effectively "wasting" the votes of minorities within each state and thus decreasing turnout. Other features of the system—for example, the possibility of faithless electors or the resolution of elections in the House of Representatives rather than by popular vote—are issues that are sometimes raised.

The District Plan

In addition to the reforms incorporated in the Twelfth and Twenty-third Amendments, several reforms have dominated discussion of the electoral college system. A popular proposal dating back to 1800 favors modifying the system along the order of a district plan. Some proposals have called for dividing each state into a number of districts equal to its total number of electors and giving each district a single elector. Others call for using existing congressional districts, with each state electing two electors on an at-large basis. Such a plan was proposed by a 22 to 9 vote in the Senate in 1813, and again in 1819 by a vote of 28 to 10. The House did not act on the first proposal, and in 1820, its 92 to 54 vote was just shy of the required two-thirds majority.

Missouri's Senator Thomas Hart Benton supported the district plan, as did Andrew Johnson. In the 1870s, Indiana Senator Oliver P. Morton supported the plan, and in the 1940s and 1950s, Representative Frederic R. Coudert Jr. of New York and South Dakota Senator Karl E. Mundt supported it. Other supporters of this plan have included South Carolina Senator Strom Thurmond, Arizona Senator Barry Goldwater, and President Harry Truman. Democratic Senators Paul Douglas of Illinois and John F. Kennedy of Massachusetts opposed it.

Whatever its merits, the district system still allows a candidate to win a majority of votes within a state and not win a majority of its electoral votes. It arguably does little to deal with the problem of "wasted" votes within districts, and it still leaves open the possibility that a president would be elected with less than a majority of popular votes (Peirce 1968, 152–68). Such a system might also encourage gerrymandering of individual districts (Hardaway 1994, 144–45).

The Proportional Plan

A second plan that has frequently been introduced is the proportional plan, under which a state's electoral votes would be divided in proportion to its popular votes. First introduced in 1848, the original plan awarded only whole delegates, but subsequent plans have carried this out to the nearest one-thousandth.

Supporters of a proportional plan have included Nebraska Senator George W. Norris, Massachusetts Senator Henry Cabot Lodge, and Texas Representative Ed Gossett. In 1950, the Senate approved such a plan by a vote of 67 to 27, but in the House, the plan was defeated by a vote of 134 for and 210 against. In 1956, the Senate subsequently voted 48 to 37 for a substitute offered by Price Daniel of Texas that would allow states to choose between the direct and the proportional plan.

Although the proportional plan takes care of the "wasted" vote problem, it does not guarantee a president elected by a majority. In the 1940s and 1950s, some opponents also feared that it would give an advantage to noncompetitive one-party states, especially those in the South, where Democrats typically racked up large majorities.

The Automatic Plan

A third alternative to the current electoral college system is often called the automatic system and appears to have first been contemplated by Thomas Jefferson. This system would eliminate the individual electors and give each state's votes to candidates who captured a majority there.

In 1934, the Senate voted 42 to 24 for such a plan, thus falling short of the required two-thirds. President Lyndon Johnson later supported this plan, as did Indiana Democratic Senator Birch Bayh before he became a supporter of the direct popular vote mechanism. The automatic plan would constitute a relatively minor change in the current system, and some may have opposed this scheme for fear that it would be an obstacle to more serious reforms (Peirce 1968, 177–81).

Direct Popular Election

By far the most popular alternative to the current electoral college system is that of the direct popular vote suggested at the Constitutional Convention of 1787 and first proposed in Congress in 1816. Andrew Jackson has been designated "the spiritual godfather of the direct vote movement" (Peirce 1968, 183). Most such plans have called for a runoff election in the event that no candidates receive 40 percent or more of the votes.

The Chamber of Commerce and the American Bar Association supported such a plan in the 1960s, and Senator Birch Bayh became a prominent supporter. The House of Representatives adopted such a proposal in 1969 by a vote of 338 to 70 (Longley and Braun 1972, 152), but the Senate killed it, twice falling short of the number needed to invoke cloture of debates intended to defeat the measure.

Other Proposals

Other plans have been introduced to give electoral representation to Guam, Puerto Rico, or other U.S. possessions; to allow the U.S. Supreme Court to resolve disputed elections; to allow both houses of Congress—rather than the House of Representatives alone—to resolve elections in which

no candidate receives a majority; to require a vote of electors; to require a runoff in cases in which no presidential candidate receives a majority of the popular vote; and so forth. Connecticut Federalist Senator James Hillhouse once suggested that U.S. senators should serve for three-year terms, with retiring senators drawing balls from a box, and the one drawing the colored ball to serve as president for a year (Peirce 1968, 194). Other plans have called for alternating presidents between the North and the South or requiring candidates to get a majority of electors in each of four sections of the nation.

Another plan, recently supported by Jesse Jackson's Rainbow Coalition, calls for majority preference voting (MPV). Under such a system, voters rank candidates in their order of preference, with the votes of last-place candidates being redistributed until one candidate has a clear majority (Richie 1995). Such a plan might well encourage third-party candidates.

Obstacles to Reform

The diversity of reform proposals has served in part as an obstacle to change, since it has made it difficult to achieve consensus on an alternative. Moreover, whereas critics charge that the current system is archaic, many defenders of the current system believe that it has been vital to achieving governmental consensus by discouraging third parties. Defenders also believe that the current system is a bastion of federalism that has worked remarkably well. It appears that it would take sustained leadership or another election like that of 1800 or 1824 to inaugurate major reform of the current system.

See also Twelfth Amendment; Twenty-third Amendment.

❖ ELEVENTH AMENDMENT ❖

The Eleventh Amendment was the first amendment adopted to overturn a

Supreme Court decision and the only adopted amendment ever to address the judicial branch of government. The amendment has spawned numerous cases that have both expanded and narrowed its apparent scope.

Article III of the Constitution extends judicial power to controversies "between a State and Citizens of another State." In arguing on behalf of the new Constitution, however, leading Federalists responded to Anti-Federalist criticisms by contending that this clause would not undermine the doctrine of sovereign immunity, according to which a sovereign—in this case, a state government—could not be sued without its consent.

Despite such assurances, in *Chisholm v. Georgia* (1793), the Supreme Court upheld a suit brought against Georgia by the executor of the estate of a South Carolina merchant who was suing for payment of goods delivered during the Revolutionary War. The success of this suit may have threatened other states with significant debts. The lower house of the Georgia legislature subsequently passed a bill providing that any federal marshal attempting to enforce the Court's judgment would be "hereby declared guilty of felony, and shall suffer death, without the benefit of the clergy, by being hanged" (cited by Jacob 1972, 57).

Congress proposed the Eleventh Amendment in 1794; it was ratified by the necessary number of states in 1795 but was not promulgated by the secretary of state until 1798, a date that is sometimes incorrectly cited as the official ratification date. The amendment provides that "the Judicial power of the United States shall not be construed to extend to any suit in law or equity, commenced or prosecuted against one of the United States by Citizens of another State, or by Citizens or Subjects of any Foreign State." In *Hollingsworth v. Virginia* (1798), the Court ruled that the original

congressional resolution did not require the president's signature for the amendment to be valid and gave the amendment retrospective application.

The Eleventh Amendment does not appear to have barred many suits during its early history. This was largely because Chief Justice John Marshall ruled in *Osborn v. Bank of the United States* (1824) that the Eleventh Amendment did not bar suits against officers of a state. Moreover, in *Cohens v. Virginia* (1821), Marshall ruled that the amendment did not bar appeals to federal courts in cases in which the states themselves initiated the suits.

By the end of Reconstruction, however, a number of southern states were repudiating debts, and after resolution of the disputed presidential election of 1876, there was little federal will to enforce such debts by force of arms. Thus, in 1883, the Supreme Court ruled in *Louisiana ex rel Elliott v. Jumel* that shareholders could not sue Louisiana for interest on bonds. In 1890, Justice Joseph P. Bradley, the same justice whose vote on the electoral commission had resulted in the election of fellow Republican Rutherford B. Hayes, authored the decision in *Hans v. Louisiana* (1890) that reinterpreted and extended the scope of the Eleventh Amendment.

Extending the literal language of the Eleventh Amendment to cover suits brought by a state citizen against its own state, Bradley broadly interpreted the Eleventh Amendment as a restatement of what he believed to be the original constitutional understanding that states could not be sued without their consent. *Ex parte New York* (1921) subsequently extended the breadth of the Eleventh Amendment to forbid admiralty cases (not technically considered cases in "law or equity") against a state without its consent. *Monaco v. Mississippi* (1934) applied the same principle to cases brought against a state by foreign governments (Orth 1987, 139–41).

State immunity has, however, been somewhat modified by *Ex parte Young* (1908), which effectively reaffirmed *Osborn v. Bank of the United States* (1824) by permitting state officials, as opposed to states themselves, to be sued. Moreover, in *Lincoln County [Nevada] v. Luning* (1890), the Court decided that state immunity was not extended to state subdivisions. Other rulings have held that federal jurisdiction in the area of interstate commerce and in enforcement of the Fourteenth Amendment may override traditional state immunities. Ironically, the concept of sovereign immunity has become so much "part of the United States unwritten constitution" that it has often predominated over "the language of the Amendment" (Orth 1987, 152).

There have been at least two attempts to amend the Eleventh Amendment, one introduced in 1883 and the other in 1913. The former provided that Congress could make provision "by appropriate legislation for the enforcement of contracts entered into by any of the States of the Union" (quoted in Orth 1987, 70).

In *Seminole Tribe v. Florida* (1996) the Supreme Court recently called renewed attention to the Eleventh Amendment by seemingly reaffirming the broad reading given to it in *Hans v. Louisiana* (1890). In a 5-to-4 ruling, the Court in the *Seminole Tribe* case ruled that the Eleventh Amendment precluded Indian tribes' suing states without their consent for failing to negotiate in good faith over the establishment of gambling casinos on Indian lands (Greenhouse 1996).

See also *Chisholm v. Georgia; Hollingsworth v. Virginia*.

❖ ELLIOTT, WILLIAM YANDELL ❖
(1896–1979)

Harvard political scientist William Yandell Elliott published a book entitled *The Need*

for Constitutional Reform (1935) during Franklin Roosevelt's first term in office. Elliott advocated a number of reforms designed primarily to strengthen both executive and legislative power and to overcome problems that Elliott perceived in the existing system of separated powers (Vile 1991c, 72–74).

Elliott offered a number of small steps that could be taken to achieve this end. These included a presidential item veto and a prohibition of riders that were not germane to the aims of a bill. The linchpin of Elliott's plan, however, was his proposal for a constitutional arrangement, borrowed from parliamentary systems, under which the president would have the power, at least once during a term, to force members of the House of Representatives to stand for election. If such an election upheld Congress over the president, the president could resign (with Congress then choosing his successor), but he would not, as in most parliamentary systems, be required to do so.

Elliott desired to cut the power of the Senate (which he associated with special interests) and advocated taking from that body "the power over bills appropriating money or raising revenue" (Elliott 1935, 32). Ideally, states would be reorganized into districts designated as "commonwealths," similar to those used for the Federal Reserve System. Elliott suggested that there might be 12 such regions, each electing eight senators. The president would be able to add 15 prominent individuals to the Senate; losing presidential candidates would also serve in this body. The vote needed to approve treaties would be changed from two-thirds of the Senate to a simple majority of both houses.

Representation in the House would continue to be based on population, but members would be elected from the new commonwealths rather than from existing states. Elliott favored a form of proportional representation for the House, with up to five representatives per district. He believed that this would help overcome the power of existing interest groups. A continuing committee of both houses would be in "perpetual residence" in Washington, D.C. (Elliott 1935, 37).

Elliott favored a new system for selecting the president. Under his plan, a joint House and Senate committee would nominate presidential candidates, and the House would choose two of these to run in a national election. The president would be selected by majority popular vote. The president would choose an executive vice president or an assistant president who would also head the administrative cabinet.

Elliott believed that although the system of judicial review was needed in the current system, such power might be modified if the legislative and executive branches were more responsible. In such a situation, he believed that the Supreme Court should be required to vote by a two-thirds vote before invalidating legislation. Generally, battles "over social reform should be fought out in party politics, not in the courts" (Elliott 1935, 179). Elliott feared that existing protections for criminal defendants—such as the prohibition against double jeopardy—were working to "aid gangsters and racketeers" (Elliott 1935, 204). He also suggested that the Supreme Court should choose the attorney general.

Elliott would strengthen the positions of governors in the new commonwealths. Like the president, they would have the power to dissolve the legislature (now to be unicameral) once during their four-year terms. Elliott would also create governor's councils and legislative steering committees. Like the president, state governors would originate the budget and would be subject to override on money bills only by a two-thirds majority.

Elliott advocated a number of administrative reforms. He wanted to create a civil service head for each department and a permanent cabinet secretariat "to propose and document Cabinet meetings" (Elliott 1935, 203). Elliott also proposed adding an advisory committee to each department consisting of "all the great interests with which it comes into normal contact" (Elliott 1935, 203), and he favored allowing cabinet members to have seats in the Senate and to appear before the House.

Elliott recognized that some of his proposals could be implemented on a piecemeal basis, but he believed that the more substantial changes—especially in regard to the Senate—could best be initiated by a constitutional convention.

❖ EMANCIPATION PROCLAMATION ❖

Abraham Lincoln often declared that although he opposed slavery, his primary goal in prosecuting the Civil War was to preserve the Union. As the war continued, Lincoln became convinced that it could best be prosecuted and the future of the Union best be guaranteed by abolishing slavery. The Emancipation Proclamation was officially issued on 1 January 1863, but Lincoln had announced his intention to do so in September of 1862 (Anastaplo 1995, 138). A war measure taken under executive authority, this proclamation declared all slaves in states adhering to the Confederacy to be free. This amounted to 74 percent of all slaves in the United States (Paludan 1994, 155).

Although Lincoln also proposed amendments containing plans for more gradual emancipation for other slaves, the momentum generated by the Emancipation Proclamation made this virtually impossible. The proclamation was extended and placed on firmer constitutional authority when, in 1865, the Thirteenth Amendment to the Constitution abolished involuntary servitude throughout the nation.

See also Lincoln, Abraham; Thirteenth Amendment.

❖ EMBARGOES, ARMS, LOANS, ❖ AND FOREIGN AID

In 1934, Republican Senator Gerald P. Nye of North Dakota held hearings indicating that bankers and manufacturers of munitions had made huge profits from their sales to the Allies in World War I (Cole 1962, 79–97). These revelations about the so-called merchants of death increased isolationist sentiment in the United States and led many to suspect that U.S. participation in the war had been engineered to continue such profit making.

Even before the hearings, Democratic Representative Ross Collins of Mississippi had introduced a resolution that would have prohibited making or renewing loans to nations engaged in war, unless the United States itself was engaged in such a war as an ally. Collins repeatedly introduced this resolution in the late 1930s, during which time Congress adopted a number of neutrality acts that were designed to prevent the United States from trading with belligerent nations or taking passage on their ships (DeConde 1971, 567). Some such laws had a "cash and carry" exemption or allowed the president some discretion whether to impose the embargo on one or both sides of a conflict. The Japanese attack on Pearl Harbor in 1941 ended U.S. isolationism.

During the cold war, the United States used foreign aid as a tool of foreign policy making, but critics charged that such aid was wasteful. In 1949, Republican Senator William Langer of North Dakota offered an amendment restricting foreign aid to times of war. Republican Representative Noah Mason of Illinois introduced similar resolutions in 1957 and 1959, extending the prohibition on foreign aid to international organizations as well as to foreign governments.

❖ EMBARGOES, TRADE ❖

When Thomas Jefferson was president, he decided to ask Congress to declare an embargo on trade with Great Britain and France rather than risk war over the seizure of American vessels and the impressment of American seamen. Such power could be justified either as an exercise of congressional power over foreign commerce or as a means of national defense. Initially defensive in nature, in time embargo became a method, albeit a fairly unsuccessful one, of exerting pressure on belligerents (Mayer 1994, 217). The embargo, which lasted from December 1807 to March 1809, was especially resented in the New England states, which were dependent on such commerce. Both during this embargo and later at the Hartford Convention that met during the War of 1812, these states issued calls to limit congressional embargo powers. The Hartford Convention called for a 60-day limit (Vile 1993c, 186).

❖ EMPLOYMENT OPPORTUNITY ❖

Unemployment continues to be a major problem, prompting governmental intervention in the form of job creation and training programs as well as unemployment insurance. Franklin Roosevelt's New Deal and Lyndon Johnson's War on Poverty stand out as high points in the national government's efforts. There continue to be sharp debates over what role the government—as opposed to private enterprise—should play in reducing unemployment and over the effectiveness of specific governmental programs (Baumer and Van Horn 1985).

At least seven times since 1983, Representative Major Owens, a Democrat from Brooklyn, New York, has introduced an amendment to guarantee the right to employment opportunity to everyone and to give Congress power to enforce the amendment with appropriate legislation. Current legislative trends point less toward work as a governmentally guaranteed right and more toward work as a duty to be performed in return for welfare and other benefits.

❖ *ENGEL V. VITALE* (1962) ❖

Few decisions have stirred more calls for a constitutional amendment than this ruling by the Supreme Court authored by Justice Hugo L. Black. At issue was a short nondenominational prayer mandated by the New York State Board of Regents for public school children to recite at the beginning of each school day. A number of parents objected on the basis that the prayer constituted an undue establishment of religion in violation of the First Amendment as applied to the states by the due process clause of the Fourteenth Amendment.

Black agreed with the challengers. Viewing the prayer as a distinctively "religious activity" (*Engel* 1962, 424), he noted that England had been torn by controversy over the Book of Common Prayer and that Americans, especially Thomas Jefferson and James Madison, were aware of the dangers of unifying church and state. Black argued that the fact that the prayer was voluntary and that students could be excused from the exercise was irrelevant. The key was the fact that "a union of government and religion tends to destroy government and to degrade religion" (*Engel* 1962, 431).

Justice William O. Douglas's concurrence focused primarily on the fact that since the schools in question were funded by the government, the state would be financing a religious exercise. In his dissent, Justice Potter Stewart argued that the New York exercise fell short of an establishment of religion and cited a variety of other connections between church and state that were accepted in modern America.

The majority decision in *Engel* was vigorously denounced. New York Republican Congressman Frank Becker called it "the most tragic decision in the history of the United States" (Becker and Feeley 1973, 24). The decision prompted 53 representatives and 22 senators to introduce anti-*Engel* amendments in the 87th Congress, and the Senate Judiciary Committee held hearings on the subject (Becker and Feeley 1973, 25–26). Congressional opposition was even more pronounced after the Court's subsequent decision extending *Engel*'s prohibitions to Bible reading in *Abington v. Schempp* (1963).

To date, the Court has not backed down. In *Wallace v. Jaffree* (1985), it struck down an Alabama law specifically designed to designate school prayer as an option during a moment of silence—a decision that may not, however, apply to moment-of-silence laws that do not put prayer in a privileged position. In *Lee v. Weisman* (1992), the Court extended the ban to prayers delivered by members of the clergy at high school graduations. Pressures for an amendment to establish prayer in school continue.

See also Prayer in Public Schools.

❖ ENGLISH LANGUAGE ❖ AMENDMENT

The issue of language is often tied to sentiments connected with nationality and race (Baron 1990, xiv). Moreover, people who speak a primary language other than the dominant one are sometimes regarded as unpatriotic. Since 1981, a score of proposals have been introduced in Congress to make English the official language of the United States. California Republican Senator Samuel I. Hayakawa, a nationally recognized linguist, introduced the first such amendment. Hearings were held in the Senate (*The English Language Amendment* 1985) and in the House (*English Language*

Constitutional Amendments 1989). The Senate version of this amendment was fairly general, whereas the House version prohibited the use of languages other than English except as a means of teaching language proficiency. Some believe that such an amendment could be used to restrict "multilingual tests, forms and ballots, as well as translators for legal and emergency services" (Baron 1990, 24–25). Some states have adopted English-language laws (Baron 1990, 201), but the impact of such legislation has varied from state to state.

Laws against teaching foreign languages have sometimes reflected nativist sentiments. In *Meyer v. Nebraska* (1923), the Supreme Court invalidated a Nebraska law prohibiting the teaching of languages other than English; in this case, the law had been enforced against a parochial school teacher teaching from a German text. In *Katzenbach v. Morgan* (1966), the Supreme Court upheld a provision of the Voting Rights Act of 1965 that struck down literacy tests for otherwise eligible voters who had completed the sixth grade in an accredited school in Puerto Rico. In *Lau v. Nichols* (1974), the Supreme Court ruled that a school system had to provide a program to deal with some 1,800 Chinese students who knew no English. Although this decision provoked considerable controversy over bilingual education, most such programs are designed to enable students to make a transition to English (Baron 1990, 11).

English is now spoken "by more than 97 percent of the people in the nation" (Baron 1990, 177). Although some individuals see the English language amendment as a way of promoting national unity, others fear that it could be used to discriminate against people for whom English is a second language.

For Further Reading:

Tatalovich, Raymond. 1995. *Nativism Reborn? The Official Language Movement and the American States*. Lexington: University Press of Kentucky.

❖ ENVIRONMENTAL ❖ PROTECTION

The text of the U.S. Constitution is silent about a number of contemporary concerns, including the right to an education and the right to a clean environment. Increasing concern over the environment in the 1960s led to a number of proposals late in that decade and thereafter to provide environmental protection.

Typical was a proposal introduced by Democratic Representative Richard Ottinger and Republican Representative Theodore Kupferman (both from New York) in 1968. They billed their proposal as "a conservation bill of rights" (*Congressional Record*, 13 July 1968, 17116). The first section of their proposal broadly guaranteed "the right of the people to clean air, pure water, [and] freedom from excessive noise and [that] the natural, scenic, historic and esthetic qualities of their environment shall not be abridged." The second section called on Congress to draw up a national inventory of "the natural, scenic, esthetic and historic resources of the United States." A third section would have prohibited action by state or federal agencies adversely affecting this heritage "without first giving reasonable notice to the public and holding a public hearing thereon" (*Congressional Record*, 17116–17). Section 1 of this proposal is especially interesting because, whereas most existing constitutional provisions offer "negative protection for individuals from government action" (Hoban and Brooks 1987, 169), this would commit the government to a more affirmative role (also see Schlickeisen 1994). Other proposals, including one by Democratic Representative Morris Udall of Arizona, whose brother served as secretary of interior in the Kennedy and Johnson administrations, followed language of the Declaration of Independence in proposing to make environmental rights "inalienable" (H.J. Res. 1205, 1970).

In 1970, the National Environmental Policy Act (NEPA) was signed. It heralded an anticipated "environmental decade," in which environmental legislation and litigation both increased immensely (Wenner 1982, 1). Although courts have never recognized the right to a clean and healthy environment as a constitutional right (Rosenberg 1991, 278), they did enforce congressional laws. Such activity suggests that although the Constitution does not affirmatively protect the environment, there are few constitutional obstacles to accomplishing this objective through legislation.

❖ EQUAL RIGHTS AMENDMENT ❖

No amendment has been introduced in Congress more frequently than the equal rights amendment (ERA). From its first introduction in 1923, the amendment has been sponsored several hundred times.

Proposals in Congress

The first time the amendment was actually voted on by a house of Congress was in 1946, when it garnered a 38 to 35 vote in the Senate. In 1950, the amendment achieved the needed two-thirds majority with a Senate vote of 65 to 19; in 1953, the Senate proposed it again by a vote of 73 to 11. In both the 1950 and the 1953 votes, the Senate accepted what was known as the Hayden rider, sponsored by Democratic Senator Carl Hayden of Arizona. This rider provided that the amendment "shall not be construed to impair any rights, benefits, or exemptions now or hereafter conferred by law upon members of the female sex" (Boles 1979, 38). In 1970, a discharge petition effectively pried the amendment from the House Judiciary Committee, where Democratic chairman Emanuel Celler had previously kept it bottled up (Boles 1979, 38). That same year, a House majority of 252 to 15 approved the amendment with no riders.

In 1972, the House again adopted the amendment, this time by a 354 to 24 vote, and the Senate followed suit in 1972 by a vote of 84 to 8 (Boles 1979, 13–16).

As finally approved, the equal rights amendment contained a seven-year deadline in its authorizing resolution. In 1979, the House voted 233 to 189 and the Senate 60 to 36 to extend the deadline until 30 June 1982 (Berry 1986, 70), but at the end of this time, only 35 of the needed 38 states had ratified, and some of these had attempted to rescind their ratifications. In January 1983, the amendment was reintroduced in the House, but the 278 to 147 vote fell shy of the required two-thirds majority (Mansbridge 1986, 187). Subsequently, the amendment has not been voted on by either house.

Content of the ERA

The equal rights amendment proposed by Congress had three sections. Its heart was Section 1, which provided simply that "equality of rights under the Law shall not be denied or abridged by the United States or by any State on account of sex." The second section invested enforcement power in Congress, and the third provided for a transitional period of two years after its ratification. Alice Paul, the original sponsor of the equal rights amendment, worded the second section of the amendment to invest enforcement power jointly in the states and the federal government. She also opposed inclusion of the seven-year ratification deadline (Hoff-Wilson 1986, 8).

A number of versions of the amendment were introduced before Congress finally settled on one. The original proposal provided that "men and women shall have equal rights throughout the United States and every place subject to its jurisdiction." In 1950, Helen Hill Weed suggested a rider (much like Carl Hayden's) that would have specified that "this article shall not be construed to impair any rights, benefits, exemptions, or prohibition conferred upon men and women equally, or conferred upon one sex alone when inapplicable to both sexes." A Senate resolution of 1953 would have provided that "whenever in this Constitution the term 'person, persons, people,' or any other personal pronoun is used the same shall be taken to include both sexes" (Boles 1979, 121–25). After the House proposed the ERA in 1971, North Carolina Democratic Senator Sam Ervin proposed a substitute that provided that "neither the United States nor any State shall make any legal distinction between the rights and responsibilities of male and female persons unless such distinction is based on physiological or functional differences between them." He also proposed amendments relating to such matters as the military draft, family support, privacy, and homosexuality (Mansbridge 1986, 12).

Debates over the ERA

Such differences in wording and proposed alterations indicate some of the tensions that surrounded the equal rights amendment debate. When it was initially proposed, the National Woman's Party, a "militant" wing of the forces that had pushed for the Nineteenth Amendment (Boles 1979, 40), was one of the few organizations that actively supported the amendment. More moderate organizations such as the League of Women Voters opposed it. They had been working for protective legislation such as minimum wage and maximum hour legislation for women and feared that an equal rights amendment might be used to undermine such gains. Over time, many more groups joined the cause, but differences in emphasis remained, as did ambiguity about precisely what results the amendment would have.

Once proposed by Congress, the ERA was initially received quite positively; 21 of 32 legislatures in session in 1972 ratified with hardly any delays (Boles 1979, 61). In time, 35 of the needed 38 states would rat-

ify, but by then, the anti-ERA forces had effectively mobilized, and some states that had given their approval attempted to rescind their ratifications. Conservative Phyllis Schlafly, founder of the Eagle Forum, appears to have been particularly successful with her Committee To Stop ERA.

Scholars still debate why the ERA failed. In part, its failure may have stemmed from disputes about what the amendment would do. Some thought that it would require women to be included in a military draft. Others thought that it would affect family law and possibly invalidate statutory rape laws. Still others charged that it might mandate unisex bathroom facilities or homosexual marriages. With recognition of a right to privacy, the latter possibilities were arguably fairly remote, but given the way that Article V requires something of a national consensus, opponents did not have to prove their position but only raise sufficient doubts to block the amendment in 13 or more states (Mansbridge 1986).

Judicial Decisions and the ERA

Ironically, progressive judicial decisions on behalf of women's rights may have served to undercut the impetus for the ERA (L. Goldstein 1987). In the nineteenth century, the Court had been unsympathetic to the issue. Thus, in *Bradwell v. Illinois* (1873), it had upheld an Illinois law barring women from the practice of law, and in *Minor v. Happersett* (1875) it had upheld women's exclusion from the ballot. As late as *Goesaert v. Cleary* (1948), the Supreme Court upheld paternalistic laws restricting women. At just about the time that Congress proposed the ERA, however, the Court began to use the equal protection clause of the Fourteenth Amendment to liberalize women's rights. In *Reed v. Reed* (1971), for example, a unanimous Court held that a state could not select the administrator of an estate on the basis that one candidate was a man and the other a woman. Similarly, in *Frontiero v.*

Richardson (1973), the Court struck down a military law that presumed that married women depended on their husbands, who were thus automatically entitled to extra monetary allowances, but made women prove that their husbands were dependent on them. Perhaps more importantly, four of the justices declared that they considered gender to be a "suspect category," thus mandating the Court's most stringent level of scrutiny (the majority of the Court later settled on an intermediate standard for gender-based classifications). In the same year as *Frontiero,* the Court declared in *Roe v. Wade* that the right of privacy gave fairly broad leeway to women in obtaining abortions.

The decisions on behalf of women's rights enabled opponents of the amendment to argue that it was no longer needed. At the same time, the abortion decision enabled them to raise fears that the courts might expand interpretations of the amendment in unforeseen directions that might bring about greater changes in social relationships than many Americans, who were committed to equality in theory, actually wanted in practice (Mansbridge 1986). It has been argued that a key reason the ERA failed to muster the required congressional majorities in 1983 stemmed from fears that it might require states to fund abortions (Craig and O'Brien 1993, 148). For their part, the ERA supporters may have played into the hands of such critics by suggesting, in their attempts to get the ERA adopted, that the amendment would bring about greater changes than it actually would have.

Controversies over the ERA Extension

As the seven-year ratification deadline approached, proponents asked for more time, and in 1979, Congress extended the deadline for another three years. This led to controversy over whether the action was legal and whether the vote should have required a two-thirds majority (Freedman and Naughton 1978).

Lower courts addressed ERA issues in two cases, both of which challenged the idea, set forth in *Coleman v. Miller* (1939) that issues concerning the amending process were "political questions" inappropriate for judicial resolution. In *Dyer v. Blair* (1975) Judge—later Supreme Court Justice—John Paul Stevens ruled that the Illinois state legislature had the power to decide that a three-fifths vote was required for ratification of the amendment. In *Idaho v. Freeman* (1981), Judge Marion Callister decided that Idaho had a right to rescind ratification of the ERA, that Congress had no power to extend the ERA deadline, and that, in any case, such a vote would have required a two-thirds majority. Although it was appealed to the Supreme Court, this case was mooted when the ERA failed to be ratified within the extension that Congress had granted. However, perhaps heartened by the belated ratification of the Twenty-seventh Amendment, a number of representatives introduced a resolution in May 1995 requiring that the House of Representatives verify ratification of the equal rights amendment if and when it received an additional three ratifications from the states.

Given the division that the fight over the ERA engendered, its current prospects appear dim. A number of states have added such amendments to their own constitutions (Gamme 1989).

See also *Idaho v. Freeman;* Nineteenth Amendment; Schlafly, Phyllis.

❖ ERVIN, SAM J., JR. (1896–1985) ❖

Sam J. Ervin Jr. of North Carolina served in the U.S. House of Representatives from 1946 to 1947 and in the Senate from 1954 to 1974. Ervin's most visible public role occurred when he served as chairman of the Senate Watergate Committee, which held televised hearings about abuses in the Nixon administration. Although he had a law degree from Harvard, Ervin was known for his down-home country charm, and he was passionately devoted to the U.S. Constitution.

Ervin participated in a number of controversies involving the constitutional amending process. Perhaps most notably, in the wake of the attempt led by fellow Senator Everett Dirksen of Illinois to call a convention to overturn Supreme Court decisions involving state legislative apportionment, Ervin introduced legislation to govern such Article V conventions. Ervin did not believe that such a convention would have to be an open, or general, convention. He believed that Congress, faced with the necessary number of applications, had a mandatory obligation to call such a convention. Ervin believed that states should be able to rescind calls for such a convention prior to a two-thirds majority or to rescind amendment ratifications prior to a three-fourths majority. Ervin proposed that state requests for a convention should be valid for four years. As to representation at a convention, Ervin proposed that a delegate be selected from each congressional district, with two at-large delegates, bringing each state's representation to its strength in the electoral college. Although he originally advocated following the precedent of 1787 by giving each state delegation a single vote, he later modified this view, proposing to allow each delegate to vote individually (Ervin 1968; Kauper 1968). Ervin's legislation was not adopted, but it might still serve as a model if an Article V convention is ever convened.

Especially in the field of criminal justice, Ervin believed that the activist Warren Court had usurped the role of the amending process. He argued that there was a rather clear line between amending and interpreting the Constitution: "The power to amend is the power to change the meaning of the Constitution, and the power to interpret is the power of determining the meaning of the Constitution as established by the Founding Fathers" (Ervin 1984, 123).

As a senator, Ervin participated in a number of amending controversies. He supported an amendment that would have permitted voluntary confessions and limited federal habeas corpus review of criminal convictions. A strong proponent of separation of church and state, Ervin opposed the amendment that would have restored voluntary prayer in public schools (Ervin 1984, 237–48). Ervin also opposed the equal rights amendment. His proposed modifications of this amendment, all unsuccessful, reflected his concerns. His proposed revisions would have allowed laws that protected women, kept child-support laws in force, protected personal privacy, maintained existing definitions of sexual offenses, recognized physiological and functional differences between males and females, and exempted women from military service (Ervin 1984, 265–66).

Summarizing his view of the sanctity of the Constitution, Ervin observed:

Constitutional amendments are "for keeps." Unlike ordinary laws, they cannot be easily repealed. Once adopted, they can be removed from the Constitution only by means of the amendatory process created by Article V. . . . Congress and the States should act cautiously, advisedly, soberly, and without emotion when they are asked to add an amendment to the Constitution. They should never adopt an amendment unless it is calculated as well as intended to promote the general welfare of the United States. (Ervin 1984, 273)

❖ EXECUTIVE OFFICES, EXCLUSION FROM ❖

Officials in the executive branch, including members of the cabinet, are selected by the president with the advice and consent of the Senate. The original Virginia plan that was introduced at the Constitutional Convention of 1787 included a provision specifying that members of Congress would be ineligible for appointments to the executive or judicial branches, but this disqualification was later applied only to offices that were created or whose salaries were increased during the term of a legislator (Sundquist 1986, 37–38). Especially in the nation's first 100 years, numerous amending resolutions were introduced with a view toward minimizing risks that such offices would be awarded simply as political favors. Proposals included exclusion of general contractors, members of Congress, relatives of members of Congress, officeholders in general, and individuals who had served as representatives in the electoral college. Periodically, there were also proposals to elect postmasters, district attorneys, and other federal functionaries.

A flurry of proposals were introduced after the presidential election of 1824. In that election, there were four candidates—Andrew Jackson, John Quincy Adams, William Crawford, and Henry Clay. None received a majority of electoral votes necessary for election, and under the terms of the Twelfth Amendment, the House of Representatives had to choose among the top three candidates. Although he had come in last in the balloting, Henry Clay had considerable influence in the House of Representatives, where he was Speaker. He used this influence to support John Quincy Adams, who won on the first ballot, despite the fact that he had received fewer popular and electoral votes than Jackson.

Jackson and his followers were furious when, three days after Adams's selection, he appointed Clay as his secretary of state. Jackson charged that a "corrupt bargain" had been struck (Boller 1984, 35–37). It is not surprising that, in his first annual message after being elected president in 1828, one of Jackson's proposed reforms of the electoral college system called for excluding members of the House who had participated in presidential selection from executive offices (J. Richardson 1908, 2:448).

See also Cabinet.

❖ EXTRACONSTITUTIONAL ❖ MEANS OF CHANGE

Although the U.S. Constitution was officially ratified in 1789, it has been formally amended only 27 times. In part, the paucity of amendments stems from the fact that, comparatively speaking, the U.S. Constitution is a relatively brief document that deals primarily with matters of governmental structure rather than with day-to-day policies (Lutz 1994, 357). A contemporary scholar has also hypothesized that "a low amendment rate associated with a long average constitutional duration strongly implies the use of some alternate means of revision to supplement the formal amendment process" (Lutz 1994, 358).

In the United States, it is not always easy to decide which issues are "constitutional" and which are not. Clearly, some changes can be made only by constitutional amendments, whereas others may or may not require such amendments, largely depending on the attitude of those who occupy the government. Judicial decisions, especially those by the Supreme Court, have a major impact on constitutional interpretation. Laws and executive orders can also modify constitutional understandings and practices. The constitutional amending process, the legislative process, and executive orders each have advantages and disadvantages and often act synergistically (Vile 1994a, 111).

In recent years, two prominent scholars have directed renewed attention to extraconstitutional changes. Focusing on the founding period, the Civil War, and the New Deal—the last of which was implemented without the use of any constitutional amendments—Bruce Ackerman has argued that periods of "higher lawmaking" may be effected by actions taken by the political branches that are later codified by the Supreme Court (Ackerman 1991, 266–67).

Working from the premise of popular sovereignty, Akil Reed Amar has argued that an Article V convention could specify that its proposals be ratified by a majority of the people. Alternatively, in a position that is very close to that advocated by supporters of a referendum amendment, Amar has argued "that Congress would be constitutionally obliged to convene a proposing convention, if a bare majority of American voters so petitioned Congress" (Amar 1988, 1065; for critique, see Vile 1990–1991; also see Torke 1994).

See also Ackerman, Bruce; Amar, Akil Reed.

F

❖ FAILED AMENDMENTS ❖

Only six amendments that Congress has proposed by the necessary majorities have subsequently failed to be ratified by the states (Keller 1987; for texts, see Anastaplo 1989, 298–99).

The Bill of Rights that Congress proposed in its first session originally contained 12 amendments. The second was putatively ratified in 1992 as the Twenty-seventh Amendment. By contrast, the first proposal, dealing with the size of Congress and the ratio of representation to population, was never ratified.

Two amendments proposed by the required congressional majorities in the nineteenth century failed to be adopted. In 1810, the so-called Reed amendment, or "phantom" amendment, was introduced to strip citizenship from individuals who accepted titles of nobility from foreign governments. Although it was mistakenly thought to have been ratified, this amendment actually fell one state short of such ratification. Making far less progress was the Corwin amendment, proposed in 1861 on the eve of the Civil War. Its intention was to reassure the South by prohibiting future amendments that might interfere with slavery. There was at least one proposal introduced in Congress to repeal this amendment, which, of course, became a nullity with the adoption of the Thirteenth Amendment.

Three amendments proposed by Congress in the twentieth century have failed to be ratified. One was the child labor amendment proposed in 1924. A second was the controversial equal rights amendment. The third such proposal, adopted by Congress in 1978, would have treated the District of Columbia as a state for purposes of congressional representation, presidential and vice presidential selection, and the amending process.

The equal rights amendment contained a ratification deadline, subsequently extended, in the congressional authorizing resolution but not in the text; the amendment dealing with representation for the District of Columbia had an internal deadline of seven years. Although none of the other amendments had internal deadlines, none appears to be a likely candidate for an attempt at ratification similar to that which resulted in the Twenty-seventh Amendment.

See also Congress, Size of; District of Columbia, Representation for.

❖ *FAIRCHILD V. HUGHES* (1922) ❖

In this companion case to *Leser v. Garnett* (1922), the Court rejected a challenge to the constitutionality of the Nineteenth Amendment by a plaintiff taxpayer and member of the American Constitutional League. The Court declared that a general citizen, in this case one who was not an elected official and who resided in a state (New York) where women already had the right to vote, had no standing "to secure by indirection a determination whether a statute if passed, or a constitutional amendment about to be adopted, will be valid" (*Fairchild* 1922, 130).

See also *Leser v. Garnett.*

❖ FAIRMAN, CHARLES (1897–?) ❖

In *Adamson v. California* (1947) and subsequent cases, Justice Hugo L. Black cited speeches by John Bingham and other supporters of the Fourteenth Amendment to argue that they had intended to overturn *Barron v. Baltimore* (1833) and incorporate all the provisions of the Bill of Rights and apply them to the states.

Fairman, a professor of law and political science at Stanford University, authored a seminal article designed to refute Black's view. Fairman drew on evidence from records of congressional debates over the Fourteenth Amendment and contemporary civil rights legislation, as well as from debates in the states over ratification of this amendment, observations about contemporary state constitutions, and judicial interpretations contemporary with the amendment's ratification (Fairman 1949). Arguing that contemporaries had not been as clear about their intention as Black attempted to portray them, Fairman ultimately concluded that Benjamin Cardozo's interpretation of the due process clause of the Fourteenth Amendment in *Palko v. Connecticut* (1937) came close to the framers' understanding of the privileges and immunities clause. In that case, Cardozo had argued that the due process clause was designed to protect only those provisions of the Bill of Rights "implicit in the concept of ordered liberty."

Fairman's study, like Black's own thesis, continues to be the subject of lively scholarly debate (see Yarbrough 1988; Curtis 1986; Morrison 1949).

See also Black, Hugo LaFayette; Incorporation.

❖ FEDERALIST PAPERS ❖

See Federalists.

❖ FEDERALISTS ❖

Soon after the U.S. Constitution was written and sent to the states for ratification, the nation split into two camps. Those who supported the document called themselves Federalists and designated their opponents as Anti-Federalists. The respective sides argued their cases in the state ratifying conventions that subsequently approved the new Constitution (see Gillespie and Lienesch 1989). The most famous product of the Federalist–Anti-Federalist debates was a series of articles defending the Constitution that was initially published in a New York newspaper and shortly thereafter collected in a book known as *The Federalist Papers.* Alexander Hamilton, James Madison, and John Jay authored these essays under the pen name of Publius. A number of their essays addressed issues related to the constitutional amending process (Vile, 1992 34–41).

Federalist No. 40 was devoted primarily to demonstrating that the authors of the Constitution had been justified in proposing a new constitution. Although admitting that the original purpose of the Constitutional Convention had been to revise the Articles of Confederation rather than to propose a new government, Madison noted that the delegates had also been commissioned to make such alterations as were necessary "to render the Constitution of the federal government adequate to the exigencies of the Union" (Hamilton, Madison, and Jay 1961, 247). Such a goal, he argued, had proved impossible to achieve by mere revisions, and the delegates had therefore pursued their higher duty, subject to approval or disapproval by the people.

In *Federalist* Nos. 39 and 43, Madison defended the amending process as a moderate mechanism. *Federalist* No. 39 noted that the amending mechanism was "neither wholly federal nor wholly national" (246). Similarly, *Federalist* No. 43 argued that the amending mechanism "guards equally against that extreme facility, which would render the Constitution too mutable, and that extreme difficulty, which might perpetuate its discovered faults" (278). Madison further defended the mechanism for allowing either the states or the national government "to originate the amendment of errors" (278).

In *Federalist* Nos. 49 and 50, Madison explained why the Constitution did not embody two contemporary amending proposals. In the first essay, Madison critiqued a proposal that Thomas Jefferson had advanced in his *Notes on the State of Virginia* (Jefferson 1964, 204–5) whereby two branches of government could call a constitutional convention. Madison's chief objection was that frequent conventions would prove destabilizing and would undermine faith in the document. He also believed that such conventions would stir popular passions and tend to aggrandize the legislative branch, whose members would be more numerous and better connected within the population. In *Federalist* No. 50, Madison further opposed Pennsylvania's scheme for periodic reviews of the Constitution by a council of censors. His discussion led into the defense of separation of powers that is found in the subsequent and better-known essay.

A key Anti-Federalist objection to the Constitution was the absence of a bill of rights. Hamilton addressed this issue in No. 84, the penultimate *Federalist* essay. Arguing that such a bill of rights was unnecessary and might even prove dangerous, Hamilton followed up in the final essay by suggesting that a second convention would be unwise and that amendment would be much easier and more prudent after adoption of the new Constitution.

Faced with increasing calls for a bill of rights and frightened by the prospect that a second convention might be called (Levinson 1990b; Weber 1989; Lash 1994), key Federalists agreed to push for a bill of rights once the Constitution was ratified. James Madison subsequently led the fight in the First Congress for what became the first 10 amendments to the Constitution.

Opposition to the Constitution appears to have dissipated relatively soon after its ratification, although the nation quickly divided on how the new document should be interpreted. One of the first two political parties organized largely by Alexander Hamilton and advocating strong powers for the national government subsequently took the Federalist label. James Madison, by contrast, identified with the Democratic Republican Party that he and Thomas Jefferson organized and that (echoing many of the themes of the original Anti-Federalists) was more suspicious of national power.

See also Anti-Federalists.

For Further Reading:
Wills, Garry. 1981. *Explaining America: The Federalist*. Garden City, NY: Doubleday.

❖ FIFTEENTH AMENDMENT ❖

Before the adoption of the Fifteenth Amendment, the matter of suffrage was purely a matter for the states. Once the Fifteenth Amendment prohibited deprivation of voting rights on the basis of "race, color, or previous condition of servitude," however, a number of other amendments—most notably the Nineteenth and Twenty-sixth—have protected the franchise.

The first resolutions introduced in Congress on African American suffrage were introduced in 1860 and 1861 as a way of averting war. In contrast to amendments that would be introduced after the Civil War, these amendments would have excluded blacks from voting or holding office. One of the supporters of such an amendment was Democratic Senator Stephen A. Douglas of Illinois, who had participated in the famous Lincoln-Douglas debates focusing on the issue of slavery.

After the war, there was considerable, albeit far from universal, sentiment among Republicans to guarantee that the franchise would not be denied on the basis of race. In addition to racist sentiment, there were also concerns that a federal guarantee would erode the American scheme of federalism. Largely as the result of compromise, Section 2 of the Fourteenth Amendment did not actually forbid disenfranchisement of blacks, but it did give Congress the right to reduce representation in states that did so. This provision was never enforced.

After ratification of the Fourteenth Amendment in 1868, there was continuing concern about voting rights for African Americans. Idealistic principles mixed with more partisan Republican concerns that the black vote might be crucial to the party's continuing electoral success. Congress adopted a number of laws granting suffrage to blacks in the District of Columbia and in the federal territories, and it conditioned the admission of Nebraska into the Union and the seating of southern state congressional delegates on those states' extending the right to vote to African Americans. Ironically, this legislation left the northern and border states as the only ones in which such suffrage had not been so guaranteed (U.S. Senate 1985, 36).

Radical Republicans preferred the statutory route, because they wanted to assert congressional power over the area of voting rights; more moderate Republicans feared that rights obtained via legislation would lack the security that an amendment could

provide (Maltz 1990, 146). Republican electoral victories in the 1868 elections gave special impetus to such efforts, which probably could not have been enacted under other circumstances.

The debates over the Fifteenth Amendment became quite complex. In the House, the original proposal introduced by Massachusetts Republican George Boutwell prohibiting abridgment of the right to vote "by reason of race, color, or previous condition of slavery" was met with unsuccessful calls to guarantee universal suffrage, thus invalidating literacy, property, and any other voting qualifications (Maltz 1990, 147–48). At least one proposal was offered to exclude "Chinamen and Indians not taxed" from the provisions of this amendment; another proposal would have prohibited any restriction of the voting rights of anyone 12 years of age or older (cited in Ames 1896, 230).

For its part, the Senate, mindful of Georgia's attempt to exclude black officeholders from the state legislature, voted on a provision by Nevada Republican Senator William Stewart that would protect both the right to vote and the right to hold office. The Senate also considered limitations on property and literacy requirements. As initially passed, the amendment also sought to guarantee the popular election of electors for president (Maltz 1990, 149).

After the House rejected this plan, a conference committee was established, from which the current language of the Fifteenth Amendment emerged. This dropped all references to officeholding rights and to qualifications other than race, color, or previous condition of servitude and included a separate enforcement section. The House approved this amendment on 25 February 1869 by a vote of 144 to 44 (35 not voting); the Senate followed the next day by a vote of 39 to 13 (U.S. Senate 1985, 37). The amendment was ratified by February 1870. A controversy over New York's attempted rescission of its ratification was nullified by an additional ratification by Nebraska and a number of other states. Georgia, Texas, Virginia, and Mississippi were required to ratify as a condition of readmission into the Union (Grimes 1978, 58).

The Fifteenth Amendment was evaded by numerous strategies, legal and otherwise. These included adoption of grandfather clauses, literacy tests and understanding clauses (often enforced in a highly arbitrary manner), poll taxes, the all-white primary, and physical intimidation. These mechanisms proved so effective that Goldwin Smith (1898, 267) suggested at the turn of the century that the amendment had become a dead letter and should be repealed. From a somewhat different vantage point, attorneys Arthur Machen (1910) and William Marbury argued that the Fifteenth Amendment violated implicit limits on the amending process. The Supreme Court ignored such arguments in voiding Maryland's grandfather clauses in *Myers v. Anderson* (1915).

Despite evasion and slack enforcement of the Fifteenth Amendment, an amending proposal was introduced as early as 1877 to restrict its application. Moreover, members of Congress from the South introduced numerous proposals from 1900 to 1915 to repeal the amendment. Perhaps they realized that although it was being narrowly interpreted at the time, it had the potential for expansive interpretation in the future. Some revival of the amendment occurred with the Supreme Court's decision in *Smith v. Allwright* (1944) invalidating the all-white primary. The amendment subsequently served as a justification for expansive voting rights legislation in the 1960s and thereafter.

See also Marbury, William.

For Further Reading:

Mathews, John M. 1909. *Legislative and Judicial History of the Fifteenth Amendment*. New York: Da Capo Press, 1971 reprint.

❖ FIFTH AMENDMENT ❖

The Fifth Amendment was proposed by the First Congress and ratified in 1791 as part of the Bill of Rights. The amendment outlines a variety of guarantees, most of which are directed toward the rights of individuals who are accused of crimes or on trial for them.

The multiple guarantees of this amendment were found in several different parts of the bill of rights that James Madison originally presented to Congress and remained separated until Senate deliberations, when they were combined. Madison's original proposals specified that no one would be subject "to more than one trial or one punishment" (Kurland and Lerner 1987, 5:262) rather than to be "twice put in jeopardy." Madison's original proposal also had a broader self-incrimination provision; the limitation to criminal cases was made during House debates.

The Fifth Amendment contains five basic guarantees. The first such guarantee requires indictment by a grand jury in "capital" (death penalty) or other "infamous" cases, with an exception for personnel in the armed services. The grand jury is distinct from the petit jury guaranteed in the Sixth Amendment. Whereas petit juries award judgments or decide on guilt or innocence and determine penalties in criminal cases, a grand jury simply ascertains whether a prosecutor has sufficient evidence to proceed with a trial. Such juries are designed to guard against prosecutorial vindictiveness. The purpose of the so-called double-jeopardy provision that follows is similar. If an initial finding of innocence were not considered final, a prosecutor could simply wear down a defendant with repeated prosecutions for the same offense.

No provision in the Fifth Amendment is better known, or more controversial, than the provision against self-incrimination. A similar guarantee was found in a number of early state constitutions and in proposals of-fered by the Virginia and North Carolina ratifying conventions (Lutz 1992, 160; for earlier origins, see Levy 1968). One scholar has identified three major purposes of this provision: "(1) maintaining a responsible accusatorial system, (2) preventing cruel and inhumane treatment of suspects, and (3) offering protection for personal privacy" (D. O'Brien 1995, 946). Modern judicial decisions have extended the meaning of this clause beyond that of prohibiting physical coercion to assuring that mental coercion is forbidden as well. In its famous decision in *Miranda v. Arizona* (1966), the Supreme Court extended this guarantee from the courtroom to the station house by ruling that police have to inform suspects of their right to remain silent.

No clause in the Fifth Amendment has been more important than the due process clause. Due process obviously relates to pro-cedural fairness, but there are times when the Court has given this clause, and its com-panion clause in the Fourteenth Amend-ment, a substantive content as well. Al-though all provisions of the Constitution are subject to judicial interpretation, this one seems to allow greater leeway than many less open-ended clauses.

Unlike the other provisions in the amendment, the last provision of the Fifth Amendment, usually dubbed the takings clause, does not deal with the rights of sus-pected criminals. Instead, it provides that the government cannot take private prop-erty without justly compensating its owners. The right of the government to condemn private property for public use, the so-called right of eminent domain, is thus assumed rather than directly stated. Significantly, in *Chicago, Burlington & Quincy Railroad Co. v. Chicago* (1897), the takings clause was the first to be applied to the states via the due process clause of the Fourteenth Amendment. All other provisions of the Fifth Amendment, except for the provision

providing for grand jury indictments, have also been so "incorporated."

There have been attempts to repeal vari-ous provisions in the Fifth Amendment. In 1958, Senator Strom Thurmond of South Carolina introduced an amendment de-signed to alter the provision against double jeopardy. In the next year, a book ques-tioned whether courts had properly inter-preted the self-incrimination provision of the amendment and suggested that the principle should not apply to pretrial investigations (although there should be protections against police use of "third degree" tactics) and that the right should apply only to an ac-cused and not to other witnesses called to testify at a trial (Mayers 1959, 229–31). Similarly, a federal judge writing in 1968 of-fered an amendment designed to change a number of judicial interpretations of the self-incrimination clause (Friendly 1968, 721–22). Some amendments have also been offered that would suspend the prohibition against the taking of private property with-out compensation during times of war.

See also Substantive Due Process.

For Further Reading:

Bodenhamer, David J. 1992. *Fair Trial: Rights of the Accused in American History.* New York: Oxford University Press.

Yandle, Bruce. 1995. *Land Rights: The 1990s' Property Rights Rebellion.* Lanham, MD: Rowman & Littlefield.

❖ FINER, HERMAN (1898–1969) ❖

Political scientist Herman Finer offered far-ranging reforms of U.S. government in a book published in 1960. Finer focused pri-marily on the presidency, believing that the job had become too awesome for one indi-vidual to handle, but he also believed that differing terms of office for the president and members of Congress contributed to the problem.

Finer offered nine major reforms of the existing system. His first and most important proposal was that the president would run on a ticket with 11 vice presidents to be named by national nominating conventions without any instructions from primaries. The president and his cabinet would serve four-year terms, and the two-term limit found in the Twenty-second Amendment would be eliminated. Vice presidents would, like current cabinet members, head executive departments, although some would not have such responsibility but "would be available as deputies to the President and concerned with the main lines of policy as well as general counseling" (Finer 1960, 304).

Finer's second proposal called for making the terms of the president, members of the House, and members of the Senate equal. He favored a four-year term but would accept a five-year stint. He believed that if the executive and legislative candidates ran at the same time and for the same term, this would promote a common platform and would serve to strengthen U.S. political parties.

The third aspect of Finer's plan provided that, to be eligible for president or vice president, an individual "must be presently a member of the House of Representatives or the Senate or must have served at least four years in either house" (1960, 309). Those elected to the cabinet would be replaced through special elections; individuals on the losing ticket "could be regarded as elected to Congress by the fact of their appearance on the presidential ticket; and they could choose in which house they wished to serve" (1960, 312).

Finer's fourth proposal called for the president to name his first vice president and designate an order of succession among the others. His fifth proposal provided that the president would assume the general direction of policy while allowing each vice president to "conduct the business of his department independently and on his own responsibility" (1960, 314).

Finer's sixth proposal would give the president the authority to dismiss and replace his vice presidents. Finer also indicated that the president and his cabinet would sit in the House of Representatives and "participate in congressional business—through messages, through debates, [and] through answering the questions" (1960, 315). Finer proposed reducing the powers of the Senate. It would lose its power to confirm appointments and ratify treaties and would no longer share power with the House in overriding presidential vetoes. Finer's seventh proposal called for maintaining the presidential veto but allowing a 55 percent vote of the House of Representatives to override it.

Although Finer did not believe that Congress should be able to oust the president and his cabinet, he did believe that the president and his cabinet should be able to resign, thus necessitating new elections for both the legislative and the executive branches. This was his eighth proposal. His ninth would have eliminated patronage and spoils, allowing civil servants to continue in office regardless of party affiliation as long as they served the government faithfully and competently.

Finer's is one of the few proposals to develop the idea of a plural executive. It does not appear to have garnered much support.

❖ FINLETTER, THOMAS ❖
(1893–1980)

Thomas Finletter, attorney and special assistant to the secretary of state, authored a book advocating constitutional reform just as World War II was coming to an end (Finletter 1945). Like Alexander Hehmeyer, Finletter was concerned about the government's ability to function effectively once the war was over (Vile 1991c, 91–93).

Finletter was especially concerned about what he perceived to be the lack of fit between governmental means under a system of checks and balances and expanded governmental ends.

Finletter dedicated much of his book to a historical overview designed to show that the existing governmental system resulted in excessive legislative-executive conflict and often led to paralysis. He favored the establishment of more executive-legislative bodies; an institution like the British question hour, where representatives of the administration could explain and justify their policies; and reform of the congressional committee system and its use of seniority. He also advocated establishment of "a joint executive-legislative cabinet" (Finletter 1945, 88). Such a cabinet would be composed of nine congressional leaders from the majority party and nine members of the executive cabinet. Finletter also believed that a majority of both houses of Congress should be able to ratify treaties.

Finletter opposed a parliamentary system, largely because he believed that the American people (and not Congress) had a right to choose their chief executive directly. Finletter believed, however, that the system of fixed election dates should be altered. He proposed that the president and members of both houses of Congress be elected for six-year terms. The president would, in turn, have the power to dissolve Congress and call new elections. Finletter believed that such a system would restore unified government, strengthen party discipline, and make parties more responsible. Finletter also believed that the residency requirement for members of Congress should be eliminated so that parties could run candidates for office outside their districts.

Finletter recognized that formidable forces of "inertia and of satisfaction with things as they are" blocked the path to reform, but he thought that without reform, the conflict between the legislative and executive branches would eventually destroy self-government in the United States (Finletter 1945, 145–47).

❖ FIRST AMENDMENT ❖

The First Amendment was proposed by the First Congress and ratified in 1791 as part of the Bill of Rights. The amendment contains two clauses related to religion. One prohibits Congress from "making a law respecting an establishment of religion," and the other prohibits Congress from "prohibiting the free exercise thereof." The amendment also provides protection for freedom of speech, press, peaceable assembly, and petition. Without the latter rights, a republican, or representative, form of government would be quite precarious. Although it was originally the third of 12 proposed amendments (the first two of which were not initially ratified), there is some rightful symbolism in the fact that this important amendment now heads the Bill of Rights.

Background

The First Amendment is a distillation of proposals that James Madison submitted to Congress after consulting state constitutions and requests from the state ratifying conventions. In the area of religion, Madison proposed that "the civil rights of none shall be abridged on account of religious belief or worship, nor shall any national religion be established, nor shall the full and equal rights of conscience be in any manner, or on any pretext, infringed" (Kurland and Lerner 1987, 5:25). In attempting to protect freedom of speech and the press, Madison proposed that "the people shall not be deprived or abridged of their right to speak, to write, or to publish their sentiments; and the freedom of the press, as one of the great bulwarks of liberty, shall be inviolable." Similarly, Madison proposed that "the people shall not be restrained from peaceably assembling and consulting for their common good; nor from applying to the Legislature by petitions, or remonstrances, for redress of their grievances" (Kurland and Lerner 1987, 5:25). Madison also proposed that "no State shall violate the equal rights of conscience, or the freedom of the press, or the trial by jury in criminal cases" (Kurland and Lerner 1987, 5:25).

It appears that Madison's wording prohibiting Congress from establishing a "national" religion was dropped largely out of concern that it would imply that the new government was "national" rather than "federal" (Kurland and Lerner 1987, 5:93). A similar concern for states' rights apparently led to the deletion of Madison's guarantee against invasions of individual rights by the states.

Religion

No provisions of the First Amendment have provoked greater controversy than the first two clauses dealing with religion. There may well be implicit tension between the idea that government should not establish religion and the guarantee that it should not interfere with its free exercise. Thus, attempts to guarantee free exercise may appear to further religion, whereas attempts to prevent an establishment may appear to infringe on religious exercise. As recently as July 1995, Congress held hearings to examine the prospect of adding a constitutional amendment to clarify this balance.

The most notable cases before the Supreme Court involving the establishment clause have involved public prayer and Bible reading in public schools. In *Engel v. Vitale* (1962), the Supreme Court ruled that the recitation of a prayer composed by the New York State Board of Regents constituted an impermissible establishment of religion that violated the rights of nonbelievers. Similarly, in *Abington v. Schempp* (1963), the Court struck down daily devotional Bible readings

and recitations of the Lord's Prayer in school. Although courts appear to be more receptive toward the idea of a moment of silence during which prayer is not mandated but may take place, the earlier Court decisions continue to bring calls for a constitutional amendment.

Under its interpretations of the establishment clause, the Supreme Court has struck down most forms of governmental aid to parochial schools. In so doing, it has formulated the three-pronged Lemon test, named after the case *Lemon v. Kurtzman* (1971), in which it was first formulated. This test requires that, to pass constitutional muster, a law must have a secular legislative purpose; must not, as its primary effect, either advance or inhibit religion; and must avoid excessive entanglement between church and state. However, the Court does not always apply this test. Thus, in *Marsh v. Chambers* (1983), it permitted continuation of the practice of a chaplain leading prayers at the beginning of a state legislative session; in *Lynch v. Donnelly* (1984), it permitted the display of a religious crèche on public property because this crèche was part of a much larger secular display (see Swanson 1990). Such decisions were written by justices who interpreted the establishment clause as permitting accommodation between the government and religion; others have taken a view of strict separation of church and state, and still others attempt to follow a path of complete neutrality (for one view, see Monsma 1993; for another, see Levy 1986).

The free exercise clause was obviously intended to guarantee a wide range of religious freedom; almost as obviously, a religious justification can rarely justify direct disobedience of a generally applicable law. In *Employment Division, Department of Human Resources of Oregon v. Smith* (1990), the Supreme Court ruled that state employees fired from their jobs for ingesting peyote as part of a Native American religious ceremony were not entitled to unemployment compensation. The outcry over the decision led to the Religious Freedom Restoration Act, designed to ensure that the Court did not override free exercise claims except in cases in which the government was able to establish a compelling state interest. In *Church of the Lukumi Babalu Aye v. City of Hialeah* (1993), even before the new law was adopted, the Court struck down a Florida law that appeared to single out acts of animal sacrifice practiced by a church native to Haiti while permitting other killings of animals.

Speech

Few freedoms are more essential to the democratic process than the freedom of speech, but acts of speech can be so related to action that the seemingly absolute prohibition in the First Amendment has been subject to numerous judicial qualifications. In an early case, *Schenck v. United States* (1919), Justice Oliver Wendell Holmes noted that even the most stringent protection accorded to speech would not protect an individual falsely shouting "fire" in a crowded theater and causing a panic. Although there has been much subsequent discussion and eventual judicial repudiation of Holmes's "clear and present danger" test, the notion that even speech has limits has remained. In *Brandenburg v. Ohio* (1969), the Court indicated that it would suppress the expression of pure speech only when it was likely to lead to imminent lawless action (Wirenius 1994).

The Court has been willing to accept reasonable restrictions on the time, place, and manner of speech, but it has been wary of laws that single out speech on the basis of its content. In recent years, the Court has also extended protection to symbolic speech. Its two most controversial cases have been *Texas v. Johnson* (1989) and *United States v. Eichman* (1990), wherein the Court respectively struck down a state law and a federal law designed to prohibit desecration of the American flag. Numerous amendments have been introduced to overturn these decisions, and support in the states is strong for such an amendment. During the cold war, amendments were also introduced to ban certain types of speech thought likely to lead to subversion of the government.

There are a number of special areas related to freedom of speech that the Supreme Court has treated somewhat differently from others. For example, the Supreme Court has never regarded obscenity as speech. In *Miller v. California* (1973), it identified three criteria for defining obscenity. Under these criteria, speech can be judged obscene if the average person applying contemporary community standards would find that a work taken as a whole appeals to a prurient (lustful) interest in sex; if a work depicts or describes in a patently offensive way sexual conduct specifically defined by law; and if such a work lacks serious literary, artistic, political, or scientific value. Not surprisingly, these criteria still leave considerable room for judicial judgment.

Libel, or defamatory speech, is another special area. Since *New York Times v. Sullivan* (1964), the Court has applied the standard of "actual malice" to cases involving "public figures." This is a stringent test designed to encourage robust criticism of such individuals. Under this test, such figures can collect libel awards only when they are able to demonstrate that information was published with knowledge that it was false or with "reckless disregard" for its veracity (see Lewis 1991).

Although it is an extremely narrow category, the Supreme Court also ruled in *Chaplinsky v. New Hampshire* (1942) that so-called fighting words are not protected by the First Amendment. Such words are derogatory words spoken in close proximity to another person and likely to evoke physical violence rather than reasoned discussion.

Press

Freedom of the press is a corollary to freedom of speech (Powe 1991). Traditionally, the core of freedom of the press was identified as the prohibition against prior restraint of publication. Although it strongly affirmed this core content in *Near v. Minnesota* (1931), the Court also insisted that the freedom was wider than this. In *New York Times v. United States* (1971), the Pentagon Papers case, the Supreme Court overruled an injunction against the *Times* and other newspapers and permitted them to publish a classified story critical of American participation in the Vietnam conflict (see Unger 1972).

Assembly and Petition

The guarantees for peaceable assembly and petition have not been adjudicated as frequently as others in the First Amendment, but like other guarantees there, they are critical to the functioning of democratic institutions. In recent years, the Court has held that these and related clauses guarantee a constitutional right of association. In *Griswold v. Connecticut* (1965), Justice William O. Douglas cited the First Amendment as one of the foundations of the constitutional right to privacy. All the provisions of the First Amendment have been applied to the states via the due process clause of the Fourteenth Amendment.

See also *Engel v. Vitale;* Flag Desecration; Religious Equality Amendment.

❖ FISHER, SIDNEY GEORGE ❖ (1809–1875)

Philadelphia lawyer Sidney George Fisher published a critique of the U.S. Constitution entitled *The Trial of the Constitution* in 1862 (Vile 1992, 97–105). Largely prompted by Fisher's perception that the rigidity of the formal constitutional amending process had been an obstacle to the satisfactory resolution of the issues that led to the Civil War, Fisher's analysis is remarkable for at least two reasons. First, in contrast to almost all previous commentators other than the Anti-Federalists, Fisher questioned the adequacy of the formal amending process. Second, Fisher proposed the British model of legislative sovereignty as an alternative. However, he also associated this model with cautious and incremental change.

Joseph Story had praised the amending process in Article V as an effective safety valve. Fisher argued that this safety valve had been ineffective in preventing revolutionary violence and that "the [constitutional] boiler has burst" (1862, 27). Using another analogy, Fisher proclaimed that Article V had become "an iron fetter" (1862, 33). In Fisher's judgment, the irony of the amending process was that it was most likely to be used at the very time when its operation was likely to be most dangerous: "To put its cumbrous machinery in motion, the people must be roused, and as the most important organic changes are generally connected with the interests of sections or of classes, the people are very likely to be roused by them, to be divided into parties, to be influenced by passion" (S. Fisher 1862, 34).

Having concluded that the existing mechanism for constitutional change was essentially unusable, Fisher proceeded to advocate a system whereby Congress would institute constitutional change subject to popular appeal at the ballot box. In this manner, the people of the current generation rather than those of the American founding would govern. Such a scheme required a substantial limitation of judicial power. Fisher would limit federal judicial review to correcting "unintentional" violations of the Constitution, to controlling state courts, and to "criminal usurpations of power by the Executive or Legislative, or a conspiracy by both to overturn the Government" (S. Fisher 1862, 79).

Although the legislative and executive branches both demonstrated by their actions in the Civil War that the Constitution was a grant of power as well as a list of restraints, Fisher's proposal for a system of legislative sovereignty was not accepted. Fisher's book was published toward the end of the longest period in U.S. history (1804–1865) during which no constitutional amendments were adopted. Ironically, the very process that Fisher criticized for its ineffectiveness was successfully utilized three times from 1865 to 1870. This period was, however, followed by more than a generation before another amendment was adopted. This period, especially the early Progressive Era, also witnessed criticism of the adequacy of the constitutional amending process.

For Further Reading:

Fisher, Sidney G. 1967. *A Philadelphia Perspective: The Diary of Sidney George Fisher Covering the Years 1834–1871*. Philadelphia: Historical Society of Pennsylvania.

Riker, William H. 1954. "Sidney George Fisher and the Separation of Powers during the Civil War." *Journal of the History of Ideas* 15 (June): 397–412.

❖ FLAG DESECRATION ❖

Few recent amendment controversies have provided a faster or more intense response than the Supreme Court's 1989 decision in *Texas v. Johnson*. This decision overturned the conviction of Gregory Johnson under the Texas Venerated Objects Law. Johnson had burned an American flag in front of the Dallas City Hall during the Republican National Convention in 1984. In an intensely argued decision, five of nine Supreme Court justices ruled that Johnson's action was a form of "symbolic speech" protected under the First Amendment. Both the House and the Senate passed resolutions expressing their concern about and disappointment with this decision, and they subsequently debated a constitutional amendment on the subject.

History of Flag Desecration Laws and Judicial Decisions

Although the decision in *Texas v. Johnson* initiated a firestorm, concern for protecting the flag dates quite far back in U.S. history. Legislation designed to protect the flag was favorably voted on by the House of Representatives in 1890 and by the Senate in 1904 and 1908. Moreover, between 1897 and 1905, 34 states adopted flag desecration laws, with most of the remaining states following suit in the period during and immediately after World War I (R. Goldstein 1990, 38). Many of these laws dealt not only with desecration of the flag but also with improper commercial usage. Thus in *Halter v. Nebraska* (1907), the U.S. Supreme Court upheld the conviction of a businessman who sold beer bottled with flag emblems. On a related matter, however, in *Stromberg v. California* (1931), the Court struck down a California law prohibiting the display of red flags on the grounds that the law was too vague.

The next two cases to reach the Supreme Court dealt not with flag desecration but with flag salutes. Before U.S. entry into World War II, many states adopted compulsory flag-salute laws in an attempt to encourage patriotism. The Court upheld such a law in *Minersville School District v. Gobitis* (1940). These laws were opposed by Jehovah's Witnesses, who interpreted the flag salute as worship of a graven image. In the aftermath of the Court's decision, Jehovah's Witnesses were victimized by mobs, and as many as 2,000 Witness children were expelled from schools (R. Goldstein 1990, 46). Subsequently, the Supreme Court used Flag Day in 1943 to reverse itself in *West Virginia Board of Education v. Barnette*, now declaring that the First Amendment protected individuals' rights not to violate their consciences by mouthing salutes they did not believe.

The Vietnam War and a televised incident of flag burning in Central Park in April

1967 brought renewed attention to the flag and precipitated the first federal legislation on the subject. This law, adopted in 1968, provided a penalty of up to $1,000, a year in jail, or both for anyone who "knowingly cast[s] contempt upon any flag of the United States by publicly mutilating, defacing, defiling, burning, or trampling upon it" (cited in R. Goldstein 1990, 49). Shortly thereafter, a number of proposals were introduced in Congress to guard voluntary flag salutes in public schools and buildings and to allow Congress to protect the flag from desecration.

In *Street v. New York* (1969), the Court struck down the conviction of a man who had burned a flag in the aftermath of James Meredith's assassination. But this case was complicated by the fact that it appeared that his conviction might have resulted from what he said when burning the flag rather than from the act itself. That same year, in *Spence v. Washington*, the Court overturned the conviction of an individual who had taped a peace symbol to the flag. In *Smith v. Goguen* (1974), the Supreme Court struck down for vagueness a Massachusetts law that had been applied to an individual who had worn a flag patch on the seat of his pants. The Supreme Court issued no further decisions on the subject between 1974 and 1989 (R. Goldstein 1990, 63).

Reactions to *Texas v. Johnson*

Scores of amendments were introduced in the wake of the Court's 1989 decision in *Texas v. Johnson;* interestingly, a number of these amendments also sought to exclude campaign spending from First Amendment restraints, thus arguably overturning the Supreme Court's 1976 decision in *Buckley v. Valeo.* President George Bush went to the Iwo Jima Monument to announce his support for an amendment introduced by Republican Representative Robert Michel of Illinois. This amendment provided that "the Congress and the states shall have power to prohibit the physical desecration of the Flag of the United States" (Vile 1989, 169).

During hearings on such an amendment, some members of Congress—relying on some equivocal language in the Court's opinion and on the testimony of some prominent law professors, including Laurence Tribe of the Harvard Law School—concluded that Congress had the power to overturn the decision in *Texas v. Johnson* by legislation. A vote for a flag desecration amendment was thus defeated in the Senate in 1989 by a vote of 51 to 48 (R. Goldstein 1990, 28). That same year, however, Congress adopted the Flag Protection Act, which was designed to punish anyone who "knowingly mutilates, physically defiles, burns, maintains on the floor or ground, or tramples upon any flag of the United States." The law exempted "any conduct consisting of the disposal of a flag when it has become worn or soiled" (R. Goldstein 1990, 85).

Accepting expedited review of the law, the Supreme Court struck it down in a 5-to-4 decision in *United States v. Eichman* (1990). It appeared, however, that both public and congressional sentiment had cooled since the earlier decision. Faced with arguments that an amendment would protect the flag at the cost of sacrificing the principles for which it stood and that it would be unwise to set the first precedent of restricting the Bill of Rights, Congress could not garner the required two-thirds majorities in 1990 (the votes for an amendment were 254 to 177 in the House and 58 to 42 in the Senate) (Biskupic 1990, 2063).

Although the amendment appeared to be dead, support began to grow again after the dramatic congressional elections of 1994. In 1995, the House of Representatives voted 312 to 120 for the amendment, which subsequently garnered 63 votes (versus 36 against) in the Senate to fall just shy of the two-thirds majority needed. Utah

Republican Senator Orrin Hatch expressed the sentiment of other amendment supporters when he vowed that "this amendment is not going to go away," and it may be an issue in the 1996 presidential campaign (Toner 1995).

Issues Raised by the Flag Desecration Amendment

One fascinating aspect of the flag desecration amendment is that it has revived arguments that there might be limits on the amending process. Thus, one scholar argued that such an amendment would violate rights protected by the Ninth Amendment and could be adopted only if language were included specifically indicating that the American people no longer considered flag burning to be a natural right (Rosen 1991). Another author argued that since the First Amendment prohibited Congress from making any law abridging the freedom of speech, such an amendment would have to be adopted by the unused convention route (Isaacson 1990; for critiques of Rosen and Isaacson, see Vile 1993b, 136–43).

If a constitutional amendment is adopted, the courts could have difficulty deciding precisely what representations are defined as flags. For example, would representations of flags in newspapers or magazines count? There is also the ironic possibility that an amendment specifically prohibiting flag desecration would actually widen protection for other forms of symbolic speech (Vile 1989).

See also Campaign Contributions and Expenditures; Constitutional Amendments, Limits on; *Texas v. Johnson*.

For Further Reading:

Bates, Stephen. 1991. "Deconstructing the Flag-Burning Debate." *This World & I* 7 (July): 523–29.

Curtis, Michael K., ed. 1993. *The Constitution and the Flag.* Vol. 2. *The Flag Burning Cases.* New York: Garland.

Dry, Murray. 1991. "Flag Burning and the Constitution." In *The Supreme Court Review, 1990,* ed.

Gerhard Casper et al. Chicago: University of Chicago Press.

Goldstein, Robert J. Forthcoming. *The American Flag Desecration Controversy: A Collection of Documents from the Civil War to 1990.* Syracuse, NY: Syracuse University Press.

———. 1995. *Burning the Flag: The Great 1989–1990 American Flag Desecration Controversy.* Kent, OH: Kent State University Press.

———. 1994. *Saving "Old Glory": The History of the American Flag Desecration Controversy.* Boulder, CO: Westview.

Kaplan, Morton A. 1991. "Freedom of Speech: Its Constitutional Scope and Function." *This World & I* 7 (July): 531–41.

McBride, James. 1991. "'Is Nothing Sacred?': Flag Desecration, the Constitution and the Establishment of Religion." *St. John's Law Review* 65: 297–324.

Tushnet, Mark. 1990. "The Flag-Burning Episode: An Essay on the Constitution." *University of Colorado Law Review* 61: 39–53.

❖ FORFEITURE OF OFFICE ❖

See Offices, Forfeiture of or Ineligibility for.

❖ FOURTEENTH AMENDMENT ❖

No provision of the Constitution has been more disputed among scholars or more litigated before courts than the Fourteenth Amendment. It was proposed by the necessary congressional majorities in June 1866 and ratified in July 1868. The Fourteenth Amendment was wedged between two other amendments that were adopted contemporaneously soon after the Civil War, and an understanding of the dilemmas faced after the war does much to explain it.

Background

Under the terms of the Thirteenth Amendment, involuntary servitude had been eliminated. Since slaves had previously counted as only three-fifths of a person for determining a state's representation in the House of Representatives and the electoral college, such freedom presented the possibility that the states of the ex-Confederacy might actually gain representation in the government. Moreover, almost as soon as the slaves were freed, many of the states that had permitted slavery enacted restrictive Black Codes that effectively stripped the former slaves of their freedom. In such circumstances, those who had led the rebellion might actually increase their political power, gaining in Congress what they had been unable to achieve on the battlefields.

Congress reacted by adopting the 1866 Civil Rights Bill, which effectively ignored the Supreme Court's decision in *Scott v. Sandford* (1857) by recognizing the citizenship of all native-born Americans (except some Native Americans) and attempting to protect their rights. Congress also adopted the Freedmen's Bureau Bill of 1866, which authorized military trials for those violating civil rights (U.S. Senate 1985, 30). Both bills were adopted over President Andrew Johnson's vetoes and in the face of arguments that they were unconstitutional. Although the Thirteenth Amendment had abolished slavery, doubts remained as to whether it provided adequate authority for the protection of other civil and political rights that had traditionally rested with the states.

Creation and Proposal

In response to this situation, in December 1865, Congress created a Joint Committee on Reconstruction composed of 15 members—five Republicans and one Democrat from the Senate, and seven Republicans and two Democrats from the House. The committee was chaired by Republicans Thaddeus Stevens (Pa.) of the House and William P. Fessenden (Maine) of the Senate (W. Nelson 1988, 48). On 12 January 1866, Representative John Bingham (R. Ohio) introduced a proposed amendment to grant Congress power to provide "equal

protection" for "all persons in every State within the Union," and eight days later, a subcommittee incorporated this provision into a proposal giving Congress power "to secure to all citizens of the United States, in every State, the same political rights and privileges; and to all persons in every State equal protection in the enjoyment of life, liberty, and property." The subcommittee also proposed that "whenever the elective franchise shall be denied or abridged in any State on account of race, creed or color, all persons of such race, creed or color, shall be excluded from the basis of representation" (W. Nelson 1988, 49).

The joint committee subsequently presented Congress with two amendments, one to reduce the representation of states restricting voting rights and the other designed to protect the rights of the newly freed slaves. The House adopted the first amendment, but it was postponed in the Senate. The other amendment did not make it through either house (W. Nelson 1988, 50).

In the meantime, the joint committee was reworking its proposals and meshing them into a single amendment. In the process, it changed the language of "political rights and privileges" into "privileges and immunities." Moreover, rather than stripping whites of suffrage in states that restricted the franchise, the committee settled on a provision—apparently first suggested by Indiana Democrat Robert Dale Owen Jr.—to reduce representation for such states and to disenfranchise those who had supported the Confederate cause (W. Nelson 1988, 50–57). It also included a provision guaranteeing the Union debt and repudiating the Confederate debt and making it clear that slaveholders would not be compensated for slaves who had been emancipated. The House accepted this revised amendment in May 1866, but the Committee of the Whole in the Senate subsequently made two important modifications.

One was to add the definition of citizenship that became the first sentence of Section 1 of this amendment. The second change was to weaken the prohibition against voting by former Confederates; it now banned from office former Confederates who had joined the cause after taking an oath of allegiance to the U.S. Constitution (W. Nelson 1988, 58). The House subsequently concurred in these revisions (for further discussion of congressional actions, see Virginia Commission on Constitutional Government 1967; James 1956; Flack 1908; Maltz 1990).

Content

As adopted, the Fourteenth Amendment is divided into five sections. Section 1 overturned *Scott v. Sandford* (1857) by extending citizenship to all persons "born or naturalized in the United States and subject to the jurisdiction thereof." It also forbade states to abridge the privileges and immunities of such citizens. More broadly, it prohibited states from denying persons "due process of law" or "equal protection of the law."

Section 2 repealed the three-fifths clause and, in a provision that has never been enforced, sought to reduce representation for states restricting the franchise "in the proportion which the number of such male citizens shall be to the whole number of citizens twenty-one years of age in such State." This was the section that was so upsetting to advocates of women's rights such as Susan B. Anthony and Elizabeth Cady Stanton, who had hoped that suffrage for women would be granted along with suffrage for African Americans. Disappointed by both the Fourteenth and the Fifteenth Amendments, they would have to wait until 1920 for the adoption of the Nineteenth Amendment granting suffrage to women.

The last three sections of the amendment dealt with incidental matters. Section 3 prohibited officeholding by those who, having taken an oath to uphold the U.S. Constitu-

tion, subsequently supported the Confederacy, but it provided that a two-thirds vote of Congress could remove such a disability, and it soon did so. Section 4 guaranteed the Union debt while repudiating that of the Confederacy and denied all claims by former slaveholders for compensation for their slaves. Finally, Section 5, like Section 2 of the Thirteenth Amendment, granted Congress power to enforce the amendment.

Ratification

The ratification of the Fourteenth Amendment was almost as controversial as the debates over its proposal (Fernandez 1966; Suthon 1953). Although the amendment met with favor in the North, most Southern states rejected it. In 1867, Congress subsequently adopted the Military Reconstruction Act, providing that states of the Confederacy could be readmitted to the Union without military rule if they ratified the Fourteenth Amendment. Several subsequently did so. At about that time, New Jersey and Ohio attempted to rescind their ratifications. Secretary of State William Seward presented the facts to Congress, which declared the amendment adopted (James 1984, 288–99). At least one other state appears to have ratified the amendment prior to the congressional votes, and other ratifications followed before any judicial decisions based on the amendment. Moreover, Congress had not previously found it necessary to take a separate step to "promulgate" an amendment.

Interpretation

Ratification of the Fourteenth Amendment was just the beginning of the controversy over its meaning. Especially difficult to resolve is the question of the extent to which the guarantees in the Fourteenth Amendment were designed to harmonize with, or supersede, earlier understandings of federalism (compare W. Nelson 1988 and Richards 1993). Much contemporary debate has also centered on the question whether the due process clause or the privileges and immunities clause in Section 1 of the amendment was designed to overrule *Barron v. Baltimore* (1833) and apply the provisions of the Bill of Rights to the states. Senator Hugo L. Black later advocated this view based on his reading of the congressional debates on the subject.

The Supreme Court majority did not initially take this position. Indeed, its decisions in the nineteenth century gave restrictive readings to most provisions of the amendment. In the *Slaughterhouse* cases (1873), the Court narrowly read the privileges and immunities of Section 1 of the amendment. In the *Civil Rights* cases (1883), the Court overturned the Civil Rights Act of 1875, which had attempted to prohibit discrimination in places of public accommodation. In a distinction that has never been repudiated, the Court reasoned that the Fourteenth Amendment applied only to state action and not to actions by individuals. Finally, in *Plessy v. Ferguson* (1896), the Supreme Court upheld racial segregation and southern Jim Crow laws by formulating the "separate but equal" doctrine, justifying segregation as long as facilities for races were equal.

Although limiting the scope of the Fourteenth Amendment in the area of civil rights, the Court increasingly began to embrace the idea of substantive due process, by which it imposed limits on governmental regulation of businesses (Cortner 1993; Gillman 1993). This posture was perhaps best epitomized in the case of *Lochner v. New York* (1905). Only in 1937, after Roosevelt introduced his court-packing plan, did the Court retreat from this area.

In contrast to the demise of economic due process, the twentieth century has witnessed the progressive expansion of the civil rights provisions of the Fourteenth Amendment. Through a process of selective incorporation, the Supreme Court has gradually applied most provisions of the Bill of Rights to the states via the due process clause of the Fourteenth Amendment. Indeed, in *Griswold v. Connecticut* (1965) and *Roe v. Wade* (1973), it ruled that additional rights not specifically stated in the Bill of Rights also apply to the states through the due process clause. In *Baker v. Carr* (1962), *Reynolds v. Sims* (1964), and subsequent cases, the Court has also expanded the equal protection clause to cover matters of state and congressional legislative apportionment, generating numerous pleas for an amendment to curb the Court's interpretation. In *Brown v. Board of Education* (1954), the Court overturned *Plessy v. Ferguson* (1896) and gave a broad reading to the equal protection clause (D. Jackson 1992). The Court has given similarly broad readings to the congressional enforcement provisions in Section 5 of the Fourteenth Amendment. It has also used the Fourteenth Amendment as a basis for limiting discrimination based on gender.

Some of the most controversial areas of modern public policy—including questions about affirmative action and school busing—continue to center on the meaning of the Fourteenth Amendment.

Proposals for Amendment or Repeal

From 1903 to 1920, several proposals were introduced—most by southern representatives—to eliminate all but the first sentence of Section 2 of the Fourteenth Amendment. Although Congress had never acted to reduce representation for states that restricted voting rights, the threat was apparently still of concern. In 1920, Democratic Senator James Phelan of California introduced an amendment restricting citizenship by birth to those who were white, African, or American Indians, presumably with the intention of excluding those of Asian backgrounds. The 1930s witnessed at least three attempts to repeal Section 1 of the Fourteenth Amendment, one by Senator William Borah of Idaho.

In March 1957, the Georgia General Assembly sent a memorializing resolution to Congress to declare both the Fourteenth and Fifteenth Amendments invalid on the basis of alleged irregularities in the procedures by which they were adopted. A supporter of this resolution argued for an amendment repealing the Fourteenth and Fifteenth Amendments, adding the word "expressly" to the Tenth Amendment, and limiting citizenship to whites. This latter provision provided in relevant part:

No person shall be a citizen of the United States unless he is a non-Hispanic White of the European race, in whom there is no ascertainable trace of Negro blood, nor more than one-eighth Mongolian, Asian, Asia Minor, Middle Eastern, Semitic, Near Eastern, American Indian, Malay or other non-European or nonwhite blood, provided that Hispanic whites, defined as anyone with an Hispanic ancestor, may be citizens if, in addition to meeting the aforesaid ascertainable trace and percentage tests, they are, in appearance, indistinguishable from Americans whose ancestral home is the British Isles or Northwest Europe. Only citizens shall have the right and privilege to reside permanently in the United States. (Pace 1986, 99)

The most recent attempt to repeal the Fourteenth Amendment appears to have been made by Democratic Representative John Rarick of Louisiana in 1973.

See also Bingham, John A.; Equal Rights Amendment; Incorporation; Promulgation of Amendments; Thirteenth Amendment.

❖ FOURTH AMENDMENT ❖

The Fourth Amendment was proposed by the First Congress and ratified in 1791 as part of the Bill of Rights. It provides that "the right of the people to be secure in their persons, houses, papers, and effects, against unreasonable searches and seizures, shall not be violated, and no Warrants shall issue, but upon probable cause, supported by Oath or affirmation, and particularly describing the place to be searched, and the persons or things to be seized."

Like the amendment that precedes it, the Fourth Amendment was largely motivated by abuses by the British. They had used general warrants, or so-called writs of assistance, in tracking down customs abuses in the colonies. A number of states subsequently adopted provisions against such warrants, and ratifying conventions in Maryland, Virginia, and North Carolina all proposed amendments dealing with the subject (Lutz 1992, 57).

The proposed bill of rights that James Madison submitted to the House of Representatives contained a provision that is quite similar to what became the Fourth Amendment. One difference was that Madison's version referred to "other property" rather than to "effects." Another difference was that Madison's version specified that the people's rights "shall not be violated by warrants issued without probable cause," whereas the text of the current Fourth Amendment leaves a greater disjunction between the prohibition against unreasonable searches and seizures and the warrant requirement (see Kurland and Lerner 1987, 5:25, 237).

The final version of this amendment presents an interpretive ambiguity—namely, that of establishing the relationship between unreasonable searches and seizures and warrants. It is obvious that the amendment outlaws searches conducted pursuant to warrants that are not supported by probable cause, that are not supported by oath or affirmation, or that do not particularly describe the person or place to be seized. What courts have had to flesh out is precisely what, if any, kinds of warrantless searches are considered to be reasonable and what kinds are "unreasonable" and therefore unconstitutional.

Currently, the courts recognize a number of circumstances in which warrantless searches are not considered to be unreasonable. These include cases involving "hot pursuit" of suspects, "exigent circumstances" in which evidence is in imminent danger of destruction, stop-and-frisk searches incident to arrest, and searches of objects in "plain view" or in "open fields" (D. O'Brien 1995, 802–10). Moreover, because automobiles are mobile, courts have fashioned a whole host of exceptions related to them (D. O'Brien 1995, 834–40).

The problems of wiretapping and other forms of electronic surveillance were obviously not contemplated by the framers of the Fourth Amendment. Perhaps just as obviously, such surveillance poses a threat that is equal to or greater than that which the framers did anticipate. In *Olmstead v. United States* (1928), the Supreme Court initially decided against applying the Fourth Amendment to this issue, but it subsequently reversed course in *Katz v. United States* (1967) and ruled that such surveillance, like other searches, requires a warrant.

Although the Fourth Amendment outlaws unreasonable searches and seizures and sets some basic guidelines for issuing warrants, it does not specify what will happen if the government proceeds to conduct illegal searches. Over time, the Court has formulated the exclusionary rule, whereby such illegally obtained evidence is barred from trials. First applied to the national government in *Weeks v. United States* (1914), this rule was subsequently extended to the states in *Mapp v. Ohio* (1961). Recent cases however, have recognized some exceptions—for example, the "good faith" exception established in *United States v. Leon* (1984) and the "inevitable discovery" exception established in *Nix v. Williams* (1984). Other provisions of the Fourth Amendment have also been extended to the states via the due process clause of the Fourteenth Amendment.

In the Connecticut birth-control case *Griswold v. Connecticut* (1965), Justice William O. Douglas cited the Fourth Amendment as one of the sources of the right of privacy. No amendments have been introduced in Congress to repeal the Fourth Amendment, but there are continuing criticisms of judicial interpretations of this amendment (Rothwax 1996).

❖ FREE ENTERPRISE ❖

The Constitution of the United States contains a number of protections for private property. These include the contracts clause in Article I, Section 10; the takings, or just compensation, clause of the Fifth Amendment; and the due process clauses of the Fifth and Fourteenth Amendments.

The Constitution does not specifically prohibit the government from creating or purchasing private enterprises. Chief Justice John Marshall's decision in *McCulloch v. Maryland* (1819) authorized the establishment of a national bank as a legitimate means of carrying out other constitutional powers—a means consistent with and not elsewhere prohibited by the Constitution. Although socialism has never been especially popular in the United States—with the Socialist Party suffering a significant decline since the 1930s (Shannon 1967, ix)—the national government has occasionally taken on projects, such as the Tennessee Valley Authority, that could be undertaken by private industry. From time to time, reformers have called on the government to take over the operation of one or another industry, railroads being a special concern toward the end of the nineteenth century.

From 1952 to 1978, more than a dozen amending proposals were introduced in Congress to prohibit the national government from engaging in any private business not specified in the Constitution (thus presumably exempting the post office) that would compete with private enterprise. A number of these proposals also called for repeal of the Sixteenth Amendment and estate or gift taxes.

❖ FREEDMEN, REDISTRIBUTION OF ❖

Democratic Senator Garrett Davis of Kentucky offered two of the more bizarre amendment proposals during debates over the Thirteenth Amendment. One would have required that slaves be removed from slave states before being given their free-dom. The second proposed distributing freedmen throughout the country proportionally to the white population.

Davis's proposals are a reminder that, as early as Thomas Jefferson, many observers thought that the past history of black-white relations in America would make it difficult for the two races to coexist if African Americans were granted freedom (Jefferson 1964, 132). Moreover, as late as Abraham Lincoln, politicians advocated slave recolonization, with Lincoln using his second annual address to advocate an amendment that would have rested on the consent of those being recolonized (J. Richardson 1908, 6:140).

See also Thirteenth Amendment.

G

GARCIA V. SAN ANTONIO ❖ METROPOLITAN TRANSIT ❖ AUTHORITY (1985)

Garcia v. San Antonio Metropolitan Transit Authority is one of the most important contemporary cases affecting judicial interpretation of the Tenth Amendment. The issue in the case was whether the San Antonio Metropolitan Transit Authority (SAMTA) was subject to the wage and overtime provisions of the Fair Labor Standards Act that Congress enacted under its authority to regulate commerce. *Garcia* overturned *National League of Cities v. Usery* (1976). In that 5-to-4 decision, written by Justice William Rehnquist, the Court had cited concerns about federalism in exempting traditional state and local governmental activities (as opposed to private enterprises) from such federal regulations.

After reviewing the history that had transpired since *Usery*, Justice Harry Blackmun wrote the 5-to-4 decision in *Garcia* in which he argued that the Court had been unable to distinguish with any degree of consistency between those governmental functions that were traditional and those that were not. He therefore concluded that this judicial attempt should be abandoned. Blackmun argued that the very fact that the federal government had appropriated grant monies to SAMTA and other state programs demonstrated that the states had clout in influencing federal decisions. He argued that the structure of the federal system—and especially the guarantee of equal state suffrage in the Senate—rather than judicial oversight would be sufficient to protect state interests.

Justices Lewis Powell, Warren Burger, William Rehnquist, and Sandra Day O'Connor dissented, putting special emphasis on the importance of the Tenth Amendment as a limit on federal power. Justice Powell noted that "the States' role in our system of government is a matter of constitutional law, not of legislative grace" (*Garcia* 1985, 567). Appealing to "the spirit of the Tenth Amendment," Justice O'Connor, a former Arizona state legislator, noted a number of changes, including the direct election of senators, that had increased the need for judicial vigilance in protecting states' rights (*Garcia* 1985, 584–85).

Congress reacted to *Garcia* by adopting a bill allowing states to substitute compensatory time off for overtime pay (Rossum and Tarr 1991, 217). To date, however, Congress has not proposed any of several amendments that have been advocated for overturning or limiting *Garcia* (see Advisory Commission on Intergovernmental Relations 1986, 43–48). Recent discussions of unfunded federal mandates and other issues may, however, indicate renewed concern over state power and renewed attention to the Tenth Amendment. This could result in further attempts to refine the constitutional allocation of powers between state and national governments.

See also Seventeenth Amendment; Tenth Amendment; Unfunded Federal Mandates.

For Further Reading:

Advisory Commission on Intergovernmental Relations. 1987. *Is Constitutional Reform Necessary To Reinvigorate Federalism? A Roundtable Discussion.* November. Washington, DC: ACIR.

❖ GARDINER, WILLIAM (1885–?) ❖

Born in Missouri, William Gardiner worked as a teacher and department store credit supervisor before earning an Ed.D. in 1942. Gardiner may well have been the oldest individual ever to offer a new U.S. constitution for consideration when he published *A Proposed Constitution for the United States of America* in 1973. His plan included an odd mix of prescription and commentary, of existing constitutional provisions and innovations.

Under Gardiner's plan, Congress would continue to be bicameral, but the House would have 200 members serving for four-year terms. Moreover, members of the House would be responsible for electing the president and vice presidents, who would also serve as cabinet members. Senators would serve eight-year terms and would be selected, as they were prior to the adoption of the Seventeenth Amendment, by state legislatures. Legislators in such bodies, like members of the House of Representatives when choosing executive officials, would have to pledge not to consult beforehand about such choices. Strict attendance would be kept by page boys and girls (to whom Gardiner's constitutional proposal makes several references), and members could be removed for missing twice in one month or three times in a year.

The president and eight vice presidents would serve for four-year terms, and the Justice Department would be elevated to a more prominent watchdog role. The Supreme Court would consist of 11 members serving to age 70. Other officials in government would be required to attend special academies.

In contrast to the existing Constitution, Gardiner's went into great length in describing the organization of state governments. All counties would have to adopt a county commissioner form of government, with the number of commissioners based on each county's population. Gardiner listed specific state officials and their methods of selection. Under his plan, local school boards would be replaced by parent-teacher associations. Schools would work with industries to provide jobs to keep juveniles from delinquency.

Gardiner proposed to prohibit political parties and lobbying. He would also eliminate campaign managers, speechwriters, and most congressional staff.

Constitutional amendments could be proposed in four ways and ratified in five; they would have a five-year deadline. Gardiner further suggested that his plan might be put into place by a president who made himself a temporary dictator.

Gardiner's greatest innovations would have been in the area of civil liberties. He would permit a speaker to lecture or pray in public schools, "provided he does not boost or condemn any church organization, or question the validity of the Bible" (Gardiner 1973, 9). He would eliminate freedom of the press so that "spoken or printed words that have a deteriorating influence on the morals and stability of the people shall be prohibited" (Gardiner 1973, 15). Gardiner specified that "any mawkish person or news medium that criticizes an apprehending officer for a justifiable killing shall be prosecuted" (Gardiner 1973, 17). Gardiner proposed to eliminate both grand and petit juries and to replace trials with "criminal proceedings" without Fifth Amendment guarantees against self-incrimination, confrontation of witnesses, and private defense attorneys. Capital punishment would be prescribed for a litany of offenses. Individuals who had received "free food" or other relief over the past four years would be prohibited from voting (Gardiner 1973, 27).

Guns and other concealed weapons would be registered but not prohibited. In place of the current Bill of Rights, people would be assured of being "treated fairly and squarely" (Gardiner 1973, 43).

Apart from this essay, Gardiner's proposal does not appear to have been the subject of other secondary literature.

❖ GENERAL WELFARE ❖

Article I, Section 8 of the Constitution grants Congress power to lay taxes "to pay the Debts and provide for the Common Defense and general Welfare of the United States." Because this general welfare clause is linked to the taxing power, Congress has "no general power" to legislate for the general welfare but only to tax for this purpose (Peltason 1994, 71).

In *United States v. Butler* (1936), however, the Supreme Court ruled that the taxing and spending powers may be exercised in addition to other grants of power in Article I, Section 8. The Court thus upheld the view originally advanced by Alexander Hamilton over the rival view advocated by James Madison, which would have limited taxing and spending powers to carrying out other specific constitutional grants.

Faced with quite restrictive judicial readings of congressional power over economic issues, members of Congress introduced amendments in 1935, 1936, and 1937 that would have expanded congressional power to legislate on behalf of the general welfare. President Franklin Roosevelt considered support of a proposal that had originally been introduced as part of the Virginia plan at the Constitutional Convention of 1787. It would have allowed Congress to "legislate in all cases for the general interests of the union, and also in those in which the states are separately incompetent, or in which the harmony of the United States may be interrupted by the exercise of indi-

vidual legislation" (cited in Kyvig 1989, 471). Beginning with *West Coast Hotel v. Parrish* (1937), its historic "switch in time that saved nine," the Supreme Court began to interpret congressional powers under the commerce clause more liberally. Proposals to expand such powers via a new general welfare clause subsequently ceased.

For Further Reading:

Engdahl, David E. 1994. "The Spending Power." *Duke Law Journal* 44 (October): 1–109.

❖ GOVERNORS, ROLE IN THE AMENDING PROCESS ❖

From time to time, observers have questioned whether the approval of a state's governor is required to legitimize either a state's ratification of an amendment or a state's application for a constitutional convention. Although no Supreme Court decision has addressed this issue directly, the answer appears to be negative (Edel 1981, 107–8).

At the national level, the Supreme Court decided in *Hollingsworth v. Virginia* (1798) that the president's approval was not required for ratification of an amendment. In *Hawke v. Smith, No. 1*, the Court further indicated that the "legislature" mentioned in Article V was the lawmaking body. Democratic North Carolina Senator Sam Ervin convincingly argued that "the term 'legislature' should have the same meaning in both the application clause and the ratification clause of Article V" (Ervin 1968, 889). Legislation that he and Utah Republican Senator Orrin Hatch proposed to deal with Article V conventions did not require such gubernatorial approval.

❖ GRAND JURY ❖

The Fifth Amendment to the U.S. Constitution specifies that "no person shall be held to answer for a capital, or otherwise infamous crime, unless on a presentment or indictment of a grand jury." This provision remains one of the few in the Bill of Rights that has not been applied to the states as well as to the national government (*Hurtado v. California* [1884]; *Gyuro v. Connecticut* [1968]). Today, less than half of the states have grand jury systems. The remaining states rely on a system of indictment by "information" that is offered in an affidavit by a prosecutor to a judge (Abraham 1993, 104).

Whereas a petit jury decides on guilt or innocence, a grand jury decides whether there is sufficient evidence for a prosecutor to bring an individual to trial. The grand jury developed in England as a means of shielding individuals from overzealous or vindictive prosecutors who might bring unwarranted indictments. Federal grand juries typically consist of 23 individuals, with 12 or more needed for an indictment. Proceedings are held in secret, without many of the due process safeguards required in an actual trial.

In 1973, Republican Congressman Charles Wiggins of California introduced an amendment that would have modified the existing Fifth Amendment requirement to allow Congress to specify whether indictments would proceed by grand jury or by use of information. Several such resolutions have subsequently been introduced, and the House of Representatives held hearings on the subject in 1976 and 1977.

In introducing his amendment, Wiggins noted that most grand jury proceedings were "dominated by the prosecutor." He further observed that "in modern society grand jurors do not ordinarily possess either the skills or the training to conduct the complex investigations that a truly independent evaluation would require" (*Congressional Record*, 1979, 32912).

See also Fifth Amendment.

❖ *GRISWOLD V. CONNECTICUT* ❖ (1965)

The scope of judicial interpretation influences the degree to which legislative action or constitutional amendment will be needed to strike down unwise laws. Few modern cases have sparked more intense debate on the subject than this case involving a longstanding state law prohibiting the use or prescription of birth-control devices.

Justice William O. Douglas's majority opinion was apparently strongly influenced by Justice William Brennan (Garrow 1994, 245–49). Douglas argued that although the Constitution did not specifically mention the right to privacy, the First, Third, Fourth, Fifth, and Ninth Amendments all had "penumbras, formed by emanations from those guarantees which help give them life and substance" (*Griswold* 1965, 484). The majority found that such penumbras, as applied to the states by the due process clause of the Fourteenth Amendment, protected the right of marital privacy.

Justice Arthur Goldberg's concurring opinion emphasized the hitherto largely neglected Ninth Amendment, arguing that it provided a textual basis for the judicial protection of unenumerated rights. In his concurring opinion, Justice John Marshall Harlan argued that the due process clause of the Fourteenth Amendment "stands . . . on its own bottom" (*Griswold* 1965, 478) rather than being intended to incorporate one or more specific provisions in the Bill of Rights. In another concurring opinion, Justice Byron White stated that prohibitions on the use of contraceptives by married couples did not deter illicit sexual activity.

In dissent, Justice Hugo Black reiterated his long-held belief, previously articulated in *Adamson v. California* (1947), that the authors of the due process clause of the Fourteenth Amendment intended to apply the specific guarantees of the Bill of Rights to the states, but no more. As such, the amendment did not authorize the Court to strike down legislation simply because it was unwise. Those who desired to keep the Constitution "in tune with the times" needed to use the amending process (*Griswold* 1965, 522). In his dissent, Justice Potter Stewart agreed that the Court had no power to invalidate a law simply because it was silly or unwise.

Griswold prepared the way for the 1973 decision in *Roe v. Wade* invalidating most state laws on abortion. This decision has prompted numerous calls for a right to life amendment.

❖ GUARANTEE CLAUSE ❖

One of the most elusive provisions of the Constitution is the clause in Article IV, Section 4 providing that "the United States shall guarantee to every State in this Union a Republican Form of Government." It further provides that the United States "shall protect each of them against Invasion; and on Application of the Legislature, or of the Executive (when the Legislature cannot be convened) against domestic Violence." The first part of this guarantee is the only specific restriction in the Constitution "on the form or structure of state governments" (Wiecek 1972, 1). Through most of U.S. history, this clause has been what Charles Sumner called "a sleeping giant" (Wiecek 1972, 290). Although some Republicans relied on this clause for authority to reconstruct the South after the Civil War, its inherent ambiguity has made it difficult to apply.

Two amending proposals have related to the guarantee clause. A proposal introduced in 1861 to give each state control over slavery within its territories also stipulated that the national government could still aid states faced with slave insurrections. In 1870, a much different proposal, aimed at Klan violence against African Americans, would have allowed Congress to authorize intervention even when a state did not apply for aid (Ames 1896, 171–72).

In *Luther v. Borden* (1849), the Supreme Court decided that the question of whether a state government was republican or not was a "political question." As such, the matter was one for Congress to resolve when it decided whether to seat a state's representatives. Alternatively, a president might make such a determination when deciding whether to send aid to a government facing domestic violence, as John Tyler had done in the case of Rhode Island.

For many years, the guarantee clause stood as an obstacle to judicial intervention in matters involving state legislative apportionment. When the Supreme Court eventually decided in *Baker v. Carr* (1962) that this issue was justiciable, it did so on the basis of the equal protection clause of the Fourteenth Amendment rather than the guarantee clause.

If either the Court or Congress were ever to give an expanded meaning to the guarantee clause, the results could be as politically far-reaching as the adoption of any amendment ratified to date.

See also Political Questions.

H

❖ HAMILTON, HUGH L. ❖

One of the most thorough and systematic plans for a new constitution was presented in a book published by Hugh L. Hamilton in 1938. Likening the Constitution to a jig-saw puzzle, Hamilton examined it section by section and concluded that "thirty-one pieces are rotted and have to be thrown away; forty-four of them are badly in need of repair; thirty-seven of them have to be re-painted; and we have to make eighteen new pieces to complete the picture. Only thirty-seven of the original pieces are left intact" (H. Hamilton 1938, 5).

Hamilton does not appear to have been motivated by a consistent ideology. His goals were fairly conventional, and he suggested that the main goal of contemporaries was "contentment—congenial occupation, adequate leisure, an absorbing hobby, a pleasant home, and wholesome recreation" (H. Hamilton 1938, 102).

Section I of the new constitution addressed general provisions. Innovations included allowing adjustments on state boundaries, with the proviso that the number of states would not be reduced below 30. Hamilton also proposed a provision—similar to contemporary neutrality legislation—limiting travel on ships of belligerent nations and restricting loans to or trade with such countries. The constitution further specified that most jobs would be filled through a civil service commission.

Section II of the proposed constitution was the bill of rights. It would deny citizenship "to the insane, the criminal, the illiterate, the non-English speaking and those who fail to comprehend the nature of our government" (H. Hamilton 1938, 112). Freedom of the press would include a provision "prohibiting control of the press in any part of the United States by individuals or groups which tends to abridge their freedom" (H. Hamilton 1938, 113). The current Fourth Amendment would be modified to make governmental officials responsible for unreasonable searches and seizures or from "publicity, initiated by their order or performed by them" (H. Hamilton 1938, 113). Hamilton would permit the use of sworn testimony by dead witnesses, outlaw capital punishment, and eliminate the due process clause, which he considered to be ambiguous.

Section III outlined states' rights and limitations. It would have required state executives to extradite criminals who had fled to their states.

Congress would be renamed the National Assembly and be divided into a Senate and a Congress; members would receive salaries of $9,000 a year and actual travel expenses. Congress would consist of from 100 to 200 members chosen for a maximum of two six-year terms. The Senate would be a similar size. Instead of representing states, senators would be chosen by "representatives of the professions, finance, service, agriculture, manufacturing, construction, trade, communication and transportation, apportioned according to the census" (H. Hamilton 1938, 122). Senators would serve a single 12-year term. The National Assembly would have power over child labor, with a provision allowing work by those over age 13 that was not injurious to their health or schooling. The National Assembly would have control over commerce but not over manufacturing. In a measure similar to some modern proposals for a balanced budget amendment, Hamilton would have required all laws mandating expenditures to "specify the method of raising said funds" (H. Hamilton 1938 120).

The president would be directly elected by the people to a single six-year term and would be paid $75,000 a year. The vice president would be designated as postmaster general and would be a member of the president's cabinet.

The number of Supreme Court justices would be specified at nine. Judges would be required to retire at age 80. The power of judicial review would be spelled out, but when the Supreme Court declared a law to be unconstitutional, Hamilton provided that it "shall include the wording of a Constitutional Amendment which would validate the legislation" (H. Hamilton 1938, 132). Hamilton would eliminate the provisions of the current Eleventh Amendment and allow a two-thirds majority of the Supreme Court to impeach the president "for non-adherence to this Constitution" (H. Hamilton 1938, 133).

Amendments would be proposed by two-thirds of both houses of the National Assembly and ratified by the electors. Every 25 years, the president could call a constitutional convention. Hamilton specified that "no amendment which would prohibit the electorate from changing any part of this Constitution by methods prescribed therein shall ever be proposed or ratified" (H. Hamilton 1938, 134).

Hamilton remains an elusive figure. Several academic journals reviewed his work, but otherwise it appears to have "faded into near oblivion" (Boyd 1992, 153).

❖ *HANS V. LOUISIANA* (1890) ❖

Hans v. Louisiana is closely tied to the Eleventh Amendment. A Louisiana citizen brought suit against that state to recover money due to him on bonds he had purchased that the state refused to honor.

In *Chisholm v. Georgia* (1793), the Supreme Court accepted jurisdiction over a similar case involving a suit brought against a state by a citizen of another state. Congress subsequently proposed and the states ratified the Eleventh Amendment in response. It stated that the judicial power of the United States would not be interpreted to extend to suits "commenced or prosecuted against one of the United States by Citizens of another State, or by Citizens or Subjects of any Foreign State."

Granting that the Eleventh Amendment did not specifically cover this contingency, Justice Joseph Bradley returned to what he believed to be the popular understanding of the Constitution prior to *Chisholm*, according to which a state, as a sovereign, could not be sued without its consent. He thereby effectively accepted Justice James Iredell's dissenting opinion in *Chisholm* over the majority ruling. Justice John Marshall Harlan agreed with the result in *Hans* but did not accept the Court's analysis of *Chisholm v. Georgia*.

Hans in effect viewed the Eleventh Amendment as a restatement rather than a true amendment of the original Constitution (Orth 1992, 251). In so doing, it specifically widened the application of the literal words of the amendment and thus might leave this amendment open to future reinterpretation.

See also Eleventh Amendment.

❖ HARDIN, CHARLES (1908–) ❖

Political scientist Charles Hardin introduced his plans for governmental reform in the midst of the Watergate crisis. His objective was summarized in the title of his book, *Presidential Power and Accountability*, but he also described his plans as covering "presidential leadership and party government" (Hardin 1974, 2). After an analysis designed to show that existing limits on the president were inadequate and that the bureaucracy was out of control, Hardin advanced nine proposals, each designed to lead to greater governmental accountability and control (Hardin 1974, 183–85).

First, Hardin proposed that the president and members of the House and Senate be elected at the same time to four-year terms, with this calendar interrupted if the government dissolved and new elections were called. Second, Hardin proposed supplementing existing single-member House districts with at-large seats—the party winning the presidency to get 100 extra seats and the losing party 50, provided that the winning party retained a majority. Party committees would select the at-large members, with the minority "shadow cabinet" having input into its party's slate of candidates.

Third, Hardin proposed that members of the House would nominate presidential candidates. These members would also replace a president who was disabled. As part of this proposal, Hardin would eliminate the vice presidency. Fourth, Hardin would significantly reduce the power of the Senate. It would neither confirm nominees to office nor ratify treaties. Moreover, if the House of Representatives waited at least 60 days and repassed a bill that the Senate had rejected, it would still go to the president for his signature. Hardin's fifth proposal allowed for the override of a presidential veto by a majority of House votes and only limited participation by the Senate.

Sixth, Hardin would allow members of Congress to serve in other offices, especially the president's cabinet. Seventh, the defeated presidential candidate would have a seat in the House and other privileges (including an official residence). Like the president, he would be subject to removal by the party committee that nominated him.

Hardin's eighth proposal provided that the presidency would go to the party winning the national plurality of votes. His ninth called for repeal of all conflicting constitutional provisions as well as of the two-term presidential limit in the Twenty-second Amendment.

Other than his last proposal, Hardin was fairly vague about how to implement his ideas (see Vile 1991c, 117). Indeed, at one point, he suggested that it would be better to allow some features of a new system to "develop by convention than to stipulate them in advance" (Hardin 1974, 182). This vagueness, as well as what many believed to be the successful resolution of the Watergate crisis, probably hindered the impact of Hardin's proposals. Nonetheless, Hardin reissued his call for reform in 1989, at which time he reiterated the need to replace "the separation of powers between the executive and the legislature by a separation between the government and the opposition" (Hardin 1989, 201).

❖ HARPER V. VIRGINIA BOARD ❖ OF ELECTIONS (1966)

In 1964, the states ratified the Twenty-fourth Amendment. Applying to both primary and general elections for national offices, it prohibited the imposition of a poll tax as a condition of voting. In *Harper v. Virginia Board of Elections*, Justice William O. Douglas wrote an opinion for the Supreme Court extending the poll tax prohibition to state elections. He relied on the equal protection clause of the Fourteenth Amendment and on his judgment that, as a fundamental right, voting should not be dependent on one's ability to pay a fine.

Justice Hugo Black wrote a striking dissenting opinion in which he stated that the Court should have upheld its earlier decisions in *Breedlove v. Suttles* (1937) and *Butler v. Thompson* (1951). Acknowledging his own personal opposition to the imposition of a poll tax, he argued that such a tax could have a rational basis. Moreover, he argued that, in making its decision, the Court was usurping the amending power:

> If basic changes as to the respective powers of the state and national government are needed, I prefer to let those changes be made by amendment as Article V of the Constitution provides. For a majority of this Court to undertake the task . . . amounts . . . to an exercise of power the Constitution makers with foresight and wisdom refused to give to the Judicial Branch of the Government. (*Harper* 1966, 676)

Citing the "concept of a written constitution," Black further suggested that "when a 'political theory' embodied in our Constitution becomes outdated," the Court was less qualified to come up with a new one "than the people of this country proceeding in the manner provided by Article V" (*Harper* 1966, 678). Black believed that Congress could, under its enforcement authority in Section 5 of the Fourteenth Amendment, outlaw the poll tax if it found that this tax was "being used as a device to deny voters equal protection of the laws" (*Harper* 1966, 679).

Justices John Marshall Harlan and Potter Stewart also dissented. They argued that the majority decision was based on "current egalitarian notions of how a modern democracy should be organized" rather than on any constitutional mandates (*Harper* 1966, 686).

See also Twenty-fourth Amendment.

❖ HARTFORD CONVENTION ❖

Early American history witnessed numerous disputes about the respective authority of the state and national governments. In the Virginia and Kentucky Resolution of 1798, James Madison and Thomas Jefferson asserted the right of states to "interpose" themselves on behalf of civil liberties, in this case, by opposing the federal Alien and Sedition Acts. Later, of course, other southerners would develop this doctrine into the doctrines of nullification and secession.

States' rights sentiment was not, however, confined to the South. Such sentiment became especially strong in New England in the years leading up to and including the War of 1812. Jefferson's proclamation of an embargo, as well as the war itself, interfered substantially with New England commerce and led to resentment, culminating in an 1815 meeting of representatives of these states known as the Hartford Convention. This convention proposed seven amendments.

The first two resolutions reflected the continuing split between free and slave states. Convention delegates proposed eliminating the clause whereby slaves were counted as three-fifths of a person; they also favored requiring a two-thirds vote in both houses of Congress for the admission of new states, thus making the admission of additional slave states less likely. The third and fourth resolutions would have limited Congress's power to impose embargoes to 60 days and would have required a two-thirds vote to do so. The fifth proposal would have required a two-thirds vote for Congress to declare war, absent the need for immediate defense. The sixth proposal would have prevented naturalized citizens from serving in Congress or holding other civil offices, and the seventh would have limited the president to one term (Ford 1898, 688–89).

Delegates from the Hartford Convention arrived in Washington, D.C., as residents were celebrating news of the American victory at the Battle of New Orleans and the signing of a peace treaty with Great Britain (Vile 1993c, 186). The close association of the Federalist Party with the Hartford Convention led to its demise, but a number of the convention's ideas continued to be topics of discussion.

❖ HAWKE V. SMITH, No. 1 (1920) ❖

This case stemmed from a petition to enjoin the Ohio secretary of state from printing ballots for voter approval of the state legislature's ratification of the Eighteenth Amendment. Ohio had added such referendum provisions to its constitution in November 1918. In January 1919, Ohio's governor sent copies of the state's legislative ratification of the Eighteenth Amendment to the U.S. secretary of state, who included Ohio's ratification in his count.

Writing for a unanimous Court, Justice William Day decided that, in specifying legislative ratification of amendments, the Constitution clearly had in mind "the representative body which made the laws of the people," rather than the people themselves (*Hawke* 1920, 227). Referring to the precedent in *Hollingsworth v. Virginia* (1798), Day argued that, when ratifying amendments, states were performing a federal rather than a legislative function. Perhaps partly motivated by concern about the possible rescission of amendments, Day noted that "any other view might lead to endless confusion in the manner of ratification of federal amendments" (*Hawke* 1920, 230).

Hawke leaves open Congress's option to specify that states ratify amendments by conventions, as in the case of the Twenty-first Amendment, which repealed the Eighteenth. Moreover, a U.S. circuit court opinion in *Kimble v. Swackhamer* (1978) permits referendums on constitutional amendments as long as they are purely advi-

sory. As long as the Court continues to recognize *Hawke*, however, those who favor actual ratification of amendments by popular referendums will have to seek a constitutional amendment.

See also Initiative and Referendum; *Kimble v. Swackhamer.*

For Further Reading:
Walroff, Jonathan L. 1985. "The Unconstitutionality of Voter Initiative Applications for Federal Constitutional Conventions." *Colorado Law Review* 85:1525–45.

❖ HAWKE V. SMITH, No. 2 (1920) ❖

A companion case to *Hawke v. Smith, No. 1,* this ruling concerned the submission of the Nineteenth rather than the Eighteenth Amendment to state voters. In a two-paragraph decision, Justice William Day ruled that, in accord with the companion opinion, the provision of Ohio's constitution requiring approval of amendments by referendum was unconstitutional.

❖ HAZLITT, HENRY (1894–1993) ❖

Henry Hazlitt was long a believer in the need for constitutional reform (Hazlitt 1931). He offered his proposal for a parliamentary system in a book first published in 1942 and subsequently reissued, in somewhat reduced form, in 1974. Throughout this period, Hazlitt continued to believe that the nation's inflexible Constitution was responsible for many of its ills. He favored a parliamentary system whereby the Congress could vote no confidence in a premier who could, in turn, dissolve Congress and call for new elections.

Hazlitt believed that the first step toward change should be reform of the amending process. He favored adoption of a system like that in Australia. Under such a plan, amendments would be proposed by absolute majorities in both houses of Congress and submitted to the people through a referendum. Ratification would require a majority of voters in a majority of states (Hazlitt 1942, 11–12).

The central reform that Hazlitt advocated was to fuse legislative and executive powers. To this end, he favored significantly reducing the power of the Senate, ending the system of fixed terms of office, and eliminating the president's veto and related powers. Hazlitt concentrated on Congress. Among his more novel suggestions was the proposal that officeholders be deprived of voting rights during their tenure; alternatively, their votes could be segregated at separate polling booths so that the public could see how their positions influenced their votes. Hazlitt thought that the House of Representatives should have about 150 members. Their first task would be to choose a premier. The president would make the ultimate selection, but only after congressional balloting. The premier would, in turn, select a cabinet of 10 to 12 men; like the premier, they would not necessarily have to be selected from Congress.

Members of the cabinet would continue to head executive departments, but undersecretaries would be designated as administrators so that cabinet members could focus on policy issues. The cabinet would formulate major bills. These would then be submitted to a legislative council of about a dozen men representing the entire legislature. Bills would then go to standing congressional committees (where seniority would have been eliminated), whose power would be that of revising and overseeing rather than formulating legislative measures (Hazlitt 1942, 140). The cabinet would subsequently set the legislative agenda, with the legislature weighted, when needed, to give the largest party a majority.

Rejecting the initiative except for amendments designed to reduce "the powers, terms or number of legislators or changing the method of election" (Hazlitt 1942, 159), Hazlitt favored the referendum mechanism only as a way of ratifying constitutional amendments. House members would serve four-year terms, subject to dissolution and new elections or to individual recall.

Ideally, Hazlitt favored a Senate of two dozen men chosen for eight-year terms by the House of Representatives, but he realized that this would conflict with the Article V provision that no state be deprived of its equal representation without its consent. He was therefore willing to settle for a Senate with a reduced role, enabling it to delay and reconsider but not block House legislation.

Although he would take away the president's veto power and his power to execute laws, make treaties, and direct military policy (Hazlitt 1942, 105), Hazlitt wanted to preserve the president as head of state. In such a position, he could perform ceremonial functions, advise the premier, and, on extraordinary occasions, dissolve the legislature on his own authority (Hazlitt 1942, 111). The president would be chosen for a 5- to 10-year term by both Houses of Congress.

Recognizing that such major changes would be difficult to adopt, Hazlitt proposed a number of less drastic expedients. These included amendments to limit the president to two terms, give the president an item veto, eliminate the requirement that members of Congress reside in the states that select them, specify that judges retire at 70 or 75 years of age, fix the membership of the Supreme Court, and allow Congress to remove up to one judge a year for usurping congressional functions. Other proposed reforms included allowing both houses of Congress to approve treaties by majority vote, eliminating the vice presidency, and reforming congressional rules (Vile 1991c, 86). In his 1974 book, Hazlitt also proposed preventing the president from serving consecutive terms and allowing state governors to appoint one member of the Supreme Court (Vile 1991c, 94 n.2). In an essay first published in 1983, Hazlitt reaffirmed his support for a presidential item veto and sought to prevent the Senate from increasing appropriations approved by the House (Hazlitt 1987).

See also Parliamentary System.

❖ HEHMEYER, ALEXANDER ❖ (1910–1993)

Attorney Alexander Hehmeyer originally prepared his proposals for constitutional revision as part of a study of domestic political reform being made in anticipation of the end of World War II (Hehmeyer 1943). He hoped to use the sense of urgency generated by the war to stimulate interest in reform (Vile 1991c, 90–91). Recognizing that the only authority a convention would have would be to propose changes, Hehmeyer favored convening a constitutional convention by a concurrent resolution of Congress.

Hehmeyer anticipated a convention of 97 members—48 to be named by the states, 16 by Congress, 16 by the president, 16 by the chief justice, and a chair appointed by Congress (Hehmeyer 1943, 38–40). He foresaw four areas where such a convention should concentrate: relations between the president and Congress, the balance between the nation and the states, liberalization of the amending process, and a reexamination of the Bill of Rights.

In reassessing Congress, Hehmeyer concluded that plans for a parliamentary system were impractical and concentrated instead on seeking "to make Congress more responsive to the President and to make the President more responsive to Congress and to do this without departing radically from existing institutional forms" (Hehmeyer 1943, 64). Initially suggesting a three-year presidential term, Hehmeyer instead rec-

ommended a plan by which members of the House of Representatives would serve four-year terms.

Hehmeyer advocated extensive cabinet reform. He proposed reorganizing the cabinet so that it would have eight members: a "Secretary Without Portfolio, Secretary for Administration, Secretary for Legislation, Secretary for International Affairs, Secretary for National Defense, Secretary for Law, Secretary of the Economy, [and a] Secretary for National Welfare" (Hehmeyer 1943, 77). Most such secretaries would not have to run departments; that task would be given to full-time administrators. The secretary of legislation would have the power to initiate legislation in Congress and participate in debates. The president could make changes in his cabinet on the basis of midterm elections. Administrators of agencies could be selected through the civil service system.

Hehmeyer proposed a number of congressional reforms, including the establishment of automatic vote recorders, more efficient parliamentary procedures, better staffing, and a joint legislative council. This council would include three presidential representatives to coordinate legislation between the two houses. Hehmeyer would also reduce the number of standing committees, eliminate the seniority rule, and alter the system of appropriations. He further advocated that treaties be proposed by a majority of both houses of Congress rather than by a two-thirds vote of the Senate.

Hehmeyer believed that there was considerable room to develop regional authorities and consolidate local governments. He also favored eliminating tax duplication and resolving conflicts between state and national taxing authorities.

Hehmeyer respected the Bill of Rights and thought that consideration should be given to including economic and social rights. He also favored a more liberalized amending process. He suggested that amendments should be introduced in one of five ways: "by a majority of the elected membership of both Houses of Congress"; "by a two-thirds majority of either House if approved in two (or perhaps three) consecutive sessions"; "by a majority of the State legislatures if within a period of five years, they approve the identical proposal"; "by a convention to be convened by Congress either on its own initiative or if requested within a period of five years by a majority of the State legislatures;" or, in a proposal reminiscent of Thomas Jefferson, "by a Convention to be convened regularly every thirty years upon the call of the President" (Hehmeyer 1943, 163–67). Such amendments would be ratified "(a) By two-thirds of the State legislatures acting within four years or (b) By a majority of the voters in two-thirds of the States and a majority of all those voting in the nation at a special election held within two years from the date of the proposal or at the next succeeding election for Representatives" (Hehmeyer 1943, 169).

Hehmeyer admired the role of the Supreme Court in applying constitutional guarantees to modern times and suggested that it might render advisory opinions. He also wanted to fix the number of Supreme Court justices at nine and eliminate federal jurisdiction in diversity of citizenship cases. Under miscellaneous reforms, Hehmeyer included such proposals as having ex-presidents serve for life in the Senate, giving the president an item veto, allowing for the postponing of national elections in times of emergency, abolishing the electoral college and the vice presidency, and abolishing state residency requirements for members of Congress.

❖ HENDERSON, YANDELL ❖ (1873–1974)

Yandell Henderson was a professor of physiology at Yale University and an active member of the newly formed Progressive Party, under whose banner he ran unsuccessfully for Congress (Vile 1991c, 54–55). He advocated three major reforms in an article in the *Yale Review* (Henderson 1913).

First, Henderson favored either fusing or otherwise bringing the legislative and executive branches into closer cooperation. He even suggested that, at the state level, legislators might be replaced by a board of directors presided over by the governor. Second, Henderson proposed that the people should be able to "recall" judicial decisions by voting on whether to give sanction to laws that the courts invalidated. Henderson suggested that this would be "a far more sensible method of amending the old and of gradually building up a new set of principles and institutions than the present method of effecting constitutional amendments" (Henderson 1913, 89). Third, Henderson believed that the time had come for the United States to "establish a real nation and a real national government instead of a Union of States and a Federal Government" (Henderson 1913, 89). Henderson favored calling a national constitutional convention to achieve these goals.

❖ HIGHWAYS ❖

Few states are more closely associated with the automobile than California. The state's clogged freeways are daily reminders of the importance of the car to the state's lifestyle. In 1952, the California legislature petitioned Congress to call a convention relative to the use of federal highway taxes. The proposed amendment specified that:

> all money, collected from any taxes now or hereafter imposed by the United States upon motor vehicles or the operation thereof, and upon the manufacture, sale, distribution, or use of motor vehicle fuels, supplies and

equipment . . . shall be apportioned by the Congress to the several States and shall be used by the States exclusively for the construction and maintenance of highways in the manner prescribed by Congress. (*Congressional Record*, 1992, 4003)

In 1956, the national government created the Highway Trust Fund, which earmarked moneys from user taxes for highway construction, including the interstate highway system. The fund succeeded in insulating expenditures on highways from competition with projects in the general budget (I. Rubin 1990, 131–41).

❖ HOLLINGSWORTH V. VIRGINIA ❖ (1798)

The Court heard the case of *Hollingsworth v. Virginia* after ratification of the Eleventh Amendment. The Court was asked to declare that the amendment had not been properly ratified. Opponents argued that Article I, Section 7 required that "every order, resolution, or vote to which the concurrence of the Senate and House of Representatives may be necessary (except on a question of adjournment) shall be presented to the President of the United States," and the president had not signed this measure. The Court was also asked to rule that, if the amendment had been ratified, it should have only a prospective effect, not applying to cases that had been brought before its adoption.

The Court unanimously rejected both arguments, with Justice Samuel Chase responding to attorneys' arguments by saying that the presidential veto applied "only to the ordinary cases of legislation" and that the president "has nothing to do with the proposition, or adoption, of amendments to the Constitution" (*Hollingsworth* 1798, 382).

Professor David Currie noted that, in dismissing a suit seemingly still authorized by Section 13 of the Judiciary Act of 1789 (now thought to be superseded by the Eleventh Amendment), the Court anticipated the exercise of judicial review of federal legislation that is more commonly traced to the Supreme Court's 1803 decision in *Marbury v. Madison* (Currie 1985, 22). In arguing that an extension of the equal rights amendment ratification deadline required a two-thirds vote of Congress and presidential approval, Yale's Charles Black (1978) warned against any further extension of the *Hollingsworth* precedent regarding the need for presidential signatures.

❖ HOPKINS, CASPAR ❖ (1826–1893)

Caspar Hopkins was a "pioneer, businessman, author, and former president of the California Immigration Union" (Vile 1991c, 38). He published an article in 1885 advocating a series of 10 constitutional amendments (Hopkins 1885). Some of the proposals were unique to Hopkins, but others reflected themes common to his era.

In Hopkins's first two proposals, he called for authorizing Congress to legislate on civil matters such as "marriage, divorce, inheritance, probate proceedings, modes and subjects of taxation, education, the tenure of real estate, and the collection of debts." He also proposed to clarify congressional jurisdiction "over interstate commerce and communication, and the exclusive regulation of banks, insurance companies, and all other corporations which transact business in more than one State of Territory" (Hopkins 1885, 388). Similarly, state powers would be curtailed in these areas.

Hopkins's third proposal called for increasing federal judicial jurisdiction over all claims against the United States. He would also have invested courts with the power to settle contested elections or cases involving the qualifications of legislators. His fourth proposal called for restricting congressional authority to the adoption of general or public measures, thus eliminating private bills.

Like Woodrow Wilson, Hopkins favored a system whereby the president could appoint cabinet members from the majority party in Congress. This was his fifth proposal. His sixth would have required legislators to undergo special education in colleges specifically designed for the purpose.

Although sentiment was already growing for a system of direct election of senators (which would eventually result in the adoption of the Seventeenth Amendment), in his seventh proposal, Hopkins took a different approach. He advocated recognizing the inevitable influence of wealth by limiting the right to vote for senators to those who had paid taxes on $100,000 or more of their incomes.

Hopkins's eighth and ninth proposals dealt with immigrants and Native Americans. He favored limiting immigration to foreigners with sufficient education, skills, or property and limiting voting to natural-born citizens. Hopkins wanted to abolish programs that treated American Indians differently from other groups.

Finally, Hopkins proposed a number of changes relative to terms of office. Under his scheme, senators would serve for ten years, the president for eight, and members of the House for six. No executive officers—presumably including the president—with the power of patronage would be eligible for reelection. Hopkins would further eliminate the electoral college and establish two or three vice presidents in case both the president and the first vice president were disabled.

Hopkins believed that the weight of inertia was working against his proposals. He feared that a convention would be "full of peril and probabilities of failure," in part because "the country is full of communists, socialists, advocates of woman suffrage, agrarians, and cranks, whose every effort would be concentrated upon such an opportunity to realize their peculiar views in the fundamental law" (Hopkins 1885, 898).

❖ HOUSING ❖

Unlike many constitutions that were formulated in the two centuries that followed its adoption, the U.S. Constitution confines itself to the protection of political rights and leaves economic and social rights largely to the political process. Although both state and national governments have made periodic attempts to provide housing for those in need, the right to housing has never been considered to be an entitlement (Salins 1987, 176).

In July 1993, Democratic Representative Charles Rangel of New York introduced an amendment designed to guarantee "that all U.S. citizens shall have a right to decent and affordable housing, which shall not be denied or abridged by the United States or any State" (H.J. Res. 64). Given the failure of the Constitution to recognize other economic rights, the short-term prospect for such an amendment appears dim.

❖ HUBBELL, JANETTE ❖

See Dolbeare, Kenneth, and Janette Hubbell.

❖ *IDAHO V. FREEMAN* (1981) ❖

One of the most fascinating recent cases involving the constitutional amending process emerged from the controversy over the proposed equal rights amendment (ERA). Judge Marion Callister, from the U.S. District Court in Idaho, delivered the verdict in *Idaho v. Freeman*.

A number of Idaho and other state legislators argued that Idaho's rescission of its prior ratification of the ERA was constitutional, that Congress had no right to extend the ERA deadline, and that, in any case, such an extension would have required a two-thirds rather than a simple majority vote. Callister agreed with all three contentions. His ruling was, however, stayed by the U.S. Supreme Court and eventually mooted by the failure of the necessary number of states to ratify the ERA, despite the deadline extension.

The most extended portion of Callister's decision, which relied heavily on the district court decision written by John Paul Stevens in *Dyer v. Blair* (1975), had to do with whether the questions the legislators raised were political questions and therefore inappropriate for judicial resolution. In *Coleman v. Miller* (1939), the Supreme Court had suggested that many amending issues, and specifically the matter of whether amendment ratifications were made contemporaneously, were committed to congressional, rather than judicial, resolution. After reviewing the criteria established in *Baker v.*

Carr (1962) for deciding whether issues were political questions, Callister decided that they were not present in this case. He argued that the Constitution had divided amending powers between Congress and the states rather than granting them exclusively to the former. Moreover, he decided that precedents surrounding the adoption of the Fourteenth Amendment had not yet established the right of a state to rescind ratifications. Callister believed that such issues "must be interpreted with the kind of consistency that is characteristic of a judicial, as opposed to political [congressional] decision making" (*Idaho* 1981, 1139).

Callister settled on a contemporary consensus model similar to the one the Court had articulated in *Dillon v. Gloss* (1921). Under this model, he decided that, prior to ratification by three-fourths of the states, a state's last action—whether ratification or rescission—should prevail. Callister further ruled that although Congress was not required to set a ratification deadline, once it did so, it would have to abide by it, since states may have ratified an amendment contingent on their understanding that other states would have to ratify within that limit. In any case, Callister believed that the congressional extension of the ERA deadline had been unconstitutional, because Congress could act in such circumstances only in its Article V rather than its Article I capacity, and Article V referred only to actions by two-thirds of that body.

Although this decision hardly settles the

issues addressed, *Idaho v. Freeman,* like *Dyer v. Blair,* could undercut *Coleman v. Miller* by providing precedents for judicial resolution of amending issues.

See also *Dyer v. Blair;* Equal Rights Amendment.

For Further Reading:

Carroll, John. 1982. "Constitutional Law: Constitutional Amendment. Rescission of Ratification. Extension of Ratification Period. *State of Idaho v. Freeman.*" *Akron Law Review* 14 (Summer): 151–61.

❖ IMPEACHMENT ❖

Article I, Section 2 of the U.S. Constitution vests the House of Representatives with the power of impeachment, or the power to bring charges against appointed governmental officials. Article II, Section 4 specifies "Treason, Bribery, or other high Crimes and Misdemeanors" as the exclusive grounds for impeachment. Article I, Section 3 further provides that trials of impeachment take place before the Senate; if the president is on trial, the chief justice presides. Conviction of any officer requires a two-thirds vote and results in removal from office.

A number of amendments have attempted to alter or clarify this process. Two proposals were introduced in 1913 by Ohio congressmen. One, offered by Democrat Atlee Pomerene, would have provided for a method other than impeachment for removing civil officers other than the president, the vice president, and members of the Supreme Court. A second, proposed by Republican Leonard Howland, would have allowed for trials of all except top officials by 12 senators. In 1945, Republican Senator William Langer of North Dakota proposed that a vote by a majority of senators present should be sufficient for an impeachment conviction.

Democratic Senator Howell Heflin of Al-abama has introduced recent amendments on the subject. One would allow Congress to remove judges from office for inability to perform their duties, as well as for infractions of the law; this proposal would also suspend officers indicted for felony offenses. A more detailed proposal offered by Heflin would provide for a seven-member judicial inquiry commission to discipline judges guilty of violating canons of judicial ethics and to suspend or place on senior status judges unable to perform their duties. A number of recent proposals have also provided that judges would lose their offices immediately upon conviction of a crime.

Such proposals may have been prompted in part by recent cases of impeachment involving U.S. District Judges Harry F. Claiborne, Alcee L. Hastings, and Walter L. Nixon (Abraham 1993, 45–46; Volcansek 1993). Claiborne refused to resign after being convicted of felonies and imprisoned. Hastings was elected to the House of Representatives after being impeached and convicted. Like Claiborne, Nixon refused to resign from office after being convicted, in his case, of perjury. Nixon objected to the procedure by which a committee of the Senate heard his case in 1989 before the full Senate voted to convict him. In *Nixon v. United States* (1993), the Supreme Court upheld the Senate conviction on the basis that Article I, Section 3 of the Constitution vested the Senate with "the sole Power to try all Impeachments," thus implying that matters of procedure were "political questions" for the Senate to resolve.

See also Judiciary, Removal of Members.

For Further Reading:

Berger, Raoul. 1973. *Impeachment: The Constitutional Problems.* Cambridge, MA: Harvard University Press.

Committee on Federal Legislation of the Bar Association of the City of New York. n.d. *The Law of Presidential Impeachment.* New York: Harrow Books.

❖ INCORPORATION ❖

Of all the twentieth-century developments in constitutional interpretation, none has been more important than the "incorporation" of prominent provisions of the Bill of Rights into the due process clause of the Fourteenth Amendment. Through this process, such rights now apply to the states as well as to the national government. Prior to the Civil War, Chief Justice John Marshall ruled in *Barron v. Baltimore* (1833) that the provisions in the Bill of Rights were intended to limit only the national government.

The language of the Fourteenth Amendment, however, was directed to the states, which were now prohibited from denying the privileges and immunities or the due process rights of their citizens. Most prominently in the *Slaughterhouse* cases (1873), the Supreme Court initially gave a narrow reading to these clauses, especially the privileges and immunities provision. In 1884, however, Justice John Marshall Harlan wrote a dissent in *Hurtado v. California* (1884), arguing that the due process guarantees in the Fourteenth Amendment were intended to apply provisions of the Bill of Rights—in this case, the provision for indictment by grand jury—to the states. With the possible exception of Fifth Amendment property rights (*Missouri Pacific Railway Co. v. Nebraska* [1896] and *Chicago, Burlington & Quincy Railway Co. v. Chicago* [1897]), the Court majority rejected Justice Harlan's stand. In 1925, however, the Court declared in *Gitlow v. New York* that freedom of speech did apply to the states, and it recognized several other exceptions in subsequent years.

In *Palko v. Connecticut* (1937), Justice Benjamin Cardozo attempted to provide some organizing principle to distinguish those guarantees in the Bill of Rights that the Court found to be applicable to the states from those—like the Fifth Amendment guarantee against double jeopardy at issue in this case—that it did not. He articulated the idea of selective incorporation, by which he suggested that those guarantees in the Bill of Rights that were implicit in the concept of ordered liberty would apply to the states, but others would not.

Few cases better exemplify the varied views on incorporation than the case of *Adamson v. California* (1947). At least four different views were articulated there. In refusing to overrule a decision on a case in which a prosecutor had commented on a defendant's failure to testify in his own defense (forbidden in federal cases by the self-incrimination provision of the Fifth Amendment), Justice Stanley Reed restated the view of selective incorporation for the Court majority. In a concurring opinion, Justice Felix Frankfurter articulated the view that the due process clause required "fundamental fairness" and that such fairness could not be mechanically ascertained simply by determining whether a provision was or was not in the Bill of Rights. Justice Hugo Black, like Justice Harlan before him, articulated the view of total incorporation. As a former U.S. senator, he based his conclusion on his own reexamination of the debates over the Fourteenth Amendment—an argument that Charles Fairman and other scholars have since disputed, albeit not without generating questions about their own scholarship. Justices Frank Murphy and Wiley Rutledge articulated the view of total incorporation plus—that is, the idea that there may be rights in addition to those in the first 10 amendments that apply to the states. This view became even more prominent in the Connecticut birth-control case, *Griswold v. Connecticut* (1965). Rounding out the picture is the position of "selective incorporation plus" (Abraham and Perry 1994, 87).

Although the view of selective incorporation has dominated most Supreme Court decision making, over the course of time, the Supreme Court has incorporated more and more guarantees from the Bill of Rights into the due process clause. Today, only five guarantees remain outside judicial protection. They are the Second Amendment right to bear arms, the Third Amendment's guarantee on quartering troops, the Fifth Amendment's guarantee of a grand jury indictment, the Seventh Amendment's right to a jury trial in a civil case, and the Eighth Amendment's guarantee against excessive fines and bail (D. O'Brien 1995, 309). The last case to incorporate a new provision in the Bill of Rights was the decision to apply the protection against double jeopardy in *Benton v. Maryland* (1969).

See also *Adamson v. California; Barron v. Baltimore;* Fourteenth Amendment; *Palko v. Connecticut.*

❖ INDIANS ❖

See Native Americans.

❖ INITIATIVE AND ❖ REFERENDUM

In *Federalist* No. 10, James Madison distinguished a direct, or pure, democracy from an indirect, or representative, democracy (Hamilton, Madison, and Jay 1961, 81–82). Although he defended the latter, there have been many subsequent advocates of more direct democracy. Among their favorite mechanisms are the initiative and referendum. The former mechanism allows citizens to initiate legislation through petitions, and the latter permits citizens to approve or disapprove legislation; sometimes both mechanisms are classified under the single term referendum (Schmidt 1989, 3).

Types of Referendums
Referendums can be limited to either legislative or constitutional change. The first American referendum was the 1788 Massachusetts referendum on the state constitution, and although the U.S. constitution makes no such provision, many American states and foreign nations have subsequently adopted a requirement for popular approval of constitutions or of amendments to them. In early 1861, the Senate apparently came but one vote shy of accepting a proposal for a national plebiscite on a series of compromises offered by Senator John C. Crittenden of Kentucky to avoid the Civil War (Shermer 1969, vii). Historically, initiatives and referendums have often been tied to the recall, a mechanism by which voters can demand the ouster of a sitting officeholder.

Direct Democracy's Three Periods of Popularity
A student of direct democracy has identified three periods during which direct democracy was particularly popular at the national level. These are "the populist and progressive movements (1890–1912); . . . the isolationist and peace movements (1914–1940); and . . . the issue activism both of the left and the right (1970–1988)" (Cronin 1989, 164).

The Populist and Progressive Eras
The movement for the initiative and referendum in the Populist and Progressive Eras began in the states, with South Dakota's adoption of this mechanism in 1898 and adoptions in 17 other states by 1917 (Musmanno 1929, 173). Perhaps because other representative institutions were less developed, this movement was successful primarily in the West—a breeding ground for other Progressive Era amendments (Grimes 1978, 65–100). Four-fifths of the states adopting the mechanism were west of the Mississippi River (Schmidt 1989, 10).

As early as 1895, Populist Kansas Senator William Peffer introduced a national amendment to allow submission of important matters to the people upon petition by one-fifth of the voters or one-fourth of the state legislatures (Musmanno 1929, 173). Other contemporary proposals varied the number of voters required to initiate such a petition—a proposal by Wisconsin Democratic Representative Lucas Miller permitted such action by as few as 1,000 inhabitants. Republican Senator Joseph Bristow of Kansas introduced a proposal allowing the president to go over the head of Congress by placing measures that he favored, but that Congress failed to enact, on the ballot (Musmanno 1929, 175).

The National Direct Legislative League was formed in the 1890s to push for a national referendum. This idea was often favored by Prohibitionists and other third-party representatives. Theodore Roosevelt and Woodrow Wilson both indicated support for such measures (Cronin 1989, 50).

The Isolationist and Peace Movements

The most popular referendum proposal from 1914 to 1940 was the war referendum, or the Ludlow amendment (after Democratic Representative Louis Ludlow of Indiana), as it was frequently called. The idea actually appears to have originated during the Civil War in a book by Robert E. Beasley (1864) in which he advocated taking a vote on whether the war should be continued. The idea was subsequently stimulated by hopes of keeping the United States out of World War I and by disillusionment with that war and suspicions that it had been engineered by arms dealers.

Most such proposed amendments specified that, except in cases of invasion, Congress could not declare war or draft citizens until such a proposal was submitted to the people for approval. Influential supporters included Democratic and Populist presidential candidate and Secretary of State William Jennings Bryan and Republican Senator Robert La Follette of Wisconsin. Both, however, subsequently supported Wilson's decision to enter World War I without such a vote (Cronin 1989, 165). In the 1930s,

the movement for a war referendum received support from 65 college and university presidents, the National Education Association, historian Charles Beard, and even Republican Congressman Everett Dirksen of Illinois (Cronin 1989, 169–70).

In 1938, the House of Representatives voted 209 to 188 not to discharge this amendment from committee. Opposition by Franklin D. Roosevelt and the approach of World War II pretty much brought an end to this proposal, although Oregon Republican Senator Mark Hatfield introduced a variant during the Vietnam War.

Issue Activism of the Right and Left

The 1960s and 1970s witnessed renewed support for the idea of a national initiative and referendum from representatives of both the political Right and the political Left. The movement received support in 1977 when Roger Telschow and John Forster, who had worked with such measures at the state level, founded a lobby group called Initiative America. Democratic Senator James Abourezk of South Dakota and Democratic Representative James Jones of Oklahoma introduced an amendment supported by at least 50 members of Congress. It would have permitted 3 percent of citizens (including at least 3 percent of the voters in 10 or more states) to initiate a referendum that would take effect when subsequently ratified by a majority (Cronin 1989, 159). Supporters included consumer advocate Ralph Nader, New York Republican Representative Jack Kemp, columnist Patrick Buchanan, then Democratic (later Republican) Texas Congressman Phil Gramm, California Republican Congressman Barry Goldwater Jr., Oregon Republican Senator Mark Hatfield, economist Arthur Laffer, and a majority of the American people as measured in public-opinion polls (Cronin 1989, 173–75). A fair number of scholars also favored this proposal (Berg, Hahn, and Schmidhauser 1976, 190–201; B. Barber

1984, 281–89). As in the past, there was wide variation as to what percentage or regional representation would be needed to propose or approve referendums, 3 and 8 percent being the most common numbers suggested for proposing a referendum.

Most referendum proposals would have exempted issues of constitutional reform or war-making matters, thus somewhat distancing advocates of this period from those of the preceding one. Many proposals would have prevented Congress from modifying laws adopted by referendum for two years, except by an extraordinary majority of two-thirds or three-fourths. Congress held hearings on the subject in 1977.

Concerns of Initiative and Referendum Supporters

Advocates of the initiative and referendum often see these mechanisms as a means of bypassing politicians who have lost touch with the people. The same concern has been shared by advocates of congressional term limits. Perhaps illustrating this tie, in 1993 and 1994, Republican Representative Peter Hoekstra of Michigan offered a bill to provide for a national advisory referendum on term limits for members of Congress.

States continue to experiment with initiative and referendum measures. Such state experiences—for example, the movement led by Howard Jarvis in 1978 to adopt Proposition 13 to limit California state property taxes and Coloradans more recent vote (voided in *Romer v. Evans* [1996]) to prohibit all state and local legislation that protects homosexuals (Baker 1995)—have led to speculation about whether conservatives or liberals would be most likely to gain if such mechanisms were adopted. One student of the subject found that the advantage tends to shift from one side to the other, depending on the issue. He therefore concluded that "the referendum is neither an unfailing friend nor an implacable enemy of either left or right" (Ranney 1978, 85).

See also Congress, Recall of Members; Judiciary, Removal of Members; President, Vote of No Confidence.

For Further Reading:

Ku, Raymond. 1995. "Consensus of the Governed: The Legitimacy of Constitutional Change." *Fordham Law Review* 64 (November): 535–86.

Sullivan, J. W. 1893. *Direct Legislation by the Citizenship*. New York: Nationalist Publishing Company.

❖ INSURANCE ❖

From 1905 through 1933, a number of proposals were introduced in Congress either to allow that body to insure the lives of U.S. citizens or to regulate the insurance industry. The latter proposals were undoubtedly stimulated by the unique position that insurance has had in relation to other industries.

Because of the nation's commitment to free enterprise, most life insurance and many other types of insurance are handled by private companies. Initially, states were responsible for most regulation of the insurance industry, and states often discriminated against companies whose headquarters were located in other states. Such regulations were challenged as a violation of the federal commerce power in *Paul v. Virginia* (1869), but the U.S. Supreme Court rejected this challenge, and state regulation continued until 1944.

In *United States v. South-Eastern Underwriters Association* (1944), in a close 4-to-3 decision written by Justice Hugo Black, the Supreme Court reversed course and applied the Sherman Antitrust Act (a federal law) to insurance companies that operated across state lines. The following year, Congress responded by passing the McCarran Act. This law left insurance regulation to the states, absent adoption of congressional laws specifically addressed to the insurance industry.

❖ INTERMARRIAGE ❖

Although amendments have been introduced periodically to vest the national government with the power to regulate marriage and divorce (especially to prohibit polygamy), such laws have been almost exclusively left to state regulation. Through most of U.S. history, many states have passed miscegenation laws limiting or prohibiting interracial marriages, especially between whites and blacks.

There have been at least three proposed amendments (1871, 1912, and 1928) to prohibit interracial marriage. The first was introduced by Missouri Democratic Representative Andrew King. The other two were introduced by Democratic Representatives Seaborn Roddenbery and Coleman Blease of South Carolina.

The issue of state miscegenation laws did not reach the U.S. Supreme Court until 1967. The case was called *Loving v. Virginia* and involved Virginia's attempt to punish a white man and a black woman who had married. In its decision, the Supreme Court decided that prohibitions against interracial marriage violated the equal protection clause of the Fourteenth Amendment and were therefore unconstitutional.

See also Marriage, Divorce, and Parenting.

❖ INTERNAL IMPROVEMENTS ❖

Under the general welfare clause in Article I, Section 8 of the Constitution, Congress may tax and spend for the general welfare. In early American history, Republicans often interpreted this provision quite restrictively. Their reading led many to question the legitimacy of federal expenditures on projects such as roads or canals. Presidents Thomas Jefferson, James Madison, James Monroe, Andrew Jackson, and James Polk all either recommended an amendment specifically to authorize federal expenditures of this nature or vetoed congressional laws for such improvements that they thought were directed chiefly to state rather than national interests (Ames 1896, 260–63). On occasion, as in Jackson's veto of the Maysville Road bill (extending a road from Maysville, Kentucky, to Henry Clay's hometown of Lexington), such concerns may also have been tied to partisan considerations (Urofsky 1988, 280). However, few early presidents took the position of John Quincy Adams, who argued for an expansive list of federal domestic expenditures (McDonald 1982, 71).

In the first half of the nineteenth century, a number of congressmen, including future president Martin Van Buren, introduced constitutional amendments to legitimize federal expenditures on internal improvements. With the expansion of federal powers over the last century and a half, the issue of federal aid to the states appears to have become chiefly a prudential rather than a constitutional issue.

See also General Welfare.

J

❖

❖ JAMESON, JOHN A. ❖
(1824–1890)

John Jameson practiced law in Chicago and served for 18 years as a judge in the chancery division of Cook County (Malone 1961, 5: 601). In 1867, he published the first edition of a work on constitutional conventions, released in a number of subsequent editions (Jameson 1887), that proved to be extremely influential. Stimulated in part by the movement for Southern secession and in part by claims by leaders of state conventions that such bodies were sovereign, Jameson was intent on establishing that a constitutional convention was subject to legal restraints.

Jameson identified four types of conventions: "the spontaneous convention, or public meeting"; "the ordinary legislative convention, or general assembly"; "the revolutionary convention"; and the "constitutional convention" (Jameson 1887, 3–4). Jameson was especially concerned with distinguishing the revolutionary convention, or the provisional government that bridges the gap from one form of government to another, from the constitutional convention, which, he argued, was "subaltern" and "never governs" (Jameson 1887, 10). Thus domesticated, a constitutional convention was unlikely to pose a threat to existing governments.

Jameson's treatment of more general amending controversies repeated familiar themes. Arguing that amending mechanisms were "in the nature of safety valves,"

he argued that such provisions needed "to reconcile the requisites for progress with the requisites for safety" (Jameson 1887, 549). Jameson believed that the methods of proposing amendments by conventions and by general assemblies were "of about equal authority," although he speculated that "as our Constitutions become riper and more perfect with time and experience, the necessity of employing the more expensive mode by Conventions will be found to be less and less" (Jameson 1887, 551–52). Jameson also suggested that the convention method was more suitable for major revisions and the method of legislative proposal more appropriate for less drastic alterations. He further argued that Sidney George Fisher had been mistaken in believing that a system of legislative sovereignty would have prevented the Civil War (Jameson 1887, 567).

In addressing specific amending issues, Jameson suggested that states had the power to ratify amendments they had previously rejected but not to rescind ratifications once given. He doubted, however, that such ratifications were perpetually valid. Arguing that "an alteration of the Constitution has relation to the sentiments of today," he said that, if not ratified in a timely fashion, an amendment "ought to be regarded as waived, and not again to be voted upon, unless a second time proposed by Congress (Jameson 1887, 634). On this basis, Jameson questioned Ohio's 1873 ratification of what in 1993 putatively became the Twenty-seventh Amendment.

❖ JEFFERSON, THOMAS ❖
(1743–1826)

Few Americans have been more receptive to the idea of change than was Thomas Jefferson, chief author of the Declaration of Independence and third president of the United States. Some of Jefferson's most important pronouncements are found in letters to friends, especially his Virginia neighbor and political ally James Madison. Jefferson was far bolder than Madison, and his thoughts generally ranged over much wider territory; Madison's thoughts were arguably both more cautious and deeper.

The view of revolution that Jefferson set forth in the Declaration of Independence was, however, moderate. Jefferson argued not for revolution upon slight provocation but for revolution after "a long train of abuses & usurpations." He noted that "governments long established should not be changed for light and transient causes." However, at a later time, when leading Americans nearly panicked over Shay's Rebellion, Jefferson—then in France—took a more positive view. He argued that "a little rebellion now and then is a good thing, & as necessary in the political world as storms in the physical" (Jefferson 1905, 5:256). Moreover, he said that "the tree of liberty must be refreshed from time to time with the blood of patriots & tyrants. It is its natural manure" (Jefferson 1905, 5:362). Faced with a more serious revolution in France, Jefferson was, however, more cautious. Writing to Lafayette in 1814, he urged the revolutionaries to "be contented with a certain portion of power, secured by formal compact with the nation, rather than grasping at more, hazard all upon uncertainty, and risk meeting the fate of their predecessor" (Jefferson 1905, 11:456).

Jefferson at once expressed faith in the people's ability to make constitutional changes and a belief, perhaps best articulated in the Declaration of Independence,

that there were certain natural rights that were morally beyond majority control. In authoring his Bill for Establishing Religious Freedom, one of three accomplishments that he asked be recorded on his gravestone, Jefferson noted that a declaration of irrevocability would not be legally binding. He nonetheless went on to declare that "the rights hereby asserted are of the natural rights of mankind, and . . . if any act shall be hereafter passed to repeal the present or to narrow its operations, such act will be an infringement of natural rights" (Jefferson 1905, 2:441).

Jefferson was serving as a diplomat in France when the Constitutional Convention of 1787 was meeting. Although he subsequently favored the Constitution as a whole, he strongly believed that a bill of rights was needed to complete the framers' work. His correspondence with Madison on the subject is often credited with helping to persuade the latter of the advisability of such protections. Madison later repeated some of Jefferson's arguments when advocating the Bill of Rights on the floor of the House of Representatives (Mason and Stephenson 1993, 349–51). Ironically, one of Jefferson's arguments for such a bill of rights was that, by being placed in the Constitution, such rights would be enforced by the judiciary. Later, however, Jefferson became concerned that John Marshall and his Federalist allies on the Supreme Court were using such power to sap democratic institutions.

Jefferson respected those who had authored his state's constitution during the Revolution, but he warned against looking at this or any other such constitutions "with sanctimonious reverence" or deeming them to be "too sacred to be touched" (Jefferson 1905, 12:11). Perhaps because of both his negative experiences at the hands of the Federalist-dominated Marshall Court and his recognition of how difficult it was to channel power within constitutional guidelines, Jefferson feared that the Constitution could be modified by liberal construction rather than by appeals directly to the people.

In the controversy over the constitutionality of the national bank, Jefferson took the view that such a bank could not be created under the existing Constitution. Jefferson has accordingly been criticized for the most daring and farsighted act of his administration—namely, the purchase of the Louisiana Territory (H. Adams 1974, 1:165–72). This purchase was not directly sanctioned in the Constitution, and Jefferson would have preferred to get sanction from an amendment for his action, but he feared that the delay might scuttle the deal, and he proceeded without such specific constitutional authorization.

Of all of Jefferson's phrases, perhaps none has provided more support for would-be constitutional reformers than a phrase he coined in a letter to James Madison in 1789. There, Jefferson introduced the principle "*that the earth belongs in usufruct to the living*'; that the dead have neither powers nor rights over it" (Jefferson 1905, 6:3–4). From this principle, Jefferson suggested that every debt and, indeed, every constitution should be renewed every 19 years.

The more sober-minded Madison, ever concerned about the effect that frequent changes might have on popular appreciation for the Constitution, subjected this proposal to withering criticism, some of which found its way into *Federalist* No. 49. Despite this critique, Jefferson continued to advocate his view. In a letter in 1813, Jefferson repeated his idea that each generation "has . . . a right to choose for itself the form of government it believes most promotive of its own happiness" and that, accordingly, "for the peace and good of mankind . . . a solemn opportunity of doing this every nineteen or twenty years should be provided by the constitution" (Jefferson 1905, 12:13). In this letter, Jefferson noted that "we might as well require a man to wear still the coat which fitted him when a boy, as civilized society to remain ever under the regimen of their barbarous ancestors" (Jefferson 1905, 12:12).

At the national level, Madison's view of cautious constitutional change has dominated. Purposely or otherwise, many states have come closer to the idea that each generation should be able to incorporate its own views into or indeed rewrite its own constitution (Vile 1992, 72–74).

See also Declaration of Independence; Madison, James.

For Further Reading:
Cunningham, Noble E. 1987. *The Pursuit of Reason: The Life of Thomas Jefferson*. Baton Rouge: Louisiana State University Press.
Mayer, David N. 1994. *The Constitutional Thought of Thomas Jefferson*. Charlottesville: University Press of Virginia.

❖ JOINT RESOLUTION ❖

Although members of Congress occasionally introduce amendments in the form of simple resolutions in a single house, the great majority of amendments in both houses are introduced as joint resolutions. This joint resolution mechanism appears to be dictated by the fact that amendments require approval by a two-thirds vote of both houses of Congress before they are sent to the states, three-fourths of which are required for ratification.

Although it often deals with somewhat narrower matters, a joint resolution has been described as "for all intents and purposes the same as a bill" (Schneier and Gross 1993, 125). Unlike other joint resolutions, resolutions proposing amendments do not require the president's signature (*Hollingsworth v. Virginia* [1798]). Joint resolutions are designated as H.J. Res. or S.J. Res. and are numbered consecutively in each house in the order they are introduced within each two-year congressional session (Kravitz 1993, 139).

❖ JUDICIAL INTERPRETATION ❖

See Constitutional Interpretation.

❖ JUDICIARY, ADVISORY OPINIONS BY ❖

Ever since the first Supreme Court headed by John Jay declined President Washington's request to define rights under a U.S. treaty, U.S. constitutional courts have declined to issue such advisory opinions. Early in the New Deal, the Supreme Court exercised a fairly obstructionist role, voiding a number of Franklin D. Roosevelt's major programs. Two members of Congress introduced resolutions in 1935, one of which was reintroduced in 1937, that would have required the Supreme Court, when so requested by the president or a set majority of Congress, to issue such an opinion.

In 1934, Congress had already adopted the Federal Declaratory Judgment Act, permitting the Court to issue declaratory judgments in some cases. Like advisory opinions, such judgments are nonbinding, but unlike advisory opinions, they involve real disputes between specific individuals. Professor Henry J. Abraham observed that "the line between advisory opinions and declaratory judgments is a thin one" (1993, 354).

❖ JUDICIARY, AGE LIMITS FOR MEMBERS ❖

The judicial branch is the only one for which the Constitution makes no provision for a minimum age (Vile and Perez-Reilly 1991). Moreover, because federal judges are appointed "during good behavior," they may serve until they are quite old without ever facing voters' judgment of their competency for continued service.

A few proposals have been introduced in Congress that would have required a minimum age for judges and justices (often from 30 to 40). Others would have required that judges have a minimum number of years of legal practice or experience in other courts. Such provisions have typically been introduced as parts of amendments designed to change the current method of judicial selection.

There have been many more proposals (often as part of amendments that also would have applied to members of Congress and other officeholders) to limit the age of sitting judges or require a mandatory retirement age. This practice is followed in many states. The most frequently proposed ages range from 65 to 75. There is reason to believe that this might have a significant impact on the composition of the courts, many of whose members continue to serve until reaching an advanced age. Thus, of the 100 Supreme Court vacancies from 1789 to 1991, 58 were created by death in office (Abraham 1993, 41). Moreover, other justices have retired from the Court only after extensive periods of disability (Cooper and Ball 1996, 354–68).

The year 1937 witnessed Franklin D. Roosevelt's court-packing plan. It proposed giving the president power to appoint one new Supreme Court justice (up to 15) for every one who remained on the Court past the age of 70; it would also have enabled him to appoint additional judges to lower courts. Although Congress rejected Roosevelt's plan, it provided a fairly generous retirement package so that judges would not be forced to continue in office simply for financial reasons.

See also Court-Packing Plan.

❖ JUDICIARY, COMPENSATION OF MEMBERS ❖

In an attempt to preserve executive independence, Article II, Section 1 of the Constitution prevents Congress from increasing or diminishing a president's pay during his term of office. The Twenty-seventh Amendment now prevents congressional salaries from being raised or lowered prior to an intervening election.

Because judges serve "during good behavior," which effectively means until they die, retire, or are impeached and convicted, their salaries could be eroded by inflation during their service. Article III, Section 1 of the Constitution thus allows Congress to raise, but not to lower, the salaries of judges during their terms of office. In the process of ratifying the Constitution, Virginia and North Carolina proposed that periodic increases or decreases in judicial salaries be enacted as part of more general salary regulations (Ames 1896, 153). No subsequent proposals have addressed this topic, although the subject of judicial raises is periodically the focus of political disputes.

❖ JUDICIARY, COURT ❖
OF THE UNION

Although the issue of judicial review of congressional legislation receives the majority of scholarly attention, the Court's exercise of judicial review of state laws might be just as important, if not more so. The Supreme Court exercised this power as early as 1810 (*Fletcher v. Peck*), and it often met with stiff resistance from proponents of states' rights.

One of the problems, particularly during the Marshall Court, was that proponents of states' rights thought that the Supreme Court was biased toward federal powers, just as state courts might be biased toward their own. There were a handful of proposals in the nineteenth century, at least two during the period of Reconstruction, to create a special tribunal to resolve questions of conflict between state and national powers. A proposal introduced in 1821, apparently stimulated by the Supreme Court's nationalistic opinion in *Cohens v. Virginia* of that

year (Levy 1995, 435), would have had the Senate serve as the appellate review body for such cases. A proposal submitted in 1867 would have vested this power in a court consisting of one member from each state (Ames 1896, 163).

Reaction to decisions by the Warren Court—especially regarding state legislative apportionment—stimulated renewed attention to this issue in the early 1960s. Among three proposals introduced and adopted at the December 1962 meeting of the General Assembly of States, sponsored by the Council of State Governments, was a resolution to create a Court of the Union composed of the chief justices of each state's highest court. This court would hear appeals when requested to do so by five noncontiguous states and would be authorized by majority vote to reverse Supreme Court decisions relative to the rights reserved to the states under the Tenth Amendment.

Alabama, Arkansas, Florida, South Carolina, and Wyoming subsequently requested a constitutional convention to deal with the topic, and at least 15 proposals for an amendment were introduced in Congress from 1963 to 1981. South Carolina Senator Strom Thurmond appears to have been the first to introduce this proposal. This, and other proposals by the Council of State Governments, encountered considerable scholarly opposition, one scholar referring to calls for a Court of the Union as "patently absurd" (C. Black 1963, 957).

See also Council of State Governments.

❖ JUDICIARY, EXERCISE OF ❖
JUDICIAL REVIEW BY

Of all the powers exercised by U.S. courts, none is more important than their exercise of judicial review. This power enables them to declare laws passed by the state legislatures or by Congress, or actions taken by the executive or governmental agencies, to be unconstitutional and hence void. The power of judicial review is not specifically stated in the Constitution, but it was forcefully asserted by Chief Justice John Marshall in *Marbury v. Madison* (1803); he defended it as a way of ensuring the supremacy of the written constitution over popular willfulness. Such review distinguishes the U.S. system from systems of parliamentary sovereignty, under which decisions of the legislative branch are final.

Although the power of judicial review is consistent with a system providing for checks and balances, it pits the judgment of the only unelected branch of the government against the judgment of the people's elected representatives. This presents what one prominent scholar described as "the counter-majoritarian difficulty" (Bickel 1986, 16–22). Judicial review also continues to spark controversy over the appropriate level of judicial activism or restraint—generally interpreted to mean deference to legislative judgments (Halpern and Lamb 1982; Wolfe 1991)—and helps fuel continuing controversies over questions of constitutional interpretation.

Many of the amending proposals that were introduced in the nineteenth century relative to the judiciary dealt with judicial jurisdiction. The Eleventh Amendment was the most visible and, to date, the only successful proposal designed specifically to limit judicial jurisdiction. A member of Congress introduced a proposal in the December–January session of the 1846–1847 Congress to take away the courts' power to declare laws unconstitutional, but proposals aimed specifically at judicial review are more characteristic of the twentieth century. The Progressive Era, the years surrounding the Court's historic "switch in time that saved nine" in 1937, and the 1960s and 1970s mark the greatest activity in this area. Most proposals did not call for the complete elimination of judicial review but would have limited its exercise by requiring supermajorities of the Supreme Court to act before it invalidated laws. In 1912, Republican Representative Fred Jackson of Kansas thus proposed that when any U.S. court declared a law to be invalid, three-fourths of the state legislatures should then decide on the law's validity (H.J. Res. 351). Numerous proposals have also been introduced to allow Congress to override judicial exercises of its review power.

At least three proposals introduced during the Progressive Era would have required the concurrence of all but two of the Supreme Court justices to declare laws to be unconstitutional. Another proposal from this period would simply have invested Congress with the power to specify the majority on the Court that would be necessary to invalidate such legislation. Republican Senator Joseph Bristow of Kansas introduced another proposal that would have submitted exercises of judicial review to voters, who would be able to reverse such decisions by a majority referendum.

A far greater number of proposals emerged during the New Deal, especially around the time of Franklin D. Roosevelt's court-packing plan. These ranged from giving explicit constitutional recognition to the right to judicial review, to eliminating the power altogether, to providing (as in proposals from the Progressive Era) for supermajority votes, most commonly set at two-thirds.

Beginning in 1958 and reaching a peak in the late 1960s, members of Congress again began introducing amendments to limit judicial review. Louisiana Democratic Representative John Rarick introduced a proposal in 1967 (H.J. Res. 384) that would have limited the power of judicial review to the Supreme Court. It would further have required a unanimous verdict in cases in which the Court decided to void a law. Far more common were proposals to require a two-thirds vote either of the Supreme Court's entire membership or of those voting in a given case. A variation introduced by Republican Representative Jesse Younger of

California (H.J. Res. 173) in 1967 would have allowed a two-thirds majority of Congress to limit the power of judicial review. Although such proposals helped register dissatisfaction with the scope of Supreme Court decision making, particularly during the New Deal and the Warren Court years, to date, none has proved successful.

See also Congress, Overriding Judicial Decisions; Constitutional Interpretation; Court-Packing Plan.

❖ JUDICIARY, JURISDICTION OF ❖

Article III, Section 2 of the Constitution outlines the jurisdiction of—that is, the types of cases to be heard by—the federal courts. In a few cases, the Supreme Court exercises original jurisdiction and hears cases for the first time, but in most instances, its jurisdiction is appellate. In such cases, it reviews the judgments of lower federal courts or decisions reaching a state's highest court that involve questions of federal law or constitutional interpretation (Abraham 1993, 171–73).

From the beginning, many advocates of states' rights feared the exercise of federal judicial power and sought to curb it. After the Court's decision in *Chisholm v. Georgia* (1793), the states succeeded in adopting the Eleventh Amendment, modifying Article III so as to preclude the Court from accepting cases brought by citizens of another state without that state's consent. A number of other proposals designed to clip federal jurisdiction were introduced from 1800 to 1810, but apart from a few proposals designed to provide for an alternative tribunal to adjudicate cases between the states and the national government, the remaining amending proposals—including one that would have repealed the Eleventh Amendment—actually sought to expand federal jurisdiction.

Twentieth-century proposals to alter judicial jurisdiction have varied. They include an attempt in 1901 to extend such jurisdiction to matters involving the use of water, attempts in the second decade to limit federal jurisdiction over matters involving corporations (considered to be citizens under the terms of the Fourteenth Amendment), and limits on the Court's exercise of judicial review of state and federal legislation.

From a somewhat different perspective, individuals who fear that congressional power might be used to undermine individual rights have proposed to limit congressional authority under Article III to make exceptions to and provide regulations for the Supreme Court's appellate jurisdiction. One proponent of the latter amendment was one-time Supreme Court Justice Owen Roberts (R. Smith 1987, 268).

Democratic Representative Robert Sikes of Florida introduced a resolution in 1959 (H.J. Res. 201) prohibiting the Supreme Court from being able to "overrule, modify, or change any prior decision of that Court construing the Constitution or Acts of Congress promulgated pursuant thereto." Given the many times that the Court has made such reversals, often in important cases (Ernst 1973), such an amendment could have a major impact on judicial decision making and might well prompt state legislators and members of Congress to introduce more changes through the amending mechanism.

See also Eleventh Amendment; Judiciary, Court of the Union; Judiciary, Exercise of Judicial Review by.

❖ JUDICIARY, LIMITS ON ❖ TAXING POWER

On 20 April 1990, Missouri Republican Senator John Danforth introduced an amendment (S.J. Res. 295) with more than 25 cosponsors. It was designed to prohibit federal courts from ordering the laying or increasing of taxes. The Senate conducted hearings on the subject in June 1990, and the amending proposal was reintroduced in 1991 and 1992.

Senator Danforth and others were apparently prompted by a Supreme Court decision rendered on 18 April 1990 in *Missouri v. Jenkins*, a desegregation case. The supervisory U.S. district court had initially ordered the Kansas City, Missouri, school district to double property taxes to pay for the construction of magnet schools designed to hasten desegregation. The U.S. Court of Appeals subsequently ruled that, rather than ordering this levy itself, the court could simply order a lifting of state restrictions on such taxes and let the Kansas City school district come up with its own funding.

In upholding this less intrusive approach, the Supreme Court rested its decision on the principle of comity, or respect for state and local initiatives, rather than on constitutional grounds. Writing for the five-person Court majority, Justice Byron White asserted, however, that "a court order directing a local government body to levy its own taxes is plainly a judicial act within the power of a federal court" (*Missouri* 1990, 55). In a vigorous concurring opinion, Justice Anthony Kennedy disagreed. He argued that "today's casual embrace of taxation imposed by the unelected, life-tenured Federal Judiciary disregards fundamental precepts for the democratic control of public institutions" (*Missouri* 1990, 58–59).

One of the last-minute modifications to the Senate version of the balanced budget amendment that came but a single vote shy of adoption in March 1995 was a provision by Democratic Senator Sam Nunn of Georgia that would have provided that "the judicial power of the United States shall not extend to any case or controversy arising under this Article except as may be specifically authorized by legislation adopted pursuant to this section" ("Text of Amendment" 1995, 705). Nunn's concern suggests that the issue raised by *Missouri v. Jenkins* is still viable.

❖ JUDICIARY, NUMBER OF SUPREME COURT JUSTICES ❖

Article III of the U.S. Constitution mentions the Supreme Court but does not specify how many justices it should have. In the Judiciary Act of 1789, Congress set this number at six, but the number alternated between five and ten before Congress settled on nine justices in 1869 (Barnum 1993, 202). In his court-packing plan of 1937, Franklin Roosevelt proposed adding one justice (up to 15) for each justice who remained on the Court over the age of 70. Ultimately defeated in Congress, this plan prompted a score of proposals from 1937 through the 1950s to set the number of justices permanently at nine.

Such proposals sometimes contained other provisions for mandatory retirement of justices at a certain age or specifying that an extraordinary majority would be needed to declare laws unconstitutional. In the 83d Congress, the Senate voted 58 to 19 to accept a proposal sponsored by Republican Senator John Marshall Butler of Maryland (S.J. Res. 44) designed to safeguard judicial independence by fixing the number of justices at nine and adopting a number of other reforms. These included setting a compulsory retirement age of 75, making justices ineligible to run for president or vice president, and preventing Congress from being able to alter the appellate jurisdiction of the Supreme Court ("Composition and Jurisdiction" 1953, 1106).

See also Court-Packing Plan.

❖ JUDICIARY, OFFICEHOLDING BY MEMBERS ❖

There is some evidence that the framers of the Constitution may have anticipated fairly close ties between the executive and judicial branches of government. Thus, although

Article I, Section 6 prohibits members of Congress from holding other offices, it contains no such prohibition for judges and justices (Scigliano 1994, 278).

Especially in early American history, members of the judiciary were sometimes appointed to serve on diplomatic missions or asked to perform other public duties. In the twentieth century, Justice Robert Jackson served as the chief U.S. prosecutor at the Nazi war crime trials in Nuremberg, and Chief Justice Earl Warren headed the commission that investigated the assassination of President John F. Kennedy. Justice Abe Fortas's continuing service as an adviser to President Lyndon Johnson was, however, one of the factors that ultimately led to his resignation from the Court (B. Murphy 1988, 114–40), and experience suggests that modern justices are likely to keep informal contacts with the executive at arm's length.

In addition to serving in executive offices, some justices have harbored presidential aspirations. John McLean, who served on the Supreme Court from 1830 to 1861, was called the "politician on the Supreme Court" and was mentioned as a possible presidential candidate for more than 30 years (Gatell 1969, 535). Charles Evans Hughes, who served as an associate Supreme Court justice from 1910 to 1916 and as chief justice from 1930 to 1941, resigned in 1916 to challenge Woodrow Wilson for the presidency. William Howard Taft was appointed chief justice of the Supreme Court after having served a term as president—the only individual to serve in both positions. More recently, in a letter released to the public, Franklin D. Roosevelt listed Justice William O. Douglas as a possible vice presidential running mate in 1944 (McCullough 1992, 304–7).

After President Washington appointed Chief Justice Oliver Ellsworth as a commissioner to France, two proposals were introduced in 1800 to restrict judges from serving in dual offices. In the 1870s, and again in

1916—the year Justice Hughes ran for president—proposals were made that would prevent justices from running for president. In the 1950s, the Senate voted positively on an amendment that would have included a prohibition on justices' running for president or vice president, among other provisions designed to guarantee judicial independence.

See also Congress, Members' Eligibility for Other Offices.

JUDICIARY, ❖ ORGANIZATION OF ❖

On a few occasions, members of Congress have introduced amendments to reorganize the federal judiciary. However, short of abolishing the Supreme Court, an institution for which the Constitution makes explicit provision, there are few alterations in the judicial system that cannot be made by ordinary acts of legislation. Article III, which describes the judiciary, is the briefest of the three distributing articles, and it does not even specify the number of Supreme Court justices.

Much of the current structure of the federal judicial system was established in a series of judiciary acts that were adopted from 1789 to 1925 (Hall 1992, 172–77). President Franklin D. Roosevelt's court-packing plan was a good example of a proposal to alter the judiciary that failed. Proposals for a Court of the Union fall into a similar category.

See also Court of the Union; Court-Packing Plan.

❖ JUDICIARY, QUALIFICATIONS ❖ OF MEMBERS

Although the Juris Doctor degree is "an unwritten prerequisite for a place on the federal bench," the Constitution does not make this qualification explicit (Abraham 1992, 49). At least one modern scholar has suggested that individuals with other types of professional training should be considered for the Supreme Court (A. Miller 1982, 286). Moreover, there is considerable scholarly debate as to whether prior judicial experience ought to be required of federal judges or Supreme Court justices. Of the first 110 justices, 42, including such luminaries as John Marshall, Joseph Story, Louis Brandeis, and Felix Frankfurter, had no prior judicial experience at all (Abraham 1992, 50–52). The latter justice was a particularly vocal advocate of the view that such previous experience should not be a prerequisite.

In addition to periodic proposals to require that judges be elected, serve for fixed terms, be subject to Senate reconfirmation, or retire at a certain age, the 1960s and 1970s witnessed a number of proposals that would have mandated judicial qualifications. Some such proposals would have mandated a specified minimum number of years of prior judicial experience; at least one would have required that judges be natural-born citizens 30 years of age or older with a law degree (see, for example, H.J. Res. 325, 1973); and at least one attempted to guarantee partisan balance on the Supreme Court.

In 1971, Democratic Representative Charles Griffin of Mississippi reintroduced a proposal (H.J. Res. 95) that he had also advocated in 1968 and 1969 prohibiting two justices from the same state from serving on the Supreme Court. Griffin may have been responding in part to President Nixon's 1970 appointment of Harry Blackmun, who, like Chief Justice Warren Burger (whom Nixon had appointed the previous year), was from Minnesota. Nixon nominated Blackmun after failing to get two southerners, Clement F. Haynesworth Jr. and Harold Carswell, confirmed.

❖ JUDICIARY, REMOVAL ❖ OF MEMBERS

Currently, the only legal mechanism that is available for removing sitting federal judges is that of impeachment by the House of Representatives and conviction by a two-thirds vote of the Senate. Article II, Section 4 of the Constitution limits impeachable offenses to "Treason, Bribery, or other high Crimes or Misdemeanors." Although this provision guards judges against being removed for political reasons, it leaves no legal means to remove judges who are incompetent.

Throughout U.S. history, members of Congress have introduced proposals to liberalize this process. The first such plan was introduced by Virginia's flamboyant Representative John Randolph, who had helped lead the unsuccessful impeachment effort against Justice Samuel Chase. Randolph's proposal would have enabled the president to remove judges, provided he gave a joint address to both houses of Congress to justify his actions. Members of Congress introduced several other proposals in the next 30 years, with others following in 1850 and 1867.

At least three proposals for removing judges were introduced in 1912. Democratic Senator Henry Ashurst of Arizona appeared to be influenced by contemporary interest in the recall. Tennessee Democratic Representative Cordell Hull introduced the other two resolutions, providing for the removal of inferior court judges by concurrent resolution in Congress.

Proposals for removing judges have been introduced at a fairly steady pace since 1941. Some such proposals would apply only to lower court judges, and others have been directed specifically to members of the Supreme Court. Louisiana Democratic Representative John Rarick introduced a proposal in 1968 (H.J. Res. 1094) that would allow 1 percent or more of the voters of two-thirds of the states to petition for the removal of a Supreme Court justice, which action would be effected by a majority vote at the next congressional election. Florida Republican Louis Frey introduced a resolution in 1976 (H.J. Res. 912) that would have allowed the Senate, with House concurrence, to remove a justice who was unable to perform his duties "by reason of a personal mental or physical disability," including "habitual intemperance." This proposal came within a year of the retirement of Justice William O. Douglas, who had remained on the Supreme Court after suffering a debilitating stroke.

Other proposals from this period would have delegated removal powers to the courts themselves, usually subject to review by the U.S. Supreme Court. Still others would have vested this power directly in the High Court.

Many states now provide for disciplinary commissions, often consisting of fellow judges and laypersons, as well as recall elections for judges thought to be incompetent or out of touch (H. Jacob 1995, 195–96). In 1980, Congress adopted the Judicial Councils Reform and Judicial Conduct and Disability Act. It permits judicial councils in the 13 federal circuits to discipline, but not to remove, lower court judges (Abraham 1993, 42).

❖ JUDICIARY, SELECTION ❖ OF MEMBERS

The judicial branch is the only branch of the federal government whose members are not elected. Instead, under the terms of Article II, Section 2 of the Constitution, the president appoints judges with the advice and consent, or approval, of the Senate. Although the framers designed this mechanism in large part to insulate judges from the political process, judicial selection and confirmation can be an extremely political process (Massaro 1990), and nomination is certainly no guarantee of confirmation.

Thus, as of the end of the Bush administration, 28 of 142 nominees to the Supreme Court had failed to be confirmed by the Senate (Abraham 1992, 39).

In contrast to the national government, many states either elect judges or use a mechanism, such as the Missouri and California plans, that combines a system of appointment and electoral confirmation (Abraham 1992, 35–39). The movement for judicial accountability was especially prominent in the Jacksonian period and again in the Progressive Era (Tarr 1994, 69). Despite the former movement, there were only four proposed changes in the method of selecting federal judges in the nation's first 90 years (Ames 1896, 146). Since then, there have been more than 65 such proposals; many seem to coincide with periods in which there was intense opposition to the Court as an institution or strong concern over controversial rulings (Nagel 1965).

The most common proposal calls simply for the election of federal judges and other appointed officeholders, for example, district attorneys, clerks, marshals, revenue collectors, and postmasters. Such elections may be proposed only for members of the Supreme Court, only for members of lower U.S. district and circuit courts, or for both the Supreme Court and the lower courts. Such proposed elections are also frequently tied to judicial terms of from 4 to 12 years and are sometimes phrased in terms of a recall.

Most proposals calling for the election of Supreme Court justices appear to foresee the creation of nine electoral districts in the United States for such elections. This might increase the role that geographic representation now plays in such appointments. Some proposals also call for changing the current practice by which the president designates the chief justice (Vile 1994b), specifying instead that the justices would choose their own chief (as is the case in many states).

Other proposals, especially prominent in the 1950s and 1960s, would have allowed the president to appoint Supreme Court justices from a list of five nominees selected by the chief justices of state supreme courts. Some other proposals have called for including members of the House of Representatives in the confirmation process. One of the most innovative such proposals, a kind of congressional court-packing plan, was introduced in 1946 by Democratic Senator James Eastland of Mississippi. It would have provided that no president could appoint more than three justices to the Supreme Court and would have required the retirement of any beyond three that had been so appointed. Such vacancies would have been filled by the U.S. House of Representatives, with the representatives of each state having a single vote.

Recent controversies over nominees to the Supreme Court have rekindled controversies about possible alternatives. Among proposals that would require an amendment are those providing for judicial term limits, for judicial elections, or for raising the current requirement for Senate confirmation to a two-thirds majority of that body (S. Carter 1994, 195–203).

❖ JUDICIARY, TERMS ❖ OF JUDGES

The president appoints federal judges and justices with the "advice and consent," or approval, of the Senate. Such judges and justices serve "during good behavior," which means that they continue in office until they die or resign or until the House of Representatives impeaches and the Senate convicts them of an impeachable offense. By contrast, many states judges are elected by the people or serve fixed terms of office (Glick 1988, 86–98).

Proposals to limit the terms of federal judges date back to 1808 and have been introduced in almost every subsequent decade. Such proposals are often tied to

mandatory retirement ages, typically somewhere between 65 and 75. In the 1850s and 1860s, Andrew Johnson was a prominent proponent of a 12-year judicial term (Ames 1896, 152).

Proposals for fixed judicial terms have been especially popular from the late 1960s to the present (with close to 200 proposals introduced in this period), but their specific provisions have varied substantially. Some such proposals would apply only to Supreme Court justices, others only to inferior federal judges, and still others to both. Although some call for a one-term limit, the overwhelming majority would allow judges to be reappointed or reelected to office. The process of presidential renomination and Senate reconfirmation appears to be the most popular.

As in recent controversies on congressional term limits, no consensus has emerged as to how long such terms should be. Proposals have varied from 4 to 18 years (Ross 1990; Levinson 1992). As part of a package of term limits for members of the House and Senate, Democratic Representative Andrew Jacobs Jr. of Indiana introduced a proposal in 1967 that would have prohibited federal judges from serving more than 10 out of any 12 years (H.J. Res. 868).

Senate confirmations of Supreme Court justices have become increasingly public affairs (S. Carter 1994), and at least one recent nominee, Justice Clarence Thomas, is reported to have likened his own confirmation to a type of death (Danforth 1994). In such circumstances, there is likely to be substantial opposition to the idea of Senate reconfirmation of sitting judges and justices.

See also Judiciary, Age Limits for Members.

❖ JURY TRIALS ❖

Article III of the Constitution provides that "the trial of all crimes, except in cases of impeachment; shall be by jury." The Sixth Amendment also guarantees "an impartial jury" in federal criminal cases, and the Seventh Amendment extends this right to federal civil cases involving more than $20. Applying its incorporation doctrine, the Supreme Court has ruled that the Sixth Amendment right to a jury trial in criminal cases applies to the states via the due process clause of the Fourteenth Amendment (*Duncan* [1968]), but it has not extended this right in civil trials. With roots deep in English common law, the jury is thought to guarantee fairness; commentators have also long argued that service on a jury provides an education in citizenship (Tocqueville 1969, 270–76; Abramson 1994).

The fact that only a few amending proposals have been introduced relative to the jury system probably indicates that, despite periodic scholarly criticism (Frank 1969, 108–25), the system continues to be held in general favor. Several proposals introduced around the time of the Civil War would have provided jury trials for escaped slaves. In 1927, another proposal, of unknown import, was introduced relative to jury trials. In 1948, a proposal was introduced to permit juries of fewer than 12 members in certain cases.

The Constitution does not specify the number of individuals who must sit on a jury, and the Supreme Court has upheld the use of six-member juries in noncapital cases (*Williams* [1970]). In *Ballew v. Georgia* (1978), however, the Supreme Court struck down the use of a five-person jury. In *Johnson v. Louisiana* (1972) and *Apodaco v. Oregon* (1972), it upheld nonunanimous jury verdicts in noncapital criminal cases, and in *Burch v. Louisiana* (1979), it ruled that six-member juries must vote unanimously to convict (D. O'Brien 1995, 1047–52). The judiciary has thus arguably adapted, or enabled the jury mechanism to adapt, to modern exigencies.

K

❖ *KIMBLE V. SWACKHAMER* ❖
(1978)

Acting as a circuit justice, Chief Justice Rehnquist upheld a 4-to-1 Nevada Supreme Court decision by refusing to enjoin the placement of an advisory referendum concerning the equal rights amendment on the upcoming Nevada ballot. Rehnquist said that *Leser v. Garnett* (1922) and *Hawke v. Smith* (1920) "stand for the proposition that the two methods for state ratification of proposed constitutional amendments set forth in Art. V of the United States Constitution are exclusive" (*Kimble* 1978, 1387). Rehnquist noted, however, that this referendum was advisory only and thus was little different from a representative seeking advice from his constituents.

❖ KRUSCH, BARRY (1958–) ❖

One of the most recent plans for a new constitution is also one of the most ambitious. Barry Krusch of New York offered this proposal in a book entitled *The 21st Century Constitution* (1992). An extensive opening chapter details current faults in the U.S. system. Krusch attributes most of these to separation of powers, to the fact that the Constitution was written prior to the modern information age, and to the fact that actual practices (what he calls the empirical constitution) no longer match the written document. In the rest of his book, Krusch outlines an alternative constitution. His alternative is, however, built around the current constitutional outline. Krusch wants to make the Constitution more responsive to public wishes and more adaptable to modern technologies, but he also has great faith in the power of experts to guide legislative decision making and identify national interests.

Under Krusch's plan, Congress would continue to consist of two branches, but with somewhat different functions. Members of both branches would be prohibited from being members of political parties and would be limited to eight years of service. Members of the new House of Representatives, consisting of a minimum of 1,000 members, would serve one-year terms and would be required to be graduates of a federal academy (also responsible for proposing congressional rules). Each state would continue to have two senators, but they would serve two-year terms. The Senate's primary function would be governmental oversight. A federal committee of 50 senators would administer "the National Database, the National Poll, the National Objectives, the National Initiative, the National Referendum, and the National Recall" (Krusch 1992, 128). The committee would also nominate candidates for the House of Representatives and the presidency, making sure that their nominees were "representative of the population . . . with regard to sex, race, national origin and other factors" (Krusch 1992, 129). The Senate would be responsible for setting up a legislative review board of nine members, serving for a single three-year term, that would compile "performance ratings" for representatives according to the degree to which they voted for bills that served the national interest. The Senate would also commission polls to ascertain the public will.

The majority necessary to pass bills—and the determination of whether a bill would need to pass one or both houses and/or be signed by the president—would be based on the evaluation that the bills received from the legislative review board. Any income taxes would have to apply to at least three-fourths of the population, with the highest tax bracket limited to 50 percent and the lowest at least half that amount (Krusch 1992, 158). Borrowing would require a sanction by a two-thirds vote of both houses and the voters. The legislative veto, declared unconstitutional in *Immigration and Naturalization Service v. Chadha* (1983), would be permitted (Krusch 1992, 165). Congress would create and regulate a national academy, a department of rights enforcement, and a federal election commission, with all electoral campaigns to be publicly financed.

The right to an education would be granted, a national database would be created to disseminate information to the citizens, and a national channel would educate people, with "one-half of the programming" to "reflect the Will of the People as determined by the June National Poll" (Krusch 1992, 179). Current principles regarding freedom of speech, religion, and other rights in the Bill of Rights would be set forth in greater detail that better reflects current case law. One fascinating provision allows for penalties for those distorting "those aspects of reality which have been or can be objectively verified as true" (Krusch 1992, 183).

The president and vice president would be selected by majority vote, with the na-tional recall taking the place of presidential impeachment. Presidential powers to commit troops without congressional authorization would be clipped.

Nine nonpartisan judges representative of the population would serve staggered nine-year terms. Although judges would no longer have the power of judicial review, they would have no obligation to enforce laws that they considered to be unconstitutional.

The current federal arrangement of the government would undergo few changes, but amendments could be proposed by a majority of both houses or two-thirds of the people. Two-thirds of the people or state legislatures could also call for a convention. Amendments would be ratified by two-thirds of the state legislatures or conventions or by three-fifths of the electorate. In a provision similar to one that Thomas Jefferson made, every 25 years, the people would be asked whether they wanted another convention (Krusch 1992, 236).

The main articles of the new constitution would be augmented by supplements that could be altered more easily. Krusch would also include a rule of constitutional construction that "strict terms such as 'no' or 'all' shall be strictly construed, and broad terms such as 'liberty' and 'justice' shall be broadly construed" (Krusch 1992, 247).

A Second Federal Convention Act would provide the rules for constitutional ratification. Krusch anticipates a convention of 1,200 delegates to write or affirm the constitution, with members of no single profession to compose more than 5 percent of its members (Krusch 1992, 249). The people would choose from among three to six such documents.

Krusch is president of Americans for a Constitutional Convention, Inc. His book includes an address for people who are interested in serving as delegates to a mock constitutional convention.

L

At least one proposal was introduced in 1883 and two in 1886 that would prohibit states from contracting out convict labor. Although no such amendment was adopted, fears by free laborers of unfair competition continue to limit the tasks that states feel that they can assign to convicts. Recently, however, Alabama and Arizona reinstituted the chain gang as a way of saving state money and deterring crime (Gavzer 1995, 6).

❖ LABOR, HOURS OF ❖

From 1884 to 1937, members of Congress introduced more than 30 proposals to give that body power to regulate the hours of labor. Some such resolutions applied specifically to factories; some proposed "uniform" hours of labor; and some combined a proposal about hours of labor with power over minimum wages, the prevention of unfair labor practices, or other regulations of labor.

Proposals for reform coincided with a period during which the federal courts often struck down state and federal regulatory legislation that they perceived to have a class bias (Gillman 1993). The due process clause of the Fourteenth Amendment—which the Court interpreted as embodying "freedom of contract"—was the tool that the courts used most frequently to accomplish this objective. The best known of these decisions was *Lochner v. New York* (1905), in which the Supreme Court struck down a New York state law regulating the hours of bakers (Kens 1990). Decisions in which the Court upheld such laws usually involved industries considered to be particularly dangerous, such as mining in *Holden v. Hardy* (1898), or individuals whom the Court thought were in need of special state protection, such as women in *Muller v. Oregon* (1908).

In *West Coast Hotel v. Parrish* (1937) and *National Labor Relations Board v. Jones & Laughlin Steel Corp.* (1937), the Supreme Court made its historic "switch in time that saved nine" and began interpreting existing congressional powers under the commerce and taxing provisions generously enough to uphold most labor-related legislation. Such interpretations negated the need for a constitutional amendment, and members of Congress ceased introducing them.

See also *Lochner v. New York*.

❖ LAND, DIVISION OF ❖

A number of amendments that have been proposed to grant or expand the national government's power over agriculture have included grants of power to tax or otherwise regulate land. Henry George (1839–1897) promoted a single-tax movement with the 1871 publication of his essay "Our Land and Land Policy," which subsequently became the basis of his influential *Progress and Poverty* (1938).

Democratic Representative John Randolph Thayer of Massachusetts offered perhaps the most drastic proposal to alter land distribution by amendment in January 1904 (H.J. Res. 83). Thayer would have allowed the national government to take land from anyone with more than 12 acres and redistribute it so that everyone would have at least eight contiguous acres. Similar distributions were to be made after each census (Musmanno 1929, 1903).

See also Agriculture.

❖ LAWRENCE, WILLIAM B. ❖ (1800–1881)

American diplomat and international law specialist William B. Lawrence published an article in 1880 in which he advocated substantial changes in the U.S. Constitution (Vile 1991c, 32–34). He was especially concerned about the treatment the South had received during Reconstruction and by the irregularities of the election of 1876. He also considered the power of the presidency to be a special threat to republican government.

Lawrence directed the majority of his article to historical critique and review rather than to suggested changes, but the suggestions he did offer were major ones. Lawrence argued that a system in which Congress selected the president would be better than the existing system because it would lead to greater legislative-executive harmony and would entrust the decision to those who were most knowledgeable. Lawrence believed that it was "impossible to conceive of any worse political machinery" than the national nominating convention (Lawrence 1880, 407).

Lawrence also called the vice presidency "altogether objectionable," noting that vice presidents were often selected "without regard to the possible succession" and that the office had been largely created so that each member of the electoral college could cast two votes (Lawrence 1880, 406). Lawrence argued that a powerful executive was dangerous in a heterogeneous nation, where he could "influence legislation, as well as the administration of the Government, in favor of his section to the prejudice of others" (1880, 408).

Lawrence favored the establishment of a parliamentary system. Passing over more familiar models, Lawrence commended the Swiss form. As he described it, this system vested executive authority in a federal council of seven members from different geographic areas who were selected by the legislature for three-year terms. This legislature chose the president and vice president annually, but neither officer had substantially more powers than members of the council, a majority of which was necessary "to sanction every deliberation (Lawrence 1880, 408–9).

❖ LAZARE, DANIEL ❖

Lazare, a freelance journalist, has authored a stinging critique of modern American government in which he argues that most American social problems are the result of an antiquated constitution that stresses checks and balances and separation of powers and produces gridlock rather than governmental accountability (1996). In almost every area he examines, Lazare finds European parliamentary systems to be better, and he condemns what he regards as American worship of a written constitution. He even compares those who admire the American Founders, the Constitution, and Federalist justifications of it to "Iranian mullahs waiving copies of the Koran" (1996, 284).

Lazare argues that Article V is the "dangling thread" (1996, 297) that could eventually unravel the existing system that he so criticizes. Lazare imagines a situation in which California threatens to secede unless the current system of equal state apportionment in the Senate is ended. In arguments similar to those raised elsewhere by Akil Reed Amar, Lazare suggests that the House of Representatives could respond in an extraconstitutional manner by voting by a simple majority to abolish equal representation in the Senate and then allowing the American people to ratify its decision in a referendum.

Although he does not go into detail about the new system this would initiate, he does say that it would not only embody the principle of legislative sovereignty but also "reduce the president to semi-figurehead status" and "effectively rob the judiciary of much of its power" (1996, 293–94)." Lazare further notes that "not just the Constitution would be toppled, but so would checks and balances, separation of powers, and the deeply inculcated habit of deferring to the authority of a group of eighteenth-century Country gentlemen. Instead of relying on previous generation's judgment and analysis, the people would have no choice than to rely on their own" (1996, 295).

That deference to the current Constitution to which Lazare makes continual reference would appear to present a major obstacle to his plans.

❖ LEGISLATION PROPOSED ❖

To date, Congress has not adopted legislation to guide a possible convention petitioned for by the states under Article V of the Constitution to propose amendments. One prominent and active supporter of such legislation was Democratic Senator Sam Ervin of North Carolina, who introduced the Federal Constitutional Convention Act in 1967. At that time, he and Republican Senator Everett Dirksen of Illinois were working for a convention to repeal the Supreme Court's reapportionment decisions. The other most prominent supporter

of such legislation has been Republican Senator Orrin Hatch of Utah, who first presented his Constitutional Implementation Act in 1979 and has been advocating it ever since. The Ervin bill passed the Senate in 1971 and 1973 but was never acted on in the House of Representatives. Hatch's bill has been approved by the Senate Judiciary Committee but not by either house of Congress (Caplan 1988, 77).

Both Ervin and Hatch believed that Congress has the power to adopt such legislation under the necessary and proper clause. Both also argued that neutral legislation should be passed that could apply to any issue rather than being tailor-made to specific conventions. Interestingly, both senators took the position that states can call either a limited or an open convention, but their legislation would apply only to the former.

The Ervin and Hatch bills are surprisingly similar. The Ervin bill originally proposed that applications for a convention would be valid for seven years, but Ervin subsequently reduced this period to four years (Ervin 1968, 891); the Hatch bill provides a period of no longer than seven years but allows state applications to specify a shorter period (Hatch 1991, S561). Because no such deadline is now specified, the Hatch bill would give an additional two-year life (absent state rescission) to proposals introduced in the last 16 years (Hatch 1991, S561). The Hatch bill also encourages, but does not require, states to list other state applications that they believe cover the same topic.

Both the Ervin and the Hatch legislation would permit Congress to specify the time, place, and (consistent with state petitions) the general subject matter of the convention. The original Ervin bill gave each state a number of delegates equal to its representation in the House but required that state delegates vote as a bloc ("Proposed Legislation" 1972, 1625). The revised bill followed the model of the electoral college in giving each state a number of votes equal to its total number of U.S. senators and representatives and allowed for majority rule. The Ervin bill provided that such delegates would be elected in the states. Hatch apparently favors such popular election but would not require it (Hatch 1991, S562). Like the Ervin bill, the Hatch bill would apportion delegates in the same manner as does the electoral college.

The Ervin bill explicitly provided that the convention could propose amendments by a majority rather than by a two-thirds vote; the Hatch bill appears to contemplate this but does not explicitly say so. Although Hatch opposed the amendment designed to treat the District of Columbia as a state for purposes of representation in Congress, his proposal explicitly provides that "the people of the District of Columbia shall elect as many delegates as the whole number of Senators and Representatives to which said District would be entitled in the Congress if it were a State" (Hatch 1991, S564).

Both Ervin and Hatch accepted the doctrine of contemporary consensus as articulated in *Dillon v. Gloss* (1921). Accordingly, in addition to limiting the time span during which convention petitions were valid, both would permit states to rescind petitions for a convention or to rescind ratification of a proposed amendment up to the point where two-thirds of the states had ratified it. If adopted as legislation, such a rule might well apply to all amendments and not simply to those that were proposed by a convention.

Although both Ervin and Hatch believed that Congress was obligated to call a convention when it received the necessary number of applications, both sought to guard against a so-called runaway convention by allowing Congress to refuse to report amendments to the states that were proposed by a convention that exceeded its mandate. The Ervin bill was criticized for attempting to preclude judicial review of important questions related to this legisla-

tion ("Proposed Legislation" 1972, 1635–44). In contrast, the Hatch legislation specifically recognizes such judicial authority. Hatch thus rejects the notion that such matters are political questions beyond judicial cognizance.

If adopted, legislation on the constitutional convention would, like constitutional statutes in England, be considered "quasi-organic" legislation (Ervin 1968, 880). Even if not adopted by Congress, such proposals might be consulted in the event that states muster sufficient petitions to call a convention. Absent adoption of such legislation, such decisions will likely be made on an ad hoc political basis.

❖ *LESER V. GARNETT* (1922) ❖

In a test of contemporary arguments that there were limits on the amending process, Leser and others brought suit to strike the names of women from the voting list in Baltimore despite the adoption of the Nineteenth Amendment. In rejecting this attempt, the Court addressed three arguments.

The first argument was that the Nineteenth Amendment exceeded implicit constitutional limitations by altering the electorates of even those states that had not ratified the amendment, such as Maryland. Justice Louis Brandeis responded by noting the similarities in the language of the Fifteenth and Nineteenth Amendments. He argued that the former could not be valid and the latter invalid. In so ruling, Brandeis rejected the contention that the former amendment was a war measure "validated by acquiescence" (*Leser* 1922, 136) rather than through legitimate amending procedures.

A second argument was that some of the states included in the secretary of state's compilation of ratifying states should not have been counted because of provisions in their constitutions preventing such ratification. Brandeis responded by noting that "the function of a state legislature in ratifying a proposed amendment to the Federal Constitution, like the function of Congress in proposing the amendment, is a federal function derived from the Federal Constitution; and it transcends any limitations sought to be imposed by the people of a State" (*Leser* 1922, 137). Brandeis cited both *Hawke v. Smith* cases (1920) and the *National Prohibition* cases (1920) to buttress this argument.

The third argument was that ratifications by Tennessee and West Virginia were illegal because they violated the states' own rules of legislative procedure. In responding, Brandeis further ruled that "official notice to the Secretary, duly authenticated," that they had ratified "was conclusive upon him, and, being certified by his proclamation, is conclusive upon the courts" (*Leser* 1922, 137).

See also Constitutional Amendments, Limits on.

❖ LIMITS ON CONSTITUTIONAL ❖ AMENDMENTS

See Constitutional Amendments, Limits on.

❖ LIMITS ON WEALTH ❖ AND INCOME

Early in the twentieth century and again during the Great Depression, a number of members of Congress proposed amendments to limit personal wealth or income. In 1933, Washington Democratic Congressman Wesley Lloyd introduced an amendment to limit annual incomes to $1 million (Pizzigati 1992, 55), and Pennsylvania Democrat John Synder introduced an amendment to limit the amount of income derived from capital. The idea was especially appealing among those who considered themselves to be socialists, as well as among those who could be classified as utopian

thinkers. Edward Bellamy's widely read novel *Looking Backward* (1968), first published in 1888, foresaw a world in the year 2000 in which there was a relative equality of wealth. Some proponents of the progressive income tax were as motivated by the redistributive possibilities of such a tax as by its potential to raise revenue.

Once the Sixteenth Amendment was adopted, it was more common to propose use of the tax code to effect equalization of wealth or income than to propose amendments to this end. Thus, in his book *My First Days in the White House*, Louisiana's flamboyant Senator Huey P. Long speculated that his own Share the Wealth Program would be upheld by the Supreme Court (Long 1935, 134–35). Although Long's plans went through several alterations, he proposed limiting individual fortunes to $5 million and annual income or inheritance to $1 million. Long also proposed a guaranteed national income of $2,000 to $3,000 a year, "homesteads" for all Americans, and free college education for deserving youth (Williams 1970, 693). Share the Wealth Clubs advocating Long's ideas were quite popular for a time, although they were largely concentrated in the South (Williams 1970, 701). Pressure from Long's followers is believed to have pushed Franklin Roosevelt's own ideas on progressive taxation leftward (Christman 1985, xiv).

In recent years, the gap between the rich and the poor in the United States appears to have widened (Bradsher 1995, 1). Labor journalist Sam Pizzigati, concerned about this increasing gap, recently advanced a "10 times rule," or maximum wage. Under such a system, individuals would be limited to earning 10 times the minimum wage, with incomes above that amount being paid in taxes. Pizzigati believes that, in such circumstances, people would find it advantageous to donate or distribute assets above that needed to generate the maximum income and that such redistribution would result in a number of societal advantages. Pizzigati advocates beginning a campaign for such a program at the state level and then using those states as a base to call for a constitutional amendment to that end (1992, 134–36).

For Further Reading:
Pizzigati, Sam. 1994. "Salary Caps for Everyone!" *New York Times*, 28 August, 15.

❖ LINCOLN, ABRAHAM ❖
(1809–1865)

The election of Abraham Lincoln as the United States' sixteenth president helped precipitate the Civil War. His election in 1860 on a Republican platform committed to the view that slavery was immoral and should not be permitted to expand convinced Southern states that their cherished institution of slavery would be jeopardized if they remained in the Union.

In the Lincoln-Douglas debates, Lincoln had questioned the finality of the Supreme Court's decision in *Scott v. Sandford* (1857), which had ruled that the Missouri Compromise was illegal and thus allowed for the expansion of slavery into the territories (Johannsen 1965, 64–66). Prior to his inauguration, Lincoln worked behind the scenes with congressional Republicans to oppose the Crittenden Compromise, which would have given some recognition to slavery in the territories. Lincoln did, however, support the Corwin amendment, which would have guaranteed Southern states that slavery would not be abolished there without their consent.

In his first inaugural address, Lincoln distinguished between the "constitutional" right of amending the Constitution and the "revolutionary" right of dismembering it (J. Richardson 1908, 6:10). He further expressed support both for the Corwin amendment and for the possibility of a constitutional convention that might propose amendments to the Constitution.

On 1 January 1863, Lincoln issued the Emancipation Proclamation, freeing slaves in states that remained loyal to the Confederacy. Lincoln had announced his intention to issue this proclamation in September, after the Union victory at Antietam Creek in Maryland. In his annual message of 1862, Lincoln also proposed three amendments. They would have compensated slave owners in states abolishing the institution before 1900, given perpetual freedom to all slaves freed by the war and compensated owners loyal to the Union, and provided for voluntary slave colonization abroad (J. Richardson 1908, 6:136). These plans were largely ignored by Congress (Paludan 1994, 164).

The changes wrought by the Emancipation Proclamation made such gradualism impossible. In January 1864, Democratic Senator John Henderson of Missouri offered the first amendment in Congress to abolish slavery. Soon a passage from the Northwest Ordinance of 1787 had been formulated into the Thirteenth Amendment (Paludan 1994, 300). Lincoln strongly supported this amendment (Donald 1995, 553–54). Contrary to the custom that had been followed with all amendments other than the Corwin amendment, this amendment was sent to him for his signature before being sent to the states for their eventual ratification. It has been suggested that Lincoln may have signed partly "to wipe out the memory of the Corwin Amendment" (Bernstein with Agel 1993, 100).

See also Emancipation Proclamation; Thirteenth Amendment.

❖ *LIVERMORE V. WAITE* (1894) ❖

Developments in state law sometimes influence federal law. *Livermore v. Waite* is a California case that is frequently cited in discussions of the amending process. It is especially relevant to the issue of whether a constitution can be changed other than by its own procedures, as well as to possible limits on the amending process. The case involved an amendment ratified by the California state legislature for approval by state voters to transfer the state capital from Sacramento to San Jose. Adoption was to be contingent upon receipt of a donation of a minimum of 10 acres (of a site approved by the governor, secretary of state, and attorney general) and $1 million.

The Court distinguished the two methods of amendment provided in the California constitution. The power of a constitutional convention to offer amendments was declared to be limited only by the U.S. Constitution. By contrast, the procedure by which amendments were proposed by two-thirds majorities of both houses of the state legislature and subsequently sent to the people for ratification was declared to be a delegated power "to be strictly construed under the limitations by which it has been conferred" (*Livermore* 1894, 117–18). The Court observed that the state's constitution "can be neither revised nor amended except in the manner prescribed by itself, and the power which it has conferred upon the legislature in reference to proposed amendments, as well as to calling a convention, must be strictly pursued" (Livermore 1894, 117).

In this case, the Court struck down the proposed amendment because it did not become operational, as the California constitution appeared to require, upon popular approval but upon considerations not specified there. The Court concluded that "the amendment proposed substitutes for, or rather superadds to, the will of the people another will or judgment, without which its own will have no effect" (*Livermore* 1894, 123).

See also Constitutional Amendments, Limits on.

❖ *LOCHNER V. NEW YORK* (1905) ❖

Few cases have more epitomized an era of Supreme Court decision making or indicated the potential scope of Supreme Court decisions in interpreting (and thus effectively amending) the written Constitution than did this 1905 decision. At issue was a New York law limiting the work hours of bakers to 10 hours a day and six days a week.

Lochner, who operated a bakery, argued that the law violated his liberty of contract as protected by the due process clause of the Fourteenth Amendment. Writing for a 5-to-4 majority, Justice Rufus Peckham upheld this idea of substantive due process. Rejecting arguments that the baking industry was unhealthy, Peckham found that the state had exceeded its police powers in legislating for adults who were capable of protecting their own interests. He referred to New York's laws as "mere meddlesome interferences with the rights of the individual" (Lochner 1905, 61).

Justice John Marshall Harlan wrote a dissenting opinion in which he argued that courts should defer to legislative judgments in cases in which policy makers might disagree and that the Court's interpretations unduly widened the scope of the Fourteenth Amendment. Referring to a contemporary proponent of laissez-faire economics, Justice Oliver Wendell Holmes Jr. wrote a dissenting opinion in which he observed that "the Fourteenth Amendment does not enact Mr. Herbert Spencer's Social Statics" (Lochner 1905, 75).

In subsequent cases, the Court expanded on the idea of substantive due process to strike down laws providing for minimum wages and prohibiting child labor. These rulings prompted numerous proposals to amend the Constitution, but after Franklin Roosevelt introduced his court-packing plan in 1937, the Court shifted course and allowed such legislation to be adopted through ordinary legislative means.

See also Substantive Due Process.

For Further Reading:

Gillman, Howard. 1993. *The Constitution Besieged: The Rise and Demise of Lochner Era Police Powers Jurisprudence.* Durham, NC: Duke University Press.

Kens, Paul. 1990. *Judicial Power and Reform Politics: The Anatomy of* Lochner v. New York. Lawrence: University Press of Kansas.

❖ LOCKWOOD, HENRY C. ❖ (1839–1902)

Henry Lockwood wrote a book in 1884 that has been described as "a bestseller and an essential reference work for publicists of his time" (Pious 1978, 4). Although the title of the book, *The Abolition of the Presidency,* focused on the institution that Lockwood believed was most in need of reform, Lockwood also proposed sweeping reforms of the Senate and of state governments. Like other prominent would-be reformers of his day, Lockwood's model was the English constitution, the workings of whose executive Lockwood described as "nearer to the ideal of a representative government than any upon the face of the earth" (Lockwood 1884, 278).

Lockwood devoted much of his book to noting the flaws in the presidency and in those who had been elected to that office. Essentially, Lockwood believed that the presidency was an unwelcome vestige of monarchy. Lockwood outlined his proposals in his last three chapters. Opposed to the idea of state sovereignty, Lockwood placed himself squarely on the side of nationalism. As such, he suggested that the Senate should be abolished, both because it was "the strongest fulcrum of the 'residuary sovereignty' of the States" (Lockwood 1884, 283) and because he did not think that the advantages of a bicameral system outweighed its disadvantages. Moreover, Lockwood saw no need for the existence of states from which the senators were chosen. He thus cited with approval the proposal that David Brearly had made at the Constitutional Convention of 1787 to abolish the existing states and to divide the country into 13 equal parts (Lockwood 1884, 282–83).

In his last chapter, Lockwood advanced plans for abolishing the presidency, now adding the Articles of Confederation to Great Britain as a model. Under Lockwood's plan, the presidency would be replaced by an executive council chosen by Congress and headed by the secretary of state. Members would have seats in Congress, where they would be entitled to debate and to initiate legislation. The council could also dissolve Congress and appeal to the people when the government was deadlocked on an important issue. Congress would, in turn, have the right to remove cabinet members. Lockwood's anticipated result would be "responsible Council Government" (Lockwood 1884, 305).

In such a system, Congress would be sovereign. Lockwood therefore favored eliminating judicial review. The power of the courts would be limited to expounding and interpreting the laws (Lockwood 1884, 308).

Although he did not elaborate at great length, Lockwood clearly thought that other reforms were also desirable. Thus, in critiquing the current system, Lockwood noted that "church property is not taxed, [and] religious laws deface the statute-books." Similarly, he noted the "tendency towards moneyed aristocracy" and the fact that the secret ballot "opens the door to stupendous frauds." Lockwood specifically pointed to the virtual disenfranchisement of African Americans in the South (Lockwood 1884, 313–14).

However popular it was in its day, Lockwood's book appears to have had little permanent impact. Rather than abolishing the presidency, the institution has arguably been strengthened in the twentieth century. Moreover, the states, the Senate, and judicial review all remain vital parts of the present system.

❖ LOTTERIES ❖

One senator and two members of the House of Representatives introduced proposals from May 1890 to January 1892 for a constitutional amendment to prohibit lotteries. State-sponsored lotteries have been prominent during three periods in U.S. history—the colonial period to the early nineteenth century, after the Civil War, and from 1964 to the present (Clotfetter and Cook 1989, 42).

Apart from a lottery in 1776 to support the Continental Army and lotteries operated to finance projects in Washington, D.C., from 1792 to 1842, such activity has been sponsored by the states rather than by the national government (Clotfetter and Cook 1989, 36). The 1890s marked a period of revulsion against lotteries that was stimulated by abuses associated with the Louisiana Lottery Company, which had been established in 1868.

Although Congress never adopted an amendment, in 1890, it prohibited use of the mails to promote lotteries, and in 1895, it outlawed interstate transportation of lottery tickets. The Supreme Court upheld the latter law in *Champion v. Ames* (1895). Recent years have witnessed a rebirth of state-sponsored lotteries, with the desire for state revenues overcoming objections based on morals and concerns about the creation by the states of social problems associated with gambling.

❖ LUDLOW AMENDMENT ❖

See Initiative and Referendum.

❖ *LUTHER V. BORDEN* (1849) ❖

Luther v. Borden was important both in addressing the relationship between constitutional and revolutionary change and in developing the political question doctrine. Chief Justice Roger B. Taney wrote the majority decision. The case arose when Martin Luther brought a suit against Luther Martin for trespassing. Luther Martin had entered Martin Luther's house under authority of a declaration of martial law issued by the original charter government of Rhode Island. This declaration had been prompted by the establishment of a new government, under the direction of Thomas W. Dorr, which Martin Luther supported.

The problem arose largely from the fact that the Rhode Island charter, which the colonists had decided to continue with only minor modifications at the time of the American Revolution, did not specify any means of constitutional change. Although the charter government had severely limited the franchise, and Dorr's government may well have had the support of a majority of the citizens of Rhode Island, the Dorr government had come into being through extralegal means, and the charter government did not recognize its legitimacy. Thus, Daniel Webster argued on Luther Martin's behalf that although American government was built upon the consent of the people, such government also secured itself "against sudden changes by mere majorities," and such government "does not draw any power from tumultuous assemblages" (*Luther* 1849, 31).

In deciding the case, Taney focused on the guarantee clause in Article IV, Section 4 of the Constitution. He ruled that this clause delegated to Congress the power to determine whether a state government was republican and whether to render military assistance to a state government. Congress, in turn, had delegated the latter power to the president. In this case, although the president (John Tyler) had not actually rendered aid, his declaration of support for the charter government had caused the Dorr government to fold. Taney thus decided that some matters "turned upon political rights and political questions," and it was the Court's duty "not to pass beyond its appropriate sphere of action, and to take care not to involve itself in discussions which properly belong to other forums" (*Luther* 1849, 47).

In *Coleman v. Miller* (1939), the Court decided that certain questions surrounding the amending process were political questions, but the current status of this opinion is in some doubt. In *Baker v. Carr* (1962), the Supreme Court agreed that the issue of whether a government was or was not republican continued to be a political question. It also ruled that the issue of a state's legislative apportionment could be decided on the basis of the equal protection clause of the Fourteenth Amendment.

See also *Coleman v. Miller;* Political Questions.

For Further Reading:

Dennison, George M. 1976. *The Dorr War: Republicanism on Trial, 1831–1861.* Lexington: University Press of Kentucky.

❖ LYNCHING ❖

Over 5,000 people, most of whom were black, were lynched from the 1890s through the 1950s, often with the complicity of state and local officials (Ferrell 1986, 1). The U.S. House of Representatives spent substantial time debating antilynching legislation from 1918 to 1921, and it adopted an antilynching law in 1921 that died the following year in the Senate (Ferrell 1986, 110–300).

A key objection to such legislation centered on the issue of whether Congress had sufficient authority under the Thirteenth and Fourteenth Amendments to adopt such legislation or whether such laws interfered with state police powers under the Tenth Amendment. Republican Representative Henry Emerson of Ohio introduced an amendment in March 1919 that would have given explicit recognition to federal power in this area. Courts have subsequently recognized substantially broader congressional powers over a variety of subjects. Even in the absence of federal legislation, in cases such as *Moore v. Dempsey* (1923) they were able to rule that mob-dominated trials violated the due process clause of the Fourteenth Amendment.

M

❖

McCulloch v. Maryland remains one of the most important decisions to have been written by Chief Justice John Marshall and, in fact, by any justice. By establishing the doctrine of implied powers and the principle of broad constitutional construction, this decision did much to obviate the need for many amendments that have been introduced to expand congressional powers. By the same token, by recognizing the broad reach of such powers, the decision has arguably enhanced the importance of explicit restraints on such powers, such as those found in the Bill of Rights and elsewhere in the Constitution.

McCulloch arose when the state of Maryland attempted to levy a tax on a branch of the national bank established in Baltimore. The Court had to decide whether the bank—first established after vigorous debate in the Washington administration and subsequently reestablished during Madison's presidency—was constitutional. The second issue centered on the legitimacy of Maryland's attempt to tax the bank.

In sanctioning the bank, Marshall developed the idea of implied powers. Although the power to incorporate a bank was not specifically granted in the Constitution, neither was it prohibited. In reserving powers to the states, the Tenth Amendment omitted the word "expressly," thus specifying that the powers "not delegated to the United States, nor prohibited to the States, are reserved to the States or to the people," and thus not precluding the idea of implied powers. Moreover, the right to create a corporation such as a bank was not an end in itself but a means to other ends, or powers, that were designated in the Constitution.

Specifying that under Article I, Section 8 of the Constitution Congress could exercise all powers that were "necessary and proper," Marshall argued that the framers had intended to expand rather than restrict such authority. In context, the word "necessary" neither denoted absolute necessity nor limited Congress to the most restrictive means. As Marshall observed, "The provision is made in a constitution intended to endure for ages to come, and, consequently, to be adapted to the various *crises* of human affairs (*McCulloch* 1819, 415). In justifying the creation of the bank, Marshall wrote, "Let the end be legitimate, let it be within the scope of the constitution, and all means which are appropriate, which are plainly adapted to that end, which are not prohibited, but consist with the letter and spirit of the constitution, are constitutional (*McCulloch* 1819, 421).

In upholding national sovereignty over state sovereignty, Marshall ruled that Maryland had no right to tax the bank. Such a power would inappropriately give parts of the Union, the states, the power to destroy the whole, the Union.

Virginia's John Taylor of Caroline and Judge Spencer Roane severely criticized

McCulloch, and the state proposed an amendment to create an institution other than the Supreme Court for resolving conflicts between the national government and the states (Levy 1995, 428). Long after this proposal has been largely forgotten, the Court continues to interpret constitutional powers broadly enough that the most important restrictions on such powers continue to be explicit constitutional restrictions rather than the lack of explicit constitutional grants of power.

See also Tenth Amendment.

❖ MACDONALD, DWIGHT ❖ (1906–1982)

On the magazine's thirty-fifth anniversary, the editors of *Esquire* asked journalist Dwight Macdonald to draw up a set of proposals to bring the Constitution up to date. His article was a mix of serious proposals and hyperbole.

Macdonald began by proposing that the presidency should be abolished in favor of a chairman to be chosen, as in a parliamentary system, by the majority party in Congress. This chairman would serve for six years or until his party lost a major vote in Congress. This proposal also would have eliminated the electoral college, the vice presidency, and the system of primaries. Macdonald also hoped that it would serve to clip the power and pretensions of the chief executive—and also the temptation to assassinate him. Macdonald proposed that terms of members of the House of Representatives should be lengthened to five years and that members of neither the House nor the Senate should be required to be residents of the states that elected them.

Macdonald proposed a number of social reforms. All males between the ages of 18 and 30 would be conscripted to two years' service either in the military or in "nonmilitary Work of Social Value"—the draftees'

choice (Macdonald 1968, 145). The government would establish a negative income tax to bring all citizens up to a "minimum Health & Decency Standard"; this tax would be paid "without regard to Work, Moral Character or any other Consideration except Need" (146). Macdonald would establish tribunes, or ombudsmen, in each congressional district. He would also set up history preservation and nature preservation commissions to protect historical and environmental sites, limit the number of U.S. soldiers overseas to one-fourth of 1 percent of the population (except by a four-fifths vote of both houses of Congress), and limit military expenditures to 3 percent of the gross national product. Macdonald also wanted to abolish the space program and reconfigure cities and states into more functional units.

An accompanying piece on the Bill of Rights by Karl E. Meyers was an eclectic mix of reforms that would not, like Macdonald's, require changes in governmental structure. He thought that the government should be responsible for providing a number of social and economic rights, such as access to dramatic performances, public parks, meals, and public transit. He also favored eliminating electronic eavesdropping and supersonic aircraft and curtailing the right to bear arms.

❖ MACDONALD, WILLIAM ❖ (1863–1938)

Journalist and college professor William MacDonald offered his proposals for constitutional reform shortly after the Wilson administration (MacDonald 1921, 1922). His central objective was the establishment of responsible parliamentary government, and toward this end, he offered a critique and a comprehensive plan of reform intended to reconfigure the federal system and all three branches of the federal government (Vile 1991c, 57–59).

Under MacDonald's scheme, the presidency would be significantly altered, with the president responsible for designating a member of Congress to form a cabinet and, if successful, to be premier. The premier and his cabinet would exercise most governmental powers, and they would resign when they lost congressional support. In cases in which a new cabinet could not be formed, the president would dissolve Congress and call for new elections.

MacDonald proposed to delete the current requirement that the president be natural born, to replace the electoral college with a system of direct election, to transfer the directorship of the military forces and the negotiation of treaties to the cabinet, to eliminate the president's power of appointment and removal, and to take away the president's power to recommend legislation. MacDonald's plan would also vest the power to execute laws in the cabinet, eliminate the presidential veto, provide for new elections in cases of presidential vacancy, and formulate a provision to deal with presidential disability (MacDonald 1922, 69–89).

MacDonald proposed maintaining a bicameral Congress but would fix uniform four-year terms and a minimum age of 25 years for members of both houses. He would eliminate the custom whereby representatives must be residents of their districts, abolish secret congressional sessions, allow both the Senate and the House to ratify treaties, and create a more structured budget system in which both bills raising revenue and those appropriating money would originate in the House. Congress would be given expanded powers over corporations, immigration and naturalization, education, marriage and divorce, the budget, economic control (including possible nationalizations), and internal improvements, and members would be subject to recall (MacDonald 1922, 90–116). MacDonald also favored a system of uniform requirements for voting in federal elections and wanted the House to represent both population and occupations and professions. MacDonald also favored the proliferation of political parties.

MacDonald wanted the Constitution to delineate more clearly the respective roles of the state and national governments. He thought that Congress should be able to ascertain whether a state government is republican and deny it representation, and he thought that state citizens should have a right to petition Congress on the subject (MacDonald 1922, 155). He wanted to guarantee protections for freedom of religion, assembly, and petition and for the right to bear arms against abridgments by the states as well as by the national government. He also thought that state militias were anachronisms that needed to be eliminated. Interestingly, MacDonald believed that the Eighteenth Amendment (prohibition) was an undue infringement on state police powers.

Under MacDonald's scheme, judges would be appointed by the premier and the cabinet and would be subject to removal not only by impeachment but also at the request of both houses (MacDonald 1922, 181). He wanted to created a system of administrative courts. He also wanted to control the exercise of judicial power over receiverships, cut back on the use of injunctions, and officially recognize the rights of the courts to declare a law to be unconstitutional.

MacDonald proposed that Congress should pass a resolution putting itself on record as favoring a constitutional convention and inviting states to send petitions to this end (MacDonald 1922, 224). Alternatively, arguing that the provisions in Article V might "properly be viewed as permissive and selective, not as exclusive" (MacDonald 1922, 227), he suggested that Congress could call a constitutional convention on its own.

❖ MCKEE, HENRY S. (1868–1956) ❖

California businessman Henry McKee presented his plans for political, economic, and educational reform in a book published in 1933. Like Karl Marx, with whom he otherwise shared little in common, McKee predicted that without reform, the next economic depression was likely to lead to complete political breakdown. Perhaps because he was a businessman, most of McKee's political solutions were borrowed from earlier thinkers such as Woodrow Wilson and Gamaliel Bradford.

McKee was an opponent of government by committee and a proponent of strong executive power. Like Wilson, McKee believed that by forcing men to articulate and defend their views publicly, a parliamentary system would attract men of greater talents. Accompanying a strengthened cabinet would be a type of "question hour," during which members of the cabinet would have to defend their views before Congress. McKee believed that such debates would expose demagogic appeals and flawed programs, in which category he placed the progressive income tax and inheritance taxes.

McKee favored more centralized governmental control over economic problems, subject again to the increased scrutiny and accountability that a parliamentary system would bring. McKee favored creating a single national bank in place of the system of 12 federal reserve institutions. The central bank should, in turn, be headed by a governor, "not by a Board or Committee" (McKee 1933, 91). McKee also favored the establishment of a cabinet department to head transportation and a similar cabinet office to deal with retailing and extractive industries. He believed that businesses would welcome such control, as long as it was accountable.

Although it would not have required a constitutional amendment, McKee's solution to the problems of poverty and unemployment was perhaps his most novel. He viewed both problems as essentially moral problems, resulting from poor personal finance. He therefore proposed that public schools should teach children to keep expenditures within income and to save at least 10 percent of their income a year. As has been observed elsewhere (Vile 1991c, 72), however modern his views of increased governmental control might seem, McKee took a dim view of the values of modern consumer society, stressing instead more traditional values of saving and thrift.

❖ MADISON, JAMES (1751–1836) ❖

Few individuals have had as profound an influence on the formation and understanding of the U.S. Constitution and the Bill of Rights as did James Madison, the nation's fourth president. Madison also wrote and thought profoundly about the constitutional amending process.

In addition to taking the most complete notes of the proceedings of the Constitutional Convention of 1787, Madison is believed to be one of the guiding forces behind the Virginia plan, the first major plan to be proposed there. This plan indicated that provision should be made for "amendment of the Articles of Union whensoever it shall seem necessary," and it specified that the consent of Congress should not be necessary, but it was otherwise nonspecific (Vile 1992, 27). Madison subsequently supported a proposal, however, that would funnel amendments through the national legislature, apparently opposing the state-requested convention mechanism largely on the basis of practical considerations (Weber 1989, 36).

At the convention's end, Madison was one of the Constitution's most outspoken and articulate defenders. When Patrick Henry argued at the Virginia state ratifying convention that the amending process in Article V was too difficult, Madison pointed out that the mechanism was much easier than the one under the Articles of Confederation.

Madison's most memorable defense of the new Constitution, however, came in his role as one of the three authors of the *Federalist Papers*, who wrote under the name of Publius. In *Federalist* No. 38, although acknowledging that it was not perfect, Madison defended the new Constitution as being infinitely better than the Articles of Confederation. In *Federalist* No. 43, Madison argued that the amending process "guards equally against that extreme facility, which would render the Constitution too mutable; and that extreme difficulty, which might perpetuate its discovered faults" (Hamilton, Madison, and Jay 1961, 278).

Federalist Nos. 49 and 50 may well constitute Madison's deepest and most original thinking on the idea of constitutional change. His reasoning there is especially interesting, because it was designed in part as a response to a proposal made by Madison's close friend, fellow Virginian and later fellow Democratic-Republican Party leader Thomas Jefferson. In *Federalist* No. 49, Madison opposed Jefferson's suggested plan that would enable two of three branches of the government to call a convention for altering the Constitution. Focusing on the advantages of stability, Madison honed in on the stabilizing advantages of inculcating "veneration" for the Constitution (Levinson 1990b). Madison noted that "as every appeal to the people would carry an implication of some defect in the government, frequent appeals would, in great measure, deprive the government of that veneration which time bestows on everything, and without which perhaps the wisest and freest governments would not possess the requisite stability" (Hamilton et al. 1961, 314). Madison offered similar arguments in private correspondence in regard to Jefferson's idea that the Constitution should be rewritten each generation (Vile 1992, 64–65). Similarly rejecting periodic appeals to the people in *Federalist* No. 50, Madison drew largely from the negative experiences that Pennsylvania had encountered with the Council of Censors.

The most persistent criticism of the new Constitution was that it lacked a bill of rights. Initially little concerned about this omission, Madison appears to have been persuaded in part by arguments from Thomas Jefferson and in part by his fear that if Federalist supporters of the Constitution did not make such a promise to the Anti-Federalists, these opponents would call a second convention before the work of the first one was ratified (Weber 1989; Finkelman 1991). Subsequently elected to the House of Representatives, Madison took the lead in formulating and shepherding the Bill of Rights through the First Congress. Madison structured the Bill of Rights so that it would focus primarily on individual rights rather than on possible structural changes to the yet untried national government.

As president, Madison recommended an amendment designed to permit the national government to undertake internal improvements. When no such amendment was adopted, he vetoed such legislation. By the same token, during his term, Madison approved the reestablishment of the national bank that he had previously argued was unconstitutional; in this case, he argued that established precedents were more important here than his own initial judgment.

In 1829–1830, Madison participated in the convention that met to redraw the Virginia state constitution. His final words to his country were an appeal that "the Union of States be cherished and perpetual" (Meyers 1973, 576).

For Further Reading:
Banning, Lance. 1995. *The Sacred Fire of Liberty: James Madison and the Founding of the Federal Republic.* Ithaca, NY: Cornell University Press.

Matthews, Richard K. 1995. *If Men Were Angels: James Madison and the Heartless Empire of Reason.* Lawrence: University Press of Kansas.

Miller, William Lee. 1992. *The Business of May Next: James Madison and the Founding*. Charlottesville: University Press of Virginia.

Morgan, Robert J. 1988. *James Madison on the Constitution and the Bill of Rights*. New York: Greenwood Press.

Rutland, Robert A. 1987. *James Madison: The Founding Father*. New York: Macmillan.

❖ MARBURY, WILLIAM ❖

During the Progressive Era, Maryland attorney William Marbury was one of the most prominent proponents of the argument that there were inherent limits on the power to amend the U.S. Constitution (Vile 1992, 157–71). Marbury presented his arguments in at least two law review articles questioning the legitimacy of the Eighteenth and Nineteenth Amendments (Marbury 1919, 1920; for response, see Frierson 1920). He also served as an attorney for the state of Maryland in *Myers v. Anderson* (1915)—unsuccessfully seeking to uphold the constitutionality of the state's grandfather clause against provisions of the Fifteenth Amendment—and *Leser v. Garnett* (1922)—also unsuccessfully questioning the legitimacy of the Nineteenth Amendment.

Marbury's arguments, like those of contemporary Selden Bacon, were built partly on now-discredited views of state sovereignty. In recent years, the idea that there might be judicially enforceable inherent limitations on the amending process has been revived by individuals such as Walter Murphy, who are more concerned about the protection of individual rights.

See also Bacon, Selden.

❖ *MARBURY V. MADISON* (1803) ❖

In Britain, Parliament is considered to be supreme. Because it exercises such legisla-tive sovereignty and because the country has no single written constitution, a formal amendment process is not necessary. By contrast, in the United States, the Constitution is supreme over ordinary acts of legislation. If Congress wishes to alter the Constitution, it must proceed via the Article V amending processes.

In large part, this system emerged because of the extraordinarily important decision that Chief Justice John Marshall authored in *Marbury v. Madison* (1803). Marbury brought his case to the Supreme Court after Thomas Jefferson's new secretary of state, James Madison, refused to deliver a commission to Marbury, who had been appointed a justice of the peace by the outgoing administration of John Adams.

Marshall agreed that Marbury was entitled to his commission and that laws provide a remedy in such circumstances. Marshall decided, however, that the remedy was not a writ of mandamus, a judicial order issued to an executive official issuing from the Court. He reasoned that the provision of the Judiciary Act of 1789 that appeared to grant this power to the Court was flawed because Article III of the Constitution clearly limited the original jurisdiction of the Supreme Court to certain circumstances, of which this was not one. In deciding that the Court had the responsibility of exercising judicial review and of striking this provision of the law, Marshall, a Federalist appointee, thus avoided a direct confrontation with the new Democratic-Republican administration.

In outlining his case for judicial construction of the Constitution, Marshall noted that the creation of a constitution was "a very great exertion," not "to be frequently repeated" (*Marbury* 1803, 176). He further said that the Constitution was "either a superior paramount law, unchangeable by ordinary means, or it is on a level with ordinary legislative acts, and like other acts, is alterable when the legislature shall please to alter it" (*Marbury* 1803, 177). Arguing that it was "emphatically the province and duty of the judicial department to say what the law is" (*Marbury* 1803, 177), Marshall thus ruled that he must be bound by the Constitution rather than by the Judiciary Act.

In assuming a power not directly stated in, but arguably implied by, the Constitution, Marshall at once limited changes that Congress could make in constitutional understandings and ensured that the judicial branch would play a big role in interpreting that document. If some institution in government did not have this power of interpretation, it might be necessary to resort to the constitutional amending process far more frequently.

See also Marshall, John.

For Further Reading:

Alfange, Dean Jr. 1994. "*Marbury v. Madison* and Original Understandings of Judicial Review: In Defense of Traditional Wisdom." In *The Supreme Court Review, 1993*. Chicago: University of Chicago Press.

Clinton, Robert L. 1989. Marbury v. Madison *and Judicial Review*. Lawrence: University Press of Kansas.

❖ MARRIAGE, DIVORCE, AND PARENTING ❖

States are responsible for enacting most laws related to domestic relations, including marriage and divorce. Article IV, Section 1 provides, however, that states shall give "Full Faith and Credit . . . to the public Acts, Records, and judicial Proceedings of every other State." Moreover, Article IV, Section 3 of the Constitution entrusts Congress with the power to "make all needful Rules and Regulations respecting the Territory or other Property belonging to the United States."

In exercise of this power, Congress adopted several laws in the nineteenth century aimed at the practice of polygamy, which, since 1852, had been sanctioned by the Mormon Church and practiced by church leaders (G. Larson 1971, 37). Congressional laws included the Morrill Act of 1862, restricting polygamy; a bill sponsored by Vermont Republican Luke Porter Poland in 1874 strengthening federal judicial power in the Utah Territory; and the Edmunds bill of 1874 (strengthened by the Tucker amendment in 1887), which was especially hard on polygamists and restricted their political participation (G. Larson 1971, 58–59; Peterson 1977, 102).

The U.S. Supreme Court unanimously upheld the constitutionality of such laws in *Reynolds v. United States* (1879), the first case in which it ever ruled on the First Amendment. In upholding Reynolds's conviction for polygamy, the Court said that although the federal government could not legislate belief, it could regulate conduct.

Judging from the number of amending proposals that were introduced in Congress, as well as by the fact that Utah was not admitted into the Union as a state until January 1896, after Mormon Church leaders had renounced polygamy (Lyman 1986), polygamy stirred substantial national concern. In part, that concern was motivated by the belief that polygamy, like slavery, was a relic of barbarism. President Ulysses S. Grant thus noted in his seventh annual message in 1875:

> That polygamy should exist in a free, enlightened, and Christian country, without the power to punish so flagrant a crime against decency and morality seems preposterous. True there is no law to sustain this unnatural vice; but what is needed is a law to punish it as a crime, and at the same time to fix the status of the innocent children, the offspring of this system, and of the possibly innocent plural wives. But as an institution polygamy should be banished from the land. (J. Richardson 1908, 7:355)

Republican Representative Julius Caesar Burrows of Michigan introduced the first amendment designed to restrict polygamy in 1879, with more than 20 such proposals following in each successive decade through the 1920s. From 1906 to 1913, 16 states applied for a convention to deal with this issue. Most amendments introduced in Congress specifically sought to outlaw polygamy, but some were phrased in terms of allowing Congress to make uniform rules on marriage and divorce or of prohibiting polygamists from assuming public office. From the 1930s on, the introduction of such proposals slowed but did not end completely.

Absent such an amendment, states continue to regulate most family matters within their jurisdictions, with none now sanctioning polygamy. A number of federal court decisions have, however, somewhat limited state regulation of domestic matters. The most notable cases have been *Griswold v. Connecticut* (1965), which recognized a right of marital privacy and provided access to contraceptives; *Loving v. Virginia* (1968), which struck down state restrictions on interracial marriage; *Roe v. Wade* (1973), which struck down most laws restricting access to abortion; and *Zablocki v. Redhail* (1978), which struck down a state law forbidding a noncustodial parent who was delinquent in child support from remarrying. Also, since passage of the Mann Act (also known as the White Slave Act) in 1910, the national government has selectively prosecuted individuals who have transported women across state lines for immoral purposes (Langum 1994).

Many states are now contemplating whether, under the "full faith and credit" clause of Article IV of the Constitution, they would have to recognize gay marriages if they are performed in states that sanction them. Such questions have been raised by the possibility that courts in Hawaii will soon use the equal protection clause of the Fourteenth Amendment to strike down that state's laws against same-sex marriages (D'Amato 1995).

On another family issue, in 1995 and 1996 "parental rights amendments" were introduced in a majority of states. Such amendments would alter state constitutions to provide that "the rights of parents to direct the upbringing and education of their children shall not be infringed" (Lawton 1996, 57). At present, proponents of such rights have focused on legislation rather than on amendment at the federal level. Republican Senator Charles Grassley of Iowa and Republican Representative Steve Largent of Oklahoma have proposed a Parental Rights and Responsibility Act to limit governmental regulation of family life absent a "compelling state interest." The bill focuses on four main areas—education, health care, discipline, and religious training (Lawton 1996, 57).

❖ MARSHALL, JOHN (1755–1835) ❖

No one has had a greater impact on the interpretation of the U.S. Constitution than John Marshall. Marshall fought during the Revolutionary War and, although he did not attend the Constitutional Convention of 1787, served as a delegate to the Virginia ratifying convention. As a prominent Federalist, Marshall served as John Adams's secretary of state and was subsequently appointed to the Supreme Court, where he was chief justice from 1801 to 1835.

Marshall significantly enhanced the prestige of the Supreme Court. During his long tenure, it became customary for the Court to issue majority opinions (most of which he authored) rather than, as previously, for each justice to write separately. Much to the frustration of the Democratic-Republicans, Marshall was generally able to mass even their appointees behind his decisions supporting strong national powers—for example, *Cohens v. Virginia* (1821)—and establishing the authority of the Court.

These are few areas of constitutional law on which Marshall did not have an impact. One of his most important contributions was in the area of judicial review. By asserting the right of the judiciary "to say what the law is" in *Marbury v. Madison* (1803), Marshall made it possible on many occasions for the Court to initiate changes in constitutional interpretation and to apply the Constitution to new circumstances without the need for constitutional amendments (Cahn 1954, 19). Indeed, in *Marbury*, Marshall specifically noted that the creation of a new government "is a very great exertion, nor can it, nor ought it, to be frequently repeated." Similarly, in *McCulloch v. Maryland* (1819), in upholding the constitutionality of the national bank, Marshall used the necessary and proper clause to argue for a broad interpretation of the Constitution. In so doing, he distinguished such a broad charter intended to endure for generations from more prolix legal codes that should be interpreted more strictly.

Marshall was a strong proponent of vested rights, most notably in cases such as *Fletcher v. Peck* (1810) and *Dartmouth College v. Woodward* (1819), in which he gave a broad reading to the contract clause. Similarly, Marshall upheld broad national authority over interstate commerce, especially in *Gibbons v. Ogden* (1824), where he used the grant of a federal license to a steamship to strike down a conflicting state monopoly over navigation in its waters.

Although Marshall generally chartered a bold course in constitutional interpretation, his decision in *Barron v. Baltimore* (1833) limited the application of the Bill of Rights to the national government. This interpretation stood until 1868, when the adoption of the Fourteenth Amendment led to renewed questions about the scope of such rights, most of which have subsequently been applied to the states via the due process clause of this amendment.

Marshall's vigorous tenure on the Court prompted numerous amending proposals to clip the federal judiciary, but like the efforts to convict Marshall's colleague Justice Samuel Chase on charges of impeachment, they came to nothing. When Marshall left the Court, it was well situated as a coordinate branch of the national government, with power to interpret the law and even to strike down laws it judged to be in conflict with the Constitution.

For Further Reading:
Beveridge, Albert J. 1916. *The Life of John Marshall.* 4 vols. Boston: Houghton Mifflin.

Newmyer, R. Kent. 1968. *The Supreme Court Under Marshall and Taney.* New York: Thomas Y. Crowell.

White, G. Edward. 1991. *The Marshall Court and Cultural Change 1815–1835.* New York: Oxford University Press.

❖ MEDICAL CARE ❖

Among advanced industrial nations, the United States is one of the few that relies primarily on private medical insurance rather than on government-financed health care. Moreover, although the Constitution guarantees many political rights, it makes no explicit provision for social and economic rights.

The 1940s, the 1970s, and the early 1990s all witnessed attempts to adopt national health insurance, but each effort failed (Laham 1993, 1–6). President Lyndon Johnson did succeed in 1965 in getting Congress to adopt programs for the poor (Medicaid) and the elderly (Medicare).

In October 1991 and again in February 1993, Democratic Representative Pete Stark of California, chair of the Health Subcommittee of the Ways and Means Committee, introduced an amendment that would have granted U.S. citizens a right to health care and granted Congress power to enforce this right. Although health care has not been so established as a constitutional right, current obstacles to national health insurance are political rather than legal.

❖ MERRIAM, CHARLES ❖
(1874–1953)

Charles Merriam was a political science professor at the University of Chicago who served from 1924 to 1925 as president of the American Political Science Association. In 1931, he published a book entitled *The Written Constitution and the Unwritten Attitude*. In this book, he discussed the process of constitutional change as well as several concrete contemporary proposals for such alterations (Vile 1991c, 65–66).

Merriam's main thesis was that provisions in constitutions were often ineffective if not supported by public opinion. The chief threat to modern government was not in "*lack of stability, but lack of mobility,* failure to make prompt adjustments to the new era in industry and science" (Merriam 1931, 25). Merriam was particularly impressed by the growth of cities, whose increases in population often were not reflected in state apportionment schemes. He also thought that states had lost significant power to the national government and suggested the feasibility of recognizing certain large cities as states.

Generally, Merriam seemed receptive to the idea of further alterations in the relation between the nation and the states. In addition, although he thought that there was little chance that the United States would adopt a parliamentary system, he did suggest that there were no obstacles to allowing members of the cabinet to appear before, or participate in debates within, Congress (Merriam 1931, 74). At a time prior to *United States v. Classic* (1941), when the Court had limited federal oversight over primary elections (*Newberry v. United States* [1921]), Merriam suggested that an amendment might be adopted to provide greater uniformity in such elections (Merriam 1931, 81). In a theme prominent in the wake of the Senate rejection of U.S. participation in the League of Nations, Merriam also favored altering the requirement that treaties be adopted by two-thirds votes of the Senate.

❖ MIGRATORY BIRDS ❖

In June 1911, Republican Senator George McLean of Connecticut introduced an amendment to give Congress power to protect migratory birds. Even without such explicit constitutional authority, in March 1913, Congress adopted legislation that McLean sponsored to regulate migratory birds (Lofgren 1975, 79). U.S. district court decisions in *United States v. Shauver* (1914) and *United States v. McCullagh* (1915) found that such legislation infringed on powers reserved to the states by the Tenth Amendment, and the federal government decided not to appeal to the Supreme Court.

Congress then entered into a treaty with Great Britain in 1916, providing for the protection of birds flying between the United States and Canada, and adopted legislation implementing this treaty in 1918. In a decision written by Justice Oliver Wendell Holmes Jr., the Court upheld the constitutionality of this treaty and accompanying legislation in *Missouri v. Holland* (1920).

Although the Court has subsequently qualified the treaty-making power in cases such as *Reid v. Covert* (1957), it has generally given more expansive readings to congressional authority under the commerce clause. Such readings suggest that no amendment is needed for Congress to continue its regulation of migratory birds.

❖ MILITIA ❖

When they ratified the Constitution, a number of states proposed amendments calling for the prohibition of standing armies or for state regulation of the militia. Despite such pleas, the only mention of militias in the Bill of Rights is contained in the Second Amendment in connection with the right to bear arms.

After some New England states declined to allow their militias to participate in the War of 1812, Ohio Representative (and later President) William Henry Harrison introduced amendments to give Congress power concurrent with the states to provide militia training (Ames 1896, 270–71). In 1864, Democratic Senator Willard Saulsburg of Delaware introduced a series of proposals that would have permitted slavery to continue in the South. One provision stated that the people should have certain rights against the militia.

See also Second Amendment.

❖ MILLER, ARTHUR S. ❖ (1917–1988)

Arthur Miller, a professor emeritus at George Washington University, presented his ideas for major constitutional change in a book published in the year of the bicentennial of the U.S. Constitution (A. Miller 1987). This book reflected views presented in an earlier article (A. Miller 1984). Miller wrote out of the conviction that there was an increasing disjunction between the United States' formal written constitution and the "secret" constitution by which it was actually governed. Much like critics from the Progressive Era, Miller believed that propertied elites wielded true power in American society (Vile 1991c, 143–45).

Miller began his chapter on proposed reforms by listing five major proposals. First,

he wanted Congress to have the power to make all laws needed "to provide for and maintain an environment conducive to the attainment of a sustainable society." This would include the power "to achieve an optimum population, to control and diffuse the threat of nuclear war, and to control environmental degradation" (A. Miller 1987, 105). Second, Congress should have authority "to provide for and maintain the reasonable satisfaction of human needs and fulfillment of human desires." Specifically, Miller wanted Congress to be responsible for providing "sufficient meaningful job opportunities for all who are able to work" (A. Miller 1987, 105). Third, Congress should be able to check excessive presidential and bureaucratic power. To this end, Miller wanted to establish a council of state with which the president would have to discuss his decisions; Miller also advocated increased use of the legislative veto. Fourth, Miller wanted to expand the Supreme Court's original jurisdiction so that any voter could bring a suit to "determine the validity of allegations that Congress had failed in any of its duties" (A. Miller 1987, 105). Fifth, Miller proposed rewriting the Constitution so that it applied not only to the government but also "to any societal group that exercises substantial power over individuals." Such groups would include "the supercorporations, the major trade unions, churches, farmers' leagues, [and] professional associations" (A. Miller 1987, 106). Miller, who was highly critical of nationalism, also wanted the Constitution altered so as to recognize the United States' close relations with other nations.

Believing that the idea of a parliamentary system was meritorious, Miller made six additional proposals. He proposed making Congress a unicameral body of 100 members; dividing the presidency into a separate head of government and head of state; strengthening political parties so that they would have greater control over members of Congress; substituting 10 or 12 regional governments for the existing 50 states; recognizing "supercorporations" in the Constitution and bringing greater power to bear against them; and, consistent with his earlier pleas for judicial activism (A. Miller 1982), expanding the role of the Supreme Court to take cases against both the two political branches and "private governments" (A. Miller 1987, 123). Miller hoped to transform the Constitution from a collection of negative prohibitions into a set of more affirmative guarantees.

There have been few proposals that are more far-reaching, or more politically unlikely, than Miller's.

❖ MILLER, JEREMY M. (1954–) ❖

In the year the nation celebrated the bicentennial of the U.S. Constitution, Jeremy M. Miller, a professor at Western State University College of Law, wrote an article offering a new constitution for consideration (J. Miller 1987). In the essay accompanying this proposal, Miller argued that the Constitution should embody natural law and that, consistent with libertarian principles, it should avoid "paternalistic legislation" (J. Miller 1987, 221). Miller also argued that the Constitution should further the values of truth, dignity, equality, and fundamental fairness.

Such values were incorporated into Miller's expanded preamble, which explicitly included a number of the principles of the Declaration of Independence and specifically invoked "the Supreme Judge of the World" (J. Miller 1987, 226). Article I of Miller's constitution was an expanded version of the Bill of Rights that applied limits to "federal, state, and municipal governments" (J. Miller 1987, 226). Much more detailed than the current Bill of Rights, the provisions for religious freedom would specifically prohibit either the use of "government monies" for or "government endorsement of any religion"

(J. Miller 1987, 227). It also distinguished between religious belief and religious conduct and specified that "a short prayer to God, as 'God,' is not a government endorsement of religion" (J. Miller 1987, 227). Similarly, provisions for freedom of speech prohibited "prior licensing" but allowed reasonable "time, place, and manner restrictions" (J. Miller 1987, 227). The right to bear arms included the right to own and carry "non-automatic pistols and non-automatic rifles" (J. Miller 1987, 228). Traffic regulations were to be entrusted to unarmed personnel; most abortions, dissections of the dead, and mechanical organ transplants were to be limited; judicial procedures and warrant requirements were to be made much more detailed; and juries were to be composed of seven persons.

Article II outlined citizen duties. These included the duty of males aged 17 and older to be subject to the military draft, the duty of families to find "gainful employment" (J. Miller 1987, 232), and the duty of losing plaintiffs to pay double a defendant's attorney's fees. Amendment procedures were also included in this section. All laws were to be open to such alterations. The exclusive method of change was to be for two-thirds of the states to call conventions (each state supplying a single delegate), proposals from which would subsequently become part of the Constitution when ratified by a majority of those voting in two-thirds of the states—a provision that appears to allow amendments to be adopted by less than a majority.

Article III outlined the three branches of government, "executive, parliamentary, and judicial" (J. Miller 1987, 233). The president would serve a three-year term, to be followed by possible reelection to a six-year term and subsequent two-year terms. The president would be elected by popular vote (with a runoff required when no one received a majority) and would share the power to nominate federal judges with the two houses of Congress and the Constitutional Court. Given increased powers over the budget, the president would have an item veto, power to hold a national lottery when bankruptcy threatened, and instructions to keep income taxes from 2 to 15 percent of individual income.

The parliament, like today's Congress, would consist of a House and a Senate, each state to have one senator and from one to three representatives, depending on its population. Members of the House would serve a maximum of two three-year terms. A four-fifths vote of both houses would be required to overturn decisions by the Constitutional Court on matters of constitutional interpretation, and majorities of both houses would ratify treaties.

The judicial system would be organized like the current one, with membership on the Constitutional Court specifically set at nine members, and judges serving 12-year terms. Given power to interpret the Constitution, the Constitutional Court was to be "bound by its letter and by its spirit" (J. Miller 1987, 237).

Miller included neither federal protections for voting rights nor an equal protection clause, and he has been criticized for writing a constitution that, because of "the undue specificity of some sections," was too much like a legal code (Knipprath 1987, 253–54). By the same token, his proposal omits a number of powers (for example, over the post office and copyrights) currently entrusted to Congress. Noting this, a critic said that Miller's plan "looks like a patchwork quilt, not a balanced, patterned tapestry" (Knipprath 1987, 256). Another critic suggested that part of the problem is that because Miller presented his ideas in an article rather than a book, he did not, like authors of numerous other proposed constitutions, have adequate space both to outline and to justify his numerous additions to and departures from the current Constitution (Vile 1991c, 148).

❖ MINIMUM WAGES ❖

Like the related problem of child labor, minimum wages were often associated with the so-called sweating system, under which laborers were employed for subsistence wages in large factories or unsanitary conditions. Such issues came into prominence with the rise of U.S. industrialization. Because of their position in the economy, women were inordinately affected by such conditions (Hart 1994, 64).

The first attempts to remedy the evils of the sweating system centered on limiting the number of hours that individuals could be asked to work. This movement faced a setback with the Supreme Court's decision in *Lochner v. New York* (1905), which declared that New York's regulation of bakers' work hours was in violation of the bakers' freedom of contract. In *Muller v. Oregon* (1908), however, future Supreme Court Justice Louis Brandeis—who had been hired by the National Consumers League (NCL)—successfully argued on behalf of a Washington state law that limited women's work to 10 hours a day. Brandeis relied chiefly on evidence, presented in his historic "Brandeis brief," showing that women were especially vulnerable to such exploitation, and the Court responded with a unanimous decision.

A number of states, often prodded by the Women's Trade Union League, subsequently adopted legislation providing minimum wages for women and children. Such a policy sometimes split feminist ranks, however. It pitted those who argued that half a loaf was better than none against those who disfavored any gender-specific legislation—an issue that would also emerge with the first introduction of the equal rights amendment in Congress in 1923 (Hart 1994, 111).

In the same year that the equal rights amendment was first introduced, the Supreme Court issued a decision in *Adkins v. Children's Hospital*. Justice George Sutherland authored this 5 to 3 decision for a divided Court. The Court struck down a minimum-wage law for women on the basis that although the Constitution permitted regulation of "incidents of employment" such as hours and working conditions, the due process clause mitigated against interferences with the "heart of the contract," that is, with wages. Interestingly, Sutherland relied in part on the equalizing effect that the ratification of the Nineteenth Amendment was alleged to have had on women's ability to enter into their own contracts.

Even prior to the decision, at least one amendment had been introduced in Congress to establish governmental powers to set minimum wages. However, most such amendments—some seeking to vest such powers in the states, some in Congress, and some in both—were introduced between 1925 and 1937, when Court decisions based on substantive due process were at their peak. As late as 1936, in *Morehead v. New York ex rel. Tipaldo*, the Court continued to strike down minimum-wage legislation.

In *West Coast Hotel v. Parish* (1937), a narrow Court majority led by Chief Justice Charles Evans Hughes overturned *Adkins* and upheld a Washington state minimum-wage law for women. This case is often called the "switch in time that saved nine," because many believe that it was a political reaction to Franklin D. Roosevelt's court-packing plan introduced earlier in the year.

Congress subsequently adopted the Fair Labor Standards Act in 1938, providing for minimum wages and maximum hours for both men and women in industries affecting interstate commerce. The Supreme Court upheld this law in *United States v. Darby* (1941), thus overturning its earlier decision in *Hammer v. Dagenhart* (1928) and sanctioning the treatment of this issue by the national government.

Calls for amendments on the subject have subsequently ceased, although renewed attention was spurred by the decision in *Garcia v. San Antonio Metropolitan Transit Authority* (1985), in which such minimum-wage laws were applied to state governments. In the United States, minimum-wage laws now apply to most industries. By contrast, in Britain, the minimum wage never applied beyond a few basic industries and was eliminated altogether in 1993. A student of the subject recently concluded that, despite claims for the flexibility of the British constitution, written constitutional guarantees ultimately strengthened U.S. minimum-wage policies in a positive direction (Hart 1994, 182). Debates periodically erupt about how high the minimum wage should be. Although benefiting those who keep their jobs, higher minimum wages are generally believed to contribute to higher unemployment rates.

See also Child Labor Amendment; Labor, Hours of.

❖ *MINOR V. HAPPERSETT* (1875) ❖

Despite the expanded recognition of rights in the Thirteenth through Fifteenth Amendments and extensions of the right to vote in the Wyoming and Utah territories, the nineteenth century did not prove to be a good time for advocates of women's rights at the national level. Declaring in *Bradwell v. Illinois* that "the law of the Creator" mandated that "the paramount destiny and mission of woman are to fulfill the noble and benign offices of wife and mother" (1873, 141), the Supreme Court refused to overturn the decision of the Illinois bar to exclude Myra Bradwell from the practice of law simply because she was a woman. Similarly, speaking through Chief Justice Waite in *Minor v. Happersett* (1875), the Court unanimously upheld a registrar's refusal to allow Virginia Minor to vote in the presidential election of 1872. Susan B. Anthony had asserted a similar privilege, but her case had not made it to the Supreme Court (Basch 1992, 57).

Minor and her husband cited a number

of constitutional arguments, all of which the Court rejected. It recognized that women were citizens of the United States both before and after adoption of the Fourteenth Amendment. However, in an interpretation similar to that advanced in the *Slaughterhouse* cases (1873), it rejected the argument that the right to vote was among the privileges and immunities guaranteed to all citizens by the Fourteenth Amendment. The Court noted that voting qualifications had been set, up to that point, by individual states. No state that had refused to grant suffrage to women had been considered to lack a "republican" government because of this omission. The Court further noted that Section 2 of the Fourteenth Amendment specifically mentioned males and that the Fifteenth Amendment did not extend the right to vote to females. Moreover, if that right had been included among the privileges and immunities protected by the Fourteenth Amendment, then the Fifteenth Amendment would have been unnecessary.

The effect of *Minor v. Happersett* was overturned with the adoption of the Nineteenth Amendment in 1920.

See also Nineteenth Amendment.

❖ *MISSOURI V. HOLLAND* (1920) ❖

Louis Henkin called this case "perhaps the most famous and most discussed case in the constitutional law of foreign affairs" (1972, 144). At issue was the constitutionality of a law passed under authority of a treaty with Great Britain whereby the U.S. government set rules for the protection of migratory birds between the United States and Canada. U.S. district courts had previously voided legislation adopted in the absence of such a treaty on the basis that such laws were a federal invasion of powers reserved to the states by the Tenth Amendment.

Writing on behalf of the Court, Justice Oliver Wendell Holmes Jr. upheld the legis-

lation. He said that "there may be matters of the sharpest exigency for the national well being that an act of Congress could not deal with but that a treaty followed by such an act could" (*Missouri* 1920, 433). Holmes further advanced the view that the Constitution was "an organism" whose life "could not have been foreseen completely by the most gifted of its begetters" (*Missouri* 1920, 322). Although Holmes cautioned that treaties could not "contravene any prohibitory words to be found in the Constitution" (*Missouri* 1920, 433), his opinion raised fears that the Constitution might be effectively amended by treaty rather than by constitutional amendment (Lofgren 1975, 93).

In the 1950s, such fears helped fuel support for the Bricker amendment, a proposal designed in part to limit the reach of federal treaties. Ironically, after 1937, the Supreme Court had already given a broad reading to other constitutional sources of federal power—especially the commerce clause and the taxing and spending clause—that seems to have undermined the importance of *Missouri v. Holland* as a source of federal authority (Lofgren 1975, 122). The Court qualified *Missouri v. Holland* in *Reid v. Covert* (1957).

See also Bricker Amendment; Migratory Birds; Tenth Amendment.

❖ MOMENT OF SILENCE ❖

See Prayer in Public Schools.

❖ MONEY ❖

See Currency.

❖ MONOPOLIES AND TRUSTS ❖

Among the restrictions that Thomas Jefferson wanted to include in a national bill of rights was a "restriction against monopolies" (Mason and Baker 1985, 285). Such a resolution was introduced in the Senate in March 1793 but was subsequently tabled, possibly in the belief that such matters were more appropriate for state control. One of the Marshall Court's most popular decisions was in *Gibbons v. Ogden* (1824) when it utilized congressional authority over interstate commerce to strike down New York's grant of a steamboat monopoly.

Concern over monopolies was renewed as the United States industrialized and industries began to combine into giant trusts. At least 18 amendments were introduced from 1889 to 1913 to give Congress power to regulate such combinations. In 1890, Congress adopted the Sherman Antitrust Act, which was followed by the Clayton Act of 1914 and the Federal Trade Commission Act of the same year (J. May 1992, 34). Initially, however, the Supreme Court interpreted the Sherman Antitrust Act narrowly. Thus, in *United States v. E. C. Knight Co.* (1895), the Court ruled that Congress could not control the acquisition of sugar refineries that led to a near monopoly because the acquisitions took place within a state and were a matter for state control.

In 1900, the House of Representatives debated an amendment submitted by Republican George Washington Ray of New York. It provided that "Congress shall have power to define, regulate, prohibit, or dissolve trusts, monopolies, or combinations, whether existing in the form of a corporation or otherwise." The unsuccessful House vote of 154 to 132 in favor of the measure has been attributed to the Republicans' inclusion of a provision, of great concern to states' rights advocates, that "the several States may continue to exercise such power in any manner not in conflict with the laws of the United States" (Musmanno 1929, 116–19). Also, many members of Congress believed that existing laws could be written and additional laws adopted to address the problem. Today, few doubt that congressional powers extend to this domain.

❖ MORRIS, HENRY O. ❖

Little is known about Henry Morris other than his authorship of the novel *Waiting for the Signal* (1897) and its publication by a socialist-leaning press (Boyd 1992, 106–9). The novel's main characters, Wesley Stearns and John McDermott, are reporters for the Chicago *Biograph*, owned by Adam Short. Short is sympathetic to the woes of the working class and gives his reporters the opportunity to report on the increasing gap between rich and poor and on the moral degradation of the plutocrats, especially those who live in New York City.

During the course of the novel, set shortly after the election of William McKinley in 1896 (Morris appears to have detested Cleveland and McKinley—and Mark Hanna—about equally but supported William Jennings Bryan's advocacy of a silver standard), a working-class revolution is initiated. The revolution results in little bloodshed except in New York City, which is almost completely burned by those trying to take advantage of the chaos.

A convention is subsequently held in Chicago, where Ignatius Donnelly heads a committee that writes a new Declaration of Independence. The convention also writes a new constitution, and William J. Lyon of Nebraska is nominated and subsequently elected president, replacing the military leader who oversaw the revolution. Adoption of the constitution leads to a new era of national peace and prosperity that haunts European plutocrats, who have reason to fear that their own revolutions will come with greater loss of life.

In his draft of a new constitution, Morris largely keeps the structure of the existing government in place, although he does propose some changes. Each state would be guaranteed at least three members in the House of Representatives, and the Speaker—Morris had particular disdain for Speaker Thomas B. Reed—would lose power to retard the progress of legislation (H. Morris 1897, 338). Members of Congress would be limited to 12 years in office. Although the president would continue to have a veto power, both houses of Congress would be able to override this veto by majority vote. In anticipation of the Sixteenth Amendment, Congress would have the power to levy income and other taxes, and, in anticipation of the Seventeenth Amendment, senators would be elected by popular vote. The president, also elected by popular vote, would serve a single eight-year term.

Morris's constitution embodied a number of socialist elements. The national government would take over most means of production, destroy monopolies and trusts, and (in the novel) limit individual wealth.

Congress would establish uniform codes of civil and criminal procedure. Indians would be treated like other citizens, and foreign immigration would be restricted to "the healthy, moral, intelligent and self-supporting" (Morris 1897, 344). Morris's novel indicates that he is generally suspicious of both Jews and foreigners. The people would vote on whether they wanted an initiative and referendum.

Morris would expand most constitutional rights, and his constitution devotes special attention to freedom of speech and of the press. Judicial powers to issue injunctions would be limited, and no one could be imprisoned for violating a court order except after a jury trial.

In Morris's scheme, a majority of both houses of Congress would be able to propose amendments or call a constitutional convention. Amendments would be ratified by a majority of the state legislatures.

In a preface to the third edition, Morris notes that he has been "deluged with letters" asking when the revolution will occur. He answers that he does not know the date but that "the revolution is sure to come—it is on the way.—I leave the reader to guess when the storm will burst" (Morris 1897, ix).

❖ MOTT, LUCRETIA COFFIN ❖ (1793–1880)

Lucretia Coffin Mott was a Quaker minister and political reformer. She provided leadership in the movement for the abolition of slavery that eventually led to the Thirteenth Amendment and in the movement for women's rights that eventually resulted in the Nineteenth Amendment.

Mott, the mother of six children, helped found the Philadelphia Female Anti-Slavery Society in the 1830s and helped establish Swarthmore College in 1864. With Elizabeth Cady Stanton, Mott helped organize the Seneca Falls Convention of 1848, where the idea of women's suffrage first emerged as an important concern. The proposed equal rights amendment was often called the Lucretia Mott amendment in her honor.

See also Equal Rights Amendment; Nineteenth Amendment; Thirteenth Amendment.

❖ MURDER AND KIDNAPPING ❖

In the U.S. federal system, most matters of criminal law are handled by the states. A number of members of Congress have proposed amendments to give Congress power to punish criminals for felonies such as murder, kidnapping, lynching, or polygamy or to invest the trials for such offenses in federal courts.

The most notorious kidnapping of this century, that of Charles Lindbergh's baby, occurred in March 1932. The baby's body was found on 12 May 1932 (Knappman 1994, 386), and a week later, Illinois

Democratic Representative Charles Karch introduced a resolution to give Congress power to punish murder and kidnapping. Although states retain primary jurisdiction over these offenses, Congress has exercised its power under the commerce clause to adopt the Lindbergh Act, making it a crime to transport a victim across state or national lines and creating a presumption that such transit has occurred when a victim is not released within 24 hours (*Black's Law Dictionary* 1969, 837).

See also Marriage, Divorce, and Parenting.

❖ MURPHY, CORNELIUS F., JR. ❖ (1933–)

In a chapter of a book published a year after the bicentennial of the Constitution, Duquesne law professor Cornelius Murphy recommended the convening of a constitutional convention (Vile 1991c, 148–49). More concerned about the positive implications that such a convention would have for democratic theory than about advocating a specific agenda, Murphy sketched four areas for possible reform.

He suggested, somewhat vaguely, that a convention might seek to "delineate the boundaries between personal freedom and social order." He favored adding "economic, social and cultural entitlements," like those recognized in the Universal Declaration of Human Rights, to the Constitution. He wanted to combine states into more functional regional units. He also thought that problems created by the separation of the legislative and executive branches and the "fractionation of power" needed to be addressed. Murphy did not believe that the reforms he proposed could be adequately addressed "within the inherited constitutional structure" or by "piecemeal amendment" (C. Murphy 1988, 70).

❖ MURPHY, WALTER F. (1929–) ❖

Walter F. Murphy recently retired as the Edward S. Corwin professor of politics at Princeton University. Murphy is one of the most articulate and persistent modern defenders of the view that there may be implicit and judicially enforceable limits on constitutional amendments within a true constitutional democracy. Murphy has defended his view in numerous essays over an extended time (W. Murphy 1978, 1980, 1987, 1990, 1992a, 1992b, 1995).

Drawing in part from judicial decisions in other constitutional governments, Murphy argued that the very notion of a constitutional democracy committed to principles of justice and the preservation of human dignity serves to limit the scope of change permitted within such a system. In a system that consists of a hierarchy of values, more important values must necessarily predominate over those with which they are in conflict. Moreover, the U.S. Constitution is informed by and based on the values of the Declaration of Independence, and the natural rights articulated there serve to limit what the Constitution can permit. The whole notion of amendments refers to those types of alterations that are consistent with the instrument being amended, not simply to changes that follow procedural guidelines.

Although Murphy's writings have not convinced all observers (Vile 1995), his work continues to provoke reflection about the scope and nature of constitutional change.

See also Constitutional Amendments, Limits on.

❖ *MYERS V. ANDERSON* (1915) ❖

In this case, a companion to *Guinn v. United States* (1915), the Supreme Court struck down provisions of a Maryland law regulating voting in Annapolis. This law, like the Oklahoma law at issue in *Guinn*, contained a grandfather clause that imposed a literacy test only on those—namely, African Americans—whose ancestors were not entitled to vote prior to 1 January 1868, that is, prior to ratification of the Fourteenth and Fifteenth Amendments.

Chief Justice Edward White struck the law down as a violation of the Fifteenth Amendment. In so doing, he implicitly rejected arguments for limits on the amending process that had been offered by William Marbury and other attorneys for the state. They had argued that "if construed to have reference to voting at state or municipal elections, the Fifteenth Amendment would be beyond the amending power conferred upon three-fourths of the States by Art V. of the Constitution" (Myers 1915, 373).

See also Constitutional Amendments, Limits on.

N

❖

❖ NATIONAL PROHIBITION ❖
CASES

Seven cases challenging the constitutionality of the Eighteenth Amendment and the Volstead Act, the lead being *Rhode Island v. Palmer,* were grouped together and decided for the Court by Justice Willis Van Devanter. Judging from the arguments that accompanied the cases, the challengers' primary hope was to convince the Court that the Eighteenth Amendment exceeded certain limits on the constitutional amending process as well as falling short of a number of procedural qualifications.

Rather than grapple directly with these arguments, Van Devanter basically stated conclusions. Thus, he simply stated that the power to regulate alcohol "is within the power to amend reserved by Article V of the Constitution" (*National Prohibition* cases 1920, 386). This prompted Justice Joseph McKenna to note that such a policy, if established, "will undoubtedly decrease the literature of the court if it does not increase lucidity" (*National Prohibition* cases 1920, 393). However, in their dissenting opinions, McKenna and John Clarke likewise focused primarily on the meaning of "concurrent powers" in Section 2 of the Eighteenth Amendment rather than providing any in-depth discussion of possible limits on the amending process.

Van Devanter decided that Congress's vote, rather than an explicit statement, was enough to show that it considered the Eighteenth Amendment to be necessary. He also noted that the two-thirds majority required by Article V was two-thirds of a quorum rather than of the entire membership. Van Devanter cited *Hawke v. Smith* (1920) as authority for excluding any state requirements that amendments also be confirmed or rejected by referendum.

On the matter of concurrent powers, which so distressed the dissenters, Van Devanter argued that the clause granting such powers to the nation and the states was intended to allow neither government "to defeat or thwart the prohibition, but only to enforce it by appropriate legislation" (*National Prohibition* cases 1920, 387). Moreover, he decided that the Eighteenth Amendment, and the accompanying Volstead Act (which applied to all beverages with 0.5 percent or more alcohol content), could be applied both to preexisting alcohol and to that manufactured or imported after its passage.

Opposition to the Eighteenth Amendment was intense. The Court would reject another legal challenge in *U.S. v. Sprague* (1931). Eventually, it was repealed by the Twenty-first Amendment.

See also Constitutional Amendments, Limits on.

❖ NATIVE AMERICANS ❖

The U.S. Constitution mentions Native Americans in few places, yet their treatment and status have been a perpetual source of shame and controversy throughout American history. Both Article I, Section 2 of the Constitution and Section 2 of the Fourteenth Amendment exclude "Indians not taxed" from the numbers used to calculate representation in the House. Article I, Section 8 further extends congressional power over commerce "with the Indian tribes."

The earliest proposed amendment related to Native Americans was introduced in 1832 when the state of Georgia petitioned Congress for a convention to clarify the rights of Indians. The state had been stung by John Marshall's decision in *Worcester v. Georgia* (1832). In that case, he had invalidated a Georgia statute requiring that a minister obtain a license to live in Cherokee country, and he had enlarged the right of Indian sovereignty. With President Andrew Jackson unwilling to enforce this judgment holding Georgia to treaties it had made, the state proceeded to remove the Cherokees in the historic evacuation known as the "trail of tears."

There appears to have been at least one attempt to include Indians within the citizenship guarantee of the Fourteenth Amendment, but in cases such as *Elk v. Wilkins* (1884), the Court did not interpret the amendment to confer citizenship on Indians. Congress finally took this action in 1924 (Wunder 1994, 50).

In 1937, a South Dakota representative proposed including Indians in apportioning the House of Representatives, and in 1940, a North Dakota representative voted to deprive Congress of the power to regulate intrastate commerce with them. When they were charged with one of a number of major crimes defined by Congress or when they were off reservations, Native Americans were governed by federal constitutional guarantees, but on the reservations, tribal courts were not bound by the Bill of Rights (Wunder 1994, 132–33). At least four proposals from 1939 through 1953

were introduced—three by Democratic Senator Patrick McCarran of Nevada—to restore the same rights to American Indians as were enjoyed by other American citizens. In 1968, Congress adopted legislation known as the Indian Bill of Rights. It applied most, but not all, provisions of the Bill of Rights to proceedings on Indian reservations (Wunder 1994, 135–44).

❖ NATURAL LAW ❖

Many of the American founders believed strongly in the idea of natural law. This idea, traceable back to ancient Greek and Roman as well as to medieval Christian philosophers, posited the existence of an unwritten set of unchanging moral principles that could be ascertained through human reason (Sigmund 1971).

Thomas Jefferson premised the Declaration of Independence on this doctrine, which he linked to the "unalienable rights" of "life, liberty, and the pursuit of happiness." Pointing to the fact that the Declaration is included at the beginning of the U.S. Code, some have argued that it is part of the organic law of the land (Jaffa 1994, 4–5) and that judges should enforce this part of the nation's "unwritten constitution" (Grey 1975). Others prefer to maintain the distinction between natural law and positive law (O'Neil 1995) and think that judges should enforce only those natural law principles that are embodied in such parts of the Constitution as the Bill of Rights, the Fourteenth Amendment, and other specific provisions.

It appears that, prior to 1787, American courts frequently resorted to natural-law concepts in justifying their decisions and that they later devoted greater attention to specific phrases and more general principles of the written Constitution (L. Goldstein 1991, 15). In *Calder v. Bull* (1798), a decision about the scope of the ex post facto provision, Justice Samuel Chase argued for judicial enforcement of such natural law principles, whereas Justice James Iredell thought that courts should base their judgments only on specific constitutional provisions. From the late nineteenth century through 1937, the Court's focus on substantive due process appeared to embody a type of natural-law reasoning that usurped the people's role in amending the Constitution. Arguably, modern opinions on the right to privacy have a similar natural-law foundation. Some advocates of limits on the amending process have based their argument on natural-rights principles said to be implicit in the Constitution (Rosen 1991, 1086).

See also Declaration of Independence.

For Further Reading:
   Corwin, Edward S. 1955. *The "Higher Law" Background of American Constitutional Law*. Ithaca, NY: Cornell University Press.
   Hamburger, Philip A. 1993. "Natural Rights, Natural Law, and American Constitutionalism." *Yale Law Journal* 102 (January): 907–60.

❖ NECESSARY AND PROPER CLAUSE ❖

The last clause in Article I, Section 8 of the Constitution grants Congress power "to make all laws which shall be necessary and proper for carrying into Execution the foregoing Powers." Often called the "elastic" or "sweeping" clause, this served as one of the central constitutional supports by which John Marshall justified the constitutionality of the national bank in *McCulloch v. Maryland* (1819). Without such a provision, many more amendments would undoubtedly have been necessary in order to expand congressional powers.

If not tied specifically to constitutional ends, however, the clause could undermine the whole notion of a constitution of enumerated powers (Engdahl 1994, 13). In 1806, John Clopton, a Democratic representative from Virginia, introduced an amendment to construe the clause so as "to comprehend only such laws as shall have a natural connection with and immediate relation to the powers enumerated in the said section, or such other powers as are expressly vested by the Constitution in the Government of the United States" (Ames 1896, 168). More recently, a participant in a law review symposium cited the ambiguity of the necessary and proper clause as a reason for nominating it as the most "stupid" provision in the current document (Graber 1995).

❖ NEW DEAL ❖

See Court-Packing Plan.

❖ NINETEENTH AMENDMENT ❖

Although they proclaimed human equality, the American Founding Fathers did little to heed Abigail Adams's plea to "remember the Ladies, and be more generous and favourable to them than your ancestors" (letter to John Adams dated 31 March 1776 in Mason and Baker 1985, 119). Only in New Jersey were women permitted to vote, and there the doctrine of coverture, by which a married couple constituted a single entity, essentially limited this right to unmarried women (Bernstein with Agel 1993, 129). Moreover, throughout most of the eighteenth and nineteenth centuries, women were subjected to a number of legal disabilities that affected their title to land, custody of their children in the case of divorce, and access to occupations (Van Burkleo 1990, 10).

Origins of the Suffrage Movement
The movement for women's suffrage is usually dated to the Seneca Falls Convention of

1848, where Elizabeth Cady Stanton drew up the Seneca Falls Declaration of Rights and Sentiments that she patterned after the Declaration of Independence. Many of the early leaders of the women's suffrage movement were also active in the abolition movement and in the movement for national alcoholic prohibition. These women were understandably upset when the Fourteenth and Fifteenth Amendments made no specific provisions for women. Indeed, the Fourteenth Amendment was the first to introduce the term "male" into the Constitution. Largely because of disputes arising over the proper stance for women to take toward these amendments, women's suffrage proponents split into two main groups. Elizabeth Cady Stanton and Susan B. Anthony, who opposed adoption of the Fourteenth Amendment, formed the National Woman Suffrage Association; Henry Ward Beecher and Lucy Stone, who favored the amendment, formed the American Woman Suffrage Association (Kraditor 1981, 3–4). This rivalry continued until the two groups joined in 1890 to become the National American Woman Suffrage Association (NAWSA).

Democratic Representative James Brooks of New York was the first to offer a women's suffrage amendment in Congress. He introduced his proposal in 1866 as an amendment to Section 2 of the Fourteenth Amendment and again in 1869 as an addition to the Fifteenth Amendment. Although Brooks was not successful, the Fifteenth Amendment subsequently became the model for the women's suffrage amendment (also called the Susan B. Anthony amendment), which was introduced regularly in Congress from 1880 until it was proposed by the necessary majorities in 1919. Few observers could have been surprised when in *Minor v. Happersett* (1875) the Supreme Court rejected the argument that the Fourteenth Amendment extended the right to vote to women.

Much of the pressure for women's suffrage came from the western states. They were motivated partly by their desire to get enough voters to qualify for statehood. The Wyoming Territory granted suffrage to women in 1869, and other states and territories followed. Some allowed women to vote in all elections, and others limited such voting to school board elections or elections for the president (Bernstein).

Debates over Women's Suffrage

As in other amending controversies, most notably the later disputes over the equal rights amendment, both sides of the women's suffrage debate claimed more radical consequences for the amendment than it would eventually generate. Opponents feared that women would be sullied by their participation in politics and forecast dire changes in family and social structures. Whereas some proponents of suffrage argued that it was simply a recognition of women's equality under the law, others anticipated that women would have an ennobling influence on political life that would inaugurate major political reforms. The argument was also advanced from time to time that the votes of educated women might help counteract the votes of African Americans and immigrants (Kraditor 1981, 14–74).

The tie between women's suffrage and other issues was sometimes a disability. Women (especially those in the Women's Christian Temperance Union) had taken such an active part in the movement for national alcoholic prohibition that those opposed to Prohibition feared that women's suffrage would lead to adoption of the Prohibition amendment. Especially in the South, fears were raised that an amendment granting women the right to vote might renew federal efforts to enforce the Fifteenth Amendment. Southerners were a major source of support for the Shafroth-Palmer amendment of 1914, which would have allowed each state to have a referendum (if so requested by 8 percent or more of the voters) on the women's suffrage issue rather than setting a single national standard (for southern views, see Wheeler 1993). Some supporters of women's suffrage wanted it limited to white women (Grimes 1978, 91).

Growing Support for the Amendment
As increasing numbers of states began to extend the right to vote in whole or in part to women, pressures for a federal amendment increased. In 1914, the Senate voted 35 to 34 for the amendment, with the House falling far shorter in 1915 with a vote of 174 to 204. That same year, under the leadership of Alice Paul, the Congressional Union for Woman Suffrage (CU)—later the Woman's Party (WP)—broke with NAWSA and advocated more militant measures, including campaigns against all Democrats, who were generally less supportive of the amendment than Republicans. The CU also led a series of parades and controversial pickets outside the White House.

The adoption of the Eighteenth Amendment probably aided the Nineteenth Amendment, in that some of those who had opposed women's suffrage for fear that it would lead to Prohibition now had nothing more to lose. World War I also mobilized increasing numbers of women into the workforce and led some to believe that their sacrifices should be acknowledged. Initially a tepid supporter of the amendment, President Woodrow Wilson addressed the Senate in 1918 in support of it (Flexnor 1974, 307–9), but it again fell short of the necessary votes, as it would in early 1919 as well. Wilson subsequently called a special session of Congress in May 1919, and the amendment finally succeeded, with the final Senate vote coming on 28 May 1919. Proposals to limit the vote to white women, to ratify the amendment by conventions rather than by state legislatures, and to entrust states with primary enforcement powers were all rejected at this time (U.S. Senate 1985, 56).

Ratification of the Amendment
The amendment was ratified in just over a year, with most opposition coming, as expected, in the South. The thirty-sixth state to ratify was Tennessee. Several prominent leaders of the women's movement, including Carrie Chapman Catt, president of the National Woman Suffrage Association, came to Nashville to lobby and were met by almost equally well-organized opponents. The Tennessee constitution contained a provision that the state legislature could not vote for a proposed amendment until after an intervening election (A. Taylor 1957, 104), but both the U.S. solicitor general and Tennessee's attorney general declared this provision invalid after the Supreme Court's two decisions in *Hawke v. Smith* (1920). The Tennessee Senate subsequently adopted the resolution by a vote of 24 to 4 and sent it to the House, where a motion to table the resolution failed by a vote of 48 to 48. When the measure came up for a vote, a 24-year-old state representative named Harry Burn switched votes because of his mother's request to adopt the amendment, and another member did the same in order to call the vote up for reconsideration. The "red rose brigade" (consisting of opponents of the amendment, whose supporters wore yellow roses) subsequently left the state for Alabama to prevent a quorum on reconsideration, but after a series of complicated maneuvers, they proved unsuccessful. The U.S. secretary of state apparently ignored a later House resolution of nonconcurrence (A. Taylor 1957, 122–24).

Subsequent Developments
The amendment was quickly implemented. In *Leser v. Garnett* (1922), the Supreme Court rejected a challenge to this amendment, and in *Adkins v. Children's Hospital* (1923), the Court cited the amendment in

striking down a minimum-wage law for women in the District of Columbia. Partly on the basis of this precedent, the author of a recent article argued that the Nineteenth Amendment might be interpreted as a broader guarantee of women's rights than has so far been the case (J. Brown 1993).

Celebrations in Tennessee and throughout the nation marked the seventy-fifth anniversary of the Nineteenth Amendment in 1995. Events in Washington, D.C., were held in the basement of the Capitol near a statue of Susan B. Anthony, Elizabeth Cady Stanton, and Lucretia Mott, because the House had failed to vote on an earlier Senate resolution to move the monument—donated by the National Woman's Party in 1921—to the main rotunda. Among the dozens of statues of American forefathers there, none depicted American women ("A Celebration" 1995, 9).

See also Anthony, Susan Brownell; Catt, Carrie Lane Chapman; Paul, Alice; Shafroth-Palmer Amendment; Stanton, Elizabeth Cady.

For Further Reading:
Stevens, Doris. 1995. *Jailed for Freedom: American Women Win the Vote.* Troutdale, OR: New Sage.

Wheeler, Marjorie S. 1995. *Votes for Women! The Woman Suffrage Movement in Tennessee, the South, and the Nation.* Knoxville: University of Tennessee Press.

Wheeler, Marjorie S., ed. 1995. *One Woman, One Vote: Rediscovering the Woman Suffrage Movement.* Troutdale, OR: New Sage.

❖ NINTH AMENDMENT ❖

One of the most elusive and controversial amendments to the Constitution is the Ninth Amendment. It was ratified in 1791 as part of the Bill of Rights. This amendment provides that "the enumeration in the Constitution of certain rights, shall not be construed to deny or disparage others retained by the people."

Arguably a reflection of the natural-rights philosophy of the Founding Fathers, this provision appears to have originated in a proposed amendment to the Virginia constitution. A similar provision had been proposed by both the Virginia and the North Carolina ratifying conventions (Lutz 1992, 53, 57, 63) before being incorporated in the Bill of Rights that James Madison proposed in the First Congress. Madison's original provision actually incorporated the ideas that would later appear in both the Ninth and the Tenth Amendments: "The exceptions here or elsewhere in the Constitution, made in favor of particular rights, shall not be so construed as to diminish the just importance of other rights retained by the people, or to enlarge the powers delegated by the Constitution; but either as actual limitations of such powers, or as inserted merely for greater caution" (Kurland and Lerner 1987, 5:25).

One of the Federalists' original objections to the inclusion of a bill of rights was that it would be impossible to make a complete list of human rights. Such a bill might prove dangerous if observers concluded that because a right was not enumerated it had therefore been forfeited. The Ninth Amendment appears to have been introduced with this problem in mind. Speaking before the House of Representatives, Madison thus noted:

It has been objected also against a bill of rights, that, by enumerating particular exceptions to the grant of power, it would disparage those rights which were not placed in that enumeration; and it might follow by implication, that those rights which were not singled out, were intended to be assigned into the hands of the General Government, and were consequently insecure. This is one of the most plausible arguments I have ever heard urged against the admission of a bill of rights into this system; but, I conceive, that it may be guarded against. I have attempted it [in the Ninth Amendment]. (Kurland and Lerner 1987, 5:399)

The only recorded debate on the subject in the First Congress centered on Elbridge Gerry's unsuccessful motion to substitute the word "impair" for "disparage" (Kurland and Lerner 1987, 5:400); other modifications were insignificant (Caplan 1983, 258).

For most of its first 150 years, the Ninth Amendment lacked the judicial gloss so typical of other provisions in the Bill of Rights. What judicial interpretations there were suggested what a leading student of the Ninth Amendment called a "rights-powers" approach to the amendment. Under this approach, courts considered unenumerated rights under the amendment to consist only of those rights that remained because the government was granted no power over them (Barnette 1989, 14). An alternative approach would be to conceive of the protections for unenumerated rights in the Ninth Amendment, like other protections in the first 10 amendments, as "power-constraints" on government (Barnette 1989, 14). This interpretation received some backing with the Supreme Court's decision invalidating Connecticut's birth-control law in *Griswold v. Connecticut* (1965). Although mentioned in Douglas's majority opinion, it was given considerably more emphasis in Justice Arthur Goldberg's concurring opinion.

The main obstacle to this "power-constraints" approach appears to be twofold. First is the difficulty of deciding precisely what unenumerated rights would be protected by the Ninth Amendment. Second is the related concern that expansive interpretation of such unenumerated rights might upset the scheme of separation of powers or federalism by unduly empowering the judiciary (DeRosa 1996).

Another way of interpreting the Ninth Amendment is to view it simply as a recognition that rights protected under state constitutions when it was adopted would continue in force "until modified or eliminated by state enactment, by federal preemption, or by a judicial determination of unconstitutionality" (Caplan 1983, 228).

With such wide disparities of interpretation, the Ninth Amendment is likely to continue to be the focus of intense scholarly debate.

For Further Reading:

DeRosa, Marshall L. 1996. *The Ninth Amendment and the Politics of Creative Jurisprudence: Disparaging the Fundamental Right of Popular Control.* New Brunswick, NJ: Transaction Publishers.

Massey, Calvin R. 1995. *Silent Rights: The Ninth Amendment and the Constitution's Unenumerated Rights.* Philadelphia: Temple University Press.

Patterson, Bennett B. 1955. *The Forgotten Ninth Amendment.* Indianapolis, IN: Bobbs-Merrill.

❖ NUMBER OF PROPOSED ❖ AMENDMENTS

When Herman Ames surveyed the amendments that had been proposed during the nation's first 100 years, he counted 1,736 proposals. He noted, however, that "it is scarcely possible that all the proposed amendments presented to Congress have been included" (Ames 1896, 11). The precision of his count is further undercut by the fact that he included some state petitions and proposals for amendments that presidents made in speeches but that were not necessarily introduced as amendments in Congress. Also, Ames sometimes split a single proposal into several components, each of which he numbered separately. Notwithstanding such limitations, his count still remains the best approximation for the nation's first 100 years.

In the next published list of amendments, the Library of Congress counted 1,316 amendments that had been introduced in Congress from 1890 through 1926 (Tansill 1926). Clearly, the rate at which amendments were being introduced was increasing. It has continued to do so.

When the last list of proposed amendments was published in 1992, the author counted 10,431 proposals. These included the 3,000-plus amendments counted by Ames and Tansill, as well as 2,340 amendments introduced from 1926 to 1962 (*Proposed Amendments* 1963; this study duplicates parts of *Proposed Amendments* 1957), 1,548 from 1963 to 1968 (*Proposed Amendments* 1969), 3,054 from 1969 to 1984 (Davis 1985), and 437 from 1985 to 1990 (D. Harris 1992, CRS-8).

Assuming that the rate of amendments from 1991 through 1996 is approximately the same as that during the preceding five years—and this seems consistent with the number of amendments taken from lists available on the Internet and provided by David Huckabee of the Library of Congress—this would mean that approximately 10,900 amendments have been introduced in Congress. The most complete list of state applications for a constitutional convention, which was published in 1993, lists 399 such proposals, some of which were included in Ames's count of the first 100 years (Paulsen 1993).

Of the thousands of proposed amendments, only 34 have been proposed by the requisite congressional majorities. Of these, six remain failed amendments, and only 27 have been adopted by the states. One such amendment (the Twenty-first) repealed another (the Eighteenth), and doubts continue as to the legitimacy of the Twenty-seventh Amendment, which was ratified in 1993, more than 200 years after first being proposed by Congress.

O

❖

❖ OBSCENITY AND ❖ PORNOGRAPHY

Laws directed toward the regulation of obscenity and pornography arouse intense emotions. Those favoring such laws believe that they help promote morality; those opposed to such laws believe that they infringe on the freedoms of speech and the press guaranteed by the First and Fourteenth Amendments. At least half a dozen proposals were introduced in Congress from 1959 to 1970 to grant that body or the states the power to enact legislation regulating obscenity. During this same period, U.S. court decisions were often criticized for being too tolerant of obscenity.

In the nineteenth century, U.S. courts gave fairly wide range to state antiobscenity statutes under the so-called Hicklin test. Under this formula, obscenity was judged according to "whether the tendency of the matter charged as obscenity is to deprave and corrupt those whose minds are open to such immoral influence and into whose hands a publication of this sort may fall" (quoted in Abraham and Perry 1994, 206). As the Court began to give increasing scrutiny to such legislation in the 1950s, it liberalized its standards in cases such as *Roth v. United States* and *Alberts v. California* (1957) but still denied that the First Amendment protected obscenity.

Since then, the Court's most difficult problem has been that of identifying obscenity. Some justices, such as William Brennan, eventually concluded that it was impossible to regulate obscenity without infringing on other First Amendment rights. But in *Miller v. California* (1973), Chief Justice Warren Burger formulated a three-part test that, with minor modifications, is still in force today. This test provided that a work is obscene if "(a) the average person, applying contemporary community standards, would find that the work, taken as a whole, appeals to the prurient; (b) the work depicts or describes, in a patently offensive way, sexual conduct specifically defined by the applicable state law; and (c) the work, taken as a whole, lacks serious literary, artistic, political, or scientific value" (*Miller* 1973, 25). Since then, the Court has permitted governments to tighten the regulation of pornography involving juveniles or directed to juveniles or nonconsenting adults. It has also allowed local governments to use zoning ordinances to regulate pornography.

❖ O'CONOR, CHARLES ❖ (1804–1888)

Charles O'Conor was a successful New York attorney who put forward proposals for constitutional reforms in the 1870s and 1880s. Like his contemporaries who were concerned with political corruption, O'Conor hoped to eliminate private legislation at both state and national levels (O'Conor 1877, 29). He also hoped to cut off the source of government graft by eliminating duties and tariffs, limiting government revenues to what could be raised by "immediate taxation," and prohibiting governments from borrowing or coining money (O'-Conor 1877, 1314–16). O'Conor also proposed to reduce the number of laws by adopting general statutes that would be suitable for each kind of political subdivision, and he thought that the invention of the telegraph made it possible to eliminate the diplomatic corps (O'Conor 1881, 1316). He favored shortening the ballot and reducing the number of elected offices, but, convinced that voting was a duty rather than a right, he also favored limiting the franchise and eliminating the secret ballot (O'Conor 1877, 6).

As a Catholic, O'Conor wanted to exclude public schools from teaching religion or other sectarian ideals. O'Conor wanted to outlaw polygamy, and he opposed liberal divorce laws. He also suggested that state autonomy could be preserved and greater uniformity could be achieved if a "court of ultimate appeal" was created to hear cases coming from both state and federal courts. It would be composed of judges selected by the states to deal with "conflicting laws" and "jarring jurisprudence" (O'Conor 1881, 1317).

O'Conor favored making both Congress and state legislatures unicameral, but his most radical proposal related to the presidency. O'Conor proposed that the office be filled each month by lot from the legislature, in his own words, "thus substantially extinguishing the great office of President" (O'Conor 1877, 35). He predicted that efforts expended on competition for this office could then be diverted to more productive private enterprises.

Largely as a result of the novelty of O'Conor's ideas and their failure "to form a coherent whole" (Vile 1991c, 27), they do not appear to have been very influential.

❖ OFFICES, FORFEITURE OF ❖ OR INELIGIBILITY FOR

The Constitution does not prohibit individuals who are convicted of crimes from serving in office, but it does provide some mechanisms for removing such individuals. Thus, Article I, Section 2 of the Constitution gives the House of Representatives the sole power of impeachment, and the subsequent section provides that the Senate shall try impeachments. Article I, Section 4 extends the prospect of impeachment to the president, vice president, "and all civil Officers of the United States" but limits the grounds of such impeachment to conviction of "Treason, Bribery, or other high Crimes and Misdemeanors." Article I, Section 3 specifies that conviction requires a two-thirds vote. Conviction is to extend no further "than to removal from Office, and disqualification to hold and enjoy any Office of honor, Trust or Profit under the United States." Of the seven impeachment convictions the Senate has rendered (all of federal judges), it has voted for disqualification to future offices in only two cases (Peltason 1994, 53).

According to Article I, Section 5, each house of Congress may "punish its Members for disorderly Behavior, and, with the Concurrence of two thirds, expel a Member." It was under such a threat that Oregon Republican Bob Packwood resigned from the Senate in 1995 after a Senate committee unanimously voted to recommend such a penalty for sexual harassment and other wrongdoing.

Congress may further exclude members by a majority vote. According to the Supreme Court's decision in *Powell v. McCormack* (1969), it can do so only when members fail to meet the constitutionally specified age, citizenship, or residence requirements.

As the framers undoubtedly intended, neither the procedure for impeaching and convicting governmental officials nor that for expelling members of Congress is a simple one. Moreover, unless the Senate so specifies when it convicts an individual of an impeachable offense, even a person removed from one office may be eligible for another. Two proposals were offered in the nineteenth century, one in 1838 and the other in 1876, to prohibit individuals convicted of embezzlement or bribery from holding office. Some of the contemporary proposals to outlaw polygamy also contained provisions designed to exclude polygamists from holding office.

Beginning in 1985, there have been about 20 more proposals directed at prohibiting convicted felons from serving as federal officials, as members of Congress, or as judges. These proposals may have been stimulated by the conduct of Harry E. Claiborne, a U.S. district court judge in Nevada, who continued to draw his salary after being convicted and imprisoned and subsequently became the fifth federal judge in history to be impeached and convicted (Abraham 1993, 45). In 1992, Florida judge Alcee Hastings was elected to Congress after having been successfully removed from office by a Senate vote of impeachment (Peltason 1994, 53).

See also Marriage, Divorce, and Parenting.

❖ *OREGON V. MITCHELL* (1970) ❖

The decision for the Court in *Oregon v. Mitchell, Texas v. Mitchell,* and *United States v. Arizona* precipitated the proposal and ratification of the Twenty-sixth Amendment. The cases also serve as classic examples of differences among the justices as to the meaning of the post–Civil War amendments and the degree to which these amendments permit legislative and judicial extensions of constitutional rights.

The Court considered three questions involving congressional authority exercised in the 1970 amendments to the 1965 Voting Rights Act. These questions involved congressional authority to lower the voting age to 18 in state and federal elections, bar the use of literacy tests, and eliminate state residency requirements in presidential elections.

Justice Hugo Black's opinion, which garnered four votes from the two major divisions of the Court, recognized congressional authority under Article I, Section 4; Article II, Section 1; and the necessary and proper clause to lower the voting age for federal elections. Black also stated that Article I, Section 2 limited federal power to lower the voting age in state and local elections. He further denied that the equal protection clause of the Fourteenth Amendment, which was directed primarily to discrimination on the basis of race, provided such authority. Black accepted the literacy-test ban on the basis of the enforcement clauses of the Fourteenth and Fifteenth Amendments, and elimination of residency requirements on the basis of congressional authority over federal elections.

Justice William O. Douglas would have relied on the authority of the equal protection and privileges and immunities clauses of the Fourteenth Amendment to lower the voting age in both state and federal elections. He would also have upheld the other provisions of the law.

Justice John Marshall Harlan accepted the congressionally imposed literacy ban on the basis of the Fifteenth Amendment. However, he used exhaustive analysis of the framing of the Fourteenth Amendment to deny that the amendment had been intended to provide authority for other federal measures at issue. Citing powers reserved to the states by the Tenth Amendment, Harlan suggested that federal authority over these other voting matters would require amendments similar to the Fifteenth, Nineteenth, and Twenty-fourth Amendments. Harlan also rejected Black's analysis of Article I, Sections 2 and 4.

Justices William Brennan, Byron White, and Thurgood Marshall disputed Harlan's narrow reading of the Fourteenth Amendment. They would have upheld all aspects of the law under the equal protection clause and congressional enforcement powers under the Civil War amendments.

Justices Potter Stewart, Warren Burger, and Harry Blackmun accepted Black's distinction between congressional power over federal elections and that over state and local elections. However, they grounded congressional power over residency requirements on the privileges and immunities of American citizens, including the right to travel.

See also Twenty-sixth Amendment.

P

❖ PACE, JAMES O. (1954–) ❖

New York attorney James Pace advanced one of the most novel and racist contemporary proposals for constitutional amendment in a book entitled *Amendment to the Constitution: Averting the Decline and Fall of America* (Pace 1986). Addressing a variety of concerns related to the decline of the family, permissive sexual relations, crime, disrespect for religion, poverty, and declining educational standards, Pace's primary concern is the nation's increasing racial diversity. He is also troubled by the way that the Fourteenth Amendment has enabled the federal courts to oversee traditional state and local controls in areas such as pornography and crime control.

Pace calls for the adoption of an amendment that would repeal the Fourteenth and Fifteenth Amendments and alter the Tenth Amendment by adding the word "expressly" before the word "delegated." This would thereby foreclose the possibility of implied congressional powers that Chief Justice Marshall recognized in *McCulloch v. Maryland* (1819). Pace would further limit citizenship to "non-Hispanic white [people] of the European race, in whom there is no ascertainable trace of Negro blood, nor more than one-eighth Mongolian, Asian, Asia Minor, Middle Eastern, Semitic, Near Eastern, American Indian, Malay or other non-European or nonwhite blood" (Pace 1986, 140). Pace would restrict the right to reside permanently in the United States to

citizens. He advocates programs for resettling noncitizens in other nations while allowing those who were needed—for example, blacks, who, "because of their physical abilities," might be employed as police officers to enforce the amendment—to get temporary work permits (Pace 1986, 118). Pace favors calling a constitutional convention to inaugurate his plans.

❖ *PALKO V. CONNECTICUT* (1937) ❖

Palko v. Connecticut remains one of the leading cases dealing with the incorporation controversy (Abraham and Perry 1994, 56–59). At issue was a Connecticut law that permitted the state to retry an individual if there had been errors in that individual's first trial. Here, the state retried a case in which Palko had been sentenced to life in prison for second-degree murder; on retrial, the state won a conviction of murder in the first degree, carrying the death penalty. If that had occurred in a federal court, it would have been considered to be double jeopardy, in violation of the Fifth Amendment. Palko argued for the view that all the prohibitions in the Bill of Rights that applied to the federal government should also apply to the states through the due process clause of the Fourteenth Amendment.

In an 8-to-1 decision for the Court, Justice Benjamin Cardozo rejected this contention. His task was complicated by the fact that, by 1937, the Court had accepted the idea that some provisions of the Bill of Rights—for example, protections for freedom of speech and the press—did apply to the states through the Fourteenth Amendment, although it had rejected the application of other rights. Cardozo attempted to reconcile these cases by articulating the doctrine of selective incorporation, or fundamental rights. According to this view, the due process clause of the Fourteenth Amendment incorporated only those provisions that are "of the very essence of a scheme of ordered liberty" or that are based on principles of justice "so rooted in the traditions and conscience of our people as to be ranked as fundamental" (*Palko* 1937, 325). Seeing this case as a legitimate state attempt to remedy past errors rather than as an attempt to wear the defendant down, Cardozo decided that no violation of due process had taken place.

The arguments in *Palko* would later be repeated in *Adamson v. California* (1947), where Justice Hugo Black advanced his support for the doctrine of total incorporation and Justice Felix Frankfurter advocated a view akin to Cardozo's. Although continuing to profess adherence to the doctrine of selective incorporation or fundamental fairness, over time, the Court ruled that most provisions in the Bill of Rights were fundamental and should be applied to the states. In *Benton v. Maryland* (1969), the Court finally applied the double-jeopardy provision to the states, thus overruling the specific decision in *Palko*.

See also Incorporation.

❖ PARDON POWER ❖

See Presidency, Pardon Power.

❖ PARLIAMENTARY SOVEREIGNTY ❖

In Great Britain, the struggle for liberty centered on the struggle for power between the Crown and Parliament. Because the Crown was a hereditary office and the Parliament was an elected body, the idea of democracy came to be identified with the latter body. Over time, the British accepted the notion that democratic rule required that Parliament be sovereign.

By contrast, in America, the struggle for independence began with the rejection of parliamentary sovereignty, especially as it related to taxation (Reid 1993). Moreover, as American constitutional theory developed, it put increasing emphasis on the idea that all three branches of the new government were limited by the written Constitution.

In consequence of these developments, Americans had to formulate a different theory of constitutional amendment than did the British. When the British refer to their constitution, they do not refer to a single document but to a host of documents, practices, and understandings that have developed over a long period. In practice, this system has adopted constitutional change fairly cautiously (Vile 1993d), but in theory, constitutional changes can be effected simply by parliamentary action. By contrast, the U.S. system is based on a written constitution that is not changeable by ordinary acts of legislation but requires extraordinary majorities at both state and national levels. Thus it is not surprising that characterizations of the U.S. Constitution as "rigid" appear to have been initiated by James Bryce, an English observer (Bryce 1905, 1906; Vile 1992, 137–38). Because the United States' written constitution is a brief outline that leaves many matters to legislative majorities, many policy changes can be initiated short of constitutional amendment.

❖ PARLIAMENTARY SYSTEM ❖

Among those who have proposed major constitutional changes, few alterations have been more popular than those designed to incorporate one or another aspect of parliamentary systems, especially as this system is practiced in Great Britain. This system generally avoids the problem of divided government, wherein the legislative majority and the chief executive are from different parties. It does so by allowing the majority party or majority coalition within the legislative branch, generally designated as the parliament, to choose the chief executive, who is usually called a prime minister.

In contrast to the U.S. system, in which members of Congress are forbidden to hold executive office, members of the British cabinet are chosen from and continue to serve in the Parliament. Fairly strict party discipline is the norm, and if Parliament rejects one of the prime minister's major bills or gives a vote of "no confidence" in the existing administration, the monarch dissolves the Parliament and calls new parliamentary elections, in which all members of the House of Commons are up for election. The parliamentary system also stresses norms of collective decision making and ministerial responsibility, and it requires the prime minister to appear before Parliament on a regular basis to answer questions—the so-called question hour. In this system, the lower house, designated as the House of Commons, has substantially greater powers than does the upper house, the House of Lords.

Although some individuals have advocated an entirely new U.S. Constitution along British lines, many members of Congress have introduced amendments to adopt one or more parts of this system. Such proposals have included plans allowing members of Congress to serve in the cabinet or permitting Congress to take a vote of no confidence in the president.

Proponents of the parliamentary model defend it as a way of making government more responsive to the people and of overcoming problems of stalemate and inaction attributed in the U.S. system to the separation of powers. One recent study, however, suggested that the problems of divided government in the United States may be exaggerated (Mayhew 1991); another study denies that separation of powers is responsible for many of the problems that have been attributed to it (Sargentich 1993). Others suggest that systems that appear from a distance to have advantages may, on closer inspection, demonstrate weaknesses. Moreover, the strengths of some such systems may result in part from greater social homogeneity and from factors other than constitutional structures (Ceaser 1986).

See also Divided Government.

❖ PAROCHIAL SCHOOLS, AID TO ❖

Long before provisions of the First Amendment's establishment clause were applied to the states through the due process clause of the Fourteenth Amendment, proponents of the Blaine amendment sought to restrict state governmental funding of parochial schools. This issue reemerged when at least four proposals were introduced from 1973 to 1975 to allow tax credits or other types of state financial assistance to parochial schools.

In several cases, most notably *Lemon v. Kurtzman* (1971), the Supreme Court has invalidated most forms of direct aid to parochial schools. It has, however, upheld the constitutionality of state payments to parents for bus fares to parochial schools (*Everson v. Board of Education* [1947]) and the provision of secular textbooks for such schools (*Meek v. Pittenger* [1973]). In *Mueller v. Allen* (1983), the Court upheld a state law that permitted tax deductions for all parents for school expenses, including tuition for parochial schools. Recent debates have shifted attention to the constitutionality of voucher systems that would allow parents to use such state-provided vouchers for publicly or privately administered schools of the parents' own choosing (Skillen 1993). The constitutionality of such plans might be on firmer footing if the proposed Religious Equality Amendment is adopted.

See also Blaine Amendment; Religious Equality Amendment.

❖ PATENTS AND COPYRIGHTS ❖

Article I, Section 8 of the Constitution grants Congress power "to promote the Progress of Science and useful Arts, by securing for limited Times to Authors and Inventors the exclusive Right to their respective Writings and Discoveries." The 1952 Patent Act grants inventors a 17-year monopoly over their inventions (Lieberman 1992, 371). Copyrights now extend 50 years beyond an author's death (*Information Please Almanac* 1993, 594–95).

In 1953, New Jersey Democratic Representative Hugh Addonizio introduced an amendment to grant copyrights and patents "in perpetuity." Although such an amendment might increase rewards for authors and inventors, it might also slow progress by retarding the free flow of ideas.

❖ PAUL, ALICE (1885–1947) ❖

Alice Paul is often identified as one of the "new suffragists" (Lunardini 1986, 17). Paul, who never married, earned a Ph.D. in political science from the University of Pennsylvania and law degrees from the Washington College of Law and American University. After taking part in suffragist demonstrations in England—where she met fellow American Lucy Burns, with whom she would subsequently work quite closely—Paul was appointed chair of the Congressional Committee of the National American Woman Suffrage Association (NAWSA) in 1912. Paul subsequently

founded the Congressional Union for Woman Suffrage, which became independent in 1914 and firmly opposed the Shafroth-Palmer amendment (which would have left women's suffrage to be determined by individual state referendums), which NAWSA representatives had initially approved.

Paul was a persistent organizer who sponsored a suffragist parade the day before Woodrow Wilson's inaugurations in 1913 and 1917 and founded the National Woman's Party in 1916. This organization, which was regarded as more radical than the NAWSA, worked to oppose candidates who did not support the Anthony amendment. It also sponsored a series of pickets in front of the Wilson White House for 18 months beginning in January 1917, the same year that the Congressional Union merged with the National Woman's Party (NWP). Picketers, including Paul, were jailed; Paul was force-fed after she declared a hunger strike. Unlike the NAWSA, the NWP refused to support Wilson's war efforts. Still, the combined pressures from the NAWSA and the NWP, along with Wilson's hopes that such a measure would help boost war morale, convinced him to endorse the Anthony amendment, which became the Nineteenth Amendment in 1920.

Thereafter, the NWP continued its push for women's rights. Initially, it was the only such women's organization to support the Lucretia Mott, or equal rights, amendment. The amendment was written and first proposed by Paul at the seventy-fifth anniversary of the Seneca Falls Convention and subsequently introduced in Congress in December 1923 by Republic Senator Charles Curtis (S.J. 21) and Republican Representative Daniel Anthony, both of Kansas.

Paul crusaded for the League of Nations in the 1920s and 1930s. She was also instrumental in getting recognition of equal gender rights in the preamble to the United Nations Charter (McHenry 1980, 320). Paul opposed the seven-year deadline for ratification of the equal rights amendment, as well as the deletion of concurrent enforcement power in the states (Fry 1986, 21).

See also Equal Rights Amendment; Nineteenth Amendment; Shafroth-Palmer Amendment.

For Further Reading:

Flexnor, Eleanor. 1974. *Century of Struggle: The Woman's Rights Movement in the United States.* New York: Atheneum.

❖ PEACE CONVENTION ❖

In February 1861, the same month that the states of the Deep South were meeting in Montgomery, Alabama, to draw up a new Confederate constitution, the state of Virginia called for a convention of the states to devise a plan of reconciliation. Such a call deviated from the convention procedure specified in Article V of the Constitution.

Twenty-one of the 34 states responded by sending delegates to Washington, D.C. (Dumond 1973, 241). Because Virginia did not specify how states would be represented, states sent anywhere from 5 to 11 delegates, and the convention ended up voting, as at the U.S. Constitutional Convention of 1787, by state (Dumond 1973, 244). Although the proceedings were secret, an account was later published by L. E. Chittenden (1864), one of the delegates. Former President John Tyler of Virginia served as president, and many other notables attended.

The convention ended up creating a committee of one delegate from each state. Its recommendations, later submitted to Congress, closely resembled the Crittenden Compromise. Under the convention plan, slavery in the territories would have been dealt with somewhat differently, with a greater role for federal courts than Crittenden would have recognized (Dumond 1973, 247–48). Also, the convention would have provided that, except in cases of discovery or acquisition of special facilities, new territories would have to be acquired by treaties approved by a majority of the senators from each section (Dumond 1973, 249).

Apparently, the convention hoped that its proposed amendments would be submitted by Congress directly to the states for their approval. This would have bypassed the requirement in Article V for a prior congressional sanction by a two-thirds vote of both houses. The convention further proposed ratification, as in the case of the original Constitution, by state conventions (Keogh 1987, 291). Never considered by the full House, the convention proposals (substituted for the Crittenden Compromise) were defeated on the closing day of the lame-duck Senate by a vote of 7 to 28. The House and Senate did adopt the Corwin amendment, which would have protected slave states from amendments interfering with that institution, but like the convention proposals, this failed to avert civil war.

❖ PEI, MARIO (1901–1978) ❖

Mario Pei, a professor of Romance languages at Columbia University, called for a constitutional convention in an article published in the late 1960s (Pei 1967–1968; Vile 1991c, 100–101). He argued that such a convention would be a better way of revising and clarifying ambiguous sections of the current document than would more piecemeal reform.

Pei presented his own agenda for reform as more of a set of suggestions than a settled scheme. His proposals included four-year terms for the members of the House of Representatives; clarification of constitutional provisions relative to declarations of war; reform of the electoral college system; and the popular election and/or confirmation of Supreme Court justices, with the possibility of limited terms of office. Other ideas included having the president run on a ticket with members of his cabinet and reconsidering Supreme Court rulings relative to the establishment clause of the First Amendment and the right of peaceable assembly. Pei would also examine existing interpretations of the Second Amendment and the relation between the nation and the states. Among his proposed tax reforms was a plan to repeal the Sixteenth Amendment and to allocate different kinds of taxes among the different levels of government.

Pei envisioned a convention that would meet for a year or two. He thought that the voters of each state should choose delegates on nonpartisan ballots, with elected delegates to resign from any other offices. He also thought that proposed reforms should require the approval of two-thirds of the delegates.

Pei argued that the convention mechanism was democratic. He suggested that one of the major parties should propose such a convention as part of its platform.

❖ PENN, WILLIAM (1644–1718) ❖

William Penn was an English Quaker. Along with parishioner William Mead, Penn had been arrested and tried in 1670 for preaching to his congregation, and he was subjected to a kangaroo judicial proceeding that led to his popular vindication (Peck 1992, 85–87). He later received a land grant in America from the king. Penn's Frame of Government for Pennsylvania (1682–1683) was the first such document to contain an amending mechanism (Beatty 1975, 61).

In the preamble to this document, Penn observed, "I do not find a model in the world that time, place, and some singular emergences have not necessarily altered" (Thorpe 1909, 5:3053–54). Here and in subsequent charters that he drew up for Delaware and Pennsylvania, Penn allowed for future charter alterations with the consent of the governor and six-sevenths of the assembly. Drawing on his view that freedom of conscience was especially fundamental, however, Penn provided that protections for this right should never be altered (Thorpe 1909, 5:3079–80). Both the required supermajorities to initiate change and the presence of entrenchment mechanisms find echoes in the amending article of the U.S. Constitution.

❖ PENSIONS ❖

The Constitution makes no explicit mention of pensions. There was no general scheme of government pensions in the nation's early history, but controversy periodically surfaced with respect to military pensions, bonuses, and land grants. These were given to compensate those who had served in the military, to provide care to those wounded in the service, or as support for the widows and children of such veterans (Glasson and Kinley 1918). In the 1880s and 1890s, members of Congress introduced amending resolutions to prevent the decrease or repeal of promised pensions, to limit pensions to those provided under law at the time an individual enlisted, or to restrict pensions to individuals or to the families of individuals actually wounded in service (Musmanno 1929, 129–31).

Although there are still occasional disputes about veterans' benefits, today, primary attention has shifted from military pensions to old-age and disability pensions provided under the Social Security system established in 1935 (Myles 1989). At least one amendment proposed in 1935 attempted to give Congress power to establish this program. Despite Supreme Court decisions upholding the taxation provisions of the act in *Steward Machine Co. v. Davis* (1937) and *Helvering v. Davis* (1937), several amendments were introduced from 1939 to 1941 to formalize this power. A handful of subsequent proposals have attempted to place limits on the extent to which Social Security and other related taxes can be raised.

There are continuing concerns that the Social Security program might become bankrupt as the number of senior citizens and the ratio of nonworking to working individuals increase. In 1964, Massachusetts submitted a petition for a constitutional convention to deal with this issue, but no other state joined in this call.

❖ PHILIPPINE INDEPENDENCE ❖

In July 1930, Democratic Senator Royal Copeland of New York introduced an amending resolution to grant independence to the Philippines, an objective subsequently accomplished by ordinary legislation. After defeating the Spanish in the Spanish-American War of 1898, the United States purchased these Pacific islands from Spain and, much to the chagrin of American anti-imperialists, forcefully overwhelmed the independence movement there.

Subsequently, the Jones Act of 1916 promised eventual independence ("Philippines" 1994). After the Filipinos rejected the provisions for independence in the 1933 Hawes-Cutting-Hare bill, Congress adopted the Tydings McDuffie Act of 1934 (Grunder and Livezey 1973, 220–23). It provided for an interim commonwealth to be followed by complete independence in 1946 ("Philippines" 1994).

This timetable was followed despite the disruptions caused by the Japanese seizure of the islands in World War II. The United States, however, continued to view the Philippines as a special area of responsibility and influence (Shalom 1981), and it maintained military bases there until quite recently.

❖ PIBURN, JOHN L. (1872–?) ❖

John Piburn was a medical doctor and author of a book published in 1932 proposing the text of a new U.S. Constitution and a revised code suitable for California and other states. Although much of his proposed constitution simply rearranged the provisions in the existing document, it also contained a number of innovative ideas.

Most prominent was the creation of the Educational Department and Educational College, the organization of which led off the document. Consisting of five recent graduates elected by each college and initially governed by the first member to be selected from the University of Missouri (Piburn 1932, 12), the department was to have extensive powers to promote and oversee education, including power to specify how grading will be done (20–24), designate what size diplomas should be (24), and set tax rates for education (14). "Religious," "denominational," and "sectarian" schools were to be prohibited, as would night classes, the use of initials on diplomas (16), and the issuance of any doctoral degrees other than in medicine (27). BS and MS degrees were to be designated as outranking BAs or MAs (27).

In Piburn's scheme, the House of Representatives would be designated as the House of Solons (32). Piburn would prohibit laws from being rewritten; any changes would have to be adopted as new laws and their predecessors repealed (39). Piburn's prohibition against "sumptuary laws" (46) was apparently designed to abolish the Eighteenth Amendment, which he described in his introduction as "a crime"— an introduction where he likewise saw the only good in the Nineteenth Amendment as the fact that "it will help to un-Christianize women." Piburn would replace the congressional power to declare war with the power to call an election for declaring war, which election would require a majority of males under age 40—presumably those most likely to serve—to approve (41). Piburn applied the restraints in the Bill of Rights directly to Congress, although he extended the establishment clause to both the nation and the states and specified that "all the promoters of religion, and their followers, are jointly and severally liable for damages, libel, and slander for their utterances and practices" (49–50). Piburn further modified what is now the First Amendment by explicitly providing for civil and criminal libel (46–47). On another matter, he would have prohibited miscegenation laws "restricting the amalgamation of the races; or the mating of the sexes" (50), a move that the U.S. Supreme Court did not make until its 1967 decision in *Loving v. Virginia*.

Piburn would have eliminated the office of vice president and provided that presidential vacancies be filled by the oldest senator from the president's party (55). Piburn also included a provision for presidential disability similar to that now found in the Twenty-fifth Amendment (55). Piburn would have explicitly provided for the exercise of judicial review (59) and would have imposed a one-term limit on all offices (66).

Piburn's constitution was to be ratified by the people in three-fourths of the states, and the amending process now in Article V would have been altered so that amendments could be ratified in the same fashion. In a scheme somewhat reminiscent of Thomas Jefferson, a nine-member committee appointed by the Educational College, the Senate, and the House of Solons was to consider revising the document in the year 2000 and "once every fifty years thereafter" (71).

A peculiar blend of the farsighted and the eccentric, of prejudice and enlightenment, Piburn's proposal does not appear to have sparked significant popular or scholarly interest.

❖ PLESSY V. FERGUSON (1896) ❖

Plessy v. Ferguson was one of the most important decisions about the meaning of the Thirteenth and Fourteenth Amendments to be handed down in the nineteenth century (Lofgren 1987). In the *Civil Rights* cases (1883), the Supreme Court had ruled that Congress did not have the power to remedy individual acts of racial discrimination that were not the result of state action. By contrast, in *Plessy v. Ferguson,* the Court upheld a Louisiana Jim Crow law requiring that white and black passengers be seated in separate train cars. This law was challenged by Homer Plessy, an individual who was seven-eighths white and one-eighth black, after he was denied seating on a car reserved for whites.

In rejecting Plessy's Thirteenth Amendment claim, Justice Henry Brown, writing the Court's 7 to 1 majority decision, cited the *Civil Rights* cases as evidence that the Thirteenth Amendment had the limited purpose of freeing the slaves. In interpreting the Fourteenth Amendment, Brown distinguished between legal and social rights and concluded that "it could not have been intended to abolish distinctions based on color, or to enforce social, as distinguished from political, equality, or a commingling of the two races upon terms unsatisfactory to either (*Plessy* 1896, 544). In response to John Marshall Harlan's dissenting opinion suggesting that racial discrimination was as arbitrary as requiring members of different races to walk on different sides of the street or to live in houses of different colors, Brown upheld Jim Crow laws as reasonable. He ascertained such reasonableness by deferring to the state's "liberty to act with reference to the established usages, customs, and traditions of the people, and with a view to the promotion of their comfort, and the preservation of the public peace and good order" (*Plessy* 1896, 550). Brown further denied that segregation was a badge of inferiority: "If this be so, it is not by reason of anything found in the act, but solely because the colored race choses [*sic*] to put that construction upon it" (*Plessy* 1896, 551).

John Marshall Harlan's dissent took a broad view of both the Thirteenth and the Fourteenth Amendments. Harlan is best known for articulating his vision of a color-blind Constitution: "But in view of the Constitution, in the eye of the law, there is in this country no superior, dominant, ruling class of citizens. Our Constitution is color-blind, and neither knows nor tolerates classes among citizens. In respect of civil rights, all citizens are equal before the law" (*Plessy* 1896, 559).

Plessy v. Ferguson remained the law of the land until it was reversed by the Supreme Court's decision in *Brown v. Board of Education* (1954).

See also *Brown v. Board of Education*.

❖ POLITICAL QUESTIONS ❖

The political questions doctrine has proved to be one of the most elusive doctrines of U.S. constitutional law. Basically, the doctrine is designed to allow courts to defer judgments on issues that they think are, for one reason or another, best left to the "political," that is, the elected, branches of government. However, the Court has sometimes equivocated as to whether this doctrine is motivated by constitutional or prudential concerns. Moreover, some issues that courts once considered to be political are no longer considered to be so (Scharpf 1966).

As early as *Marbury v. Madison* (1803), Chief Justice John Marshall had asserted that the Court dealt with individual rights and that "questions in their nature political . . . can never be made in this Court" (168). The major nineteenth-century case involving the political questions doctrine, however, was *Luther v. Borden* (1849). Asked to determine which of two rival Rhode Island

governments was "republican" under the guarantee clause in Article IV, Section 4 of the Constitution, the Court deferred to the decisions already made by the president and Congress.

Although it had previously answered a number of important amending issues, in *Coleman v. Miller* (1939), the Supreme Court applied the political questions doctrine to the amending process. It proclaimed itself "equally divided" on the issue of whether a state's lieutenant governor could break a tie on a state's ratification of an amendment. On the issue of whether a state could ratify an amendment it had previously rejected, however, the Court decided that this question, as well as the related question of whether a state could rescind a ratification once it was given, was a political question for Congress to decide. Similarly, it decided that Congress had the responsibility for ascertaining whether amendments were ratified in a timely fashion (Vile 1993b, 24–35).

A number of developments have affected the political questions doctrine since *Coleman*. Most significantly, in *Baker v. Carr* (1962), the Supreme Court reversed course on the justiciability of state legislative apportionment. Whereas in *Colegrove v. Green* (1946) it had decided that such issues fell under the guarantee clause and were nonjusticiable, in *Baker v. Carr* it decided that such issues could be reached under the equal protection clause of the Fourteenth Amendment. In *Powell v. McCormack* (1969), the Court subsequently decided that the question of qualifications of a member of Congress was not a political question but was one that the Court could decide. By contrast, in *Nixon v. United States* (1993), the Court decided that the Constitution vested the issue of impeachment proceedings exclusively in Congress.

In *Dyer v. Blair* (1975), a U.S. district court decided that it was not precluded under the political questions doctrine from deciding that a state legislature (albeit not a state constitution) had the right to set an extraordinary majority requirement for ratification of an amendment. Similarly, in *Idaho v. Freeman* (1981), another district court called into question the application of the political questions doctrine as it related to a number of issues surrounding ratification of the equal rights amendment.

Justice William Brennan offered the most complete catalog of questions that are considered political in *Baker v. Carr*, where he cited six:

[1] a textually demonstrable constitutional commitment of the issue to a coordinate political department; [2] or a lack of judicially discoverable and manageable standards for resolving it; [3] or the impossibility of deciding without an initial policy determination of a kind clearly for nonjudicial discretion; [4] or the impossibility of a court's undertaking independent resolution without expressing lack of the respect due coordinate branches of government; [5] or an unusual need for unquestioning adherence to a political decision already made; [6] or the potentiality of embarrassment from multifarious pronouncements by various departments on one question. (1962, 217)

Applying these principles, especially in light of precedents that have been written since *Coleman v. Miller*, a number of scholars have argued that the Supreme Court has considerable leeway in deciding modern amending controversies (Dellinger 1983; Rees 1986; Vile 1993b).

See also *Coleman v. Miller*; Guarantee Clause.

❖ POLL TAXES ❖

See Twenty-fourth Amendment.

❖ POLLOCK V. FARMERS' LOAN & TRUST CO. (1895) ❖

In one of the most controversial rulings in its day, the Supreme Court first invalidated taxes on income from state and municipal bonds and on income from property (*Pollock* 1 [1895]); on reargument, it invalidated the federal tax on personal and corporate income (*Pollock* 2 [1895]). Although the decisions appeared to conflict with earlier rulings, including dicta in *Hylton v. United States* (1796) and a decision upholding a Civil War income tax in *Springer v. United States* (1881), in the second *Pollock* decision, Chief Justice Melville Fuller stated that the Court was doing no more than reading the constitutional language about direct taxes in its "obvious sense" (1895, 618). He further noted that if the people desired to change this language, "the ultimate sovereignty may be . . . called into play by a slow and deliberate [constitutional amending] process, which gives time for mere hypothesis and opinion to exhaust themselves, and for the sober second thought of every part of the country to be asserted" (1895, 635).

In one of four dissenting opinions, Justice John Marshall Harlan criticized the majority for departing from precedents. He stated, "If this new theory of the Constitution . . . is justified by the fundamental law, the American people cannot too soon amend their Constitution" (1895, 674).

Harlan's advice was heeded when the Sixteenth Amendment was ratified in 1913, effectively overturning the *Pollock* decision. This was only the third such amendment in U.S. history to have such an effect.

See also Sixteenth Amendment.

❖ POST OFFICE ❖

Throughout much of U.S. history, the post office has been a major source of political patronage. In 1829, President Andrew Jackson made the postmaster general a cabinet official, albeit "not so much to honor the Post Office as to control it" (Cullinan 1968, 44). The president subsequently exercised the right to both appoint (subject to Senate confirmation) and fire first-, second-, and third-class postmasters (Cullinan 1968, 221). The president's power to fire such officials without Senate approval was confirmed in *Myers v. United States* (1926).

There have been a number of proposals throughout U.S. history to make the positions of postmasters and other presidential appointees (for example, revenue assessors) elective. Although most such proposals came in the nineteenth century, Democratic Texas Representative Olin Teague offered several such proposals in the 1960s. The Postal Reorganization Act of 1970 removed the postmaster general from the cabinet and made the U.S. Postal Service into a public corporation with its own civil service system. It thus dried up what has been called the "last great pool of patronage" (M. Nelson 1989, 854). Calls to make postmasters' positions elective appear to have ceased.

In 1973, Democratic Representative Tom Bevill of Alabama proposed an amendment prohibiting the use of U.S. mails for "the transmission, carriage, or delivery of communications hostile to or subversive of this Constitution and the laws and form of government of the U.S. or of any State" (H.J. Res. 131). This proposal could be in conflict with the free speech provision of the First Amendment.

❖ PRAYER IN PUBLIC SCHOOLS ❖

Since 1962, several hundred amendments have been introduced to allow spoken prayer in public schools, making this one of the most frequently offered proposals in U.S. history.

Catalysts for the Prayer Amendment

The proposals began in the aftermath of the Supreme Court's decision in *Engel v. Vitale* (1962), in which it struck down a nondenominational prayer composed by the New York State Board of Regents for public schools. In an 8-to-1 decision written by Justice Hugo Black, the Court found that the prayer constituted an impermissible establishment of religion in violation of the First Amendment. In *Abington v. Schempp* (1963), in an 8-to-1 decision written by Justice Tom Clark, the Court subsequently extended its ruling to prohibit devotional readings from the Bible and recitation of the Lord's Prayer.

These two cases, especially the first, hit like bombshells and provoked numerous cries of outrage. One congressman noted that "we ought to impeach these men in robes who put themselves up above God," and another commented that "they put the Negroes in the schools and now they've driven God out" (cited in Laubach 1969, 2). Although Congress did not act on one member's proposal to buy a Bible "for the personal use of each justice," the House voted, in September 1962, to put the words "In God We Trust" behind the Speaker's desk (Laubach 1969, 3).

Congressional Amending Efforts

Early efforts to overturn the Supreme Court's decisions centered on a proposal offered by New York Democratic Representative Frank J. Becker of New York. A devout Roman Catholic who was not running for reelection, Becker devoted much of his effort toward getting a majority of his colleagues in the House to vote for a discharge petition to pry the amendment from the House Judiciary Committee, where fellow New York Democrat Emanuel Celler was trying to keep it bottled up.

Becker's proposal, as modified in conjunction with other House sponsors, had four sections, the last of which contained a seven-year ratification deadline. The other three sections were as follows:

Sec. 1: Nothing in this Constitution shall be deemed to prohibit the offering, reading from, or listening to prayers or Biblical scriptures, if participation therein is on a voluntary basis, in any governmental or public school, institution or place.

Sec. 2: Nothing in this Constitution shall be deemed to prohibit making reference to, belief in, reliance upon, or invoking the aid of God or a Supreme Being in any governmental or public document, proceeding, activity, ceremony, school, institution, or place, or upon any coinage, currency, or obligation of the United States.

Sec. 3: Nothing in this article shall constitute an establishment of religion. (Beaney and Beiser 1973, 32)

Celler reluctantly called for hearings, but an increasing number of scholars and religious leaders began to raise questions about the implications of this amendment—for example, which version of the Bible would be used—and others questioned the wisdom of altering the Bill of Rights. Becker's discharge petition failed.

In 1964, the Republican platform called for an amendment to permit prayer and Bible reading in schools. In 1966, Illinois Republican Senator Everett Dirksen (who had also been active in trying to repeal the Supreme Court's reapportionment decisions) introduced such an amendment, the heart of which provided that "nothing contained in this Constitution shall prohibit the authority administering any school, school system, educational institution or other public building supported in whole or in part through the expenditure of public funds from providing for or permitting the voluntary participation by students or others in prayer" (Laubach 1969, 142).

Indiana Democratic Senator Birch Bayh subsequently presided over hearings on this amendment. Again, scholars and religious leaders raised questions. Dirksen subsequently brought his amendment to the floor without the support of the Senate Judiciary Committee. The vote of 49 to 37 fell short of the required two-thirds (Laubach 1969, 149).

In 1967, Dirksen revised his amendment to provide that "nothing in this Constitution shall abridge the rights of persons lawfully assembled, in any public building which is supported in whole or in part through the expenditure of public funds, to participate in non-denominational prayer" (Laubach 1969, 149). Again the amendment proved unsuccessful, as did a similar amendment sponsored in 1970 by Tennessee Republican Senator Howard Baker. A 1971 vote in the House of Representatives on a similar measure garnered 240 votes to 163, again falling short of the necessary two-thirds (Keynes with Miller 1989, 194).

In 1979, Ronald Reagan made prayer in school part of his platform for the presidency. The year before, hearings had been held on a proposal by North Carolina Republican Senator Jesse Helms to curb the jurisdiction of the Supreme Court over such issues. Helms's proposal was eventually stopped by a filibuster (R. Smith 1987, 276).

Congress subsequently considered Reagan's amendment. It provided that "nothing in this Constitution shall be construed to prohibit individual or group prayer in public schools or other public institutions. No person shall be required by the United States or by any state to participate in such prayer" (R. Smith 1987, 276). In March 1984, the amendment received a vote of 56 to 44 in the Senate, again falling short of the required two-thirds majority (R. Smith 1987, 278). However, that same year, Congress adopted the Equal Access Act, designed to allow religious groups to meet on high school property if noncurricular nonreligious groups were also permitted to meet there.

In *Wallace v. Jaffree* (1985), the Supreme Court struck down an Alabama law that specifically allowed students to use a moment of silence for the purpose of prayer (a decision that does not, however, resolve the issue of whether a moment of silence that does not specifically endorse prayer might be valid). Utah Republican Senator Orrin Hatch subsequently introduced an amendment providing that "nothing in this Constitution shall be construed to prohibit individual or group silent prayer or reflection in public schools. Neither the United States nor any state shall require any person to participate in such prayer or reflection, nor shall they encourage any particular form of prayer or reflection" (R. Smith 1987, 188). Again, hearings were held, with the Judiciary Committee favorably reporting out the amendment. More recently, although the amendment was not included in the Contract with America, congressional Republicans promised another vote on it.

Current Developments

To date, no such amendment has been adopted. Doubts remain as to both the proper wording of such an amendment and the wisdom of modifying any part of the Bill of Rights. Some proponents of greater religious freedom retain the hope that the Supreme Court will eventually ease the tension by officially sanctioning some existing moment-of-silence laws. In 1995, President Clinton attempted to fend off a prayer amendment by stressing religious rights that schoolchildren already have under the Equal Access Act and other judicial decisions. Some versions of the proposed Religious Equality Amendment specifically provide for reinstitution of public prayer in schools.

See also *Abington v. Schempp; Engel v. Vitale;* Religious Equality Amendment.

For Further Reading:

Schotten, Peter, and Dennis Stevens. 1996. *Religion, Politics and the Law: Commentaries and Controversies.* Belmont, CA: Wadsworth.

❖ PREAMBLE TO THE CONSTITUTION ❖

The first paragraph of the Constitution is called the preamble. In elegant language, it delineates the primary purposes of the document. The preamble has an "aspirational tone" (S. Barber 1984, 34). The Supreme Court, however, has held that, taken alone, the preamble "has never been regarded as the source of any substantive power conferred on the government of the United States, or on any of its departments" (*Jacobson* 1905, 22).

There have been at least four proposals to alter the preamble, one in 1869 and three in the 1960s. At least one wanted to incorporate the principles of the Declaration of Independence there. Many of those who have proposed texts of new constitutions have also altered the preamble to reflect new or widened purposes for government to achieve. The Confederate constitution altered the preamble to reinforce Southern claims of state sovereignty (a matter that the opening words of the preamble, "We the people of the United States," arguably left ambiguous). In a move later advocated by proponents of the Christian amendment, the Confederate constitution preamble also mentioned "Almighty God" (DeRosa 1991, 135).

❖ PRESIDENCY, AGE LIMITS FOR ❖

The Constitution sets a minimum age of 35 for the president but does not specify a maximum age. When Ronald Reagan was inaugurated for his first term in 1981, he was just shy of his seventieth birthday, and the "age issue" had already emerged when he first sought the Republican nomination five years earlier (Ceaser 1988, 183). Republican Bob Dole of Kansas began his third attempt for the Republican nomination for president in 1995 at the age of 72.

A number of amending proposals introduced in the 1970s would have made Reagan ineligible for a second term or Dole ineligible for a first because they would have denied eligibility to presidential or vice presidential candidates who had reached the age of 70. Most would have provided that the president serve for a single six-year term.

❖ PRESIDENCY, APPOINTMENT ❖ AND REMOVAL POWERS OF

Article II, Section 2 of the Constitution outlines the power to appoint executive officials and vests this power largely in the president, who must operate with the "Advice and Consent of the Senate." The Constitution does not specify who has the power to remove executive officials. This issue was an especially controversial issue in the nineteenth century and was a major bone of contention between President Andrew Johnson and the Reconstruction Congress; Johnson's secretary of war Edwin M. Stanton refused to accept Johnson's authority to fire him until the impeachment effort against Johnson failed in the Senate.

In *Myers v. United States* (1926), Chief Justice (and ex-president) William Howard Taft authored a decision upholding President Wilson's authority to fire a first-class postmaster, without Senate concurrence. Taft argued that the framers intended to vest this power in the president, who would best be able to ascertain the capabilities and performance of his subordinates. Taft further argued that "the power to remove inferior executive officers, like that to remove superior officers, is an incident of the power to appoint them, and is in its nature an executive power" (*Myers* 1926, 161).

Two subsequent cases have somewhat qualified this power. In *Humphrey's Executor v. United States* (1935), the Court unanimously ruled that a president could not fire a member of the Federal Trade Commission—considered a quasi-legislative and quasi-judicial body. Similarly, in *Wiener v. United States* (1958), the Court denied that President Eisenhower could remove without cause a member of the War Claims Commission, also described by the Court as a quasi-judicial body.

Most proposals for altering or clarifying presidential appointment and removal powers came in the nineteenth century. Some were designed to give Congress the power to appoint and remove the secretary of the Treasury Department, members of the post office department, or various other members of the cabinet; some proposed including the House of Representatives in the advice and consent function and in removals; some would have permitted cabinet officers (rather than the president) to select officers under them; others attempted to set specific terms for executive officials; and still others attempted to exclude various individuals—members of Congress, for example—from executive offices (Ames 1896, 134–38). The nineteenth century also witnessed the development of the civil service system.

Judicial decisions have clarified the appointment and removal power in the twentieth century, and the executive's power to remove members of his administration is generally accepted. Periodically, members of Congress have introduced proposals to provide a means, in addition to impeachment and conviction, to remove judicial officers.

See also Civil Service Reform.

❖ PRESIDENCY, COMPENSATION FOR ❖

Article II, Section 1 of the Constitution provides that "the President shall, at stated

Times, receive for his Services, a Compensation, which shall neither be increased nor diminished during the period for which he shall be elected, and he shall not receive within that Period any other Emolument from the United States, or any of them."

The first Congress set the president's salary at $25,000 a year (although Washington, and later Kennedy, refused such compensation), a figure that was doubled in 1873. As of 1969, the president receives $200,000 annually, but there are other perquisites, such as travel, expense accounts, use of the White House, and the like (Bledsoe 1989, 830).

In 1808, Federalist Senator James Hillhouse of Connecticut introduced an amendment to cut the president's salary to $15,000 a year, and in 1822, Democrat Timothy Fuller of Massachusetts proposed that such compensation be fixed—along with that of members of Congress—every 10 years. Amendments introduced in 1882 and 1884 to limit the president to one term also had a provision to grant him a pension (Ames 1896, 129). The United States did not provide such pensions until 1958. Today, ex-presidents receive a salary equal to that of a cabinet secretary (Bledsoe 1989, 839). After 200 years, it appears that further adjustments in presidential compensation or perquisites are likely to continue to be resolved by ordinary legislation rather than by constitutional amendment.

❖ PRESIDENCY, CREATION OF ❖
A SEPARATE CHIEF OF STATE

In Great Britain, the prime minister serves as chief of government, and the monarch serves as ceremonial chief of state. In the United States, by contrast, the president carries out both sets of responsibilities. Although ceremonial tasks can be wearisome, a president can also manipulate them to increase his visibility and prestige. President

Richard M. Nixon was especially fond of the ceremonial aspects of his office.

In 1975, after the collapse of Nixon's presidency, Democratic Representative Henry Reuss of Wisconsin proposed a constitutional amendment to create a ceremonial chief of state who would be confirmed by a majority vote of both houses of Congress. The chief of state could serve an unlimited number of four-year terms and would receive the same salary as the president. Terms of the chief of state would overlap with those of presidents, the first to be appointed two years into the president's term. Reuss's proposal generated little support (Diller 1989, 594).

PRESIDENCY, MEMBERSHIP
❖   IN SENATE FOR   ❖
EX-PRESIDENTS

In a parliamentary system, unsuccessful candidates for prime minister generally continue to lead their party in that body, assuming that they are reelected to the parliament. In contrast, once U.S. presidents leave office, they have no official governmental post, although the visibility and government-provided financial support for such individuals have grown fairly dramatically in recent years. As early as 1875, proposals were introduced to make ex-presidents lifetime at-large or ex officio nonvoting members of the U.S. Senate (M. Nelson 1989, 1079–80). A resolution introduced in 1917 would have given ex–vice presidents at-large membership in the House of Representatives. The period from 1960 to 1963 witnessed at least seven proposals to give ex-presidents ex officio status in the Senate. At least one of these proposals, offered by Democratic Representative Morris Udall of Arizona, would apply to all unsuccessful candidates for president.

In 1963, the Senate altered its rules to provide that "former presidents of the

United States shall be entitled to address the Senate upon appropriate notice to the presiding officer who shall thereupon make the necessary arrangements." The next year, Truman made some remarks to the Senate, but to date, no ex-president has delivered a formal address there (M. Nelson 1989, 1080).

For Further Reading:

Clark, James C. 1985. *Faded Glory: Presidents out of Power*. New York: Praeger.

❖ PRESIDENCY, OATH OF ❖

The only oath specifically included in the U.S. Constitution is the oath of the president. He swears or affirms faithfully to "execute the office of President . . . and . . . preserve, protect, and defend the Constitution of the United States."

A number of the practices currently associated with the oath—for example, swearing on a Bible and having the oath administered by the chief justice of the United States—are not specified in the Constitution (Euchner and Maltese 1989, 262). The words "so help me God" are not included in the Constitution either, although President Washington began the practice of adding them. Several proposals—the most persistent being that of Democrat John Rarick of Louisiana—have called for these words to be added to the text of the Constitution. If they were so added, it would be the first explicit mention of God in the document, a longtime objective of supporters of the Christian amendment.

See also Christian Amendment.

❖ PRESIDENCY, PARDON POWER ❖

Since 1974, more than 25 amending proposals have been introduced in Congress to modify the president's pardon power. This power is delineated in Article II, Section 2 of the Constitution, which grants him "Power to grant Reprieves and Pardons for Offenses against the United States, except in Cases of Impeachment."

In *Federalist* No. 74, Alexander Hamilton defended this provision not simply as a way of mitigating individual injustices but also as a means of restoring domestic peace. Hamilton noted that "in seasons of insurrection or rebellion, there are often critical moments when a well-timed offer of pardon to the insurgents or rebels may restore the tranquillity of the commonwealth: and which if suffered to pass unimproved, it may never be possible afterwards to recall" (Hamilton, Madison, and Jay 1961, 449).

The Supreme Court has interpreted the pardon power broadly. In *Ex Parte Garland* (1867), upholding a pardon to a former Confederate issued by President Andrew Johnson, the Court said that the executive pardon "extends to every offense known to the law, and may be exercised at any time after its commission, either before legal proceedings are taken, or during their pendency, or after conviction and judgment" (380). Similarly, in *Schick v. Reed* (1974), upholding a condition to a pardon issued by President Eisenhower, the Court said that the purpose of the power was "to allow plenary authority in the President to 'forgive' the convicted person in part or entirely, to reduce a penalty in terms of a specified number of years, or to alter it with conditions which are themselves constitutionally unobjectionable" (266). The pardon power includes the authority to issue general amnesties, which several presidents have granted. President Carter made such provision for Vietnam-era draft evaders.

President Ford issued the most controversial pardon in U.S. history in 1974 when he extended a "full, free, and absolute pardon" to former President Nixon "for all offenses against the United States which he had committed or may have committed or taken part in" (McDonald 1992, 620). This pardon appears to have been the catalyst for most amendment proposals that followed. Most such proposals, including one introduced by Minnesota Democratic Senator Walter Mondale, would have allowed Congress to disapprove such pardons by a two-thirds vote within 180 days (Duker 1977, 537). Other proposals would have limited the president to pardoning only those convicted of crimes or, like a proposal offered by California's Democratic Senator Barbara Boxer, would have prohibited the president from pardoning individuals employed in his own administration.

<hr>

❖ PRESIDENCY, PLURAL ❖
EXECUTIVE

One of the most important decisions that the delegates to the Constitutional Convention made was to fashion the presidency as a singular office rather than to entrust such powers in a dual executive or executive council. Pennsylvania's James Wilson defended a singular executive to those who feared that it would assume monarchical powers; he argued that a single individual would be better able to assume responsibility for executive tasks (M. Nelson 1989, 23). In *Federalist* No. 70, Alexander Hamilton further defended a singular executive as a means of achieving "energy" and "unity" in government (Hamilton, Madison, and Jay 1961, 423–34).

As the slavery controversy grew, however, some began to fear that a single president might tilt the resolution of this issue toward the interest of a single section of the nation. Indeed, the election of Abraham Lincoln eventually prompted the Southern secession movement. Picking up on an earlier idea of John C. Calhoun's, Virginia Democratic Representative Albert Jenkins introduced a resolution in 1860 to create a dual executive; that same year, Democratic Represen-

tative John Noell of Missouri proposed replacing the president with a three-person executive council. In 1878, Ohio Democratic Representative Milton Southard, who feared that the presidency was becoming too monarchical, proposed creating a presidency of three men representing the western, eastern and middle, and southern states (Ames 1896, 69–70). In 1975, Democratic Representative Henry Reuss of Wisconsin introduced proposals for the creation of a separate chief of state to perform ceremonial functions now assumed by the president.

From a somewhat different perspective, political scientist Matthew Holden Jr. advocated an amendment to create a plural executive, with the prospect of guaranteeing that at least one of the vice presidents forming the resulting executive would be an African American (Holden 1973b, 252–53). Herman Finer proposed adding 11 vice presidents, who, with the president, would exercise collective responsibility in much the same way as the cabinet in Great Britain (Finer 1960, 304).

<hr>

❖ PRESIDENCY, ❖
QUALIFICATIONS FOR

The Constitution requires that the president be at least 35 year old and have resided in the United States for 14 years or more. Article II, Section 1 of the U.S. Constitution further specifies that the president must be "a natural born Citizen" or citizen when the Constitution was adopted. This provision was apparently designed to ease fears that the delegates to the Constitutional Convention of 1787 might be planning to invite a European monarch to serve as chief executive (M. Nelson 1987, 395).

The term "natural born citizen" has been subject to some dispute and could one day be clarified by an amendment. Meanwhile, it probably already includes individuals—such as George Romney, who ran unsuccessfully for the 1968 Republican nomination—born overseas to parents who were American citizens (Gordon 1968).

Members of Congress have proposed a number of amendments to alter presidential qualifications, many in the first 100 years of the nation's history. These included proposals to raise the age of eligibility from 35 to 45, to exclude former secessionists from the office (a qualified version of which appeared in Section 3 of the Fourteenth Amendment), and to bar members of Congress or those who are holding office or have held office within two or four years of a presidential election from the job (Ames 1896, 74–75).

In 1976, House Minority Leader John Rhodes and Senator Barry Goldwater, both Arizona Republicans, sponsored a version of this last proposal that would have barred members of Congress from the presidency for two years after they left office. Their primary intention was to avoid excessive absences by members of Congress running for chief executive. As the 1964 Republican presidential candidate, Goldwater could testify from personal experience to the difficulty of pursuing both tasks. Their proposal would not have affected the provisions for appointing vice presidents under the Twenty-fifth Amendment.

The most popular proposal affecting presidential qualifications, first offered in the 1860s and periodically introduced from the 1940s to the present, would alter the requirement that a president be a natural-born citizen. This would allow foreign-born citizens to be eligible after being American citizens and residents for a certain number of years. Although sponsors of this proposal have included Missouri Senator Thomas Eagleton (S.J. Res. 72, 1983), who was George McGovern's initial Democratic nominee for vice president in 1972, the idea has not received much attention (Gordon 1968, 27).

❖ PRESIDENCY, ROLE IN THE AMENDING PROCESS ❖

Article V of the Constitution does not designate a role for the president in the amending process. However, Article I, Section 7 specifies that "every order, resolution, or vote to which the concurrence of the Senate and the House of Representatives may be necessary (except on the question of adjournment) shall be presented to the President of the United States" for his approval or veto. This clause has led to questions whether the president's signature is needed for an amendment to be valid.

Historically, the answer has been negative. A review of the deliberations of the Constitutional Convention of 1787 indicates that the veto power was discussed in the context of legislation rather than with respect to constitutional amendments (Edel 1981, 33–38). Since amendments must already have been proposed by the same majority needed to override a presidential veto, it is not likely that presidential vetoes would have any significant effect. Moreover, in an early decision in *Hollingsworth v. Virginia* (1798), the U.S. Supreme Court declared that the president's signature was not necessary. Even a critic of this decision, who wants it confined as narrowly as possible, does not appear to advocate reversal of the ruling (C. Black 1978).

On two occasions, presidents have signed amendments before they were sent to the states for approval. The first such signature occurred in 1861, when outgoing President James Buchanan signed the Corwin amendment (which was not subsequently ratified), designed to prevent any congressional interference with the institution of slavery; the second occurred in 1865, when President Abraham Lincoln signed the Thirteenth Amendment abolishing slavery (Bernstein with Agel 1993, 91, 100).

Although their signatures are not required, presidents frequently take positions on constitutional amendments. Article II, Section 3 of the Constitution grants the president power to "recommend" to Congress "such Measures as he shall judge necessary and expedient." Presidents from George Washington to the present have recognized that this right encompasses power to recommend constitutional amendments (Sidak 1989, 2085).

See also *Hollingsworth v. Virginia.*

❖ PRESIDENCY, SEIZURE POWERS OF ❖

In April 1952, President Harry Truman issued Executive Order 10340, which directed the secretary of commerce to seize and operate U.S. steel mills. Truman took this action, which he immediately reported to Congress, to avert a threatened strike that might interfere with U.S. war efforts in Korea (Westin 1990). In so acting, Truman decided against simply delaying the strike by calling for a cooling-off period under the Taft-Hartley Act of 1947. Instead, he relied on the broad grants of executive power within the Constitution itself. As a consequence, at least three resolutions were introduced that April and May in the House of Representatives calling for a constitutional amendment to limit executive seizure powers.

Such an amendment proved to be unnecessary. On 2 June 1952, the Supreme Court ruled in *Youngstown Sheet & Tube Co. v. Sawyer* (often known simply as the steel seizure case) that the president had exceeded his constitutional powers. Justice Hugo Black authored the 6-to-3 decision, which was especially skeptical of the president's broad claim of inherent executive authority. The equally celebrated concurring opinion of Justice Robert Jackson, however, suggested that the president's actions would have been constitutional if Congress had authorized them.

❖ PRESIDENCY, VETO POWER OF ❖

Of all the domestic powers exercised by the president, few are as formidable as the veto, which is outlined in Article I, Section 7 of the Constitution. Qualified rather than absolute, the presidential veto can be overridden by a two-thirds vote of both houses of Congress. The veto's placement within Article I of the Constitution indicates that the framers understood it to be a legislative power and that it therefore represents a departure from strict separation of powers (Spitzer 1988, 18). The threat of such a veto can give a president considerable influence over the formulation of pending legislation. Although presidents may use the veto to void laws they consider to be unconstitutional, the Constitution did not limit use of the mechanism to such circumstances.

President Andrew Jackson reflected his view of the presidency as an embodiment of popular will by exercising the veto 12 times, more than all his predecessors combined (Spitzer 1988, 33). Jackson's administration also marked the introduction of the first of at least 11 proposals introduced in the nineteenth century that would have allowed Congress to override such vetoes by a simple majority vote (Spitzer 1988, 38). Former president John Quincy Adams and perpetual presidential candidate Henry Clay both offered such proposals during the administration of John Tyler, who was especially criticized for his use of the veto power. The House of Representatives voted 99 to 90 in favor of one such bill in 1842, thus falling substantially below the two-thirds majority required (Ames 1896, 132). Proposals to override presidential vetoes by majority vote were reintroduced in Congress in 1912 and 1913 and from 1943 to 1945.

There were two proposals in the first half of the nineteenth century to eliminate the presidential veto. A number of other proposals later in the century would have required vetoes to be overriden by two-thirds of the members elected in each house rather than by two-thirds of a quorum. The latter was a long-standing practice that was eventually legitimated in *Missouri Pacific Railway Co. v. Kansas* (1919).

New York Democratic Representative Jonathan Bingham introduced an amendment resolution in the House in 1975 that would have allowed Congress to override a veto by a three-fifths vote of both houses, but it applied only in the case of an un-elected president (such as Gerald Ford, who was then serving) appointed under the Twenty-fifth Amendment (H.J. Res. 529). After the Supreme Court's opinion in *Immigration and Naturalization Service v. Chadha* (1983), in which it declared the so-called legislative veto to be unconstitutional, at least two resolutions were introduced to restore this mechanism, one coming a week after the decision. Such a veto, a part of about 200 laws, allowed Congress to delegate to the president certain powers, with the understanding that one or both houses could later veto his action. The Court found that such legislative vetoes violated the presentment clause (requiring bills to be presented to the president for a possible veto) and, in some cases, the requirement that legislation be passed by both houses of Congress.

A president exercises a pocket veto by deciding not to sign a bill presented to him within 10 days of a congressional adjournment. In early American history, questions were raised as to whether a president could sign a bill once Congress had adjourned. President Ulysses S. Grant accordingly proposed an amendment that would have forbidden Congress to pass any laws in its final 24 hours (Spitzer 1988, 110).

By far the most popular proposed reform of the veto power has been the proposal to give the president a so-called line-item veto, similar to that exercised by many state governors. Such a power was entrusted to, but never exercised by, the president of the Confederate States of America (Spitzer 1988, 126) and has been advocated by members of Congress from both parties and from both ends of the political spectrum. Georgia's Republican Senator Mack Mattingly introduced a bill that received substantial support in the Senate in 1985; it provided that all major spending proposals would be divided into separate bills before being presented to the president (Cronin and Weill 1985, 127).

Most proposed amendments dealing with item vetoes have been limited specifically to appropriations bills. The 1880s witnessed the introduction of at least two such item-veto proposals for rivers and harbors bills. A number of nineteenth-century presidents, including James Madison, vetoed legislation on the basis that Congress had no constitutional authority to pass legislation for internal improvements.

President Grant asked for an item veto in his annual message of 1873, and the first such proposal was introduced in Congress three years later by West Virginia Congressman James Faulkner. Since then, more than 150 item-veto amendments have been introduced, but only once—in 1884—has such an amendment been favorably reported out of committee, and this was not acted on by the Senate (Spitzer 1988, 127). Modern advocates of the item veto have included Presidents Harry S. Truman, Dwight D. Eisenhower, Gerald Ford, Ronald Reagan, George Bush, and Bill Clinton. Indeed, all three presidential candidates in the 1992 election endorsed this proposal. The only presidents on record against such an item veto are William Howard Taft (Ross and Schwengel 1982, 72), who later served as chief justice of the United States, and Jimmy Carter, who initially supported the proposal but later changed his mind (Cronin and Weill 1985, 130).

Advocates of the item veto believe that it represents a return to the founders' original intention, which has been subverted by the increased use of "riders," or nongermane amendments, that Congress often adds to appropriations bills (Best 1984a). There have been at least half a dozen proposals in U.S. history to prevent such riders or to limit each bill to a single subject. Proponents also see the item veto as a way of trimming the federal budget, which has itself been the subject of numerous proposed amendments. Critics of the item veto doubt that it would have a significant effect on the budget and fear that it might unduly increase presidential powers. Some critics even suggest that it might ultimately result in greater spending, as members of Congress add items in the expectation of some presidential vetoes and as presidents accept such items in exchange for support of other bills.

The item veto was one of the proposals in the Republicans' Contract with America. In March 1996, Republicans agreed on a "functional equivalent of the line-item veto" by means of legislation rather than amendment (Taylor 1996, 637). This bill, whose constitutionality may be challenged, allows presidential rescissions of individual budget items to stand unless Congress disapproves within 30 days. It also contains a "lockbox mechanism" designed to dedicate any savings from the item veto to a reduction of the national debt (Taylor 1996b, 866).

See also Congress, Legislative Veto of.

For Further Reading:
Sidak, J. Gregory. 1995. "The Line-Item Veto Amendment." *Cornell Law Review* 80 (July): 1498–1505.

❖ PRESIDENCY, VOTE OF ❖
NO CONFIDENCE

U.S. presidents serve for fixed terms of office. In contrast, new elections are called in parliamentary systems when parliament votes "no confidence" in the prime minister. Commended for making government responsive to the people, such a mechanism has been proposed as part of a number of plans to rewrite the Constitution. Although his attorney general eventually convinced him that the idea was not feasible, during debates over the League of Nations, Democratic President Woodrow Wilson proposed that senators opposing the plan resign and put themselves up for reelection, with the understanding that if a majority were reelected, Wilson would resign and allow a Republican to assume office (Link 1963, 70–71).

Congressional amending proposals for a vote of no confidence in the president have been clustered in two periods—the early 1950s and the early 1970s. Republican Representatives Frederick Coudert of New York and Charles Kersten of Wisconsin and Republican Senator Robert Hendrickson of New Jersey offered the first set of proposals, perhaps in reaction to the fact that the presidency had been occupied by Democrats from 1933 to 1953. Democrat Edith Green of Oregon introduced a resolution in July 1973 (H.J. Res. 666) tied to concerns over President Nixon's abuse of office. It provided that Congress could, by a two-thirds vote of both houses, adopt a resolution stating that the president had failed to execute the laws, had willfully exceeded his powers, or had violated individual rights. In such a case, Congress could call for a new publicly funded election to be held within 90 days. With a view to the situation at hand, Green further specified that such an election would not preclude use of the impeachment procedure.

Democratic Representative Henry Reuss of Wisconsin, who also advocated creation of a separate chief of state and a number of other reforms (Vile 1991c, 119–21), was another supporter of such a mechanism. In 1974, he proposed that a three-fifths vote of both houses of Congress should be able to declare no confidence in the president and institute an election within 90 to 110 days. His initial proposal contemplated that the vice president would serve during the interim period, but a subsequent proposal left the president in office during this time and required that all members of Congress also stand for reelection. Reuss's resolution was the subject of deliberation, both in a special law review symposium ("Symposium on the Reuss Resolution" 1975) and in subsequent congressional hearings (*Political Economy and Constitutional Reform* 1982).

Interest in the no-confidence vote appears to have waned with Nixon's resignation.

❖ PRICE FIXING ❖

In 1932 and 1933, at least four amendments were proposed to allow Congress to fix prices and prevent profiteering during war. Especially during wartime, power to control prices already appears to have been well established when these amendments were introduced. During World War I, over a dozen federal agencies regulated prices, with the Food and Fuel Administrations having primary control over consumer prices (C. May 1989, 95). During World War II, the Court also upheld the Emergency Price Control Act of 1942 in *Yakus v. United States* (1944). At the state level, the Court had already sanctioned New York's regulation of milk prices in *Nebbia v. New York* (1934).

❖ PRIOR STATE REJECTION OF AMENDMENTS

Article V of the Constitution does not specifically address whether a state legislature or convention can ratify an amendment that it has previously rejected. Precedents indicate that this practice is on far firmer ground than a state's power to rescind its ratification of a pending amendment (Edel 1981, 47–48).

One basis on which Kansas's ratification of the proposed child labor amendment was challenged in *Coleman v. Miller* (1939) was that the legislature had previously rejected this amendment. In that decision, although acknowledging "that Article V says nothing of rejection but speaks only of ratifications," the Court ultimately grounded its refusal to intervene in the matter on the idea that the issue was a political question for Congress to resolve (*Coleman* 1939, 447–50).

Although subsequent cases have called into question the application of the political questions doctrine to some amending issues, it seems doubtful that the Supreme Court would deny a state the right to ratify an amendment it has previously rejected. Without such authority, the Fourteenth Amendment would probably not have been ratified, and the amending process would be even more difficult than it is now. Most proposed legislation on the subject has recognized such a right.

See also *Coleman v. Miller*; Legislation Proposed.

❖ PRIVACY, RIGHT TO ❖

See *Griswold v. Connecticut; Roe v. Wade.*

❖ PROGRESSIVE ERA ❖

Amendments have not been adopted at a uniform pace in U.S. history but have tended to be adopted in clusters. The Bill of Rights was adopted as a unit, three amendments were ratified in the five years that followed the end of the Civil War, and four more were adopted from 1913 to 1920.

This latter period corresponds roughly with the end of the Progressive Era, a time during which reformist sentiments were strong and reformers were optimistic about their ability to solve social problems (Ekirch 1974; Gould 1974; Link and McCormick 1983). Prominent Progressives included Herbert Croly, Theodore Roosevelt, and—to a lesser degree—Woodrow Wilson.

Many Progressives, undoubtedly influenced by the long hiatus of the amending process, started out with fairly critical views of the U.S. Constitution and its possibility for change. Progressives were also especially critical of the political party system—with its bosses, patronage, and vote buying—that had developed in the wake of Jacksonian politics. Progressives wanted to transfer power from the parties to the people, but this desire was combined with the desire to elevate and reform individuals as well.

The four amendments ratified from 1913 to 1920 illumine different aspects of Progressive thought. The Sixteenth Amendment, which legalized the income tax, is, in a sense, the foundation of the powers of the modern national government. Without this or an equivalent revenue source, the national government simply could not take on all its modern functions. The fact that this tax can also be made progressive, so that it takes a higher percentage of the income of the rich than of the poor, means that it has the ability to redistribute income, the disparities of which concerned Progressive reformers.

The Seventeenth Amendment, providing for the direct election of senators, was a strike at the party politics that had dominated senatorial selection in the state legislatures, as well as a more direct expression of the voice of the people. The Eighteenth Amendment, providing for national alcoholic prohibition, seems more problematic, especially in retrospect, but it was tied to Progressive strands of Protestant moralism and to a desire to combat a genuine social evil. Finally, the Nineteenth Amendment capped more than half a century of reform efforts on behalf of women's suffrage, which many believed would not only promote fairness but also

serve to bring women's elevated moral sensibilities to bear at the ballot box.

In addition to these amendments, Progressive leaders advocated numerous other reforms, many of which still influence U.S. politics. These include the direct primary; the initiative, referendum, and recall (also closely associated with midwestern Populism, with at least indirect ties to Progressivism); compulsory schooling; and such economic reforms as antitrust measures, protections against child labor, maximum-hours legislation, and minimum wages (Eisenach 1994, 8–9).

❖ PROMULGATION ❖ OF AMENDMENTS

In *Coleman v. Miller* (1939), the Supreme Court indicated that most issues surrounding the constitutional amending process were "political questions" for Congress to resolve. In so ruling, the Court appears to have been influenced in large part by the actions of the Reconstruction Congress regarding the dispute whether the Fourteenth Amendment had been ratified. The situation was a messy one, but on that occasion, faced with attempts by Ohio and New Jersey to rescind their ratifications of the amendment, Congress adopted a joint resolution counting those states in the final total and stating that the Fourteenth Amendment was "hereby declared to be a part of the Constitution of the United States, and it shall be duly promulgated by the Secretary of State" (quoted in Dellinger 1983, 397). More recently, Congress adopted a similar resolution declaring that the Twenty-seventh Amendment had been ratified.

Article V of the Constitution makes no mention of the need for congressional promulgation of amendments. Moreover, the Supreme Court's decision in *Dillon v. Gloss* (1921) indicated that amendments become part of the law of the land when ratified by the necessary number of states rather than when acknowledged, or promulgated, by the secretary of state, or, in later practice, the administrator of the General Services Administration or the archivist of the Library of Congress.

Law professor Walter Dellinger has argued that congressional promulgation can neither add to nor detract from the legitimacy of an amendment. Believing that such a mechanism is likely to be "an unwieldy, uncertain and unpredictable mechanism for resolving amendment disputes" (1983, 392), he thinks that such matters can better be resolved through the exercise of judicial review.

❖ PROPOSAL OF AMENDMENTS ❖

Article V of the Constitution divides the amending process into two steps, proposal and ratification. Although more controversies have arisen with regard to the ratification of amendments than their proposal, both areas have been fields for controversy.

In the *National Prohibition* cases (1920), the Supreme Court declared that when Congress proposed an amendment by the requisite two-thirds majorities, there was no need for it to adopt a separate resolution stating its judgment that such an amendment was necessary. In the same decision, the Court decided that the required two-thirds majority vote "is a vote of two-thirds of the members present—assuming the presence of a quorum—and not a vote of two-thirds of the entire membership, present and absent" (1920, 386). On at least some occasions, such majorities have been ascertained by voice vote rather than by roll call.

The most controversial issue involving the proposal of amendments centers on the still untried Article V mechanism for a convention to propose amendments, which Congress is supposed to call when it receives petitions from two-thirds of the state legislatures. As is the case with the ratification of amendments, the Constitution does not specify how contemporaneous such applications must be; it also does not specify whether such calls have to center on the same topic.

Some scholars argue that the states can call for only a general convention and that other calls are invalid (C. Black 1979; Dellinger 1979). Others scholars believe that states may call a convention on a single topic or subject area (Rees 1986; Van Alstyne 1978; for discussion of this issue, see Vile 1993b, 54–73). Some scholars argue that, based on the nature of petitions it has received, Congress is already bound to call such a convention (Paulsen 1993, 1995; Van Sickle and Boughey 1990). Absent some catalytic event, it seems unlikely that this view will prevail.

See also *National Prohibition* Cases.

PUERTO RICO, ❖ REPRESENTATION IN ❖ ELECTORAL COLLEGE

In 1961, the states ratified the Twenty-third Amendment granting Washington, D.C., representation in the electoral college equivalent to that of the least populous state—presently three votes. In the two years that followed, representatives from New York, Texas, and New Mexico, all states with sizable Hispanic populations, introduced amendments to grant similar representation for Puerto Rico, a U.S. commonwealth acquired from Spain in the Spanish-American War of 1898.

The commonwealth now holds presidential primaries and sends delegates to both major party conventions. It remains unrepresented, however, in the electoral college. Either the adoption of a constitutional amendment or Puerto Rico's admission as a state, a long-discussed option (Melendez 1988), appears to be a prerequisite to such representation.

R

❖ RATIFICATION OF AMENDMENTS ❖

Article V of the Constitution specifies the manner in which amendments are proposed and ratified. After being proposed either by the necessary congressional majorities or by a special convention, they become part of the Constitution "when ratified by the Legislatures of three fourths of the several States, or by Conventions in three fourths thereof, as the one or the other Mode of Ratification may be proposed by the Congress." Acknowledging the difficulty of amendment, one author noted that "ratification isn't beanbag" (Vose 1979, 113), yet to date, the states have failed to ratify only 6 of 33 amendments that Congress has submitted to them. State legislatures ratified 26 amendments; special state conventions ratified the Twenty-first Amendment.

A number of legal questions have arisen concerning the process of ratification. In an early case, *Hollingsworth v. Virginia* (1798), the Supreme Court decided that the president's signature was not required for amendment ratifications. In *Hawke v. Smith* (1920), it subsequently decided that a state could not require such amendments to be approved by referendums—although the Supreme Court later ruled in *Kimble v. Swackhamer* (1978) that a nonbinding referendum to ascertain state sentiment was not unconstitutional. In *Dillon v. Gloss* (1921), the Court declared that ratification must be soon enough after Congress has

proposed an amendment to reflect a contemporary consensus of the states; it also held that such ratification was complete on the date that the last of the necessary number of states approved rather than on the date that the secretary of state declared such ratification complete. In *United States v. Sprague* (1931), the Court affirmed that Congress had the responsibility of designating which of the two modes specified in the Constitution the states would follow when ratifying an amendment.

Coleman v. Miller (1939) subsequently raised additional issues, including whether prior rejection of an amendment precluded subsequent ratification, whether a state's lieutenant governor could cast a tie-breaking vote in the state legislature in favor of an amendment, and whether a state's ratification had been made within a reasonable length of time. In this case, the Court declared that it was "equally divided" on the issue of the lieutenant governor's veto and decided that the other issues were "political questions" for Congress to resolve.

The equal rights amendment subsequently brought renewed attention to ratification issues. A lower court case, *Dyer v. Blair* (1975), raised the issue of whether a state could require the ratification of amendments by supermajority—in this case, a three-fifths vote. Future Supreme Court Justice John Paul Stevens ruled that this issue was justiciable and that the state ratifying bodies should ascertain the majority that would be required; he did, however, rule that any requirements found in a state's constitution on the subject were invalid.

Another district court decision in *Idaho v. Freeman* (1981) also focused on the proposed equal rights amendment. At issue was a state's right to rescind ratification of an amendment that had not yet been ratified by the necessary three-fourths of the states. Also at issue was the right of Congress to extend the ratification deadline. Like the issues that Stevens had examined, these issues were deemed justiciable by the district judge. Working from the principle of contemporary consensus, the judge declared that a state should be able to rescind ratification of a pending amendment. He further argued that Congress had no power to extend the original deadline for the equal rights amendment, and even if it did, such action would require a two-thirds vote of both houses (Vile 1993b, 49–51). This decision became moot when the equal rights amendment failed to be adopted. A seemingly surefire way to avoid future controversies over ratification deadlines is to include them within the text of proposed amendments (as was done in the case of the Eighteenth, Twentieth, Twenty-first, and Twenty-second Amendments), where they will be self-executing (Dellinger 1983, 409).

The proposal that putatively became the Twenty-seventh Amendment did not have such a deadline. Considerable controversy was generated by the decision of the national archivist—subsequently affirmed by Congress—to accept this amendment that was originally proposed in 1789 but not ratified by the necessary majority of states until 1992.

❖ RECALL ❖

See Congress, Recall of Members; Judiciary, Removal of Members; Presidency, Vote of No Confidence.

❖ REFERENDUM ❖

See Initiative and Referendum.

❖ *REID V. COVERT* (1957) ❖

This case set aside the convictions by courts-martial of Clarice Covert and Dorothy Smith, wives of U.S. military personnel stationed overseas who had killed their husbands. The courts-martial had been held under putative authority of executive agreements that had been reached with the nations involved.

Writing for Chief Justice Earl Warren and for Justices William O. Douglas, William Brennan, and himself, Justice Hugo Black ruled that provisions of the Bill of Rights—including Fifth and Sixth Amendment guarantees of grand jury indictment and trial by a petit jury—applied to U.S. citizens abroad. Black argued that "no agreement with a foreign nation can confer power on Congress, or on any other branch of Government, which is free from the restraints of the Constitution" and that allowing agreements with foreign governments to override the Constitution would be to "permit amendment of that document in a manner not sanctioned by Article V" (*Reid* 1957, 16 and 17).

Although Black denied that his decision was in conflict with *Missouri v. Holland* (1920), his opinion helped ease fears that that case had raised. In easing such fears, the Reid decision may well have undercut support for the Bricker amendment, designed to limit the scope of federal treaties.

See also Bricker Amendment.

❖ RELIGIOUS EQUALITY ❖ AMENDMENT

For decades, members of some religious groups have complained that they have been treated unfairly. They believe that, in attempting to enforce the First Amendment's prohibition against an establishment of religion, courts and other governmental agencies have often denied the legitimate free exercise and free speech rights of those with strong religious beliefs (Reed 1995, 1–12; but see Foltin 1996).

In *Employment Division, Department of Human Services v. Smith* (1990), the Supreme Court denied unemployment compensation to state employees who had been fired from their jobs for ingesting peyote as part of their Native American religious practice. In so doing, the Court apparently abandoned the strict scrutiny it had previously extended to laws impinging on free exercise rights. Although this decision was blunted by subsequent adoption of the Religious Freedom Restoration Act (Vile 1994a, 61), concerns were renewed with the federal court of appeals decision in *Rosenberger v. Rector and Visitors of the University of Virginia* (1994). This ruling upheld the University of Virginia's decision to deny expenditure of student activity fee funds to an evangelical Christian publication while funding similar publications that did not have such an evangelical orientation. Although the Supreme Court overturned this ruling in 1995 and decided that the university could not deny funding to a group simply because it was religious, concerns remained that the free exercise clause of the First Amendment was not being fully honored. These concerns led to a number of individuals to advocate a religious equality amendment (Casey 1995; Goodstein 1995).

In November 1995, two Republicans introduced separate amending resolutions in Congress. Representative Henry Hyde of Illinois proposed in H.J. Res. 121 that

neither the United states nor any state shall deny benefits to or otherwise discriminate against any private person or

group on account of religious expression, belief, or identity; nor shall the prohibition on laws respecting an establishment of religion be construed to require such discrimination.

In contrast to Hyde's proposal, the proposal introduced by Representative Ernest Istook Jr. of Oklahoma (H.J. Res. 127) specifically mentioned prayer in the public schools:

To secure the people's right to acknowledge God according to the dictates of conscience: Nothing in this Constitution shall prohibit the acknowledgements of the religious heritage, beliefs, or traditions of the people, or prohibit student-sponsored prayer in public schools. Neither the United States nor any State shall compose any official prayer or compel joining in prayer, or discrminate against religious expression or belief.

Although Istook's proposal specifically permits student-sponsored prayer in schools, advocates of a religious equality amendment generally note that it differs from earlier proposals to permit public prayer in schools or to acknowledge God in the Constitution. One advocate specifically asserts that the proposal "is not a 'school prayer' amendment (as that term is commonly understood) because it does not permit state-sponsored teacher-led prayer." He further notes, however, that "if a school board sets aside a time for a student message at a graduation ceremony, the student speaker would have the right to say a prayer under the proposed amendment." Moreover, although the amendment would not permit "special funding of religious schools and social service providers," under such an amendment, "the Constitution would no longer prohibit religious entities from participating in neutrally available government funding programs" including a school voucher system (Baylor 1995, 4–5).

The Religious Equality Amendment was the first of 10 proposals included in the Christian Coalition's Contract with the American Family—a take-off of the earlier Republican Contract with America (Reed 1995, 1–12).

In a related vein, in 1995, Republican Senator Thad Cochrane of Mississippi introduced an amendment prohibiting the state or national governments from abridging the free exercise of religion and granting Congress power to enforce this amendment. Cochrane noted on the Senate floor that the First Amendment already contained a free exercise clause, but he feared that the adoption of the Religious Freedom Restoration Act might have shifted the protection of religious liberty from the Constitution, where it had been secure, to Congress, where it might be more vulnerable (Cochrane 1989, S6867).

See also Christian Amendment; Prayer in Public Schools.

❖ REPRODUCTIVE RIGHTS ❖

Since the Supreme Court's decision in *Roe v. Wade* (1973), American women have had the legal right to obtain abortions. Abortion opponents have introduced numerous calls for a right to life amendment to overturn this decision. Although such an amendment has not been adopted, in cases such as *Webster v. Reproductive Health Services* (1989) and *Planned Parenthood of Southeastern Pennsylvania v. Casey* (1992), the Supreme Court has permitted states to impose greater restrictions on this procedure.

Perhaps with a view to such restrictions, in April 1993, Democratic Representative Patsy Mink of Hawaii introduced an amendment to protect the rights of individuals "to have full control over reproductive decisions affecting their own bodies" (H.J.

Res. 176). If the Supreme Court ever reversed its decision in *Roe v. Wade*, there might be considerable support for such an amendment.

See also Right to Life.

❖ RESCISSION OF RATIFICATION OF PENDING AMENDMENTS ❖

Periodically, questions have arisen about the states' power to rescind their ratifications of pending constitutional amendments. The Constitution is silent on this point. Congress has yet to adopt legislation to deal with the subject, although legislation proposed by North Carolina Democratic Senator Sam Ervin and Utah Republican Senator Orrin Hatch would have accepted the legitimacy of such rescissions.

In dealing with ratification of the Fourteenth Amendment, Congress indicated that it did not accept the legitimacy of two attempted rescissions, but the precedent is a muddy one, and it is not clear whether the congressional judgment was actually essential to the amendment's ratification (Vile 1990, 112). Moreover, when the issue of rescissions reemerged during the controversy over the equal rights amendment, a U.S. district court ruled in *Idaho v. Freeman* (1981) that such rescissions are permissible. This precedent is complicated, however, by the fact that Congress had extended the original ratification deadline. Also, the decision was eventually mooted when the amendment failed to receive the necessary number of state ratifications.

One argument for permitting states to rescind ratification of pending amendments is an argument from balance, since states have been permitted to ratify amendments that they have previously rejected (Grinnell 1959, 1164). The doctrine of contemporary consensus that the Court articulated in *Dillon v. Gloss* (1921) also suggests that states should not be included in a consensus they no longer share. It has also been argued that the ability to rescind is a guard against hasty change.

Arguments against rescission include the value of finality (Orfield 1942, 70). Some also fear that if state legislators knew that a vote to ratify an amendment would not be final they might be tempted to treat their votes less seriously (Freedman and Naughton 1978, 11). It can also be argued that the process of amendment is difficult enough without allowing states additional leeway in rejecting amendments.

In the absence of clear precedents, it appears likely that Congress will resolve this issue on a case-by-case basis. Although this is consistent with the Supreme Court's decision in *Coleman v. Miller* (1939) that amending issues were "political questions," such discretion continues the uncertainty about a matter that should arguably be covered by preordained rules (Dellinger 1983, 395–96).

See also *Idaho v. Freeman.*

For Further Reading:

Baker, A. Diane. 1979. "ERA: The Effect of Extending the Time for Ratification on Attempts To Rescind Prior Ratifications." *Emory Law Journal* 28: 71–110.

Burke, Yvonne B. 1976. "Validity of Attempts To Rescind Ratification of the Equal Rights Amendment." *University of Los Angeles Law Review* 8: 1–22.

Ginsberg, Ruth B. 1969. "Ratification of the Equal Rights Amendment: A Question of Time." *Texas Law Review* 57: 919–45.

Kanowitz, Leo, and Marilyn Klinger. 1978. "Can a State Rescind Its Equal Rights Amendment Ratification: Who Decides and How?" *Hastings Law Journal* 28 (March): 969–1009.

Planell, Raymond M. 1974. "The Equal Rights Amendment: Will States Be Allowed To Change Their Minds?" *Notre Dame Lawyer* 49 (February): 657–70.

Vierra, Norman. 1981. "The Equal Rights Amendment: Rescission, Extension and Justiciability." *Southern Illinois Law Journal* 1981: 1–29.

❖ REVENUE SHARING ❖

In the early 1960s, the national government appeared to have a much stronger revenue base than did the states. Between 1965 and 1971, 14 states petitioned Congress to call a constitutional convention to amend the Constitution to provide for federal revenue sharing.

In contrast to more traditional categorical grant-in-aid programs and block grants, revenue sharing was designed to give maximum leeway to state funding decisions. Georgia Republican Representative Standish Thompson introduced amendments providing for revenue sharing in 1967 and 1969. Under his plan, the national government would eventually have provided 10 percent of the money it collected through income taxes to the states, based on their populations and with no strings other than an antidiscrimination provision.

Although little progress was made on proposed amendments, in 1972, the Nixon administration successfully launched revenue sharing for state and local governments. State governments were dropped from the program in 1980, and the entire program—under which some $85 billion had been funneled to states and localities—was terminated in 1986 during the Reagan administration (Harrigan 1994, 41).

❖ REVOLUTION ❖

In modern times, the term *revolution* has been used to denote violent political changes, such as those associated with the French Revolution of 1789 or the Russian Revolution of 1917. Originally, however, the term appears to have derived from astronomy, where it referred to the more orderly processes that could be observed in the heavens (Wills 1978, 51). Moreover, although they were not bloodless, it can be argued that revolutions like those in Great

Britain in 1688 and America in 1776 were qualitatively different from those that followed (Diamond 1976).

Whatever distinctions there might be among different types of revolutions, they all resort to change from outside the existing legal framework. By contrast, formal amending processes are designed as means of effecting change within the system. Although the Declaration of Independence proclaimed that the people had a right to revolution, such revolution, as Thomas Jefferson described it, was a last resort, not to be undertaken "for light and transient Causes."

The seeming inability of the British constitution to accommodate to change was doubtless on the minds of delegates at the Constitutional Convention of 1787. Thus, Virginia's George Mason noted that change was inevitable and that it would be better to provide for amendments "in an easy, regular and Constitutional way than to trust to chance and violence" (Farrand 1966, 1:203).

Although he stated a moderate view of revolution in the Declaration of Independence, Thomas Jefferson elsewhere blurred the lines between constitutional and revolutionary change. At a time when many countrymen were horrified by Shays's Rebellion, Jefferson calculated that, with 13 colonies that had been independent for 11 years each, Shays's Rebellion amounted to but one revolution in a century and a half. He further asked, "What signify a few lives lost in a century or two? The tree of liberty must be refreshed from time to time with the blood of patriots & tyrants. It is its natural manure" (Jefferson 1905, 5:362).

The tie between amendment and revolution was forcefully demonstrated during the Dorr war in Rhode Island. The forceful attempt to replace Rhode Island's charter government with a more democratic scheme arose largely from the charter government's failure to provide a means of peaceful change. Defending the charter government as the legitimate government in the case of *Luther v. Borden,* Daniel Webster argued that "our American mode of government does not draw any power from tumultuous assemblages" and that "when it is necessary to ascertain the will of the people, the legislature must provide the means of ascertaining it" (*Luther* 1849, 31). A political opponent on many other subjects, South Carolina Senator John C. Calhoun agreed. He said, "It would be the death-blow of constitutional democracy, to admit the right of the numerical majority, to alter or abolish constitutions at pleasure,—regardless of the consent of the Government, or the forms prescribed for their amendment" (Calhoun 1851–1856, 6: 229–30).

The safety-valve analogy, often used to describe a formal amending process, also highlights the manner in which peaceful mechanisms for change help avert the need for violence.

See also *Luther v. Borden;* Safety-valve Analogy.

❖ REYNOLDS, EUSTACE ❖

In 1915, a New Yorker named Eustace Reynolds published a modified constitution for consideration. Aside from the fact that a number of his ideas were similar to those advocated by William Jennings Bryan, who was then secretary of state (Boyd 1992, 129), and that Reynolds promised to use any money from reprints of his constitution for the cause of international peace (Reynolds 1915, 18), no biographical information is available. Most of Reynolds's plan is simply a reprint of the existing Constitution with proposed changes highlighted in bold type. Although most changes involved the conduct of foreign affairs, some other alterations were also proposed.

"Sex qualifications" for voting were to be eliminated (as they soon would be in the

Nineteenth Amendment), but the voting age was to be raised to 25 and limited to those who could read and write (Reynolds 1915, 1–2). The vice president, who would serve with the president in a single six-year term, was assigned to represent the United States in a council of other viceroys and vice presidents. With approval of another body consisting of "under-secretaries of state and deputy-ministers for foreign affairs," this council would have power to "make and promulgate decrees in all matters affecting international intercourse, commerce, affairs, or relations"; to "regulate commerce with foreign nations"; and to punish "offenses against the law of nations" (Reynolds 1915, 2–3). Such regulations would be recognized in Article VI as the supreme law of the land (Reynolds 1915, 13). Congress would, in turn, lose its power to "enter into any agreement or contract with another state, or with a foreign power, to engage in war," except in cases of "invasion" or "imminent danger" (Reynolds 1915, 7).

The judicial power would have been altered in Reynolds's scheme so as to require the chief justice to appoint another Supreme Court justice to sit en banc with members of judiciaries from other nations "and pass upon international questions as they come properly before the court for adjudication" (Reynolds 1915, 10–11). This international court would have appellate jurisdiction in cases involving controversies between American states or their citizens and foreign citizens, and it would have original jurisdiction when the United States and foreign governments were involved. U.S. courts would be given explicit authority to disregard unconstitutional laws and decrees.

Reynolds would have maintained the guarantees in the Bill of Rights, but he would have permitted a prosecutor to comment, and a jury to weigh this fact, when a defendant chose to exercise the right against self-incrimination. He would also have restricted the national government's right to collect income tax on state securities. The impact of Reynolds's work, if any, on the public is unknown (Boyd 1992, 131).

❖ *REYNOLDS V. SIMS* (1964) ❖

This case was one of the most important and controversial cases decided by the Warren Court. It established that the equal protection clause of the Fourteenth Amendment required that both houses of a state legislature—in this case, Alabama's—need to be apportioned according to the one-person one-vote standard.

In so ruling, Chief Justice Earl Warren extended the earlier decision in *Baker v. Carr* (1962), which had established that state legislative apportionment schemes were justiciable under the equal protection clause but had not specified the standard to be utilized. Over the objections of dissenting Justice John Marshall Harlan that the Court was misinterpreting the Fourteenth Amendment, Warren argued that "the right of suffrage can be denied by a debasement or dilution of the weight of a citizen's vote just as effectively as by wholly prohibiting the free exercise of the franchise" (*Reynolds* 1964, 555).

Together, *Baker v. Carr* and *Reynolds v. Sims* provoked numerous calls for an amendment to give states greater leeway. Illinois Republican Senator Everett Dirksen led the call for a constitutional convention on the subject. These efforts failed, and both decisions remain in effect. As the Court indicated in the *Reynolds* case, however (1964, 578), it is willing to accept somewhat greater population disparities among state legislative districts than it permits with respect to state-drawn congressional districts.

See also *Baker v. Carr;* States, Legislative Apportionment.

❖ *RHODE ISLAND V. PALMER* ❖

See *National Prohibition* Cases.

❖ RICE, ISAAC L. (1850–1915) ❖

Isaac Rice was a gifted man who was born in Bavaria and educated at Columbia Law School, where he stayed an additional six years to study and teach before going into the practice of law (Malone 1963, 3:541). In 1884, Rice published an article in which he advocated calling a constitutional convention to address a number of problems, most of which he attributed to the U.S. system of separation of powers and checks and balances. Rice believed that this system was "both weak and irresponsible" (Rice 1884, 534) and that it led to political corruption. In its place, he hoped to establish a parliamentary system (Vile 1991c, 37–38).

Rice proposed three major reforms. The first was to expand the powers of Congress to enable it "to settle all questions of national concern" (Rice 1884, 540). Specifically, he wanted to institute "a uniform code of commerce for the whole country" so that "powerful combinations" would be unable to hide behind artificial state boundaries (Rice 1884, 540). Second, Rice proposed ending the separation of legislative and executive powers. In his words, "the executive must be entitled to propose laws necessary for the preservation of the public welfare, and the legislative must be enabled to control the execution of all laws passed" (Rice 1884, 540). As in a parliamentary system, Rice wanted the heads of executive agencies to serve in Congress; although he did not use the term, he also appears to have contemplated the creation of a prime minister. Third, Rice proposed making the legislature "the sole and responsible judge of the constitutionality of its acts," leaving the judiciary to "interpret" congressional will rather than "to control it" (Rice 1884, 540).

One of numerous reformers who have looked to parliamentary systems for guidance, Rice does not appear to have stirred much contemporary interest with his proposal for a convention.

❖ RIGHT TO LIFE ❖

Few issues have proved to be more emotionally wrenching or politically divisive than the issue of abortion (Tribe 1990; Epstein and Kobylka 1992; Hunter 1994). From the time shortly after *Roe v. Wade* was first argued in 1971 to the present, more than 325 proposals have been introduced in Congress to restrict abortions, and at least 19 states have called for a constitutional convention to address this issue. The fact that most such proposals have been made by those opposed to abortion is not a sign that congressional opinion on the subject is uniform but rather an indication that, throughout this period, those who accept a woman's right to choose an abortion have had the weight of the courts on their side and thus had no need to introduce such amendments.

Background to *Roe v. Wade*

Prior to 1973, the issue of abortion was largely a state matter. Most states had adopted laws restricting abortions in the second half of the nineteenth century, at which time abortions were often medically dangerous for women. By 1972, 19 states had liberalized their laws to permit therapeutic abortions, but this meant that, in most states, such procedures were still illegal (Keynes with Miller 1989, 249).

In 1965, the Supreme Court ruled in *Griswold v. Connecticut* that there was a constitutional right to privacy granted by various penumbras of the Bill of Rights and the Fourteenth Amendment. This decision, in turn, served as the basis for the Court's decision in *Roe v. Wade* (1973), in which it overturned a Texas abortion law. Written by Justice Harry Blackmun for a 7-to-2 majority of the Court, the opinion stated that the constitutional right to privacy was sufficient to permit a woman to choose to have an abortion without state interference, at least through the first two trimesters (the first six months) of pregnancy. Thereafter, a state could legislate on behalf of the life of the fetus, except in cases in which the life or health of the mother was threatened (see Garrow 1994).

Reactions to *Roe v. Wade*

Perhaps because *Roe v. Wade* was thrust so suddenly into the public consciousness (Glendon 1987), it engendered strong responses from both supporters and opponents. Undoubtedly, the decision galvanized public opinion in a way that would not have occurred in the face of state liberalization of abortion laws and the ever-increasing number of legal abortions that were being performed in the years leading up to the decision (Rosenberg 1991, 178–80). Subsequent developments have proceeded on a number of different fronts.

Legislatively, opponents of abortion have followed four distinct strategies—attempts to adopt amendments; limit judicial jurisdiction over the subject of abortion; restrict abortion funding; and adopt other laws, including laws defining the moment that human life begins, providing for informed consent, establishing waiting periods, regulating clinics, or otherwise restricting abortion access without outlawing it completely (Keynes with Miller 1989, 247). Such strategies are sometimes pursued independently and sometimes in tandem.

It should be noted that the idea of restricting judicial jurisdiction has also been advocated by opponents of prayer in school and school busing. Republican Representative Philip Crane of Illinois introduced such a proposal relative to abortion in 1979. It provided that:

[T]he Supreme Court shall not have jurisdiction to review, by appeal, writs of certiorari, or otherwise, any case arising out of any State statute, ordinance, rule, regulation or any part thereof, or arising out of any Act interpreting, applying, or enforcing a State statute, ordinance, rule or regulation, which relates to abortion. The district courts shall not have jurisdiction of any case or question which the Supreme Court does not have jurisdiction to review. (Keynes with Miller 1989, 292)

Much of the controversy over attempts to restrict abortion funding have focused on the Hyde amendment, named after its sponsor, Republican Representative Henry Hyde of Illinois. The Supreme Court upheld this law, which limits federal funding for nontherapeutic abortions, in *Harris v. McRae* (1980). It decided that the right to an abortion did not include the right to government funding for such an abortion. In *Beal v. Doe* (1977), the Court had previously decided that states did not have to provide such funding either.

Judicial Responses to Legislation

The Court's reactions to other legislative attempts to regulate abortions have arguably zigged and zagged with the mood of the nation, the nature of the specific controversy, and the individuals who have occupied the judiciary. For example, the Court struck down laws that require spousal consent for abortions or that absolutely mandate parental consent for minors to obtain abortions. It has been more sympathetic, however, to laws providing for parental consent when such laws permit some form of judicial bypass. In *Webster v. Reproductive Health Services* (1989) and in *Planned Parenthood of Southeast Pennsylvania v. Casey* (1992), the Court accepted various other state-imposed restrictions on abortion. The latter case is especially significant; the majority, although arguing that such restrictions should not impose an "undue burden" on a woman's right to choose an abortion, appeared largely to scuttle the trimester analysis that was a significant part of the Court's decision in *Roe v. Wade* (for short summaries of cases since *Roe v. Wade*, see D. O'Brien 1995).

Amendments Designed To Overturn *Roe v. Wade*

Amendments on abortion have been divided into four categories:

Those amendments [that] would (1) restore the states' authority to restore the status quo ante, (2) authorize Congress and the states to protect human life at every stage of biological development, (3) prohibit Congress and the states from interfering with human life at every stage of development, or (4) define the fetus as a person within the meaning of the Fifth and Fourteenth amendment's due process clauses and extend due process rights to the unborn child. (Keynes with Miller 1989, 280)

It should be noted that North Carolina Republican Senator Jesse Helms pushed for legislation in 1982 that would accomplish the last of these four objectives. The law was based on the premise that, since the Court had stated in *Roe v. Wade* that it did not know when human life began, it might defer to congressional judgments and congressional enforcement powers under Section 5 of the Fourteenth Amendment. His attempt was unsuccessful.

At times, abortion opponents have been split between those who want to use the amending process to restrict or prohibit abortion throughout the nation and those who are willing to settle for returning this matter to the states. In 1981, Utah Repub-

lican Senator Orrin Hatch sponsored legislation that would give both Congress and the states concurrent authority to restrict abortions. The Senate subsequently voted 49 to 50 against a substitute amendment offered by Missouri Democratic Senator Thomas Eagleton that provided simply that "a right to abortion is not secured by the Constitution." Most recent proposals to restrict abortion have mandated exceptions in cases when a woman's life is at stake. Rather than focusing on a constitutional amendment, the Christian Coalition's recent Contract with the American Family advocates legislation protecting states that do not choose to fund abortion, limiting late-term abortions, and eliminating federal funding of groups that support abortion (Reed 1995, 63–84).

Other Consequences of *Roe v. Wade*

The abortion controversy has been a major bone of contention in a number of congressional confirmation hearings, including the unsuccessful confirmations of Judge Robert Bork (who was thought to be unsympathetic to a constitutional right to privacy) to the Supreme Court in the Reagan administration and of Dr. Henry Foster (who had performed abortions) to be surgeon general in the Clinton administration. Presidents have also used executive orders to permit or restrict fetal tissue research and abortion counseling (Vile 1994a, 58). Although more than 20 years have elapsed since the Court's historic attempt to resolve the abortion issue in *Roe v. Wade*, emotional debates continue in Congress and elsewhere (Fraley 1995).

See also Reproductive Rights; *Roe v. Wade*.

For Further Reading:
O'Connor, Karen. 1996. *No Neutral Ground? Abortion Politics in an Age of Absolutes*. Boulder, CO: Westview.

❖ RIGHT TO WORK ❖

A major piece of legislation that covers U.S. labor relations is the Taft-Hartley Act of 1947. This law permits states to adopt a so-called closed, or union, shop requiring all workers to belong to unions that a majority has selected (Tomlins 1985, 282–316). It also permits states to adopt open shops, or right-to-work laws, allowing individuals to choose whether to belong to such unions. Union advocates argue that the open shop is unfair because it allows nonmembers to benefit from contract negotiations made by an organization to which they did not contribute. Some civil libertarians respond that a closed shop violates individual freedom of association.

In the years immediately prior to the Taft-Hartley Act, a number of amendments were proposed that would guarantee an open shop. The most persistent supporter of such an amendment was Democratic Representative Wilbert O'Daniel of Texas. In July 1955, Indiana Representative William Jenner introduced another resolution that would guarantee the rights of workers for hire "to receive their earnings in full"; Jenner probably thereby intended also to prohibit a union shop under which workers must pay dues to the union.

❖ RIGID CONSTITUTION ❖

In his acclaimed book on American politics (Bryce 1906, 1: 370), as well as in an essay (Bryce 1905), Lord James Bryce of England developed a distinction between flexible and rigid constitutions. This distinction was a frequent point of reference in the early years of the twentieth century and a basis for many of the criticisms of the amending process that were made by reformers of the Progressive Era.

Bryce offered his classification as an alternative to early distinctions between written and unwritten constitutions. Like this earlier scheme, however, Bryce's distinguished between constitutions that had developed by customs and usages, like that of Great Britain, and constitutions that were considered to be paramount law unchangeable by ordinary legislative means, like the United States.

Although Bryce noted that rigid constitutions "mark a comparatively advanced stage in political development, when the idea of separating fundamental laws from other laws has grown familiar, and when considerable experience in the business of government and in political affairs generally has been accumulated" (Bryce 1905, 46), the designation of such a constitution as "rigid" may not have been an altogether impartial designation (Vile 1992, 138). At one point likening a rigid constitution to an iron bridge, Bryce noted that "the fact that it is very strong and all knit tightly into one fabric, while enabling it to stand firm under small oscillations or disturbances, may aggravate small ones" (Bryce 1905, 68), and he cited the U.S. Civil War as an example. Moreover, writing in the time between the post–Civil War amendments and the Progressive Era amendments, Bryce identified the U.S. Constitution as "the most difficult to change" (Bryce 1905, 61).

Today, the older distinction between written and unwritten constitutions is more common than Bryce's distinction between flexible and rigid constitutions. A recent article suggested a classification of constitutions into those formulated by a single lawgiver, those based on immemorial customs and usages, and those formulated by a constitutional convention (Vile 1993d). Whatever scheme is used, it is important not to let labels obscure complexities and to recognize that most systems blend characteristics of more than one ideal type. Also, a constitution that may seem relatively rigid in one period might prove quite susceptible to change in other circumstances.

❖ ROBINSON, DONALD L. ❖
(1936–)

Donald Robinson, a professor of political science at Smith College, has been closely associated with the Committee on the Constitutional System (CCS). Robinson has published two books designed to elicit discussion about reforms considered and proposed by this committee (Robinson 1985, 1989; for discussion, see Vile 1991c, 129–31).

In an article reflecting his own views, Robinson advocated three constitutional reforms: lengthening the terms of members of the House of Representatives to four years and those of senators to eight, allowing members of Congress to head executive agencies, and allowing the president and one-third of both houses of Congress or a majority of either house to call an election (Robinson 1987).

❖ *ROE V. WADE* (1973) ❖

Roe v. Wade is one of the most controversial and far-reaching decisions of the twentieth century, and it stimulated numerous efforts to adopt a right to life amendment. In *Roe*, a 7-to-2 majority of the Court, led by Justice Harry Blackmun, struck down state abortion laws for the first time. It based its decision on the constitutional right of privacy, which it had recognized in *Griswold v. Connecticut* (1965) and other cases.

Blackmun argued that most U.S. abortion laws had been enacted in the second half of the nineteenth century. He traced the origins of such laws to three causes: the desire to discourage illicit sexual activity, protect women's health, and guard prenatal life. In this case, the state did not assert the first interest. Blackmun further found that the state's interest in prohibiting abortion to protect women's health was not as pressing as it had been before the discovery of antiseptics, when abortion was a far riskier procedure. As to the protection of prenatal life, Blackmun argued that no consensus had emerged as to when human life begins. However, the common law generally did not punish abortions that were performed prior to "quickening," and even then, the offense was not generally regarded as murder.

In an attempt to balance the state's concern with the potential life of the fetus and the health of the mother, Blackmun formulated different rules for each of the three trimesters of pregnancy. During the first, the decision of the woman and her doctor was to be decisive. In the second trimester, the state could set forth requirements as to the licensing and qualifications of doctors, types of facilities, and the like, which were designed to ensure that the abortion procedure was safe for the woman. In the third trimester, the outset of which generally marked the period of "viability," that is, the point at which a fetus could survive outside its mother's womb, Blackmun said that the state could pass laws protecting the fetus. He made an exception, however, when abortion might be "necessary to preserve the life or health of the mother" (*Roe* 1973, 164).

In addition to stimulating calls for an amendment, *Roe v. Wade* has stirred considerable controversy. The Supreme Court has subsequently faced numerous issues related to its first decision (D. O'Brien 1995, 1199–1203). Prominent cases have included *Harris v. McRae* (1980), upholding the constitutionality of the Hyde amendment, which prohibits federal funding of nontherapeutic abortions; *Webster v. Reproductive Health Services* (1989), upholding a number of restrictions imposed by the state of Missouri; and *Planned Parenthood of Southeastern Pennsylvania v. Casey* (1992), upholding several state-imposed restrictions on abortion—including a 24-hour waiting period and a requirement for a parent's or judge's consent for a minor to obtain an abortion—that it claimed were not substantial enough to impose an "undue burden." In the *Planned Parenthood* opinion written by Justices Sandra Day O'Connor, Anthony Kennedy, and David Souter, the Court professed to be upholding the central holding of *Roe* even while rejecting much of its rigid trimester analysis.

See also *Griswold v. Connecticut;* Right to Life.

For Further Reading:

Garrow, David J. 1994. *Liberty and Sexuality: The Right to Privacy and the Making of* Roe v. Wade. New York: Macmillan.

❖ SAFETY-VALVE ANALOGY ❖

Consistent with the parallels that were often drawn in early American history between the Constitution and a machine (Kammen 1987), one of the most frequently repeated analogies used for the amending process was that of a safety valve. It is possible that the specific analogy was coined by Justice Joseph Story when he wrote that the amending process was "the safety valve to let off all temporary effervescences and excitements; and the real effective instrument to control and adjust the movements of the machinery, when out of order, or in danger of self-destruction" (Story 1987, 680).

In critiquing this analogy, Sidney George Fisher later claimed that Article V had been more like an "iron fetter" than a safety valve; "the efficacy of a safety-valve depends on the promptness with which it can be opened and the width of the throttle. If defective in either of these, when the pressure of steam is too high the boiler will burst" (S. Fisher 1862, 33). Attorney Frederic B. Johnstone later criticized the amending process during the Progressive Era by noting that the difficulty of constitutional amendment made the Constitution like a dangerous boiler that "becomes a source of danger under pressure in the absence of a safety valve" (1912, 282).

However mechanical, the safety-valve analogy highlights the way in which a method for peaceful and legal change helps alleviate pressures that might otherwise be channeled into violence and revolution.

❖ SCHLAFLY, PHYLLIS (1924–) ❖

Phyllis Schlafly is the individual most frequently associated with the defeat of the equal rights amendment. As the 1972 founder and current president of the conservative Eagle Forum, Schlafly continues to take credit for leading "the pro-family movement to victory over the principal legislative goal of the radical feminists, called the Equal Rights Amendment" (1995 biographical data sheet provided by the Eagle Forum). Her views on the subject are more thoroughly explained in an Eagle Forum video entitled "What's Wrong with ERA?"

Schlafly has a master's degree in political science from Harvard University as well as undergraduate and law degrees from Washington University. She continues to be a prominent conservative spokesperson on college campuses, writes a widely distributed syndicated column, publishes the *Phyllis Schlafly Report,* and has authored or edited 16 books. These include *A Choice Not an Echo* (1964), which supported Republican Senator Barry Goldwater's bid for the presidency in 1964, and books on U.S. foreign policy, illiteracy, and education.

Schlafly is a strong believer in the U.S. Constitution and in Article V, which outlines the amending process. She recently opposed plans by the Council of States for a conference of the states, fearing that it might develop into an open-ended convention to rewrite the U.S. Constitution (*Phyllis Schlafly Report* April 1995, May 1995). She also opposes an amendment to make the District of Columbia a state. The mother of six children, Schlafly was named 1992 Illinois Mother of the Year.

See also Equal Rights Amendment.

❖ SCHOOL BUSING ❖

In the wake of the Supreme Court's decision in *Brown v. Board of Education* (1954), which called for an end to school segregation, a number of congressmen from the South proposed amendments that would give states exclusive administrative control over public schools. Over time, most proposed amendments came to focus specifically on the assignment of students to schools on the basis of race and the use of busing to achieve racial balance.

On this issue, individuals who supported the decision in *Brown* were divided. Praise for the effectiveness of busing as a means of promoting desegregation was balanced by concerns about the associated costs, the impact of busing on the quality of education and the idea of community schools, and the resulting creation of private one-race schools and the "white flight" that sometimes resulted from forced busing.

There were about 25 amending proposals introduced in Congress dealing with busing in the 1960s, over 225 in the 1970s, and more than 20 in the 1980s. Congressional sponsors from outside the South increased in the late 1970s and the 1980s. Ten states, including Michigan (1971) and Massachusetts (1974, 1976), also petitioned Congress for a convention on this issue during the 1960s and 1970s.

Contrary to the hopes of President Richard Nixon, the Burger Court unanimously upheld the use of busing as a tool to remedy past cases of de jure (legalized) segregation in *Swann v. Charlotte-Mecklenburg Board of Education* (1971). The Court's decision indicated that there were limits to the use of busing, however, and in *Milliken v. Bradley* (1974), in a 5-to-4 decision also written by Chief Justice Burger, the Supreme Court refused to uphold a district court mandate providing for an interdistrict remedy for an intradistrict case of de jure segregation. This and subsequent decisions appeared to limit the scope of busing in cases of de facto segregation that resulted from voluntarily chosen housing patterns rather than from discriminatory governmental actions.

A summary of amending proposals has divided them into five categories:

[those] that would prohibit (1) the federal courts from assigning students to public schools on the basis of their race, (2) *any* governmental authority from assigning students to public schools on the basis of their race, (3) governmental authorities from assigning students on the basis of their race to any public school other than the one closest to their residence, (4) governmental authority from assigning students to schools other than the one closest to their residence, without exception, and (5) governmental interference with parents' or guardians' rights to chose a public school for their children. (Keynes with Miller 1989, 225)

In the 1970s, both the House and Senate Judiciary Committees held hearings on antibusing amendments. A proposed amendment by Democratic Representative Ronald M. Mottl of Ohio was discharged from committee, but it was defeated in 1979 by a vote of 209 to 206 in the House of Representatives (Keynes with Miller 1989, 226). There were other attempts to limit busing through restrictions on the Department of Health, Education, and Welfare; through restrictions on the Justice Department; and through controversial and unsuccessful congressional attempts to restrict judicial jurisdiction over this issue (Keynes with Miller 1989, 219).

See also *Brown v. Board of Education.*

For Further Reading:

Schwartz, Bernard. 1986. *Swann's Way: The School Busing Case and the Supreme Court.* New York: Oxford University Press.

Wilkinson, J. Harvie III. 1979. *From Brown to Bakke: The Supreme Court and School Integration: 1954–1978.* New York: Oxford University Press.

❖ SCHOOLS, PUBLIC ❖

The U.S. Constitution does not say anything directly about education. Many states provided for public education in constitutional reforms made in the 1840s and 1850s (Butts 1978, 81). Others, especially in the South, lagged behind in establishing public school systems. In the decades immediately following the Civil War, several members of Congress introduced national amendments calling on states to provide public education for their citizens. In his annual message of December 1875, President Ulysses S. Grant tied this proposed amendment to a restriction on aid to parochial schools (J. Richardson 1908, 8: 334), which resulted in the proposal of the unsuccessful Blaine amendment.

All states eventually established public schools. The Supreme Court endorsed racial segregation in *Plessy v. Ferguson* (1896), and this policy extended to schools and did not change until the Court's decision in *Brown v. Board of Education* (1954). Modern amending proposals have attempted to limit the use of school busing and to permit prayer and Bible reading in public schools.

See also Blaine Amendment; Prayer in Public Schools; School Busing.

❖ SCOTT V. SANDFORD (1857) ❖

Few cases in American history have stirred more controversy that did the majority opinion in this case. It was written by Chief Justice Roger B. Taney—a Jackson appointee from Maryland who served on the Court from 1836 to 1864. Dred Scott, a slave, had been taken by his master Dr. Emerson, an army surgeon, to a free state and a free territory and back to Missouri, which was a slave state. Scott and his wife Harriet sued Sanford (incorrectly spelled by the Court reporter as Sandford), the executor of Emerson's estate, for their freedom on the basis of their residence on free soil.

Taney ruled against the Scotts. He declared that however states might choose to define state citizenship, the Constitution limited national citizenship to whites. He interpreted the Declaration of Independence and other founding documents as applying only to whites. Taney cited both the slave importation clause and the fugitive slave clause (omitting the three-fifths clause from his discussion) to indicate that the American framers had regarded African Americans as an inferior class not entitled to the privileges of citizenship. Taney further held it to be the Court's duty to interpret the Constitution with the same words and meaning it had when it was adopted. In a reference to the amending provisions, Taney noted that if parts of the Constitution were thought to be unjust, "there is a mode prescribed in the instrument itself by which it may be amended, but while it remains unaltered, it must be construed now as it was understood at the time of its adoption." As a noncitizen, Scott therefore had no right to appear in a federal court.

Taney went on, however, to examine the Missouri Compromise of 1820, by which slavery had been excluded from much of the Louisiana Territory. Again, Taney gave a narrow construction to the Constitution. He claimed that the provision related to the governance of territories referred only to territories in possession of the government in 1789 and not to territory that was subsequently purchased. People in such territory were guaranteed the same constitutional protections as other citizens, including the Fifth Amendment right not to be deprived of their property (slaves) without their consent. This interpretation served as the basis for the notion of substantive due process that would so affect constitutional interpretation during the next 75 years of Court history.

As to Scott's claim to have become free by reason of his residence in a free state, Taney ruled that such matters were governed by state law. He thus accepted the judgment of the Missouri Supreme Court that such residence in Illinois had not given Scott his freedom.

This case served as a catalyst to civil war rather than, as Taney had hoped, providing a solution to a vexing national problem. *Scott* was subsequently overturned by the Thirteenth and Fourteenth Amendments. The former abolished slavery, and the latter defined citizenship to apply to all persons born in the United States. Ironically, however, in the *Slaughterhouse* cases (1873), the first Supreme Court decision to interpret the Fourteenth Amendment, the Court continued to rely on the distinction between state and federal citizenship that Taney had developed in *Scott* to give a restrictive reading of the amendment.

See also Fourteenth Amendment; Substantive Due Process.

❖ SECESSIONISTS, LIMITING THE RIGHTS OF ❖

After the Civil War, numerous attempts were made to exclude individuals who had been active in or had given support to the Confederate States of America from holding office, voting, or participating in certain professions. Some of these attempts took the form of legislation, and some were proposed as amendments.

In *Cummings v. Missouri* (1867), the Supreme Court invalidated a Missouri law requiring individuals in certain professions to swear that they had never supported the Confederacy. Similarly, in a companion case, *Ex parte Garland* (1867), it struck down a similar oath required of attorneys practicing in federal courts. In both cases, the Court decided that such laws were unconstitutional ex post facto laws (retroactive criminal laws) and bills of attainder (legislative punishments without benefit of a trial).

Numerous amendment proposals were introduced in Congress to exclude former members of the Confederacy from civil office or from voting. Republican Senator Jacob Howard of Michigan eventually introduced the resolution that became Section 3 of the Fourteenth Amendment. This section provided:

> No person shall be a Senator or Representative in Congress, or elector of President and Vice President, or hold any office, civil or military, under the United States, or under any State, who, having previously taken an oath, as a member of Congress, or as an officer of the United States, or as a member of any State legislature, or as an executive or judicial officer of any State, shall have engaged in insurrection or rebellion against the same, or given aid or comfort to the enemies thereof.

This section also gave Congress the power to remove this disability by a two-thirds vote, and it did so on behalf of most southerners in a vote in 1872 (Grimes 1978, 55).

See also Fourteenth Amendment

❖ SECOND AMENDMENT ❖

Few, if any, provisions of the Constitution are more controversial than the Second Amendment. It was ratified in 1791 as part of the Bill of Rights. It provides that "a well regulated Militia, being necessary to the security of a free State, the right of the people to keep and bear Arms, shall not be infringed."

Several states that had ratified the Constitution proposed such an amendment (Vandercoy 1994, 1029–32), and such a proposal was among those that James Madison proposed in the First Congress in 1789. His original proposal contained a related provision that would have established a right of conscientious objection for religious reasons (see Kurland and Lerner 1987, 5:25), but the Senate deleted it.

In recent years, the Second Amendment has drawn renewed scholarly attention (S. Heller 1995) and has even prompted a full-page advertisement signed by scholars who believe that the amendment has been too narrowly interpreted (Academics for the Second Amendment 1995, A23). Interpretations of the Second Amendment differ radically. The National Rifle Association has argued for an absolutist view of this amendment in opposing legislation that would ban certain types of guns, including handguns and assault rifles. By contrast, the American Civil Liberties Union has supported gun regulations and has interpreted the amendment to refer to the protection of collective state militia rather than of individual rights (for contrasting positions, see Levinson 1989).

The difficulty of interpreting the Second Amendment centers in part on the fact that it is the only amendment to contain a statement of purpose. Interpreters have to decide whether the purpose limits the meaning of the entire amendment or whether the right to "keep and bear Arms" that follows has independent meaning.

Even a resolution of this issue does not necessarily solve the interpretive problems, because it can and has been argued that the framers interpreted the idea of the militia quite broadly, believing that an armed citizenry was a guard against tyranny. Thus, during debates in the First Congress, Elbridge Gerry noted that the proposal that became the Second Amendment "is intended to secure the people against the maladministration of the Government." He further connected the militia with the desire "to prevent the establishment of a standing army" (Kurland and Lerner 1987, 5:210). Thus, some proponents of original intent argue that the amendment should be interpreted quite expansively (see Halbrook 1994; Cramer 1994).

By contrast, others argue that the basic thrust of the amendment was simply to ensure "that citizens have a constitutionally protected right to serve in militia in defense of state and country" (Spitzer 1995, 35). Under this interpretation, "the Second Amendment is founded on *federalism,* balancing powers between the federal government and the states; and *military necessity,* developing a political compromise between politically popular militias and a politically unpopular but militarily necessary national professional army." Such a view would denigrate arguments on behalf of "hunting, sporting, recreation, or even personal protection" (Spitzer 1995, 35–36). Since state militias have for all practical purposes ceased, those who hold this view also hold that "the Second Amendment has been rendered essentially irrelevant to modern American life" (Spitzer 1995, 38). Moreover, under such an interpretation, both state and federal governments have the power to regulate gun ownership, which is blamed by many for the rising tide of violence in the nation.

To date, the Supreme Court has rarely ventured into the gun-control controversy. In *United States v. Miller* (1939), the

Supreme Court unanimously upheld a federal law against the use of sawed-off shotguns by ruling that the Second Amendment protected only weapons that could be used as part of a militia. Ironically, this principle would make regulation of assault weapons quite difficult. In *Quilici v. Village of Morton Grove* (1983), the Court refused to review a lower court decision upholding a ban on the ownership of handguns. To date, the Second Amendment remains one of the few guarantees in the Bill of Rights that has not been applied to the states via the due process clause of the Fourteenth Amendment.

Two proposed amendments were introduced in 1913 to authorize Congress to regulate the carrying of concealed weapons in the District of Columbia and the territories. The next proposal appears to have been the one that New York Democratic Representative Major Owens introduced in 1992; he offered another appeal for an amendment designed to clarify the Second Amendment in June 1995.

The paucity of proposed amendments certainly does not stem from disinterest in the Second Amendment. The likely explanation is that most proponents and opponents of gun control have preferred to battle over the meaning of the existing constitutional provision rather than to introduce a new one.

For Further Reading:

Cottrol, Robert J., ed. 1994. *Gun Control and the Constitution: Sources and Explorations on the Second Amendment.* New York: Garland.

Cottrol, Robert J., ed. 1993. *Gun Control and the Constitution: Sources and Explorations of the Second Amendment.* 3 vols. New York: Garland.

Second Amendment Symposium. 1995. *Tennessee Law Review* 62 (Spring): 443–821.

❖ SECRETARY OF STATE ❖

The secretary of state served until 1818 by custom, and from then until 1951 by statute, as the person responsible for certifying and proclaiming the ratification of constitutional amendments. Congress transferred this function to the administrator of the General Services Administration in 1951 and to the archivist of the Library of Congress in 1984 (Bernstein with Agel 1993, 246).

The action of certifying amendments is generally routine, but Secretary William Seward faced anything but a routine situation when deciding what to do about the Fourteenth Amendment. Although one more than the necessary 28 states had ratified, North and South Carolina had done so in the face of prior rejections of the amendment, and Ohio and New Jersey had subsequently voted rescissions (Dellinger 1983, 389). Seward reported these facts to Congress, directing particular attention to the attempted rescissions, and it subsequently voted to promulgate the amendment, which Seward did (James 1984, 289–304). The issue is further confused, however, by the fact that a telegram had been introduced in congressional debates, indicating that Georgia had also ratified. This provided the necessary three-fourths majority whether the two rescissions were counted or not (A. Baker 1979, 79–80).

Walter Dellinger has argued that the congressional promulgation of the Fourteenth Amendment was unique, unwarranted, and unnecessary. In his view, an amendment becomes effective the moment it is ratified by the necessary states, whether it is so noted at the time by the official responsible or not (Dellinger 1983, 402).

The controversial ratification of the Twenty-seventh Amendment brought renewed attention to the role of the official responsible for certifying amendments. In that case, the decision by the archivist of the Library of Congress to certify the amendment was confirmed by a vote in Congress. In the minds of critics concerned about the possible absence of a contemporary consensus, however, this did little to justify the ratification of an amendment more than 200 years after it had been proposed.

❖ SEGREGATION ❖

One of the Supreme Court's most important decisions of the twentieth century was its ruling in *Brown v. Board of Education* (1954). In this decision, it unanimously declared an end to the system of state-mandated segregation that it had previously sanctioned in *Plessy v. Ferguson* (1896).

In 1948, even before the *Brown* decision, Democratic Representative Oren Harris of Arkansas had introduced an amendment designed to allow individuals to segregate themselves from others voluntarily. He reintroduced this amendment in 1958 and 1961. Three days after the *Brown* decision, Democratic Representative John Bell Williams of Mississippi introduced an amendment designed to allow states to maintain racial segregation in schools. Other proposals with a similar aim were introduced to limit federal interference with state police powers. Numerous other proposals have been introduced specifically to limit the use of school busing to achieve racial balance.

See also *Brown v. Board of Education; Plessy v. Ferguson;* School Busing; States, Police Powers.

❖ SELF-INCRIMINATION ❖

The Fifth Amendment provides that no person "shall be compelled in any criminal case to be a witness against himself." In *Malloy v. Hogan* (1964), the Supreme Court reversed earlier rulings and decided that this guarantee applied to state as well as federal trials. The right was further expanded by the Warren Court in *Miranda v.*

Arizona (1966) to preclude the use of confessions made in the absence of warnings about self-incrimination and the right to an attorney. Although *Miranda* significantly expanded the right against self-incrimination, this right has deep roots in English common law and has variously been defended as a way of promoting fairness in an accusatorial legal system, as a way to prevent cruel and inhumane treatment of defendants, and as a way of protecting personal privacy (D. O'Brien 1995, 946–49).

A number of congressmen have proposed modifications of the Fifth Amendment. Among the most prominent advocates of a modification from 1968 to the present has been Democratic Representative Andrew Jacobs Jr. of Indiana, who worked as a police officer while in law school (Barone and Ujifusa 1994, 464). His proposal has three parts: it would stipulate that individuals could not be compelled to incriminate themselves "except in open court"; it would prevent the introduction of prior criminal convictions, "except where they are an element of the crime charged"; and it would alter the Sixth Amendment so that defendants would be informed not only of the nature and cause of the accusations against them but also of the evidence (H.J. Res. 314, 1979). In 1971, Republican Representative Carleton King of New York introduced a proposal (H.J. Res. 903) prohibiting the use of physical or mental torture to extract confessions but permitting inferences that might be made from failure to testify. King would also have permitted "the reasonable in-custody questioning of suspects by police."

❖ SEVENTEENTH AMENDMENT ❖

The American framers considered bicameralism, the division of Congress into two branches, to be quite important. Anticipating that the legislative body would be the most powerful in a republic, the framers hoped that the Senate would be a somewhat smaller, wiser body capable of tempering "the sudden and violent passions" thought to be more characteristic of larger legislative chambers (Hamilton, Madison, and Jay 1961, 379).

The Framers' Scheme

Whereas members of the House of Representatives were apportioned according to population, each state was guaranteed two senators. This provision, part of the Great Compromise that was necessary at the Constitutional Convention of 1787 to reconcile the interests of the large and small states (Vile 1993a, 16), was further entrenched by a provision in Article V providing that no state shall be deprived of its equal Senate representation without its consent. In an attempt to give the Senate a different electoral base than the House, the framers specified in Article I, Section 3 that it would be composed of "two Senators from each State, chosen by the Legislature thereof, for six Years."

Calls for Change

Beginning in 1826, there were increasing calls to change this method of selection to popular election, a movement notably supported by Tennessee Senator and later President Andrew Johnson. This movement hit full stride at the end of the nineteenth century. By the time the amendment was ratified in 1913, there had been close to 200 proposals introduced in Congress to this effect, including over 50 petitions (some redundant) from 31 states. The threat of a convention appears to have been a strong motive that finally prompted the Senate to act.

Early in American constitutional history, there had been considerable controversy about how state legislatures were to make their choices. Congress adopted legislation on the subject on 25 July 1866, but the legislation proved singularly ineffective in solving many of the problems (Haynes 1960, 85). Many thought that the system allowed money and influence to control the political system (Grimes 1978, 79).

A close scholar of the subject identified the following problems: deadlocks, stampeded elections, bribery and corruption, unfilled vacancies depriving states of their constitutionally entitled equal representation, misrepresentation of popular wishes, interference with the state's regular legislative business, and confusion and corruption of state politics (Haynes 1960, 86–95). In one notorious example in Missouri in 1904, representatives attempted to stop the legislative clock to give time for a senatorial election. Tactics included hoisting a ladder, fistfighting, and throwing books. It was reported that "the glass of the clock front was broken, but the pendulum still persisted in swinging until, in the midst of a yelling mob, one member began throwing ink bottles at the clock, and finally succeeded in breaking the pendulum" (Haynes 1960, 90).

Action by the States

After the Senate's repeated refusal to act, a number of states began to take matters into their own hands. Most popular was a method, initially adopted in Oregon by popular referendum, whereby candidates for the state legislature were asked to pledge their votes for the candidate who won the party primary (Haynes 1960, 101–4). Senators so selected naturally felt obligated to support an amendment for popular election. As Idaho Senator Borah remarked, "I should not be here if it [election by the legislature under direct instructions of a popular vote] had not been practiced, and I have great affection for the bridge which carried me over" (Haynes 1960, 108).

Proposal and Ratification

An amendment providing for the direct election of senators was first adopted in the

House on 21 July 1894. The House was also successful in votes taken in 1898, 1900, and 1902. The Senate's first vote in 1911 proved unsuccessful, and there was considerable friction between the two houses about the so-called race rider, introduced by Republican Representative Horace Young of Michigan and largely supported by southern Democrats. Although accepting the direct election of senators, this rider would have removed such elections from federal supervision, including protections offered to black voters by the Fifteenth Amendment. Eventually, Republican Senator Francis Bristow of Kentucky succeeded in invalidating the race rider by adding an amendment to the resolution that became the Seventeenth Amendment (Grimes 1978, 79–81). On 11 April 1911, Socialist Representative Victor Berger of Wisconsin introduced a resolution for abolition of the Senate (H.J. Res. 79). Like petitions for a convention, it seems likely that this proposal was designed to pressure senators. Both houses finally agreed on the Seventeenth Amendment in May 1912.

The amendment was ratified by the necessary number of states on 8 April 1913, Massachusetts being the first and Connecticut the thirty-sixth to ratify (U.S. Senate 1985, 46). As ratified, the amendment calls for the direct election of senators by state voters with the qualifications "requisite for electors of the most numerous branch of the State legislatures." These were the same qualifications previously introduced in Article I, Section 2 of the Constitution for voting for members of the House of Representatives. The amendment also provides that state executives may temporarily fill vacancies until the people vote. Thus, when Democratic Senator Al Gore Jr. of Tennessee became vice president in 1993, Democratic Governor McWherter appointed Democrat Harlan Matthews until state voters chose Republican Fred Thompson in the next regular congressional election in 1994.

Critiques and Implications of the Amendment

The Seventeenth Amendment has been called "the most drastic alteration in the system of federalism since the Civil War Amendments" (Bernstein with Agel 1993, 122). Although it is difficult to imagine its repeal, one such proposal was introduced in June 1939 by a Montana representative. The amendment is occasionally criticized for weakening political parties and for reducing the proper influence of the states in the federal system. With the increasingly high costs of political campaigns and the lack of any limits on what an individual can contribute to his own efforts, the goal of seeing that the Senate is not a "millionaires club" may also have been thwarted (R. Peters 1990).

In her dissenting opinion in *Garcia v. San Antonio Metropolitan Transit Authority*, a case involving congressional authority to set wage regulations for state and local governments, Justice Sandra Day O'Connor, a former Arizona legislator, referred to the direct election of senators as one factor that may have "lessened the weight Congress gives to the legitimate interests of States as States" (1985, 584). It is possible that increased concerns about federalism could eventually result in another constitutional amendment to redress a perceived imbalance.

Citing the implications of the Seventeenth Amendment as "unchartered waters," one author recently criticized a U.S. circuit court opinion in *Trinsey v. Pennsylvania* (1991). This case dealt with the procedures used to select party nominees for the election of a successor to Republican Senator John Heinz of Pennsylvania, who died in a plane crash. The author of the article argued that the amendment should be interpreted to prohibit a state from selecting candidates for senatorial vacancies without following normal primary election procedures (Little 1991).

For Further Reading:

Hoebeke, C. H. 1995. *The Road to Mass Democracy: Original Intent and the Seventeenth Amendment.* New Brunswick, NJ: Transaction.

❖ SEVENTH AMENDMENT ❖

The Seventh Amendment was proposed by the First Congress and ratified as part of the Bill of Rights in 1791. The amendment provides that "in suits at common law, when the value in controversy shall exceed twenty dollars, the right of trial by jury shall be preserved, and no fact tried by a jury, shall be otherwise re-examined in any Court of the United States, than according to the rules of common law."

The absence of a guarantee of juries in civil cases was a prominent Anti-Federalist criticism of the new document, and the ratifying conventions of Massachusetts, Maryland, Virginia, and North Carolina all called for guarantees of juries in civil cases (Lutz 1992, 57). Accordingly, when James Madison offered his proposal for a bill of rights, he included a provision that "in suits at common law, between man and man, the trial by jury as one of the best securities to the rights of the people, ought to remain inviolate" (Kurland and Lerner 1987, 5:26).

Supreme Court decisions have extended guarantees for jury trials to federal statutory law, as well as to common, or judge-made, law cases. As in the case of the Sixth Amendment, however, the Court has not required that such juries consist of the traditional 12 members. Whereas the Sixth Amendment provision for a jury trial in criminal cases has been applied to the states via the due process clause of the Fourteenth Amendment, the provision in the Seventh Amendment has not so been applied. States are therefore free to dispense with such requirements in their civil proceedings.

In the past decade, at least two individuals have advocated repeal of the Seventh Amendment (Antieau 1995; Kennedy 1991).

❖ SHAFROTH-PALMER AMENDMENT ❖

Sometimes simply referred to as the Shafroth amendment, this proposal was introduced in Congress in March 1914 and was sponsored by Democratic Senator John F. Shafroth of Colorado and Democratic Representative Mitchell Palmer of Pennsylvania (Kraditor 1981, 204–9). Initially, the amendment also had the support of Ruth Hanna McCormick of the National American Woman Suffrage Association (NAWSA).

The amendment proposed allowing 8 percent of a state's voters to petition to place women's suffrage on the state ballot, the issue subsequently to be decided by a state referendum. This would have left the issue of women's suffrage a matter for state rather than for federal action (Lunardini 1986, 55). NAWSA's endorsement of the proposal was dropped in 1915 when Carrie Chapman Catt was elected its president, and the organization directed renewed attention to the alternative Anthony amendment, which became the Nineteenth Amendment in 1920 (Lunardini 1986, 182).

See also Initiative and Referendum; Nineteenth Amendment.

❖ SHERMAN, ROGER (1721–1793) ❖

Roger Sherman was an American Founding Father from Connecticut who served on the committee that drafted the Declaration of Independence; he also signed the Articles of Confederation and attended the Constitutional Convention of 1787 (M. Bradford 1994, 21–28). Sherman was an active member of the convention who helped formulate the Connecticut Compromise, providing that states would be represented by population in the House of Representatives (as the Virginia plan had proposed) and equally in the Senate (as the New Jersey plan had advocated). At the convention, Sherman suggested inclusion of the provision in Article V that the states could not be deprived of their equal representation in the Senate without their consent.

Although he eventually gave his support, Sherman initially opposed the Bill of Rights on the theory that such a bill would allow the national government to control the acts of individuals within the states (M. Bradford 1994, 26). As a member of the first House of Representatives, Sherman raised the initial objection to James Madison's plan to incorporate new amendments within the text of the document rather than adding such amendments, as Congress eventually decided to do, at the end of the document. Sherman observed, "We ought not to interweave our propositions into the work itself, because it will be destructive of the whole fabric. We might as well endeavor to mix brass, iron, and clay, as to incorporate such heterogeneous articles; the one contradictory to the other" (Kurland and Lerner 1987, 5:34).

❖ SIXTEENTH AMENDMENT ❖

The Sixteenth Amendment provides that "the Congress shall have power to lay and collect taxes on incomes, from whatever source derived, without apportionment among the several States, or without regard to any census or enumeration." By giving sanction to the income tax, this amendment has had a profound effect on everyday life (Carson 1973). Coming 43 years after the adoption of the Fifteenth Amendment, the Sixteenth Amendment also restored faith in the efficacy of the constitutional amending process and initiated a seven-year period in which three additional amendments were proposed and ratified (Kyvig 1988).

Although the U.S. Supreme Court narrowly decided to void the income tax law of 1894 in *Pollock v. Farmers' Loan & Trust Co.* (1895), it had previously accepted a wartime income tax in *Springer v. United States* (1881). Not only had war ceased in the interim, but the rhetoric had also been raised by those—including New York attorneys Joseph H. Choate and William D. Guthrie—who argued against the income tax in *Pollock*. They charged that the tax, with its potential for redistributing income by charging higher rates on higher incomes, smacked of populism and socialism (Kyvig 1988, 187).

In addition to Populists, Democrats generally favored the income tax, as did the Theodore Roosevelt–William Howard Taft wing of the Republican Party. Support was especially strong in the South, Midwest, and West, with greater opposition in the Northeast industrial states, which could be expected to bear a greater percentage of the tax. When the Payne-Aldrich Tariff Bill was debated in Congress in 1909, a number of individuals, including Tennessee's Democratic Representative Cordell Hull, wanted to include an income tax provision in the hope that the Supreme Court would reconsider its decision in *Pollock*. Others, including President (and future chief justice) William Howard Taft, feared the impact that a judicial turnabout might have on the prestige of the Supreme Court (Kyvig 1988, 191–92).

The leader of the Senate Republicans, Conservative Rhode Island millionaire Nelson Aldrich, sought to stymie the so-called Bailey-Cummins income tax addition by proposing an income tax amendment in its place. It seems clear that Aldrich's proposal was a tactical maneuver based on the premise, supported by more than 40 years of Article V quiescence, that such an amendment would never be adopted. Voting 77 to 0, however, the Senate approved the amendment in July 1909, and the House followed by a 318 to 14 majority that same month. The necessary number of states ratified the amendment in 1913. Ironically, such ratification closely followed a unanimous Supreme Court decision that upheld a corporate tax adopted in 1909 (*Flint v. Stone Tracy Co.* [1911]).

At least one commentator argued that the Sixteenth Amendment was invalid. Relying on arguments from the Tenth Amendment, similar to those advanced by Selden Bacon and others that the Court would soon dismiss, the commentator argued that the Sixteenth Amendment was the type of amendment that only the people of a state—as opposed to its legislature—could ratify (R. Brown 1920).

In the 1930s, opponents of big government often focused their wrath on the income tax, and the American Taxpayers Association and the Committee for Constitutional Government both proposed to repeal the amendment or provide for a maximum limit of 25 percent. Although this proposal got some support in Congress (see *Hearings* 1954, 1956), where it was introduced by, among others, Democratic Representative Emanuel Celler of New York, its proponents were far more successful in mobilizing calls from the states for a convention. Apparently, 34 states filed such petitions, although 12 of these also appear to have rescinded their calls (Caplan 1988, 69).

See also *Pollock v. Farmers' Loan & Trust Co.*

For Further Reading:

Schrader, George D. 1970. "Constitutional History of the Income Tax." *Georgia State Bar Journal* 7 (August): 39–55.

❖ SIXTH AMENDMENT ❖

The Sixth Amendment was proposed by the First Congress as part of the Bill of Rights and ratified in 1791. It contains multiple guarantees, all of which relate to the rights of an accused in criminal proceedings:

In all criminal prosecutions, the accused shall enjoy the right to a speedy and public trial, by an impartial jury of the State and district wherein the crime shall have been committed; which district shall have been previously ascertained by law, and to be informed of the nature and cause of the accusation; to be confronted with the witnesses against him; to have compulsory process for obtaining witnesses in his favor, and to have the assistance of counsel for his defense.

Most of the provisions of the Sixth Amendment were found in the Bill of Rights that James Madison presented to the First Congress (Kurland and Lerner 1987, 5:25). He, in turn, drew from provisions in existing state constitutions and proposals made by the state conventions that ratified the Constitution.

Each of the provisions of the Sixth Amendment has been fleshed out in judicial decisions. Although the guarantees in the Bill of Rights applied initially only to the national government, all the provisions of the Sixth Amendment have subsequently been made applicable to the states via the due process clause of the Fourteenth Amendment. The provisions of the Sixth Amendment that have evoked the most attention and controversy in recent years are those related to jury trials and the right to counsel.

The jury specified in the Sixth Amendment is known as a petit jury. Unlike the grand jury required by the Fifth Amendment, a petit jury is one that determines guilt or innocence and, in some instances, decides on an appropriate penalty. In recent years, the issues of jury size and unanimity have dominated discussion of this institution. In *Williams v. Florida* (1970), the Supreme Court ruled that juries of six persons were appropriate in noncapital criminal cases. Similarly, in *Johnson v. Louisiana* (1972) and *Apodaca v. Oregon* (1972), the Court upheld the use of nonunanimous juries, although it decided in *Burch v. Louisiana* that juries of six did have to be unanimous.

The right to counsel has also undergone substantial reevaluation in recent years. Originally, it was interpreted merely to guarantee that an individual had the right to employ an attorney. However, in the famous trial of the Scottsboro Boys, a group of black youths arrested in Alabama and charged with the rape of two white girls, the Court decided that certain extraordinary situations called for state-appointed counsel when individuals could not afford to defend themselves (*Powell v. Alabama* [1932]; D. Carter 1964). Then, in *Gideon v. Wainwright* (1973), the Supreme Court extended the right to court-appointed counsel to indigents in all felony cases (see Lewis 1974). *Argersinger v. Hamlin* (1972) extended the guarantee to all cases in which imprisonment was possible. In *Miranda v. Arizona* (1966), the Court required police officers to inform suspects being interrogated of this right.

As concerns about law enforcement have increased in recent years, some scholars have expressed concern that Supreme Court decisions have eroded some of the guarantees in the Sixth Amendment (Garcia 1992), but this very debate may reflect the continuing relevance of the rights of criminal defendants (Bodenhamer 1992, 138). Although members of Congress have often reacted angrily to Supreme Court decisions expounding the rights of criminal defendants, they have offered no provisions to repeal this amendment.

❖ *SLAUGHTERHOUSE* CASES ❖ (1873)

The *Slaughterhouse* cases, the first adjudicated under the Thirteenth and Fourteenth Amendments, have had a profound impact on the interpretation of these amendments and their subsequent legal evolution. At issue was a series of regulations that the state of Louisiana had imposed on those who butchered animals in New Orleans and surrounding parishes. Apparently motivated by a combination of noble concerns about health and crass political considerations (Labbe 1983), the law limited butchering to the facilities of a single privately owned company; these facilities were to be open to all, with both price and safety regulations.

Butchers with their own facilities sued and challenged this law as a violation of the Thirteenth and Fourteenth Amendments, with special emphasis on the privileges and immunities clause of the latter. Writing for a majority of five, Justice Samuel Miller rejected these claims. In looking at the postwar amendments, Miller stated that "the one pervading purpose found in them all" was "the freedom of the slave race." Although acknowledging that the amendments might also forbid "Mexican peonage or the Chinese coolie labor system," he found that their central purpose needed to be kept in view.

Miller interpreted the privileges and immunities clause as requiring states to extend the same rights to citizens of other states within their jurisdiction as they extended to their own citizens. Noting that the Fourteenth Amendment distinguished between state and national citizenship, Miller argued that it intended to leave the protection of most citizen privileges and immunities where it had always been, that is, at the state level. In rejecting the idea of broad nationally based rights, Miller stated that this would make courts "a perpetual censor upon all legislation of the States" and would be inconsistent with American notions of federalism:

The argument, we admit, is not always the most conclusive which is drawn from the consequences urged against the adoption of a particular construction of an instrument. But when, as in the case before us, these consequences are so serious, so far-reaching and pervading, so great a departure from the structure and spirit of our institutions; when the effect is to fetter and degrade the State governments by subjecting then to the control of Congress, in the exercise of powers hithertofore universally conceded to them of the most ordinary and fundamental character; when in fact it radically changes the whole theory of the relations of the State and Federal Governments to each other and of both these governments to the people; the argument has a force that is irresistible, in the absence of language which expresses such a purpose too closely to admit of doubt (1873, 78).

Miller also rejected pleas based on the Thirteenth Amendment and on the due process and equal protection clauses of the Fourteenth Amendment.

In dismissing Miller's narrow reading of the Fourteenth Amendment, Justice Stephen Field said in his dissent that if the privileges and immunities guaranteed by the amendment were so limited, the Fourteenth Amendment "was a vain and idle enactment, which accomplished nothing, and most unnecessarily excited Congress and the people on its passing" (1873, 96). Similarly, in his dissent, Justice Noah Swayne said that the post–Civil War amendments had been designed "to rise to the dignity of a new Magna Charta." He further noted that the Fourteenth Amendment was designed to "embrace equally all races, classes and condition of men" and that, however novel such power might seem, "the novelty was known and the measure deliberately adopted" (1873, 125, 129).

The due process and equal protection clauses of the Fourteenth Amendment have subsequently been interpreted quite broadly, but the privileges and immunities clause has never rebounded from the narrow reading it received in this case. Scholars are still divided as to whether the decision appropriately recognized necessary state police powers and the continuity with the federal system that the authors of the postwar amendments intended, or whether the decision represented a judicial "amendment" of these additions in the guise of interpretation.

For Further Reading:

Agnes, Richard L. 1994. "Constricting the Law of Freedom: Justice Miller, the Fourteenth Amendment, and the *Slaughter-House Cases.*" Chicago-Kent Law Review 70: 627–88.

❖ SLAVERY, AND COLONIZATION ❖

One of the obstacles to slave emancipation was the fear that the white and black races would find it difficult to live together. Thus, in favorably reporting a proposed plan in Virginia to alter the laws so as to free slaves born after the act and to colonize them "to such place as the circumstances of the time should render most proper," Thomas Jefferson noted the problem with allowing them to stay: "Deep-rooted prejudices entertained by whites; ten thousand recollections, by the blacks, of the injuries they have sustained; new provocations; the real distinctions which nature has made; and many other circumstances, will divide us into parties and produce convulsions, which will probably never end but in the extermination of the one or the other race" (Jefferson 1964, 132–33).

An American Colonization Society was founded in December 1816–January 1817, with the hope that the colonization of free blacks might eventually be followed by complete emancipation (see letter of Robert G. Harper in Pease and Pease 1965, 18–59). In 1832, Whig Representative

William Archer of Virginia introduced an amendment calling on Congress to aid the colonization movement from the sale of public lands, a resolution seconded that same congressional session by the Maryland state legislature.

A number of similar plans were introduced in the early 1860s, one of which was part of a series of proposals by Democratic Senator Stephen A. Douglas of Illinois in 1860. In his annual message of 1862, President Abraham Lincoln recommended three amendments, one of which called on Congress to provide money for the recolonization of free blacks who were willing to relocate (J. Richardson 1908, 6:136). With the final emancipation of all African Americans by the Thirteenth Amendment, the financial and other practical obstacles to such a plan became overwhelming, and calls for such an amendment ceased.

SLAVERY, COMPENSATION FOR

A critical obstacle to slave emancipation was the financial loss that such emancipation represented to the owners. In his annual message of 1862, President Abraham Lincoln proposed a scheme of compensation for states that abolished slavery by January 1900 (J. Richardson 1908, 6:136).

Instead, Lincoln later issued the Emancipation Proclamation freeing slaves behind enemy lines, and the Thirteenth Amendment abolished the remnants of this institution in 1865. Fearful that slaveholders might later press their claims for compensation, a number of congressmen introduced resolutions to prohibit such compensation. Section 4 of the Fourteenth Amendment subsequently incorporated a provision prohibiting the United States from assuming any debts incurred by those in rebellion "or any claim for the loss or emancipation of any slave."

See also Thirteenth Amendment.

SLAVERY, DISTRICT OF COLUMBIA

The existence of slavery in the District of Columbia caused special consternation among representatives of the free states. In 1839, former President John Quincy Adams, then serving as a Whig representative from Massachusetts, proposed the abolition of slavery and the slave trade in the nation's capital after 1845. The Compromise of 1850 subsequently abolished the slave trade in that city.

A number of proposals relating to slavery in the District of Columbia were among the wave of amendments introduced in Congress beginning in 1860. Some sought to guarantee the continuing legality of slavery in the District, and some sought to abolish it. Others sought to have the question determined by practices in nearby Virginia and Maryland or in the latter state alone, and still others sought to guarantee the right of federal officers who owned slaves to bring them into the District with them. Congress abolished slavery in the District in April 1862 (prior to the Thirteenth Amendment) and provided for the compensation of owners who were loyal to the Union (Urofsky 1988, 419).

SLAVERY, FOREIGN COMMERCE

Even many slave owners who attended the Constitutional Convention of 1787 appear to have had antipathy for the slave trade. Largely at the insistence of the South Carolina delegation, however, Article I, Section 9 of the Constitution withheld power over this trade from Congress until 1808.

In the years immediately preceding this date, seven state legislatures, the first of which was North Carolina's, petitioned for amendments to end the slave trade. In 1807, when Thomas Jefferson was president, Congress adopted legislation outlawing American participation in slave trade beginning the following January. This legislation was later strengthened in 1818 (Finkelman 1992, 792).

U.S. law did not, of course, apply internationally. Thus, the Supreme Court had to deal with a number of subsequent cases, most notably *The Antelope* (1825), involving slaves who had come ashore from other nations. It generally took the position that the slave trade, although contrary to natural law, was not contrary to international law but was rather subject to the rules adopted by individual nations. Moreover, the continuing submission of amendments to end the slave trade right up to the Civil War was an indication that existing laws on the subject were not always effective.

It is fascinating that although the constitution of the Confederate States of America was in many ways a slave document, it banned the importation of additional slaves, thus effectively reaching beyond the U.S. Constitution on this point. The adoption of the Thirteenth Amendment ended any incentive to bring slave ships to the United States.

For Further Reading:

Rawley, James A. 1981. *The Transatlantic Slave Trade: A History*. New York: W. W. Norton.

Reynolds, Edward. 1985. *Stand the Storm: A History of the Atlantic Slave Trade*. London: Allison & Busby.

❖ SLAVERY, INSURRECTIONS ❖

One of the catalysts to the Civil War was the raid that John Brown led on Harpers Ferry. He hoped that this action would trigger a general slave revolt. Although his hope was not realized, his raid renewed fears among southern slaveholders.

Three proposals were offered in 1861 to give Congress power to pass penal laws to punish individuals who incited or aided such insurrections or conspiracies, and another was proposed in 1864 as a substitute for the Thirteenth Amendment (Ames 1896, 206). Ironically, federal powers under the Fourteenth Amendment would later be evoked in cases such as *U.S. v. Guest* (1966) and *U.S. v. Price* (1966) to punish conspiracies against the rights of African Americans.

See also Brown, John.

❖ SLAVERY, INTERSTATE COMMERCE ❖

Article I, Section 9 granted Congress the power to limit the foreign slave trade after 1808, but it did not directly address congressional control of the interstate slave trade. Although Congress never attempted to restrict slavery through use of this mechanism, southerners appeared to regard such a use as a real possibility. Several amendments proposed on the eve of the Civil War, including those by Tennessee's Democratic Representative (and future president) Andrew Johnson, Kentucky's Unionist Representative John Crittenden, and Illinois' Democratic Senator Stephen Douglas, attempted expressly to guarantee the right to engage in such interstate trade.

Long before, in 1823, Georgia had proposed an amendment supported by three other states that had been designed to keep any part of the Constitution from being interpreted "to authorize the importation or ingress of any person of color into any one of the United States contrary to the law of such State" (quoted in Ames 1896, 210). This proposal was prompted by the South Carolina Seaman Act of 1822. The original law, later modified, had provided for the jailing and possible enslavement of free blacks who left their ships for shore. In his role as a circuit court judge, Associate Justice William Johnson described the law as being in conflict with both federal commerce power and a treaty with Great

Britain. William Wirt, President John Quincy Adams's attorney general, subsequently reaffirmed Johnson's opinion. President Andrew Jackson's attorney generals, John Macpherson Berrien and future Chief Justice Roger B. Taney, later reversed Wirt's opinion, and the issue continued to be contested until the Thirteenth Amendment abolished slavery (Wiecek 1977, 133–39).

❖ SLAVERY, PROTECTION FOR ❖

Slavery was an issue long before the Civil War (Lively 1992, 11–37). One of the South's greatest fears, a fear that eventually led to secession, was that the more populous northern states might one day use the law or the constitutional amending process to abolish slavery.

In 1850, Democratic Representative John Daniels of North Carolina introduced an amendment to prevent such abolition. Beginning in 1860, there were a number of similar proposals (one introduced by Mississippi Democratic Representative Jefferson Davis, future president of the Confederacy) designed to protect slavery by specifically recognizing the institution or prohibiting any federal interference with it.

The best known of these proposals, designed to be unalterable, was the Corwin amendment, which had the support of President Abraham Lincoln, at least for a time. Southern secession marked the failure of this proposal and prepared the way for the very thing that the southerners had feared. In 1865, the Thirteenth Amendment abolished slavery.

See also Corwin Amendment.

❖ SLAVERY, RETURN OF FUGITIVES ❖

One of the most persistent problems engendering controversy between northern and southern states prior to the Civil War concerned the pursuit and capture of slaves who fled north to obtain their freedom.

Article IV, Section 2 of the Constitution provided that "no Person held to Service or Labour in one State, under the Laws thereof, escaping into another, shall, in Consequence of any Law or Regulation therein, be discharged from such Service or Labour, but shall be delivered upon Claim of the Party to whom such Service or Labour shall be due." This provision did not, however, explicitly designate whose obligation it was to return fugitives. High-handed actions by some southern slave catchers—who tended to presume that all blacks were escaped slaves—led many northern states to adopt personal liberty laws designed to provide legal protections against false kidnappings.

Congress adopted a fugitive slave law in 1793, which it later strengthened in 1850 as part of the compromise adopted that year, but as abolitionist sentiment grew, northern states became increasingly uncooperative. Court decisions written by Joseph Story in *Prigg v. Pennsylvania* (1842) and by Chief Justice Roger Taney in *Abelman v. Booth* (1859) attempted to uphold the rights of slaveholders, but sentiment in some northern states remained uncooperative, and southerners were unsatisfied. In his annual message of 1860, President James Buchanan proposed what he termed an "explanatory amendment" recognizing "the right of property in slaves." He further proposed "a like recognition of the right of the master to have his slave who has escaped from one State to another restored and 'delivered up' to him, and the validity of the fugitive-slave law enacted for this purpose, together with a declaration that all State laws impairing or defeating this right are violations of the Constitution, and are consequently null and void" (J. Richardson 198, 5:638).

For his part, incoming President Abraham Lincoln was willing to enforce the fugitive slave law against any conflicting state legislation, but he did not think that a constitutional amendment was necessary (T. Morris 1974, 205).

About 30 amending resolutions followed in the year after Buchanan's speech. Most would have affirmed or strengthened the fugitive slave law. Some would have struck down conflicting state legislation. Some, like a proposal by Tennessee's Andrew Johnson, would have had the government provide compensation for fugitive slaves who were not returned. A few, reflecting the sentiments that had led to the personal liberty laws, provided that fugitive slaves would be entitled to a jury or to other procedural protections of regular criminal trials.

In June 1864, Congress repealed the fugitive slave law, and subsequent adoption of the Thirteenth Amendment ended this controversy. One writer believes that the Thirteenth and Fourteenth Amendments "carried forward the commitment that had been embodied in the Personal Liberty Laws" (T. Morris 1974, 218).

❖ SLAVERY, RIGHT TO TRAVEL WITH SLAVES ❖

In the early years of the Republic, northern free states generally made provision for slave owners to travel there with their slaves. By 1860, however, most northern states explicitly denied this right (Finkelman 1981, 340).

A notorious case was initiated in 1852 when a Virginia slave owner, Jonathan Lemmon, came by ship to New York with his slaves, intending to take a steamboat to New Orleans. When Lemmon came ashore with his slaves, New York courts, including New York's highest tribunal, held that the slaves had become free (*Lemmon* [1860]). Many slavery opponents subsequently feared, however, that *Scott v. Sandford* (1857) signaled an increased willingness on the part of the U.S. Supreme Court to protect slavery, even in the northern states (Finkelman 1981, 313–38).

In attempts to reduce the friction that this issue was causing, four amendments were introduced on 12 December 1860 with provisions that would have protected the rights of slave owners to travel with their slaves. A substitute for the Thirteenth Amendment, which was introduced in 1864, would have limited the right to such travel to other slave states. For its part, the Constitution of the Confederate States of America granted citizens "the right to travel and sojourn in any State of this Confederacy, with their slaves and other property," thus attempting to guarantee the kind of comity that had ended in the North (Finkelman 1981, 21).

❖ SLAVERY, THE TERRITORIES AND ❖

Numerous amending proposals were introduced just before the outbreak of the Civil War to resolve the issue of slavery in the territories. This issue was important because these territories were the breeding ground for new states and because such states threatened the precarious balance that had been established in the early years of the Republic between free states and slave states, which eventually ended with the admission of California.

The Northwest Ordinance of 1787, adopted under the Articles of Confederation and reauthorized by the new government in 1789, had prohibited slavery in that area. Subsequent congressional legislation regarding the Southwest Territory and the Louisiana and Missouri Territories had prohibited the federal government from interfering with the institution there. Slavery was, however, later forbidden in the Illinois, Indiana, and Michigan Territories (Lively 1992, 12).

The divergent policy for northern and southern territories was formalized with the Missouri Compromise of 1820. Under this plan, Missouri was admitted as a slave state, Maine was admitted as a free state, and slavery was forbidden in the Louisiana Territory north of a line at 36' 30''. The failed Wilmot Proviso, which was introduced during the Mexican-American War, subsequently stirred passions by proposing to abolish slavery in any territories acquired from Mexico. Moreover, the Kansas-Nebraska Act of 1854 effectively repealed the Missouri Compromise line by specifying that Kansas and Nebraska, both north of the line, would decide for themselves whether they wanted to be slave or free. This law embodied the principle of popular sovereignty championed by Illinois Democratic Senator Stephen Douglas. Similarly, in 1857, Chief Justice Roger Taney decided in *Scott v. Sandford* that the provisions of the Missouri Compromise that restricted slavery in the northern territories were unconstitutional.

Members of the newly formed Republican Party were especially concerned about the Kansas-Nebraska Act and the *Scott* decision. Both actions appeared to open the prospect for the expansion of slavery, and Republicans were committed to the principle that slavery could be tolerated only if it were placed on a course of ultimate extinction (Foner 1970). Many southern Democrats were just as concerned that, as the balance of the Union tipped toward the free states, their peculiar institution would be jeopardized.

Proposed constitutional amendments reflected national divisions. In an apparent attempt to reaffirm the much-criticized *Scott* decision, President James Buchanan called for federal protection of slavery in the territories in his 1860 annual message. Other proposals repeated Buchanan's call for federal protection of slavery in the territories, called for resurrection of the 36' 30" line drawn by the Missouri Compromise, proposed to take away any authority of the federal government or the territorial legislatures regarding slavery, or called for states to decide whether they wanted to have slaves at the time they joined the Union.

Ultimately, no compromises proved successful, and the nation plunged into the Civil War. The Thirteenth Amendment subsequently prohibited slavery not only in the northern territories but also in those southern states where the institution had been so entrenched.

See also *Scott v. Sandford*.

❖ SMITH, GOLDWIN (1823–1910) ❖

British-born Goldwin Smith, a barrister and professor who eventually settled in Canada, presented his views on the need for American constitutional reform in an article published in 1898. His thoughts appear to have been largely stimulated by the threat of "Bryanism" in the previous presidential contest, and like others of his day, his solution was that of a cabinet, or parliamentary, government (Vile 1991c, 40–42).

Smith favored reducing the power of the Senate; he thought that some states, such as Nevada, had been introduced prematurely in the Senate, and he thought that small states had inordinate influence. He also considered the two-year term for members of the House of Representatives to be too short to allow members to gain the requisite knowledge or perform as statesmen. In Smith's judgment, however, the most urgent weakness in U.S. government was "the want of initiative and control in legislation and, still more palpably, in finance, arising from the exclusion of the responsible ministers of state from the assembly which makes the laws, regulates the expenditure, and imposes the taxes" (G. Smith 1898, 262).

Smith also believed that the change of administration every four years needlessly destroyed continuity in the State Department.

Because he was especially concerned about the Supreme Court's acceptance of inconvertible paper money, Smith thought that the Court should be limited to interpreting, rather than modifying, the Constitution. Pointing to the sectional strife that disputes over tariff policy had spawned throughout American history, Smith advocated "an equal *ad valorem* duty on all imports, variable in amount with the necessities of the treasury" (G. Smith 1898, 266).

Believing that the Fifteenth Amendment had become a dead letter, Smith favorably cited a petition by Louisiana and two other states for a convention to repeal it. He also believed that immigration (and possibly suffrage) restrictions were needed, especially in the case of "the Russian or Hungarian Jew" (G. Smith 1898, 267). Anticipating that Cuba might be annexed to the United States, he also favored an amendment to regulate the governing of such dependencies.

Elsewhere, Smith speculated that "a union of this Northern Continent" might be an appropriate occasion for revising the Constitution (G. Smith 1906, 851). Sharing the common belief of his day that it was extremely difficult to change the U.S. Constitution, Smith did not, however, hold out much prospect for the reforms he advocated.

❖ SMITH V. UNION BANK OF GEORGETOWN (1831) ❖

Smith v. Union Bank of Georgetown involved the disposition of an estate. The specific question was whether debts should be paid according to the laws where the decedent had been domiciled or according to the laws of the state where he held his property. The Supreme Court decided that the latter rule should govern.

In so ruling, Justice William Johnson noted, "Whether it would or would not be politic to establish a different rule by a convention of the States, under constitutional

sanction, is not a question for our consideration" (*Smith* 1831, 528). A modern scholar who believes that constitutional conventions may be limited to a single subject has cited this decision as support for his view (Caplan 1988, 45–46).

❖ SOCIALIST PARTY OF AMERICA ❖

Although Socialist candidates for president such as Eugene Debs and Norman Thomas have occasionally attracted national attention, unlike many Western European democracies, the United States has never had a strong Socialist Party (Shannon 1967). This may reflect the comparative weakness of organized labor in the United States, but it may also stem from the fact that Americans have often associated the agenda of the Socialists with that of the Communists. Although both parties are traditionally committed to governmental ownership of major industries, Socialists favor reform through the ballot box and are committed to other democratic methods. By contrast, Communists are traditionally committed to revolutionary violence and show little respect for democracy.

Of all their platforms, the Socialist platform of 1932 focused the most on constitutional reforms. Many of these reforms showed clear consistency with those of earlier Progressivists (Vile 1991c, 67–68) and included provisions for "proportional representation" (presumably in Congress), "direct election of the President and Vice President," and adoption of "the initiative and referendum" (Porter and Johnson 1966, 353). The platform also called for the elimination of the Supreme Court's power to declare laws unconstitutional and liberalization of the amending process. In addition, the platform called for repeal of the Eighteenth Amendment and national alcoholic prohibition.

❖ SOUTH CAROLINA V. BAKER ❖ (1988)

This case involved a section of the Tax Equity and Fiscal Responsibility Act of 1982, which had removed the federal tax exemption for interest earned on unregistered state bonds. South Carolina argued that this provision violated both the Tenth Amendment and the doctrine of intergovernmental tax immunities.

Writing for a 7 to 1 majority of the Court, Justice William Brennan upheld the law. Working from the precedent in *Garcia v. San Antonio Metropolitan Transit Authority* (1985), Brennan dealt with the Tenth Amendment argument by ruling that states "must find their protection from congressional regulation through the national political process, not through judicially defined spheres of unregulated state activity" (*South Carolina* 1988, 512). On the related matter of the national government's authority to force states to adopt regulations on behalf of federal interests (an issue also raised by the amendment to prohibit unfunded federal mandates), Brennan found that the law in question did not significantly differ from other such laws that the Court had upheld.

The issue of intergovernmental tax immunity dated back to the decision in *Pollock v. Farmers' Loan & Trust Co.* (1895), which immunized interest earned on state bonds from federal taxation. Even after the adoption of the Sixteenth Amendment, the Court had upheld this exemption, prompting numerous amending proposals to permit the taxation of state securities. Noting that the *Pollock* decision regarding state bonds represented but one of a number of intergovernmental tax immunities that were recognized at that time, Brennan pointed out that most such immunities had since been abandoned. He therefore decided that the *Pollock* decision was no longer valid on this point, and he overturned it.

Justices John Paul Stevens, Antonin Scalia, and William Rehnquist each wrote concurring opinions. Justice Sandra Day O'Connor dissented. She believed that the existing tax immunity doctrine, which accepted taxes that were not directly imposed on—or discriminatory with regard to—state governments, was inadequate to protect state sovereignty.

Delaware Republican Senator William Roth has since proposed an amendment to limit federal taxation of state and local obligations issued to finance governmental activities or public purposes. Cosponsors included South Carolina Republican Senator Strom Thurmond, South Carolina Democratic Senator Ernest Hollings, and Kansas Republican Senator Bob Dole.

See also *Garcia v. San Antonio Metropolitan Transit Authority*; Tenth Amendment.

❖ SOVEREIGNTY ❖

Once at the center of much of the discussion of law and politics, the idea of sovereignty is often traced back to the French philosopher Jean Bodin and the English philosophers Thomas Hobbes and John Austin. A modern writer noted that "sovereignty was an attribute of a determinate person or body to whom the generality of the society gave habitual obedience and who or which was not itself habitually obedient to any other person or body. Within that society the sovereign had ultimate power to lay down the law" (Walker 1980, 1163).

It is difficult to identify the sovereign in a system like that of the United States, in which state and national powers are divided in a federal system and in which the powers of both sets of governments are further divided into three major branches. There is, however, considerable warrant for suggesting that the ultimate sovereign—what one writer called the "pro-sovereign" (Radin 1930) to distinguish it from the regularly functioning government—is the amending mechanism. Lester B. Orfield noted that "in the last analysis, one is brought to the conclusion that sovereignty in the United States, if it can be said to exist at all, is located in the amending body" (1942, 154). Orfield further noted that "the sovereign is a real sovereign, though one fluctuating in its composition" (1942, 159).

The idea that the amending process is sovereign is sometimes called into question by the entrenchment provision providing for equal state representation in the Senate. However, since this limit can be overridden with the states' consent, it is not absolute, and in any case, it has little "practical significance" (Orfield 1942, 162).

The idea advanced by some writers that there are implicit limits on the amending process suggests that sovereignty rests elsewhere, namely, in whatever body or bodies—perhaps the courts—have responsibility for ascertaining or enforcing such limits. It might also be argued on the basis of the preamble and the Ninth and Tenth Amendments that "the people" are the sovereign. It is largely on this basis that Akil Amar argued that the people have the power to amend the Constitution outside of the specific procedures designated by Article V.

❖ SPECIAL PROSECUTOR ❖

Although the Watergate scandal did not mark the first use of a special prosecutor, this position has assumed increased visibility and has been more frequently utilized since this historic event. Great concern was raised over the independence of this office on 20 October 1973 when, in the so-called Saturday night massacre, President Richard Nixon fired Watergate special prosecutor Archibald Cox. After the consequent public uproar, Nixon appointed Leon Jaworski to this post on 1 November 1973.

Shortly thereafter, Missouri Democrat

William Randall offered what he called "the Executive Investigation and Prosecution Amendment." Randall wanted to alleviate questions—later largely resolved in favor of the arrangement in *United States v. Nixon* (1974)—about the propriety of one executive official, namely, the president, appointing another officer to investigate other executive officials. Randall therefore proposed giving this authority to Congress.

The Ethics in Government Act of 1978—subsequently revised and reauthorized in 1982, 1987, and 1992—now provides that a special court appoints such prosecutors at the request of the attorney general, who can remove them only for cause. The Supreme Court upheld this arrangement in *Morrison v. Olson* (1988). Concerns over possible abuses of the present scheme are balanced by its acknowledged role as an auxiliary check and balance to possible executive abuses (Harriger 1992, 199–217).

❖ STANTON, ELIZABETH CADY ❖ (1815–1902)

Elizabeth Cady Stanton was one of the nation's foremost proponents of women's rights and women's suffrage. Her husband, Henry Brewster Stanton, whom she married in 1840, was then an executive of the abolitionist American Anti-Slavery Society. Elizabeth was a proponent of abolition and temperance when she met Lucretia Mott at the London Anti-Slavery Convention in 1840 and became more active in feminist issues.

In 1848, Stanton and Mott helped organize the historic Seneca Falls Women's Rights Convention in New York. In what has been described as "a brilliant propagandistic stroke" (Banner 1980, 41), delegates chose to pattern their plea for women's equality on the language of the Declaration of Independence. At the time, many citizens regarded Stanton's call for women's suffrage as radical. This label often stuck with her, despite the fact that she was married and raised seven children.

Stanton is often associated with Susan B. Anthony. Stanton made Anthony's acquaintance in 1851, and she worked with her (sometimes envying the unmarried Anthony's greater mobility) for much of her remaining life. In 1863, Stanton and Anthony helped gather 300,000 petitions for the emancipation of slaves, an objective accomplished with the Thirteenth Amendment. In 1866, Stanton became the first woman to run for the U.S. House of Representatives. In 1868, Stanton and Anthony founded the Workingwoman's Association, and in 1869, they founded the National Woman Suffrage Association. They did so after having opposed women who had supported the Fourteenth and Fifteenth Amendments despite the failure of these amendments to extend legal protections to women. When Stanton and Anthony's group merged with the rival American Woman Suffrage Association to form the National American Woman Suffrage Association (NAWSA) in 1890 and to push for what was to become the Nineteenth Amendment, Stanton became the first president. She served until Anthony became president in 1892.

Stanton generally kept little distance between herself and those espousing radical causes. Stanton's *Woman's Bible*, which she published in 1895 and which reflected her own religious skepticism, provoked considerable controversy, and NAWSA disavowed any tie with the work the following year. A list of causes Stanton supported in addition to suffrage includes "coeducation, girls' sports, job training, equal wages, labor unions, birth control, cooperative nurseries and kitchens, property rights for wives, child custody rights for mothers, and reform of divorce laws" (Griffith 1984, xiv). The decision to acknowledge Anthony rather than Stanton as the mother of the

Nineteenth Amendment appears to have been part of a conscious strategy to avoid what was perceived to be Stanton's more radical stigma (Griffith 1984, xv).

See also Anthony, Susan Brownell; Nineteenth Amendment.

❖ STATE-FEDERAL RELATIONS ❖

Political scientists recognize three basic forms of government: confederal, federal, and unitary. In confederal governments, such as the Articles of Confederation, power is divided between the states and a national government, but since the latter must operate through the former—in raising taxes and armies, for example—the former is more powerful. In a unitary government, like that in Great Britain, there are no permanent state governments. By contrast, a federal government retains states but allows both state and national governments to operate directly upon individuals. In both confederal and federal governments, written constitutions are necessary. Otherwise, there would be no clear way to allocate power between the two levels of government (Vile 1993a, 91–92).

By its very nature, a federal government is complex. Even with a written constitution, there are likely to be disputes about the appropriate allocation of authority between the nation and the states, and adjustments may be needed. A number of constitutional amendments have addressed federal concerns. These include the Bill of Rights; the Eleventh, Fourteenth, and Seventeenth Amendments; and amendments (for example, the Fifteenth, Nineteenth, and Twenty-sixth) that have set national standards for voting rights.

Of all the conflicts over federalism in the United States, none proved more irreconcilable than the one that led to the Civil War. This conflict, in turn, reflected tensions in the original debates between the

Federalists and the Anti-Federalists (Mason 1964) and had roots in the conflict from 1828 to 1832 over federal tariff policies. This tariff controversy led to a number of proposals, some for a constitutional convention, to deal with the situation.

The period from 1860 to 1861, just before the outbreak of the Civil War, led to a virtual avalanche of proposals. Many were designed to deal specifically with the issue of slavery and its many ramifications, but others were directed more generally to state-federal relations. Proposals included defining those powers that were reserved to the states or denied to the national government, guaranteeing state equality, providing that states should be permitted to appoint federal officers within their boundaries, creating a plural executive or otherwise guaranteeing that legislation could not be adopted without the concurrence of each section of the nation, providing a legal means for states to secede, prohibiting such secession, or recognizing federal law as supreme.

Within five years of the end of the Civil War, the nation had adopted three amendments (the Thirteenth, Fourteenth, and Fifteenth Amendments), and in *Texas v. White* (1869), the Supreme Court declared that the Constitution had created "an indestructible Union of indestructible States" (725). The vigorous debates reflected in the *Slaughterhouse* cases (1873), however, indicated that even the postwar amendments had not resolved federalism issues. State-federal conflict was especially prominent in the wake of the Supreme Court's ruling in *Brown v. Board of Education* (1954), which declared de jure segregation to be illegal. This decision subsequently led to calls for protection of state police powers. More recently, the belief that federal regulations have become stifling has led to renewed attention to the Tenth Amendment and to calls for adjusting state-federal relations by amendment ("Conference of the States" 1995.

❖ STATES, ADMISSION OF NEW ❖

The framers of the Constitution were far-sighted enough to provide in Article IV, Section 3 that "new states may be admitted by Congress into the Union." This was subject to the reservation that new states would be formed neither within existing states nor by joining two or more states or parts of states without their consent. In cases such as *Coyle v. Smith* (1911), involving Oklahoma's authority to move its capital after it became a state, the Supreme Court has established that new states enter on an equal basis with older ones.

The admission of new states was especially controversial in the nation's early history, when both North and South examined each new candidate for statehood with a view to its impact on the respective balance that free and slave states would have in the Senate. Apparently with this issue in mind, in 1815, Senator Joseph Varnum of Massachusetts introduced a resolution to prevent the admission of new states except by a two-thirds vote. In 1839, former President John Quincy Adams, then serving as a Whig in the House of Representatives, sought an amendment to impose a flat ban on the admission of new slave states.

Controversy shifted but continued after the Civil War, when the admission of Utah became especially controversial. In 1871, Democratic Representative Abram Comingo of Missouri introduced an amendment requiring that a new state have at least enough population to entitle it to one member in the House of Representatives under the ratio for representation then in use.

In 1896, Ohio Republican Representative Lucien Fenton introduced an amendment to prohibit the admission of states from any territories south of 30' north latitude, thus excluding Hawaii from future statehood. Several other proposed amendments sought either to prevent the acquisition of any noncontiguous territories, several of which the United States acquired as a result of the Spanish-American War, or to require the admission of such territories by approval of two-thirds votes of both houses of Congress and three-fourths of the state legislatures.

Close to 30 amending resolutions were introduced in Congress from 1953 to 1961 regarding the admission of new states. These amendments were apparently aimed at Alaska and Hawaii. Concerns were raised about the nation's ability to defend these areas and, especially in the case of Hawaii, about the Americanization of an area with such a large Asian population (Bell 1984).

Most of the proposals introduced in the 1950s resurrected the idea that new states should be admitted only by the procedures and majorities needed to amend the federal Constitution. Almost as if their sponsors feared that such a policy might be applied retroactively, a number of such resolutions specifically exempted the procedure under which the Republic of Texas (which joined as a republic rather than as a prior territory) had been admitted as a state. Perhaps as a way of highlighting population disparities, especially in the case of Alaska, some resolutions in the 1950s would have allowed Congress to limit the representation of new states in the U.S. Senate.

See also Marriage, Divorce, and Parenting.

For Further Reading:

Onuf, Peter. 1984. "Territories and Statehood." In *Encyclopedia of American Political History: Studies of Principal Movements and Ideas*, ed. Jack P. Greene, 3: 1283–1304. New York: Charles Scribner's Sons.

❖ STATES, BOUNDARIES OF ❖

Numerous proponents of a new constitution for the United States have suggested that state boundaries need to be redrawn along more functional lines. Rexford Tugwell, for example, wanted to divide existing states into approximately 20 "newstates"; Leland Baldwin called for approximately 15 states, with Alaska being permitted to join Oregon or become a commonwealth. Charles Merriam also thought that state boundaries needed to be redrawn, with some large cities being given status as states; he noted that the *Chicago Tribune* received some 3,000 proposed maps when it held a contest for redrawing the boundaries of existing states (Merriam 1931, 58).

More recently, Matthew Holden Jr. suggested giving statehood to the 19 cities with populations over 500,000, thereby ensuring greater representation to African Americans and urban interests (Holden 1973b, 245–52). In a related vein, radical African Americans such as Detroit's Brother Imari (formerly Richard B. Henry) have argued for setting aside five Gulf Coast states to create a special black nation (Holden 1973a, 69; Imari 1968, 30–31).

The fact that members of Congress are elected from states may account for the paucity of proposals that have been introduced there for redrawing state boundaries. Several proposals introduced before the Civil War attempted to ensure that legislation would require the consent of the nation's major regions, and others called for a plural executive representing the nation's major sections.

Whig Senator Garrett Davis of Kentucky also introduced two proposals in 1864 for a new division of New England. One such proposal would have combined Maine and Massachusetts into East New England and the other states in the region into West New England, leaving the latter state composed of two noncontiguous parts. Apparently, Davis's proposal was designed to express his disdain for Massachusetts; he believed that its leaders' rhetoric had been largely responsible for the Civil War (Ames 1896, 215–16).

❖ STATES, CONSTITUTIONAL ❖ REVISION

The federal amending mechanism developed in large part from the experience with such provisions in state constitutions and charters, but the traditions of state and federal reform now differ significantly.

The federal Constitution is a brief document that has been in force since 1789 and has been formally amended only 27 times. By contrast, state constitutions are often codelike documents and are much more frequently amended and revised. The constitutions of the southern states have been revised and replaced particularly frequently. This difference between federal and state constitutions has led one observer to comment on what he calls "the Dual American Constitutional Tradition" (Cornwell 1981, 9). The fact that the guarantee clause in Article IV of the U.S. Constitution provides only that a state have a "republican" form of government gives states considerable leeway in initiating constitutional reforms.

State constitutions may be altered in one of three ways. Like the national Constitution, they may be altered by interpretation, especially by the judicial branch. They may also be altered by piecemeal amendments or through wholesale constitutional reform (Cornwell, Goodman, and Swanson 1975, 8–9). Such reforms are often initiated by either constitutional conventions or constitutional commissions.

Piecemeal amendments usually follow two stages—initiation and ratification. Unlike the national government, where this reform has been the subject of amending proposals, a number of states permit amendments to be introduced by popular initiatives (J. May 1987, 158–60). More commonly, however, amendments to state constitutions are introduced by constitutional conventions, by constitutional commissions, or by the state legislatures (Cornwell et al. 1975, 8–9). Most states require that the state leg-

islature propose amendments by extraordinary majorities; some require votes in successive sessions of the legislature. All states except Delaware require ratification of amendments by popular vote. Most states require ratification by a simple majority, but at least two require extraordinary majorities (Cornwell et al. 1975, 8–9).

Constitutional conventions are the most frequent vehicle for complete state constitutional overhauls, and most state constitutions explicitly provide for them. Although the topic is one over which there has been considerable disagreement (compare Jameson 1887 and Dodd 1910), in most states, such conventions are subject to at least some legislative control. Like regular amendments proposed at the state level, most new constitutions must be approved by the voters. In a proposal reminiscent of a proposal by Thomas Jefferson that was rejected at the national level, a number of states require the people to vote periodically on constitutional revision (Sturm and May 1982, 122).

See also Initiative and Referendum.

❖ STATES, CONTROL OVER ❖ NATURAL RESOURCES

In *United States v. California* (1947) and related cases, the U.S. Supreme Court decided that offshore oil was the property of the national government. In 1953, Congress enacted the Submerged Lands Act to vest ownership of lands within three miles of the coast in the states.

Beginning in the 1950s, the national government has become increasingly active in environmental regulation, an area previously left largely to state control. In March 1956, even before the adoption of much federal legislation on the subject, Democratic Representative Walter Rogers of Texas introduced an amendment to allow states "to conserve and regulate the exploration, production, and distribution of their petroleum products, water, sulfur, and all other minerals and natural resources" (H.J. Res. 588). Although no subsequent amendments on the topic have been introduced, controversy continues over the extent to which federal regulation is appropriate in this area.

See also Environmental Protection.

❖ STATES, LEGISLATIVE APPORTIONMENT ❖

One of the most influential and disputed areas in which the Warren Court intervened was the area of state legislative apportionment; it also issued decisions on the apportionment of congressional districts. The Constitution provides for reapportionment of House seats after each census. From 1842 to 1929, Congress required states to establish "contiguous equal districts," a requirement that it omitted in its 1929 and subsequent apportionment laws (D. O'Brien 1991, 387).

Throughout most of the nineteenth century, states entering the Union were also required to guarantee representation in their state legislatures based on population. At the turn of the century, however, states began to react to the flood of new immigrants and the rise of large cities by refusing to reapportion their legislatures (D. O'Brien 1991, 670). The result was that thinly populated rural areas often had the same representation within states as did urban areas with many times the population.

In *Colegrove v. Green* (1946), the Supreme Court refused to accept a challenge brought under the guarantee clause of the Constitution and overturn an Illinois legislative apportionment scheme in which population discrepancies were fairly large. Pointing to *Luther v. Borden* (1849), the Court decided that such matters were political questions, more appropriate for resolu-

tion by other branches of government. In *Gomillion v. Lightfoot* (1960), the Court seemed to open the door when it struck down a clear scheme of racial gerrymandering in Tuskegee, Alabama, but the case in which the Court truly reversed the course it had proclaimed in *Colegrove* was *Baker v. Carr* (1962). This case challenged the system of representation in Tennessee, which had last reapportioned itself in 1902. In a decision authored by Justice William Brennan, the Court decided that the matter of state legislative apportionment was justiciable under the equal protection clause of the Fourteenth Amendment.

In *Gray v. Sanders* (1963), the Court invalidated Georgia's system of primary elections, and Justice William O. Douglas articulated the principle of "one person one vote" that would be evoked in future cases. Most notably, in *Reynolds v. Sims* (1964), the Court applied this standard to both houses of a state legislature, and in *Wesberry v. Sanders* (1964), it applied it to house congressional districts. The principles of both decisions were reiterated in a series of related rulings (D. O'Brien 1991, 674–77).

Few decisions have led to sharper criticisms than those dealing with the apportionment question. Senate Minority Leader Everett Dirksen led a personal crusade to overturn *Reynolds v. Sims,* and more than 200 proposals were introduced in Congress on the subject from the decision in *Baker v. Carr* through the 1960s. The Council of State Governments pushed for amendments to overturn the reapportionment decisions, make the amending process easier, and clip the power of the Supreme Court. Twice failing to win a Senate vote for an amendment to permit states to apportion at least one house on a basis other than population (Urofsky 1988, 835), proponents of such an amendment pushed for a constitutional convention. By 1969, 33 states had applied for such a convention ("33 States Ask Congress" 1969).

As more and more states were being reapportioned, however, and urban areas were beginning to receive fairer representation, there was increasing support for the Court's rulings. A few more proposals were introduced in the 1970s, but the issue now appears largely to have faded from public consciousness.

Even while equalizing district populations, many states continue to show themselves adept at gerrymandering, that is, in configuring district boundaries to advantage particular parties or candidates. In recent cases such as *Shaw v. Reno* (1993) and *Miller v. Johnson* (1995), attention has gradually shifted to this issue, with special focus on whether districts can be gerrymandered in ways designed to increase representation for racial minorities.

See also *Baker v. Carr;* Council of State Governments; *Reynolds v. Sims.*

❖ STATES, POLICE POWERS ❖

Throughout U.S. history, scholars and politicians have argued about the proper allocation of power between the state and national governments. Powers reserved to the states by the Tenth Amendment are often referred to as state police powers. Such powers typically involve regulation of morality, of marriage and family matters, of health and safety, and of property, but the term police powers is amorphous and clearly resists easy definition (Scheiber 1992, 639).

Although the national government does not have direct constitutional authority over most such matters, it may affect them in the course of exercising its powers over interstate commerce, taxation, and the like (Curry, Riley, and Battistoni 1989, 250–52). Thus, in *Champion v. Ames* (1903), the Supreme Court upheld the federal government's prohibition of the interstate sale of lottery tickets.

Beginning with a resolution introduced on 24 May 1954 by Democratic Senator James Eastland and continuing through 1973, about 25 proposals were introduced in Congress to limit interference with state powers over health, morals, education, marriage, and good order; to give states the right to manage their own internal affairs; or to protect the reserved rights of the states. Almost without exception, the sponsors of these amendments were southerners, most from the Deep South. This suggests that most of these proposals were in response to the Supreme Court's decision in *Brown v. Board of Education,* issued on 17 May 1954, and subsequent cases that called for an end to racial segregation. Interestingly, a key rationale for *Plessy v. Ferguson* (1896)—the Supreme Court decision mandating the doctrine of separate but equal that *Brown* overturned—had been the states' right to follow local custom and preserve public order.

See also Tenth Amendment.

❖ STICKNEY, ALBERT ❖ (1839–1908)

Albert Stickney was a New York lawyer who published a book in 1879 advocating major constitutional changes (Vile 1991c, 27–29). Stickney's central objective was to create a system that would secure in each governmental department the "best men" and see that they gave "their best work" (Stickney 1879, 15). In Stickney's view, the primary obstacle to such objectives was the political party system, which he linked to a system of limited terms in office. He associated both parties and fixed terms with political corruption. In contrast to those who advocated a pure parliamentary system, however, Stickney favored neither the fusion of the legislative and executive branches nor the system of calling for a vote of no confidence by the majority.

Stickney began his description of proposed reforms by focusing on the judiciary. In a sense, this branch of government provided a model for the other branches in that its members already serve during good behavior. Believing that such tenure provided security against abuse, Stickney thought that judges, even at the federal level, could be elected rather than appointed. Stickney believed that voters would take their cues from the legal profession in making their selections.

Stickney advocated lodging executive power in one man with the power to appoint all heads of departments. These heads would, in turn, have authority over their subordinates. The president would serve during good behavior and would be responsible to the legislature, which could remove him only by a two-thirds vote. Stickney proposed to revive the electoral college as a deliberative body, free of partisanship, that would choose the president.

Initially, Stickney indicated that the real work of the legislature should not be making and revising laws—a task for judges—but rather "supervision and control" (Stickney 1879, 214). Specialists within departments would submit spending plans, and then the legislature would look them over, approve, authorize, and supervise them. Stickney favored a legislature (presumably unicameral) of 500 men who would devote their full time to their duties and would not have fixed terms. The legislature would have "absolute control of the money," power of "making *all necessary laws*," power to remove any governmental official by a two-thirds vote, but no power over appointments (Stickney 1879, 218). Stickney clearly believed that there were many areas of legislation, including the laws of marriage and divorce, where Congress should have greater authority. Believing that there must be a supreme power within the state, Stickney proposed eliminating the executive veto, but in its place, he proposed that all legislation

would have to be adopted by a two-thirds majority—a majority that would presumably be easier to obtain.

Stickney thought that the vice presidency should be eliminated. In cases of presidential vacancies, he would allow the senior cabinet officer to serve until the electoral college could choose a new president. Believing that only men with established reputations would be selected to legislative office, Stickney thought that the average member would serve about 12 years. Moreover, freed from party influence, such legislators would be able to serve the public. Legislatures would exercise greater wisdom than the people could exercise on their own behalf.

Stickney acknowledged that his plan would establish an aristocracy, but it would be an aristocracy of talent rather than of heredity. Whereas the American founders had sought the solution to government in institutions, Stickney professed to find the key in selecting men of good character to govern (Stickney 1879, 258). Perhaps because his plan was so novel, it appears to have had little contemporary influence, but Woodrow Wilson did cite Stickney's criticism of political parties in arguing for responsible cabinet government (Wilson 1882, 208–10).

❖ STORY, JOSEPH (1779–1845) ❖

In addition to serving as an associate justice of the U.S. Supreme Court from 1811 to 1845, Joseph Story was one of the most influential legal commentators of the nineteenth century. His analysis of the amending process reflected the general esteem with which the process was held, at least until the criticisms initiated by Sidney George Fisher at the time of the Civil War and the later criticisms that were raised during the Progressive Era.

Story commended the founders for recognizing the need for an amending process and also recognizing that "a government forever changing and changeable, is, indeed, in a state bordering upon anarchy and confusion" (Story 1987, 678–79). Summarizing his view, Story observed that "the great principle to be sought is to make the changes practicable, but not too easy; to secure due deliberation, and caution; and to follow experience, rather than to open a way for experiments, suggested by mere speculation or theory" (Story 1987, 679).

Story went on to describe the amending process as "the safety valve to let off all temporary effervescences and excitements; and the real effective instrument to control and adjust the movements of the machinery, when out of order, or in danger of self-destruction" (Story 1987, 680). Although the analogy of the Constitution to a machine was frequently evoked in the nineteenth century (Kammen 1987), Story appears to have been the first to use the safety-valve analogy in reference to the amending process.

❖ SUBSTANTIVE DUE PROCESS ❖

Both the Fifth Amendment and the Fourteenth Amendment contain clauses prohibiting deprivation of "life, liberty, or property, without due process of law." The guarantee in the Fifth Amendment applies to the national government, and the guarantee in the Fourteenth Amendment applies to the states. Through the latter clause, the courts have applied most of the guarantees in the Bill of Rights to state governments.

Although the language of the clauses in both the Fifth and the Fourteenth Amendments focus on *process*, at various times the Court has also given them a substantive meaning (Abraham and Perry 1994, 92–153). Indeed, the courts have interpreted these clauses so flexibly that their decisions have approached the kinds of changes usually reserved for constitutional amendments.

The Supreme Court's first use of substantive due process appears to have been in *Scott v. Sandford* (1857) and the *Slaughterhouse* cases (1873). Especially from the end of the nineteenth century until the shift in judicial emphasis and philosophy in 1937, the Supreme Court used the idea of substantive due process to strike down state and federal regulations believed to interfere unreasonably with liberty of contract. *Lochner v. New York* (1905), striking down hours regulations for bakers, and *Adkins v. Children's Hospital* (1923), voiding federal minimum-wage laws for women in the District of Columbia, epitomized this judicial philosophy. More recently, critics have alleged that the Court's decisions in *Griswold v. Connecticut* (1965), striking down Connecticut's prohibition of birth-control devices, and in *Roe v. Wade* (1973), legalizing abortion, were based primarily on substantive ideas of justice not found within the constitutional text.

Numerous amendments, including those attempting to regulate child labor, provide minimum wages, limit workers' hours, and the like, were proposed to overturn decisions by the Court when it was using the due process clause to strike at such economic regulations. More recently, the right to life amendment has been intended to strike down the Court's decisions on abortion.

See also *Lochner v. New York; Scott v. Sandford.*

❖ SUBVERSION ❖

The fear of subversion dates at least as far back as the Alien and Sedition Laws of 1798. Such fear was heightened by suspicions directed at the Communist Party during the cold war that followed World War II.

Initially, federal courts proved fairly deferential to legislation designed to register and control communists. Focusing specifically on decisions in *Dennis v. United States*

(1951) and *Communist Party v. Subversive Activities Control Board* (1961), one observer said that such decisions demonstrated "deference to legislative judgments about the existence of a subversive conspiracy, minimal rationality standards for review of the means chosen to suppress subversion, and a balancing of the rights of individuals to freedom of political expression versus the state's interest in maintaining its power" (Wiecek 1992, 847).

As it began to give greater attention to individual rights, however, the Warren Court began to examine such legislation more closely for possible conflicts with the First Amendment and other constitutional protections. Thus, in *United States v. Robel* (1967), the Supreme Court struck down a provision of the Subversive Activities Control Act of 1950 that prohibited members of the Communist Party from working at defense facilities.

This decision prompted a bevy of amending proposals, most from southern representatives, to allow Congress to exclude from employment at defense facilities individuals who knowingly became or remained a member of any organization committed to overthrowing the government by force. Even before *Robel*, an Alabama representative had introduced an amendment designed to allow public schools to exclude subversives from the classroom. Subsequent proposals also sought to extend federal power to control the transmission of subversive materials through the U.S. mails.

❖ SUNDQUIST, JAMES (1915–) ❖

Political scientist James Sundquist has authored one of the most historically informed surveys of constitutional reforms in the United States (1986). He is at once aware of the reasons that the American founders settled on a system of checks and balances and convinced that the framers may have solved the problem of tyranny by creating a system that results in excessive deadlock and stalemate (Vile 1991c, 131–33).

As a scholar, Sundquist devotes most of his attention to a discussion of past reform proposals, but he concludes by advocating consideration of nine constitutional amendments. Many overlap with proposals offered by the Committee on the Constitutional System, for which one edition of his book was published.

Sundquist's recommendations are as follows: combine the president and his running mate on a team ticket with members of the House and Senate, so voters would be unable to split their votes; raise terms of members of the House of Representatives to four years and terms of senators to eight; allow either the president or a majority of either house of Congress to call special elections in which all members of the legislative and executive branches would be up for election; remove the constitutional prohibition that prevents members of Congress from serving in the executive branch; create a limited presidential item veto, subject to an override by a majority of both houses of Congress; restore the legislative veto, albeit only when both houses of Congress concur; add an amendment effectively incorporating the provisions of the War Powers Resolution of 1973 into the Constitution; allow majorities of both houses of Congress (rather than two-thirds of the Senate) to approve treaties; and provide for a national referendum to break legislative-executive deadlocks (Sundquist 1986, 241–42).

See also Committee on the Constitutional System.

T

❖ TARIFFS ❖

In a book first published in 1902, a scholar identified the tariff as "the most persistent issue in American politics" (Stanwood 1963, 1:1). Yet during the first hundred years of the nation's history, only three amending proposals dealt with this issue. After the Nullification Crisis of 1828–1832—largely centering on southern objections to the sectional character of existing tariff policies, which tended to benefit northern industrial states at the expense of the more agrarian South—Georgia and Alabama petitioned for a constitutional convention to resolve the issue. An 1864 substitute for the Thirteenth Amendment would have permitted the use of tariffs for raising revenue as long as they were not excessive; a third proposal, offered in 1871, would have substituted direct taxes for tariffs (Ames 1896, 252).

The Payne-Aldrich Tariff Bill of 1907 gave Congress the power to establish a tariff board to give advice on tariff rates, but by the language of Article I, Section 8 of the Constitution, Congress continues to have the duty to set tariff rates. From 1916 to 1922, three proposals were introduced to transfer the power of setting tariff rates to a nonpartisan board or tariff commission. Recent debates over the North American Free Trade Agreement indicate that trade and tariff issues can still stir considerable political controversy.

For Further Reading:
Taylor, George R., ed. 1993. *The Great Tariff Debate, 1820–1830*. Boston: D. C. Heath.

❖ TAXATION, DIRECT ❖

In an attempt to protect the least populous states, Article I, Section 9 of the Constitution specifies that "no Capitation, or other direct, Tax shall be laid, unless in Proportion to the Census." However, the document does not define what direct taxes are.

In 1793, an amending resolution was introduced to define direct taxes, and three years later, in upholding a federal tax on carriages as an indirect tax, the Supreme Court indicated in *Hylton v. United States* that only taxes on persons and land fell into the direct tax category. *Pollock v. Farmers' Loan & Trust Co.* (1895) subsequently included income taxes in this category but was overturned by the Sixteenth Amendment.

Eighteen provisions were introduced in the nation's first century relative to the apportionment of direct taxes. Some would have overturned the three-fifths clause (as the Fourteenth Amendment eventually did) to require that only free individuals be counted in such apportionment. Others would have apportioned direct taxes according to property values (Ames 1896, 143–44).

Today the issue is moot because the national government relies on the income tax that was sanctioned by the Sixteenth

Amendment and on various other excise taxes that are considered to be indirect.

See also Sixteenth Amendment.

❖ TAXATION, EXPORT ❖

In a provision meant to protect the agricultural states, Article I, Section 9 of the Constitution prohibits Congress from levying a tax "on Articles exported from any State." In addition, Article I, Section 10 specifies that "no State shall, without the Consent of Congress, lay any Imposts or Duties on Imports or Exports, except what may be absolutely necessary for executing its inspection Laws."

From 1812 to 1914, 12 attempts were made to repeal the ban on congressional export levies. Most grouped around three periods—the War of 1812, the Civil War, and World War I—when governmental resources were down (Musmanno 1929, 112). Two proposals introduced in 1866 and one in 1884 would have applied specifically to exports of cotton, suggesting a possible intent to retaliate against the South.

In 1974, Michigan Republican Representative Robert Huber renewed the call to grant Congress power to levy export fees. It is difficult to imagine such a proposal, adverse to the interests of so many states, gaining the necessary majorities.

❖ TAXATION, INHERITANCE ❖

The Supreme Court upheld the constitutionality of a federal inheritance tax in *New York Trust Co. v. Eisner* (1916). Still, at least 10 amendment proposals have contained provisions designed explicitly to recognize such a power in the Constitution, with at least two such proposals declaring that such taxes could be levied only on estates valued at $50,000 or $100,000 or more (Musmanno 1929, 164). Some of the proposals

to repeal the Sixteenth Amendment have also called for limits on, or abolition of, inheritance taxes.

❖ TAXATION, LAND ❖

At least two proposals have been introduced, one by Democratic Representative Horace Voorhis of California in 1942 and the other by Democratic Representative Herman Eberharter of Pennsylvania in 1944, to allow Congress to tax land values. From a somewhat different perspective, Democratic Senator Morris Sheppard of Texas introduced three resolutions from 1937 to 1941 that would provide for a homestead exemption of up to $5,000 for a head of a household. Since Sheppard's proposal, an increasing number of states have exempted such property from taxes (Roemer 1983, 110); it is unclear whether Sheppard intended to universalize such exceptions against state taxation or whether he intended to guard against a future federal tax on land.

❖ TAXATION, MAJORITIES ❖ NEEDED TO INCREASE

Some proponents of a balanced budget amendment foresee reaching the balanced budget goal by cuts in spending, but others anticipate that federal taxes will also need to be raised to accomplish this. Opponents of such taxes believe that they simply encourage the government to increase spending.

The Constitution does not set any special majorities for the passage of tax legislation. In the last two decades, several members of Congress have proposed a constitutional amendment that would require a two-thirds vote of both Houses to raise taxes, the same vote now required to override a presidential veto. In December 1994, Republican members of the House of Representatives proposed a change in House rules that would require a three-fifths vote of the House to enact tax increases. Although the constitutionality of this measure has been questioned (Ackerman et al. 1995; Soller 1995 [but see McGinnis and Rappaport 1995]), the House adopted it in January 1995 by a 279-to-152 vote. Fifteen House members and a number of other parties have subsequently brought a suit challenging this rule change. Others have accused the Republicans of applying the new rule inconsistently (A. Rubin 1995).

See also Balanced Budget Amendment.

❖ TAXATION, RETROACTIVE ❖

As part of the Revenue Reconciliation Act of 1993, Congress retroactively raised taxes on high incomes and estates. The Supreme Court has subsequently upheld the constitutionality of such provisions ("Retroactive Tax Increases" 1994, 1588). Since the adoption of the 1993 law, however, numerous members of Congress—mostly Republicans—have sponsored what they call a "Citizens Tax Protection Amendment" designed to make such retroactive taxes illegal.

❖ TAXATION, STATE AND FEDERAL EMPLOYEES ❖

The Constitution does not specifically prohibit the national government from taxing the states or the states from taxing the federal government, but limitations can easily be surmised based on considerations of federalism. As early as *McCulloch v. Maryland* (1819), Chief Justice John Marshall ruled that the states could not tax a branch of the national bank.

In *Dobbins v. Erie County* (1842), the Court extended this rather sensible prohibition to the more problematic cases of states taxing the salaries of federal officials. In *Col-*

lector v. Day (1871), the prohibition was made reciprocal, and it stayed so until *Graves v. New York ex rel. O'Keefe* (1939). There, the Supreme Court repudiated its earlier prohibitions on the taxation of the salaries of governmental officials, now insisting only that such salaries not be singled out for special taxation.

From 1932 to two weeks prior to the *Graves* decision, at least four proposals were introduced in Congress that would have permitted state and federal taxation of governmental officials' incomes. *Graves* made such an amendment unnecessary, and Congress subsequently amended its tax laws in accord with this new precedent.

❖ TAXATION, STATE INCOME TAX OF NONRESIDENTS ❖

From 1953 to 1965, about 50 proposals were introduced in Congress to prohibit states or localities from taxing the income of nonresidents or from discriminating against nonresidents. In 1958, Connecticut also submitted a request to Congress for a convention to deal with this issue.

Most of the resolutions introduced in Congress were introduced by representatives of states surrounding New York. New York is one of those states that taxes all income earned within the state as well as income that its residents earn in other states (Penniman 1980, 13). Thirteen states permit local governments to levy income or payroll taxes on all who work there, and Philadelphia even applies this law to visiting athletes (Christensen 1995, 273).

❖ TAXATION, STATE SECURITIES ❖

Throughout most of American history, the U.S. Supreme Court has upheld a doctrine of intergovernmental tax immunity that prevented both state and national governments from taxing the interest on bonds issued by one another. This prohibition was articulated, among other places, in *Pollock v. Farmers' Loan & Trust Co. (1)* (1895).

From 1920 to 1943, more than 100 amendments were introduced that would either allow Congress to tax the interest on state securities or allow both state and national governments to tax interest on bonds issued by one another. Some such proposals were linked to proposals for the taxation of state and federal employees' income. Others would apply only when such income exceeded a set amount, such as $12,500.

Although Congress still does not tax revenues from registered state securities, its decision in *South Carolina v. Baker* (1988) indicates that the Supreme Court does not see any constitutional barriers preventing it from doing so.

See also Taxation, State and Federal Employees.

❖ TENTH AMENDMENT ❖

The Tenth Amendment was ratified in 1792 as the last provision of the Bill of Rights. The amendment provides that "the powers not delegated to the United States by the Constitution, nor prohibited by it to the states, are reserved to the States respectively or to the people."

One of the major concerns of Anti-Federalist opponents of the new Constitution centered on the scope of powers of the new central government. Five of the seven states that proposed amendments in the process of ratifying the Constitution suggested an amendment to protect the rights of the states under the new system. James Madison made such a provision part of the Bill of Rights that he offered in the First Congress. His first version of this provision mixed guarantees that are now found in the Ninth and Tenth Amendments.

The primary debate over the Tenth Amendment in the First Congress centered on whether to include the word "expressly" before the word "delegated" (Kurland and Lerner 1987, 5:403–4). Had Congress done so, the provision would have closely resembled article 2 of the Articles of Confederation, which had provided that "every state retains its sovereignty, freedom, and independence, and every Power, Jurisdiction and right, which is not by this confederation expressly delegated to the United States, in Congress assembled" (Kurland and Lerner 1987 5: 400). James Madison opposed this emendation, believing that "there must necessarily be admitted powers by implication, unless the Constitution descended to recount every minutia" (Kurland and Lerner 1987, 5: 403). His view was eventually validated by a vote of 32 to 17.

Even before the Tenth Amendment was ratified, Thomas Jefferson used it as part of his "strict construction" argument against the constitutionality of the national bank. The rival view of Alexander Hamilton was eventually vindicated in *McCulloch v. Maryland* (1819), where Chief Justice John Marshall cited the omission of the word "expressly" as a justification for the doctrine of implied powers.

The great difficulty in interpreting the Tenth Amendment stems from the fact that it does not specify precisely what powers are delegated to the national government. Moreover, those parts of the Constitution that do enumerate such powers—most notably, Article I, Section 10—allow for implied powers.

Early Supreme Court decisions referred to state "police powers" over such matters as education, health, welfare, land management, and the policing of its citizens' activities. However, after the Civil War, the national government asserted full control over most such functions in the states of the former Confederacy, and the Fourteenth Amendment subsequently raised the possibility that the old relationship between the states and the national government had been drastically altered (McDonald 1992, 863).

Initially reluctant to interpret the Fourteenth Amendment so expansively, the Court adopted somewhat contradictory lines of opinion on the matter from roughly the turn of the century until 1937. In some notable cases, particularly those involving the regulation of activities such as gambling, prostitution, and the consumption of alcoholic beverages, which the Court regarded as moral evils, it generally recognized broad federal authority under the commerce clause and other federal powers. On other occasions, the Court invalidated legislation. Most notably, in *Hammer v. Dagenhart* (1918), the Court invalidated a federal child labor law adopted under putative authority of the commerce clause; it thought that the law invaded state police powers or interfered with free market forces. In a classic error that showed seeming ignorance of the decision at the Constitutional Convention of 1787 to omit the word "expressly" from the amendment, Justice William Day declared that "to them [the states] and to the people the powers not expressly delegated to the national government are reserved" (275).

In 1937, shortly after Franklin D. Roosevelt's court-packing plan, the Supreme Court reversed course in this second area of cases and began interpreting the commerce clause and other grants of federal powers more liberally. In *United States v. Darby* (1941), Justice Harlan Fiske Stone pronounced that the Tenth Amendment "states but a truism that all is retained which has not been surrendered" (124). With only a few exceptions, the amendment has been relatively dormant since then.

In *National League of Cities v. Usery* (1976), the Supreme Court relied on the Tenth Amendment to overturn the application of federal minimum-wage laws to certain state employees, but this decision was subsequently overturned in *Garcia v. San Antonio Metropolitan Transit Authority*

(1985), in which the Court indicated that the states should look to their representatives in Congress rather than to the courts for protection. The Supreme Court's recent decision in *United States v. Lopez* (1995), declaring that the federal law prohibiting the carrying of guns within 1,000 feet of a school zone exceeded federal authority under the commerce clause, suggests, however, that the idea of states' rights articulated in the Tenth Amendment continues to be a concern.

Concern for such rights was reflected in reactions to the Supreme Court's reapportionment decisions in the 1960s, in recent proposals for an amendment to forbid unfunded federal mandates, and in increased references to the Tenth Amendment, especially among Republican officeholders. Kansas Senator Bob Dole, for example, often carries a copy of the Tenth Amendment with him and has promised to "dust off the 10th Amendment and restore it to its rightful place in our Constitution" (quoted in Moore 1996, 1940). Many believe that the national government has gone too far in the direction of consolidation and has paid too little attention to the powers reserved to the states.

See also *Garcia v. San Antonio Metropolitan Transit Authority; McCulloch v. Maryland;* States, Police Powers.

❖ TERM LIMITS ❖

See Congress, Term Limits.

❖ TERRITORIES ❖

Article IV, Section 3 grants Congress power to "make all needful Rules and Regulations respecting the Territory or other Property belonging to the United States." Surprisingly, it makes no specific provision for the acquisition of new territories.

This omission presented a dilemma for President Thomas Jefferson in 1803. Although he favored a strict construction of the Constitution, and therefore wanted a constitutional amendment to legitimize his purchase of Louisiana, he eventually acquiesced with congressional leaders of his party who thought that such an amendment was unnecessary and feared that it might complicate the diplomatic situation (Vile 1992, 70–71).

In the early years of the Republic, most issues relating to the territories centered on the issue of slavery. Ironically, at least one amendment introduced in 1866 sought to reduce the states that had participated in the rebellion to territories.

Issues involving territories often centered on the admission of new states, requiring a certain population before this occurred or seeking to prevent certain territories (especially those that were not contiguous with existing states) from being admitted into statehood. A resolution introduced by a California representative in 1872 sought to provide that public lands in the territories be given only to those who actually settled there. At least three resolutions introduced from 1875 to 1880 proposed that territories should have at least one member in the House of Representatives and one vote in the electoral college. In an idea more fully implemented with the adoption of the Twenty-third Amendment in 1961, at least one such proposal would also have given one electoral vote to the District of Columbia. Since 1975, there have been a number of proposals to provide representation in the electoral college for U.S. territories.

See also Slavery, the Territories and.

For Further Reading:
Onuf, Peter. 1984. "Territories and Statehood." In *Encyclopedia of American Political History: Studies of Principal Movements and Ideas*, ed. Jack P. Greene. 3: 1283–1304. New York: Charles Scribner's Sons.

❖ *TEXAS V. JOHNSON* (1989) ❖

Texas v. Johnson was one of the Supreme Court's most controversial decisions in recent years. It prompted numerous calls for a constitutional amendment to prohibit flag desecration.

The case involved the actions of Gregory Johnson, who took part in a "Political War Chest Tour" at the Republican National Convention of 1984. At one point in this demonstration, he publicly burned an American flag and was subsequently arrested and convicted under a Texas statute prohibiting desecration of a venerated object. Prior to being appealed to the U.S. Supreme Court, one Texas court of appeals upheld his conviction and another struck it down.

In this case, Justice William Brennan led a 5-to-4 majority affirming that Johnson's conduct was a form of symbolic speech protected by the First and Fourteenth Amendments. The Court ruled that the value of such speech outweighed the two interests advanced by Texas.

The majority rejected Texas's argument that prosecution was needed to prevent a breach of the peace, since no such breach occurred or appeared imminent. Along these lines, the majority further rejected the idea that Johnson's words fell into the small class of "fighting words" that it had recognized in prior cases, most notably *Chaplinsky v. New Hampshire* (1942).

As to Texas's desire to preserve the flag as a symbol of national unity, Brennan noted that the law in question did not prohibit all types of destruction of the flag but only that which would be offensive to others. As such, the restriction on speech was "content based" and subject to special scrutiny (*Texas* 1989, 412). Brennan argued that "government may not prohibit the expression of an idea simply because society finds the idea itself offensive or disagreeable" (*Texas* 1989, 414). Government could adopt precatory, or recommendatory, regulations, but it must use persuasion rather than force when attempting to curb symbolic speech.

Chief Justice William Rehnquist and Justice John Paul Stevens wrote dissenting opinions focusing on the uniqueness of the flag as a national symbol. They argued that Johnson was not being prosecuted for what he said but rather for what he did.

Congress responded to the decision by adopting the Flag Protection Act of 1989 rather than by proposing a constitutional amendment. The Court subsequently struck down this new law in *United States v. Eichman* (1990), and debate over the wisdom of a flag desecration amendment continues.

See also Flag Desecration; *United States v. Eichman*.

❖ THIRD AMENDMENT ❖

The Third Amendment is part of the Bill of Rights and is among the least controversial amendments to the U.S. Constitution. The amendment grew out of some of the abuses by Great Britain that led to the Revolutionary War. The amendment provides that, "no Soldier shall, in time of peace be quartered in any house, without the consent of the Owner, nor in time of war but in a manner to be prescribed by law."

A similar provision was contained in the English Petition of Rights of 1628. In addition, at the time the U.S. Constitution was written, four state constitutions had such a provision, and three state ratifying conventions proposed such a guarantee before James Madison incorporated it in the list of rights he presented to the First Congress (Lutz 1992, 52, 56, 64).

The amendment was little debated in the House of Representatives and was unaltered by either it or the Senate. It has never been the subject of a Supreme Court decision or the subject of a proposed constitutional amendment. The Third Amendment remains one of the few provisions of the Bill of Rights that the Supreme Court has not applied to the states via the due process clause of the Fourteenth Amendment. However, Justice William O. Douglas did cite this amendment in *Griswold v. Connecticut* (1965) as one of a number of amendments that serve as a foundation for a right to privacy.

❖ THIRTEENTH AMENDMENT ❖

The Constitution of 1787 circumspectly omitted direct mention of slavery. Still, a number of clauses—most notably the three-fifths clause (Article I, Section 2), the migration and importation clause (Article IV, Section 9), and the fugitive from labor clause (Article IV, Section 2)—gave implicit sanction to the institution in states where it already existed. The predominant attitude about slavery even in the South was that it was at best a necessary evil, and a number of prominent southerners were among those who supported the idea of freeing slaves and colonizing them in Liberia.

Surprisingly, prior to 1860, there were few proposals to eliminate slavery by constitutional amendment. Arthur Livermore, a Democratic representative from New Hampshire, introduced one such proposal in 1818; another was introduced by Whig Representative (and former president) John Quincy Adams of Massachusetts in 1839. The latter would have abolished hereditary slavery after 1842, prohibited the admission of further slave states into the Union, and abolished slavery and the slave trade in the District of Columbia after 1845.

Just prior to the Civil War, there were more proposals—including the Corwin amendment and the Crittenden Compromise—relative to slavery, but most sought to reassure the southern states that were about to secede by guaranteeing that slavery would be perpetual. In 1861 and 1862, Congress adopted confiscation laws relating to slaves who had been used in the rebellion or those who had escaped to or been captured by the Union armies. In 1862, Congress provided for compensated emancipation in the District of Columbia and—despite the 1857 decision in *Scott v. Sandford*—outlawed slavery in the federal territories (Maltz 1990, 13). In September 1862, President Abraham Lincoln issued his preliminary Emancipation Proclamation. Officially proclaimed on 1 January 1863, it freed all slaves held in areas of rebellion and was justified as a war measure (Maltz 1990, 14).

Although there was some sentiment to abolish slavery by statute, there was general agreement that Congress lacked such power. In December 1863, Republican Representatives James M. Ashley of Ohio and James F. Wilson of Iowa introduced emancipation amendments. Senator John B. Henderson, a Missouri Democrat, introduced a similar amendment in the Senate in January 1864, with Republican Charles Sumner of Massachusetts offering a somewhat different version the next month (Maltz 1990, 15). Such amendments were justified both on the grounds of morality and as a means of securing future peace by eliminating the situation of the nation being half slave and half free (Maltz 1990, 15–16).

Although the amendment had broad Republican support, some of the congressional Democrats who were left after the secession of the southern states argued that Article V could not legally be used to effect such a major change. Although the amendment passed the Senate by a vote of 38 to 6 in August 1864, the 93 to 65 vote it received in the House in June fell 13 votes shy of the required two-thirds majority (Maltz 1990, 19). Republican James Ashley of Ohio then switched his vote—in a maneuver mimicked by Kansas Republican

Senator Bob Dole after the 1995 Senate defeat of the balanced budget amendment—to allow him room to reintroduce the amendment in the second session of the 38th Congress (Maltz 1990, 19).

The Republicans won substantial victories in the election of 1864. This election, along with fears that Democrats might forever be saddled with the onus of slavery, led to another vote in January 1865, when the House adopted the amendment by a vote of 119 to 56 (Maltz 1990, 20). The states ratified the amendment this same year.

The Thirteenth Amendment is divided into two parts. The first section prohibits "slavery" and "involuntary servitude, except as a punishment for crime." This language was taken almost directly from the Northwest Ordinance of 1787. Section 2 grants Congress power to enforce the amendment. Questions would subsequently be raised as to whether Section 1 was intended to grant any rights other than freedom from bondage (see, for example, *Civil Rights* cases of 1883) and precisely what powers Congress was intended to have under Section 2. Such issues are difficult to resolve on the basis of contemporary debates (Maltz 1990, 21–28). In *Jones v. Alfred H. Mayer Co.* (1968), the Supreme Court upheld a ban on racial discrimination in housing on the basis of a law adopted under authority of the amendment.

See also *Civil Rights* Cases; Emancipation Proclamation.

❖ THREE-FIFTHS CLAUSE ❖

At the Constitutional Convention of 1787, representatives of northern and southern states had different interests with respect to taxation and representation. Northerners wanted any direct taxes to be apportioned to include the slave population, but they did not want slaves to figure in the formula for apportioning seats in the U.S. House of

Representatives. By contrast, southern representatives did not want their slaves to be taxed, but they did want them counted for representation purposes (Vile 1993a, 28–29).

The delegates settled on an expedient compromise. It was based on a formula used under the Articles of Confederation and was incorporated in Article I, Section 2 of the Constitution. This compromise provided that both taxation and representation would be based on the "whole Number of free Persons" and "three fifths of all other Persons."

Prior to the Civil War, a number of congressmen, including former President John Quincy Adams, proposed modifying the Constitution so that both taxes and representation would be based solely on the number of free persons. With the adoption of the Thirteenth Amendment, slavery was eliminated. This meant that southern states, and the Democratic Party, might actually gain representation in the House of Representatives. Section 2 of the Fourteenth Amendment subsequently specified that representation would now be apportioned "counting the whole number of persons in each State, excluding Indians not taxed." In an ultimately futile attempt to prevent southern states from disenfranchising the newly freed slaves, this amendment further provided that if states denied such voting rights, "the basis of representation therein shall be reduced in the proportion which the number of such [disenfranchised] male citizens shall bear to the whole number of male citizens twenty-one years of age in such State."

See also Fourteenth Amendment.

❖ TIEDEMAN, CHRISTOPHER ❖ (1857–1904)

It is common to distinguish the written Constitution of the United States from the unwritten constitution of Great Britain. However, law professor Christopher Tiedeman wrote a book in 1890 that pointed to the similarities of the two constitutions and the way that they change. He argued that law necessarily arose from the legal and moral habits of a people and what he called the "prevalent sense of right" (Tiedeman 1890, 7).

Tiedeman argued that regardless of what the written words of a constitution appear to say, courts use interpretation and construction to see that laws comport with popular understandings. Moreover, in the United States, the written Constitution provides only a skeleton, with most governmental operations less determined by what is written that by what is unwritten. Tiedeman argued that the flesh and blood of a constitution is "not to be found in the instrument promulgated by a constitutional convention, but in the decisions of the courts and acts of the legislature, which are published and enacted in the enforcement of the written Constitution" (Tiedeman 1890, 43).

Much of Tiedeman's book was devoted to a development of this thesis. Changes in the operation of the electoral college, the understanding by which presidents served no more than two terms, and changing interpretations of the contracts clause and of the doctrine of natural rights provided some of his illustrations. Whereas some scholars would criticize judges for going against the original intent of those who wrote the Constitution, Tiedeman praised them for interpreting law in accord with the needs and desires of the present generation.

Nowhere was this clearer than in Tiedeman's discussion of the Fourteenth Amendment. Tiedeman agreed with those who thought that this amendment was intended to have a broad scope. Still, Tiedeman praised the Court for "keeping the operation of this amendment within the limits which they felt assured would have been imposed by the people, if their judgment had not been blinded with passion, and which in their cooler moments they would ratify" (Tiedeman 1890, 108).

Because the unwritten constitution so frequently limits the written words, Tiedeman was led to inquire into the value of a written constitution. His response was that the Constitution enabled judges with power "to serve as a check upon the popular will in the interest of the minority" (Tiedeman 1890, 163).

For Further Reading:

Halper, Louise A. 1990. "Christopher G. Tiedeman, 'Laissez-Faire Constitutionalism' and the Dilemma of Small-Scale Property in the Gilded Age." *Ohio State Law Journal* 51: 1349–84.

Mayer, David N. 1990. "The Jurisprudence of Christopher G. Tiedeman: A Study in the Failure of Laissez-Faire Constitutionalism." *Missouri Law Review* 55 (Winter): 93–161.

Vile, John R. 1992. *The Constitutional Amending Process in American Political Thought.* New York: Praeger.

❖ TIME LIMITS ON AMENDMENTS ❖

The Constitution does not specify the length of time during which a proposed amendment can be ratified. When the Eighteenth Amendment was being debated in 1917, however, Republican Senator (later president) Warren G. Harding of Ohio proposed that a deadline for ratification be set at 1 January 1923, apparently in the hope of putting an obstacle in the amendment's path (Bernstein with Agel 1993, 173–74). Similar deadlines were included in the Twentieth Amendment, the Twenty-first Amendment, and the Twenty-second Amendment. Deadlines were also included in the amendment proposed in 1978 to treat the District of Columbia as a state for purposes of representation in Congress, presidential elections, and the amending process.

In *Dillon v. Gloss,* the Supreme Court ruled that the Constitution implied that ratification must "reflect the will of the people in all sections at relatively the same period" (1921, 375). It thus upheld the constitutionality of the seven-year deadline in the Eighteenth Amendment.

The amendment proposed in 1924 that would have given Congress the power to regulate child labor did not contain such a time limit. In *Coleman v. Miller* (1939), the Court examined Kansas's attempt to ratify the amendment 13 years after it was proposed and ruled that the determination of the contemporaneousness of such a ratification was a "political question" for Congress to resolve.

When Congress proposed the equal rights amendment in 1972, it included a seven-year deadline. This deadline was not included in the text of the proposed amendment itself, where it would presumably be self-enforcing, but in an accompanying resolution. In 1978, Congress extended the ratification deadline of the equal rights amendment to 1982. This action was successfully challenged in a U.S. district court in *Idaho v. Freeman* (1981), but the issue became moot when the amendment failed to meet even this new deadline.

The amendment that has done the most to stretch the idea of contemporary consensus expressed in *Dillon v. Gloss* is the putative ratification of the Twenty-seventh Amendment relative to congressional pay raises. Despite concerns raised by scholars (Vile 1991a), Congress accepted the legitimacy of this amendment, first proposed as part of the Bill of Rights in 1789, even though the necessary number of states did not ratify until 1992.

The last two controversies make it a virtual certainty that Congress will place ratification deadlines within the texts of future proposals. Still, there is no apparent legal barrier to keep Congress from departing from the seven-year formula.

See also *Coleman v. Miller; Dillon v. Gloss;* Twenty-Seventh Amendment.

❖ TITLES OF NOBILITY ❖

One of the earliest proposed amendments that would have provided for the loss of citizenship would have supplemented the restrictions on titles of nobility already found in Article I, Section 9 of the Constitution by further proposing that

> [i]f any citizen of the United States shall accept, claim, receive or retain any title of nobility or honour or shall, without the consent of Congress, accept and retain any present, pension, office or emolument of any kind whatever, from any emperor, king, prince or foreign power, such person shall cease to be a citizen of the United States, and shall be incapable of holding any office of trust or profit under them, or either of them. (Bernstein with Agel 1993, 178)

Republican Senator Philip Reed of Maryland introduced this amendment in January 1810, and it was ratified by 1 May by a vote of 87 to 3 in the House and 19 to 5 in the Senate.

Sometimes called the Reed amendment, or the "phantom amendment," this proposal was included as part of a Constitution printed for the House of Representatives in 1817 (a mistake subsequently copied in a number of other places). However, it was soon discovered that the proposed amendment had come a single vote shy of ratification (Earle 1987, 33).

Long a mystery to historians, who found that contemporary debates did little to illumine its purpose, it now appears that the proposal might have been motivated by fears that the son of Jerome Bonaparte (brother to Napoleon) and his one-time Baltimore wife, Elizabeth Patterson, might one day try to claim an American throne. Apparently, Republicans—who were closer on foreign policy matters to France than to England—introduced the measure to defuse criticisms raised by Patterson's pretensions and her associations with top party officials. Federalists had little choice but to concur or face charges that they were hoping to get titles from England (Earle 1987, 37). One historian noted that, with Napoleon's defeat in Europe, "by the time of the amendment's bizarre reappearance in the House of Representatives [in the form of the printed Constitution that included it], it was an anachronism" (Earle 1987, 37).

This proposal remains one of six amendments proposed by Congress but never ratified by the requisite number of states.

See also Citizenship, Loss of.

❖ TRADEMARKS ❖

Article I, Section 8 grants Congress power "to promote the Progress of Science and useful Arts, by securing for limited Times to Authors and Inventors the exclusive Right to their respective Writings and Discoveries." In the *Trade Mark* cases (1879), however, the Supreme Court unanimously ruled that this provision did not grant Congress power over trademarks. The Court ruled that the exercise of any such congressional power would have to be restricted to transactions in interstate or foreign commerce.

Almost immediately, Iowa Republican Representative Moses McCoid introduced an amendment to grant Congress power to regulate trademarks. Similar proposals were introduced in 1911 and 1913 and in the late 1940s and early 1950s. As early as 1881, however, Congress had adopted new legislation on trademarks under the authority of its commerce powers, and since 1937, the Supreme Court has interpreted such powers broadly.

Congress has exercised such powers over trademarks in the U.S. Trademark Act of 1946, generally known as the Lanham Act, as well as in the Trademark Counterfeiting Act of 1984. Trademarks are registered with the U.S. Trademarks Office.

❖ TREASON ❖

Article III, Section 3 of the Constitution specifies that "treason against the United States, shall consist only in levying War against them, or in adhering to their Enemies, giving them Aid and Comfort." It further specifies that conviction of treason requires either a confession in open court or the testimony of two or more witnesses to an overt act. Although entrusting Congress with the power "to declare the punishment of Treason," the Constitution prevents such penalties from being passed from one generation to another.

In addition to the grounds for treason listed in the U.S. Constitution, the British permitted conviction for "compassing or imagining the death of the king (Chapin 1964, 3). Clearly, the framers feared the impact that such a broad definition might have on freedom of expression. With this in mind, the courts have construed the treason clause strictly throughout most of U.S. history (Hurst 1971, 192).

There have been about 25 proposals introduced in Congress relative to treason. Two such proposals, both introduced in 1901 after the assassination of President William McKinley, would have broadened the definition of treason to include such assassination attempts.

In 1924, Missouri Democratic Representative Joseph Wolff introduced a measure that would make it treason to defraud the government with respect to war materials and equipment. That same year, Pennsylvania Republican George Washington Edmonds would have extended the definition of treason to include any efforts to establish a new form of government except by constitutional amendment.

Most proposals that have been introduced since the end of World War II have attempted to expand the definition of treason to include adherence to or support of groups advocating the overthrow of the government by force; some have specifically mentioned the Communist Party. A 1968 proposal by Louisiana Democratic Representative John Rarick would have defined treason against the United States to include "levying war against them or in adhering to their enemies, giving them aid or comfort, or engaging in acts of subversion." Reflecting his distrust of the courts, Rarick further specified "that the judicial power shall not extend to limit, transfer or negate the powers granted herein, exclusively to the Congress or to alter or amend by interpretation or otherwise the commonly accepted meaning of the language imployed [*sic*] by Congress in laws enacted pursuant to such powers" (H.J. Res. 1213).

❖ TREASURY, DEPARTMENT OF ❖

Congress is the branch of government most frequently associated with the power of the purse. Under the Constitution, however, the president appoints all cabinet members, including the secretary of the treasury.

Although the Constitution does not specify who has the power to remove such officials, court decisions, most notably that in *Myers v. United States* (1926), have confirmed that the power of such officials is vested in the president. The Court noted that the president was responsible for enforcing the laws and would presumably be best informed about the performance of his subordinates.

Chief Justice (and former president) William Howard Taft, who wrote the decision in *Myers*, relied heavily on debates in the First Congress, where James Madison had been a strong advocate of the president's removal power. During these debates, however, Madison had suggested that there might be a reason to treat the secretary of the treasury differently from other officials (D. O'Brien 1991, 286). In the nation's early years, at least three members of Congress—States' Rights Democratic Representative John Barbour of Virginia (1828) and Whig Representatives John Underwood (1836, 1838) and Henry Clay (1841) of Kentucky—proposed amendments to vest either the appointment or the appointment and removal of the treasury secretary in Congress.

In *Bowsher v. Synar* (1986), the Supreme Court reaffirmed presidential authority over budget cuts when it struck down a provision of the Balanced Budget and Emergency Deficit Control Act of 1985. That provision had entrusted the specification of such cuts to the comptroller general, who was subject to removal by Congress rather than by the president.

❖ TREATIES, RATIFICATION OF ❖

As disputes about the Bricker amendment demonstrate, the treaty-making power has been a subject of intense debate. Article II, Section 2 of the Constitution provides that the president "shall have Power, by and with the Advice and Consent of the Senate, to make Treaties, provided two-thirds of the Senators present concur."

Early in American history, the House of Representatives threatened to annul this constitutional provision by failing to appropriate funds needed to carry out the Jay Treaty. The Virginia legislature subsequently proposed that the House of Representatives share in approving treaties, a proposal that was not introduced again until 1884. In 1899, there were two proposals, probably stimulated by the Spanish-American War, to provide for treaty ratification by a majority vote of the Senate.

The two world wars both provoked proposals to alter the treaty power. President Woodrow Wilson's failure to get the Treaty of Versailles ratified by the necessary two-thirds of the Senate (the vote was 49 to 35) appears to have triggered several proposals that were introduced from 1919 to 1925. Some proposed that such treaties should become effective by a majority vote in the Senate, some wanted treaties to be ratified by a majority vote in both the House and the Senate, and at least one representative wanted treaties to be ratified by a national referendum.

Such proposals took on a new urgency with U.S. entry into World War II. In May 1945, the House of Representatives voted 288 to 88 (with 56 members abstaining) for an amendment to enable a majority of both houses to ratify treaties, but the Senate was not keen on giving up its prerogative (Ackerman and Golove 1995, 865, 889). In the meantime, the lines between treaties ratified by the Senate, executive agreements entered into by the president, and other international agreements negotiated by the president with the approval of both houses of Congress were being obscured. The Senate appears to have accepted this situation in part as an alternative to formal constitutional change.

By 1954, the agreement between the United States and Canada regarding the St. Lawrence Seaway, which had previously been sent to the Senate for approval as a treaty, was adopted by a simple majority of both houses of Congress (Ackerman and Golove 1995, 893). In 1993, a similar procedure, negotiated under the Trade Act of 1974, was used to ratify the North American Free Trade Agreement (NAFTA). This bill was put on a legislative "fast track" in exchange for constant presidential-legislative collaboration during the negotiating process. Bruce Ackerman, a prominent theorist on the amending process, has cited this development as an example of constitutional innovation outside the Article V amending process and praised it for its "efficacy, democracy [and] legitimacy" (Ackerman and Golove 1995, 916).

Proposals to alter the formal treaty-making process continued throughout the 1950s, 1960s and 1970s. A number of the later proposals, undoubtedly stimulated by the United States' experience in Vietnam, would have required the involvement of both houses of Congress in any treaty committing U.S. forces abroad.

See also Bricker Amendment.

❖ TUGWELL, REXFORD ❖
(1891–1979)

No modern would-be constitutional reformer has worked longer or more diligently than Rexford Tugwell. One of the three members of Franklin Roosevelt's original "brain trust," Tugwell had an active life as both a college professor and a public servant before joining the Center for the Study of Democratic Institutions (headed by Robert Hutchins) as a senior fellow (Ashmore 1970).

In his first six years there, Tugwell initiated discussions that led him to draft 37 successive versions of a proposed constitution. This draft was published in a special issue of the center's magazine in 1970. Tugwell continued his revisions and offered his fortieth version in a book published in 1974 (for analysis, see Vile 1991c, 106–10).

Tugwell's proposals were quite complex, and they were such a departure from the existing constitutional scheme that they are not easily summarized. Certainly, Tugwell put great emphasis on governmental planning, adding numerous new boards, commissions, and positions. He also believed that existing state governments were antiquated and needed to be altered radically.

Unlike many twentieth-century reformers, however, Tugwell would have maintained the system of separated powers and did not advocate a parliamentary system.

Tugwell's fortieth constitution differed significantly in organization from his thirty-seventh and consisted of 12 articles. Article I dealt with rights and responsibilities. In addition to most guarantees now found in the Bill of Rights and various amendments, this section contained protections for individual privacy, guarantees against discrimination based on "race, creed, color, origin, or sex," prohibitions against any public support for religion, a guarantee that those unable to "contribute to productivity shall be entitled to a share of the national product," and a guarantee of education "at public expense" for those establishing eligibility (1974, 595–96). Citizen responsibilities included respecting the rights of others, participating in democratic processes, and avoiding violence; to promote the latter goal, and in contrast to the Second Amendment of the existing Constitution, Tugwell would reserve the bearing of arms to "the police, members of the armed forces, and those licensed under law" (1974, 597).

Tugwell designated the government under his fortieth constitution the "Newstates of America" (the thirty-seventh version referred instead to the "United Republic of America"). Article II dealt with these newstates, none of which was to contain less than 5 percent of the existing population. Each would have its own constitution as well as its own "governors, legislatures, and planning, administrative, and judicial systems" (1974, 598). Like present states, they would exercise "police powers"; all rights and responsibilities applied at the national level would also apply to the states.

Article III established an "electoral branch" of government supervised by an "overseer" selected by the Senate. The overseer would "supervise the organization of national and district parties, arrange for discussion among them, and provide for the nomination and election of candidates for public office" (1974, 599). Duties would include assisting in the nomination of candidates and in arranging and supervising elections. All costs would be paid from public funds, and all private personal expenditures would be prohibited.

Article IV delineated a planning branch headed by a national planning board of 15 members. It would be responsible for submitting 6- and 12-year plans.

Article V described the president, who was designated as "the head of government, shaper of its commitments, expositor of its policies, and supreme commander of its protective forces" (1974, 604). He would serve a nine-year term subject to recall by 60 percent of the voters after three years. He would be served by two vice presidents, one for internal affairs and the other for general affairs. The latter would supervise "Chancellors of External, Financial, Legal, and Military Affairs" (1974, 604). Treaties negotiated by the president would go into effect unless rejected by a majority of the Senate. The president would appoint a public custodian in charge of governmental property and an intendant to supervise intelligence and investigation offices.

Article VI described a drastically altered Congress. A Senate of 70 to 80 members would be appointed by various groups and individuals, and members would serve for life terms. The Senate's main function would be to consider, and at times delay, but not initiate legislation. It would also select a three-person national security council to consult with the president about the deployment of American troops abroad. The Senate would also select the national watchkeeper, a type of ombudsman. Members of the House of Representatives would be selected from 100 districts, each of which would select three members for three-year terms; to give the body a more national orientation, there would be another 100 at-

large members. The House would be "the original lawmaking body of the Newstates of America" (1974, 609). In contrast to the current Constitution, which is silent on such matters, Tugwell's document outlined the selection of committees and their chairs and included a much longer list of congressional powers, including powers over banking, insurance, communications, transportation, space exploration, welfare, education, libraries, the conservation of natural resources, and civil service.

Article VII established a regulatory branch headed by a national regulator to be selected by the Senate and to serve as head of a regulatory board of 17 members. The regulator would charter corporations, regulate industrial mergers, and supervise the marketplace.

The judicial branch was delineated in Article VIII in considerable more complexity than the current Constitution. Section 1 of this article began as follows: "There shall be a Principal Justice of the Newstates of America; a Judicial Council; and a Judicial Assembly. There shall also be a Supreme Court and a High Court of Appeals; also Courts of Claims, Rights and Duties, Administrative Review, Arbitration Settlements, Tax Appeals, and Appeals from Watchkeeper's Findings" (1974, 614). The principal justice would preside over the system and appoint all members of the national courts; he would serve an 11-year term and would share with the president the power to grant reprieves and pardons. Although Tugwell criticized the extent of judicial review as currently exercised, the Supreme Court would continue to exercise such power under his plan.

Article IX dealt with general provisions, Article X with governmental arrangements, and Article XII with transition to the new government. Article XI dealt with the amending process. The judicial council would have the power to formulate amendments to be approved by the Senate and president and submitted to the people and adopted by majority vote. Every 25 years, the overseer would conduct a referendum on whether a new constitution was needed. If approval was given, the judicial council would draw up a constitution to go into effect if not disapproved by a majority.

Tugwell's plan was the topic of considerable discussion and criticism (Kelly 1981, 650), but it generated little in the way of practical results.

❖ TULLER, WALTER (1886–1939) ❖

California attorney Walter Tuller wrote an article in 1911 that advocated the calling of a constitutional convention to propose an amendment for the direct election of U.S. senators. Although he devoted most of the article to showing that Congress was obligated to call such a convention when requested to do so by two-thirds of the states and that the Court could enforce such a responsibility (see Vile 1991c, 53–54), Tuller also advanced two subjects that he wanted a convention to handle.

First, Tuller wanted to reduce the number of states required to call such a convention from two-thirds to one-half. At a time when many regarded the amending process as too rigid, Tuller saw such a reduction as a way of keeping the Constitution from becoming "too far removed from the people." Second, Tuller wanted an amendment granting the national government power "to regulate corporations or monopolies in any form" (Tuller 1911, 385).

Tuller anticipated a convention of "the strongest and ablest men in the nation" (Tuller 1911, 386). Contrary to most modern convention proposals, Tuller anticipated that each state would be represented equally, but he was willing to let the convention decide whether members would vote individually or by state.

See also Seventeenth Amendment.

❖ TWELFTH AMENDMENT ❖

There have been hundreds of proposals to alter the process of presidential and vice presidential selection, but the Twelfth Amendment is the only substantial change that has been made in this procedure. This amendment grew out of America's early experience, which showed that the original manner of selecting the executive as specified in Article II of the Constitution had some unintended consequences. Many of these were hastened and exaggerated by a development that most of the framers neither anticipated nor easily welcomed, namely, the development of political parties (Turner 1973; Bernstein 1993).

Operation of the Electoral College

The electoral college is a system of indirect election whereby state-designated electors choose the president and vice president. The discovery of this mechanism was a major development at the Constitutional Convention of 1787, because the electoral college provided a way for the executive to act independently of Congress and thus furthered the idea of a system of separated powers.

Alan Grimes identified six defining features of the electoral college system: it allowed states to determine whether electors would be chosen by the people or by the state legislatures; it gave each state a number of electors equal to its total representation in the House and Senate, thus somewhat advantaging both large states (with the greatest number of representatives) and small states (guaranteed at least three votes); electors met within each state and cast two ballots for president; members of Congress were prohibited from serving as electors; other federal officeholders were also excluded from the job; and electors had to cast at least one of their two votes for someone from another state (Grimes 1978, 20).

The framers thought that such an election would avoid the tumult and possible uncertainties of popular election at a time when technology was more primitive. The framers also anticipated that electors would have a better knowledge of candidates from other states than would the populace as a whole.

Early Presidential Elections

Although it is sometimes asserted that the framers anticipated that electors would perform a deliberative function, from the very first election in 1788, electors came ready to cast predetermined votes (Kuroda 1994, 31). Some states selected delegates by direct election (now the universal procedure) and others by legislative appointment; similarly, some used an at-large system of election, and others chose electors by district. In the first election, all 69 delegates who participated—New York was unable to settle on the method of selecting electors and did not cast ballots—voted for George Washington. Other votes were split among 11 other men, with John Adams's 34 votes putting him in second place and earning him the vice presidency, a position that one representative, knowing Adams's penchant for titles, called "His Superfluous Excellency" (Kuroda 1994, 24).

By the election of 1792, the Federalist and Democratic-Republican Parties had begun to emerge. Once again, however, Washington was selected unanimously, this time with 132 votes. Adams came in second. The fact that Adams had only 77 votes indicated that the party "ticket" had not yet completely emerged.

Washington decided to retire after his second term, so the election of 1796 was the first without his candidacy. This election saw a closer contest between the top two party candidates and greater cohesion in voting combinations. Because some Federalists who voted for Adams did not vote for Thomas Pinckney, however, the person with the second highest number of votes

was Thomas Jefferson, head of the emerging Democratic-Republican Party. This meant that the president and vice president would be from different parties.

The Election of 1800

Although having a president and vice president from different parties was far from a desirable situation, the election of 1800 was the one that finally galvanized action by revealing yet another flaw in the original electoral system. In this election, all 73 electors who cast a vote for Jefferson also voted for Aaron Burr, in an attempt to avoid the different-party problem of the previous election. Since the Constitution did not provide separate designations for presidential and vice presidential candidates, the result was a tie in the electoral college, which threw the election into the House of Representatives, where each state had one vote and where the outgoing Federalists effectively had the ability to make the choice. In the initial ballot, Jefferson got the votes of eight states and Burr of six, with two states divided. Since the Constitution required a president to get a majority, more ballots had to be taken. It took about a week of balloting, and 36 ballots, before enough Federalists abstained (in part at the urging of Alexander Hamilton, who distrusted Burr even more than he distrusted Jefferson) to give the election to Jefferson.

Proposal and Ratification of the Twelfth Amendment

The years immediately following produced scores of proposals, including an automatic plan (supported for a time by Thomas Jefferson) whereby the office of electors would be eliminated and the person receiving the plurality of a state's votes would get all its electoral votes. Other plans proposed eliminating the vice presidency and reconsidering the three-fifths compromise under which electors were allocated to southern states; specifically designating votes for president and vice president; and requiring district elections both for electors and for members of Congress (Kuroda 1994, 107–26).

The election of 1802 brought substantial gains to the Democratic-Republicans in Congress and renewed pressure for a constitutional amendment. In October 1803, the House voted 88 to 39 for an amendment that would have had electors designate which ballot they were casting for president and which for vice president and would have reduced from five to three the number of candidates the House would choose among if no candidate received a majority.

The Senate then began its own debate, which resulted in the current language of the Twelfth Amendment. Like the version accepted in the House, this proposal specified that when no one received a majority, the House of Representatives would choose from among the top three candidates, rather than the top five. It also provided that if the House did not choose a candidate by 4 March (subsequently changed by the Twentieth Amendment to 20 January), the vice president would act as president. The amendment stirred highly partisan debate. Federalists, who purported to represent the interests of the small states, fought the reduction from five candidates to three. Others felt that any constitutional changes might dangerously lower the floodgates to reform (Kuroda 1994, 141).

There was also debate whether amendments required a two-thirds vote of all members or only of those members present. On 2 December 1803, the amendment was narrowly carried by a vote of 22 to 10—although this was short of two-thirds of the entire membership of 34 (Kuroda 1994, 142–43).

The new Senate version then went back to the House, where, on 8 December 1803, after an initial count of 83 to 41, Speaker Nathaniel Macon cast his vote with the majority to give it precisely the two-thirds majority needed. New Hampshire attempted to become the necessary thirteenth state to ratify in June 1804, but the governor created a state of confusion with a veto, and the honor apparently went to Tennessee in late July. The new amendment set the framework for the 1804 presidential election. In this contest, Jefferson was elected on a ticket that included New York's George Clinton.

Consequences and Implications of the Twelfth Amendment

Although it did not specifically mention them, the amendment affirmed the role that political parties had come to play in designating candidates. It also arguably denigrated the vice presidency. The individual in this position was now clearly recognized as second fiddle; subsequently, he would often be chosen more for regional or ideological balance than for his qualifications to be president (Kuroda 1994, 172).

The parties subsequently acquired a share in the system that was reaffirmed as large and small states both continued their overrepresentation under the new plan. Despite numerous subsequent proposals, including many calls for complete abolition of the electoral system, it has not been substantially altered by constitutional amendment since 1804.

See also Electoral College Reform.

❖ TWENTIETH AMENDMENT ❖

Although it is separated by more than a dozen years from its four immediate predecessors, like them, the Twentieth Amendment grew from the democratic sentiment spawned by the Progressive Era. Progressive Republican Senator George Norris of Nebraska was a key architect of the amendment that altered the dates that members of the national legislative and executive branches took office (Grimes 1978, 104–5). Adoption followed about 30 proposals made prior to 1900 and about 90 more in the early twentieth century. The first two proposals were introduced by famous New Yorkers, Aaron Burr (1795) and Millard Fillmore (1840). These and other proposals suggested that the inauguration date be set as early as December and as late as May.

The Congress under the Articles of Confederation set things in motion when it provided that the first Congress under the new Constitution would begin on 4 March. Although this date was not specified in the Constitution, it was perpetuated both by custom and by concern that moving it forward would unconstitutionally shorten terms (Bernstein with Agel 1993, 154). Prior to the adoption of the Seventeenth Amendment, the 4 March date also gave time to state legislatures, which typically did not begin sessions until January, to make their selections (Grimes 1978, 105). Article I, Section 4 of the Constitution, however, specified that the annual meeting of Congress should begin on the first Monday in December. This meant that a new Congress would not come into regular session until 13 months after it was elected in November. In the meantime, the outgoing lame-duck legislature could adopt legislation without being accountable to the voters. To cite but one example, in a series of events that eventually led to the Supreme Court's historic decision in *Marbury v. Madison* (1803), an outgoing Federalist Congress adopted the Judiciary Act of 1801, adding fellow Federalists to the judiciary, much to the consternation of the newly elected Republican administration.

Whereas progressives viewed the situation as undemocratic, many congressional conservatives, including Republican House Speaker Nicholas Longworth, actually "preferred a cooling-off period before the new Congress came into session" (Grimes 1978, 106). Some also liked the short congres-

sional session (from December through March) in alternate years. Thus, although the amendment passed the Senate in 1923, 1924, and 1926, it failed to receive the necessary majority of votes when first voted on in the House in 1928. In 1929, a conference committee failed to resolve differences between the two houses. A 1930 Democratic landslide broke the deadlock and resulted in the elevation of Democrat John N. Garner of Texas, who favored the amendment, as House Speaker. Although the House of Representatives initially adopted a provision that would have required at least one house of the ratifying state legislatures to be elected before ratifying the amendment, this provision was dropped in conference committee (Grimes 1978, 108). The Senate subsequently voted for the amendment by a vote of 63 to 7 (with 25 abstaining) on 6 January 1932; the House followed with a 336 to 56 vote (1 answering present and 38 not voting) on 16 February 1932. Virginia was the first state to ratify on 4 March 1932; Utah put the amendment over the top on 23 January 1933, and the last of the existing 48 states (Florida) ratified on 26 April of that year (U.S. Senate 1985, 62).

The Twentieth Amendment has six sections. The first, and most important, sets the beginning of congressional terms on 3 January and those of the president and vice president on 20 January. Section 2 provides that the annual session of Congress begins on 3 January. Anticipating some of the problems later addressed in the Twenty-fifth Amendment, Section 3 specifies that if the president-elect dies prior to inauguration, the vice president–elect becomes president. It also allows the vice president–elect to serve if no one has received a majority of the electoral college and the House of Representatives has not yet chosen among the finalists. It further allows Congress to provide by law for an interim in cases in which neither officer has been selected. Section 4 grants the same power in the case of the death of a candidate during congressional deliberations. Section 5 provides that the amendment would become effective on 15 October after its ratification, and Section 6 makes the Twentieth Amendment the second to contain a seven-year ratification deadline.

A number of subsequent proposals have been introduced to modify the Twentieth Amendment. In a sense, however, they are in the same spirit, since they are designed to move inauguration dates even further back to November or December (see Levinson 1995, 185).

Several other amending proposals have been made to end congressional sessions in July, probably with a view to shortening the period in which Congress can legislate. In a less hurried time (1878), an amendment was even offered to provide for biennial congressional sessions. Five years earlier, in a speech on 2 December 1873, President Ulysses S. Grant had proposed that when the president called special sessions of Congress (as permitted in Article II, Section 3), such sessions should be limited to subjects the president proposed (J. Richardson 1908, 7:242–43). A number of subsequent proposals would have enabled Congress to call itself into special session. Proposals introduced in 1920 and 1923 by House Republican Edward Browne of Wisconsin, precipitated by President Woodrow Wilson's debilitating stroke, would have enabled Congress to provide for cases of such presidential disability, an issue later addressed in the Twenty-fifth Amendment.

❖ TWENTY-FIFTH AMENDMENT ❖

Amendments have been introduced throughout American history to deal with presidential disability and with vacancies in the office of vice president.

Although a number of early vice presidents died in office and one, John C. Calhoun, resigned to become a senator, no president died until 1841, when the elderly William Henry Harrison passed away shortly after his inauguration. His successor, John Tyler, made it clear that he considered himself to be the president and not simply an "acting" president until a reelection could be called. Despite ambiguity about the framers' intentions on this matter, this precedent became standard practice for other vice presidents who replaced chief executives. Tyler's precedent, however, neither addressed the issue of what would happen in cases of presidential disability nor made provision for filling vice presidential vacancies.

Laws Dealing with Presidential Succession

Congress addressed the issue of vice presidential vacancies in a number of laws, but their diversity demonstrated the lack of consensus on how the issue was best resolved. In 1792, Congress adopted legislation putting the president pro tempore of the Senate and the Speaker of the House of Representatives behind the vice president in the line of succession, but this arrangement made it possible that, in cases of a double vacancy, the presidency might change political parties without an intervening election. After a period during which both the president pro tempore and the Speaker positions were vacant, Congress revised the law in 1886 to provide that the heads of the executive departments, beginning with the secretary of state and the secretary of the treasury, would be in the line of succession. Because it is possible that such officials may never have held elective office (a particular concern of President Harry S. Truman), however, this law was altered in 1947 to place the Speaker and the president pro tempore ahead of cabinet officers in the line of succession (Feerick 1992, 37–47).

Presidential Disability

In the meantime, the issue of presidential disability remained. In 1881, President

James A. Garfield lingered for 80 days before dying from an assassin's bullet. President William McKinley also lived several days before dying of another assassin's bullet in 1901, and President Woodrow Wilson suffered a debilitating stroke in 1919. The problem of such disabilities became especially acute with the invention of nuclear weapons. President Dwight D. Eisenhower suffered a number of health problems during his tenure, and he eventually drew up a letter of understanding allowing Vice President Richard Nixon to assume his duties during such times as President Eisenhower might be disabled.

Adoption of the
Twenty-fifth Amendment

Especially after President John F. Kennedy's assassination, there were calls to formulate informal arrangements into a viable constitutional procedure. Shortly after the assassination, Indiana Democratic Senator Birch Bayh, who chaired the Senate Judiciary Committee's Subcommittee on Constitutional Amendments, held hearings on the subject. The Senate subsequently approved a proposed amendment in 1964 by a 64 to 0 vote. In 1965, it again approved an amendment by a 72 to 0 vote, with the House concurring by a vote of 368 to 29. A conference committee version was subsequently adopted by voice vote in the House and by a vote of 68 to 5 in the Senate, with the latter vote occurring on 6 July 1965. Ratification by the necessary number of states was completed on 10 February 1967 (Feerick 1992, 95–111).

Provisions of the
Twenty-fifth Amendment

The Twenty-fifth Amendment has five sections. An observer noted that it "rivals the Fourteenth in length, and surpasses all other amendments in wordage" (Young 1974, 395). The first section officially confirms John Tyler's 1841 precedent by specifying that when the president dies or resigns, "the Vice President shall become president."

Section 2 provides for filling vice presidential vacancies. It rejected earlier proposals that had been introduced to provide for multiple vice presidents (New York Senator Kenneth Keating wanted to created separate executive and legislative vice presidents) or to provide that vice presidential vacancies be filled by a vote of the last electoral college (a position advocated for a time by Richard Nixon). Instead, this section provides that the president shall nominate a replacement when the vice presidency is vacant. Such nominations are confirmed by a majority vote of both houses of Congress.

Although they do not specifically define it, Sections 3 and 4 of the twenty-fifth Amendment deal with the problem of presidential disability. Section 3 provides that when the president informs the president pro tempore of the Senate and the Speaker of the House that he is unable to perform his duties, "such powers and duties" shall be performed by the vice president until such time as the president sends a letter stating that his disability is over.

Section 3 handles an ideal case, but what happens if the president fails to recognize or acknowledge that he has a disability? Section 4 sets up a complicated system of checks and balances. Rejecting earlier proposals to require a special commission to deal with such matters or to entrust such decisions to the Supreme Court, Section 4 outlines another route. Under this provision, the vice president assumes the president's duties if the vice president and a majority "of the principal officers of the executive departments or such other body as Congress may by law provide" transmit a written declaration to the president pro tempore of the Senate and the Speaker of the House that the president is unable to carry out his duties. The president may subsequently submit his own written declaration that his disability has ended and resume his duties, assuming that the vice president and members of the cabinet or other congressionally designated body do not disagree within four days. If there is such a disagreement, the vice president continues to exercise presidential duties. Congress, in turn, assembles within 48 hours. If, within 21 days, two-thirds of both houses of Congress affirm that the president is disabled, the vice president continues in office. If Congress reaches no such agreement, the president resumes his duties.

Operation of the Twenty-fifth Amendment

After being wounded in an attempted assassination, President Ronald Reagan was reluctant to invoke the disability provisions of the Twenty-fifth Amendment, apparently fearing that it would cause popular alarm (Feerick 1992, xiii–xiv; also see Abrams 1994). Although he later declared that he was not invoking provisions of this amendment when he underwent cancer surgery, he appears to have adhered fairly closely to the amendment's procedures (Feerick 1992, xvi–xvii).

The provision of the Twenty-fifth Amendment that has been most frequently exercised is the section dealing with filling vice presidential vacancies. President Nixon nominated, and Congress subsequently confirmed, Gerald Ford when Vice President Spiro Agnew resigned in 1973 after being charged with accepting bribes while in the Maryland government. When Ford was subsequently elevated to the presidency after Nixon resigned in the wake of the Watergate scandal, he selected, and Congress confirmed, former New York governor Nelson Rockefeller as vice president.

Proposals To Alter the Twenty-fifth Amendment

There have been several proposals to repeal either Section 2 (dealing with filling vice presidential vacancies) or the entire Twenty-fifth Amendment. Some such proposals appear to stem from concerns that the existing disability provision is too complex and might be abused by an overly ambitious vice president. Other proposals stem from concern that the Twenty-fifth Amendment allows the office of both president and vice president to be filled by individuals who have not been popularly elected.

Focusing in part of the latter concern and in part on the putative failure of the office to attract strong characters from the adoption of the Twelfth Amendment through the Nixon administration, historian Arthur M. Schlesinger Jr. (1974) has advocated eliminating the vice presidency. He proposes allowing the secretary of state or another eligible cabinet officer to serve in cases of a presidential vacancy (assuming there is more than a year until the next regularly scheduled election) until a new election can be held. A Twentieth Century Fund Task Force Report on the Vice Presidency (1988) opposed this recommendation.

For Further Reading:
"The Twenty-fifth Amendment: Preparing for Presidential Disability." 1995. *Wake Forest Law Review* 30 (Fall): 427–648.

❖ TWENTY-FIRST AMENDMENT ❖

The Twenty-first Amendment is distinctive in at least two ways. It is the only amendment ever to have repealed another, and to date, it is the only amendment ever to be ratified by state conventions rather than by state legislatures.

The Eighteenth Amendment, ratified in 1919, represented a great social experiment in its attempt to outlaw the consumption of alcoholic beverages. Although the amendment appears to have cut the consumption of alcohol, it was far from successful in eliminating it. Organized crime and its accompanying violence received a major boost, providing a product that so many wanted and were willing to break the law to get. Speakeasies, where one could drink in social settings, flourished. Many feared that true temperance was less likely to be achieved by the flaunting of such complete prohibition than by less invasive governmental regulations.

Moreover, almost from the time that the Eighteenth Amendment was adopted, it was challenged as an unconstitutional interference with state police powers. Although the Supreme Court rejected this argument in the *National Prohibition* cases (1920), critics continued to believe that the amendment represented an unwarranted federal intrusion into an area of personal relations best left to state control.

Supporters of the Eighteenth Amendment included Democratic Senator Morris Sheppard of Texas, who boasted that "there is as much chance of repealing the Eighteenth Amendment as there is for a hummingbird to fly to the planet Mars with the Washington Monument tied to its tail" (Kyvig 1985, 14). Despite such predictions, the year that the Eighteenth Amendment was ratified, Captain William H. Slayton founded the Association Against the Prohibition Amendment (AAPA), which lobbied throughout the next decade for repeal of the Eighteenth Amendment (Kyvig 1979, 39–52). A prominent supporter was New York Republican Senator James W. Wadsworth. In the mid-1920s, the organization also received important support from the Du Pont family, especially Pierre. He enlisted the aid of John J. Raskob, who would later exert considerable influence for the repeal amendment after being appointed by Al Smith—the Democratic candidate for president in 1928—to chair the Democratic National Committee (Kyvig 1979, 101). Also important was the foundation in 1929

of the Women's Organization for National Prohibition Reform (WONPR). It provided something of a counterweight to the Women's Christian Temperance Union, which had been so influential in mustering support for the Eighteenth Amendment.

Almost from the adoption of the Eighteenth Amendment until its repeal, proposals were periodically introduced to modify it. Proposals included plans to repeal the amendment, hold a referendum on the question of repeal of the amendment, permit beverages with alcohol below a certain percentage (the Volstead Act, which enforced the Eighteenth Amendment, had applied even to beer with 3.2 percent alcohol content), or allow the federal government to tax and license alcoholic beverages.

Two events—the Great Depression, which began in 1929, and the election of 1932—eventually gave impetus to adoption of the Twenty-first Amendment. The first event encouraged the government to look at alcohol as a potential source of revenue as well as a source of employment. The second brought the Democratic Party into power. Whereas the Republican Convention of 1932 merely proposed allowing voters to consider repeal of the Eighteenth Amendment, the Democrats took a clear stand against Prohibition.

The vote for Democrats was so overwhelming that the lame-duck Congress ended up repealing the amendment even before the new one came into office. Initially, the Senate version contained four sections: Section 1 would have repealed the Eighteenth Amendment; Section 2 reserved to the states and territories powers to regulate alcohol; Section 3 granted Congress concurrent power to regulate the consumption of alcohol at places of sale (an antisaloon provision); and Section 4 set a seven-year ratification deadline. Section 3 was subsequently deleted, and Section 4 was modified to provide for ratification by state conventions rather than state legislatures.

This move may have been stimulated in part by discussion generated by the decision in *Hawke v. Smith* (1920), in which the Supreme Court had struck down Ohio's attempt to decide on the ratification of the Eighteenth Amendment by a state referendum; the convention mechanism also helped bypass state legislatures that were believed to be dominated by dry forces.

The Senate voted 63 to 23 (10 not voting) for this amendment on 16 February 1933, and the House followed with a vote of 289 to 121 (with 16 not voting) on 20 February (U.S. Senate 1985, 67–68). In the absence of federal guidelines, states set up their own ratifying conventions (see E. Brown 1935, 1938). These bodies served more as referendums on Prohibition than deliberative assemblies, and the amendment was ratified in a record (for then) of 10 months. Of some 21 million Americans who voted on the subject, 72.9 percent expressed support of repeal (Kyvig 1979, 178). Ironically, it was the predominantly Mormon Utah that jockeyed its deliberations to provide the thirty-sixth ratification needed to put the amendment over the top (Kyvig 1979, 182).

On at least five occasions from 1935 to 1939, Texas Democratic Senator Morris Sheppard, author of the Eighteenth Amendment, introduced resolutions to repeal the Twenty-first Amendment, thereby reinstating national alcoholic prohibition. In 1938, Democratic Representative Gomer Smith of Oklahoma introduced an amendment prohibiting drunkenness in the United States and its territories.

It should be noted that the Twenty-first Amendment recognizes that states have explicit power over alcohol. Many states use a local option system that gives individual cities and counties considerable autonomy to decide what regulation of alcohol is appropriate. In her dissenting opinion in *South Carolina v. Dole* (1987), Justice Sandra Day O'Connor argued that the amendment

gave states authority to set their own minimum drinking age free of federal threats to cut state highway budgets. In 1996 the U.S. Supreme Court decided in *44 Liquormart v. Rhode Island* that the Twenty-first Amendment does not negate First Amendment free speech rights; the Court thus voided a state law prohibiting the advertisement of liquor prices in newspapers or on billboards.

See also Eighteenth Amendment.

❖ TWENTY-FOURTH ❖ AMENDMENT

Initially intended to serve as a means of ascertaining that voters had a financial stake in the community, the poll tax was increasingly used after the Civil War as a means of keeping African Americans from voting. In *Breedlove v. Shuttles* (1937), the Supreme Court unanimously upheld such a state law against a challenge under the equal protection clause of the Fourteenth Amendment.

In 1941, Democratic Representative Lee Geyer of California introduced legislation to repeal state poll taxes; Geyer also founded the short-lived National Committee to Abolish the Poll Tax (Lawson 1976, 61). The next year, the House of Representatives voted favorably on the bill, but it was killed in the Senate by a filibuster. By the late 1950s, the House had voted favorably on such legislation on five occasions, but the Senate had never approved it (Ogden 1958, 243).

In part because of continuing questions about the constitutionality of such legislation, opponents of the poll tax increasingly began to focus on proposals for a constitutional amendment that had first been introduced in 1941. Florida Democratic Senator Spessard Holland was a persistent and forceful advocate of this amendment. By June 1961, his proposal (S.J. Res. 58) had 67 cosponsors, but it was tied up in the Senate Judiciary Committee by the committee chair, Democrat James O. Eastland of Mississippi. In order to break this logjam, the Committee on Interior and Insular Affairs subsequently introduced a resolution (S.J. Res. 29) to make Alexander Hamilton's house a national monument. By prearrangement, this resolution instead became the focus of the poll tax issue. After 10 days, debate was cut off, and thereafter, the Holland amendment was successfully offered as a substitute and approved by a vote of 77 to 16 on 27 March 1961. Leaders of the House suspended the rules to limit debate, and it approved the amendment 294 to 86 (with 54 not voting and 1 voting present) on 27 August 1961 (U.S. Senate 1985, 75–76). The necessary number of states ratified by February 1964, but by then, only five states still retained such a tax (Bernstein with Agel 1993, 138). In a telling demonstration of the symbolic power of amendments, a group of high school students subsequently organized a successful effort to add North Carolina's ratification during the celebration of the bicentennial of the U.S. Constitution ("North Carolina Ratifies the 24th Amendment" 1989).

The Twenty-fourth Amendment provides that "the right of citizens of the United States to vote in any primary or other election for President or Vice President, or for Senator or Representative in Congress, shall not be denied or abridged by the United States or any State by reason of failure to pay any poll tax or other tax." Section 2 vests enforcement authority in Congress.

The language of the amendment covers only federal elections, but in *Harper v. Virginia State Board of Elections* (1966), the Supreme Court overturned *Breedlove v. Shuttles* (1937) and held that such a tax violated the equal protection clause of the Fourteenth Amendment. At least in retrospect, this decision suggests that the Supreme Court might have accepted a legislative rather than a constitutional solution to the poll tax problem.

❖ TWENTY-SECOND ❖ AMENDMENT

One of the most persistent proposals for reform in U.S. history was the one that ultimately resulted in the Twenty-second Amendment. Exempting the current presidential officeholder (President Harry S. Truman) from its provisions, this amendment limited all subsequent persons from being elected as president more than twice or, in the case of a vice president who succeeded to the presidency, from serving a total of more than 10 years.

Proposals for Reform
At least 270 proposals for term limits were introduced in Congress from 1789 to 1947, with the average frequency increasing from just over one per session in the first 100 years, to two from 1890 to 1928, and to three thereafter (Willis and Willis 1952, 469). Although it is probably true that the American people "show little sign of wanting to abandon the Twenty-second Amendment" (M. Nelson 1989, 48), numerous proposals have been introduced in Congress both to lift the two-term limit and to substitute a single six-year presidential term.

The Constitutional Convention and Early Practices
At the Constitutional Convention of 1787, the original Virginia plan, which contemplated that Congress would select the president, proposed a single term of unspecified length (Padover 1962, 53). Delegates apparently feared that separation of powers might be undermined if a president attempted to bargain with legislators to gain reelection. With the invention of the electoral college mechanism—in which members would meet only once within individual states and then dissolve—this fear largely evaporated, and the delegates decided not to impose any term limits. Indeed, Alexander Hamilton defended the president's

"duration in office" as a key to executive energy and firmness. Writing in *Federalist* No. 72, Hamilton noted that "nothing appears more plausible at first sight, nor more ill founded upon close inspection, than a scheme . . . of continuing the Chief Magistrate in office for a certain time, and then excluding him from it, either for a limited period, or forever after" (Hamilton, Madison, and Jay 1961, 437).

President George Washington decided to retire after two terms, and President John Adams was defeated in his bid for a second term. In responding to a request from the Vermont state legislature encouraging him to run for a third term, President Thomas Jefferson elevated Washington's prudent decision not to run for a third term into a political principle (M. Nelson 1989, 46–47). President Andrew Jackson later urged Congress to propose an amendment limiting the president to a single four- or six-year term (J. Richardson 1908, 2:519, 3:117). The Senate approved two term limits in 1824 and 1826, but both died in the House; the constitution of the Confederate States of America provided for a single six-year term (Stathis 1990, 63). Presidents Ulysses S. Grant and Woodrow Wilson were tempted to run for third terms. The House dampened Grant's hopes when, in December 1875, it passed a resolution stating that the "precedent established by Washington and other presidents of the United States, in retiring from the presidential office after their second term, has become, by universal concurrence, a part of our republican scheme of government" (quoted in Stathis 1990, 64). Theodore Roosevelt, who had served a full second term and all but six months of his first term, when he took office after William McKinley's assassination, ran as a third-party candidate for president in 1912, after waiting out four years. The election of 1912 led to a favorable Senate vote on a single six-year term, but the measure died after incoming President Woodrow Wilson announced his opposition to it (Sundquist 1986, 46). The two-term tradition seemed so well fixed by 1925 that Herbert Horwill cited it as part of the United States' customs and usages that rose to the level of constitutional principles.

Adoption of the Twenty-second Amendment

Faced with the outbreak of World War II in Europe, President Franklin D. Roosevelt consented to renomination in 1940 and was eventually elected to four terms, his last being cut short by his death. Republican frustrations with his multiple terms appear to have accounted in large part for adoption of the Twenty-second Amendment (Statis 1991). The Twenty-second Amendment passed the House by a vote of 285 to 121 in February 1947 and the Senate by a vote of 59 to 23 the following month. By a vote of 82 to 1, the Senate rejected a substitute amendment that would have fixed the terms of all federal officeholders at six years (Willis and Willis 1952, 478). The partisan aspects of support for the amendment were demonstrated by the fact that Republicans supported the amendment unanimously in both the House (238 to 0) and the Senate (46 to 0), whereas Democrats opposed it by respective votes of 121 to 47 and 23 to 13. President Harry S. Truman basically stayed on the sidelines, and the amendment took almost four full years to be ratified, a record prior to the putative ratification of the Twenty-seventh Amendment in 1993 (M. Nelson 1989, 47–48). Of thousands of Republican state legislators whose votes were recorded, only 83 voted against the amendment (Stathis 1990, 70).

Issues and Consequences

Some of the debates over presidential term limits were surprisingly similar to more modern debates over congressional term limits, with which such proposals were often conjoined. Proponents argued that long terms threaten a system of separated powers and checks and balances. Perhaps remembering that Franklin Roosevelt's decision to seek a third term had been a prominent campaign issue, opponents said that the people decided whether to impose term limits when they voted (Willis and Willis 1952, 476–78).

Prior to the adoption of the Twenty-second Amendment, there were actually more proposals for a single presidential term—ranging from four to eight years, with four- and six-year proposals being most common—than there were for a two-term limit. A two-term limit appears to have tilted some power away from the president and toward Congress, but a one-term limit would arguably have had a much greater impact, effectively making every elected president a lame duck and thereby increasing congressional control over lawmaking (Willis and Willis 1952, 480). The one-term proposal continues to be introduced, sometimes along with proposals for direct popular election or proposals for limiting other officeholders. Supporters of a single six-year presidential term have included Republican Senator Jesse Helms of North Carolina (1977), Democratic Representative John Conyers of Michigan (1980), Democratic Senator Lloyd Bentsen of Texas (1981), and Republican Senator Strom Thurmond of South Carolina (1981).

Despite the Republican role in ratification of the amendment, to date, its effects have been felt by only two Republican presidents, Dwight D. Eisenhower and Ronald Reagan. Interestingly, 24 of 29 scholars who responded to a survey in 1957 indicated their belief that the amendment ought to be repealed (Stathis 1990, 73). While in office, Reagan lobbied for repeal of the amendment, and resolutions to this effect continue to be introduced in Congress. In the lead essay in a book published after he left office, Reagan described the Twenty-second Amendment as "a perversion of the Constitution's sound design for a limited but energetic government" (Reagan et al. 1990, 1). He was particularly concerned about the effect the amendment had on a president's effectiveness during his second term.

See also Congress, Term Limits; Electoral College Reform.

❖ TWENTY-SEVENTH AMENDMENT ❖

Article I, Section 6 of the U.S. Constitution provides that "the Senators and Representatives shall receive a Compensation for their Services, to be ascertained by Law, and paid out of the Treasury of the United States." The latter part of this clause is especially important because it enabled legislators to gain an independence that they might not have had if their salaries had been dependent on the states (Bernstein 1992, 502).

The fact that members of Congress are elected could be a plausible argument for protection against congressional aggrandizement, but when the Constitution was being debated, three states sensed enough danger that they proposed amendments to limit congressional pay raises. In compiling a bill of rights in the First Congress in 1789, James Madison proposed an amendment specifying that "no law, varying the compensation for the services of the Senators and Representatives, shall take effect, until an election of Representatives shall have intervened." This was originally the second of 12 amendments submitted to the states, but since only six states ratified it, it did not become part of the Bill of Rights.

In the nineteenth century, congressional pay increases twice provoked renewed pleas for ratification of the congressional pay-raise amendment. In 1817, Congress passed a compensation bill switching its salary from $6 a day to $1,500 a year and provoking such controversy that the bill was repealed—albeit not retroactively. Many members, including Daniel Webster (then representing New Hampshire), were voted out of office (Miller and Dewey 1991, 98). Similarly, in 1873, Congress adopted the Salary Grab Act, retroactively increasing salaries by $2,500 a year and provoking such outrage that it was repealed (Bernstein 1992, 534). The original second amendment was reintroduced in Congress, and Ohio ratified it 82 years after the last ratification (Strickland 1993, 716).

Congress twice voted to cut its salary during the Great Depression, but the twentieth century has otherwise witnessed a steady progression of congressional salary increases. Salaries went from $10,000 a year in 1935 to $125,100 in August 1991 (Bernstein 1992, 535). Moreover, Congress invented a number of mechanisms by which pay raises could be recommended by special commissions and go into effect without a direct vote. In 1978, 105 years after Ohio's ratification, Wyoming became the eighth state to ratify the pay-raise amendment. During this same period, faith in Congress appeared to decline, as members were caught in check-kiting controversies involving the congressional credit union and in questions of undue influence involving the failure of prominent savings and loan institutions (Vile 1992, 15–16).

In 1982, Gregory Watson, a student at the University of Texas at Austin, wrote a term paper for a government course in which he examined the congressional pay-raise amendment and concluded that it could still be ratified. Although he received a C from his skeptical instructor (Bernstein 1992, 537), he launched a one-man effort and spent over $5,000 of his own money to persuade additional state legislatures to ratify. The effort was not a very public one, but from 1983 to 1992, an additional 32 states ratified. On 14 May 1992, Don Wilson, the national archivist, certified the amendment as part of the Constitution, a decision that was approved shortly thereafter by votes of 99 to 0 in the Senate and 414 to 3 in the House (Bernstein 1992, 542).

Wilson's certification and the congressional votes have not necessarily settled the legitimacy issue. In *Dillon v. Gloss* (1921), the Supreme Court indicated that, to be valid, ratifications of amendments should be contemporaneous with their proposal. In *Coleman v. Miller* (1939), the Court later ruled that the issue of contemporaneousness was a political question for Congress to solve, but subsequent cases appear to have eroded this precedent. Not surprisingly, the putative ratification of the Twenty-seventh Amendment has stirred considerable rethinking of the amending process (Dalzell and Beste 1994; Paulsen 1993; Levinson 1994; Spotts 1994; Van Alstyne 1993).

See also Watson, Gregory.

❖ TWENTY-SIXTH AMENDMENT ❖

Under the Constitution, voting qualifications are set by the states, subject to any restrictions incorporated in constitutional amendments. Prior to 1971, there were no constitutional age restrictions for voting, although Section 2 of the Fourteenth Amendment had implicitly sanctioned the widespread 21-year minimum (as well as all male suffrage, which was not eliminated until adoption of the Nineteenth Amendment in 1920) by specifying that state representation in Congress could be reduced only when states denied the vote to men 21 years of age or older.

World War II marks the beginning of interest in reducing the voting age to 18. This reduction was tied to the fact that many men were being drafted for military service at that age, and it seemed ironic that one could be called upon to defend a nation in which one could not vote. In 1942, at least four members of Congress introduced resolutions to reduce the voting age to 18. They were Republican Senator Arthur Vanderberg of Michigan and Democratic Representatives Jennings Randolph of West Virginia and Jed Johnson and Victor Wickersham of Oklahoma. More than 150 proposals were subsequently introduced between 1942 and 1971, with an occasional proposal to set the age at 19 rather than 18, and with New York Democratic Representative Emanuel Celler of New York introducing at least one proposal in 1954 to freeze the age at 21. In 1953, the Senate debated a resolution to lower the voting age to 18, but it failed by a vote of 34 to 24 (U.S. Senate 1985, 89).

Support for the amendment increased during the Vietnam War, and Congress held hearings on the subject in 1968 and 1970. The public and some members of Congress—a number of whom had proposed extending the vote to active-duty military personnel regardless of age—may have been focusing on the link between military service and voting. The hearings, however, tended to put greater emphasis on the increased educational levels of modern youth (perhaps in recognition that only men could be drafted). The hearings also cited other responsibilities and privileges that 18- to 21-year-olds were exercising—including driving automobiles, drinking alcohol (an age that most states have subsequently raised), holding jobs, having families, being tried as adults in court, and attending college. Although some witnesses pointed to antiwar demonstrations as evidence that 18- to 21-year-olds were immature, others, including future Republican Senator Samuel I. Hayakawa, joined those who attributed such demonstrations to a small group of radicals rather than to the age group as a whole (*Hearings* 1970, 36–43).

After the hearings, Massachusetts Democratic Senator Edward Kennedy focused on the Supreme Court's decision in *Katzenbach v. Morgan* (1966) upholding federal suspension of state literacy tests. He suggested bypassing the amending process and lowering the voting age by statute, and such a provision was subsequently added to the Voting Rights Act of 1970. The testimony of Assistant Attorney General (later chief justice) William Rehnquist that this could be accomplished only through amendment (*Hearings* 1970, 233–49) proved prescient. In *Oregon v. Mitchell* (1970), a narrow Court majority, with Justice Hugo Black holding the balance, decided that Congress could lower the voting age in federal but not in state elections.

Only three states had voting ages of 18, with three others setting the age at 19, three at 20, and the rest at 21 (Grimes 1978, 142–43). This meant that absent repeal of the Voting Rights provision or adoption of an amendment, most states would have to create a dual voting system. This created the impetus for Jennings Randolph, then a West Virginia senator, to reintroduce the 18-year-old vote as an amendment. Accepted on 10 March 1971 by a vote of 94 to 7 in the Senate and on 23 March by a vote of 401 to 19 (with 12 not voting) in the House (U.S. Senate 1985, 90), the amendment was ratified within three months, the fastest ratification in U.S. history. Altogether, 42 states ratified. Ironically, the 18-to-21 age group has subsequently had one of the lowest voting rates in the general population.

In 1992, Minnesota Democratic Farm-Labor Representative Timothy Penny introduced a proposal to repeal the Twenty-sixth Amendment and lower the voting age to 16, but this proposal did not garner significant support. The 18-year age requirement seems unlikely to be changed in the near future.

See also *Oregon v. Mitchell.*

❖ TWENTY-THIRD AMENDMENT ❖

Because Article II, Section 1 of the Constitution limited the selection of presidential electors to states, Washington, D.C., had no input in presidential elections up to 1961. At that time, its population exceeded that of the 13 least populous states (U.S. Senate 1985, 75). As early as 1883, Republican Representative Henry Blair of New Hampshire introduced an amendment to remedy this situation by granting the District representation in the electoral college. More than a dozen such proposals were introduced in Congress between 1915 and 1923, with others following from 1945 and thereafter.

In 1959, Tennessee Democratic Senator Estes Kefauver introduced S.J. Res. 39 to provide for the emergency functioning of Congress by granting state governors the right to fill mass vacancies. When the Senate Committee on the Judiciary reported this amendment favorably to the Senate floor, Florida Democrat Spessard Holland proposed an amendment to abolish the poll tax (a proposal that later became the Twenty-fourth Amendment), and New York Republican Kenneth B. Keating introduced an amendment to grant the District of Columbia both the right to select presidential electors and the right to representation in the House of Representatives (Grimes 1978, 127; U.S. Senate 1985, 76–77). The Senate voted favorably on all three proposals and sent them to the House.

The House decided to concentrate on H.J. Res. 757, a proposal introduced by Democrat Emanuel Celler of New York containing the current language of the Twenty-third Amendment. It grants the District "a number of electors of President and Vice President equal to the whole number of Senators and Representatives in Congress to which the District would be entitled if it were a State, but in no event more than the least populous state [which is entitled to three]." Although this proposal was criticized for being too narrow, Celler argued that his proposal was more likely to be ratified and indicated that he had agreed to

support Holland's poll tax amendment separately (Grimes 1978, 129).

The House approved the Celler amendment by voice vote on 14 June 1960, and the Senate concurred, also by voice, on 16 June 1960. The amendment was ratified in nine months, with New Hampshire rescinding its 29 March ratification and readopting it the next day to become the thirty-eighth state to approve, providing the necessary three-fourths (U.S. Senate 1985, 77).

The Twenty-third Amendment did not completely equalize the District of Columbia's weight in the electoral college, since the District still has no role in the event that the House or Senate has to decide an electoral deadlock. Rhode Island Democrat Claiborne Pell introduced amendments in 1963 and 1967 to remedy this situation. The unratified amendment that Congress proposed in 1978 to treat the District of Columbia as a state for purposes of representation in Congress, presidential and vice presidential electors, and the amending process contained an explicit repeal of the Twenty-third Amendment. In 1990, Virginia Republican Representative Stanford Parris introduced an amendment to remove electors for the District of Columbia from the electoral college.

❖ TWO-THIRDS MAJORITY TO PROPOSE AMENDMENTS ❖

Article V of the Constitution specifies that two-thirds majorities are required in both houses of Congress to propose constitutional amendments. Alternatively, two-thirds of the states may petition Congress for a constitutional convention. In the *National Prohibition* cases (1920), the Supreme Court ruled that the two-thirds majority of Congress that is specified in Article V "is a vote of two-thirds of the members present—assuming the presence of a quorum—and not a vote of two-thirds of the entire membership, present and absent" (386). The Court's earlier decision in *Hollingsworth v. Virginia* (1798), in which it decided that amendments did not require a president's signature, may have been predicated in part on the fact that amendments are already proposed by the same majority required to overrule a presidential veto.

The two-thirds requirement for proposing amendments, like the three-fourths requirement for ratifying them, indicates that the amending process was not designed to incorporate all changes favored by the majority but only those with an unusually strong consensus behind them. In effect, the requirement for such majorities gives a veto to strong minority interests.

See also *National Prohibition* Cases.

U

❖

The relation between the nation and the states was a concern even before the adoption of the U.S. Constitution, and it has continued to be so ever since. As the Supreme Court has recognized increasingly broad congressional powers under the provisions in Article I, Section 8 related to federal taxation and regulation of commerce between the states (see, for example, the analysis under Child Labor Amendment), some advocates of states' rights have argued that state powers have been unduly eroded in violation of the language and spirit of the Tenth Amendment.

The Supreme Court registered this concern when, in *National League of Cities v. Usery* (1976), it decided by a 5-to-4 vote that the wage and hour provisions of the Fair Labor Standards Act that applied to private industries should not apply to traditional state functions. In 1985, however, in another 5-to-4 decision, the Court reversed course in *Garcia v. San Antonio Metropolitan Transit Authority* and decided that the line between traditional and nontraditional state functions was too difficult for the Court to draw. It further decided that the Constitution gave states adequate representation within Congress and other parts of the national government to protect their own interests.

States have subsequently complained not only about such wage and hour regulations

(indeed, states have actually succeeded in having some such regulations repealed) but also about unfunded congressional mandates that pass costs on to states and localities without providing federal funding for such requirements. The U.S. Conference of Mayors even sponsored a National Unfunded Mandate Day to protest what the mayors regarded as the unfair burden and the displacement of local choices that such mandates were imposing on states and localities (Gillmor and Eames 1994, 397).

Ohio Republican Congressman Paul Gillmor has proposed an amendment that would prohibit Congress from enacting unfunded mandates but would not prohibit states from voluntarily spending their own funds as a condition to receiving federal funds. Gillmor is especially concerned that the adoption of a balanced budget amendment "could increase the pressure for Congress to impose unfunded mandates" (Gillmor and Eames 1994, 410). Estimates of the cost of such mandates run up to $11 billion a year (Pear 1994, 20).

In March 1995, President Bill Clinton signed the Unfunded Mandate Reform Act, which had received a boost from the Republican congressional elections of 1994 (Hosanky 1995, 40). This act, which appears to undercut the need for a constitutional amendment, makes it more difficult for Congress to adopt unfunded mandates, requires more information about the projected costs of federal regulations, and restricts unfunded or underfunded federal mandates (Conlan, Riggle, and Schwartz 1995, 23).

See also Balanced Budget Amendment; Child Labor Amendment.

❖ UNITED NATIONS ❖

The United Nations was created at the end of World War II in the hope of promoting international cooperation. Some individuals feared that such an organization might undermine the sovereignty of individual nations. This appears to have been the concern of Republican Stephen Day of Illinois, who introduced an amending resolution in May 1944 intended to preserve "the independence and sovereignty of the United States" (H.J. Res 277). Similarly, a proposal introduced by North Dakota Democratic Representative Quentin Burdick in 1957 to prohibit the service of United States citizens under any banner other than the stars and stripes (H.J. Res 20) may have been aimed at U.S. participation in UN peacekeeping missions.

A key component of the organization is the Security Council. Originally composed of 11 members, 5 of which (including the United States) were permanent, the council has subsequently expanded to 15 members.

The president appoints the U.S. ambassador to the United Nations with the advice and consent of the Senate. The year after the United Nations was established, Connecticut Republican Congresswoman Clare Boothe Luce introduced a resolution relative to the election of U.S. representatives to the Security Council. The proposal is otherwise obscure and does not appear to have elicited further congressional debate or support.

For Further Reading:

Claude, Inis L. Jr. 1971. *Swords into Plowshares: The Problems and Progress of International Organization.* 4th ed. New York: Random House.

❖ UNITED STATES OF AMERICA, PROPOSED NAME CHANGES ❖

Radical Republican Representative George Washington Anderson of Missouri proposed an amendment shortening the nation's name to America in 1866 (H.R. 61). Similarly, Wisconsin Democratic Representative Lucas Miller introduced an amendment in 1893 to rename the nation the United States of the World (H.J. Res. 208). This latter name corresponded with that proposed by Victoria Chaflin Woodhull in 1870 (Stern 1974). After first suggesting that it be called "the United Republic of America," Rexford Tugwell wrote a proposed constitution for what he designated the "Newstates of America."

❖ UNITED STATES V. EICHMAN (1990) ❖

After the U.S. Supreme Court invalidated a Texas statute preventing flag desecration in *Texas v. Johnson* (1989), members of Congress who opposed the decision had to decide whether to respond with a flag burning amendment or with legislation. A majority adopted the latter course, passing the Flag Protection Act of 1989. Protesters in Seattle and Washington, D.C., immediately challenged this law.

The Flag Protection Act asserted an interest in preserving the nation's flag without making reference to explicit content-based limitations on speech. Still, the Court found that "it is nevertheless clear that the Government's asserted *interest* is 'related "to the suppression of free expression"'" . . . and concerned with the content of such expression" (*Eichman* 1990, 315). As in *Texas v. Johnson,* the Court found that the law "suppresses expression out of concern for its likely communicative impact" (*Eichman* 1990, 317) and must be subject to strict scrutiny under the First Amendment. In exercising such scrutiny, a majority of five justices led by Justice William Brennan refused to overrule its earlier decision and thus struck down the new law. Justice John Paul Stevens authored the dissenting opinion, restating his stance in the earlier case. The push for a flag desecration amendment gained renewed momentum after the historic elections of 1994.

See also Flag Desecration; *Texas v. Johnson*.

❖ UNITED STATES V. SPRAGUE ❖ (1931)

This case arose, like the *National Prohibition* cases (1920), from a challenge to the Eighteenth Amendment. Although citing its own rationale, the U.S. district court accepted the conclusion of Seldon Bacon and other opponents of the Prohibition amendment, who argued that no matter what Congress specified, such an amendment restricting the rights of the people could not be appropriately ratified by state legislatures. Instead, it required ratification by state conventions.

In writing the unanimous opinion for the Court, in which Chief Justice Charles Evans Hughes did not participate, Justice Owen Roberts argued that the "plain language of Article V" should take priority over any hypothesized "intent of its framers" (*Sprague* 1931, 729). Citing the language of Article V of the Constitution, Roberts argued that the choice between the two means of ratification "rests solely in the discretion of Congress" (*Sprague* 1931, 732). Since Congress, in making this selection, acts "as the delegated agent of the people in the choice of the method of ratification," it is not limited (as Bacon had argued) by the Tenth Amendment, which refers to powers "not delegated to the United States" rather than to powers specifically delegated to Congress (*Sprague* 1931, 733).

Roberts further argued that, contrary to Bacon's argument, a number of prior amendments—most notably "the Thirteenth, Fourteenth, Sixteenth, and Nineteenth," all of which the Court had accepted—also touched on the rights of individual citizens (*Sprague* 1931, 734). The Court's acceptance of the lawfulness of their ratifications was an additional argument for accepting the lawfulness of the Eighteenth Amendment.

Ironically, the Eighteenth Amendment would be repealed (by the Twenty-first Amendment) in the very manner—namely, by state conventions—by which its opponents said that it should have been ratified.

❖ UNWRITTEN CONSTITUTION ❖

See Customs and Usages.

❖ UPHAM, THOMAS CARLYLE ❖

About the only biographical information that is known about Thomas C. Upham is the proposal for a new constitution that he apparently composed in large part in 1937 and 1938 and offered in a book published in 1941 (Boyd 1992, 176). In this proposal, Upham provided a bit of biographical insight when he noted that part of his antipathy to charity derived from the fact that "I have had to take charity myself a few times" (Upham 1941, 56).

Upham aimed to "retain much of the framework, some of the contents, and all of the spirit—plus—of the old constitution" (Upham 1941, 32). While building on the existing document, Upham proposed a number of utopian and socialistic features, and he was particularly concerned about promoting greater equality. His preamble lists, among other objectives, that of forming a society "of mutual co-operation, human brotherhood, general kindliness, common welfare, equal rights, economic security, material prosperity, and universal peace" (Upham 1941, 67).

Upham's constitution begins with the executive branch, consisting of a president nominated by petition and elected by a plurality of voters for a single six-year term. A senator would succeed him in case of vacancy or incapacity. The president's power as commander in chief would be subject to override by a three-fourths vote of Congress. The president would have the right to submit legislation directly to Congress or to the people for approval and would be subject to recall by petition and a vote of two-thirds of the population.

The Senate would consist of 17 nonpartisan citizens elected for a maximum of two six-year terms. Each would also head one of 17 departments, including one dealing with "cultural security" and another with "private relations" (Upham 1941, 77). Members of the House would be chosen from 24 newly created districts that would take the place of the existing state and local governments, which Upham would eliminate. Congressional laws would be subject to an item veto. The people would have the right of petition, referendum, and recall.

The Supreme Court would be maintained, with justices retiring at age 75. There would also be district courts and criminal boards. Petit juries would consist of six local citizens and six citizens from another part of the country, with a guarantee that at least one juror would be "of the same, race, color, sex, and religious persuasion as the accused" (Upham 1941, 91). Government attorneys would serve both as defense counsel and as prosecutors.

At age 18, every citizen would have the obligation to register for citizenship. Citizens would be required to work from age 21 to 70. They could not be required to work more than five days and 35 hours a week and would be guaranteed a two-week vacation. All would be paid on a standard wage scale ranging (for those aged 24 to 60) from $1,000 a year to $10,000 a year so that the maximum wage would be no more than 10 times the minimum. Although individuals would be permitted to own small businesses, the government would own major industries, and individuals would be limited to owning $100,000 of private property. Strikes would be outlawed, medical care and education would be guaranteed to all, charity would be forbidden, and all citizens would be required to learn English. A "work and wages" standard would replace the gold standard (Upham 1941, 113). Rights would be protected against both governmental and private action, with existing rights preserved and occasionally expanded.

Wars would be outlawed, some exception apparently being made for defense and for actions within the Western Hemisphere (Upham 1941, 61). The United States would seek to form an international union that would work for "the attainment of Christian or other good ideals in the world" (Upham 1941, 115).

Upham favored calling a convention of 84 individuals to write the constitution, its work to become effective when ratified by the people. Future amendments would be instituted by two-thirds of both houses of Congress and ratified by two-thirds of those voting. The president would also have the right to take proposed changes to the people.

❖ *U.S. TERM LIMITS V. THORNTON* (1994) ❖

In this case, the U.S. Supreme Court struck down a term limit provision in the Arkansas state constitution. By implication, the Court also voided laws and constitutional provisions limiting the terms of national legislators that had been adopted in 22 other states.

Thornton centered on the provisions of Article I, Sections 2 and 3 of the U.S. Constitution setting forth age, citizenship, and residency requirements for members of the U.S. House and Senate. Arkansas had attempted to keep candidates off the ballot when they had served three terms in the House or two terms in the Senate.

Relying in large part on the decision in *Powell v. McCormack* (1969), the Court majority of five, led by Justice John Paul Stevens, held that the qualifications established in Article I were designed to be exclusive and that the Arkansas constitution added another qualification. Stevens argued that such additional state-imposed qualifications were "inconsistent with the framers' vision of a uniform national legislature, representing the people of the United States." He further opined that "if the qualifications set forth in the text of the Constitution are to be changed, the text must be amended."

By contrast, Justice Clarence Thomas, who wrote the dissenting opinion, said that although the Constitution established minimum qualifications for legislators, it was silent about additional qualifications. In Thomas's view, such restrictions were thus reserved, under provisions of the Tenth Amendment, to the people of the states. Noting that "the Constitution simply does not recognize the mechanism for action by the undifferentiated people of the Nation," Thomas observed that the amending process "calls for amendments to be ratified not by a convention of the national people, but by conventions in each state or by the state legislatures elected by these people."

At least one senator, Republican Hank Brown of Colorado, announced a plan to get around this decision by passing legislation defining the term "inhabitant" to exclude members of Congress who had been gone from their districts for more than half a year for 12 consecutive years (Seelye 1995, A11). Other supporters of term limits renewed calls for a constitutional amendment on the subject.

See also Congress, Term Limits.

V

❖ VICE PRESIDENT ❖

There is no other U.S. constitutional office that has been subjected to greater scorn than that of the vice presidency (Twentieth Century Fund Task Force 1988, 21; also see Young 1974). Especially in recent years, however, this office has increased in power and visibility and has become a major springboard to the presidency.

The Constitution of 1787 assigns only two functions to the vice president. One is to be available in case the president dies. The second, mixing executive and legislative powers, is to preside over and break tie votes in the U.S. Senate.

In large part, the vice presidency appears to have been created as a concomitant of the electoral college (Schlesinger 1974, 490). Under the original electoral scheme, each elector was to cast two votes. The person with the greatest number would become president, and the runner-up would become vice president. With the emergence of political parties, this scheme hit two major snags. First, it permitted a president and vice president to be elected from different parties; Federalist John Adams thus had a Democratic-Republican vice president, Thomas Jefferson. Second, there was the possibility of a tie in the electoral college. Such a tie occurred in the election of 1800, when all the Democratic-Republican electors for Thomas Jefferson also cast their votes for fellow party member Aaron Burr, and the election had to be resolved by the

U.S. House of Representatives. The Twelfth Amendment was subsequently adopted and specified that electors would cast separate votes for the two offices.

After adoption of this amendment, the vice presidency declined in stature, and some members of Congress began to introduce resolutions to abolish the institution. Alternatively, there were proposals to establish multiple vice presidencies or to permit Congress to fill vice presidential vacancies.

Although the institution was generally weak, in 1841, John Tyler established an important precedent. In succeeding William Henry Harrison, who died in office, Tyler insisted that he was the real and not simply an "acting" president.

The Twentieth Amendment settled one issue surrounding the vice presidency when it specified that if a president is not chosen in time for his term, the vice president–elect should be president. The amendment simply allowed Congress to legislate in cases in which neither the president nor the vice president had been so selected, but to date, Congress has yet to adopt such legislation.

The two greatest problems with the vice presidency were that the Constitution did not establish a procedure whereby a vice president could take over in cases of presidential disability, and it made no provision for filling vice presidential vacancies. The Twenty-fifth Amendment addressed both problems; it established a complex procedure whereby the vice president and cabinet could declare a president disabled, and it allowed a president to nominate, and a majority of Congress to confirm, vice presidential replacements.

Adoption of the Twenty-fifth Amendment has not ended calls for amendments to abolish the vice presidency or for further clarification of procedures to be followed in cases of presidential disability. Some questions also remain about the manner in which vice presidents are chosen by presidential candidates, with concerns being expressed that considerations of ticket balancing sometimes outweigh fitness to assume the presidency. Perhaps with such problems in mind, proposals were introduced in 1956 and 1957 to elect the vice president separately from the president. Since adoption of the Twenty-fifth Amendment, there have also been occasional calls to fill vice presidential vacancies by special elections rather than by presidential appointment and congressional confirmation.

See also Twelfth Amendment; Twentieth Amendment; Twenty-fifth Amendment.

❖ VICTIMS' RIGHTS ❖

As courts have extended broader protection to the rights of criminal defendants, attention has begun to focus as well on the rights of victims. Thus, in *Payne v. Tennessee* (1991), the Supreme Court overturned two earlier decisions and upheld the use of victim impact statements in the penalty phase of capital trials.

Florida Republican Representative Ileana Ros-Lehtinen, the first Cuban-born American to serve in such a capacity, introduced amending resolutions in 1990 and 1991 to guarantee victims' rights. Her proposal would grant crime victims and their next of kin "the right to be informed, to be present, and to be heard, when relevant, at all crucial stages of the prosecution, except to the extent that the constitutional rights of the accused are infringed" (H.J. Res. 247, 1991).

A similar amendment was introduced on Victim Rights Day in April 1996.

For Further Reading:

Cassell, Paul G., and Steven J. Twist. 1996. "A Bill of Rights for Crime Victims." 127 *Wall Street Journal* (24 April): A15.

Kyl, John. 1996. "Why Victims Need a Bill of Rights." *Washington Times* (22 April): A21.

❖ VOTING RIGHTS, LITERACY TESTS ❖

Literacy tests were among the tools used by whites in southern states to discriminate against African Americans. Although the idea that voters should be able to read and write can be justified under democratic theory, literacy and "understanding" tests were frequently administered in a way that permitted illiterate whites to vote but excluded highly educated blacks (Lawson 1976, 86–88).

In *Lassiter v. North Hampton County Board of Elections* (1959), the Supreme Court ruled that state power over suffrage included the right to set literacy requirements. That same year, at least two amendments were introduced to limit state voting restrictions to those concerned with age, residence, or imprisonment. From 1961 through 1963, several amendments were introduced either to establish free and universal suffrage throughout the United States or specifically to abolish the use of literacy tests in federal elections.

In the Voting Rights Act of 1965, Congress decided to address this issue through legislation instead. In *South Carolina v. Katzenbach* (1966), the Court held that congressional power under Section 2 of the Fifteenth Amendment was sufficient to uphold a literacy test ban in states identified as having low registration and voting rates. Similarly, in *Katzenbach v. Morgan* (1966), the Court upheld a provision of the law granting the right to vote to anyone who had completed a sixth-grade education in an accredited Puerto Rican school. In 1970, Congress banned literacy tests completely. Relying on the enforcement provisions of the Fourteenth and Fifteenth Amendments, the Court upheld this ban in *Oregon v. Mitchell* (1970).

See also Fifteenth Amendment.

❖ VOTING RIGHTS, RESIDENCY REQUIREMENTS ❖

More than 30 proposals were introduced from 1959 to 1971 seeking to address state residency requirements for voting. None was adopted.

In *Oregon v. Mitchell* (1970), however, the Supreme Court upheld a provision in the 1970 revision of the Voting Rights Act of 1965 that standardized such requirements for federal elections at 30 days. Similarly, in *Dunn v. Blumstein* (1972), the Court struck down a Tennessee residency requirement of one year in the state and three months in the county as a violation of the equal protection clause of the Fourteenth Amendment and impairment of the right to travel. In *Marston v. Lewis* (1973), the Supreme Court upheld a 50-day requirement designed to allow states to prepare accurate voting lists.

W

❖ WALLACE, WILLIAM KAY ❖
(1886–?)

American diplomat William Kay Wallace offered his critique of the U.S. Constitution and proposals for reform during the Great Depression (see Vile 1991c, 68–70). Wallace believed that the Constitution had been built on such ideas as individualism, natural rights, the social contract, and a geographically based state that were now seriously outdated. He further believed that economic reorganization was as important as political change.

Wallace advocated what he identified as "scientific capitalism" and declared it to be "the one best way, or the method of efficiency" (Wallace 1932, 104). Here, as elsewhere, Wallace seemed to assume that readers had as clear a view of what was required as he did. His initial description of the state as "the directive agency of social control, a clearing-house that will expedite and adjust public affairs" (137) also seemed vague, although he did articulate his belief that a new government should outlaw war. Initially, he indicated that the form, but not the substance, of the existing three branches of government could be maintained.

Wallace presented his specific proposals, which he hoped to initiate through a constitutional convention, in a chapter near the end of his book. There he outlined five broad guarantees that the new government should assume. The first was a guarantee of economic liberty. He included specific rights "to the full fruits of one's labor," "to economic security," "to education," and "to leisure" (1932, 182).

The second was a guarantee of social security designed to cover "all of the contingencies and possible caprices of fortune in the life of the individual." More specific guarantees included "social insurance" covering old age and unemployment, "child welfare and training," adjusted work schedules, and "adult education" (1932, 183).

Wallace's third guarantee was that of a "more effective government." To this end, he proposed replacing the current states with nine regional states, each with four to six representatives. These representatives would form a national board of directors (presumably unicameral) that would select from its members a president, appoint all governmental officials from the civil service, and exercise legislative functions.

To implement his fourth guarantee of "personal liberty and property," Wallace advocated transferring all corporate enterprises from private to public ownership and paying current holders of such property in governmental bonds. The new industries would be "scientifically regulated," with the profit motive being replaced; individuals would, however, still be able to own other forms of private property "in order to stimulate the creative ingenuity of all the citizens" (1932, 188).

Wallace's fifth guarantee was for a "planned national economy" (1932, 189). To this end, the state would become the "supreme economic arbiter," with power to conscript citizens in war and peace. The state would further coordinate economic activities and organize credit "as a public not a private function" (1932, 191).

Wallace's proposal was unique in its rejection of natural rights and in its almost complete embrace of a planned socialistic economy. Perhaps for this reason, his calls for a constitutional convention had no significant impact, and his proposals have been largely unknown to or ignored by subsequent reformers.

❖ WAR, DECLARATION OF ❖

When New York and Rhode Island ratified the U.S. Constitution, they proposed that Congress should not be able to declare war except by a two-thirds vote. This proposal was reintroduced at the Hartford Convention of 1815. Beginning about the time of World War I, a number of proposals were introduced either to require supermajorities of two-thirds or three-fourths or to prohibit Congress from declaring war except in cases of invasion. Some proposals for a national initiative and referendum would also have required voter initiation or approval of such declarations.

World War II marks the last occasion that the United States officially declared war, yet the nation has subsequently been involved in costly conflicts in Korea and Vietnam as well as in a host of other minor engagements for which congressional approval was either tepid or lacking. Congress attempted to rein in presidential powers in the War Powers Resolution of 1973, but the law has not proved altogether successful (J. H. Ely 1993).

Beginning in 1986, Democratic Representative Andy Jacobs Jr. of Indiana, a veteran of the Korean War, introduced several proposals to repeal the provision in Article I, Section 8 that grants Congress the power to declare war. According to one of his legislative aides, Jacobs's proposals were designed to call attention to the manner in which presidential foreign policy decisions have encroached on congressional powers (Tom Runge, telephone conversation with author, 15 June 1995).

See also Hartford Convention; Initiative and Referendum.

❖ WAR, OPPOSITION TO GOVERNMENT DURING ❖

The U.S. Constitution protects dissent even in times of war. The Supreme Court has ruled, however, that speech that is normally permissible might be suppressed during wartime when such speech creates a "clear and present danger" that Congress has a right to prevent (*Schenck* 1919, 52).

Public opposition to U.S. participation in the Vietnam War was particularly intense. Although the Supreme Court upheld a federal law prohibiting the destruction of draft cards (*O'Brien* [1968]), it was otherwise fairly protective of political protesters during this period.

Between 1966 and 1969, Democratic Representative Olin (Tiger) Teague of Texas, a World War II veteran who chaired the Veterans' Affairs Committee, introduced at least three resolutions that would have made it unlawful to aid or encourage the United States' enemies during a war. His proposal, in obvious tension with the free speech and press guarantees of the First Amendment, would have included restrictions on "public demonstrations, public writings, [and] public speeches" (H.J. Res. 102, 1967).

❖ WAR, POWER DURING ❖

Constitutional provisions have provided legal authority for extensive expansion of federal war powers, especially in this century. During World War I, such powers were utilized as a basis for seizing the nation's railroads and telephone and telegraph systems. Concern with winning the war also fueled the drive for national alcoholic prohibition (C. May 1989, 26, 60–93).

From 1922 to 1939, at least 25 amendments sought to grant the government power not only to conscript soldiers but also to conscript property during times of war (sponsors included Indiana Democratic Representative Louis Ludlow and North Dakota Republican Senator Gerald Nye). At least some of these proposals were motivated by a desire to take any profits out of war. Some proposals specifically sought to exempt governmental takings in wartime from the Fifth Amendment requirement that the government provide just compensation.

Short of this requirement, there appear to be few constitutional obstacles to governmental seizures and operation of industries during times of war. In *Youngstown Sheet & Tube Co. v. Sawyer* (1952), however, the Supreme Court invalidated President Harry S. Truman's seizure of the steel mills during the Korean War, but the justices focused on the lack of congressional authority for such a seizure (Congress had decided against such authority when it adopted the Taft-Hartley Act of 1947) rather than on any inherent constitutional limitations on the subject.

❖ WAR, PROHIBITION OF ❖

Republican Senator Lynn Frazier of North Dakota consistently introduced amending proposals from 1926 to 1939 to prohibit war by declaring it to be illegal. New York Republican (and later American Laborite) Representative Vito Marcantonio also submitted such a proposal in 1936.

Although the scope of these proposals was unusual and arguably utopian, the 1920s and 1930s saw substantial growth in

antiwar sentiment and an American Committee for the Outlawry of War was established in December 1921. In August 1928, representatives of the United States and 14 other nations signed the Kellogg-Briand Pact renouncing the use of war, but the Senate's 85-to-1 ratification of this treaty in January 1929 was predicated on reserving the nation's right to self-defense (Ellis 1961, 212). Not surprisingly, the treaty proved ineffective in preventing World War II and subsequent conflicts.

For Further Reading:

Morrison, Charles C. 1972. *The Outlawry of War: A Constructive Policy for World Peace*. New York: Garland Publishing.

❖ WARREN COURT ❖

Earl Warren served as chief justice of the United States from 1953 to 1969, and the Court during this period is generally referred to as the Warren Court. A former district attorney, attorney general, three-term California governor, and Republican vice presidential candidate, Warren proved to be a far more liberal and activist justice than President Eisenhower, who appointed him to the position, had anticipated. Moreover, although not nearly as intellectual as his strong-minded colleagues Hugo Black, William O. Douglas, Felix Frankfurter, John Marshall Harlan, and William Brennan, Warren proved to be an effective leader who could often achieve a greater degree of consensus than might otherwise have been expected.

Shortly after Warren assumed the reins of the Court, it issued its unanimous decision in *Brown v. Board of Education* (1954), declaring an end to 60 years of de jure racial discrimination in the United States. In numerous subsequent decisions, the Court showed some flexibility in the implementation of desegregation decisions but never deviated from the central principle articulated in *Brown.*

In 1962, the Court issued its decision in *Baker v. Carr,* declaring that state legislative apportionment was not a political question but was justiciable under the equal protection clause of the Fourteenth Amendment. In a follow-up case, *Reynolds v. Sims* (1964), the Court applied the "one person one vote" standard to both houses of state legislatures. These decisions stirred considerable sentiment for a constitutional amendment to give states greater leeway. Focusing on the apportionment decisions and other liberal rulings, the conservative John Birch Society launched an effort to impeach Earl Warren. Such attempts had little apparent effect on the Supreme Court's liberal decisions related to the First Amendment and in other areas of the law.

The Warren Court's rulings on the Fourteenth Amendment contained some of its most influential constitutional interpretations. Before Warren came to the Court, it had already begun the process of incorporating some of the important limitations on the national government that were found in the Bill of Rights and applying them to the states. The Warren Court rapidly accelerated this process, especially with respect to the rights of criminal defendants. Thus, in *Mapp v. Ohio* (1961), it applied the exclusionary rule to the states; in *Gideon v. Wainwright* (1963), it extended the right to appointed counsel for indigents; and in *Miranda v. Arizona* (1966), it extended a whole panoply of rights previously required only at the federal level. In *Griswold v. Connecticut* (1965), the Court struck down a Connecticut law proscribing birth control by holding that the provisions in the Bill of Rights had penumbras that encompassed the right to privacy, thus laying a foundation for the Court's liberal abortion decision in the following decade. In his last major decision from the bench, *Powell v. McCormack* (1969), Warren further narrowed the political questions doctrine, with possible implications for future amending cases.

Many of the Warren Court's decisions led to proposed amendments, but none proved successful. The Court did, however, encounter considerable political opposition. When Warren first expressed his desire to resign, many of the criticisms of the Court as being too liberal and too activist fell on President Lyndon Johnson's choice of Justice Abe Fortas, who withdrew from consideration for chief justice and later resigned from the Court. President Richard Nixon subsequently had the chance to appoint Warren Burger to this position. Both Burger and his successor, William Rehnquist, have issued more conservative decisions, in many cases not so much reversing as slowing earlier trends (Funston 1977). The Warren Court stands as one of the clearest examples of the way the Supreme Court can inaugurate a constitutional revolution without the adoption of new amendments.

For Further Reading:

Schwartz, Bernard. 1988. *Super Chief: Earl Warren and His Supreme Court—A Judicial Biography.* New York: New York University Press.

❖ WASHINGTON, GEORGE ❖
(1732–1799)

George Washington served as leader of American forces during the Revolutionary War, as the president of the Constitutional Convention of 1787, and as the nation's first president. Although he was not as intellectually gifted as John Adams, Thomas Jefferson, or James Madison, he articulated a vision of America's destiny that was remarkably prescient (Bradley 1945), and his role at the Constitutional Convention and as first president was critical to the forging of the Union. His farewell address, in which he warned about the dangers of encroachments by one governmental branch over others and of the danger of entangling foreign alliances, is an important state paper.

The Bill of Rights was proposed and ratified during Washington's first term. Much like James Madison, Washington appears to have believed that although not all the amendments were absolutely necessary, they could do no harm and would help quiet the fears that opponents of the new Constitution had stirred (Vile 1992, 50).

In his farewell address and elsewhere, Washington drew the obligation to obedience to government from the presence of a means of peaceful change:

> The Government . . . containing within itself a provision for its own amendment, has a just claim to your confidence and support. Respect for its authority, compliance with its laws, acquiescence in its measures, are duties enjoined by the fundamental maximums of true liberty. The basis of our political system is the right of the people to make and to alter their constitution of government. But the constitution which at any time exists till changed by an explicit and authentic act of the whole people is sacredly obligatory upon all. (quoted in Kaufman 1969, 21)

On many other occasions, Washington referred to the amending process as a "constitutional door" (Norham 1988). Thus, in arguing that the new Constitution was not perfect but was a distinct improvement over the Articles of Confederation, Washington noted that it was one in which "a Constitutional door is left open for its amelioration" (Fitzpatrick 1931–1944, 29:411).

❖ WATSON, GREGORY ❖

Gregory Watson served as an aide to Texas state senator Ric Williamson. As a sopho-more economics major at the University of Texas at Austin, Watson wrote a paper for a government class in which he examined the amendment to delay congressional pay raises until an election intervened, which had been introduced in 1789 as part of the original Bill of Rights. He concluded that this proposal was still a viable subject for state ratification.

Despite receiving a C on this paper, Watson launched a one-man campaign, financed with his own funds, for ratification of this amendment (Bernstein 1992, 537). Watson's efforts were rewarded in 1992 (Watson was then 30 years old) with the putative ratification of the Twenty-seventh Amendment.

See also Twenty-seventh Amendment.

For Further Reading:
"The Man Who Would Not Quit." 1992. *People* 37 (1 April): 72

❖ WEDGWOOD, WILLIAM B. ❖ (?–1883)

William B. Wedgwood was a Maine native who moved to New York, where he joined the bar in 1841. He favored numerous reforms during his life, including civil service reform and the emancipation and recolonization of the slaves and the compensation of their owners (Boyd 1992, 22). An author and educator as well as a lawyer, Wedgwood wrote books on New York law and the U.S. Constitution and helped found the City University of New York School of Law (Boyd 1992, 29). Wedgwood's most novel contribution to thinking about constitutional change was a new constitution included in his 1861 book entitled *The Reconstruction of the Government of the United States of America*.

Wedgwood's immediate aim was to halt the progression of the Civil War, and his solution was to allow North and South to form two republics, joined together as the "Democratic Empire." Believing that the United States was heir to the blessings that had once been bestowed on ancient Israel, Wedgwood described his proposed plan as a "theocratic Democracy" (Wedgwood 1861, 15). As did the future constitution for the Confederate states, Wedgwood's contained an acknowledgment of God in the preamble. He also stated that the primary purpose of government was to "develop and arrange" natural law principles into "a written code, under the sanction of legislative enactment" (Wedgwood 1861, 17). Early articles of Wedgwood's constitution elaborately described the flag and seal of the Democratic Empire, the former to contain 7 colors and 13 stripes in a double rainbow containing, among other things, the otherwise unexplained symbolical letters W.C.P.P.

Wedgwood's constitution contained a number of novel features. In several places it went into detail about the relationship between natural rights and political rights. It guaranteed a good education to all and required that all citizens labor (Wedgwood 1861, 16). Although protecting the right to worship, it prohibited "the worship of idols and the sacrifice of human beings" (Wedgwood 1861, 17). Several times it sanctioned the government's right to exercise eminent domain.

Wedgwood would have set up three degrees, or levels, of government—state, national, and imperial. Each would comprise officeholders "of high moral and religious character" (Wedgwood 1861, 18). States would fall naturally into "Labor States" and "Capital States," with Wedgwood advocating extension of the Missouri Compromise line "west until it reaches the Atlantic [sic] Ocean" (Wedgwood 1861, 19). Each of the three levels of government would be divided into legislative, executive, and judicial branches, with terms in the respective Houses of Representatives being one, two,

and four years and those in the respective Senates being two, four, and six years. Similarly, state governors would serve for two years, the president for four years, and the emperor for six years.

Wedgwood went into surprising detail in describing the powers of state governments. State powers would include regulation of property, education, and highways; providing employment for the needy; and enacting laws for domestic relations. National powers seemed to be designed to handle problems between and among the states. The imperial government (headquartered in New York) would deal with matters of defense and diplomacy, with the emperor serving as commander in chief of the army and navy.

Wedgwood believed that the impending Civil War had been brought on in large part by those who had spoken contemptuously, sometimes from the pulpit, of the old Constitution and of those who owned slaves. He accordingly proposed that "slanderous words, coming from whatever source they may come, must be suppressed and punished. All unkind language, by which the feelings of a fellow-citizen may be injured, should be carefully avoided" (Wedgwood 1861, 26).

Wedgwood hoped that Canada, Mexico, and other Central and South American republics would eventually join the new empire, "triumphantly" vindicating the Monroe Doctrine (Wedgwood 1861, 27). Wedgwood ended his discourse with reference to the four horses of the biblical book of Revelation. Clearly, Wedgwood's primary, and unsuccessful, hope was to avoid the impending conflict.

❖ WELFARE PAYMENTS, ❖ RIGHT TO

Although it is generally accurate to say that "welfare benefits are legislative choices, not constitutional commands" (Lieberman 1992, 574), courts have surrounded welfare recipients with certain constitutional protections. Thus, in *Shapiro v. Thompson* (1969), the Supreme Court ruled that a Connecticut one-year residency requirement for welfare recipients violated the right to travel. Similarly, in *Goldberg v. Kelly* (1970), the Court ruled that a New York law that did not provide welfare recipients with a hearing before terminating benefits was unconstitutional.

In 1971, Republican Representative Edwin Eshleman of Pennsylvania introduced an amendment related to welfare rights. It declared that welfare was "not a right, but is to be determined in accordance with the specific provisions of . . . laws, duly enacted by the Congress of the United States or by the State or political subdivision involved" (H.J. Res. 206). On a related topic, a proposal by Rhode Island's ratifying convention in 1790 would have specified "that Congress should have power to establish a uniform rule of inhabitancy and settlement of the poor of the different States throughout the United States" (Ames 1896, 189).

❖ WEST, JAMES C. (?–1946) ❖

One of the least accessible proposals for a new constitution was contained in a book published by James C. West in Springfield, Missouri, in 1890. The only known copy is now a fragile document in the Library of Congress, but fortunately, the proposal has recently been reprinted (Boyd 1992).

West served as a clerk, a newspaper editor, and a prosecuting attorney, and although he was a Democrat, his ideology was close to that of the Populists (Boyd 1992, 68–69). The historian who reprinted West's constitution noted that it reflected "the limited horizon of a midwestern small town political observer" (Boyd 1992, 70).

Although most of West's proposals followed the outline of the Constitution of 1787, he added several features that made his proposal unique.

Congress remained fairly similar, but West added a requirement that members be natural born and sought to guarantee one representative for every 175,000 persons. He also would have excluded individuals from the House who were worth more than $25,000 and senators who were worth more than $50,000. The terms of senators would be reduced to four years, and no person would be eligible to either house who had "not labored five years, after he had attained the age of ten years, at either agricultural or some mechanical arts" (Boyd 1992, 74). Members would have to attend all congressional sessions except in cases of sickness. Their oath would obligate them to seek "the greatest good of the greatest number," and they would swear not to "approve of anything contrary to the spirit of the Constitution, either impress or implied" or risk "the vengeance of God . . . and the universal detestation of mankind" (Boyd 1992, 74). The wages of members of Congress were not to exceed 15 times the wage of laboring farmhands. West attempted to guard against committee changes in a bill contrary to its sponsor's intentions and appeared to make provision for the House of Representatives to act alone to override a presidential veto of a finance bill.

In listing the powers of Congress, West attempted to prevent the government from collecting surplus revenue. However, he favored introduction of "a tax on the sumptuousness of the people" as well as taxes on land and income. He also sought to limit borrowing except in cases of war and not until "the circulating medium has been increased to $60 sixty dollars per capita" (Boyd 1992, 78). Generally, he wanted the circulating capital to be maintained at $40 per person. West wanted to make it a crime for persons or corporations to "engage in any pool, combine, trust or rebate system," and he hoped to prevent the immigration of persons who "Congress thinks are detrimental" (Boyd 1992, 78, 81).

West wanted the president to be elected by popular vote. The president's salary could not exceed 125 times the average wage for a laboring farmhand. His powers, like those of the judiciary, remained unchanged.

After repeating the core of the current amending process, West went on to suggest that amendments "which will render null and void any provision of this Constitution" would require consent by three-fourths of the House and a majority of voters, whereas amendments adding to the Constitution would require only the former. West proposed that his constitution would go into effect when ratified by two-thirds of the states. His document included all 15 amendments that were then part of the Constitution, except for the Twelfth, which he omitted in recognition that the president would, under his system, be elected by popular vote.

❖ WILSON, THOMAS WOODROW ❖ (1856–1924)

In addition to serving as twenty-eighth president of the United States, Thomas Woodrow Wilson was an influential critic of the constitutional amending process and the U.S. system of checks and balances. He was also a strong advocate of the British parliamentary system and was more influential than many merely academic critics of the U.S. system.

In an early work, *Congressional Government*, Wilson noted that "it would seem that no impulse short of the impulse of self-preservation, no force less than the force of revolution, can nowadays be expected to move the cumbrous machinery of formal amendment erected in Article V" (1885,

242). Similarly, in a later work, Wilson contrasted the Newtonian system outlined in the U.S. Constitution with the Darwinian system of the natural world: "The trouble with the [Newtonian] theory is that government is not a machine, but a living thing. It falls, not under the theory of the universe, but under the theory of organic life. It is accountable to Darwin, not to Newton" (1908, 56).

Wilson was a strong admirer of the English governmental system and of responsible cabinet government. He believed that parliamentary debates refined and enlarged public views and attracted gifted and principled men to involvement in politics. In a work that was not published in his lifetime, Wilson advocated two constitutional changes to advance the nation closer to such a system. One would allow the president to choose members of Congress for his cabinet. They would, in turn, be permitted to initiate legislation and lead debate (1882, 202). Elsewhere, Wilson indicated that such a system would also require "ministerial responsibility," under which the cabinet would resign if Congress rejected "any important part of their plans" (1879, 498). Wilson's second proposal called for lengthening the terms of both the president and members of Congress (1882, 202).

Although Wilson's early focus was on congressional government, he increasingly advocated presidential leadership. Competently leading the nation through World War I, Wilson was unable to get the nation to join the League of Nations after the war, and he ruined his health in the process of trying.

The Progressive Era, during which he served as president, witnessed the addition of four constitutional amendments, somewhat undermining Wilson's own observations about constitutional inflexibility. The Sixteenth and Seventeenth Amendments were ratified almost simultaneously with Wilson's inauguration. Wilson opposed the

Eighteenth Amendment but was eventually persuaded to support the Nineteenth Amendment. Both amendments were ratified toward the end of his second term.

❖ WOMEN'S CHRISTIAN ❖ TEMPERANCE UNION

Like the struggle for women's suffrage that culminated in the adoption of the Nineteenth Amendment, the movement that led to national alcoholic prohibition and the ratification of the Eighteenth Amendment was decades in the making. The Women's Christian Temperance Union (WCTU) was among the most important groups in the early struggle for Prohibition. The WCTU was founded in Lake Chautauqua, New York, in August 1874, the year after lectures in Ohio by Dr. Diocletion Lewis sparked the Women's Crusade to force the closure of saloons.

By the 1880s, the WCTU was "the largest organization of women the United States had yet known" (Bordin 1981, xvi). Indeed, the WCTU has been described as "unquestionably the first mass movement of American women" (Bordin 1981, 156). At its first national convention held in Cleveland, Ohio, in 1874, it elected Annie Wittmyer, founder of the Methodist Home Missionary Society and editor of the *Christian Woman,* as its first president. The WCTU selected Frances Willard of Illinois, a college educator, as corresponding secretary. Willard would head the WCTU in its glory days from 1879 until her death in 1898. She was succeeded by Lillian M. Stevens, who served as president from 1898 to 1914.

The WCTU succeeded in mobilizing large numbers of women—mostly, but not exclusively, middle- and upper-class white evangelical Protestants—under the banner of "home protection." Such women were thus able to engage in political action in defense of what had traditionally been regarded as women's chief sphere—a sphere often threatened when the male breadwinner became an alcoholic. Moreover, following Willard's "do everything" philosophy, the organization sponsored a variety of political programs, with state and local chapters being given considerable discretion in choosing where they would focus their energies. WCTU concerns included women's suffrage, prison reform, the establishment of kindergartens and Sunday schools, Sabbath observance, temperance education, proposals for moral purity and the elevation of prostitutes, labor reforms, eugenics, and antismoking. For a time during the 1880s, the WCTU was closely allied with the National Prohibition Party. Some, but by no means all, members embraced contemporary antinativist and anti–Roman Catholic sentiments. The *Union Signal* was the main WCTU newspaper.

Most WCTU members did not join in Willard's espousal of Christian socialism in the 1890s. By the time of her death, the organization had begun a slow decline as women increasingly joined the National Federation of Women's Clubs, the National American Woman Suffrage Association, and other such organizations (Bordin 1981, 149–59). During Lillian Stevens's presidency, the WCTU's earlier broad agenda gradually narrowed. An analyst noted that the WCTU's image changed from that of containing "the best, most respected, most forward-looking women in town to narrow-minded antilibertarians riding a hobbyhorse" (Bordin 1981, 155).

See also Eighteenth Amendment.

For Further Reading:

Epstein, Barbara L. 1981. *The Politics of Domesticity: Women, Evangelism, and Temperance in Nineteenth-Century America*. Middletown, CT: Wesleyan University Press.

❖ WOODHULL, VICTORIA CHAFLIN (1838–1927) ❖

Victoria Chaflin Woodhull led an active life. She was a stockbroker and one-time protégé of Cornelius Vanderbilt; a reformer, lecturer, spiritualist, and sometime advocate of free love; a proponent of woman's suffrage who split with Susan B. Anthony's National Woman Suffrage Association; and an editor of *Woodhull and Chaflin's Weekly* and later the *Humanitarian*. Woodhull was also a thrice-married member of an eccentric family; her sister was the vivacious Tennessee Celeste Chaflin. Victoria Woodhull was the primary catalyst for charges of adultery against popular preacher Henry Ward Beecher (see McHenry 1980, 451–52; Marberry 1967; Arling 1972). Woodhull proposed a Constitution of the United States of the World in a speech in 1870, two years before her first of five bids for the presidency.

Her proposed constitution was a unique blend of old and new provisions. Congress would continue to be bicameral, with senators serving terms of 10 years and members of the House serving for 5 years; all bills would originate in the House (Stern 1974, 6), with the possibility of abolishing the Senate if three-fifths of the House and the American people concurred (Stern 1974, 22). Moreover, the House could override presidential vetoes by a simple majority vote (Stern 1974, 6). Congress would prescribe a common form of constitution for each state (Stern 1974, 7) and would exercise expanded powers to guarantee equal rights; establish a uniform criminal code, a common law, a system of welfare-workfare, prison discipline, inheritance and other progressive taxes, and a system of national railroads; and propose a world tribunal (Stern 1974, 8–11).

The president and his ministerial cabinet of 16 designated officers would be selected by an electoral college and serve 10-year nonrenewable terms (Stern 1974, 12–16).

Judges would also be selected by the electoral college, with a judicial system consisting of district courts, a three-judge Supreme Court of the States, and a five-person Supreme Court of the United States (Stern 1974, 18).

The franchise would extend to all 18-year-old citizens other than "idiots and the insane" (Stern 1974, 19), thus anticipating both the Nineteenth and the Twenty-sixth Amendments. Woodhull's constitution further provided for the recall, the initiative, and the referendum, with amendments to be adopted by three-fifths of the voters either on their own or in response to proposals made by a three-fifths vote of the House of Representatives (Stern 1974, 22–23).

Although there were a number of provisions for equality, no bill of rights was included. Woodhull's proposal received little publicity and "had little discernible impact on the American political process or the condition of women in American life" (Boyd 1992, 43).

In 1893, Congressman Lucas Miller of Wisconsin offered a resolution to change the name of the United States to the United States of the World (H.J. Res. 208). This proposal, which he presented by request, contained a number of whimsical features (Musmanno 1929, 185–86), some of which resembled features of the Woodhull plan.

See also Anthony, Susan Brownell; Nineteenth Amendment.

❖ WOODWARD, AUGUSTUS B. (1775?–1827) ❖

Augustus Woodward provided one of the earliest comprehensive analyses of the U.S. Constitution and its operation in an 1825 publication called *The Presidency of the United States*. Woodward concentrated a great deal of attention on the emerging cabinet system, whose history he described before he enumerated 20 "evils" that needed solutions.

The problems Woodward identified were as follows (Woodward 1825, 43–67):

1. The exclusion of the vice president from cabinet councils that would better familiarize him with the job to which he might succeed;

2. The conflict among cabinet members for the presidential post;

3. The difficulty that noncabinet officers had in becoming presidential candidates;

4. The misuse of patronage;

5. The problems caused by party opposition that was often fueled by sectional jealousies;

6. Variations in the methods of selecting presidential electors;

7. Problems arising when the House of Representatives had to choose among the top candidates for the presidency;

8. Problems arising when presidential electors were not chosen on the same day as the general election;

9. The need for a presidential secretary;

10. The failure of Washington, D.C., to have representatives either in the electoral college (a problem not addressed until 1961 by adoption of the Twenty-third Amendment) or in Congress;

11. Corruption of Congress brought about by inadequate attention to the doctrine of separation of powers;

12. Providing the president with a furnished residence without explicit constitutional sanction and despite the constitutional provision preventing additional emoluments for that office;

13. The need for a mechanism whereby the president could establish a committee of investigators;

14. The failure to standardize rules of presidential etiquette;

15. The need for a method whereby various regions of the country would be granted an opportunity to fill the presidency;

16. The need to acquaint the vice president with presidential duties and relieve him of responsibility for presiding over the Senate;

17. The lack of a cabinet office relating to domestic affairs;

18. Concern that cabinet meetings might detract from cabinet officers' attention to their respective departments;

19. Concern that cabinet officers, fearful of losing their jobs, might fail to provide the president with independent counsel; and

20. Concern that the cabinet system lacked adequate constitutional sanction.

Woodward did not elaborate on how all these problems should be solved or provide specific language for constitutional amendments. He did provide an outline for a Department of Domestic Affairs that would include branches for advancing sciences and the arts; for agriculture, commerce, and internal improvements; for preservation of public documents; and so forth. Woodward also proposed dividing the Department of Foreign Affairs into eight bureaus, each to deal with a different area of the world.

Many of the problems Woodward addressed are dated. Other concerns—representation for the District of Columbia, the electoral college, and the role of the president in a republican system—remain.

❖ WORKERS' COMPENSATION LAWS ❖

In the nineteenth century, several common-law principles limited employer liability for on-the-job accidents. The fellow-servant rule allowed employers to evade responsibility when other employees were negligent; contributory negligence exempted employers when the injured person shared in the fault; and the assumption-of-risk doctrine presumed that employees who knew of workplace dangers assumed the risks (Urofsky 1988, 558).

At the turn of the century, states began

creating insurance pools and requiring employees either to participate or to secure private insurance coverage for on-the-job injuries. Beginning in 1906, the national government adopted legislation to cover industries engaged in interstate commerce. In 1908, the Supreme Court struck down the federal law as overly broad, and in *Ives v. South Buffalo Railway Co.* (1911), the New York Court of Appeals invalidated a state law granting compensation for injured workers (Urofsky 1988, 560–61).

That year, Illinois Democratic Representative Frank Buchanan introduced an amendment giving Congress the power to pass laws granting compensation to injured workers. Within months of the *Ives* decision, however, state courts began ruling favorably on other state laws (Hall 1989, 244), and the Supreme Court upheld a revised Federal Employers' Liability Act of 1908 in the *Second Employers' Liability* case of 1912. Amending proposals on the topic subsequently ceased.

❖ WORLD GOVERNMENT ❖

One proposed solution to the problem of international conflict is the establishment of international organizations or a world government. Colorado Democratic Senator John Safroth offered an amendment in 1916 to authorize the creation of an international peace tribunal. Despite the intense efforts of Woodrow Wilson, the United States never joined the League of Nations, which was established at the end of World War I. The United States was, however, a founding member of the United Nations, which emerged at the end of World War II.

Allowing each nation-state to preserve its sovereignty and independence, the United Nations fell far short of the world government that many thought was necessary to preserve peace and halt the spread of nuclear weapons. This idea appears to have had special support in the 1940s and early 1950s (see Johnsen 1947; Mangone 1951), with prominent advocates including President Harry Truman, General Douglas MacArthur, and Supreme Court Justice Owen Roberts (Johnsen 1948, 65).

In 1949, Democratic Representative Charles Bennett of Florida introduced an amendment to permit U.S. participation in a limited world government. That same year, five states (California, Connecticut, Maine, New Jersey, and North Carolina) petitioned for a convention to propose amendments authorizing U.S. participation in such a body. Although international organizations have been strengthened in recent years, the idea of a world government is still a distant dream.

APPENDIX A

The Constitution of the United States

Preamble

We the People of the United States, in Order to form a more perfect Union, establish Justice, insure domestic Tranquility, provide for the common defence, promote the general Welfare, and secure the Blessings of Liberty to ourselves and our Posterity, do ordain and establish this Constitution for the United States of America.

Article I

Section 1. All legislative Powers herein granted shall be vested in a Congress of the United States, which shall consist of a Senate and House of Representatives.

Section 2. The House of Representatives shall be composed of Members chosen every second Year by the People of the several States, and the Electors in each State shall have the Qualifications requisite for Electors of the most numerous Branch of the State Legislature.

No Person shall be a Representative who shall not have attained to the age of twenty five Years, and been seven Years a Citizen of the United States, and who shall not, when elected, be an Inhabitant of that State in which he shall be chosen.

Representatives and direct Taxes shall be apportioned among the several States which may be included within this Union, according to their respective Numbers, which shall be determined by adding to the whole Number of free Persons, including those bound to Service for a Term of Years, and excluding Indians not taxed, three fifths of all other Persons [changed by Section 2 of the Fourteenth Amendment]. The actual Enumeration shall be made within three Years after the first Meeting of the Congress of the United States, and within every subsequent Term of ten Years, in such Manner as they shall by Law direct. The Number of Representatives shall not exceed one for every thirty Thousand, but each State shall have at Least one Representative; and until such enumeration shall be made, the State of New Hampshire shall be entitled to choose three, Massachusetts eight, Rhode-Island and Providence Plantations one, Connecticut five, New-York six, New Jersey four, Pennsylvania eight, Delaware one, Maryland six, Virginia ten, North Carolina five, South Carolina five, and Georgia three.

When vacancies happen in the Representation from any State, the Executive Authority thereof shall issue Writs of Election to fill such Vacancies.

The House of Representatives shall choose their Speaker and other Officers; and shall have the sole Power of Impeachment.

Section 3. The Senate of the United States shall be composed of two Senators from each State, *chosen by the Legislature thereof* [changed by the Seventeenth Amendment], for six Years; and each Senator shall have one Vote.

Immediately after they shall be assembled in Consequence of the first Election, they shall be divided as equally as may be into three Classes. The seats of the Senators of the first Class shall be vacated at the Expiration of the second Year, of the second Class at the Expiration of the fourth Year, and of the third Class at the Expiration of the sixth Year, so that one third may be chosen every second Year; *and if Vacancies happen by Resignation, or otherwise, during the Recess of the Legislature of any State, the Executive thereof may make temporary Appointments until the next Meeting of the Legislature, which shall then fill such Vacancies* [changed by Section 2 of the Twentieth Amendment].

No Person shall be a Senator who shall not have attained to the Age of thirty Years, and been nine Years a Citizen of the United States, and who shall not, when elected, be an Inhabitant of that State for which he shall be chosen.

The Vice President of the United States shall be President of the Senate, but shall have no Vote, unless they be equally divided.

The Senate shall choose their other Officers, and also a President pro tempore, in the Absence of the Vice President, or when he shall exercise the Office of President of the United States.

The Senate shall have the sole Power to try all Impeachments. When sitting for that Purpose, they shall be on Oath or Affirmation. When the President of the United States is tried the Chief Justice shall preside: And no Person shall be convicted without the Concurrence of two thirds of the Members present.

Judgment in Cases of Impeachment shall not extend further than to removal from Office, and disqualification to hold and enjoy any Office of honor, Trust or Profit under the United States: but the Party convicted shall nevertheless be liable and subject to Indictment, Trial, Judgment and Punishment, according to Law.

Section 4. The Times, Places and Manner of holding Elections for Senators and Representatives, shall be prescribed in each State by the Legislature thereof; but the Congress may at any time by Law make or alter such Regulations, except as to the Places of choosing Senators.

The Congress shall assemble at least once in every Year, and such Meeting shall be *on the first Monday in December* [changed by Section 2 of the Twentieth Amendment], unless they shall by Law appoint a different Day.

Section 5. Each House shall be the Judge of the Elections, Returns and Qualifications of its own Members, and a Majority of each shall constitute a Quorum to do Business; but a smaller Number may adjourn from day to day, and may be authorized to compel the Attendance of absent Members, in such Manner, and under such Penalties as each House may provide.

Each House may determine the Rules of its Proceedings, punish its Members for disorderly Behaviour, and, with the Concurrence of two thirds, expel a Member.

Each House shall keep a Journal of its Proceedings, and from time to time publish the same, excepting such Parts as may in their Judgment require Secrecy; and the Yeas and Nays of the Members of either House on any question shall, at the Desire of one fifth of those Present, be entered on the Journal.

Neither House, during the Session of Congress, shall, without the Consent of the other, adjourn for more than three days, nor to any other Place than that in which the two Houses shall be sitting.

Section 6. The Senators and Representatives shall receive a Compensation for their Services, to be ascertained by Law, and paid out of the Treasury of the United States. They shall in all Cases, except Treason, Felony and Breach of the Peace, be privileged from Arrest during their Attendance at the Session of their respective Houses, and in going to and returning from the same; and for any Speech or Debate in either House, they shall not be questioned in any other Place.

No Senator or Representative shall, during the Time for which he was elected, be appointed to any civil Office under the Authority of the United States, which shall have been created, or the Emoluments whereof shall have been increased during such time; and no Person holding any Office under the United States, shall be a Member of either House during his Continuance in Office.

Section 7. All Bills for raising Revenue shall originate in the House of Representatives; but the Senate may propose or concur with amendments as on other Bills.

Every Bill which shall have passed the House of Representatives and the Senate, shall, before it be-come a Law, be presented to the President of the United States; If he approve he shall sign it, but if not he shall return it, with his Objections to that House in which it shall have originated, who shall enter the Objections at large on their Journal, and proceed to reconsider it. If after such Reconsideration two thirds of that House shall agree to pass the Bill, it shall be sent, together with the Objections, to the other House, by which it shall likewise be reconsidered, and if approved by two thirds of that House, it shall become a Law. But in all such Cases the Votes of both Houses shall be determined by yeas and Nays, and the Names of the Persons voting for and against the Bill shall be entered on the Journal of each House respectively. If any Bill shall not be returned by the President within ten Days (Sunday excepted) after it shall have been presented to him, the Same shall be a Law, in like Manner as if he had signed it, unless the Congress by their Adjournment prevent its Return, in which Case it shall not be a Law.

Every Order, Resolution, or Vote to which the Concurrence of the Senate and House of Representatives may be necessary (except on a question of Adjournment) shall be presented to the President of the United States; and before the Same shall take Effect, shall be approved by him, or being disapproved by him, shall be repassed by two thirds of the Senate and House of Representatives, according to the Rules and Limitations prescribed in the Case of a Bill.

Section 8. The Congress shall have Power To lay and collect Taxes, Duties, Imposts and Excises, to pay the Debts and provide for the common Defence and general Welfare of the United States; but all Duties, Imposts and Excises shall be uniform throughout the United States;

To borrow Money on the credit of the United States;

To regulate Commerce with foreign Nations, and among the several States, and with the Indian Tribes;

To establish a uniform Rule of Naturalization, and uniform Laws on the subject of Bankruptcies throughout the United States;

To coin Money, regulate the Value thereof, and of foreign Coin, and fix the Standard of Weights and Measures;

To provide for the Punishment of counterfeiting the Securities and current Coin of the United States;

To establish Post Offices and post Roads;

To promote the Progress of Science and useful Arts, by securing for limited Times to Authors and Inventors the exclusive Right to their respective Writings and Discoveries;

To constitute Tribunals inferior to the Supreme Court;

To define and punish Piracies and Felonies committed on the high Seas, and Offences against the Law of Nations;

To declare War, grant Letters of Marque and Reprisal, and make Rules concerning Captures on Land and Water;

To raise and support Armies, but no Appropriation of Money to that Use shall be for a longer Term than two Years;

To provide and maintain a Navy;

To make Rules for the Government and Regulation of the land and naval Forces;

To provide for calling forth the Militia to execute the Laws of the Union, suppress Insurrections and repel Invasions;

To provide for organizing, arming, and disciplining the Militia, and for governing such Part of them as may be employed in the Service of the United States, reserving to the States respectively, the Appointment of the Officers, and the Authority of training the Militia according to the discipline prescribed by Congress;

To exercise exclusive Legislation in all Cases whatsoever, over such District (not exceeding ten Miles square) as may, by Cession of Particular States, and the Acceptance of Congress, become the Seat of the Government of the United States, and to exercise like Authority over all Places purchased by the Consent of the Legislature of the State in which the Same shall be, for the Erection of Forts, Magazines, Arsenals, dock-Yards, and other needful Buildings; And

To make all Laws which shall be necessary and proper for carrying into Execution the foregoing Powers, and all other Powers vested by this Constitution in the Government of the United States, or in any Department or Officer thereof.

Section 9. The Migration or Importation of such Persons as any of the States now existing shall think proper to admit, shall not be prohibited by the Congress prior to the Year one thousand eight hundred and eight, but a Tax or duty may be imposed on such Importation, not exceeding ten dollars for each Person.

The Privilege of the Writ of Habeas Corpus shall not be suspended, unless when in Cases of Rebellion or Invasion the public Safety may require it.

No Bill of Attainder or ex post facto Law shall be passed.

No capitation, or other direct, Tax shall be laid, unless in Proportion to the Census of Enumeration herein before directed to be taken [changed by the Sixteenth Amendment].

No Tax or Duty shall be laid on Articles exported from any State.

No Preference shall be given by any Regulation of Commerce or Revenue to the Ports of one State over those of another; nor shall Vessels bound to, or from,

one State, be obliged to enter, clear or pay Duties in another.

No Money shall be drawn from the Treasury, but in Consequence of Appropriations made by Law; and a regular Statement and Account of the Receipts and Expenditures of all public Money shall be published from time to time.

No Title of Nobility shall be granted by the United States: And no Person holding any Office of Profit or Trust under them, shall, without the Consent of the Congress, accept of any present, Emolument, Office, or Title, of any kind whatever, from any King, Prince or foreign State.

Section 10. No State shall enter into any Treaty, Alliance, or Confederation; grant Letters of Marque and Reprisal; coin Money; emit Bills of Credit; make any Thing but gold and silver Coin a Tender in Payment of Debts; pass any Bill of Attainder, ex post facto Law, or Law impairing the Obligation of Contracts, or grant any Title of Nobility.

No State shall, without the Consent of the Congress, lay any Imposts or Duties on Imports or Exports, except what may be absolutely necessary for executing it's inspection Laws: and the net Produce of all Duties and Imposts, laid by any State on Imports or Exports, shall be for the Use of the Treasury of the United States; and all such Laws shall be subject to the Revision and Control of the Congress.

No State shall, without the Consent of Congress, lay any Duty of Tonnage, keep Troops, or Ships of War in time of Peace, enter into any Agreement or Compact with another State, or with a foreign Power, or engage in War, unless actually invaded, or in such imminent Danger as will not admit of delay.

Article II

Section 1. The executive Power shall be vested in a President of the United States of America. He shall hold his Office during the Term of four Years, and, together with the Vice President, chosen for the same Term, be elected, as follows.

Each State shall appoint, in such Manner as the Legislature thereof may direct, a Number of Electors, equal to the whole Number of Senators and Representatives to which the State may be entitled in the Congress: but no Senator or Representative, or Person holding an Office of Trust or Profit under the United States, shall be appointed an Elector.

The Electors shall meet in their respective States, and vote by Ballot for two Persons, of whom one at least shall not be an Inhabitant of the same State with themselves. And they shall make a List of all the Persons voted for, and of the Number of Votes for each; which List they shall sign and certify, and transmit sealed to the Seat of the Government of the United States, directed to the President of the Senate. The President of the Senate shall, in the Presence of the Senate and House of Representatives, open all the Certificates, and the Votes shall then be counted. The Person having the greatest Number of Votes shall be the President, if such Number be a Majority of the whole Number of Electors appointed; and if there be more than one who have such Majority, and have an equal Number of Votes, then the House of Representatives shall immediately choose by Ballot one of them for President; and if no Person have a Majority, then from the five highest on the list the said House shall in like Manner choose the President. But in choosing the President, the Votes shall be taken by States, the Representation from each State having one Vote; a quorum for this Purpose shall consist of a Member or Members from two thirds of the States, and a Majority of all the States shall be necessary to a Choice. In every Case, after the Choice of the President, the Person having the greatest Number of Votes of the Electors shall be the Vice President. But if there should remain two or more who have equal Votes, the Senate shall choose from them by Ballot the Vice President [changed by the Twelfth Amendment].

The Congress may determine the Time of choosing the Electors, and the Day on which they shall give their Votes; which Day shall be the same throughout the United States.

No Person except a natural born Citizen, or a Citizen of the United States, at the time of the Adoption of this Constitution, shall be eligible to the Office of President; neither shall any Person be eligible to that Office who shall not have attained to the Age of thirty five Years, and been fourteen Years a Resident within the United States.

In Case of the Removal of the President from Office, or of his Death, Resignation, or Inability to discharge the Powers and Duties of the said Office, the Same shall devolve on the Vice President, and the Congress may by Law provide for the Case of Removal, Death, Resignation or Inability, both of the President and Vice President, declaring what Officer shall then act as President, and such Officer shall act accordingly, until the Disability be removed, or a President shall be elected [changed by the Twenty-fifth Amendment].

The President shall, at stated Times, receive for his Services, a Compensation, which shall neither be increased nor diminished during the Period for which he shall have been elected, and he shall not receive within that Period any other Emolument from the United States, or any of them.

Before he enter on the Execution of his Office, he shall take the following Oath or Affirmation: "I do solemnly swear (or affirm) that I will faithfully execute the Office of President of the United States, and will to the best of my Ability, preserve, protect and defend the Constitution of the United States."

Section 2. The President shall be Commander in Chief of the Army and Navy of the United States, and of the Militia of the several States, when called into the actual Service of the United States; he may require the Opinion, in writing, of the principal Officer in each of the executive Departments, upon any Subject relating to the Duties of their respective Offices, and he shall have Power to grant Reprieves and Pardons for Offenses against the United States, except in Cases of Impeachment.

He shall have Power, by and with the Advice and Consent of the Senate, to make Treaties, provided two thirds of the Senators present concur; and he shall nominate, and by and with the Advice and Consent of the Senate, shall appoint Ambassadors, other public Ministers and Consuls, Judges of the Supreme Court, and all other Officers of the United States, whose Appointments are not herein otherwise provided for, and which shall be established by Law: but the Congress may by Law vest the Appointment of such inferior Officers, as they think proper, in the President alone, in the Courts of Law, or in the Heads of Departments.

The President shall have Power to fill up all Vacancies that may happen during the Recess of the Senate, by granting Commissions which shall expire at the End of their next Session.

Section 3. He shall from time to time give to the Congress Information of the State of the Union, and recommend to their Consideration such Measures as he shall judge necessary and expedient; he may, on extraordinary Occasions, convene both Houses, or either of them, and in Case of Disagreement between them, with Respect to the Time of Adjournment, he may adjourn them to such Time as he shall think proper; he shall receive Ambassadors and other public Ministers; he shall take Care that the Laws be faithfully executed, and shall Commission all the Officers of the United States.

Section 4. The President, Vice President and all Civil Officers of the United States, shall be removed from office on Impeachment for, and Conviction of, Treason, Bribery, or other high Crimes and Misdemeanors.

Article III

Section 1. The judicial Power of the United States shall be vested in one Supreme Court, and in such inferior Courts as the Congress may from time to time ordain and establish. The Judges, both of the supreme and inferior Courts, shall hold their Offices during good Behaviour, and shall, at stated Times, receive for their Services, a Compensation, which shall not be diminished during their Continuance in Office.

Section 2. The judicial Power shall extend to all Cases, in Law and Equity, arising under this Constitution, the Laws of the United States, and Treaties made, or which shall be made, under their Authority; to all Cases affecting Ambassadors, other public Ministers and Consuls; to all Cases of admiralty and maritime Jurisdiction; to Controversies to which the United States shall be a Party; to Controversies between two or more States; *between a State and Citizens of another State* [changed by the Eleventh Amendment]; between Citizens of different States; between Citizens of the same State claiming Lands under Grants of different States, *and between a State, or the Citizens thereof, and foreign States, Citizens or Subjects* [changed by the Eleventh Amendment].

In all Cases affecting Ambassadors, other public Ministers and Consuls, and those in which a State shall be Party, the Supreme Court shall have original Jurisdiction. In all the other Cases before mentioned, the Supreme Court shall have appellate Jurisdiction, both as to Law and Fact, with such Exceptions, and under such Regulations as the Congress shall make.

The Trial of all Crimes, except in cases of Impeachment, shall be by Jury; and such Trial shall be held in the State where the said Crimes shall have been committed; but when not committed within any State, the Trial shall be at such Place or Places as the Congress may by Law have directed.

Section 3. Treason against the United States shall consist only in levying War against them, or in adhering to their Enemies, giving them Aid and Comfort. No Person shall be convicted of Treason unless on the Testimony of two Witnesses to the same overt Act, or on Confession in open Court.

The Congress shall have Power to declare the Punishment of Treason, but no Attainder of Treason shall work Corruption of Blood, or Forfeiture except during the Life of the Person attainted.

Article IV

Section 1. Full Faith and Credit shall be given in each State to the public Acts, Records, and judicial Proceedings of all other States. And the Congress may by general Laws prescribe the Manner in which such Acts, Records and Proceedings shall be proved, and the Effect thereof.

Section 2. The Citizens of each State shall be entitled to all Privileges and Immunities of Citizens in the several States.

A Person charged in any State with Treason, Felony, or other Crime, who shall flee from Justice, and be found in another State, shall on Demand of the executive Authority of the State from which he

fled, be delivered up, to be removed to the State having Jurisdiction of the Crime.

No Person held to Service or Labour in one State, under the Laws thereof, escaping into another, shall, in Consequence of any Law or Regulation therein, be discharged from such Service or Labour, but shall be delivered up on Claim of the Party to whom such Service or Labour may be due [changed by the Thirteenth Amendment].

Section 3. New States may be admitted by the Congress into this Union; but no new State shall be formed or erected within the Jurisdiction of any other State; nor any State be formed by the Junction of two or more States, or Parts of States, without the Consent of the Legislatures of the States concerned as well as of the Congress.

The Congress shall have Power to dispose of and make all needful Rules and Regulations respecting the Territory or other Property belonging to the United States; and nothing in this Constitution shall be so construed as to Prejudice any Claims of the United States, or of any particular State.

Section 4. The United States shall guarantee to every State in this Union a Republican Form of Government, and shall protect each of them against Invasion; and on Application of the Legislature, or of the Executive (when the Legislature cannot be convened) against domestic Violence.

Article V

The Congress, whenever two thirds of both Houses shall deem it necessary, shall propose Amendments to this Constitution, or, on the Application of the Legislatures of two thirds of the several States, shall call a Convention for proposing Amendments, which, in either Case, shall be valid to all Intents and Purposes, as Part of this Constitution, when ratified by the Legislatures of three fourths of the several States, or by Conventions in three fourths thereof, as the one or the other Mode of Ratification may be proposed by the Congress; Provided that no Amendment which may be made prior to the Year One thousand eight hundred and eight shall in any Manner affect the first and fourth Clauses in the Ninth Section of the first Article; and that no State, without its Consent, shall be deprived of its equal Suffrage in the Senate.

Article VI

All Debts contracted and Engagements entered into, before the Adoption of this Constitution, shall be as valid against the United States under this Constitution, as under the Confederation.

This Constitution, and the Laws of the United States which shall be made in Pursuance thereof; and all Treaties made, or which shall be made, under the Authority of the United States, shall be the supreme Law of the Land; and the Judges in every State shall be the supreme Law of the Land; and the Judges in every State shall be bound thereby, any Thing in the Constitution or Laws or any State to the Contrary notwithstanding.

The Senators and Representatives before mentioned, and the Members of the several State Legislatures, and all executive and judicial Officers, both of the United States and of the several States, shall be bound by Oath or Affirmation, to support this Constitution; but no religious Test shall ever be required as a Qualification to any Office or public Trust under the United States.

Article VII

The Ratification of the Conventions of nine States, shall be sufficient for the Establishment of this Constitution between the States so ratifying the Same.

❖ AMENDMENTS ❖

Amendment I
[First ten amendments ratified 15 December 1791]

Congress shall make no law respecting an establishment of religion, or prohibiting the free exercise thereof; or abridging the freedom of speech, or of the press; or the right of the people peaceably to assemble, and to petition the Government for a redress of grievances.

Amendment II

A well regulated Militia, being necessary to the security of a free State, the right of the people to keep and bear Arms, shall not be infringed.

Amendment III

No Soldier shall, in time of peace be quartered in any house, without the consent of the Owner, nor in time of war, but in a manner to be prescribed by law.

Amendment IV

The right of the people to be secure in their persons, houses, papers, and effects, against unreasonable searches and seizures, shall not be violated, and no Warrants shall issue, but upon probable cause, supported by Oath or affirmation, and particularly describing the place to be searched, and the persons or things to be seized.

Amendment V

No person shall be held to answer for a capital, or otherwise infamous crime, unless on a presentment or indictment of a Grand Jury, except in cases arising in the land or naval forces, or in the Militia, when in actual service in time of War or public danger; nor shall any person be subject for the same offence to be twice put in jeopardy of life or limb; nor shall be compelled in any criminal case to be a witness against himself, nor be deprived of life, liberty, or property, without due process of law; nor shall private property be taken for public use, without just compensation.

Amendment VI

In all criminal prosecutions, the accused shall enjoy the right to a speedy and public trial, by an impartial jury of the State and district wherein the crime shall have been committed, which district shall have been previously ascertained by law, and to be informed of the nature and cause of the accusation; to be confronted with the witnesses against him; to have compulsory process for obtaining witnesses in his favor, and to have the Assistance of Counsel for his defence.

Amendment VII

In Suits at common law, where the value in controversy shall exceed twenty dollars, the right of trial by jury shall be preserved, and no fact tried by a jury, shall be otherwise re-examined in any Court of the United States, than according to the rules of the common law.

Amendment VIII

Excessive bail shall not be required, nor excessive fines imposed, nor cruel and unusual punishments inflicted.

Amendment IX

The enumeration in the Constitution, of certain rights, shall not be construed to deny or disparage others retained by the people.

Amendment X

The powers not delegated to the United States by the Constitution, nor prohibited by it to the States, are reserved to the States respectively, or to the people.

Amendment XI
[Ratified 7 February 1795]

The Judicial power of the United States shall not be construed to extend to any suit in law or equity, commenced or prosecuted against one of the United States by Citizens of another State, or by Citizens or Subjects of any Foreign State.

Amendment XII
[Ratified 15 June 1804]

The Electors shall meet in their respective states and vote by ballot for President and Vice-President, one of whom, at least, shall not be an inhabitant of the same state with themselves; they shall name in their ballots the person voted for as President, and in distinct ballots the person voted for as Vice-President, and they shall make distinct lists of all persons voted for as President, and of all persons voted for as Vice-President, and of the number of votes for each, which lists they shall sign and certify, and transmit sealed to the seat of the government of the United States, directed to the President of the Senate; The President of the Senate shall, in the presence of the Senate and House of Representatives, open all the certificates and the votes shall then be counted; The person having the greatest number of votes for President, shall be the President, if such number be a majority of the whole number of Electors appointed; and if no person have such majority, then from the persons having the highest numbers not exceeding three on the list of those voted for as President, the House of Representatives shall choose immediately, by ballot, the President. But in choosing the President, the votes shall be taken by states, the representation from each state having one vote; a quorum for this purpose shall consist of a member or members from two-thirds of the states, and a majority of all the states shall be necessary to a choice. *And if the House of Representatives shall not choose a President whenever the right of choice shall devolve upon them, before the fourth day of March next following, then the Vice-President shall act as President, as in the case of the death or other constitutional disability of the President* [superseded by Section 3 of the Twentieth Amendment]. The person having the greatest number of votes as Vice-President, shall be the Vice-President, if such number be a majority of the whole number of Electors appointed, and if no person have a majority, then from the two highest numbers on the list, the Senate shall choose the Vice-President; a quorum for the purpose shall consist of two-thirds of the whole number of Senators, and a majority of the whole number shall be necessary to a choice. But no person constitutionally ineligible to the office of President shall be eligible to that of Vice-President of the United States.

Amendment XIII
[Ratified 6 December 1865]

Section 1. Neither slavery nor involuntary servitude, except as a punishment for crime whereof the party shall have been duly convicted, shall exist within the United States, or any place subject to their jurisdiction. Section 2. Congress shall have power to enforce this article by appropriate legislation.

Amendment XIV
[Ratified 9 July 1868]

Section 1. All persons born or naturalized in the United States and subject to the jurisdiction thereof, are citizens of the United States and of the State wherein they reside. No State shall make or enforce any law which shall abridge the privileges or immunities of citizens of the United States; nor shall any State deprive any person of life, liberty, or property, without due process of law; nor deny to any person within its jurisdiction the equal protection of the laws.

Section 2. Representatives shall be apportioned among the several States according to their respective numbers, counting the whole number of persons in each State, excluding Indians not taxed. But when the right to vote at any election for the choice of electors for President and Vice President of the United States, Representatives in Congress, the Executive and Judicial officers of a State, or the members of the Legislature thereof, is denied to any of the male inhabitants of such State, being twenty-one years of age, and citizens of the United States, or in any way abridged, except for participation in rebellion, or other crime, the basis of representation therein shall be reduced in the proportion which the number of such male citizens shall bear to the whole number of male citizens twenty-one years of age in such State.

Section 3. No person shall be a Senator or Representative in Congress, or elector of President and Vice President, or hold any office, civil or military, under the United States, or under any State, who, having previously taken an oath, as a member of Congress, or as an officer of the United States, or as a member of any State legislature, or as an executive or judicial officer of any State, to support the Constitution of the United States, shall have engaged in insurrection or rebellion against the same, or given aid or comfort to the enemies thereof. But Congress may by a vote of two-thirds of each House, remove such disability.

Section 4. The validity of the public debt of the United States, authorized by law, including debts incurred for payment of pensions and bounties for services in suppressing insurrection or rebellion, shall not be questioned. But neither the United States nor any State shall assume or pay any debt or obligation incurred in aid of insurrection or rebellion against the United States, or any claim for the loss or emancipation of any slave; but all such debts, obligations and claims shall be held illegal and void.

Section 5. The Congress shall have power to enforce, by appropriate legislation, the provisions of this article.

Amendment XV
[Ratified 3 February 1870]

Section 1. The right of citizens of the United States to vote shall not be denied or abridged by the United States or by any State on account of race, color, or previous condition of servitude.

Section 2. The Congress shall have power to enforce this article by appropriate legislation.

Amendment XVI
[Ratified 3 February 1913]

The Congress shall have power to lay and collect taxes on incomes, from whatever source derived, without apportionment among the several States, and without regard to any census or enumeration.

Amendment XVII
[Ratified 8 April 1913]

The Senate of the United States shall be composed of two Senators from each State, elected by the people thereof, for six years; and each Senator shall have one vote. The electors in each State shall have the qualifications requisite for electors of the most numerous branch of the State legislatures.

When vacancies happen in the representation of any State in the Senate, the executive authority of such State shall issue writs of election to fill such vacancies: Provided, That the legislature of any State may empower the executive thereof to make temporary appointments until the people fill the vacancies by election as the legislature may direct.

This amendment shall not be so construed as to affect the election or term of any Senator chosen before it becomes valid as part of the Constitution.

Amendment XVIII
[Ratified 16 January 1919; repealed by the Twenty-first Amendment]

Section 1. After one year from the ratification of this article the manufacture, sale, or transportation of intoxicating liquors within, the importation thereof

into, or the exportation thereof from the United States and all territory subject to the jurisdiction thereof for beverage purposes is hereby prohibited.

Section 2. The Congress and the several States shall have concurrent power to enforce this article by appropriate legislation.

Section 3. This article shall be inoperative unless it shall have been ratified as an amendment to the Constitution by the legislatures of the several States, as provided in the Constitution, within seven years from the date of the submission hereof to the States by the Congress.

Amendment XIX
[Ratified 18 August 1920]

The right of citizens of the United States to vote shall not be denied or abridged by the United States or by any State on account of sex.

Congress shall have power to enforce this article by appropriate legislation.

Amendment XX
[Ratified 23 January 1933]

Section 1. The terms of the President and Vice President shall end at noon on the 20th day of January, and the terms of Senators and Representatives at noon on the 3rd day of January, of the years in which such terms would have ended if this article had not been ratified; and the terms of their successors shall then begin.

Section 2. The Congress shall assemble at least once in every year, and such meeting shall begin at noon on the 3d day of January, unless they shall by law appoint a different day.

Section 3. If, at the time fixed for the beginning of the term of the President, the President elect shall have died, the Vice President elect shall become President. If a President shall not have been chosen before the time fixed for the beginning of his term, or if the President elect shall have failed to qualify, then the Vice President elect shall act as President until a President shall have qualified; and the Congress may by law provide for the case wherein neither a President elect nor a Vice President elect shall have qualified, declaring who shall then act as President, or the manner in which one who is to act shall be selected, and such person shall act accordingly until a President or Vice President shall have qualified.

Section 4. The Congress may by law provide for the case of the death of any of the persons from whom the House of Representatives may choose a President whenever the right of choice shall have devolved upon them, and for the case of the death of any of the persons from whom the Senate may choose a Vice President whenever the right of choice shall have devolved upon them.

Section 5. Sections 1 and 2 shall take effect on the 15th day of October following the ratification of this article.

Section 6. This article shall be inoperative unless it shall have been ratified as an amendment to the Constitution by the legislatures of three-fourths of the several States within seven years from the date of its submission.

Amendment XXI
[Ratified 5 December 1933]

Section 1. The eighteenth article of amendment to the Constitution of the United States is hereby repealed.

Section 2. The transportation or importation into any State, Territory or possession of the United States for delivery or use therein of intoxicating liquors, in violation of the laws thereof, is hereby prohibited.

Section 3. This article shall be inoperative unless it shall have been ratified as an amendment to the Constitution by conventions in the several States, as provided in the Constitution, within seven years from the date of the submission hereof to the States by the Congress.

Amendment XXII
[Ratified 27 February 1951]

Section 1. No person shall be elected to the office of the President more than twice, and no person who has held the office of President, or acted as President, for more than two years of a term to which some other person was elected President shall be elected to the office of the President more than once. But this Article shall not apply to any person holding the office of President when this Article was proposed by the Congress, and shall not prevent any person who may be holding the office of President, or acting as President, during the term within which this Article becomes operative from holding the office of President or acting as President during the remainder of such term.

Section 2. This Article shall be inoperative unless it shall have been ratified as an amendment to the Constitution by the legislatures of three-fourths of the several States within seven years from the date of its submission to the States by the Congress.

Amendment XXIII
[Ratified 29 March 1961]

Section 1. The District constituting the seat of Government of the United States shall appoint in such manner as the Congress may direct:

A number of electors of President and Vice President equal to the whole number of Senators and Representatives in Congress to which the District would be entitled if it were a State, but in no event more than the least populous State; they shall be in addition to those appointed by the States, but they shall be considered, for the purposes of the election of President and Vice President, to be electors appointed by a State; and they shall meet in the District and perform such duties as provided by the twelfth article of amendment.

Section 2. The Congress shall have power to enforce this article by appropriate legislation.

Amendment XXIV
[Ratified 23 January 1964]

Section 1. The right of citizens of the United States to vote in any primary or other election for President or Vice President, for electors for President or Vice President, or for Senator or Representative in Congress, shall not be denied or abridged by the United States or any State by reason of failure to pay any poll tax or other tax.

Section 2. The Congress shall have power to enforce this article by appropriate legislation.

Amendment XXV
[Ratified 10 February 1967]

Section 1. In case of the removal of the President from office or of his death or resignation, the Vice President shall become President.

Section 2. Whenever there is a vacancy in the office of the Vice President, the President shall nominate a Vice President who shall take office upon confirmation by a majority vote of both Houses of Congress.

Section 3. Whenever the President transmits to the President pro tempore of the Senate and the Speaker of the House of Representatives his written declaration that he is unable to discharge the powers and duties of his office, and until he transmits to them a written declaration to the contrary, such powers and duties shall be discharged by the Vice President as Acting President.

Section 4. Whenever the Vice President and a majority of either the principal officers of the executive departments or of such other body as Congress may by law provide, transmit to the President pro tempore of the Senate and the Speaker of the House of Representatives their written declaration that the President is unable to discharge the powers and duties of his office, the Vice President shall immediately assume the powers and duties of the office as Acting President.

Thereafter, when the President transmits to the President pro tempore of the Senate and the Speaker of the House of Representatives his written declaration that no inability exists, he shall resume the powers and duties of his office unless the Vice President and a majority of either the principal officers of the executive department or of such other body as Congress may by law provide, transmit within four days to the President pro tempore of the Senate and the Speaker of the House of Representatives their written declaration that the President is unable to discharge the powers and duties of his office. Thereupon Congress shall decide the issue, assembling within forty-eight hours for that purpose if not in session. If the Congress,

within twenty-one days after receipt of the latter written declaration, or, if Congress is not in session, within twenty-one days after Congress is required to assemble, determines by two-thirds vote of both houses that the President is unable to discharge the powers and duties of his office, the Vice President shall continue to discharge the same as Acting President; otherwise, the President shall resume the powers and duties of his office.

Amendment XXVI
[Ratified 1 July 1971]

Section 1. The right of citizens of the United States, who are eighteen years of age or older, to vote shall not be denied or abridged by the United States or by any State on account of age.

Section 2. The Congress shall have power to enforce this article by appropriate legislation.

Amendment XXVII
[Ratified 8 May 1992]

No law, varying the compensation for the services of the Senators and Representatives, shall take effect, until an election of Representatives shall have intervened.

APPENDIX B

Dates Amendments Were Proposed and Ratified

Amendment Number	Date Congress Proposed	Date Ratified
1-10	26 September 1789	15 December 1791
11	Senate: 4 March 1794	7 February 1795
	House: 4 March 1794	
12	Senate: 3 December 1803	15 June 1804
	House: 9 December 1803	
13	Senate: 8 April 1864	6 December 1865
	House: 31 January 1865	
14	Senate: 8 June 1866	9 July 1868
	House: 13 June 1866	
15	Senate: 26 February 1869	3 February 1870
	House: 25 February 25 1869	
16	Senate: 5 July 5 1909	3 February 1913
	House: 12 July 1909	
17	Senate: 9 June 1911	8 April 1913
	House: 13 April 1911	
18	Senate: 18 December 1917	16 January 1919
	House: 17 December 1917	
19	Senate: 4 June 1919	18 August 1920
	House: 21 May 1919	
20	Senate: 6 January 1932	23 January 1933
	House: 16 February 1932	
21	Senate: 16 February 1933	5 December 1933
	House: 20 February 1933	
22	Senate: 12 March 1947	27 February 1951
	House: 6 February 1947	
23	Senate: 2 February 1960	29 March 1961
	House: 14 June 1960	
24	Senate: 27 March 1962	23 January 1964
	House: 27 August 1962	
25	Senate: 19 February 1965	10 February 1967
	House: 13 April 1965	
26	Senate: 10 March 1971	1 July 1971
	House: 23 March 1971	
27	26 September 1787	8 May 1991

Most of this information was adapted from information found in an appendix entitled "Congressional Votes on Amendments" in U.S. Senate, Subcommittee on the Constitution, Committee on the Judiciary. *Amendments to the Constitution: A Brief Legislative History* (Washington D.C.: U.S. Government Printing Office, 1985), pp. 99–133.

APPENDIX C

Number of Amendments by Decade

Decade	Amendments Proposed (Approximate)	Amendments Adopted
1780s	196	0
1790s	42	1
1800s	65	1
1810s	93	0
1820s	111	0
1830s	102	0
1840s	59	0
1850s	22	0
1860s	518	3
1870s	177	0
1880s	264	0
1890s	265	0
1900s	269	0
1910s	467	3
1920s	393	1
1930s	646	2
1940s	404	0
1950s	793	1
1960s	2,598	3
1970s	2,019	1
1980s	827	0
1990s*	—	1

*As of mid-1996.

APPENDIX D

Most Popular Amending Proposals by Year &
Key Events and Publications Related to Constitutional Amendments

Year	Number of Proposals[1]	Key Events[2]	Most Frequent Proposals Introduced in Congress[3]
1683		William Penn includes amending provision in charter	
1775		American Revolution begins	
1776		Declaration of Independence written defending Revolution States begin writing constitutions	
1777		Continental Congress proposes Articles of Confederation	
1781		Articles of Confederation ratified Battle of Yorktown marks defeat of British forces	
1786		Annapolis Convention meets to discuss commercial problems Shays's Rebellion stirs fear of governmental collapse	
1787		Continental Congress adopts Northwest Ordinance regulating settlement in the territories Constitutional Convention meets in Philadelphia	
1788	124	Federalists and Anti-Federalists debate merits of new Constitution	Bill of Rights
1789	173	George Washington assumes presidency Congress decides to add new amendments to the end of the Constitution rather than incorporating them in the text After an effort led by James Madison, Congress proposes 12 amendments, 10 of which will become the Bill of Rights and 1 of which will be putatively ratified in 1992	Bill of Rights
1791	15	States ratify Bill of Rights Washington accepts Hamilton's proposal for national bank	The judiciary
1793	8	*Chisholm v. Georgia* allows states to be sued by out-of-state citizens	Judiciary (suits against the states)
1794	6	Congress proposes Eleventh Amendment limiting suits against states	Judicial jurisdiction

Year	Number of Proposals[1]	Key Events[2]	Most Frequent Proposals Introduced in Congress[3]
1795	4	States ratify Eleventh Amendment	Legislative terms
1797	1		Selection of executive
1798	5	*Hollingsworth v. Virginia* decides that president's signature not needed for amendment Federalist-dominated Congress passes Alien and Sedition Acts Madison and Jefferson write Virginia and Kentucky resolutions	Officeholding restricted to native-born
1799	2		Electors to designate choice of president
1800	7	Realigning presidential election passes control from Federalists to Democratic-Republicans and results in Jefferson-Burr tie	Selection of president
1801	1	John Marshall becomes chief justice of United States	Uniform method of selecting president
1802	12		Choice of executive
1803	7	John Marshall issues decision in *Marbury v. Madison* establishing judicial review Congress proposes Twelfth Amendment altering electoral college Louisiana is purchased without adoption of constitutional amendment	Choice of executive
1804	4	States ratify the Twelfth Amendment	Slave importation
1805	4	Samuel Chase brought to trial before Senate on impeachment charges but not convicted	Judicial jurisdiction and removal of judges
1806	10		Slave importation
1807	2	Jefferson imposes embargo in attempt to avert war with European powers	Judicial jurisdiction and compensation
1808	16	American participation in slave trade ended	Judicial, legislative, executive reforms
1809	2		Duration of embargoes
1810	3	Congress proposes amendment limiting titles of nobility; never ratified	Titles of nobility Exclusion of congressmen from executive offices
1811	2		Removal of judges Executive appointments

Year	Number of Proposals[1]	Key Events[2]	Most Frequent Proposals Introduced in Congress[3]
1812	2	U.S. and Britain engage in War of 1812	Export duties Removal of judges Legislative terms
1813	9		Choice of executive and legislators by districts
1814	9		Internal improvements National bank Legislative terms
1815	8	Hartford Convention meets Americans hear of end of war of 1812 after Jackson routs British troops at New Orleans	Slavery War-power issues
1816	30	American Colonization Society founded with intention of settling African Americans abroad	War and embargo powers Choice of executive and legislators by districts
1817	8		Choice of executive and legislators by districts
1818	19		Choice of executive and legislators by districts
1819	3	*McCulloch v. Maryland* upholds constitutionality of U.S. bank	Choice of executive and legislators by districts
1820	10	Congress adopts Missouri Compromise, limiting slavery in the territories	National bank prohibited
1821	8		Choice of executive and legislators by districts
1822	9		Choice of executive Compensation of Congress Internal improvements
1823	18	President James Monroe announces the Monroe Doctrine to deter European expansion in Western Hemisphere	Choice of executive and legislators
1824	5	Election of 1824 results in no winner; contest goes to U.S. House of Representatives, where John	Choice of executive by districts

Year	Number of Proposals[1]	Key Events[2]	Most Frequent Proposals Introduced in Congress[3]
1825	9	Quincy Adams is selected Augustus B. Woodward publishes *The Presidency of the United States*	No third term Choice of executive by districts
1826	30	Thomas Jefferson and John Adams both die on the fiftieth anniversary of the Declaration of Independence	Choice of executive
1827	5		Choice of executive
1828	6	Andrew Jackson elected president Next four years mark controversy over national tariffs	Choice of executive
1829	11		Choice of executive
1830	5		Choice of executive
1831		Anti-Mason Party holds first national nominating convention; other parties follow, replacing "King Caucus" in Congress	Choice of executive
1832	19		Choice of executive Division of state and federal powers
1833	4	*Barron v. Baltimore* says that Bill of Rights limits only the national government	Choice of executive
1834	6		Choice of executive
1835	12	Roger B. Taney is appointed chief justice of United States	Choice of executive Terms and removal of judges
1836	18		Choice of executive
1837	7		Choice of executive
1838	16		Choice of executive
1839	12		Executive powers
1840	5		One term for executive
1841	12	William Henry Harrison dies in office and is succeeded by Vice President John Tyler	One term for executive
1842	14		Executive powers
1843	3		Executive choice and term

Year	Number of Proposals[1]	Key Events[2]	Most Frequent Proposals Introduced in Congress[3]
1844	8		Choice of executive
1845	1		Choice of executive
1846	6	U.S. enters two-year war with Mexico	Executive selection and term
1847	1		Limit judicial review of state legislation
1848	4	Seneca Falls Convention calls for women's suffrage	Executive powers
1849	5	*Luther v. Borden* clarifies political questions doctrine	Executive offices
1850	9	Congress adopts Compromise of 1850 in unsuccessful attempt to heal growing sectional divisions	Executive powers and offices
1851	4		Assorted
1852	4		Direct election of senators
1853	1		Choice of executive by districts
1854	3	Kansas-Nebraska Act opens decision about slavery in the territories to "popular sovereignty" Republican Party is founded in Ripon, Wisconsin	Executive and legislative branches
1857	0	*Scott v. Sandford* invalidates Missouri Compromise and declares that African Americans cannot become citizens	
1858	1	John Brown and his followers adopt a new provisional constitution	Qualification to vote for Congress
1859	0	John Brown and his followers launch unsuccessful raid at Harper's Ferry	
1860	74	Abraham Lincoln becomes first Republican elected president	Slavery-related issues
1861	121	Congress proposes Corwin Amendment, which is never ratified by the states Unsuccessful "Peace Convention" is convened The Civil War starts The Southern states draw up their own constitution William B. Wedgewood publishes *The Reconstruction of the Government of the United States*	Slavery-related issues
1862	8	Sidney George Fisher publishes *Trial of the Constitution*, commending British model of constitutional change	Slavery and chief executive

Year	Number of Proposals[1]	Key Events[2]	Most Frequent Proposals Introduced in Congress[3]
1863	2	Congress abolishes slavery in District of Columbia Emancipation Proclamation goes into effect but applies only behind enemy lines	Slavery prohibited
1864	57	Senate proposes Thirteenth Amendment abolishing slavery Robert Beasley publishes *A Plan to Stop the Present and Prevent Future Wars*, proposing new constitution	Slavery prohibited
1865	26	House proposes and states ratify Thirteenth Amendment Civil War ends Lincoln is assassinated	Slavery Representation Suffrage
1866	129	Congress proposes Fourteenth Amendment extending rights of citizenship Southern Reconstruction begins John A. Jameson publishes first edition of *Treatise on Constitutional Conventions* denying that such conventions are sovereign	Apportionment of representatives Suffrage Equal rights
1867	29		Citizenship Executive term and selection
1868	25	U.S. Senate impeaches President Andrew Johnson; House falls a single vote short of majority needed to convict him	Executive choice and qualifications Suffrage
1869	76	Congress proposes Fifteenth Amendment extending suffrage to blacks Susan B. Anthony and Elizabeth Cady Stanton found the National Woman Suffrage Association; their rivals found the American Woman Suffrage Association The Anti-Prohibition Party founded Congress establishes number of Supreme Court justices at nine	Suffrage
1870	6	States ratify Fifteenth Amendment Victoria C. Woodhull proposes a Constitution of the United States of the World	Suffrage
1871	13		Executive eligibility and terms
1872	16		Executive choice, eligibility, term
1873	19	*Slaughterhouse Cases* restrict privileges and immunities clause of the Fourteenth Amendment	Executive choice and term Legislative compensation
1874	10	Women's Christian Temperance Union is founded	Direct election of

Year	Number of Proposals[1]	Key Events[2]	Most Frequent Proposals Introduced in Congress[3]
1875	11	Decision in *Minor v. Happersett* declares that women are not entitled to vote under the Fourteenth Amendment	senators Single six-year executive term
1876	34	Disputed election of 1876 goes to U.S. House of Representatives Centennial of the Declaration of Independence	No establishment of religion Executive choice and terms
1877	22	End of congressional Reconstruction; federal troops leave the South	Choice of executive
1878	20		War claims prohibited
1879	26	Centennial of George Washington's inauguration Albert Stickney publishes *A True Republic*	War claims Item veto
1880	13		Choice of executive
1881		Supreme Court upholds constitutionality of income tax in *Springer v. United States*	Alcoholic prohibition
1882	35		Item veto
1883	29	*Civil Rights Cases of 1883* restrict Fourteenth Amendment by focusing on distinction between state and federal action Pendleton Act establishes civil service system	Item veto
1884	33	Henry C. Lockwood publishes *The Abolition of the Presidency*	Congressional powers
1885	14		Direct election of senators
1886	35		Prohibition of polygamy
1887	12	Centennial of U.S. Constitution	Dates of congressional sessions
1888	42		Regulation of polygamy
1889	30		Uniform laws on marriage and divorce Beginning of sessions of Congress and

Year	Number of Proposals[1]	Key Events[2]	Most Frequent Proposals Introduced in Congress[3]
1890	19	Christopher Tiedeman publishes *The Unwritten Constitution of the United States* Rival women's suffrage associations merge into the National American Woman Suffrage Association (NAWSA) *Hans v. Louisiana* effectively interprets the Eleventh Amendment as a restatement rather than an amendment of the Constitution	Popular election of senators
1891	7		Popular election of senators
1892	57	Columbian Exposition in Chicago marks 400th anniversary of Columbus's discovery of the New World	Popular election of senators
1893	27		Popular election of senators
1894	18		Limit president to one term
1895	23	*Pollock v. Farmers' Loan & Trust* outlaws income tax	Direct election of senators
1896	26	*Plessy v. Ferguson* endorses "separate but equal" Herman Ames publishes first list and analysis of constitutional amendments in nation's first century Frederick Upham Adams publishes *President John Smith* with proposed text of new constitution Utah is admitted to the Union after extensive debates about the need for an amendment outlawing polygamy. William McKinley defeats William Jennings Bryan in critical presidential election	Direct election of senators Women's suffrage
1897	31	Henry O. Morris publishes *Waiting for the Signal: A Novel*	Income tax
1898	14	U.S. fights Spain in a war that leads to acquisition of overseas territories	Income tax
1899	43		Uniform marriage and divorce laws; prohibit polygamy
1900	27		Uniform marriage and divorce laws Income tax
1901	42		Direct election of senators

Year	Number of Proposals[1]	Key Events[2]	Most Frequent Proposals Introduced in Congress[3]
1902	20		president Income tax Regulation of trusts
1903	25		Direct election of senators Income tax
1904	9		Assorted proposals
1905	25	*Lochner v. New York* invalidates New York's limits on the hours of bakers and highlights growth of substantive due process	Direct election of senators
1906	18		Direct election of senators Six-year presidential term
1907	45		Direct election of senators Election of federal judges
1908	20	Woodrow Wilson publishes *Constitutional Government in the United States*	Direct election of senators
1909	38	Congress proposes Sixteenth Amendment legitimizing income tax	Direct election of senators
1910	25	Walter Dodd publishes *The Revision and Amendment of State Constitutions*	Change date that Congress convenes
1911	47	Congress proposes Seventeenth Amendment providing for direct election of senators The size of the U.S. House of Representatives is capped at 435	Direct election of senators
1912	42		Change presidential term length and limit terms Election and terms for judges
1913	74	States ratify Sixteenth Amendment States ratify Seventeenth Amendment	Change presidential term length and limit terms Popular election of president Prohibition of alcohol
1914	38	World War I begins in Europe Alice Paul forms the Congressional Union for	Prohibition of alcohol

Year	Number of Proposals[1]	Key Events[2]	Most Frequent Proposals Introduced in Congress[3]
1915	39	Woman Suffrage Eustace Reynolds publishes *The New Constitution: A Suggested Form of Modified Government*	Women's suffrage
1916	48	Jones Act promises eventual independence to Philippines	Election of president by popular vote
1917	75	U.S. enters World War I Congress proposes Eighteenth Amendment providing for national alcoholic prohibition	Women's suffrage
1918	23	*Hammer v. Dagenhart* invalidates use of federal commerce power to regulate child labor	Restricting voting to citizens
1919	56	States ratify Eighteenth Amendment Congress proposes Nineteenth Amendment extending suffrage to women President Wilson suffers stroke during unsuccessful attempt to secure U.S. participation in League of Nations "Red scare" reflects fear of communism in aftermath of the Russian Revolution of 1917 Roger Hoar publishes *Constitutional Conventions: Their Nature, Powers and Limitations*	Women's suffrage
1920	20	States ratify Nineteenth Amendment *National Prohibition* cases declare that "two-thirds" means two-thirds of a quorum *Hawke v. Smith* overturns state requirement that amendments be ratified by state referendum *Missouri v. Holland* raises fears that treaties might take away individual rights	Treaty ratification Presidential disability Amendment ratification
1921	61	*Dillon v. Gloss* expresses need for amendments to reflect contemporary consensus U.S. House of Representatives adopts anti-lynching law that is subsequently defeated in the Senate	Changes in amending procedure
1922	39	*Bailey v. Drexel Furniture Company* invalidates use of federal taxing power to regulate child labor William MacDonald publishes *A New Constitution for a New America*	Child labor amendment
1923	86		Child labor
1924	30	Congress proposes child labor amendment; never ratified	Child labor Income tax
1925	31	Herbert Horwill publishes *The Usages of the American Constitution*, stressing role of customs and usages	Dates of terms for president and Congress
1926	20	*Myers v. United States* upholds broad presidential removal	Dates of terms for

Year	Number of Proposals[1]	Key Events[2]	Most Frequent Proposals Introduced in Congress[3]
1926 (cont.)		powers	president and Congress Repeal Eighteenth Amendment
1927	42	Charles Lindbergh crosses the Atlantic in *Spirit of St. Louis*	Repeal or modify Eighteenth Amendment
1928	30		Amending procedures
1929	34	Stock market crash leads to Great Depression M. A. Musmanno publishes second analysis of amendments	Modify Eighteenth Amendment
1930	31		Modify or repeal Eighteenth Amendment
1931	61	*United States v. Sprague* says Congress has choice of how amendments are ratified and refuses to accept implicit limits on the amending process	Modify or repeal Eighteenth Amendment
1932	100	Franklin D. Roosevelt is elected president William Kay Wallace publishes *Our Obsolete Constitution*	Repeal Eighteenth Amendment
1933	62	FDR launches his ambitious New Deal programs	Provide for taxation of income from securities
1934	28		Provide for taxation of income from securities
1935	69	William Yandell Elliott publishes *The Need for Constitutional Reform*, advocating parliamentary mechanisms *Schechter Poultry Corp. v. United States* invalidates FDR's National Industrial Recovery Act; other decisions invalidate other New Deal programs U.S. Supreme Court moves into its own building, across from the Capitol	Provide for taxation of income from securities
1936	29		Minimum wage Regulation of agriculture
1937	154	U.S. Constitution has its sesquicentennial FDR introduces "court-packing" plan Court inaugurates historic "switch in time that saves nine" in *West Coast Hotel v. Parrish* and *N.L.R.B. v. Jones & Laughlin Steel Corp.* *Palko v. Connecticut* articulates "selective incorporation"	Reform of judiciary Taxation of securities War-related issues

Year	Number of Proposals[1]	Key Events[2]	Most Frequent Proposals Introduced in Congress[3]
1937 (cont.)		of the Bill of Rights to the states Ralph Cram publishes *The End of Democracy*, advocating an iconoclastic scheme of constitutional reform	
1938	24	Justice Stone authors famous footnote in *Carolene Products* case Hugh Hamilton publishes *A Second Constitution for the United States of America*	War-related issues
1939	88	*Coleman v. Miller* declares that most amending issues are "political questions" World War II begins in Europe	War-related issues Old-age assistance
1940	4	FDR runs for unprecedented third term	Two-term presidential limit
1941	45	Japanese attack Pearl Harbor; U.S. enters World War II Thomas Upham publishes *Total Democracy: A New Constitution for the United States, a Democratic Ideal for the World*	Limit terms of president
1942	12	Henry Hazlitt advocates a parliamentary system in *A New Constitution Now* Lester Orfield publishes *The Amending of the Federal Constitution*	Suffrage for 18-year-olds
1943	46	Alexander Hehmeyer publishes *Time for Change: A Proposal for a Second Constitutional Convention*	Ratification of amendments 18-year-old vote Presidential term limits
1944	22	FDR successfully runs for unprecedented fourth term	Limit presidential terms
1945	116	Thomas Finletter publishes *Can Representative Government Do the Job?* FDR Dies and Harry Truman assumes presidency World War II ends after U.S. drops two atomic bombs on Japan; cold war follows	Presidential terms Treaty ratification Equal rights amendment
1946	10		Organization of judiciary
1947	78	Congress proposes Twenty-second Amendment, limiting president to two terms *Adamson v. California* reveals diverse judicial views on incorporation controversy	Limit presidential terms
1948	7		Assorted
1949	64		Change or abolish electoral college Equal rights

Year	Number of Proposals[1]	Key Events[2]	Most Frequent Proposals Introduced in Congress[3]
1950	11	U.S. comes to aid of South Korea under UN flag	amendment Electors for District of Columbia
1951	73	States ratify Twenty-second Amendment	Change or abolish electoral college Equal rights amendment Limit treaties
1952	31	*Steel Seizure* cases invalidate Truman's takeover of steel industry	Treaties in conflict with Constitution
1953	120	President Eisenhower appoints Earl Warren as chief justice	Limit treaties and executive agreements Reform electoral college Equal rights amendment
1954	43	*Brown v. Board of Education* calls for desegregation and overturns *Plessy v. Ferguson* U.S. Senate narrowly defeats a version of the Bricker amendment designed to limit scope of treaties	Amending procedures
1955	115	Dr. Martin Luther King Jr. leads Montgomery bus boycott after Rosa Parks refuses to give up her seat	Change electoral college Scope of treaties Equal rights amendment
1956	27		Electoral college reform
1957	141		Electoral college reform Treaties Equal rights amendment Admission of new states Tax limits
1958	38	President Eisenhower sends troops to Little Rock, Arkansas, to uphold authority of federal law against southern defiance	Limit state collection of taxes on nonresidents Presidential disability
1959	194	Alaska and Hawaii become 49th and 50th states admitted to the Union	Equal rights amendment
1960	28	Congress proposes Twenty-third Amendment granting electors to District of Columbia	Alter electoral college

Year	Number of Proposals[1]	Key Events[2]	Most Frequent Proposals Introduced in Congress[3]
1961	291	States ratify Twenty-third Amendment	Equal rights amendment Direct election of president
1962	105	Congress proposes Twenty-fourth Amendment abolishing use of poll tax in federal elections *Engel v. Vitale* outlaws public prayer in public schools *Baker v. Carr* decides that state legislative apportionment is a justiciable issue Council of State Governments calls for liberalization of the amending process Cuban missile crisis stimulates fears about the emergency functioning of the government	Prayer in schools
1963	395	Dr. Martin Luther King Jr. delivers famous "I Have a Dream" speech at March on Washington, D.C. President John F. Kennedy is assassinated	Prayer in schools Equal rights amendment Electoral college reform
1964	130	Civil Rights Act of 1964 outlaws racial discrimination in places of public accommodation States ratify Twenty-fourth Amendment *Reynolds v. Sims* extends one-person, one-vote principle to both houses of state legislatures; *Wesberry v. Sanders* applies standard to House congressional districts	State legislative apportionment
1965	411	Congress proposes Twenty-fifth Amendment on presidential disability Congress adopts Voting Rights Act of 1965 *Griswold v. Connecticut* establishes a constitutional right to privacy and strikes down Connecticut birth-control law	State legislative apportionment Equal rights amendment Presidential disability Prayer in schools
1966	88	*Harper v. Virginia State Board of Education* strikes down use of poll tax in state elections *Miranda v. Arizona* expands rights of criminal defendants and stirs criticisms of the Supreme Court	Equal rights amendment Prayer in schools
1967	403	States ratify Twenty-fifth Amendment Senator Sam Ervin introduces the Federal Constitutional Convention Act, but it is not adopted President Johnson appoints Thurgood Marshall, the first African American to serve on the U.S. Supreme Court	Equal rights amendment Right to vote Prayer in schools Electoral college
1968	122	States appear on verge of calling a constitutional convention on state legislative apportionment Martin Luther King Jr. and Robert Kennedy are assassinated	Appointment, tenure, removal of judges Equal rights amendment

Year	Number of Proposals[1]	Key Events[2]	Most Frequent Proposals Introduced in Congress[3]
1968 (cont.)		George Wallace makes impressive showing in three-way race for president that Richard Nixon wins	Electoral college
1969	625	Nixon appoints Warren Burger as chief justice to replace retiring Earl Warren American astronauts take first walk on the moon Number of amendments proposed in Congress is the most in any year since the nation's founding	Equal rights amendment Direct election of president Prayer in public places
1970	149	*Oregon v. Mitchell* rules that Congress can lower voting ages for federal but not for state elections Black Panthers meet in Philadelphia in a "Revolutionary People's Convention"	Equal rights amendment Voting rights School busing
1971	453	Congress proposes Twenty-sixth Amendment extending vote to 18-year-olds; states ratify amendment Supreme Court upholds limited use of school busing in *Swann v. Charlotte–Mecklenburg County*	Equal rights amendment School busing Prayer in schools Electoral college
1972	73	Congress proposes equal rights amendment; states do not ratify Leland Baldwin publishes *Reframing the Constitution: An Imperative for Modern America* *Furman v. Georgia* outlaws death penalty as then administered	Nomination and election of president School busing
1973	326	Decision in *Roe v. Wade* extends privacy rights to protect most cases of abortion *Miller v. California* sets standards for regulation of pornography *Frontiero v. Richardson* indicates increasing judicial sensitivity to women's rights Congress adopts war powers resolution to limit future overseas involvements without congressional support Last U.S. troops withdrawn from South Vietnam; it falls to North Vietnamese two years later	School busing Prayer in schools Electoral college Right to life
1974	56	Supreme Court rejects claim of executive privilege in *U.S. v. Nixon* President Nixon resigns from office after Watergate scandal and is pardoned by incoming President Ford Charles Hardin publishes *Presidential Power and Accountability: Toward a New Constitution* Rexford Tugwell publishes *The Emerging Constitution*, advancing the most complete scheme of constitutional reform ever offered in the U.S.	State jurisdiction over abortion Pardon power Balanced budget
1975	273	Lower court decision in *Dyer v. Blair* upholds Illinois' requirement for amendment ratification by a three-fifths majority	Right to life Balanced budget Electoral college

Year	Number of Proposals[1]	Key Events[2]	Most Frequent Proposals Introduced in Congress[3]
1976	58	Bicentennial of Declaration of Independence celebrated	Right to life Congressional tenure
1977	300		Right to life Balanced budget Electoral college
1978	70	Congress proposes amendment to treat District of Columbia as state in Congress; states do not ratify Justice Rehnquist upholds a Nevada advisory referendum on the equal rights amendment in *Kimble v. Swackhamer* Supreme Court rules on affirmative action in Bakke case Alan P. Grimes publishes *Democracy and the Amendments to the Constitution*	Balanced budget Right to life
1979	261	Congress extends seven-year deadline on equal rights amendment for an additional three years	Balanced budget Right to life Direct election of president
1980	29		Right to life
1981	186	Lower court decision in *Idaho v. Freeman* calls into question extension of equal rights amendment and raises possibility of state rescissions President Reagan appoints Sandra Day O'Connor as the first woman to serve on the U.S. Supreme Court	Balanced budget Right to life
1982	35		Balanced budget Equal rights amendment
1983	148	Walter Dellinger publishes influential article in *Harvard Law Review* entitled "The Legitimacy of Constitutional Change: Rethinking the Amending Process"	Balanced budget Right to life Prayer in schools
1984	13	Congress designates the administrator of the General Services Administration to certify the ratification of amendments, a task previously entrusted to the secretary of state and the archivist of the Library of Congress	Item veto Prayer in public places
1985	113	*Garcia v. San Antonio Metropolitan Transit Authority* appears to withdraw judiciary from most federalism issues	Balanced budget
1986	17	James Sundquist publishes Constitutional Reform and Effective Government President Reagan appoints William Rehnquist to replace retiring Chief Justice Warren Burger Challenger space shuttle explodes, killing its crew and temporarily halting further shuttle flights	Assorted issues

Year	Number of Proposals[1]	Key Events[2]	Most Frequent Proposals Introduced in Congress[3]
1987	108	Bicentennial celebrations of U.S. Constitution Committee on the Constitutional System issues proposals for constitutional reform Reagan's nomination of Robert Bork to Supreme Court is rejected but initiates renewed debate about role of the court	Balanced budget Right to life
1988	10	Russell Caplan publishes Constitutional Brinkmanship, a book on the constitutional convention option	Assorted issues
1989	168	Texas v. Johnson upholds constitutional right of flag burning Congress adopts the Flag Protection Act	Flag desecration Balanced budget
1990	16	United States v. Eichman reaffirms constitutional right of flag burning and overturns Flag Protection Act Missouri v. Jenkins stimulates fears that courts might order tax increases	Assorted issues
1991	117	American Operation "Desert Storm" forces Iraqi troops from Kuwait, where they had positioned themselves in a surprise invasion the previous year Bicentennial of the ratification of the Bill of Rights Bruce Ackerman publishes We the People, Foundations, stressing unofficial amending mechanisms John Vile publishes Rewriting the United States, the first of a number of books on proposed new constitutions and the amending process	Balanced budget Term limits Item veto
1992	34	States ratify putative Twenty-seventh Amendment limiting timing of congressional pay raises Barry Krusch publishes The 21st Century Constitution Steven Boyd publishes Alternative Constitutions for the United States In Planned Parenthood v. Casey, the Supreme Court modifies but does not overturn abortion decision in Roe v. Wade	Electoral college Balanced budget
1993	144	Immigration and Naturalization Service v. Chadha strikes down the legislative veto Richard Bernstein and Jerome Agel publish Amending America, a comprehensive history of the amending process in the U.S.	Balanced budget Congressional term limits
1994	12 (List may be incomplete)	House Republicans agree to Contract with America, including a number of proposed amendments Midterm elections end 50-year domination of Congress by Democrats	Congressional tenure
1995	List incomplete	U.S. Term Limits, Inc. v. Thornton indicates that states cannot limit terms of members of Congress	

Year	Number of Proposals[1]	Key Events[2]	Most Frequent Proposals Introduced in Congress[3]
1995 (cont.)		*U.S. v. Lopez* recognizes limits on congressional powers under the commerce clause Senate narrowly rejects flag desecration amendment after House approves it Sanford Levinson publishes book of essays on the amending process entitled *Responding to Imperfection* Chester J. Antieau publishes *A U.S. Constitution for the Year 2000*	
1996	List incomplete	Presidential election highlights many of the issues in the Contract with America, especially a balanced federal budget Kenneth Dolbeare and Janette Hubbell publish *USA 2012: After the Middle-Class Revolution*	

[1]These numbers were compiled from the following lists of amendments:

For the years 1787 through 1889, Herman Ames, *The Proposed Amendments of the Constitution of the United States During the First Century of Its History* (New York: Burt Franklin, 1979; reprint of 1896 edition). (Numbers in 1788–1789 reflect proposals of state ratifying conventions.)

For the years 1889 through 1926, *Proposed Amendments of the Constitution of the United States Introduced in Congress from December 4, 1889, to July 2, 1926,* arranged by Charles C. Tansil (Washington, DC: U.S. Government Printing Office, 1926).

For the years 1927 through 1962, *Proposed Amendments to the Constitution of the United States of America Introduced in Congress from the 69th Congress, 2d Session Through the 87th Congress, 2d Session, December 6, 1926, to January 3, 1963* (Washington, DC: U.S. Government Printing Office, 1963).

For the years 1963 through 1968, *Proposed Amendments to the Constitution of the United States of America Introduced in Congress from the 88th Congress, 1st Session Through the 90th Congress, 2d Session, January 9, 1963, to January 3, 1969* (Washington, DC: U.S. Government Printing Office, 1969).

For the years 1969 through 1984, Richard Davis, *Proposed Amendments to the Constitution of the United States of America Introduced in Congress from the 91st Congress, 1st Session, Through the 98th Congress, 2d Session, January 1969–December 1984,* Congressional Research Service Report No. 85-36 GOV (Washington, DC: Congressional Research Service, 1985).

For the years 1985 through 1990, Daryl B. Harris, *Proposed Amendments to the U.S. Constitution: 99th–101st Congress (1985–1990)* (Washington, DC: Congressional Research Service, Library of Congress, 1992).

For the years from 1990 to the present, lists taken from the Internet by David Huckabee of the Library of Congress.

The list used for the first 100 years includes some proposals that were introduced in state legislatures. Petitions for conventions that occurred in the second 100 years are not included in this survey. Any mistakes made in counting the proposals from each year are mine.

[2]Most events were chosen because of their relation to the amending process, but some are presented merely as markers of contemporaneous events.

[3]I read through each list of amendments and prepared this survey with as much completeness as possible, but with no pretense to absolute accuracy. In a few years marked "assorted," no amendment proposal predominated. In years in which numerous amendments were proposed, the proposals are listed according to their frequency. The number of times that amendments were offered does not necessarily indicate which ones had the most support, since a single amendment might have had multiple cosponsors.

Abraham, Henry J. 1993. *The Judicial Process: An Introductory Analysis of the Courts of the United States, England, and France,* 6th ed. New York: Oxford University Press.

———. 1992. *Justices and Presidents: A Political History of Appointments to the Supreme Court,* 3d ed. New York: Oxford University Press.

Abraham, Henry J., and Barbara Perry. 1994. *Freedom and the Court: Civil Rights and Liberties in the United States,* 6th ed. New York: Oxford University Press.

Abrams, Herbert. 1994. *The President Has Been Shot: Confusion, Disability and the Twenty-fifth Amendment.* Stanford, CA: Stanford University Press.

Abramson, Jeffrey. 1994. *We the Jury: The Jury System and the Ideal of Democracy.* New York: Basic Books.

Academics for the Second Amendment. 1995. "An Open Letter on the Second Amendment." *Chronicle of Higher Education* 41 (11 August): A23.

Ackerman, Bruce. 1996. *We the People: Transformation.* Cambridge, MA: Harvard University Press.

———. 1991. *We the People: Foundations.* Cambridge, MA: Belknap.

———. 1989. "Constitutional Politics/Constitutional Law." *Yale Law Journal* 99 (December): 453–547.

———. 1988. "Transformative Appointments." *Harvard Law Review* 101: 1164–84.

———. 1984. "The Storrs Lectures: Discovering the Constitution." *Yale Law Journal* 93: 1013–72.

———. 1979. "Unconstitutional Convention." *New Republic* 180 (3 March): 8–9.

Ackerman, Bruce, et al. 1995. "An Open Letter to Congressman Gingrich." *Yale Law Journal* 104 (April): 1539–44.

Ackerman, Bruce, and David Golove. 1995. "Is NAFTA Constitutional?" *Harvard Law Review* 108 (February): 799–929.

Ackerman, Bruce, and Ned Katyal. 1991. "Our Unconventional Founding." *University of Chicago Law Review* 62 (Spring): 475–573.

Adams, Frederick U. 1986. *President John Smith: The Story of a Peaceful Revolution.* Chicago: Charles H. Kerr & Company; reprint New York: Arno Press, 1970.

Adams, Henry. 1974. *The Formative Years,* ed. Herbert Agar. 2 vols. Westport, CT: Greenwood Press.

Adler, Mortimer J. 1987. *We Hold These Truths: Understanding the Ideas and the Ideals of the Constitution.* New York: Macmillan.

Advisory Commission on Intergovernmental Relations. 1987. *Is Constitutional Reform Necessary To Reinvigorate Federalism? A Roundtable Discussion.* November. Washington, DC: ACIR.

———. 1986. *Reflections on Garcia and Its Implications for Federalism.* February. Washington, DC: ACIR.

Affirmative Action and Equal Protection. 1981. Hearings before the Subcommittee on the Constitution of the Committee of the Judiciary, U.S. Senate, 97th Cong., 1st Sess., on S.J. 41, 4 May, 11, 18 June, and 16 July. Washington, DC: U.S. Government Printing Office.

Agar, Herbert. 1942. *A Time for Greatness.* Boston: Little, Brown.

Agnes, Richard L. 1994. "Constricting the Law of Freedom: Justice Miller, the Fourteenth Amendment, and the *Slaughter-House Cases.*" *Chicago-Kent Law Review* 70: 627–88.

Alderman, Ellen, and Caroline Kennedy. 1991. *In Our Defense: The Bill of Rights in Action.* New York: William Morrow.

Alexander, Herbert E. 1992. *Financing Politics: Money, Elections and Political Reform,* 4th ed. Washington, DC: Congressional Quarterly Press.

Alfange, Dean, Jr. 1994. "*Marbury v. Madison* and Original Understandings of Judicial Review: In

Defense of Traditional Wisdom." In *Supreme Court Review, 1993*. Chicago: University of Chicago Press.

Amar, Akil R. 1994. "The Consent of the Governed: Constitutional Amendment Outside Article V." *Columbia Law Review* 94 (March): 457–508.

———. 1992. "The Bill of Rights as a Constitution." *Yale Law Journal* 100 (Winter): 1131–1210.

———. 1988. "Philadelphia Revisited: Amending the Constitution Outside Article V." *University of Chicago Law Review* 55 (Fall): 1043–1104.

Ambrose, Stephen E. 1966. *Duty, Honor, Country: A History of West Point*. Baltimore: Johns Hopkins University Press.

American Political Science Association, Committee on Political Parties. 1950. *Toward a More Responsible Two-Party System*. New York: Rinehart.

Ames, Herman. 1896. *The Proposed Amendments to the Constitution of the United States during the First Century of Its History*. New York: Burt Franklin; 1970 reprint.

Anastaplo, George. 1995. *The Amendments to the Constitution: A Commentary*. Baltimore: Johns Hopkins University Press.

———. 1989. *The Constitution of 1787: A Commentary*. Baltimore: Johns Hopkins University Press.

Antieau, Chester J. 1995. *A U.S. Constitution for the Year 2000*. Chicago: Loyola University Press.

Arling, Emanie. 1972. *The Terrible Siren: Victoria Woodhull*. New York: Arno Press.

Ashmore, Harry S. 1970. "Rexford Guy Tugwell: Man of Thought, Man of Action." *Center Magazine* 3 (September/October): 2–7.

Babson, Jennifer. 1995. "House Rejects Term Limits: GOP Blames Democrats." *Congressional Quarterly Weekly Reports* 53 (1 April): 918–19.

Bacon, Margaret H. 1980. *Valiant Friend: The Life of Lucretia Mott*. New York: Walker and Company.

Bacon, Selden. 1930. "How the Tenth Amendment Affected the Fifth Article of the Constitution." *Virginia Law Review* 16 (June): 771–91.

Baker, A. Diane. 1979. "ERA: The Effect of Extending the Time for Ratification on Attempts To Rescind Prior Ratifications." *Emory Law Journal* 28: 71–110.

Baker, Richard A. 1992. "Congress, Arrest and Immunity of Members of." In *The Oxford Companion to the Supreme Court of the United States*, ed. Kermit L. Hall. New York: Oxford Universtiy Press.

Baker, Thomas E. 1995a. "Can Voters Exclude Homosexuals and Their Interests from the Legislative Process?" *Preview of United States Court Cases* (20 September), 11–18.

———. 1995b. "Exercising the Amendment Power To Disapprove of Supreme Court Decisions: A Proposal for a 'Republican Veto.'" *Hastings Constitutional Law Quarterly* 22 (Winter): 325–57.

"The Balanced Budget Amendment: An Inquiry into Appropriateness." 1983. *Harvard Law Review* 96 (May): 1600–20.

Baldwin, Leland. 1972. *Reframing the Constitution: An Imperative for Modern America*. Santa Barbara, CA: ABC-CLIO.

Banner, Lois W. 1980. *Elizabeth Cady Stanton: A Radical for Women's Rights*. Boston: Little, Brown.

Banning, Lance. 1995. *The Sacred Fire of Liberty: James Madison and the Founding of the Federal Republic*. Ithaca, NY: Cornell University Press.

Barber, Benjamin. 1984. *Strong Democracy*. Berkeley: University of California Press.

Barber, Sotirious A. 1984. *On What the Constitution Means*. Baltimore: Johns Hopkins University Press.

Barnette, Randy E., ed. 1989. *The Rights Retained by the People: The History and Meaning of the Ninth Amendment*. Fairfax, VA: George Mason University Press.

Barnum, David G. 1993. *The Supreme Court and American Democracy*. New York: St. Martin's Press.

Baron, Dennis. 1990. *The English-Only Question: An Official Language for America?* New Haven, CT: Yale University Press.

Barone, Michael, and Grant Ujifusa. 1994. *The Almanac of American Politics 1994*. Washington, DC: National Journal.

Basch, Norma. 1992. "Reconstructing Female Citizenship: *Minor v. Happersett*." In *The Constitution, Law, and American Life: Critical Aspects of the Nineteenth Century Experience*, ed. Donald G. Nieman. Athens: University of Georgia Press.

Bates, Stephen. 1991. "Deconstructing the Flag-Burning Debate." *This World & I* 7 (July): 523–29.

Baumer, Donald C., and Carl E. Van Horn. 1985. *The Politics of Employment*. Washington, DC: Congressional Quarterly Press.

Baylor, Gregory S. 1995. "The Religious Equality Amendment." *Christian Legal Society Quarterly* 16 (Summer): 4–5.

Beaney, William M., and Edward N. Beiser. 1973. "Prayer and Politics: The Impact of *Engel* and *Schempp* on the Political Process." In *The Impact of Supreme Court Decisions: Empirical Studies*, 2d ed., ed. Theodore L. Becker and Malcolm M. Feeley. New York: Oxford University Press.

Beasley, Robert. 1864. *A Plan To Stop the Present and Prevent Future Wars: Containing a Proposed Constitution for the General Government of the Sovereign States of North and South America.* Rio Vista, CA: Robert Beasley.

Beatty, Edward C. 1975. *William Penn as Social Philosopher.* New York: Octagon Books.

Beauregard, Erving E. 1989. *Bingham of the Hills: Politician and Diplomat Extraordinary.* New York: Peter Lang.

Becker, Carl L. 1970. *The Declaration of Independence: A Study in the History of Political Ideas.* New York: Vintage Books.

Becker, Theodore L. 1976. *American Government: Past—Present—Future.* Boston: Allyn and Bacon.

Becker, Theodore L., and Malcolm M. Feeley, eds. 1973. *The Impact of Supreme Court Decisions: Empirical Studies,* 2d ed. New York: Oxford University Press.

Belknap, Michael R. 1992. "Communism and the Cold War." In *The Oxford Companion to the Supreme Court of the United States,* ed. Kermit L. Hall. New York: Oxford University Press.

Bell, Roger. 1984. *Last Among Equals: Hawaii Statehood and American Politics.* Honolulu: University of Hawaii Press.

Bellamy, Edward. 1968. *Looking Backward.* New York: Magnum Books.

Benjamin, Gerald, and Michael J. Malbin, eds. 1992. *Limiting Legislative Terms.* Washington, DC: Congressional Quarterly Press.

Benson, Paul R., Jr. 1970. *The Supreme Court and the Commerce Clause, 1937–1970.* New York: Denellen.

Berg, Larry L., Harlan Hahn, and John R. Schmidhauser. 1976. *Corruption in the American Political System.* Morristown, NJ: General Learning Press.

Berger, Raoul. 1973. *Impeachment: The Constitutional Problems.* Cambridge, MA: Harvard University Press.

Berke, Richard L. 1995. "Epic Political Realignments Often Aren't." *New York Times,* 1 January, E-3.

Berns, Walter., ed. 1992. *After the People Vote: A Guide to the Electoral College,* rev. ed. Washington, DC: AEI Press.

Bernstein, Richard B. 1993. "Fixing the Electoral College." *Constitution* 5 (Winter): 42–48.

———. 1992. "The Sleeper Wakes: The History

and Legacy of the Twenty-seventh Amendment." *Fordham Law Review* 56 (December): 497–557.

Bernstein, Richard B., with Jerome Agel. 1993. *Amending America: If We Love the Constitution So Much, Why Do We Keep Trying To Change It?* New York: Random House.

Berry, Mary F. 1987. "How Hard It Is To Change." *New York Times Magazine,* 13 September, 93–98.

———. 1986. *Why ERA Failed: Politics, Women's Rights, and the Amending Process of the Constitution.* Bloomington: Indiana University Press.

Best, Judith. 1984a. "The Item Veto: Would the Founders Approve?" *Presidential Studies Quarterly* 14 (Spring): 183–88.

———. 1984b. *National Representation for the District of Columbia.* Frederick, MD: University Publications of America.

———. 1971. *The Case against Direct Election of the President: A Defense of the Electoral College.* Ithaca, NY: Cornell University Press.

Betts, James T. 1967. "The Scope of Immunity for Legislators and Their Employees." *Yale Law Journal* 77 (December): 366–89.

The Bible in the Public Schools. 1967. Introduction by Robert G. McCloskey. New York: Da Capo Press; reprint of Cincinnati, OH: Robert Clarke & Co., 1870.

"A Bicentennial Analysis of the American Political Structure." 1987. Washington, DC: Report and Recommendations of the Committee on the Constitutional System. January.

Bickel, Alexander. 1986. *The Least Dangerous Branch: The Supreme Court at the Bar of Politics,* 2d ed. New Haven, CT: Yale University Press.

"The Bill of Rights." 1991. Bicentennial issue of *Life* (Fall).

Birkby, Robert H. 1973. "The Supreme Court and the Bible Belt: Tennessee Reaction to the 'Schempp' Decision." In *The Impact of Supreme Court Decisions: Empirical Studies,* 2d ed., ed. Theodore L. Becker and Malcolm M. Feeley. New York: Oxford University Press.

"The Birthright Citizenship Amendment: A Threat to Equality." 1994. *Harvard Law Review* 107: 1026–43.

Biskupic, Joan. 1990. "Critics of Measure Win Fight, but Battle Scars Run Deep." *Congressional Quarterly Weekly Report* 48 (30 June): 2063–64.

Black, Charles L. Jr. 1979. "Amendment by a National Constitutional Convention: A Letter to a Senator." *Oklahoma Law Review* 32: 626–44.

———. 1978. "Correspondence: On Article I, Section 7, Clause 3—and the Amendment of the Constitution." *Yale Law Journal* 87: 896–900.

———. 1963. "The Proposed Amendment of Article V: A Threatened Disaster." *Yale Law Journal* 72 (April): 957–66.

Black, Hugo L. 1969. *A Constitutional Faith*. New York: Alfred A. Knopf.

Black's Law Dictionary. 1969. 5th ed. St. Paul, MN: West.

Bledsoe, Craig W. 1989. "Executive Pay and Perquisites." In *Guide to the Presidency*, ed. Michael Nelson. Washington, DC: Congressional Quarterly Press.

Blocker, Jack S., Jr. 1976. *Retreat from Reform: The Prohibition Movement in the United States, 1890–1916*. Westport, CT: Greenwood Press.

Bobbit, Philip. 1992. "Constitutional Interpretation." In *The Oxford Companion to the Supreme Court of the United States*, ed. Kermit L. Hall. New York: Oxford University Press.

Bodenhamer, David J. 1992. *Fair Trial: Rights of the Accused in American History*. New York: Oxford University Press.

Bodenhamer, David J., and James W. Ely Jr., eds. 1993. *The Bill of Rights in Modern America After 200 Years*. Bloomington: Indiana University Press.

Boles, Janet K. 1979. *The Politics of the Equal Rights Amendment: Conflict and the Decision Process*. New York: Longman.

Boller, Paul E., Jr. 1984. *Presidential Campaigns*. New York: Oxford University Press.

Bonfield, Arthur E. 1968. "The Dirksen Amendment and the Article V Convention Process." *Michigan Law Review* 66 (March): 949–1000.

Borden, Morton. 1979. "The Christian Amendment." *Civil War History* 25 (June): 156–67.

Bordin, Ruth. 1981. *Women and Temperance: The Quest for Power and Liberty, 1873–1900*. Philadelphia: Temple University Press.

Bork, Robert H. 1990. *The Tempting of America: The Political Seduction of the Law*. New York: Free Press.

Bowen, Catherine Drinker. 1966. *Miracle at Philadelphia: The Story of the Constitutional Convention May to September 1787*. Boston: Little, Brown.

Bowen, James W. 1994. "Enforcing the Balanced Budget Amendment." *Constitutional Law Journal* 4 (Spring): 565–620.

Bowling, Kenneth R. 1991. *The Creation of Washington D.C.: The Idea and Location of the American Capital*. Fairfax, VA: George Mason University Press.

Boyd, Steven R., ed. 1992. *Alternative Constitutions for the United States: A Documentary History*. Westport, CT: Greenwood Press.

Bradford, Gamaliel. 1893. "Congress and the Cabinet—II." *Annals of the American Academy of Political and Social Sciences* 4 (November): 289–99.

———. 1891. "Congress and the Cabinet." *Annals of the American Academy of Political and Social Sciences* 4 (November): 404–24.

Bradford, M. E. 1994. *Founding Fathers: Brief Lives of the Framers of the United States Constitution*, 2d ed. Lawrence: University Press of Kansas.

Bradley, Harold W. 1945. "The Political Thinking of George Washington." *Journal of Southern History* 11 (November): 469–86.

Bradsher, Keith. 1995. "Gap in Wealth in U.S. Called Widest in West." *New York Times*, 17 April, 1, C4.

Brandon, Mark E. 1995. "The 'Original' Thirteenth Amendment and the Limits to Formal Constitutional Change." In *Responding to Imperfection: The Theory and Practice of Constitutional Amendment*, ed. Sanford Levinson. Princeton, NJ: Princeton University Press.

Brasseau, Carl A. 1989. "Four Hundred Years of Acadian Life in North America." *Journal of Popular Culture* 23 (Summer): 3–22.

Bridwell, R. Randall and William J. Quirk. *Judicial Dictatorship*. New Brunswick, New Jersey: Transaction Publishers.

Brown, Everett S. 1938. *Ratification of the Twenty-first Amendment to the Constitution of the United States; State Convention Records and Laws*. Ann Arbor: University of Michigan Press.

———. 1935. "The Ratification of the Twenty-first Amendment." *American Political Science Review* 29 (December): 1005–17.

Brown, Jennifer K. 1993. "The Nineteenth Amendment and Women's Equality." *Yale Law Journal* 102 (June): 2174–2204.

Brown, Raymond G. 1920. "The Sixteenth Amendment to the United States Constitution." *American Law Review* 54: 843–54.

Bryant, Irving. 1965. *The Bill of Rights: Its Origin and Meaning*. Indianapolis, IN: Bobbs-Merrill.

Bryce, James. 1906. *The American Commonwealth*, 3d ed. 2 vols. New York: Macmillan.

———. 1905. "Flexible and Rigid Constitutions." In *Constitutions*. Germany: Scientia Verlag Aalen; 1980 reprint of New York and London edition.

Burke, Yvonne B. 1976. "Validity of Attempts To

Rescind Ratification of the Equal Rights Amendment." *University of Los Angeles Law Review* 8: 1–22.

Burnham, Walter D. 1995. "Realignment Lives: The 1994 Earthquake and Its Implications." In *The Clinton Presidency: First Appraisals,* ed. Colin Campbell and Bert Rockman. Chatham, NJ: Chatham House.

———. 1970. *Critical Elections and the Mainsprings of American Politics.* New York: W. W. Norton.

Butler, David, and Bruce Cain. 1992. *Congressional Redistricting: Comparative and Theoretical Perspectives.* New York: Macmillan.

Butts, R. Freeman. 1978. *Public Education in the United States: From Revolution to Reform.* New York: Holt, Rinehart, and Winston.

Cahn, Edmond. 1954. "An American Contribution." In *Supreme Court and Supreme Law.* Bloomington: Indiana University Press.

Calhoun, John C. 1953. *A Disquisition on Government and Selections from the Discourse,* ed. C. Gordon Post. Indianapolis, IN: Bobbs-Merrill.

———. 1851–1856. *The Works of John C. Calhoun,* ed. Richard K. Cralle. New York: Russell and Russell; 1968 reprint.

Calmes, Jackie. 1996. "In Symbolical Gesture, House Is To Vote Today on Amendment Making It Harder To Boost Taxes." *Wall Street Journal* 127 (April 15): A20.

Caplan, Russell L. 1988. *Constitutional Brinkmanship: Amending the Constitution by National Convention.* New York: Oxford University Press.

———. 1983. "The History and Meaning of the Ninth Amendment." *Virginia Law Review* 69 (March): 223–68.

Carroll, John. 1982. "Constitutional Law; Constitutional Amendment. Rescission of Ratification. Extension of Ratification Period. *State of Idaho v. Freeman.* " *Akron Law Review* 14 (Summer): 151–61.

Carson, Gerald. 1973. "The Income Tax and How It Grew." *American Heritage* 25 (December): 5–9, 79–88.

Carter. Dan T. 1964. *Scottsboro: A Tragedy of the American South.* New York: Oxford University Press.

Carter, Stephen L. 1994. *The Confirmation Mess: Cleaning Up the Federal Appointments Process.* New York: Basic Books.

Casey, Samuel B. 1995. "Religious Freedom Makes Good Neighbors." *Christian Legal Society Quarterly* 16 (Summer): 3.

Ceaser, James W. 1988. "The Reagan Presidency and American Public Opinion." In *The Reagan Legacy: Promise and Performance,* ed. Charles O. Jones. Chatham, NJ: Chatham House.

———. 1986. "In Defense of Separation of Powers." In *Separation of Powers—Does It Still Work?* ed. Robert A. Goldwin and Art Kaufman. Washington, DC: American Enterprise Institute.

"A Celebration of Women's Right To Vote." 1995. *New York Times,* 27 August, 9.

Chapin, Braley. 1964. *The American Law of Treason: Revolutionary and Early National Origins.* Seattle: University of Washington Press.

Chittenden, Lucius E. 1864. *A Report of the Debates and Proceedings in the Secret Sessions of the Conference Convention for Proposing Amendments to the Constitution of the United States.* New York: D. Appleton & Company, 1864; New York: Da Capo Press, 1971 reprint.

Christman, Henry M., ed. 1985. *Kingfish to America: Share Our Wealth: Selected Senatorial Papers of Huey P. Long.* New York: Shocken Books.

Christensen, Terry. 1995. *Local Politics: Governing at the Grassroots.* Belmont, CA: Wadsworth.

Clark, James C. 1985. *Faded Glory: Presidents Out of Power.* New York: Praeger.

Clark, Walter. 1906. "Some Defects of the Constitution of the United States." In *The Papers of Walter Clark.* Vol. 2, *1902–1924,* ed. Aubrey L. Brooks and Hugh T. Lefler. Chapel Hill: University of North Carolina Press, 1950.

Clem, Alan L. 1989. *Congress: Powers, Processes, and Politics.* Pacific Grove, CA: Brooks/Cole.

Clotfetter, Charles T., and Phillip Cook. 1989. *Selling Hope: State Lotteries in America.* Cambridge, MA: Harvard University Press.

Clymer, Adam. 1996. "Senator Still Plans To Push Amendment on Tax Increase." *New York Times* 145 (April 17): A12.

Cobb, Frank. 1924. "A Twentieth Amendment." In *Cobb of "The World": A Leader in Liberalism,* ed. John L. Heaton. New York: E. P. Dutton.

Cochrane, Thad. 1994. "Constitutional Amendment Restoring the Right to the Free Exercise of Religion." *Congressional Record,* U.S. Senate, 14 June.

Coit, Margaret L. 1961. *John C. Calhoun: American Portrait.* Boston: Houghton Mifflin.

Cole, Wayne S. 1962. *Senator Gerald P. Nye and American Foreign Relations.* Minneapolis: University of Minnesota Press.

Coleman, Charles. 1938. *The Constitution Up to Date*. Bulletin no. 10. Cambridge, MA: National Council for Social Studies.

Coleman, Peter J. 1992. "Bankruptcy and Insolvency Legislation." In *The Oxford Companion to the Supreme Court of the United States*, ed. Kermit L. Hall. New York: Oxford University Press.

———. 1974. *Debtors and Creditors in America: Insolvency Imprisonment for Debt, and Bankruptcy, 1607–1900*. Madison: State Historical Society of Wisconsin.

Committee on Federal Legislation of the Bar Association of the City of New York. n.d. *The Law of Presidential Impeachment*. New York: Harrow Books.

Committee on Federal State Relations. 1963. "Amending the Constitution To Strengthen the States in the Federal System." *State Government* 10 (Winter): 10–15.

"Composition and Jurisdiction of the Supreme Court—Proposed Constitutional Amendment." 1953. In *Congressional Record*, U.S. Senate, 16 February, 1106–8.

"Conference of the States: An Action Plan To Restore Balance in the Federal System." 1995. Concept paper adopted by the Council of State Governments, the National Governors' Association, and the National Conference of State Legislatures. 1 February.

"Congressional Bomb Shelter Revealed." 1992. *Facts on File* 52: 681.

Congressional Quarterly. 1991. *Guide to Congress*, 4th ed. Washington, DC: Congressional Quarterly.

———. 1985. *Members of Congress since 1789*, 3d ed. Washington, DC: Congressional Quarterly.

Conlan, Timothy J., James D. Riggle, and Donna E. Schwartz. 1995. "Deregulating Federalism? The Politics of Mandate Reform in the 104th Congress." *Publius: The Journal of Federalism* 25 (Summer): 23–40.

Conley, Patrick T., and John P. Kaminski, eds. 1992. *The Bill of Rights and the States: The Colonial and Revolutionary Origins of American Liberties*. Madison, WI: Madison House.

"Constitution for a United Republics of America, Followed by an Index." 1970. *Center Magazine* 3 (September/October): 24–49.

Cooper, Phillip, and Howard Ball. 1996. *The United States Supreme Court from the Inside Out*. Upper Saddle River, NJ: Prentice Hall.

Cornwell, Elmer E., Jr. 1981. "The American Constitutional Tradition: Its Impact and Development." In *The Constitutional Convention as an Amending Device*, ed. Kermit L. Hall, Harold M. Hyman, and Leon V. Sigal. Washington, DC: American Historical Association.

Cornwell, Elmer E., Jr., Jay S. Goodman, and Wayne R. Swanson. 1975. *State Constitutional Conventions: The Politics of the Revision Process in Seven States*. New York: Praeger.

Cortner, Richard C. 1993. *The Iron Horse and the Constitution: The Railroads and the Transformation of the Fourteenth Amendment*. Westport, CT: Greenwood Press.

Corwin, Edward S. 1981. "The Constitution as Instrument and as Symbol." In *Corwin on the Constitution*, Vol. 1, ed. Richard Loss. Ithaca, NY: Cornell University Press.

———. 1955. *The "Higher Law" Background of American Constitutional Law*. Ithaca, NY: Cornell University Press.

Cottrol, Robert J., ed. 1993. *Gun Control and the Constitution: Sources and Explorations of the Second Amendment*. 3 vols. New York: Garland.

"Covenant, Polity, and Constitutionalism." 1980. Special issue of *Publius: The Journal of Federalism* (Fall).

Craig, Barbara H. 1988. *Chadha: The Story of an Epic Constitutional Struggle*. New York: Oxford University Press.

Craig, Barbara H., and David M. O'Brien. 1993. *Abortion and American Politics*. Chatham, NJ: Chatham House.

Cram, Ralph. 1937. *The End of Democracy*. Boston: Marshall Jones Company.

———. 1935. *Convictions and Controversies*. Freeport, NY: Books for Libraries Press; 1970 reprint.

Cramer, Clayton E. 1994. *For the Defense of Themselves and the State: The Original Intent and Judicial Interpretation of the Right To Keep and Bear Arms*. Westport, CT: Praeger.

Croly, Herbert. 1965. *The Promise of American Life*. Indianapolis: Bobbs-Merrill.

———. 1914. *Progressive Democracy*. New York: Macmillan.

Cronin, Thomas E. 1989. *Direct Democracy: The Politics of Initiative, Referendum, and Recall*. Cambridge, MA: Harvard University Press.

Cronin, Thomas E., and Jeffrey J. Weill. 1985. "An Item Veto for the President?" *Congress & the Presidency* 12 (Autumn): 127–51.

Cullinan, Gerald. 1968. *The Post Office Department*. New York: Praeger.

Cunningham, Noble E. 1987. *The Pursuit of Reason: The Life of Thomas Jefferson*. Baton Rouge: Louisiana State University Press.

Currie, David P. 1985. *The Constitution in the Supreme Court: The First One Hundred Years, 1789–1888*. Chicago: University of Chicago Press.

Curry, James A., Richard B. Riley, and Richard M. Battistoni. 1989. *Constitutional Government: The American Experience*. St. Paul, MN: West.

Curtis, Michael K., ed. 1993. *The Constitution and the Flag*. Vol. 2. *The Flag Burning Cases*. New York: Garland.

Curtis, Michael K. 1986. *No State Shall Abridge: The Fourteenth Amendment and the Bill of Rights*. Durham, NC: Duke University Press.

Dalzell, Stewart, and Eric J. Beste. 1994. "Is the Twenty-seventh Amendment 200 Years Too Late?" *George Washington Law Review* 62 (April): 501–45.

D'Amato, A. D. 1995. "Conflict of Laws Rules and the Interstate Recognition of Same-Sex Marriages." *University of Illinois Law Review* 1995: 911–43.

Danforth, John C. 1994. *Resurrection: The Confirmation of Clarence Thomas*. New York: Viking.

Daniels, Roger. 1968. *The Politics of Prejudice*. New York: Antheneum.

Davidson, Elizabeth H. 1939. *Child Labor Legislation in the Southern Textile States*. Chapel Hill: University of North Carolina Press.

Davidson, James D. 1992. "Yes, To Save Congress from Itself." *The World & I* 7 (August): 110, 112–15.

Davidson, Roger H., and Walter J. Oleszek. 1994. *Congress and Its Members*, 4th ed. Washington, DC: Congressional Quarterly.

Davis, Richard. 1985. *Proposed Amendments to the Constitution of the United States of America Introduced in Congress from the 91st Congress, 1st Session, through the 98th Congress, 2nd Session, January 1969—December 1984*. Washington, DC: Congressional Research Service Report no. 85-36 GOV.

Davis, William C. 1994. *"A Government of Our Own": The Making of the Confederacy*. New York: Free Press.

DeConde, Alexander. 1971. *A History of American Foreign Policy*, 2d ed. New York: Charles Scribner's Sons.

Dellinger, Walter. 1983. "The Legitimacy of Constitutional Change: Rethinking the Amending Process." *Harvard Law Review* 97 (December): 380–432.

———. 1979. "The Recurring Question of the 'Limited' Constitutional Convention." *Yale Law Journal* 88: 1623–40.

Dennison, George M. 1976. *The Dorr War: Republicanism on Trial, 1831–1861*. Lexington: University Press of Kentucky.

DeRosa, Marshall L. 1996. *The Ninth Amendment and the Politics of Creative Jurisprudence: Disparaging the Fundamental Right of Popular Control*. New Brunswick, NJ: Transaction Publishers.

———. 1991. *The Confederate Constitution of 1861: An Inquiry into American Constitutionalism*. Columbia: University of Missouri Press.

Diamond, Martin. 1976. "The Revolution of Sober Expectations." In *America's Continuing Revolution*. Garden City, NY: Anchor Press.

Diller, Daniel C. 1989. "Chief of State." In *Guide to the Presidency*, ed. Michael Nelson. Washington, DC: Congressional Quarterly.

Dillon, Conley. 1977. "American Constitutional Review: Are We Preparing for the 21st Century?" *World Affairs* 140 (Summer): 5–24.

———. 1974. "Recommendation for the Establishment of a Permanent Commission of Constitutional Review." *Bureaucrat* 3 (July): 211–24.

Dillon, Merton L. 1974. *The Abolitionists: The Growth of a Dissenting Minority*. De Kalb: Northern Illinois University Press.

Dirksen, Everett M. 1968. "The Supreme Court and the People." *Michigan Law Review* 66 (March): 837–74.

Dodd, Walter F. 1921. "Amending the Federal Constitution." *Yale Law Journal* 30 (February): 3211–54.

———. 1910. *The Revision and Amendment of State Constitutions*. Baltimore: Johns Hopkins University Press.

Dolbeare, Kenneth M., and Janette K. Hubbell. 1996. *USA 2012: After the Middle-Class Revolution*. Chatham, NJ: Chatham House Publishers.

Donald, David H. 1995. *Lincoln*. New York: Simon & Schuster.

Dow, David R. 1990. "When Words Mean What We Believe They Say: The Case of Article V." *Iowa Law Review* 76 (October): 1–66.

Dry, Murray. 1991. "Flag Burning and the Constitution." In *The Supreme Court Review, 1990*, ed. Gerhard Casper et al. Chicago: University of Chicago Press.

Dubois, Ellen C. 1978. *Feminism and Suffrage: The Emergence of an Independent Women's Movement in*

America, 1848–1869. Ithaca, NY: Cornell University Press.

Duker, William F. 1977. "The President's Power To Pardon: A Constitutional History." *William and Mary Law Review* 18 (Spring): 475–538.

Dumond, Dwight L. 1973. *The Secession Movement, 1860–1861*. New York: Octagon Books.

Dunne, Gerald T. 1977. *Hugo Black and the Judicial Revolution*. New York: Simon and Schuster.

Earle, W. H. 1987. "The Phantom Amendment and the Duchess of Baltimore." *American History Illustrated* 22 (November): 32–39.

Eastland, Terry, and William J. Bennett. 1979. *Counting by Race*. New York: Basic Books.

Edel, Wilbur. 1981. *A Constitutional Convention: Threat or Challenge?* New York: Praeger.

Ehrlich, Walter. 1965. *They Have No Rights: Dred Scott's Struggle for Freedom* Westport, CT: Greenwood Press.

Eidelberg, Paul. 1968. *The Philosophy of the American Constitution: A Reinterpretation of the Intentions of the Founding Fathers*. New York: Free Press.

Eiselen, Malcolm R. 1941. "Can We Amend the Constitution?" *South Atlantic Quarterly* 40 (October): 333–41.

———. 1937. "Dare We Call a Federal Convention? *North American Review* 244 (Autumn): 27–28.

Eisenach, Eldon J. 1994. *The Lost Promise of Progressivism*. Lawrence: University Press of Kansas.

Ekirch, Arthur A., Jr. 1974. *Progressivism in America: A Study of the Era from Theodore Roosevelt to Woodrow Wilson*. New York: New Viewpoints.

Elliott, Ward. 1974. *The Rise of Guardian Democracy*. Cambridge, MA: Harvard University Press.

Elliott, William Y. 1935. *The Need for Constitutional Reform: A Program for National Security*. New York: Whittlesey House.

Ellis, L. Ethan. 1961. *Frank B. Kellogg and American Foreign Relations, 1925–1929*. New Brunswick, NJ: Rutgers University Press.

Ely, James W. 1992. *The Guardian of Every Other Right: A Constitutional History of Property Rights*. New York: Oxford University Press.

Ely, John Hart. 1993. *War and Responsibility: Constitutional Lessons of Vietnam and Its Aftermath*. Princeton, NJ: Princeton University Press.

———. 1980. *Democracy and Distrust*. Cambridge, MA: Harvard University Press.

Engdahl, David E. 1994. "The Spending Power." *Duke Law Journal* 44 (October): 1–109.

The English Language Amendment. 1985. Hearings before the Subcommittee on the Constitution of the Committee on the Judiciary, U.S. Senate. Washington, DC: U.S. Government Printing Office.

English Language Constitutional Amendments. 1989. Hearings before the Subcommittee on the Judiciary, House of Representatives. Washington, DC: U.S. Government Printing Office.

Epstein, Barbara L. 1981. *The Politics of Domesticity: Women, Evangelism, and Temperance in Nineteenth-Century America*. Middletown, CT: Wesleyan University Press.

Epstein, Lee, and Joseph F. Kobylka. 1992. *The Supreme Court and Legal Change: Abortion and the Death Penalty*. Chapel Hill: University of North Carolina Press.

Erdman, Sol, and Lawrence Susskind. 1995. *Reinventing Congress for the 21st Century: Toward a Politics of Accountability, Participation and Consensus*. New York: Frontier Press.

Ernst, Morris L. 1973. *The Great Reversals: Tales of the Supreme Court*. New York: Weybright and Talley.

Ervin, Sam J., Jr. 1984. *Preserving the Constitution: The Autobiography of Sam J. Ervin Jr.* Charlottesville, VA: Michie.

———. 1968. "Proposed Legislation To Implement the Convention Method of Amending the Constitution." *Michigan Law Review* 66 (March): 875–902.

Eskridge, William N., Jr. November 1991. "Overriding Supreme Court Statutory Interpretations Decisions." *Yale Law Journal* 101 (November): 331–455.

Estaville, Lawrence E. 1990. "The Louisiana French Language in the Nineteenth Century." *Southeastern Geographer* 30 (November): 107–20.

Euchner, Charles C., and John A. Maltese. 1989. "The Electoral Process." In *Guide to the Presidency*, ed. Michael Nelson. Washington, DC: Congressional Quarterly.

Fairman, Charles. 1949. "Does the Fourteenth Amendment Incorporate the Bill of Rights? The Original Understanding." *Stanford Law Review* 2 (December): 5–139.

Farrand, Max, ed. 1966. *The Records of the Federal Convention*. 4 vols. New Haven, CT: Yale University Press.

Feerick, John D. 1992. *The Twenty-fifth Amendment: Its Complete History and Applications*. New York: Fordham University Press.

Fehrenbacher, Don E. 1978. *The Dred Scott Case: Its Significance for American Law and Politics*. New York: Oxford University Press.

Fernandez, Ferdinand F. 1966. "The Constitutionality of the Fourteenth Amendment." *Southern California Law Review* 39: 378–407.

Ferrell, Claudine L. 1986. *Nightmare and Dream: Anti-Lynching in Congress 1917–1922.* New York: Garland.

Finer, Herman. 1960. *The Presidency, Crisis and Regeneration: An Essay in Possibilities.* Chicago: University of Chicago Press.

Fink, Richard H., and Jack C. High, eds. 1987. *A Nation in Debt: Economists Debate the Federal Budget Deficit.* Frederick, MD: University Publications of America.

Finkleman, Paul. 1992. "Slavery." In *The Oxford Companion to the Supreme Court of the United States,* ed. Kermit L. Hall. New York: Oxford Universisty Press.

———. 1991. "James Madison and the Bill of Rights: A Reluctant Paternity." In *The Supreme Court Review, 1990.* Chicago: University of Chicago Press.

———. 1981. *An Imperfect Union: Slavery, Federalism and Comity.* Chapel Hill: University of North Carolina Press.

Finletter, Thomas K. 1945. *Can Representative Government Do the Job?* New York: Reynal and Hitchcock.

Fiscus, Ron. 1992. The Constitutional Logic of Affirmative Action. Durham, NC: Duke University Press.

Fisher, Louis. 1993. "The Legislative Veto: Invalidated, It Survives." *Law and Contemporary Problems* 56 (Autumn): 273–92.

———. 1991. *Constitutional Conflicts between Congress and the President,* 3d ed. Lawrence: University Press of Kansas.

Fisher, Sidney G. 1967. *A Philadelphia Perspective: The Diary of Sidney George Fisher Covering the Years 1834–1871.* Philadelphia: Historical Society of Pennsylvania.

———. 1862. *The Trial of the Constitution.* New York: Da Capo Press; 1972 reprint.

Fitzpatrick, John C. 1931–1944. *The Writings of George Washington.,* 39 vols. Washington, DC: U.S. Government Printing Office.

Flack, Horace E. 1908. *The Adoption of the Fourteenth Amendment.* Gloucester, MA: Peter Smith; 1965 reprint.

Flexnor, Eleanor. 1974. *Century of Struggle: The Woman's Rights Movement in the United States.* New York: Atheneum.

Fogleson, Robert M., and Richard E. Rubenstein. 1969. *Mass Violence in America: Invasion at Harper's Ferry.* New York: Arno Press.

Foley, Michael. 1989. *The Silence of Constitutions: Gaps, "Abeyances" and Political Temperament in the Maintenance of Government.* London: Routledge.

Folton, Richard T. 1996. "Horror Stories." *Liberty* (March/April): 6–8.

Foner, Eric. 1970. *Free Soil, Free Labor, Free Men: The Ideology of the Republican Party before the Civil War.* New York: Oxford University Press.

Ford, Paul L., ed. 1898. *The Federalist.* New York: Henry Holt.

Fowler, Robert B. 1986. *Carrie Catt: Feminist Politician.* Boston: Northeastern University Press.

Fraley, Colette. 1995. "House Opponents Savor Gains; Senate Outlook Is Unclear." *Congressional Quarterly Weekly Report* 53 (29 July): 2276–77.

Frank, Jerome. 1969. *Courts on Trial: Myth and Reality in American Justice.* New York: Atheneum.

Frankfurter, Felix. 1974. *The Commerce Clause under Marshall, Taney and Waite.* Chicago: Quadrange Books.

Freedman, Russell. 1994. *Lewis Hine and the Crusade against Child Labor.* New York: Clarion Books.

Freedman, Samuel S., and Pamela J. Naughton. 1978. *ERA: May a State Change Its Vote?* Detroit: Wayne State University Press.

Frenzel, Bill. 1992. "Term Limits and the Immortal Congress." *Brookings Review* 10 (Spring): 18–22.

Freyer, Tony. 1990. *Hugo L. Black and the Dilemma of American Liberalism.* Glenville, IL: Scott Foresman.

Friendly, Henry J. 1968. "The Fifth Amendment Tomorrow: The Case for Constitutional Change." *University of Cincinnati Law Review* 37 (Fall): 671–726.

Frierson, Wm. 1920. "Amending the Constitution of the United States: A Reply to Mr. Marbury." *Harvard Law Review<D. 33 (March): 659–66.*

Fry, Amelia R. 1986. "Alice Paul and the ERA." In *Rights of Passage: The Past and Future of the ERA,* ed. Joan Hoff-Wilson. Bloomington: Indiana University Press.

Funston, Richard Y. 1977. *Constitution Counterrevolution? The Warren Court and the Burger Court: Judicial Policy Making in Modern America.* New York: Schenkman.

Gammie, Beth. 1989. "State ERA's: Problems and Possibilities." *University of Illinois Law Review* 1989: 1123–59.

Garcia, Alfredo. 1992. *The Sixth Amendment in Modern American Jurisprudence: A Critical Perspective*. New York: Greenwood Press.

Gardiner, William. 1973. *A Proposed Constitution for the United States of America*. Summerfield, FL: William Gardiner.

Garrow, David J. 1994. *Liberty and Sexuality: The Right to Privacy and the Making of* Roe v. Wade. New York: Macmillan.

Gatell, Frank O. 1969. "John McLean." In *The Justices of the United States Supreme Court, 1789–1969: Their Lives and Major Opinions*, Vol. 1, ed. Leon Friedman and Fred L. Israel. New York: R. R. Bowker.

Gavzer, Bernard. 1995. "Life behind Bars." *Parade Magazine*, 13 August, 4–7.

George, Henry. 1938. *Progress and Poverty: An Inquiry into the Cause of Industrial Depressions and of Increase of Want with Increase of Wealth, the Remedy*, 50th anniversary ed. New York: Robert Schalkenback Foundation.

Gerber, Scott D. 1995. *To Secure These Rights: The Declaration of Independence and Constitutional Interpretation*. New York: New York University Press.

Gettlinger, Stephen. 1994. "New Filibuster Tactics Imperil Next Senate." *Congressional Quarterly* 52 (5 November): 3198.

Gillespie, Ed, and Bob Schellhas, eds. 1994. *Contract with America: The Bold Plan by Rep. Newt Gingrich, Rep. Dick Armey, and the House Republicans To Change the Nation*. New York: Random House.

Gillespie, Michael L., and Michael Lienesch, eds. 1989. *Ratifying the Constitution*. Lawrence: University Press of Kansas.

Gillman, Howard. 1993. *The Constitution Besieged: The Rise and Demise of Lochner Era Police Powers Jurisprudence*. Durham, NC: Duke University Press.

Gillmor, Paul, and Fred Eames. 1994. "Reconstruction of Federalism: A Constitutional Amendment To Prohibit Unfunded Mandates." *Harvard Journal on Legislation* 31 (Summer): 395–413.

Ginsburg, Ruth B. 1989–1990. "On Amending the Constitution: A Plea for Patience." *University of Arkansas at Little Rock Law Journal* 12: 677–94.

———. 1969. "Ratification of the Equal Rights Amendment: A Question of Time." *Texas Law Review* 57: 919–45.

Glasson, William H., and David Kinley. 1918. *Federal Military Pensions in the United States*. New York: Oxford University Press.

Glendon, Mary A. 1991. *Rights Talk: The Impoverishment of Political Discourse*. New York: Free Press.

———. 1987. *Abortion and Divorce in Western Law*. Cambridge, MA: Harvard University Press.

Glick, Henry R. 1988. *Courts, Politics, and Justice?* 2d ed. New York: McGraw-Hill.

Goldstein, Leslie F. 1991. *In Defense of the Text: Democracy and Constitutional Theory*. Savage, MD: Rowman and Littlefield.

———. 1987. "The ERA and the U.S. Supreme Court." In *Research in Law and Policy Studies*, ed. Stuart S. Nagel. Greenwich, CT: JAI.

Goldstein, Robert J. Forthcoming. *The American Flag Desecration Controversy: A Collection of Documents from the Civil War to 1990*. Syracuse: Syracuse University Press.

———. 1995. *Burning the Flag: The Great 1989–1990 American Flag Desecration Controversy*. Kent, OH. Kent State University Press..

———.1994. *Saving "Old Glory": The History of the American Flag Desecration Controversy*. Boulder, CO: Westview.

———. 1990. "The Great 1989–1990 Flag Flap: An Historical, Political, and Legal Analysis." *University of Miami Law Review* 45 (September): 19–106.

Goodnow, Frank J. 1911. *Social Reform and the Constitution*. New York: Burt Franklin; 1970 reprint.

Goodstein, Laurie. 1995. "Religious Freedom Amendment Passed." *Washington Post*, 9 June, A-12

Gordon, Charles. 1982. "The Power of Congress To Terminate United States Citizenship." *Connecticut Law Review* 4 (Spring): 611–32.

———. 1968. "Who Can Be President of the United States: The Unresolved Enigma." *Maryland Law Review* 28 (Winter): 1–32.

Gould, Lewis L., ed. 1974. *The Progressive Era*. Syracuse, NY: Syracuse University Press.

Graber, Mark A. 1995. "Unnecessary and Unintelligible." *Constitutional Commentary* 12 (Summer): 167–70.

Green, Steven K. 1992. "The Blaine Amendment Reconsidered." *American Journal of Legal History* 36 (January): 38–69.

Greenhouse, Linda. 1996. "Justices Curb Federal Power To Subject States to Lawsuits." *New York Times* 115 (28 March): A1, A12.

Grey, Thomas C. 1975. "Do We Have an Unwritten Constitution?" *Stanford Law Review* 27 (February): 703–18.

Griffin, Stephen M. 1996. *American Constitutionalism: From Theory to Practice*. Princeton, NJ: Princeton University Press.

Griffith, Elisabeth. 1984. *In Her Own Right: The*

Life of Elizabeth Cady Stanton. New York: Oxford University Press.

Grimes, Alan P. 1978. *Democracy and the Amendments to the Constitution*. Lexington, MA: Lexington Books.

Grinnell, F. W. 1925. "Finality of State's Ratification of a Constitutional Amendment." *American Bar Association Journal* 11 (March): 192–93.

Grinnell, Frank W. 1959. "Petitioning Congress for a Convention: Cannot a State Change Its Mind?" *American Bar Association Journal* 45: 1164–65.

Grodzins, Morton, 1966. *The American System: A New View of the Government in the United States*. Chicago: Rand McNally.

Grunder, Garel A., and William E. Livezey. 1973. *The Philippines and the United States*. Westport, CT: Greenwood Press.

Hahn, Jeanne. 1987. "Neo-Hamiltonianism: A Democratic Critique." In *The Case against the Constitution from Anti-Federalists to the Present*, ed. John F. Manley and Kenneth M. Dolbeare. New York: M. E. Sharpe.

Halbrook, Stephen D. 1994. *That Every Man Be Armed: The Evolution of a Constitutional Right*. Oakland, CA: Independent Institute.

Hall, Kermit L., ed. 1992. *The Oxford Companion to the Supreme Court of the United States*. New York: Oxford University Press.

———, ed. 1991. *By and for the People: Constitutional Rights in American History*. Arlington Heights, IL: Harlan Davidson.

———. 1989. *The Magic Mirror: Law in American History*. New York: Oxford University Press.

Halper, Louise A. 1990. "Christopher G. Tiedeman, 'Laissez-Faire Constitutionalism' and the Dilemma of Small-Scale Property in the Gilded Age." *Ohio State Law Journal* 51: 1349–84.

Halpern, Stephen C., and Charles M. Lamb, eds. 1982. *Supreme Court Activism and Restraint*. Lexington, MA: Lexington Books.

Hamburger, Phillip A. 1993. "Natural Rights, Natural Law, and American Constitutionalism." *Yale Law Journal* 102 (January): 907–60.

Hamilton, Alexander, James Madison, and John Jay. 1961. *The Federalist Papers*. New York: New American Library.

Hamilton, Hugh L. 1938. *A Second Constitution for the United States of America*. Richmond, VA: Garrett and Massie.

Hamilton, Robert W. 1987. *The Law of Corporations*. St. Paul, MN: West.

Hamm, Richard F. 1995. *Shaping the 18th Amendment: Temperance Reform, Legal Culture and the Polity, 1880–1920*. Chapel Hill: University of North Carolina Press.

Handy, Robert T. 1971. *A Christian America: Protestant Hopes and Historical Realities*. New York: Oxford University Press.

Hardaway, Robert M. 1994. *The Electoral College and the Constitution: The Case for Preserving Federalism*. Westport, CT: Praeger.

Hardin, Charles M. 1989. *Constitutional Reform in America: Essays on the Separation of Powers*. Ames: Iowa State University Press.

———. 1974. *Presidential Power and Accountability Toward a New Constitution*. Chicago: University of Chicago Press.

Hare, Lloyd C. 1970. *The Greatest American Woman: Lucretia Mott*. New York: Negro Universities Press.

Harrigan, John J. 1994. *Politics and Policy in States and Communities*, 5th ed. New York: HarperCollins College Publishers.

Harriger, Katy J. 1992. *Independent Justice: The Federal Special Prosecutor in American Politics*. Lawrence: University Press of Kansas.

Harris, Daryl B. 1992. *Proposed Amendments to the U.S. Constitution: 99th–101st Congresses (1985–1990)*. Washington, DC: Congressional Research Service, Library of Congress.

Harris, William F. II. 1993. *The Interpretable Constitution*. Baltimore: Johns Hopkins University Press.

Hart, Vivien. 1994. *Bound by Our Constitution: Women, Workers, and the Minimum Wage*. Princeton, NJ: Princeton University Press.

Hatch, Orrin. 1991. "Constitutional Convention Implementation Act." *Congressional Record*, U.S. Senate, 15 January, S559–65.

———. 1979. "Should the Capital Vote in Congress? A Critical Analysis of the Proposed D.C. Representation Amendment." *Fordham Urban Law Journal* 7: 479–539.

Haynes, George H. 1960. *The Senate of the United States, Its History and Practice*. New York: Russell and Russell.

Hazlitt, Henry. 1987. "A Proposal for Two Constitutional Amendments." In *A Nation in Debt: Economists Debate the Federal Budget Deficit*, ed. Richard H. Fink and Jack H. High. Frederick, MD: University Publications of America.

———. 1974. *A New Constitution Now*. New Rochelle, NY: Arlington House.

———. 1942. *A New Constitution Now.* New York: Whittlesey House.

———. 1931. "Our Obsolete Constitution." *Nation* 132 (4 February): 124–25.

Hearings before a Subcommittee of the Committee on the Judiciary, United States Senate, Eighty-Third Congress, Second Session on S.J. Res. 23 Proposing an Amendment to the Constitution of the United States Relative to Taxes on Incomes, Inheritance, and Gifts. 1954. Washington, DC: U.S. Government Printing Office.

Hearings before a Subcommittee of the Committee on the Judiciary, United States Senate, Eighty-Fourth Congress, Second Session on S.J. Res 23 Proposing an Amendment to the Constitution of the United States Relative to Taxes on Incomes, Inheritance, and Gifts. 1956. Washington, DC: U.S. Government Printing Office.

Hearings before the Subcommittee on Constitutuional Amendments of the Committee on the Judiciary: Lowering the Voting Age to 18. 1968. U.S. Senate, 90th Cong., 2d Sess., 14, 15, 16 May.

Hearings before the Subcommittee on the Judiciary: Lowering the Voting Age to 18. 1970. U.S. Senate, 91st Cong., 2d Sess., 16, 17 February, 9, 10 March.

Hehmeyer, Alexander. 1943. *Time for Change: A Proposal for a Second Constitutional Convention.* New York: Farrar and Rinehart.

Heller, Francis H. 1982. "Limiting a Constitutional Convention: The State Precedents." *Cardozo Law Review* 3: 563–79.

Heller, Scott. 1995. "The Right To Bear Arms." *Chronicle of Higher Education* 41 (21 July): A8, A12.

Henderson, Yandell. 1913. "The Progressive Movement and Constitutional Reform." *Yale Review* n.s. 3: 78–90.

Henkin, Louis. 1972. *Foreign Affairs and the Constitution.* Mineola, NY: Foundation Press.

Hoban, Thomas M., and Richard O. Brooks. 1987. *Green Justice: The Environment and the Courts.* Boulder, CO: Westview Press.

Hoebeke, C.H. 1995. *The Road to Mass Democracy: Original Intent and the Seventeenth Amendment.* New Brunswick, N.J.: Transaction

Hoffman, Joseph L., and William J. Stuntz. 1994. "Habeas After the Revolution." In *Supreme Court Review.* Chicago: University of Chicago Press.

Hoff-Wilson, Joan, ed. 1986. *Rights of Passage: The Past and Future of ERA.* Bloomington: Indiana University Press.

Holden, Matthew Jr. 1973a. *The Politics of the Black Nation.* New York: Chandler.

———. 1973b. *The White Man's Burden.* New York: Chandler.

Holmes, Stephen. 1995. *Passions and Constraint: On the Theory of Liberal Democracy.* Chicago: University of Chicago Press.

Hook, Janet, and Donna Cassata. 1995. "Low-Key Revolt May Spur Thurmond To Give Colleagues Freer Hand." *Congressional Quarterly Weekly Report* 53 (11 February): 466.

Hopkins, Caspar T. 1885. "Thoughts Toward Revising the Federal Constitution." *Overland Monthly* n.s. 6 (October): 388–98.

Horn, Dottie. 1990. "Another Star for the Stripes?" *Endeavors* 8 (Fall): 4–6.

Horwill, Herbert W. 1925. *The Usages of the American Constitution.* Port Washington, NY: Kennikat Press; 1969 reprint.

Hosanky, David. 1995. "Mandate Bill Is More Moderate Than Proposed in 'Contract.'" *Congressional Quarterly Weekly Report* 53 (7 January): 40.

Hunter, James D. 1994. *before the Shooting Begins: Searching for Democracy in America's Culture War.* New York: Free Press.

Hurst, James W. 1971. *The Law of Treason in the United States: Collected Essays.* Westport, CT: Greenwood Press.

Imari, Brother (Richard B. Henry). 1968. *War in America: The Malcolm X Doctrine.* Detroit: Malcolm X Doctrine.

Information Please Almanac: Atlas and Yearbook. 1993. 43d ed. Boston: Houghton Mifflin.

Irons, Peter. 1989. *Justice Delayed: The Record of the Japanese Internment Cases.* Middletown, CT: Wesleyan University Press.

———. 1983. *Justice at War.* New York: Oxford University Press.

Irons, Peter, and Stephanie Guitton, eds. 1993. *May It Please the Court.* New York: New Press.

Isaacson, Eric A. 1990. "The Flag Burning Issue: A Legal Analysis and Comment." *Loyola of Los Angeles Law Review* 23 (January): 535–600.

Jackson, Donald W. 1992. *Even the Children of Strangers: Equality under the U.S. Constitution.* Lawrence: University Press of Kansas.

Jackson, Robert H. 1941. *The Struggle for Judicial Supremacy.* New York: Vintage Books.

Jacob, Clyde E. 1972. *The Eleventh Amendment and Sovereign Immunity.* Westport, CT: Greenwood Press.

Jacob, Herbert. 1995. *Law and Politics in the United States,* 2d ed. New York: HarperCollins College Publishers.

Jacoby, Steward O. 1984. *The Religious Amendment Movement: God, People and Nation in the Gilded Age.* 2 vols. Ph.D. dissertation, University of Michigan.

Jaffa, Harry V. 1994. *Original Intent and the Framers of the Constitution: A Disputed Question.* Washington, DC: Regnery Gateway.

James, Joseph B. 1984. *The Ratification of the Fourteenth Amendment.* Macon, GA: Mercer University Press.

———. 1956. *The Framing of the Fourteenth Amendment.* Urbana: University of Illinois Press.

Jameson, John A. 1887. *A Treatise on Constitutional Conventions: Their History, Powers, and Modes of Proceeding,* 4th ed. Chicago: Callaghan and Company.

Jaschik, Scott, and Douglas Lederman. 1996. "Appeals Court Bars Racial Preference in College Admissions." *Chronicle of Higher Education* 43 (29 March): A26–A27.

Jefferson, Thomas. 1964. *Notes on the State of Virginia.* New York: Harper and Row.

———. 1905. *The Works of Thomas Jefferson,* ed. Paul Leicester Ford. 12 vols. New York: G. P. Putnam's Sons, Knickerbocker Press.

———. 1791. "Opinion of the Constitutionality of a National Bank." Printed in Urofsky, Melvin I., ed. *Documents of American Constitutional and Legal History.* New York: Alfred A. Knopf, 1989.

Jensen, Merrill. 1966. *The Articles of Confederation.* Madison: University of Wisconsin Press.

Johannsen, Robert W., ed. 1965. *The Lincoln-Douglas Debates of 1858.* New York: Oxford University Press.

Johnsen, Julia E., ed. 1948. *Federal World Government.* Vol. 19, no. 5 of the Reference Shelf. New York: H. W. Wilson.

———. 1947. *United Nations or World Government.* Vol. 20, no. 5 of the Reference Shelf. New York: H. W. Wilson.

Johnstone, Frederic B. 1912. "An Eighteenth Century Constitution." *Illinois Law Review* 7 (December): 265–90.

Kammen, Michael. 1987. *A Machine That Would Go of Itself: The Constitution in American Culture.* New York: Alfred A. Knopf.

Kanowitz, Leo, and Marilyn Klinger. 1978. "Can a State Rescind Its Equal Rights Amendment Ratification: Who Decides and How?" *Hastings Law Journal* 28 (March): 969–1009.

Kaplan, Morton A. 1991. "Freedom of Speech: Its Constitutional Scope and Function." *This World & I* 7 (July): 531–41.

Kaufman, Burton I. 1969. *Washington's Farewell Address: The View from the 20th Century.* Chicago: Quadrangle Books.

Kauper, Paul G. 1968. "The Alternate Amending Process: Some Observations." *Michigan Law Review* 66 (March): 903–20.

Kay, Richard S. 1987. "The Illegality of the Constitution." *Constitutional Commentary* 4 (Winter): 57–80.

Keller, Morton. 1987. Failed Amendments to the Constitution." *The World & I* 9 (September): 87–97.

Kelly, Frank K. 1981. *Court of Reason: Robert Hutchins and the Fund for the Republic.* New York: Free Press.

Kennedy, Devin C. 1991. "We Need a Fresh Start; Repeal the Seventh Amendment." *Detroit College of Law Review* (Winter): 1289–1301.

Kens, Paul. 1990. *Judicial Power and Reform Politics: The Anatomy of* Lochner v. New York. Lawrence: University Press of Kansas.

Kenyon, Cecelia, ed. 1985. *The Antifederalists.* Boston: Northeastern University Press.

Keogh, Stephen. 1987. "Formal and Informal Constitutional Lawmaking in the United States in the Winter of 1860–1861." *Journal of Legal History* 8 (December): 275–99.

Kerr, K. Austin. 1985. *Organized for Prohibition: A New History of the Anti-Saloon League.* New Haven, CT: Yale University Press.

Kershen, Drew L. 1992. "Agriculture." In *The Oxford Companion to the Supreme Court of the United States,* ed. Kermit L. Hall. New York: Oxford University Press.

Kesler, Charles R. 1990. "Bad Housekeeping: The Case against Congressional Term Limits." *Policy Review* 53 (Summer): 20–25.

Keynes, Edward, with Randall K. Miller. 1989. *The Court vs. Congress: Prayer, Busing, and Abortion.* Durham, NC: Duke University Press.

Kirwan, Albert D. 1962. *John J. Crittenden: The Struggle for the Union.* n.p.: University of Kentucky Press.

Klinkhammer, Marie C. 1965. "The Blaine Amendment of 1875." *Catholic Historical Review* 21: 15–49.

Kluger, Richard. 1975. *Simple Justice: The History of Brown v. Board of Education and Black America's Struggle for Equality.* 2 vols. New York: Alfred A. Knopf.

Knappman, Edward W., ed. 1994. *Great American Trials.* Detroit: Visible Ink Press.

Knipprath, Joerg W. 1987. "To See the Trees, but Not the Forest in Constitution-Making: A Commentary on Professor Miller's Proposed Constitution." *Southwestern University Law Review* 17: 239–56.

Kraditor, Aileen S. 1981. *The Idea of the Woman's Suffrage Movement, 1890–1920.* New York: W. W. Norton.

Kramnick, Isaac, and R. Laurence Moore. 1996. *The Godless Constitution: The Case against Religious Correctness.* New York: W. W. Norton.

Kravitz, Walter, 1993. *American Congressional Dictionary.* Washington, DC: Congressional Quarterly.

Krusch, Barry. 1992. *The 21st Century Constitution: A New America for a New Millennium.* New York: Stanhope Press.

Ku, Raymond. 1995. "Consensus of the Governed: The Legitimacy of Constitutional Change." *Fordham Law Review* 64 (November): 535–86.

Kuic, Vukan. 1983. "John C. Calhoun's Theory of the 'Concurrent Majority.'" *American Bar Association* 69: 482–86.

Kurland, Philip B., and Ralph Lerner, eds. 1987. *The Founders' Constitution.* 5 vols. Chicago: University of Chicago Press.

Kuroda, Tadahisa. 1994 *The Origins of the Twelfth Amendment: The Electoral College in the Early Republic, 1878–1804.* Westport, CT: Greenwood Press.

Kyvig, David E. 1995. "Reforming or Resisting Modern Government? The Balanced Budget Amendment to the U.S. Constitution." *Akron Law Review* 28 (Fall/Winter): 97–124.

———. 1989. "The Road Not Taken: FDR, the Supreme Court and Constitutional Amendment." *Political Science Quarterly* 104 (Fall): 463–81.

———. 1988. "Can the Constitution Be Amended? The Battle Over the Income Tax, 1895–1913." *Prologue* 20 (Fall): 181–200.

———. 1979. *Repealing National Prohibition.* Chicago: University of Chicago Press.

Kyvig, David E., ed. 1985. *Alcohol and Order: Perspectives on National Prohibition.* Westport, CT: Greenwood Press.

Labbe, Donald M. 1983. "New Light on the Slaughterhouse Monopoly of 1869." In *Louisiana's*

Legal Heritage, ed. Edward F. Haas. Pensacola, FL: Peridido Bay Press.

Laham, Nicholas. 1993. *Why the United States Lacks a National Health Insurance Program.* Westport, CT: Greenwood Press.

Landry, Thomas K. 1993. "Constitutional Invention: A Patent Perspective." *Rutgers Law Journal* 25 (Autumn): 67–104.

Langum, David J. 1994. *Crossing Over the Line: Legislating Morality and the Mann Act.* Chicago: University of Chicago Press.

Larson, Edward J. 1993. "The 'Blaine Amendment' in State Constitutions." In *The School-Choice Controversy: What Is Constitutional?* ed. James W. Skillen. Grand Rapids, MI: Baker Books.

Larson, Gustive O. 1971. *The "Americanization" of Utah for Statehood.* San Marino, CA: Huntington Library.

Lash, Kurt T. 1994. "Rejecting Conventional Wisdom: Federalist Ambivalence in the Framing and Implementation of Article V." *American Journal of Legal History* 38 (April): 197–231.

Laubach, John H. 1969. *School Prayers: Congress, the Courts and the Public.* Washington, DC: Public Affairs Press.

Lawrence, William B. 1880. "The Monarchical Principle in Our Constitution." *North American Review* 288 (November): 385–409.

Lawson, Steven F. 1976. *Black Ballots: Voting Rights in the South, 1944–1969.* New York: Columbia University Press.

Lawton, Kim A. 1996. "'The Right To Parent': Should It Be Fundamental?" *Christianity Today* 40 (29 April): 57.

Lee, Calvin B. T. 1967. *One Man One Vote: WMCA and the Struggle for Equal Representation.* New York: Charles Scribner's Sons.

Lee, Charles Robert Jr. 1963. *The Confederate Constitutions.* Chapel Hill: University of North Carolina Press.

Lee, R. Alton. 1961. "The Corwin Amendment in the Secession Crisis." *Ohio Historical Quarterly* 70 (January): 1–26.

Legislative Reference Service of the Library of Congress. 1936–1996. *Digest of Public General Bills and Resolutions.* Washington, DC: Library of Congress.

Leish, Kenneth W., ed. 1968. *The American Heritage Pictorial History of the Presidents of the United States.* 2 vols. n.p.: American Heritage.

Leuchtenburg, William E. 1995. *The Supreme Court*

Reborn: The Constitutional Revolution in the Age of Roosevelt. New York: Oxford University Press.

Levinson, Sanford. 1996. "The Political Implications of Amending Clauses," *Constitutional Commentary* 13 (Spring): 107–23.

———. 1995. "Presidential Elections and Constitutional Stupidities." *Constitutional Commentary* 12 (Summer): 183–86.

———. 1994. "Authorizing Constitutional Text: On the Purported Twenty-seventh Amendment." *Constitutional Commentary* 11 (Winter): 101–13.

———. 1992. "Contempt of Court: The Most Important 'Contemporary Challenge to Judging.'" *Washington and Lee Law Review* 49 (Spring): 339–43.

———. 1990a. "On the Notion of Amendment: Reflections on David Daube's 'Jehovah the Good.'" *S'vara: A Journal of Philosophy and Judaism* 1 (Winter): 25–31.

———. 1990b. "'Veneration' and Constitutional Change: James Madison Confronts the Possibility of Constitutional Amendment." *Texas Tech Law Review* 21: 2443–61.

———. 1989. "The Embarrassing Second Amendment." *Yale Law Journal* 99 (December): 637–60.

Levinson, Sanford, ed. 1995. *Responding to Imperfection: The Theory and Practice of Constitutional Amendment.* Princeton, NJ: Princeton University Press.

Levy, Leonard W. 1995. *Seasoned Judgments: The American Constitution, Rights, and History.* New Brunswick, NJ: Transaction Publishers.

———. 1988. *Original Intent and the Framers' Constitution.* New York: Macmillan.

———. 1986. *The Establishment Clause and the First Amendment.* New York: Macmillan.

———. 1968. *Origins of the Fifth Amendment: The Right against Self-Incrimination.* New York: Oxford University Press.

Lewis, Anthony. 1991. *Make No Law: The Sullivan Case and the First Amendment.* New York: Random House.

———. 1974. *Gideon's Trumpet.* New York: Vintage Books.

Lieberman, Jethro K. 1992. *The Evolving Constitution: How the Supreme Court Has Ruled on Issues from Abortion to Zoning.* New York: Random House.

Lind, Michael. 1966. "Pat Answers." *New Republic* 214 (February 19): 13–14.

Linder, Douglas. 1981. "What in the Constitution Cannot Be Amended?" *Arizona Law Review* 23: 717–31.

Link, Arthur S. 1963. *Woodrow Wilson: A Brief Biography.* Cleveland: World.

Link, Arthur S., and Richard L. McCormick. 1983. *Progressivism.* Arlington Heights, IL: Harlan Davidson.

Little, Laura E. 1991. "An Excursion into the Uncharted Waters of the Seventeenth Amendment." *Temple Law Review* 674 (Fall): 629–58.

Lively, Donald E. 1992. *The Constitution and Race.* New York: Praeger.

Lockwood, Henry C. 1884. *The Abolition of the Presidency.* New York: R. Worthington; 1978 reprint, Farmingdale, NY: Darbor Social Science Publications.

Lofgren, Charles A. 1987. *The Plessy Case: A Legal-Historical Interpretation.* New York: Oxford University Press.

———. 1975. "*Missouri v. Holland* in Historical Perspective." In *The Supreme Court Review.* Chicago: University of Chicago Press.

Long, Huey P. 1935. *My First Days in the White House.* Harrisburg, PA: Telegraph Press.

Longley, Lawrence D., and Alan G. Braun. 1972. *The Politics of Electoral College Reform.* New Haven, CT: Yale University Press.

Lundardini, Christine A. 1986. *From Equal Suffrage to Equal Rights: Alice Paul and the National Woman's Party, 1910–1928.* New York: New York University Press.

Lutz, Donald S. 1994. "Toward a Theory of Constitutional Amendment." *American Political Science Review* 88 (June): 355–70.

———. 1992. *A Preface to American Political Theory.* Lawrence: University Press of Kansas.

———. 1988. *The Origins of American Constitutionalism.* Baton Rouge: Louisiana State University Press.

Lyman, Edward L. 1986. *Political Deliverance: The Mormon Quest for Utah Statehood.* Urbana: University of Illinois Press.

McBride, James. 1991. "'Is Nothing Sacred?' Flag Desecration, the Constitution and the Establishment of Religion." *St. John's Law Review* 65: 297–324.

McConnell, Michael W. May 1995. "Originalism and the Desegregation Decisions." *Virginia Law Review* 81 (May): 947–1140.

McCullough, David. 1992. *Truman.* New York: Simon and Schuster.

Macdonald, Dwight. 1968. "The Constitution of

the United States Needs To Be Fixed." *Esquire* 70 (October): 143–46, 238, 240, 243–44, 246, 252.

McDonald, Forrest. 1992. "Pardon Power." In *The Oxford Companion to the Supreme Court of the United States,* ed. Kermit L. Hall. New York: Oxford University Press.

———. 1982. *A Constitutional History of the United States.* New York: Franklin Watts.

MacDonald, William. 1922. *A New Constitution for a New America.* New York: B. W. Heubsch.

———. 1921. "A New American Constitution." *Proceedings of the American Antiquarian Society* 2 (October): 439–47.

McGinnis, John O., and Michael B. Rappaport. 1995. "The Constitutionality of Legislative Supermajority Requirements: A Defense." *Yale Law Journal* 105 (November): 483–511.

Machen, Arthur W., Jr. 1910. "Is the Fifteenth Amendment Void?" *Harvard Law Review* 23 (January): 169–93.

McHenry, Robert, ed. 1980. *Liberty's Women.* Springfield, MA: G. and C. Merriam.

McIntyre, Robert S. 1992. "No, It Would Wreck the Economy." *The World & I* 7 (August): 111, 116–17, 119.

McKee, Henry S. 1933. *Degenerate Democracy.* New York: Thomas Y. Crowell.

MacPherson, Peter. 1995. "Contested Winners Seated; Challengers in Pursuit." *Congressional Quarterly Weekly Report* 53 (7 January): 28.

Main, Jackson T. 1961. *The Antifederalists: Critics of the Constitution, 1781–1788.* Chicago: Quadrangle Books.

Malone, Dumas, ed. 1961. *Dictionary of American Biography.* 10 vols. New York: Charles Scribner's Son.

Maltz, Earl M. 1995. "The Impact of the Constitutional Revolution of 1937 on the Dormant Commerce Clause—A Case Study in the Decline of State Autonomy." *Harvard Journal of Law & Public Policy* 19 (Fall): 121–45.

———. 1990. *Civil Rights, the Constitution, and Congress, 1863–1869.* Lawrence: University Press of Kansas.

"The Man Who Would Not Quit." 1992. *People* 37 (April 1): 72.

Mangone, Gerald J. 1951. *The Idea and Practice of World Government.* New York: Columbia University Press.

Mann, Thomas E. 1992. "The Wrong Medicine." *Brookings Review* 10 (Spring): 23–25.

Mansbridge, Jane J. 1986. *Why We Lost the ERA.* Chicago: University of Chicago Press.

Marberry, M. M. 1967. *Vicky: A Biography of Victoria C. Woodhull.* New York: Funk and Wagnalls.

Marbury, William L. 1920. "The Nineteenth Amendment and After." *Virginia Law Review* 7 (October): 1–29.

———. 1919. "The Limitations upon the Amending Power." *Harvard Law Review* 33 (December): 223–35.

Marduke, P. G. 1970. *The CASCOT System for Social Control of Technology.* Silver Spring, MD: Citizens' Association for Social Control of Technology.

Masei, David. 1995. "Flag Resolution's Future Murky in More Divided Senate." *Congressional Quarterly Weekly Report* 53 (22 July): 2195.

Mason, Alpheus T. 1964. *The States Rights Debate: Antifederalism and the Constitution.* Englewood Cliffs, NJ: Prentice-Hall.

Mason, Alpheus T., and Gordon E. Baker. 1985. *Free Government in the Making: Readings in American Political Thought,* 4th ed. New York: Oxford University Press.

Mason, Alpheus T., and Donald G. Stephenson Jr. 1993. *American Constitutional Law: Introductory Essays and Selected Cases,* 9th ed. Englewood Cliffs, NJ: Prentice-Hall.

Massaro, John. 1990. *Supremely Political: The Role of Ideology and Presidential Management in Unsuccessful Supreme Court Nominations.* Albany: State University of New York Press.

Massey, Calvin R. 1995. *Silent Rights: The Ninth Amendment and the Constitution's Unenumerated Rights.* Philadelphia: Temple University Press.

Mathis, Doyle. 1967. "*Chisholm v. Georgia:* Background and Settlement." *Journal of American History* 54: 19–29.

Mathews, John M. 1908. *Legislative and Judicial History of the Fifteenth Amendment.* New York: Da Capo Press; 1971 reprint.

Matthews, Richard K. 1995. *If Men Were Angels: James Madison and the Heartless Empire of Reason.* Lawrence: University Press of Kansas.

May, Christopher N. 1989. *In the Name of War.* Cambridge, MA.: Harvard University Press.

May, James. 1992. "Antitrust." In *The Oxford Companion to the Supreme Court of the United States,* ed. Kermit L. Hall. New York: Oxford University Press.

May, Janice C. 1987. "Constitutional Amendment and Revision Revisited." *Publius: The Journal of Federalism* 17 (Winter): 153–79.

Mayer, David N. 1994. *The Constitutional Thought of Thomas Jefferson*. Charlottesville: University Press of Virginia.

———. 1990. "The Jurisprudence of Christopher G. Tiedeman: A Study in the Failure of Laissez-Faire Constitutionalism." *Missouri Law Review* 55 (Winter): 93–161.

Mayers, Lewis. 1959. *Shall We Amend the Fifth Amendment?* New York: Harper and Brothers.

Mayhew, David R. 1991. *Divided We Govern: Party Control, Lawmaking, and Investigations, 1946–1990*. New Haven, CT: Yale University Press.

Meador, Lewis H. 1898. "The Council of Censors." *Pennsylvania Magazine of History and Biography* 22: 265–300.

Melendez, Edgardo. 1988. *Puerto Rico's Statehood Movement*. New York: Greenwood Press.

Meltsner, Michael. 1974. *Cruel and Unusual: The Supreme Court and Capital Punishment*. New York: William Morrow.

Merriam, Charles E. 1931. *The Written Constitution and the Unwritten Attitude*. New York: Richard R. Smith.

Meyer, Alfred W. 1951. "The Blaine Amendment and the Bill of Rights." *Harvard Law Review* 64: 939–45.

Meyer, Karl E. 1968. "So Does the Bill of Rights." *Esquire* 70 (October): 147–48.

Meyers, Marvin, ed. 1973. *The Mind of the Founder: Sources of the Political Thought of James Madison*. Indianapolis, IN: Bobbs-Merrill.

Miller, Arthur S. 1987. *The Secret Constitution and the Need for Constitutional Change*. Westport, CT: Greenwood Press.

———. 1984. "The Annual John Randolph Tucker Lecture: Taking Needs Seriously: Observations on the Necessity for Constitutional Change." *Washington and Lee Law Review* 41 (Fall): 1243–306.

———. 1982. *Toward Increased Judicial Activism: The Political Role of the Supreme Court*. Westport, CT: Greenwood Press.

Miller, Jeremy. 1987. "It's Time for a New Constitution." *Southwestern University Law Review* 17: 207–37.

Miller, Robert S., and Donald O. Dewey. 1991. "The Congressional Salary Amendment: 200 Years Later." *Glendale Law Review* 10: 92–109.

Miller, William L. 1992. *The Business of May Next: James Madison and the Founding*. Charlottesville: University Press of Virginia.

Monaghan, Henry P. 1996. "We the People[s], Original Understanding, and Constitutional Amendment." *Columbia Law Review* 96 (January): 121–77.

Monsma, Stephen V. 1993. *Positive Neutrality: Letting Religious Freedom Ring*. Westport, CT: Greenwood Press.

Moore, John. July 29, 1995. "Pleading the 10th." *National Journal* 28 (July 29): 1940–44.

Moore, Trevor W. 1970. "A Rumbling in Babylon: Panthers Host a Parley." *Christian Century* 87 (28 October): 1296–1300.

Moore, W. S., and Rudolph G. Penner, eds. 1980. *The Constitution and the Budget: Are Constitutional Limits on Tax, Spending and Budget Powers Desirable at the Federal Level?* Washington, DC: American Enterprise Institute for Public Policy Research.

Morehead, Joe. 1985. "Private Bills and Private Laws: A Guide to the Legislative Process." *Serials Librarian* 9 (Spring): 115–25.

Morgan, Thomas J. 1963. "Seventeen States Vote To Destroy Democracy As We Know It." *Look* 27 (3 December): 76–88.

Morris, Henry O. 1897. *Waiting for the Signal, a Novel*. Chicago: Schulte.

Morris, Thomas D. 1974. *Free Men All: The Personal Liberty Laws of the North, 1780–1861*. Baltimore: Johns Hopkins University Press.

Morrison, Charles C. 1972. *The Outlawry of War: A Constructive Policy for World Peace*. New York: Garland Publishing.

Morrison, Stanley. 1949. "Does the Fourteenth Amendment Incorporate the Bill of Rights? The Judicial Interpretation." *Stanford Law Review* 2 (December): 140–73.

Morton, Robert K. 1933. *God in the Constitution*. Nashville: Cokesbury Press.

Murphy, Bruce A. 1988. *Fortas: The Rise and Ruin of a Supreme Court Justice*. New York: William Morrow.

Murphy, Cornelius F., Jr. 1988. "Constitutional Revision." In *Philosophical Dimensions of the Constitution*, ed. Diana T. Meyers and Kenneth Kipnis. Boulder, CO: Westview Press.

Murphy, Walter F. 1995. "Merlin's Memory: The Past and Future Imperfect of the Once and Future Polity." In *Responding to Imperfection*, ed. Sanford Levinson. Princeton, NJ: Princeton University Press.

———. 1992a. "Consent and Constitutional Change." In *Human Rights and Constitutional Law: Essays in Honour of Brian Walsh*, ed. James O'Reilly. Dublin: Found Hall Press.

———. 1992b. "Staggering Toward the New Jerusalem of Constitutional Theory: A Response to Ralph F. Graebler." *American Journal of Jurisprudence* 37: 337–57.

———. 1990. "The Right to Privacy and Legitimate Constitutional Change." In *Constitutional Bases of Political and Social Change in the United States,* ed. Shlomo Slonin. New York: Praeger.

———. 1987. "*Slaughterhouse, Civil Rights,* and Limits on Constitutional Change." *American Journal of Jurisprudence* 23: 1–22.

———. 1980. "An Ordering of Constitutional Values." *Southern California Law Review* 53: 703–60.

———. 1978. "The Art of Constitutional Interpretation: A Preliminary Showing." In *Essays on the Constitution of the United States,* ed. M. Harmon. Port Washington, NY: Kennikat Press.

———. 1962. *Congress and the Court.* Chicago: University of Chicago Press.

Murphy, Walter F., James E. Fleming, and Sotirious Barber. 1995. *American Constitutional Interpretation,* 2d ed. Westbury, NY: Foundation Press.

Musmanno, M. A. 1929. *Proposed Amendments to the Constitution.* Washington, DC: U.S. Government Printing Office.

Myles, John. 1989. *Old Age in the Welfare State: The Political Economy of Public Pensions.* Lawrence: University Press of Kansas.

Nagel, Stuart S. 1965. "Court-Curbing Proposals in American History." *Vanderbilt Law Review* 18: 925–44.

Nelson, Michael. 1987. "Constitutional Qualifications for President." *Presidential Studies Quarterly* 17 (Spring): 383–99.

Nelson, Michael, ed. 1989. *Guide to the Presidency.* Washington, DC: Congressional Quarterly.

Nelson, William E. 1988. *The Fourteenth Amendment: From Political Principle to Judicial Doctrine.* Cambridge, MA: Harvard University Press.

Newman, Roger K. 1994. *Hugo Black: A Biography.* New York: Pantheon Books.

Niven, John. 1988. *John C. Calhoun and the Price of Union: A Biography.* Baton Rouge: Louisiana State University Press.

Norham, George W. 1988. "A Constitutional Door Is Opened for Amendment." *Texas Bar Journal* 51 (September): 804–6.

"North Carolina Ratifies the 24th Amendment." 1989. *We the People: A Newsletter of the Commission on the Bicentennial of the United States Constitution* 5 (July): 10.

Oates, Stephen B. 1970. *To Purge This Land with Blood: A Biography of John Brown.* New York: Harper and Row.

O'Brien, David M. 1995. *Civil Rights and Civil Liberties,* 2d ed. Vol. 2 of *Constitutional Law and Politics.* New York: W. W. Norton.

———. 1991. *Struggles for Power and Governmental Accountability.* Vol. 1 of *Constitutional Law and Politics.* New York: W. W. Norton.

O'Brien, F. William. 1965. "The States and 'No Establishment': Proposed Amendments to the Constitution since 1798." *Washburn Law Journal* 4: 183–210.

———. 1963. "The Blaine Amendment, 1875–1876." *University of Detroit Law Journal* 41 (December): 137–205.

O'Connor, Karen. 1996. *No Neutral Ground? Abortion Politics in an Age of Absolutes.* Boulder, CO: Westview.

O'Conor, Charles. 1881. "Democracy." In *Johnson's New Universal Cyclopaedia: A Treasury of Scientific and Popular Treasure of Useful Knowledge.* Vol. 1, Part 2. New York: A. J. Johnson.

———. 1877. *Address by Charles O'Conor Delivered before the New York Historical Society at the Academy of Music.* 8 May. New York: Anson D. F. Randolph.

Ogden, Frederic D. 1958. *The Poll Tax in the South.* University: University of Alabama Press.

O'Neil, Patrick M. 1995. "The Declaration as Ur-Constitution: The Bizarre Jurisprudential Philosophy of Professor Harry V. Jaffa." *Akron Law Review* 28 (Fall/Winter): 237–52.

Onuf, Peter. 1984. "Territories and Statehood." In *Encyclopedia of American Political History: Studies of Principal Movements and Ideas,* ed. Jack P. Greene. Vol. 3. New York: Charles Scribner's Sons.

Orfield, Lester B. 1942. *The Amending of the Federal Constitution.* Ann Arbor: University of Michigan Press.

Ornstein, Norman J. 1994. "Congress Inside Out." *Roll Call* 39 (10 March): 5–6.

Ornstein, Norman J., and Amy L. Schenhenberg. 1995. "The 1995 Congress: The First Hundred Days and Beyond." *Political Science Quarterly* 110 (Summer): 183–206.

Orth, John V. 1992. "Eleventh Amendment." In *The Oxford Companion to the Supreme Court of the United States,* ed. Kermit L. Hall. New York: Oxford University Press.

———. 1987. *The Judicial Power of the United States: The Eleventh Amendment in American History.* New York: Oxford University Press.

O'Toole, Lawrence J., Jr., ed. 1985. *American Intergovernmental Relations: Foundations, Perspectives, and Issues.* Washington, DC: Congressional Quarterly.

Pace, James O. 1986. *Amendment to the Constitution: Averting the Decline and Fall of America.* Los Angeles: Johnson, Pace, Simmons and Fennell.

Padover, Saul K. 1962. *To Secure These Blessings.* New York: Washington Square Press/Ridge Press.

Paludan, Phillip S. 1994. *The Presidency of Abraham Lincoln.* Lawrence: University Press of Kansas.

"Panthers Plan New Convention." 1971. In *Facts on File Yearbook, 1970.* Vol. 30. New York: Facts on File.

Paschal, Richard A. 1991. "The Continuing Colloquy: Congress and the Finality of the Supreme Court." *Journal of Law and Politics* 8 (Fall): 143–226.

Patrick, John J. 1994. *The Young Oxford Companion to the Supreme Court of the United States.* New York: Oxford University Press.

Patterson, Bennett B. 1955. *The Forgotten Ninth Amendment.* Indianapolis, IN: Bobbs-Merrill.

Paulsen, Michael S. 1995. "The Case for a Constitutional Convention." *Wall Street Journal* 3 May, A-15.

———. 1994. "Is Lloyd Bentsen Unconstitutional?" *Stanford Law Review* 46 (April): 907–18.

———. 1993. "A General Theory of Article V: The Constitutional Issues of the Twenty-seventh Amendment." *Yale Law Journal* 103: 677–789.

Pear, Robert. 1994. "State Officials Worry That a Federal Budget Will Be Balanced on Their Books." *New York Times,* 11 December, 34

Pearson, Hugh. 1994. *The Shadow of the Panther: Huey Newton and the Price of Black Power in America.* Reading, MA: Addison-Wesley.

Pease, William H., and June H. Pease, eds. 1965. *The Antislavery Argument.* Indianapolis, IN: Bobbs-Merrill.

Peck, Robert S. 1992. *The Bill of Rights and the Politics of Interpretation.* St. Paul, MN: West.

Pei, Mario. 1967–1968. "The Case for a Constitutional Convention." *Modern Age* 12 (Winter): 8–13.

Peirce, Neal R. 1968. *The People's President: The Electoral College in American History and the Direct-Vote Alternative.* New York: Simon and Schuster.

Peltason, Jack W. 1994. *Corwin and Peltason's Understanding the Constitution,* 13th ed. Fort Worth, TX: Harcourt Brace College Publishers.

Penney, Annette C. 1968. *The Golden Voice of the Senate.* Washington, DC: American Enterprise Institute for Public Policy Research.

Penniman, Clara. 1980. *State Income Taxation.* Baltimore: Johns Hopkins University Press.

Peters, Ronald M., Jr. 1990. "Repeal the Seventeenth!" *Extensions* 2 (Spring): 16–17.

Peters, William. 1987. *A More Perfect Union: The Making of the United States Constitution.* New York: Crown.

Peterson, Charles S. 1977. *Utah: A Bicentennial History.* New York: W. W. Norton.

"Philippines, Republic of the." 1994. *Microsoft Encarta Multimedia Encyclopedia.*

Piburn, John L. 1932. *A Constitution and a Code.* San Diego: Bowman Printing Company.

Pious, Richard M. 1978. "Introduction." In *The Abolition of the Presidency.* Farmingdale, NY: Darbor Social Science Publications.

Pizzigati, Sam. 1994. "Salary Caps for Everyone!" *New York Times,* 28 August, 15.

———. 1992. *The Maximum Wage: A Common-Sense Prescription for Revitalizing America—By Taxing the Very Rich.* New York: Appex Press.

Planell, Raymond M. 1974. "The Equal Rights Amendment: Will States Be Allowed To Change Their Minds?" *Notre Dame Lawyer* 49 (February): 657–70.

Political Economy and Constitutional Reform. 1982. Hearings before the Joint Economic Committee of the Congress of the United States. 97th Cong., 2nd Sess.

Porter, Kirk H., and Donald B. Johnson. 1966. *National Party Platforms, 1840–1964.* Urbana: University of Illinois Press.

Powe, Lucas A., Jr. 1991. *The Fourth Estate and the Constitution: Freedom of Press in America.* Berkeley: University of California Press.

Prinz, Timothy S. 1992. "Term Limitation: A Perilous Panacea." *The World & I* 7 (January): 143–53.

Proposals for a Constitutional Convention To Require a Balanced Federal Budget. 1979. Washington, DC: American Enterprise Institute for Public Policy Research.

Proposed Amendments to the Constitution of the United States, Introduced in Congress from the 69th Congress, 2d Session through the 84th Congress, 2d Session, December 6, 1926, to January 3, 1957. 1957. Washington, DC: U.S. Government Printing Office.

Proposed Amendments to the Constitution of the United States of America Introduced in Congress from the 69th Congress, 2d Session through the 87th

Congress, 2d Session, December 6, 1926, to January 3, 1963. 1963. Washington, DC: U.S. Government Printing Office.

Proposed Amendments to the Constitution of the United States of America Introduced in Congress from the 88th Congress, 1st Session through the 90th Congress, 2d Session, January 9, 1963, to January 3, 1969. 1969. Washington, DC: U.S. Government Printing Office.

"Proposed Legislation on the Convention Method of Amending the United States Constitution." 1972. *Harvard Law Review* 85: 1612–48.

Pullen, William R. 1948. *Applications of State Legislatures to Congress for the Call of a National Constitutional Convention, 1788–1867.* Master's thesis, University of North Carolina at Chapel Hill.

Radin, Max. 1930. "The Intermittent Sovereign." *Yale Law Journal* 30: 514–31.

Rakove, Jack N., ed. 1990. *Interpreting the Constitution: The Debate over Original Intent.* Boston: Northeastern University Press.

Ranney, Austin. 1978. "The United States of America." In *Referendums: A Comparative Study of Practice and Theory,* ed. David Butler and Austin Raney. Washington, DC: American Enterprise Institute for Public Policy Research.

Rasmussen, Jorgen S., and Joel C. Moses. 1995. *Major European Governments,* 9th ed. Belmont, CA: Wadsworth.

Raven-Hansen, Peter. 1975. "Congressional Representation for the District of Columbia: A Constitutional Analysis." *Harvard Journal of Legislation* 12: 167–92.

Rawley, James A. 1981. *The Transatlantic Slave Trade: A History.* New York: W. W. Norton.

Reagan, Ronald, et al. 1990. *Restoring the Presidency: Reconsidering the Twenty-second Amendment.* Washington, DC: National Legal Center for Public Interest.

Records of the Council of Censors. 1783–1784. Journal vols. 1–3. Division of Archives and Manuscripts, Pennsylvania Historical and Museum Commission.

Reed, Ralph. 1995. *Contract with the American Family: A Bold Plan by Christian Coalition To Strengthen the Family and Restore Common-Sense Values.* Nashville, TN: Moorings.

Rees, Grover, III. 1986. "The Amendment Process and Limited Constitutional Conventions." *Benchmark* 2: 67–108.

Reid, John P. 1993. *Constitutional History of the American Revolution. The Authority of Law.* Madison: University of Wisconsin Press.

Reidinger, Paul. 1996. "The Faltering Revolution." *ABA Journal* 82 (February): 56–59.

Renehan, Edward J., Jr. 1995. *The Secret Six: The True Tale of the Men Who Conspired with John Brown.* New York: Crown.

Report on the Condition of Women and Children as Wage Earners. 1910–1913. U.S. Department of Labor. 19 vols. Washington, DC: U.S. Government Printing Office.

Report to the Attorney General. 1987. *The Question of Statehood for the District of Columbia.* 3 April. Washington, DC: U.S. Government Printing Office.

"Retroactive Tax Increases: No Problem, Say Justices." 1994. *Congressional Quarterly Weekly Report* 52 (18 June): 1588.

Reynolds, Edward. 1985. *Stand the Storm: A History of the Atlantic Slave Trade.* London: Allison and Busby.

Reynolds, Eustace. 1915. *A New Constitution: A Suggested Form of Modified Constitution.* New York: Nation Press.

Rice, Isaac. 1884. "Work for a Constitutional Convention." *Century Magazine* 28 (August): 534–40.

Rich, Bennett M. 1960. *Major Problems in State Constitutional Revision,* ed. W. Brooke Groves. Chicago: Public Administration Service.

Richards, David A. J. 1993. *Conscience and the Constitution: History, Theory, and Law of the Reconstruction Amendments.* Princeton, NJ: Princeton University Press.

Richardson, James E., ed. 1908. *A Compilation of the Messages and Papers of the Presidents, 1789–1908.* 11 vols. n.p.: Bureau of National Literature and Art.

Richardson, Sula. 1991. *Congressional Terms of Office and Tenure: Historical Background and Contemporary Issues.* Washington, DC: Congressional Research Service, Library of Congress.

———. 1989. *Congressional Tenure: A Review of Efforts To Limit House and Senate Service.* Washington, DC: Congressional Research Service, Library of Congress.

Richie, Robert. 1995. "Democracy and Majority Preference Voting." *Rainbow* 3, no. 30 (27 July).

Riker, William H. 1954. "Sidney George Fisher and the Separation of Powers During the Civil War." *Journal of the History of Ideas* 15 (June): 397–412.

"Rising Clamor for Black Separatism." 1970. *U.S. News and World Report* 69 (21 September): 82.

Robinson, Donald. 1989. *Government for the Third American Century.* Boulder, CO: Westview Press.

———. 1987. "Adjustments Are Needed in the System of Checks and Balances." *Polity* 19: 660–66.

———. 1985. *Reforming American Government: The Bicentennial Papers of the Committee on the Constitutional System.* Boulder, CO: Westview Press.

Roemer, Arthur C. 1983. "Classification of Property." In *The Property Tax and Local Finance,* ed. C. Lowell Harris. New York: Proceedings of the Academy of Political Science.

Rohde, David W. 1994. "The Fall Elections: Realignment or Dealignment." *Chronicle of Higher Education* 41 (14 December): B1–B2.

Rosen, Jeff. 1991. "Was the Flag Burning Amendment Unconstitutional?" *Yale Law Review* 100: 1073–92.

Rosen, Jeffrey. 1996. "Just a Quirk." *New Republic* 214 (March 18): 16–17.

Rosenberg, Gerald N. 1991. *The Hollow Hope: Can Courts Bring About Social Change?* Chicago: University of Chicago Press.

Rosenbloom, David H. 1971. *Federal Service and the Constitution: the Development of the Public Employment Relationship.* Ithaca, NY: Cornell University Press.

Ross, Russell M., and Fred Schwengel. Winter 1982. "An Item Veto for the President?" *Presidential Studies Quarterly* 12 (Winter): 66–79.

Ross, William G. 1990. "The Hazards of Proposals To Limit the Tenure of Federal Judges and To Permit Judicial Removal Without Impediment." *Villanova Law Review* 35 (November): 1063–1138.

Rossiter, Clinton. 1987. *1787: The Grand Convention.* New York: W. W. Norton.

Rossum, Ralph A., and G. Alan Tarr. 1991. *American Constitutional Law,* 3d ed. New York: St Martin's Press.

Rothwax, Harold J. 1996. *Guilty: The Collapse of Criminal Justice.* New York: Random House.

Rousseau, Jean-Jacques. 1978. *On the Social Contract with Geneva Manuscript and Political Economy,* ed. Roger D. Masters. New York: St. Martin's Press.

Rubin, Alissa J. 1995. "Democrats Hope Tax-Raising Rule Will Come Back To Haunt GOP." *Congressional Quarterly Weekly Report* 53 (15 July): 2045–46.

Rubin, Irene S. 1990. *The Politics of Public Budgeting: Getting and Spending, Borrowing and Balancing.* Chatham, NJ: Chatham House.

Salins, Peter D., ed. 1987. *Housing America's Poor.* Chapel Hill: University of North Carolina Press.

Sargentich, Thomas O. 1993. "The Limits of the Parliamentary Critique of the Separation of Powers." *William and Mary Law Review* 34 (Spring): 679–739.

Sartori, Giovanni. 1994. *Comparative Constitutional Engineering: An Inquiry into Structures, Incentives and Outcomes.* New York: New York University Press.

Savage, James D. 1988. *Balanced Budgets and American Politics.* Ithaca, NY: Cornell University Press.

"Sawing a Justice in Half." 1939. *Yale Law Journal* 48: 1455–58.

Schapsmeier, Edward L., and Frederick H. Schapsmeier. 1985. *Dirksen of Illinois: Senatorial Statesman.* Urbana: University of Illinois Press.

Scharpf, Fritz W. 1966. "Judicial Review and the Political Question: A Functional Analysis." *Yale Law Journal* 75 (March): 517–97.

Scheiber, Harry N. 1992. "Police Power." In *The Oxford Companion to the Supreme Court of the United States,* ed. Kermit L. Hall. New York: Oxford University Press.

Schlesinger, Arthur M., Jr. 1974. "On the Presidential Succession." *Political Science Quarterly* 89 (Fall): 475–505.

Schlickeisen, Rodger. 1994. "Protecting Biodiversity for Future Generations: An Argument for a Constitutional Amendment." *Tulane Environmental Law Journal* 8 (Winter): 181–221.

Schmidt, David D. 1989. *Citizen Law Makers: The Ballot Initiative Revolution.* Philadelphia: Temple University Press.

Schneier, Edward V., and Bertram Gross. 1993. *Legislative Strategy.* New York: St. Martin's Press.

Schotten, Peter, and Dennis Stevens. 1996. *Religion, Politics, and the Law: Commentaries and Controversies.* Belmont, CA: Wadsworth.

Schouler, James. 1908. "A New Federal Constitution." In *Ideals of the Republic,* ed. James Schouler. Boston: Little, Brown.

Schrader, George D. 1970. "Constitutional History of the Income Tax." *Georgia State Bar Journal* 7 (August): 39–55.

Schrag, Philip G. 1985. *Behind the Scenes: The Politics of a Constitutional Convention.* Washington, DC: Georgetown University Press.

Schubert, Glendon. 1954. "Politics and the Constitution: The Bricker Amendment During 1953." *Journal of Politics* 16 (May): 257–98.

Schuck, Peter H., and Rogers M. Smith. 1985. *Citizenship Without Consent: Illegal Aliens in the American Polity.* New Haven, CT: Yale University Press.

Schwartz, Bernard. 1992. *The Great Rights of Mankind: A History of the American Bill of Rights.* Madison, WI: Madison House.

———. 1988. *Super Chief: Earl Warren and His Supreme Court—A Judicial Biography.* New York: New York University Press.

———. 1986. *Swann's Way: The School Busing Case and the Supreme Court.* New York: Oxford University Press.

Schwartz, Bernard, ed. 1980. *The Roots of the Bill of Rights.* 5 vols. New York: Chelsea House.

Scigliano, Robert. 1994. "The Two Executives: The President and the Supreme Court." In *The American Experiment: Essays on the Theory and Practice of Liberty,* ed. Peter A. Lawler and Robert M. Schoefar. Lanham, MD: Rowman and Littlefield.

Second Amendment Symposium. 1995. *Tennessee Law Review* 62 (Spring): 443–821.

Seelye, Katharine Q. 1995." Congress Members Off Hook on Re-election, but Not Issue." *New York Times,* 23 May, A-1, A-11.

Seitz, Don C. 1929. *Famous American Duels: With Some Account of the Causes That Led up to Them and the Men Engaged.* Freeport, NY: Books for Libraries Press; 1966 reprint.

Shalom, Stephen R. 1981. *The United States and the Philippines: A Study of Neocolonialism.* Philadelphia: Institute for the Study of Human Issues.

Shand-Tucci, Douglass. 1995. *Boston Bohemia, 1881–1990: Ralph Adams Cram: Life and Architecture.* Amherst: University of Massachusetts Press.

———. 1975. *Ralph Adams Cram: American Medievalist.* Boston: Boston Public Library.

Shannon, David A. 1967. *The Socialist Party of America: A History.* Chicago: Quadrangle Books.

Shermer, Matt. 1969. *"The Sense of the People" or the Next Development in American Democracy.* New York: American Referendum Association.

Sidak, J. Gregory. 1995. "The Line-Item Veto Amendment." *Cornell Law Review* 80 (July): 1498–1505.

———. 1989. "The Recommendation Clause." *Georgetown Law Journal* 77 (August): 2070–2135.

Sigler, Jay A. 1969. *Double Jeopardy: The Development of a Legal and Social Policy.* Ithaca, NY: Cornell University Press.

Sigmund, Paul E. 1971. *Natural Law in Political Thought.* Cambridge, MA: Winthrop Publishers.

Silva, Edward J. 1970. "State Cohorts and Amendment Clusters in the Process of Federal Constitutional Amendments in the United States,

1869–1931." *Law and Society Review* 4 (February): 445–66.

Skillen, James W., ed. 1993. *The School Choice Controversy: What Is Constitutional?* Grand Rapids, MI: Baker Books.

Smith, Goldwin. 1906. "Chief Justice Clark on the Defects of the American Constitution." *North American Review* 183 (1 November): 845–51.

———. 1898. "Is the Constitution Outworn?" *North American Review* 166 (March): 257–67.

Smith, Page. 1995. *Democracy on Trial: The Japanese American Evacuation and Relocation in World War II.* New York: Simon and Schuster.

Smith, Rodney K. 1987. *Public Prayer and the Constitution: A Case Study in Constitutional Interpretation.* Wilmington, DE: Scholarly Resources.

Smith, Steven. 1989. "Taking It to the Floor." In *Congress Reconsidered,* ed. Lawrence C. Dodd and Bruce I. Oppenheimer. Washington, DC: Congressional Quarterly.

Solberg, Winton, ed. 1958. *The Federal Convention and the Formation of the Union.* Indianapolis, IN: Bobbs-Merrill.

Soller, Christopher J. 1995. "*Newtonian* Government: Is the Contract with America Unconstitutional?" *Duquesne Law Review* 33 (Summer): 959–84.

Sorauf, Frank J. 1988. *Money in American Elections.* Glenview, IL: Scott, Foresman.

Spitzer, Robert J. 1995. *The Politics of Gun Control.* Chatham, NJ: Chatham House Publishers.

———. 1988. *The Presidential Veto: Touchstone of the American Presidency.* Albany: State University of New York Press.

Spotts, JoAnne D. 1994. "The Twenty-seventh Amendment: A Late Bloomer or a Dead Horse?" *Georgia State University Law Review* 10 (January): 337–65.

Stanwood, Edward. 1903. *American Tariff Controversies in the Nineteenth Century.* 2 vols. New York: Russell and Russell; 1967 reprint.

Stathis, Stephen. 1990. "The Twenty-second Amendment: A Practical Remedy or Partisan Maneuver?" *Constitutional Commentary* 7 (Winter): 61–88.

Steamer, Robert J. 1992. "Commerce Power." In *The Oxford Companion to the Supreme Court of the United States,* ed. Kermit L. Hall. New York: Oxford University Press.

Stern, Madeline B., ed. 1974. *The Victoria Woodhull Reader.* Weston, MA: M & S Press.

Stevens, Doris. 1995. *Jailed for Freedom: American Women Win the Vote.* Troutdale, OR: New Sage.

Stickney, Albert. 1879. *A True Republic.* New York: Harper and Brothers.

Stone, Geoffrey R., Richard A. Epstein, and Cass R. Sunstein, eds. 1992. *The Bill of Rights in the Modern State.* Chicago: University of Chicago Press.

Stoner, James R., Jr. 1995. "Amending the School Prayer Amendment." *First Things* 51 (May): 16–18.

Storing, Herbert, ed. 1981. *The Complete Anti-Federalist.* 7 vols. Chicago: University of Chicago Press.

———, ed. 1970. *What Country Have I? Political Writings by Black Americans.* New York: St. Martin's Press.

Story, Joseph. 1987. *Commentaries on the Constitution of the United States.* Durham, NC: Carolina Academic Press.

———. 1833. *Commentaries on the Constitution of the United States.* New York: Da Capo Press; 1970 reprint of Hilliard, Gray.

Stowe, Steven M. 1987. *Intimacy and Power in the Old South: Ritual in the Lives of the Planters.* Baltimore: Johns Hopkins University Press.

Strickland, Ruth A. 1993. "The Twenty-seventh Amendment and Constitutional Change by Stealth." *P.S. Political Science and Politics* 26 (December): 716–22.

———. 1989. *The Ratification Process of U.S. Constitutional Amendments: Each State Having One Vote as a Form of Malapportionment.* Ph.D. dissertation, University of South Carolina.

Sturm, Albert L., and Janice May. 1982. "State Constitutions and Constitutional Revision: 1980–81 and the Past 50 Years." In *The Book of the States: 1982–1983.* Lexington, KY: Council of State Governments.

Suber, Peter. 1990. *The Paradox of Self-Amendment: A Study of Logic, Law, Omnipotence, and Change.* New York: Peter Lang.

———. 1987. "Population Changes and Constitutional Amendments: Federalism versus Democracy." *Journal of Law Reform* 20 (Winter): 409–90.

Sullivan, J. W. 1893. *Direct Legislation by the Citizenship.* New York: Nationalist Publishing Company.

Sullivan, Kathleen M. 1995. "Constitutional Constancy: Why Congress Should Cure Itself of Amendment Fever." *Record of the Bar of the City of New York* 50 (November): 724–35.

Sundquist, James L. 1986. *Constitutional Reform and Effective Government.* Washington, DC: Brookings Institution.

Suthon, Walter J., Jr. 1953. "The Dubious Origin of the Fourteenth Amendment." *Tulane Law Review* 28: 22–44.

Swanson, Wayne R. 1990. *The Christ Child Goes to Court.* Philadelphia: Temple University Press.

Swindler, William. 1963. "The Current Challenge to Federalism: The Confederating Proposals." *Georgetown Law Review* 52 (Fall): 1–41.

"Symposium on the Reuss Resolution: A Vote of No Confidence in the President." 1975. *George Washington Law Review* 43 (January): 328–500.

Taft, Henry. 1930. "Amendment of the Federal Constitution: Is the Power Conferred by Article V Limited by the Tenth Amendment?" *Virginia Law Review* 16 (May): 647–58.

Tananbaum, Duane. 1988. *The Bricker Amendment Controversy: A Test of Eisenhower's Political Leadership.* Ithaca, NY: Cornell University Press.

Tansill, Charles C. 1926. *Proposed Amendments of the Constitution of the United States Introduced in Congress from December 4, 1889, to July 2, 1926.* Washington, DC: U.S. Government Printing Office.

Tarr, G. Alan. 1994. *Judicial Process and Judicial Policymaking.* St. Paul, MN: West.

Tatalovich, Raymond. 1995. *Nativism Reborn? The Official English Language Movement and the American States.* Lexington: University Press of Kentucky.

Taylor, A. Elizabeth. 1957. *The Woman Suffrage Movement in Tennessee.* New York: Bookman Associates.

Taylor, Andrew. 1996a. "Congress Hands Presidency a Budgetary Scalpel." *Congressional Quarterly Weekly Report* 54 (30 March): 864–67.

———. 1996b. "Republicans Break Logjam on Line-Item Veto Bill." *Congressional Quarterly Weekly Report* 54 (16 March): 687.

Taylor, George R., ed. 1993. *The Great Tariff Debate, 1820–1830.* Boston: D. C. Heath.

Taylor, Joe Gray. 1976. *Louisiana: A Bicentennial History.* New York: W. W. Norton.

Ten Broek, Jacobus. 1951. *The Antislavery Origins of the Fourteenth Amendment.* Berkeley: University of California Press.

"Text of Amendment." 1995. *Congressional Quarterly Weekly Report* 53 (4 March): 673.

"33 States Ask Congress for Constitutional Convention." 1969. *Congressional Quarterly Weekly Report* 27 (1 August): 1372–73.

Thorpe, Francis N. 1909. *The Federal and State Constitutions Colonial Charters and Other Organic Laws of the States, Territories, and Colonies Now or*

Heretofore Forming the United States of America. 7 vols. Washington, DC: U.S. Government Printing Office.

Tiedeman, Christopher G. 1890. *The Unwritten Constitution of the United States*. New York: G. P. Putnam's Sons.

Timberlake, James H. 1970. *Prohibition and the Progressive Movement, 1900–1920*. New York: Atheneum.

Tocqueville, Alexis de. 1969. *Democracy in America*, ed. J. P. Mayer. Garden City, NY: Anchor Books.

Tolchin, Mark. 1990. "Fifteen States Rally behind Calls for Amendment To Gain More Powers." *New York Times*, 26 June, A-12, col. 3–6.

Tomlins, Christopher L. 1985. *The State and the Unions: Labor Relations, Law, and the Organized Labor Movement in America, 1880–1960*. Cambridge: Cambridge University Press.

Toner, Robin. 1995. "Flag Burning Amendment Fails in Senate, but Margin Narrows." *New York Times* 115 (December 13): 1.

Torke, James W. 1994. "Assessing the Ackerman and Amar Theses: Notes on Extratextual Constitutional Change." *Widener Journal of Public Law* 4: 229–71.

Trattner, Walter I. 1970. *Crusade for the Children: A History of the National Child Labor Committee and Child Labor Reform in America*. Chicago: Quadrangle Books.

Traynor, Roger J. 1927. *The Amending System of the United States Constitution, an Historical and Legal Analysis*. Ph.D. dissertation, University of California.

Tribe, Laurence H. 1990. *Abortion: The Clash of Absolutes*. New York: W. W. Norton.

———. 1983. "A *Constitution* We Are Amending: In Defense of a Restrained Judicial Role." *Harvard Law Review* 97 (December): 433–45.

Tribe, Laurence H., and Michael C. Dorf. 1991. *On Reading the Constitution*. Cambridge, Mass.: Harvard University Press.

Tugwell, Rexford. 1974. *The Emerging Constitution*. New York: Harper and Row.

Tuller, Walter K. 1911. "A Convention to Amend the Constitution—Why Needed—How It May Be Obtained." *North American Review* 193: 369–87.

Turner, John J., Jr. 1973. "The Twelfth Amendment and the First American Party System." *Historian* 35: 221–37.

Tushnet, Mark. 1990. "The Flag-Burning Episode: An Essay on the Constitution." *University of Colorado Law Review* 61: 39–53.

Twentieth Century Fund Task Force on the Vice Presidency. 1988. *A Heartbeat Away*. New York: Printing Press Publications.

The Twenty-Fifth Amendment: Preparing for Presidential Disability. 1995. *Wake Forest Law Review* 30 (Fall): 427–648.

Unger, Sanford J. 1972. *The Paper and the Papers*. New York: E. P. Dutton.

United States Senate, Subcommittee on the Constitution, Committee on the Judiciary. 1985. *Amendments to the Constitution: A Brief Legislative History*. Washington DC: U.S. Government Printing Office.

Upham, Thomas C. 1941. *Total Democracy: A New Constitution for the United States. A Democratic Ideal for the World*. New York: Carlyle House.

Urofsky, Melvin I. 1988. *A March of Liberty: A Constitutional History of the United States*. New York: Alfred A. Knopf.

Van Alstyne, William. 1993. "What Do You Think About the Twenty-seventh Amendment?" *Constitutional Commentary* 10 (Winter): 9–18.

———. 1979. "The Limited Constitutional Convention—The Recurring Answer." *Duke Law Journal* 1979 (September): 985–1001.

———. 1978. "Does Article V Restrict the States to Calling Unlimited Conventions Only?—A Letter to a Colleague." *Duke Law Journal* 1978 (January): 1295–1306.

Van Burkleo, Sandra F. 1990. "No Rights but Human Rights." *Constitution* 2 (Spring-Summer): 4–19.

Vandercoy, David E. 1994. "The History of the Second Amendment." *Valparaiso University Law Review* 28 (Spring): 1007–39.

Van Deusen, Glyndon. 1937. *The Life of Henry Clay*. Boston: Little, Brown.

Van Doren, Carl. 1948. *The Great Rehearsal: The Story of the Making and Ratifying of the Constitution of the United States*. New York: Viking Press.

Van Riper, Paul P. 1958. *History of the United States Civil Service*. Evanston, IL: Row, Peterson.

Van Sickle, Bruce M., and Lynn M. Boughey. 1990. "Lawful and Peaceful Revolution: Article V and Congress' Present Duty To Call a Convention for Proposing Amendments." *Hamline Law Review* 14 (Fall): 1–115.

Vierra, Norman. 1981. "The Equal Rights Amendment: Rescission, Extension and Justiciability." *Southern Illinois Law Journal* 1981: 1–29.

Vile, John R. 1995. "The Case against Implicit Limits on the Constitutional Amending Process." In *Re-*

sponding to Imperfection, ed. Sanford Levinson. Princeton, NJ: Princeton University Press.

———. 1994a. *Constitutional Change in the United States: A Comparative Study of the Role of Constitutional Amendments, Judicial Interpretations, and Legislative and Executive Actions.* Westport, CT: Praeger.

———. 1994b. "The Selection and Tenure of Chief Justices." *Judicature* 78 (September-October): 96–100.

———. 1993a. *A Companion to the United States Constitution and Its Amendments.* Westport, CT: Praeger.

———. 1993b. *Contemporary Questions Surrounding the Constitutional Amending Process.* Westport, CT: Praeger.

———. 1993c. *The Theory and Practice of Constitutional Change in America: A Collection of Original Source Materials.* New York: Peter Lang.

———. 1993d. "Three Kinds of Constitutional Founding and Change: The Convention Model and Its Alternatives." *Political Research Quarterly* 46: 881–95.

———. 1992. *The Constitutional Amending Process in American Political Thought.* New York: Praeger.

———. 1991a. "Just Say No to 'Stealth' Amendment." *National Law Journal* 14 (22 June): 15–16.

———. 1991b. "Proposals To Amend the Bill of Rights: Are Fundamental Rights in Jeopardy?" *Judicature* 75 (August-September): 62–67.

———. 1991c. *Rewriting the United States Constitution: An Examination of Proposals from Reconstruction to the Present.* New York: Praeger.

———. 1990–1991. "Legally Amending the United States Constitution: The Exclusivity of Article V's Mechanisms." *Cumberland Law Review* 21: 271–307.

———. 1990. "Permitting States To Rescind Ratifications of Pending Amendments to the U.S. Constitution." *Publius: The Journal of Federalism* 20 (Spring): 109–22.

———. 1989. "How a Constitutional Amendment Protecting the Flag Might Widen Protection of Symbolic Expression." *Louisiana Bar Journal* 37 (October): 169–72.

———. 1985. "Limitations on the Constitutional Amending Process." *Constitutional Commentary* 2 (Summer): 373–88.

Vile, John R., and Mario Perez-Reilly. 1991. "The U.S. Constitution and Judicial Qualifications: A Curious Omission." *Judicature* 74 (December-January): 198–202.

Virginia Commission on Constitutional Government. 1967. *The Reconstruction Amendments Debates.* Richmond: Virginia Commission on Constitutional Government.

Volcansek, Mary L. 1993. *Judicial Impeachment: None Called for Justice.* Urbana: University of Illinois Press.

Voorhis, Jerry. 1947. *Confessions of a Congressman.* Westport, CT: Greenwood Press; 1970 reprint.

Vose, Clement E. 1979. "When District of Columbia Representation Collides with the Constitutional Amendment Institution." *Publius: The Journal of Federalism* 9 (Winter): 105–25.

———. 1972. *Constitutional Change: Amendment Politics and Supreme Court Litigation since 1900.* Lexington, MA: D. C. Heath.

Walker, David M. 1980. *The Oxford Companion to Law.* Oxford: Clarenden Press.

Wallace, William Kay. 1932. *Our Obsolete Constitution.* New York: John Day.

Walroff, Jonathan L. 1985. "The Unconstitutionality of Voter Initiative Applications for Federal Constitutional Conventions." *Colorado Law Review* 85: 1525–45.

Watson, Richard A. 1985. *Promise and Performance of American Democracy,* 5th ed. New York: John Wiley & Sons.

Weber, Paul. 1989. "Madison's Opposition to a Second Convention." *Polity* 20 (Spring): 498–517.

Weber, Paul J., and Barbara A Perry. 1989. *Unfounded Fears: Myths and Realities of a Constitutional Convention.* New York: Praeger.

Wedgwood, William B. 1861. *The Reconstruction of the Government of the United States of America: A Democratic Empire Advocated and an Imperial Constitution Proposed.* New York: John H. Tingley.

Weeks, Kent M. 1971. *Adam Clayton Powell and the Supreme Court.* New York: Dunellen.

Weiser, Philip J. 1993. "Ackerman's Proposal for Popular Constitutional Lawmaking: Can It Realize His Aspirations for Dualist Democracy?" *New York University Law Review* 68 (October): 907–59.

Welch, Susan, et al. 1993. *Understanding American Government,* 2d ed. Minneapolis–St. Paul: West.

Wenner, Lettie M. 1982. *The Environmental Decade in Court.* Bloomington: Indiana University Press.

Westin, Alan. 1990. *The Anatomy of a Constitutional Law Case: Youngstown Sheet and Tube Co. v. Sawyer; the Steel Seizure Decision.* New York: Columbia University Press.

Wheeler, Margorie S. 1993. *New Women of the New South: The Leaders of the Woman Suffrage Movement in the Southern States*. New York: Oxford University Press.

Wheeler, Marjorie S., ed. 1995a. *One Woman, One Vote: Rediscovering the Woman Suffrage Movement*. Troutdale, OR: New Sage.

———. 1995b. *Votes for Women! The Woman Suffrage Movement in Tennessee, the South, and the Nation*. Knoxville: University of Tennessee Press.

Whitaker, L. Paige. 1992. *The Constitutionality of States Limiting Congressional Terms*. Washington, DC: Congressional Research Service, Library of Congress.

White, Welsh S. 1991. *The Death Penalty in the Nineties: An Examination of the Modern System of Capital Punishment*. Ann Arbor: University of Michigan Press.

Whitman, Alden, ed. 1985. *American Reformers*. New York: H. W. Wilson.

Wiecek, William. 1992. "Subversion." In *The Oxford Companion to the Supreme Court of the United States*, ed. Kermit L. Hall. New York: Oxford University Press.

———. 1977. *The Sources of Antislavery Constitutionalism in America, 1760–1848*. Ithaca, NY: Cornell University Press.

———. 1972. *The Guarantee Clause of the U.S. Constitution*. Ithaca, NY: Cornell University Press.

Wilcox, Clyde. 1995. *The Latest American Revolution? The 1994 Elections and Their Implications for Governance*. New York: St. Martin's Press.

Wilkinson, J. Harvie, III. 1979. *From Brown to Bakke: The Supreme Court and School Integration: 1954–1978*. New York: Oxford University Press.

Williams, T. Harry. 1970. *Huey Long*. New York: Alfred A. Knopf.

Willis, Paul G., and George L. Willis. 1952. "The Politics of the Twenty-second Amendment." *Western Political Quarterly* 5 (September): 469–82.

Wills, Garry. 1981. *Explaining America: The Federalist*. Garden City, NY: Doubleday.

———. 1978. *Inventing America: Jefferson's Declaration of Independence*. New York: Doubleday.

Wilson, James G. 1992. "American Constitutional Conventions: The Judicially Unenforceable Rules That Combine with Judicial Doctrine and Public Opinion To Regulate Political Behavior." *Buffalo Law Review* 40 (Fall): 645–738.

Wilson, (Thomas) Woodrow. 1908. *Constitutional Government in the United States*. New York: Columbia University Press; reprinted in 1961.

———. 1885. *Congressional Government: A Study in American Politics*. Boston: Houghton Mifflin.

———. 1882. *Government by Debate: Being a Short View of Our National Government as It Is and as It Might Be*. In *The Papers of Woodrow Wilson*, Vol. 2, ed. Arthur S. Link. Princeton, NJ: Princeton University Press, 1967.

———. 1879. *Cabinet Government in the United States*. In *The Papers of Woodrow Wilson*, Vol. 1, ed. Arthur S. Link. Princeton, NJ: Princeton University Press, 1966.

Wirenius, John F. 1994. "The Road to *Brandenburg*: A Look at the Evolving Understanding of the First Amendment." *Drake Law Review* 43: 1–49.

Wolfe, Christopher. 1991. *Judicial Activism: Bulwark of Freedom or Precarious Security?* Pacific Grove, CA: Brooks/Cole.

Wood, Gordon S. 1969. *The Creation of the American Republic, 1776–1787*. New York: W. W. Norton.

Wood, Stephen B. 1968. *Constitutional Politics in the Progressive Era: Child Labor and the Law*. Chicago: University of Chicago Press.

Woodward, Augustus B. 1825. *The Presidency of the United States*. New York: J. & J. Harper.

Wright, Benjamin F. 1938. *The Contract Clause of the Constitution*. Cambridge, MA: Harvard University Press.

Wright, R. George. 1991. "Could a Constitutional Amendment Be Unconstitutional?" *Loyola University of Chicago Law Review* 22: 741–64.

Wunder, John R. 1994. *"Retained by the People": A History of American Indians and the Bill of Rights*. New York: Oxford University Press.

Wyatt-Brown, Bertram. 1948. *Southern Honor: Ethics and Behavior in the Old South*. New York: Oxford University Press.

Yandle, Bruce. 1995. *Land Rights: The 1990's Property Tax Rebellion*. Lanham, Maryland: Rowman & Littlefield.

Young, Donald. 1974. *American Roulette: The History and Dilemma of the Vice Presidency*. New York: Viking Press.

Yarbrough, Tinsley E. 1988. *Mr. Justice Black and His Critics*. Durham, NC: Duke University Press.

Zuckerman, Edward. 1984. *The Day after World War III*. New York: Viking Press.

❖ LIST OF CASES ❖

Abington School District v. Schempp. 1963, 374 U.S. 203

Adamson v. California. 1947. 332 U.S. 46

Adkins v. Childrens' Hospital. 1923. 261 U.S. 525

Afroyim v. Rusk. 1967. 387 U.S. 253

Apodaco v. Oregon. 1972. 406 U.S. 404

Argersinger v. Hamlin. 1972. 407 U.S. 25

Bailey v. Drexel Furniture Company. 1922. 259 U.S. 20

Baker v. Carr. 1962. 369 U.S. 186

Ballew v. Georgia. 1978. 635 U.S. 223

Barron v. Baltimore. 1833. 32 U.S. 243

Beal v. Doe. 1977. 432 U.S. 438

Benton v. Maryland. 1968. 392 U.S. 925

Benton v. Maryland. 1969. 395 U.S. 784

Bolling v. Sharpe, 1954, 347 U.S. 497

Bowsher v. Synar. 1986. 478 U.S. 714

Buckley v. Valeo. 1976 424 U.S. 1

Bradwell v. Illinois. 1873. 83 U.S. 130

Brandenburg v. Ohio. 1969. 395 U.S. 444

Breedlove v. Suttles. 1937. 302 U.S. 277

Brown v. Board of Education (1). 1954. 347 U.S. 483

Brown v. Board of Education II, 1955, 349 U.S. 294

Burch v. Louisiana. 1979. 441 U.S. 130

Butler v. Thompson. 1951. 341 U.S. 937

Calder v. Bull. 1798. 3 Dall. (3 U.S.) 386

Champion v. Ames. 1903. 188 U.S. 321

Chandler v. Wise. 1939. 307 U.S. 474

Chaplinsky v. New Hampshire. 1942. 315 U.S. 568

Chaplinsky v. New Hampshire. 1942. 215 U.S. 468

Chicago, Burlington & Quincy Railway Co. v. Chicago. 1897. 166 U.S. 226

Chisholm v. Georgia. 1793. 2 Dall. (2 U.S.) 419

Church of the Lukumi Babalu Aye v. City of Haleah. 1993. 113 S.Ct. 2217

Civil Rights Cases. 1883. 109 U.S. 3

Cohens v. Virginia. 1821. 6 Wheat (19 U.S.) 264

Colegrove v. Green. 1946. 328 U.S. 549

Coleman v. Miller. 1939. 307 U.S. 433

Collector v. Day. 1871. 78 U.S. 113

Communist Party v. Subversive Activities Control Board. 1961. 367 U.S. 1

Cooley v. Board of Wardens of the Port of Philadelphia. 1852. 53 U.S. 299

Coyle v. Smith. 1911. 221 U.S. 559

Cummings v. Missouri. 1867. 71 U.S. 277

Dartmouth College v. Woodward. 1819. 17 U.S. (4 Wheat) 518

Dennis v. United States. 1951. 341 U.S. 494

Dillon v. Gloss. 1921. 256 U.S. 368

Dobbins v. Commissioners of Erie County. 1842. 41 U.S. 435

Dodge v. Woolsey. 1856. 18 How. (59 U.S.) 331.

Duncan v. Louisiana. 1968. 391 U.S. 145

Dunn v. Blumstein. 1972. 405 U.S. 330

Dyer v. Blair. 1975. 390 F. Supp. 1291

Elk v. Wilkins. 1884. 112 U.S. 94

Employment Division, Department of Human Resources of Oregon v. Smith. 1990. 494 U.S. 872

Engel v. Vitale. 1962. 370 U.S. 421

Everson v. Board of Education. 1947. 330 U.S. 1

Ex parte Garland. 1867. 71 U.S. 333

Ex parte New York. 1921. 256 U.S. 490

Ex parte Young. 1908. 209 U.S. 123

Fairchild v. Hughes. 1922. 258 U.S. 126

Fletcher v. Peck. 1810. 6 Cranch (10 U.S.) 87

Flint v. Stone Tracy Co. 1911. 220 U.S. 107

44 Liquormart v. Rhode Island. 1995. No. 94-1194.

Frontiero v. Richardson. 1973. 411 U.S. 677

Fujii v. State of California. 1950. 217 Pac. (2nd) 481

Furman v. Georgia. 1972. 408 U.S. 238

Garcia v. San Antonio Metropolitan Transit Authority. 1985. 469 U.S. 528

Gertz v. Robert Welch, Inc. 1974. 418 U.S. 323

Gibbons v. Ogden. 1824. 22 U.S. 1

Gideon v. Wainwright. 1963. 372 U.S. 335

Gitlow v. New York. 1925. 268 U.S. 652

Goesaert v. Cleary. 1948. 335 U.S. 464

Goldberg v. Kelly. 1970. 397 U.S. 254

Gomillion v. Lightfoot. 1960. 364 U.S. 339

Gravel v. United States. 1972. 408 U.S. 606

Graves v. New York ex rel. O'Keefe. 1939. 306 U.S. 466

Gray v. Sanders. 1963. 372 U.S. 368

Green v. United States. 1957. 355 U.S. 184

Gregg v. Georgia. 1976. 428 U.S. 153

Griffin v. California. 1965. 380 U.S. 609

Griswold v. Connecticut. 1965. 381 U.S. 479

Guinn and Beal v. United States. 1915. 238 U.S. 347

Gyuro v. Connecticut. 1968. 393 U.S. 937

Halter v. Nebraska. 1907. 205 U.S. 34

Hammer v. Dagenhart. 1918. 247 U.S. 251

Hans v. Louisiana. 1890. 134 U.S. 1

Harper v. Virginia State Board of Elections. 1966. 383 U.S. 663

Harris v. McRae. 1980. 448 U.S. 297

Hawke v. Smith (No. 1). 1920. 253 U.S. 221

Hawke v. Smith (No. 2). 1920. 253 U.S. 231

Heart of Atlanta Motel v. United States. 1964. 379 U.S. 241

Helvering v. Davis. 1937. 301 U.S. 619

Hepburn v. Griswold. 1870. 75 U.S. 603

Hirabayashi v. United States. 1943. 320 U.S. 81

Holden v. Hardy. 1898. 169 U.S. 366

Hollingsworth v. Virginia. 1798. 3 U.S. (3 Dall.) 379

Home Building and Loan Association v. Blaisdell. 1934. 290 U.S. 398

Humphrey's Executor v. United States. 1935. 295 U.S. 602

Hurdado v. California. 1884. 110 U.S. 516

Hutchinson v. Proxmire. 1979. 443 U.S. 111

Hylton v. United States. 1796. 3 Dall. (3 U.S.) 171

Idaho v. Freeman. 1981. 529 F. Supp. 1107

Immigration and Naturalization Service v. Chadha. 1983. 462 U.S. 919

Ives v. South Buffalo Railway Co. 1911. 201 N.Y. 271

Jacobson v. Massachusetts. 1905. 197 U.S. 11

Johnson v. Louisiana. 1972. 406 U.S. 356

Jones v. Alfred H. Mayer Co. 1968. 392 U.S. 409

Katz v. United States. 1967. 389 U.S. 346

Katzenbach v. McClung. 1964. 379 U.S. 294

Katzenbach v. Morgan. 1966. 384 U.S. 641

Kimble v. Swackhamer. 1978. 439 U.S. 385

Knox v. Lee. 1871. 79 U.S. 457

Korematsu v. United States. 1944. 323 U.S. 214

Lau v. Nichols. 1974. 414 U.S. 5376

Lassiter v. North Hampton County Board of Elections. 1959. 360 U.S. 45

Lee v. Weisman. 1992. 112 S. Ct. 2649

Lemon v. Kurtzman. 1971. 403 U.S. 602

Lemmon v. The People. 1860. 20 N.Y. 562

Leser v. Garnett. 1922. 258 U.S. 130

Lincoln County [Nevada] v. Luning. 1890. 133 U.S. 529

Livermore v. Waite. 1894. 102 Cal. 113

Lochner v. New York. 1905. 198 U.S. 45

Louisiana ex rel. Elliott v. Jamel. 1883., 107 U.S. 711

Louisville Joint Stock Land Bank v. Radford. 1935. 295 U.S. 555

Loving v. Virginia. 1967. 388 U.S. 1

Luther v. Borden. 1849. 7 How. (48 U.S.) 1

Lynch v. Donnelly. 1984. 465 U.S. 688

Malloy v. Hogan. 1964. 378 U.S. 1

Mapp v. Ohio. 1961. 367 U.S. 643

Marbury v. Madison. 1803. 1 Cranch (5 U.S.) 137

Marsh v. Chambers. 1983. 463 U.S. 783

Marston v. Lewis. 1973. 410 U.S. 679

McCulloch v. Maryland. 1819. 4 Wheat (17 U.S.) 316

Meek v. Pittenger. 1973. 413 US. 349

Meyer v. Nebraska. 1923. 262 U.S. 390.

Miller v. California. 1973. 413 U.S. 15

Miller v. Johnson. 1995. 63 LW 4726

Milliken v. Bradley, 1974, 418 U.S. 717

Minor v. Happersett. 1875. 21 Wall. (88 U.S.) 162

Minersville School District v. Gobitis. 1940. 310 U.S. 586

Miranda v. Arizona. 1966. 384 U.S. 457

Missouri v. Holland, 1920, 252 U.S. 416

Missouri v. Jenkins. 1990. 495 U.S. 33

Missouri Pacific Railway Co. v. Kansas, 1919, 248 U.S. 276

Missouri Pacific Railway Co. v. Nebraksa. 1896. 164 U.S. 403

Monoca v. Mississippi. 1934. 292 U.S. 313

Moore v. Dempsey. 1923. 261 U.S. 86

Morehead v. New York ex rel. Tipaldo. 1936. 298 U.S. 587

Morrison v. Olson. 1988. 487 U.S. 654

Mueller v. Allen. 1983. 463 U.S. 388

Mulford v. Smith. 1939. 307 U.S. 38

Muller v. Oregon. 1908. 208 U.S. 412

Murray v. Curlett. 1963. 374 U.S. 203

Myers v. Anderson. 1915. 238 U.S. 368

Myers and Others v. Anderson. 1915. 238 U.S. 368

Myers v. United States. 1926. 272 U.S. 52

National Association for the Advancement of Colored People v. Alabama ex rel. Patterson. 1958. 356 U.S. 449

National Labor Relations Board v. Jones & Laughlin Steel Corp. 1937. 301 U.S. 1

National League of Cities v. Usery. 1976. 426 U.S. 833

National Prohibition Cases. 1920. 253 U.S. 350

Naturalization Service v. Chadha. 1993. 462 U.S. 919

Near v. Minnesota. 1931. 283 U.S. 697

Nebbia v. New York. 1934. 291 U.S. 502

Newberry v. United States. 1921. 256 U.S. 232

New York v. Quarles. 1984. 467 U.S. 649

New York Times Co. v. Sullivan. 1964. 376 U.S. 254

New York Times Co. v. United States. 1971. 403 U.S. 713

New York Trust Co. v. Eisner. 1916. 256 U.S. 345

Nix v. Williams. 1984. 467 U.S. 431

Norman v. Baltimore & Ohio Railroad Co. 1935. 294 U.S. 240

Nortz v. United States. 1935. 294 U.S. 317

Ogden v. Saunders. 1827. 12 Wheat (25 U.S.) 213

Olmstead v. United States. 1928. 277 U.S. 438

Oregon v. Mitchell, Texas v. Mitchell, United States v. Arizona. 1970. 400 U.S. 112

Osborn v. Bank of the United States. 1824, 9 Wheat (22 U.S.) 738

Palko v. Connecticut. 1937. 302 U.S. 319

Paul v. Virginia. 1869. 8 Wall. (75 U.S.) 168

Payne v. Tennessee. 1991. 111 S. Ct. 2597

Perez v. Brownell. 1958. 356 U.S. 44

Perry v. United States. 1935. 294 U.S. 330

Planned Parenthood of Southeastern Pennsylvania v. Casey. 1992. 112 S. Ct. 2791

Plessy v. Ferguson. 1896. 163 U.S. 537

Pollock v. Farmers' Loan & Trust Co. (1). 1895. 157 U.S. 429

Pollock v. Farmers' Loan & Trust Co. (2). 1895. 158 U.S. 601

Powell v. Alabama. 1932. 287 U.S. 45

Powell v. McCormack. 1969. 395 U.S. 486

Pyler v. Doe. 1982. 457 U.S. 202

Quilici v. Village of Morton Grove. 1983. 464 U.S. 863

Reed v. Reed. 1971. 404 U.S. 71

Reid v. Covert. 1957. 354 U.S. 1

Regents of the University of California v. Bakke. 1978. 438 U.S. 265

Reid v. Covert, 1957, 354 U.S. 1

Reynolds v. Sims. 1964. 377 U.S. 533

Reynolds v. United States. 1879. 98 U.S. 145

Rice v. Sioux City Memorial Park. 1955. 348 U.S. 880, 349 U.S. 70

Roe v. Wade. 1973. 410 U.S. 113

Romer v. Evans. 1996. U.S. Supreme Court. Docket No. 94-1039

Rosenberger v. Rector and Visitors of the University of Virginia. 1994. 18 F.3rd 269

Rosenberger v. Rector and Visitors of the University of Virginia. 1995. Slip Opinion. No. 94-329

Roth v. United States, Alberts v. California. 1957. 354 U.S. 476

San Mateo County v. Southern Pacific R.R. 1883. 116 U.S. 138

Schechter Poultry Corporation v. United States. 1935. 295 U.S. 495

Schenck v. United States. 1919. 249 U.S. 47

Schick v. Reed. 1974. 419 U.S. 256

Scott v. Sandford. 1857. 19 How. (60 U.S.) 393

Second Employers' Liability Case. 1912. 223 U.S. 1

Shapiro v. Thompson. 1969. 394 U.S. 618

Shaw v. Reno. 1993. 61 LW 4818

The Slaughterhouse Cases. 1873. 16 Wall. (83 U.S.) 36

Smith v. Allwright. 1944. 321 U.S. 649

Smith v. Goguen. 1974. 415 U.S. 566

Smith v. Union Bank of Georgetown. 1831. 30 U.S. (5 Pet.) 518

South Carolina v. Baker. 1988. 485 U.S. 505

South Dakota v. Dole. 1987. 483 U.S. 203

South Carolina v. Katzenbach. 1966. 383 U.S. 301

Spence v. Washington. 1974. 418 U.S. 405

Sprague v. United States. 1931. 282 U.S. 716

Springer v. United States. 1881. 102 U.S. 586

Steward Machine Co. v. Davis. 1937. 301 U.S. 548

Stone v. Powell. 1976. 428 U.S. 465

Street v. New York. 1969. 394 U.S. 576

Stromberg v. California. 1931. 283 U.S. 359

Sturges v. Crowinshield. 1819. 4 Wheat (17 U.S.) 122

Swann v. Charlotte-Mecklenburg Board of Education, 1971, 402 U.S. 1.

Texas v. Johnson. 1989. 491 U.S. 397

Texas v. White. 1869. 74 U.S. 700

Tinker v. Des Moines Independent Community School District. 1969. 393 U.S. 503

Trade-Mark Cases. 1879. 100 U.S. 82

Trinsey v. Pennsylvania. 1991. 766 F. Supp. 1338 (E.E. Pa), *rev'd* 941 F. 2d 223 (3d Cir.)

Trono v. United States. 1905. 199 U.S. 521

Trop v. Dulles. 1958. 356 U.S. 86

Twining v. New Jersey. 1908. 211 U.S. 78

U. S. Department of Commerce v. Montana. 1992. 503 U.S. 442.

U.S. Term Limits v. Thornton. 1995. 115 S. Ct. 1842

United States v. Anthony, 24 F.Cas. 829 (No. 14,459) (N.D.N.Y., 1873)

United States v. Brewster. 1972. 408 U.S. 501

United States v. Butler. 1936. 297 U.S. 1

United States v. California. 1947. 332 U.S. 19

United States v. Carolene Products Co. 1938. 304 U.S. 144

United States v. Classic. 1941. 313 U.S. 299

United States v. Darby Lumber Company. 1941. 312 U.S. 100

United States v. E.C. Knight Co. 1895. 156 U.S. 1

United States v. Eichman. 1990. 496 U.S. 310

United States v. Guest. 1966. 383 U.S. 745

United States v. Leon. 1984. 468 U.S. 897

United States v. Lopez. 1995. 63 LW 4343

United States v. McCullagh. 1915. 221 F.228 (D.C.D. Kan.)

United States v. Miller. 1939. 307 U.S. 174

United States v. Nixon. 1974. 418 U.S. 683

United States v. O'Brien. 1968. 391 U.S. 367

United States v. Pink. 1942. 315 U.S. 204

United States v. Price. 1966. 383 U.S. 787

United States v. Robel. 1967. 389 U.S. 258

United States v. Shauver. 1914. 214 F. 154 (D.C.E. Ark.)

United States v. South-Eastern Underwriters Association. 1944. 322 U.S. 533

United States v. Sprague. 1931. 282 U.S. 716

United States v. Wong Kim Ark. 1898. 169 U.S. 649

Wallace v. Jaffree. 1985. 472 U.S. 38

Walter L. Nixon v. United States. 1993. 61 LW 4069

Watkins v. United States. 1957. 354 U.S. 178

Webster v. Reproductive Health Services. 1989. 492 U.S. 490

Weeks v. United States. 1914. 232 U.S. 383

Wesberry v. Sanders. 1964. 376 U.S. 1

West Coast Hotel v. Parrish. 1937. 300 U.S. 379

West Virginia Board of Education v. Barnette. 1943. 319 U.S. 624

Wickard v. Filburn. 1942. 317 U.S.

Wiener v. United States. 1958. 357 U.S. 349

Williams v. Florida. 1970. 399 U.S. 78

Woodson v. North Carolina. 1976. 428 U.S. 280

Worcester v. Georgia. 1832. 6 Pet. (31 U.S.) 515

Yakus v. United States. 1944. 321 U.S. 414

Youngstown Sheet & Tube Co. v. Sawyer. 1952. 343 U.S. 579

Zablocki v. Redhail. 1978. 434 U.S. 374

❖ INDEX ❖

Page numbers in bold type denote main entries.

Abelman v. Booth (1859), 281
Abeyances, 92–93
Abington v. Schempp (1963), **1–2**, 36, 117, 133, 237. *See also* Blaine amendment; Christian amendment; *Engel v. Vitale;* First Amendment; Prayer in Public Schools.
Abolition of the Presidency (Lockwood), 192
Abolitionists, **2–3**, 50
Abortions. *See* Right to life.
Abourezk, James, 165
Abraham, Henry J., 172
Ackerman, Bruce, **3**
 alternative to treaty-making, 309–310
 constitutional moments, x, 87, 89
 higher lawmaking, 124
 proposed amendment for referendum, 10
Adams, Abigail, 217
Adams, Charles Francis, 84
Adams, Frederick Upham, **3**
Adams, John, 95
Adams, John Quincy
 favored amendments related to slavery, 1, 179, 279, 288, 303, 305
 introduced amendment to override vetoes, 245
 pushed for internal improvements, 167
 resigned Senate seat, 71
Adamson v. California (1947), **4–5**, 34, 126, 163, 228
Addonizio, Hugh, 230
Adkins v. Children's Hospital (1923), 207–208, 219–220, 294

Administrator of the General Services Administration, 5, 15, 270
Affirmative action, **5–6**, 39
Afroyim v. Rusk (1967), 53
Agar, Herbert, **6–7**
Agel, Jerome, x
Agnew, Spiro, 318
Agricultural Adjustment Act, 7–8, 56, 86
Agriculture, **7–8**
Air Force, **8**
Alaska, 35, 289
Alberts v. California (1957), 223
Alcoholic prohibition. *See* Eighteenth Amendment.
Aldrich, Nelson, 275
Alexander, John, 50
Alien and Sedition Acts of 1798, 8, 53, 154, 294
Alien Land Law (CA), 37
Aliens, **8–9**
All-white primary, 129
Amar, Akil Reed, x, **9**, 10, 18, 101, 124, 187, 286
Amending process. *See* Article V of U.S. Constitution.
Amending process, proposals for changing, **9–11**
Amendment, **12**
Amendment to the Constitution: Averting the Decline and Fall of America (Pace), 227
American Anti-Slavery Society, 286
American Bar Association, 37, 48, 108, 112
American Civil Liberties Union (ACLU), 269
American Colonization Society, 278
American Committee for the Outlawry of War, 341

American Constitutional League, 125
American Economic Association, 108
American Political Science Association (APSA), 108
American Society for Public Administration (ASPA), 96
American Taxpayers Association, 276
American Woman Suffrage Association, 218, 287
Americans for a Constitutional Convention, Inc., 184
Americans To Limit Congressional Terms (ALCT), 74
Ames, Herman, ix, **12**, 221
Anderson, George Washington, 330
Anderson, John, 51
Annapolis Convention, 78
Antelope, The (1825), 280
Anthony, David, 230
Anthony, Susan B., **12–13**, 46, 140, 208, 218, 287
Antieau, Chester, **13–14**
Antietam Creek, 190
Anti-Federalists, **14–15**, 30, 74, 274, 300
Antipolygamy laws. *See* Marriage, divorce, and parenting.
Anti-Prohibition Party, 15
Anti-Saloon League, **15**, 106
Antitrust measures, 249
Apodaco v. Oregon (1972), 181, 276
Appellate jurisdiction, 175
Archer, William, 279
Archivist, Library of Congress, 5, 10, **15–16**, 270
Argersinger v. Hamlin (1972), 277
Article V of the U.S. Constitution, **16–18**

Articles of Confederation, **18–19**
asked to add bill of rights to
constitution, 30
Constitutional Convention
called to revise, 78
formula for slave taxation and
representation, 305
method for amendments, 14,
16
no authority over interstate
commerce, 63
Northwest Ordinance, 282
state representation in, 71
state sovereignty under, 300
term limits, 74
threat to nation's capital during, 98
Ashurst, Henry, 178
Association Against the Prohibition Amendment (AAPA),
319
Association, freedom of, 13,
19–20
Assumption-of-risk doctrine, 349
Austin, John, 285
Australian amending process,
155–156
Automatic plan for electoral college, 111

Bacon, Selden, **21**, 77, 200,
276, 331
*Bailey v. Drexel Furniture Com-
pany* (1922), 48
Baker, Howard, 238
Baker v. Carr (1962), 11,
21–22, 66, 85–86, 98, 141,
149, 161, 194, 235, 257,
291, 342
Bakewill, Claude, 8
Bakke case, 6
Balanced budget amendment,
22–24, 81–82
Balanced Budget and Emergency
Deficit Control Act of
1985, 24, 309
Baldwin, Leland, **25**, 289
Ballew v. Georgia (1978), 181
Banking, **26**, 171, 195–196,
198, 199
Bankruptcy, **26**
Barbour, James, 73, 309
Barenblatt v. United States
(1959), 60
Barrett, William, 41
Barron v. Baltimore (1833), 5,
26–27, 32, 126, 141, 163,
203

Bayh, Birch, 112, 238, 317
Beal v. Doe (1977), 259
Beard, Charles, 165
Beasley, Robert, **27–28**, 165
Becker, Frank, 117, 237
Becker, Theodore L., **28–29**
Beecher, Henry Ward, 218, 348
Bellamy, Edward, 189
Bennett, Charles, 19, 350
Benton, Thomas Hart, 111
Benton v. Maryland (1968), 102,
164, 228
Bentsen, Lloyd, 69, 323
Berger, Victor, 273
Bernstein, Richard, x
Berrien, John Macpherson, 281
Bevill, Tom, 237
Bible reading in schools, 36, 51.
See also A*bington v. Schempp;
Engel v. Vitale;* Prayer in
public schools.
Bicameralism, 271–272
Bickel, Alexander, 69
Bill of Rights, xv, 5, 14, 17,
29–32, 170, 220. *See also
individual amendments
(First through Tenth).*
Billboards on interstate highways,
56
Bills of attainder, 14
Bingham, John, 5, 31, **32–33**,
34, 139
Bingham, Jonathan, 246
Birthright citizenship amendment, **33**, 52
Black, Charles, 86, 159
Black codes, 139
Black, Hugo, **34-35**
advocates total incorporation,
27, 141
comments on John Bingham,
32
opinion in *Adamson v. California*, 5, 126, 163, 228
opinion in *Chandler v. Wise,*
47
opinion in *Coleman v. Miller,*
57
opinion in *Engel v. Vitale,* 117,
237
opinion in *Griswold v. Connecticut,* 148
opinion in *Harper v. Virginia
Board of Elections,* 154
opinion in *Oregon v. Mitchell,*
225, 325
opinion in *Reid v. Covert,* 37,
252

opinion in steel seizure cases,
245
opinion in *U.S. v. S.E. Under-
writers,* 166
Black Monday, 86
Black Panthers, **35**
Blackmun, Harry, 44, 52, 145,
178, 259
Blaine amendment, 1, **35–36,**
50, 229
Blaine, James G., 36
Blair, Henry, 36, 105, 326
Blair, Robert, 103
Blease, Coleman, 167
Block grants, 255
Bodin, Jean, 285
Bolling v. Sharpe (1954), 39
Bomb shelters, 66
Borah, William, 107, 141, 272
Bork, Robert, 3, 81, 260
Boutwell, George, 128
Bowsher v. Synar (1986), 309
Boxer, Barbara, 243
Boyd, Steven, xii
Bradford, Gamaliel, 41, 198
Bradley, Joseph P., 53, 113, 152
Bradwell v. Illinois (1873), 120
Brandeis, Louis, 188–89, 207
Brandeis brief, 207
Brandenburg v. Ohio (1969), 134
Brearly, David, 192
Breaux, John, 91
Breedlove v. Suttles (1937), 154,
320–21
Brennan, William
debate over original intent, 81
influence on *Griswold v. Con-
necticut,* 148
opinion in *Abingdon v.
Schempp,* 1
opinion in *Baker v. Carr,*
21–22, 236, 291
opinion in *South Carolina v.
Baker,* 285
opinion in *Texas v. Johnson,*
302
opinion in *U.S. v. Eichman,*
331
opposition to death penalty, 44
views on obscenity, 223
Bricker amendment, **37**, 209,
309
Bricker, John, 37
Bristow, Francis, 273
Bristow, Joseph, 165, 174
Brooks, James, 218
Brother Imari (Richard B.
Henry), 289

Brown, Hank, 333
Brown, Henry, 234
Brown, John, 2, **38,** 380
Brown v. Board of Education I
  (1954), 5, 20, **38–39,** 59,
  141, 235, 266, 267, 271,
  288, 292, 341
Brown v. Board of Education II
  (1955), 39
Browne, Edward, 316
Bryan, William Jennings, 165,
  256
Bryce, James, 228, 261
Buchanan, Frank, 350
Buchanan, James
  cited fears of slave insurrection,
    102
  endorsed Crittenden Compro-
    mise, 90
  favored slave protection in ter-
    ritories, 283
  proposed explanatory amend-
    ment, 83, 281
  signed Corwin Amendment,
    84, 244
Buchanan, Patrick, 168
Buckley v. Valeo (1976), 43, 137
Budget process, 6–7
Budget surpluses, 22
Burch v. Louisiana (1979), 181,
  277
Burdick, Aventin, 330
Burger, Warren, 62, 145, 223,
  266, 342
Burlison, Bill, 84, 96
Burn, Harry, 219
Burns, Lucy, 230
Burr, Aaron, 201, 313, 315
Bush, George, 24, 237, 246
Busing. *See* School busing.
Butler Marshall, 176
Butler v. Thompson (1951), 154
Byrd, Robert, 16

Cabinet, **41**
  officers to appear before or be
    seated in Congress, 7, 108,
    153, 160, 204, 258, 262,
    295, 346
  proposals for altering, 41, 157
Calder v. Bull (1789), 216–17
Calhoun, John C., **42,** 61, 77,
  90, 243, 256
California Plan, 179
Callister, Marion, 121
Campaign contributions and ex-
  penditures, **43,** 59, 101
Capital crimes, 44

Capital, new location proposed,
  28
Capital punishment, 14, **43–44,**
  62, 108
Caplan, Russell, x
Cardozo, Benjamin, 4, 126, 163,
  227–28
Carolene Products case, 69
Carter, Jimmy, 242, 246
CASCOT System for Social Con-
  trol of Technology, **45–46**
Cassell, Henry, 44
Categorical grants-in-aid, 255
Catt, Carrie Lane Chapman, 13,
  46–47, 219, 274
Ceaser, James, 59
Celler, Emanuel, 119, 237–38,
  276, 325, 326
Centennial Exposition, 50
Center for the Study of Democ-
  ratic Institutions, 310
Chamber of Commerce, 112
Champion v. Ames (1903), 47,
  193, 292
Chandler v. Wise (1939), 47
Chandler, Walter, 11
Chaplinsky v. New Hampshire
  (1942), 134, 302
Chase, Samuel, 159, 178, 203,
  217
Chicago, Burlington & Quincy
  Railroad Co. v. Chicago
  (1897), 130
Chief justices, 25, 179
Child labor amendment, **47–49,**
  57, 87, 125, 249
Chilton, William, 67
Chisholm v. Georgia (1793), **49,**
  113, 175
Chittenden, L. E. 231
Choate, Joseph H., 275
Christian Amendment, 1,
  49–51, 239, 242
Christian Coalition, 81
Christian Statesman, 50
Church of the Lukumi Babalu
  Aye v. City of Hialeah
  (1993), 134
Cilley, Jonathan, 102
Cities, 204
Citizen Representative Reform
  Act New Blood Provision,
  75
Citizens Tax Protection Amend-
  ment, 299
Citizens, teaching of derogatory
  material to, 51
Citizenship, 5, 8–9, 151, 227

See also Fourteenth Amend-
  ment.
Citizenship, definition of, **51–52**
Citizenship, dual, **52**
Citizenship, loss of, **52–53**
Citizenship, officeholding rights,
  53, 154, 244
Civil Rights Act of 1875, 53,
  141
Civil Rights Act of 1964, 5, 54
Civil Rights Bill (1866), 139
Civil Rights cases of 1883, 5,
  53–54, 234, 304
Civil service reform, **54,** 89, 151
Civil War, 2, 3, 50, 169
  plan for avoiding, 343–44
  plan for referendum on, 27,
    164
  proposals to limit war claims
    from, 54
Claiborne, Harry F., 161, 224
Claims against the United States,
  54–55, 159
Clark, David, 48
Clark, Tom C., 1, 22, 237
Clark, Walter, **55–56**
Clay, Henry, 245, 309
Clayton Act of 1914, 210
Clinton, Bill, 69, 239, 329
Clopton, John, 217
Closed shop, 261
Cloture votes, 66–67
Cochrane, Thad, 254
Coercive use of federal funds, **56**
Cohens v. Virginia (1821), 113,
  173, 203
Colegrove v. Green (1946), 66,
  235, 291
Coleman, Charles H., **56–57**
Coleman v. Miller (1939), xiii,
  10, 18, 34, 48, 57, **57–58,** 97,
  103, 121, 161, 194, 235,
  248, 249, 251, 255, 306,
  324
Collector v. Day (1871), 299
Collins, James, 6
Collins, Ross, 116
Colonial charters, **58**
Comingo, Abram, 288
Commander in chief, 8, 38
Committee for Constitutional
  Government, 276
Committee for Government of
  the People (CGP), 98
Committee of Detail, 78
Committee of Eleven, 30
Committee of the Whole, 70
Committee of Twelve, 61

Committee on the Constitutional System, **59**, 262, 295
Committee To Stop ERA, 120
Communism, **59–60**, 284, 295, 308
Communist Party v. Subversive Activities Control Board (1961), 295
Comparative liability, 101
Compromise of 1850, 279
Compulsory schooling, 249
Compulsory voting, 29
Concurrent majorities, 42
Concurrent powers, **60**, 107, 215
Confederal governments, 287
Confederate debt, **60–61**
Confederate States of America, Constitution, **61–62**
  acknowledgment of God, 50, 61, 239
  admission of new states, 61
  cabinet officers appear in Congress, 61
  convention mechanisms of, 61
  impeachment provisions, 61
  importation of slaves banned, 280
  recognition of slavery, 61
  right to travel with slaves recognized, 282
  six-year presidential term, 61, 322
  state sovereignty in, 61, 239
  stimulated fears of runaway convention, 62
Conference of the States, 86, 266
Confessions, **62**, 122
Congress
  age of members, **63**
  attendance of members, **63**, 146
  commerce powers, 8, **63–64**, 159
  committee composition, **65**
  district representation, **65–66**
  emergency functioning, **66**, 76
  filibuster in Senate, **66**
  immunity of members, **66–67**
  legislative veto of, **68**
  members' eligibility for other offices, **68–69**
  overriding judicial decisions, **69–70**, 153
  powers proposed, 57, 64, 197
  private bills, **70**, 223
  quorum, **70**
  recall of members, **70–71**

representation in, **71–72**
size of, **72–73**, 205
special elections, 73
term lengths, **73–74**, 146
term limits, 63, **75–76**, 82
vacancies in, **76**
Congressional Government (Wilson), 346
Congressional practices, 18
Congressional Record, xi
Congressional Union for Woman Suffrage (CU), 219, 230
Conkling, Roscoe, 83
Connecticut Compromise, 71, 76, 110, 272, 274–75
Conscience, freedom of, 133
Conscientious objection, 14, 169
Constitutional amendments, limits on, 16, **76–77**, 138, 191, 212, 286
Constitutional commissions, 77
Constitutional Convention of 1787, **77–79**
  Article V as alternative to revolution, 256
  approach to Articles of Confederation, 19
  and bill of rights, 14, 30
  electoral college created, 109, 312
  entrenchment clauses established, 76
  formulation of Article V, 16–17, 21, 77–79
  national university and, 105
  presidential terms, 321
  ratification of proposed constitution, 16, 19
  veto power discussed, 244
Constitutional conventions, **79–80**, 250
  calls for, 7, 22, 23, 42, 55, 56, 98, 108, 157, 158, 212, 232, 312, 339
  four types identified, 169
  issue of whether must be general, 79, 250
  periodic, 11, 59, 171, 199, 234
  provisions for in Article V, 17, 79
  ratification by, 11
  "runaway" concern, 79
Constitutional interpretation, 12, **80–81**
Contemporary consensus. *See Dillon v. Gloss.*
Continental Congress, 18, 95

Contract with America, x, **81–82**
  balanced budget, 23
  item veto, 247
  prayer in schools, 239
  term limits, 74
Contract with the American Family, 82, 254
Contracts clause, **82–83**, 143
Contributory negligence, 101, 349
Conyers, John, 323
Cooley v. Board of Wardens (1852), 64
Copeland, Royal, 233
Corporations, 26, **83**, 175
Corwin amendment, 76–77, **83–84**, 125, 190, 231, 244, 281, 303
Corwin, Edwin S., xiv, 87
Corwin, Thomas, 84
Cost-of-living adjustments (COLAs), **84**
Cotton, 298
Coudert, Frederic R., Jr., 111, 247
Council of censors, 16, **85**
Council of State Governments, 11, 22, **85–86**, 173, 291
Court of the Union. *See* Judiciary, Court of the Union.
Court-packing Plan, 69, **86–88**, 172, 176, 177, 208, 301
Covenants, 58
Coverture, 217
Cox, Archibald, 286
Coyle v. Smith (1911), 288
Cram, Ralph, **88–89**
Crane, Philip, 259
Criminal justice system, 29, 35, 46, 115, 122, 146–47, 271, 277
Critical elections, **89–90**
Crittenden, John, 164, 280
Crittenden Compromise, 83–84, **90–91**, 190, 231, 303
Croly, Herbert, **91**, 249
Cultural and linguistic rights, **91**
Cummings, Homer, 87
Cummings v. Missouri (1967), 268
Curbs on judicial jurisdiction advocated, 56, 85–86
Currency, **91–92**
Currie, David, 159
Curtis, Charles, 230
Customs and usages, xv, 18, **92–93**, 261
Cutler, Lloyd N., 59

Danforth, John, 175
Daniel, Price, 111
Daniels, John, 281
Dartmouth College v. Woodward (1819), 82, 83, 203
Davis, Garrett, 51, 289
Davis, Jefferson, 281
Day, Rufus, 47–48
Day, Stephen, 330
Day, William, 155, 301
Debs, Eugene, 284
Declaration of Independence, 2, 16, 32, 55, 77, **95**, 170, 212, 239, 256, 267, 274
Defamation, **96**
Deliberation, 17
Dellinger, Walter, x, 79, 250, 270
Democratic-Republican Party, 26, 307
Dennis v. United States (1951), 294–95
Dickinson, John, 18
Dickstein, Samuel, 8
Dies Committee on Un-American Activities, 51
Difficulty of amending process, 14, 17
Dillon, C. Douglas, 59
Dillon, Conley, 77, **96–97**
Dillon v. Gloss (1921), 10, 18, 47, 57, 97, 161, 188, 249, 251, 254, 306, 324
Direct primary, 249
Dirksen, Everett, **97–98**
    constitutional convention to overturn apportionment decision, 22, 187, 257, 291
    voluntary prayer in schools, 122, 238
    war referendum, 165
Direct vs. indirect effect, 64
Discourse on the Constitution and Government of the United States (Calhoun), 42
Disquisition on Government (Calhoun), 42
Dissolution of Congress, 132
District of Columbia, Representation for, **98–99**, 125, 266
District plan for electoral college reform, 111
Divided government, **99–100**, 229
Divorce. *See* Marriage, divorce, and parenting.
Dobbins v. Erie County (1842), 299

Dodd, Walter F., **100**
Dodge v. Woolsey (1856), **100–101**
Dolbeare, Kenneth, **101**
Dole, Robert, 23, 240, 301
Domestic violence, protection against, **101–2**
Doolittle, James, 11
Dorr, Thomas W., 193
Dorr's Rebellion, 256
Double jeopardy, **102**
Douglas, Paul, 111
Douglas, Stephen A., xv, 128, 279, 280, 283
Douglas, William O.
    opinion in *Adamson v. California*, 5
    opinion in *Baker v. Carr*, 22
    opinion in *Chandler v. Wise*, 47
    opinion in *Engel v. Vitale*, 117
    opinion in *Gray v. Sanders*, 291
    opinion in *Griswold v. Connecticut*, 135, 143, 148, 303
    opinion in *Harper v. Virginia Board of Elections*, 153
    opinion in *Oregon v. Mitchell*, 225
    possible F.D.R. running-mate, 177
    retirement, 179
Douglass, Frederick, 2
Drinan, Robert, 63
Dueling, **102**
Duncan v. Louisiana (1968), 181
Dunn v. Blumstein (1972), 337
Dupont, Pierre, 319
Duties. *See* Tariffs; Taxation, export.
Dyer v. Blair (1975), **103**, 121, 161, 235, 251

Eagle Forum, 120, 265
Eagleton, Thomas, 244, 260
Eastland, James, 180, 292, 321
Eberharter, Herman, 298
Economic system, 45
Edmonds, George Washington, 308
Edmunds Bill of 1874, 201
Education department, 233
Education, establishment of a national university, **105**
Education, right to, 13, 184
Eighteenth Amendment, 7, 15,

21, 51, 60, 98, 100, **105–7**, 155, 164, 233, 149, 306. *See also* Twenty-first Amendment.
Eighth Amendment, 13, 44, **107–8**
Eiselen, Malcolm, **108**
Eisenhower, Dwight D., 37, 246, 317, 341
Elections, **108–9**
    1788, 313
    1796, 313
    1800, 313, 335
    1802, 314
    1824, 68, 110, 123
    1828, 89
    1860, 2, 89
    1868, 128
    1876, 110
    1888, 110
    1896, 89, 210
    1932, 89, 319
    1936, 86
    1960, 110
    1994, 89
Electoral college reform, **109–12**
    automatic plan, 111
    calls for abolition, 4, 108, 115, 160, 196, 197, 206
    district plan, 111
    eliminate electors, 57
    proportional plan, 55, 111
    vice-president's role, 335
Eleventh Amendment, 49, **112–14**, 152, 174
Elk v. Wilkins (1884), 216
Elliott, William Yandell, 89, **114–15**
Ellsworth, Oliver, 177
Emancipation Proclamation, 2, **115**, 190
Embargoes, arms, loans, and foreign aid, **116**
Embargoes, trade, **116**, 154
Emergency Price Control Act of 1942, 248
Emerson, Henry, 194
Eminent domain, 4, 130
Employment Division, Department of Human Resources v. Smith (1990), 133, 253
Employment opportunity, **116–17**, 205
End of Democracy, The (Cram), 88–89
Engel v. Vitale, 1, 34, 36, 98, **116**, 133, 237

English language amendment, **117–18**

English Petition of Rights of 1628, 303

Enterprise, freedom of, 13

Entrenchment clauses, 76, 286

Environmental protection, 13, 45–46, **118–19**, 205, 290

Equal Access Act, 238–239

Equal proportions method of congressional apportionment, 72

Equal Rights Amendment, x, **119–21**

as failed amendment, 125

Dyer v. Blair, 103

Idaho v. Freeman, 161–62

opposed by Ervin, 122

parallel to child labor ratification, 48

ratification issues, 251–52

Ervin, Sam, 62, 80, 120, **121–22**, 147, 187–88, 254

Eshleman, Edwin, 345

Establishment clause. *See* First Amendment.

Ethics in Government Act of 1978, 286

Eutopia, 29

Everson v. Board of Education (1947), 229

Exclusionary rule, 143

Executive offices, exclusion from, **122**

Exigent circumstances, 143

Ex parte Garland (1867), 242, 268

Ex parte New York (1921), 113

Ex parte Young (1908), 114

Ex post facto laws, 14

Extraconstitutional means of change, **123–24**

Failed amendments, 31, 72–73, **125**

Fair Labor Standards Act of 1938, 48, 209, 329

Fairchild v. Hughes (1922), **125–26**

Fairman, Charles, **126**

Faithless electors, 110

Faulkner, James, 246

Fauntroy, Walter, 98

Federal Constitutional Convention Act of 1967, 187

Federal Declaratory Judgment Act, 172

Federal diversity jurisdiction, 13, 158

Federal Election Campaign Act of 1971, 43

Federal Employers' Liability Act of 1908, 350

Federalism

as embodied in Article V, 17

comity, 176

Seventeenth Amendment, 273

See also Tenth Amendment.

Federal Register, 15

Federal Trade Commission Act of 1914, 210

Federalist Papers, 14, 126–27, 199

Federalist Party

and aliens, 8

and national bank, 26

association with Hartford Convention, 155

support for Alien and Sedition Acts, 53

Federalists (supporters of Constitution), 14, 49, 79, 113, **126–27**

Fellow-servant rule, 349

Felons, office holding by, 225

Fenton, Lucien, 288

Fessenden, William P., 139

Field, Stephen, 278

Fifteenth Amendment, 2, 8, 12, **127–29**, 227, 284

Fifth Amendment, **129–30**

double jeopardy clause, 227

due process clause, 43, 83, 92, 130, 143, 268

grand jury provision, 129, 148, 164

self-incrimination clause, 4–5, 129, 257

takings clause, 27, 130, 143

Fighting words, 96, 134, 301

Fillmore, Millard, 315

Finer, Herman, **130–31**, 243

Finletter, Thomas, **131–32**

Finney, Charles G., 2

First Amendment, **132–35**

access to information, 13

alterations suggested, 206

assembly and petition, 135

campaign financing and expenditures, 43

libel, 96

obstacle to Christian amendment, 51

press, 135

religion, 133–34

speech, 134

wording applied to national government, 31

Fisher, Sidney George, **135–36**, 169, 265

Flag desecration amendment, xv, 16, 32, 77, **136–38**

Flag design, 38, 344

Flag Protection Act of 1989, 137, 303, 330

Flag salutes, compulsory, 136

Fletcher v. Peck (1810), 82, 173, 203

Flint v. Stone Tracy Co. (1911), 276

Florence, Thomas, 51, 102

Food and Fuel Administration, 248

Forbes, Steve, 43

Ford, Gerald R., 242, 246, 318

Forfeiture of office. *See* Offices, Forfeiture of or ineligibility to.

Fortas, Abe, 177, 342

Foster, John, 165

44 Liquormart v. Rhode Island (1996), 320

Foster, Henry, 260

Four Horsemen, 87

Fourteenth Amendment, **138–42**

citizenship, 52, 227

due process clause, 4–5, 7, 14, 27, 31, 43, 83, 96, 143, 181

equal protection clause, 95, 257

interpretation of, 305–6. *See also individual court decisions.*

overturned *Dred Scott,* 5, 268

privileges and immunities clause, 53

promulgation of, 249, 270

repeal advocated, 56, 227

Section 1, 32, 33

Section 2, 8, 71, 128, 209, 305, 324

Section 3, 244, 268

Section 4, 60–61, 279

segregation and, 38–39

state and private action distinction, 53–54

woman's suffrage, 12, 218

Fourth Amendment, **142–43**, 151

Frame of Government for Pennsylvania, 232

Frankfurter, Felix, 22, 81, 163
Franking privilege, 75
Franklin, Benjamin, 95
Frazier, Lynn, 341
Free enterprise, **143–44**
Free exercise clause. *See* First
  Amendment.
Freedman's Bureau Bill of 1866,
  139
Freedmen, redistribution of, **144**
Freedom of contract, 185
Free-Soil Party, 2
French language, 91
Frey, Louis, 179
Frontiero v. Richardson (1973),
  120–21
Fugii v. California (1950), 37
Fugitive slave laws, 90, 281
Full faith and credit clause, 201
Fuller, Melville, 236
Fuller, Timothy, 241
Fundamental fairness, 163
Furman v. Georgia (1972), 44,
  108

Gallegly, Ellen, 33
*Garcia v. San Antonio Metropoli-
  tan Transit Authority*
  (1985), 64, 86, **145**, 208,
  273, 285, 301, 329
Gardiner, William, **146–47**
Garfield, James, 54, 317
Garner, John N., 315
Garrett, Finis J., 10
Garrison, William Lloyd, 2
General Agreement on Tariffs
  and Trade (GATT), 101
General Assembly of States, 85
General welfare, **147**
George III, 19
George, Henry, 185
George, Walter, 37
Gerry, Elbridge, 78, 221, 269
Gerrymandering, 292
Getz v. Robert Welch, Inc. (1964),
  96
Geyer, Lee, 320
Gibbons v. Ogden (1824), 64,
  203, 210
Gideon v. Wainwright (1963),
  277, 342
Gillmor, Paul, 329
Gingrich, Newt, 81
Gitlow v. New York (1925), 163
God, 49–51, 61, 239
Goesaert v. Cleary (1948), 120
Gold and silver, 92
Gold Clause cases (1935), 92

Goldberg, Arthur, 148
Goldberg v. Kelly (1970), 345
Goldwater, Barry, 111, 244
Goldwater, Barry, Jr., 165
Gomillion v. Lightfoot (1960),
  291
Gonzalez, Henry, 44
Gore, Albert, Jr., 273
Gore, Thomas, 26
Gossett, Ed, 111
Governors, role in the amending
  process, **147**
Graham, Howard Jay, 83
Grain elevators, 7
Gramm, Phil, 165
Gramm-Rudman-Hollings Law,
  24
Grand jury, **147–48**. *See also*
  Fifth Amendment.
Grandfather clause, 129, 213
Grant, Ulysses
  advocated free public schools
    and opposed aid to
    parochial schools, 36, 267
  appointment of new justices,
    92
  limit work of Congress to sub-
    ject of call, 316
  opposition to polygamy, 201
  proposal to prevent passage of
    bills on last day, 246
  tempted to run for third term,
    322
Grassley, Charles, 16, 202
Gravel v. United States (1972),
  67
*Graves v. New York ex rel.
  O'Keefe* (1939), 299
Graves, William, 102
Gray v. Sanders (1963), 291
Great Depression, 7, 26, 189,
  319
Green, Edith, 247
Green, Steven, 36
Green v. United States (1957),
  102
Gregg v. Georgia (1976), 44
Griffin, Charles, 178
Griffin, Stephen, x
Griffin v. California (1965), 5
Grimes, Alan P., x, 312
Griswold v. Connecticut, 34, 135,
  141, 143, **148–49**, 202,
  221, 258, 262, 294, 303,
  342
Grodzins, Morton, 60
Guarantee clause, **149**, 193, 290
Gubser, Charles, 67

Guinn v. United States (1915),
  212
Gun-Free School Zones Act, 64
Guthrie, William D., 275
Gyuro v. Connecticut (1968), 148

Habeas corpus, writ of, 27, 62
Hahn, Jeanne, 59
Halter v. Nebraska (1907), 136
Hamilton, Alexander
  at constitutional convention,
    17, 78
  duel, 102
  Federalist Papers, 127
  house as national monument,
    321
  not allowed on floor of Con-
    gress, 7
  plan to pay Revolutionary War
    debts, 98
  support for national bank, 26,
    300
  support for public debt, 24
  support for single executive,
    243
  view of general welfare clause,
    147
  view of pardon power, 242
  view of president's term,
    321–22
  views on taxing and spending
    powers, 56
Hamilton, Hugh L., **151–52**
Hammer v. Dagenhart (1918),
  47–49, 64, 208, 301
Hans v. Louisiana (1890),
  113–14, **152**
Hardin, Charles, **153**
Harding, Warren G., 306
Harlan, John Marshall
  (1833–1911)
  favored application of bill of
    rights to states, 27, 163
  favored expansive interpreta-
    tions of Thirteenth and
    Fourteenth Amendments,
    53–54
  in *Hans v. Louisiana,* 152
  Lochner dissent, 191
  Plessy dissent, 234–35
Harlan, John Marshall
  (1899–1971), 19, 22, 81,
  148, 154, 225
*Harper v. Virginia Board of Elec-
  tions* (1966), 34, **153–54,**
  321
Harpers Ferry, 38
Harris, Oren, 271

Harris, William, II, x
Harris v. McRae (1980), 259, 262
Harrison, William Henry, 205, 316
Hartford Convention, 116, **154–55,** 340
Hastings, Alcee L., 162, 225
Hatch, Orrin
  abortion legislation proposed, 260
  opposition to affirmative action, 6
  proposed convention legislation, x, 80, 147, 187–88, 239
  proposed prayer amendment, 239
  support for flag desecration amendment, 138
Hatfield, Mark, 165
Hawaii, 288–89
Hawes-Cutting-Hare bill, 233
Hawke v. Smith (No. 1) (1920), 10, 103, 107, 147, **155,** 183, 189, 215, 219, 251, 326
Hawke v. Smith (No. 2) (1920), 10, **155**
Hayakawa, Samuel I., 117, 325
Hayden Rider, 119
Hayes, Jimmy, 91
Hazlitt, Henry, **155–57**
Heart of Atlanta Motel v. United States (1964), 55, 64
Heflin, Howell, 162
Hehmeyer, Alexander, 131, **157–58**
Helms, Jesse, 238, 260, 323
Helvering v. Davis (1937), 232
Henderson, John, 190
Henderson, Yandell, 158
Hendrickson, Robert, 247
Henry, Patrick, 14, 198
Henry, Richard B. (Brother Imari), 289
Hepburn v. Griswold (1870), 91
Herrick, Manuel, 109
Hicklin test, 223
Higher lawmaking, 3
Highway Trust Fund (1956), 159
Highways, **158–59**
Hillhouse, James, 112, 241
Hilliard, David, 35
Hirabayashi v. United States (1943), 52
Hobbes, Thomas, 285
Hoekstra, Peter, 166

Holden, Matthew, Jr., 243, 289
Holden v. Hardy (1898), 185
Holland, Spessard, 320, 326
Hollings, Ernest, 285
Hollingsworth v. Virginia (1798), 18, 113, 147, 155, **159,** 171, 244, 251, 327
Holman, Rufus, 52
Holmes, Oliver Wendell, Jr., 48, 134, 191, 204, 209
Home Building and Loan Association v. Blaisdell (1934), 82
Homestead exemption, 298
Hopkins, Caspar, **159–60**
Horwill, Herbert, 92, 322
Hot pursuit, 143
House of Representatives, terms for members of
  five years, 196
  four years, 57, 59, 74, 131, 146, 153, 156, 157
  one year, 183
  six years, 160
Housing, **160**
Howard, Jacob, 268
Howland, Leonard, 162
Hubbell, Janette, **101**
Huber, Robert, 198
Huber, Walter, 44
Huckabee, David, 222
Hughes, Charles Evans, 47, 57, 177, 208
Hull, Cordell, 178, 275
Humanitarian, 348
Humphrey's Executor v. United States (1935), 86, 240
Huntington, Edward, 72
Hurtado v. California (1884), 148, 163
Hutchins, Robert, 310
Hutchinson v. Proxmire (1979), 67
Hyde, Henry, 75, 253, 259
Hyde amendment, 259, 262
Hylton v. United States (1796), 236, 297

Idaho v. Freeman (1981), 58, 121, **161–62,** 236, 252, 254, 306
Imari, Brother (Henry, Richard B.), 289
Immediatism, 2
Immigration, 33, 160, 211, 284
Immigration and Naturalization Service v. Chadha (1983), 68, 184, 246

Impeachment, 13, 27, **162,** 178, 224–225
Implied powers, 195, 201
Incorporation (of Bill of Rights), 25, 27, 36, **163**
Indian Bill of Rights, 216
Indians. *See* Native Americans.
Initiative and referendum, 9, 10, 13, 18, 29, 71, 108, **164–66**
Insurance, **166**
Intergovernmental tax immunities, 285
Intermarriage, **167,** 234
Internal improvements, **167**
International Woman Suffrage Alliance, 46
Internet, ix
Interpretivism/noninterpretivism, 80–81
Iredell, James, 217
Isaacson, Eric, 77
Isolationist and peace movements, 164–65
Istook, Ernest, Jr., 253
Ives v. South Buffalo Railway Co. (1911), 350

Jackson, Andrew
  asserts national authority, 42
  association with spoils system, 54
  duels, 102
  favored direct election of president, 112, 123
  internal improvements, 167
  Native Americans, 216
  Post Office, 237
  proposed banning members of Congress from civil offices, 68
  veto exercises, 26, 245
Jackson, Fred, 174
Jackson, Robert, 177, 245
Jacobs, Andrew, Jr., 180, 271, 340
Jameson, John, 100, **169**
Japanese immigrants, 9, 33, 52
Jarvis, Howard, 166
Jaworski, Leon, 286
Jay, John, 172
Jay Treaty, 309
Jefferson, Thomas, **170–71**
  advocacy of Bill of Rights, 30
  borrowing ban favored, 22
  certified Bill of Rights, 31
  church and state, 117

Declaration of Independence, 95, 216, 256
embargo, 116
favored automatic plan for electoral college, 112
favored federal austerity, 24
Kentucky Resolution, 154
Louisiana Purchase, 302
opposition to monopolies, 209–10
opposition to national bank, 26, 300
periodic reform favored, 11, 17, 127
Shays's Rebellion, 256
slave trading outlawed, 279–80
slavery, 144, 278
two-term precedent, 322
universities, 105
Jenkins, Albert, 243
Jenner, William, 261
Jenner bill, 60
Jim Crow laws, 5, 234
John Birch Society, 342
Johnson, Andrew
favored 12-year judicial term, 180
pardon power, 242
popular Senate election favored, 272
proposed prewar compromises, 90, 280, 282
removal of Stanton, 240
support for district plan, 111
vetoes, 139
Johnson, Jed, 325
Johnson, Lyndon B., 98, 112, 203
Johnson v. Louisiana (1972), 181, 276
Johnson, William, 280–81, 284
Johnstone, Frederic B., 265
Joint Committee of Fifteen on Reconstruction, 32
Joint Committee on Reconstruction, 139
Joint resolution, **171**
Jones, James, 165
Jones Act of 1916, 233
Jones v. Alfred H. Mayer Co. (1968), 304
Judges, terms for, 29
Judicial activism/judicial restraint, 80, 174
Judicial Councils Reform and Judicial Conduct and Disability Act (1980), 179

Judicial interpretation, 18. *See also* Constitutional interpretation.
Judicial review, 4, 11, 55, 69, 108, 135, 158, 203. *See also Marbury v. Madison.*
Judiciary
advisory opinions by, 4, 13, 89, **172**
age limits for members, **172**
compensation for members, **172**
Court of the Union, 11, 86, **173**, 177
exercise of judicial review by, **173–75**
jurisdiction of, **175**, 259
limits on taxing power, **175–76**
number of Supreme Court justices, 29, 152, **176**
officeholding by members, **176–77**
organization of, 177
qualifications of members, **177–78**
removal of members, 97, **178–79**
selection of members, **179–80**
terms of judges, 29, 87, 146, **180**
Judiciary Act of 1789, 176, 177, 200
Juries, petit, 29, 148, 276, 332. *See also* Sixth Amendment; Seventh Amendment.
Jury trials, **180–81**
Jus sanguinis, 52
Jus soli, 52

Kansas-Nebraska Act of 1854, 283
Karch, Charles, 212
Kassebaum, Nancy Landon, 59
Katz v. United States (1968), 34, 143
Katzenbach v. McClung (1964), 54, 64
Katzenbach v. Morgan (1966), 118, 325, 337
Keating, Kenneth, 317, 326
Keating-Owen bill, 47–48
Kefauver, Estes, 66, 326
Kellogg-Briand Pact, 341
Kemp, Jack, 165
Kennedy, Anthony, 176, 263
Kennedy, Edward, 325
Kennedy, John F., 111–12, 317
Kersten, Charles, 247
Keynes, John Maynard, 24

Kimble v. Swackhamer (1978), 155, **183**, 251
King, Andrew, 167
King, Carleton, 271
King of England, 58
Knox v. Lee (1871), 92
Korematsu v. United States (1944), 52
Krutsch, Barry, 29, **183–84**
Ku Klux Klan, 102, 149
Kupferman, Theodore, 118
Kyvig, David, 87–88

Labor
convict, **185**
hours of, **185**, 249
Laffer, Arthur, 165
LaFollette, Robert, 10, 91, 165
LaGuardia, Fiorello, 7
Land, division of, **185–86**
Langer, William, 116, 162
Lanham Act, 308
Largent, Steve, 202
Lassiter v. North Hampton County Board of Elections (1959), 336
Lau v. Nichols (1974), 118
Lawrence, William B., **186**
Lazare, Daniel, **186–87**
League of Nations, 204, 230, 247, 350
League of Women Voters, 46, 120
Lee, Richard Henry, 30
Lee v. Weisman (1992), 2, 117
Legal Tender Act of 1862, 91
Legislation, proposed, **187–88**
Legislative veto, 205, 246, 295
Leisy v. Hardin (1890), 106
Lemmon v. The People (1860), 282
Lemon test, 133
Lemon v. Kurtzman (1971), 133, 229
Leser v. Garnett (1922), 77, 125, 183, **188–89**, 200, 219
Lever Food Control Act, 106
Levinson, Sanford, x
Lewis, Diocletion, 347
Lewis, William, 41
Libel, 134
Liberator, 2
Liberty League, 87
Lieutenant governor's role, 57
Limits on constitutional amendments. *See* Constitutional amendments, limits on.
Limits on wealth and income, **189–90**

Lincoln, Abraham, **190**
  and alcohol, 105
  and Christian amendment, 50
  and Corwin amendment, 77,
    83–84
  election of, 2
  Emancipation Proclamation,
    115, 279, 304
  on *Scott* decision, xv
  on slave colonization, 144
  signed Thirteenth Amend-
    ment, 244
*Lincoln County [Nevada] v. Lun-
  ing* (1890), 114
Library of Congress, Legislative
  Reference Service, xi
Lindbergh Act, 212
Line-item veto, 246
Literacy tests. *See* Voting rights,
  literacy tests.
Livermore, Arthur, 303
Livermore, Samuel, 107–108
Livermore v. Waite (1894),
  190–91
Livingston, Robert, 95
Lloyd, Wesley, 189
Lochner v. New York (1905), 55,
  83, 141, 185, **191–92,**
  207, 294
Lockwood, Henry C., **192–93**
Lodge, Henry Cabot, 111
Logrolling, 98
London Anti-Slavery Convention
  (1840), 286
Long, Huey P., 189
Longworth, Nicholas, 315
Looking Backward (Bellamy),
  189
Lotteries, **193**
Louisiana, French language in,
  91
Louisiana ex rel. Elliott v. Jamel
  (1883), 113
Louisiana Lottery Company, 193
Louisiana Purchase, 22
*Louisville Joint Stock Land Bank
  v. Radford* (1935), 86
Loving v. Virginia (1967), 167,
  202, 234
Luce, Clare Boothe, 330
Lucretia Mott amendment, 211.
  See Equal Rights Amend-
  ment.
Ludlow amendment, 165. *See
  also* Initiative and referen-
  dum.
Ludlow, Louis, 165, 341
Luther v. Borden (1849), 9, 102,

149, **193–94,** 235, 256,
  291
Lutz, Donald
  analysis of constitutional
    amendments, x
  characteristics of charters, 58
  on origins of bill of rights, 30
  relation between amendment
    and interpretation, 123
Lynch v. Donnelly (1984), 133
Lynching, **194**

MacArthur, Douglas, 30
McCarran, Patrick, 216
McCarran Act, 166
McCoid, Moses, 307
McCormick, Ruth Hanna, 274
McCulloch v. Maryland, 26, 143,
  195–96, 203, 217, 227,
  299, 300
McDermott, Allan, 83
Macdonald, Dwight, **196**
MacDonald, William, **196–97**
Machen, Arthur, 129
McKee, Henry, **198**
McKenna, Joseph, 215
McKinley, William, 317
McLean, John, 177
Macon, Nathaniel, 314
McReynolds, James, 87
Madison, James, xiv, **198–200**
  Bill of Rights, 14, 30, 95
  borrowing for War of 1812, 22
  church and state, 117
  concern over convention
    mechanism, 17, 78
  Eighth Amendment, 107
  favored amendments limiting
    states, 27, 30
  Federalist Papers, 42, 85,
    126–27, 164, 171
  First Amendment, 132–33
  on internal improvements,
    167, 246
  Ninth Amendment, 220–21
  representative democracy,
    164
  Second Amendment, 269
  Seventh Amendment, 274
  Tenth Amendment, 300
  Treasury Department, 309
  Twenty-seventh Amendment,
    323
  view of general welfare clause,
    147
  Virginia Resolution, 154
Magna Carta, 30, 107

Mails, use of, 237
Majority preference voting
  (MPV), 112
"Majority Rule Club," 4
Malloy v. Hogan (1964), 271
Mann Act (1910), 202
Mansfield, Mike, 67
Manufacturing vs. commerce, 64
Mapp v. Ohio (1961), 143, 342
Marbury v. Madison (1803), 49,
  69, 159, 174, **200–201,**
  203, 235, 315
Marbury, William, 77, 129, **200,**
  213
Marcantonio, Vito, 341
Marduke, P.G., 45
Marriage, divorce, and parenting,
  38, 45, 159, **201–2,** 224
Marsh v. Chambers (1983), 133
Marshall, John, **202–3**
  banks and bankruptcy, 26
  Barron v. Baltimore, 26–27,
    31, 167
  Gibbons v. Ogden, 64
  McCulloch v. Maryland, 143,
    217
  Marbury v. Madison, 49, 69,
    174
Marshall, Thurgood, 44
Marston v. Lewis (1973), 337
Mason, Alpheus, 86
Mason, George, 17, 30, 78, 256
Mason, Noah, 116
Massachusetts Body of Liberties,
  107
Matthews, Donald, 19
Mattingly, Matt, 246
Maximum wage, 189, 332
Maysville Road Bill, 167
Medicaid, 203
Medical care, 45, **203–4**
Medicare, 203
Meek v. Pittenger (1973), 229
Meese, Edwin, 81
Merriam, Charles, **204,** 289
Meyer v. Nebraska (1923), 118
Meyers, Karl E., 196
Michel, Robert, 95, 137
Migratory birds, **204**
Military Reconstruction Act
  (1867), 140
Militia, **205**
Miller, Arthur S., **205–6**
Miller, Jeremy M., **206–7**
Miller, Lucas, 165, 330, 348
Miller, Samuel, 277
Miller v. California (1973), 134,
  223

Miller v. Johnson (1995), 292
Milliken v. Bradley (1974), 266
Minersville School District v. Gobitis (1940), 136
Minimum wages, **207–8,** 249
Ministerial responsibility, 230, 346
Mink, Patsy, 254
Minor v. Happersett (1875), **208–9,** 219
Miranda v. Arizona (1966), 62, 130, 271, 277, 342
Missouri Compromise (1820), 90, 267–68, 283
Missouri Pacific Railway Co. v. Kansas (1919), 246
Missouri Pacific Railway Co. v. Nebraska (1896), 163
Missouri Plan, 179
Missouri v. Holland (1920), 37, 204, **209,** 252
Missouri v. Jenkins (1990), 176
Modally, Walter, 243
Moment of silence. *See* Prayer in public schools.
Monaco v. Mississippi (1934), 113
Money. *See* Currency.
Monopolies and trusts, **209–10**
Monroe Doctrine, 28
Monroe, James, 105, 167
Moore v. Dempsey (1923), 194
Morehead v. New York ex rel. Tipaldo (1936), 208
Mormon Church, 201
Morris, Gouverneur, 76, 78
Morris, Henry O., **210–11**
Morrison v. Olson (1988), 286
Morton, Oliver P., 111
Mott, Lucretia Coffin, **211,** 230, 286
Mottl, Ronald M., 266
Movement, freedom of, 13–14
Mueller v. Allen (1983), 229
Mulford v. Smith (1939), 8
Muller v. Oregon (1908), 185, 207
Mundt, Karl E., 111
Murder and kidnapping, **211–12**
Murphy, Cornelius F., Jr, **212**
Murphy, Frank, 5, 163
Murphy, Walter, x, 77, **212**
Murray v. Curlett (1963), 1
Musmanno, M. A., ix
My First Days in the White House (Long), 189
Myers v. Anderson (1915), 77, 129, 200, **212–13**

Myers v. United States (1926), 237, 240, 308

Nader, Ralph, 165
National American Woman Suffrage Association (NAWSA), 13, 46, 218, 274, 287, 347, 348
National appeals court, 29
National Association for the Advancement of Colored People v. Alabama ex rel. Patterson (1958), 19
National Association of Evangelicals (NAE), 51
National Association To Secure the Religious Amendment of the Constitution, 50
National Bituminous Coal Act, 86
National Child Labor Committee (NCLC), 47
National Committee to Abolish the Poll Tax, 320
National Consumers League (NCL), 207
National Council for the Social Studies, 56
National database, 184
National Direct Legislative League, 165
National Education Association, 165
National Environmental Policy Act (NEPA), 119
National Federation of Women's Clubs, 347
National Industrial Recovery Act, 7, 48, 86
National Labor Relations Board v. Jones & Laughlin Steel Corporation (1937), 87, 185
National League for the Protection of American Institutions, 36
National League of Cities v. Usery (1976), 145, 301, 329
National Liberty Party, 2
National presidential primary, 29
National Prohibition cases (1920), 60, 77, 100, 103, 107, 189, **215,** 250, 319, 326
National Prohibition Party, 347
National Reform Association, 50
National Rifle Association, 269
National Taxpayers Union, 23
National Temperance League, 15

National Unfunded Mandate Day, 329
National Woman Suffrage Association, 12, 218–19, 230, 287
National Woman's Party (NWP), 120, 229, 230
Nationality Act of 1940, 53
Native Americans, 160, **215–16**
Natural law, **216–17**
Natural rights, 2, 95, 138, 170, 220, 339–40
Near v. Minnesota (1931), 135
Nebbia v. New York (1934), 248
Necessary and proper clause, 195, **217**
The Need for Constitutional Reform (Elliott), 114–15
Negative income tax, 196
New Deal, 3, 7, 23, 48, 64, 86–87
New England Anti-Slavery Society, 2
New Jersey Plan, 71, 78
New Times, 4
New York state income tax, 299
New York State Woman Suffrage Party, 46
New York Times v. Sullivan (1964), 34, 96, 134
New York Times v. United States (1971), 135
New York Trust Co. v. Eisner (1916), 298
New York v. Quarles (1984), 62
Newberry v. United States (1921), 109, 204
"Newstates of America," 310–11, 330
Newton, Huey, 35
Nineteenth Amendment, **217–20**
  Anthony and, 13
  Catt and, 46–47
  cited in *Adkins* decision, 208
  grassroots effort, xii
  Hawke v. Smith (2) and, 155
  Mott and, 211
  overturned *Minor,* 209
  Shafroth-Palmer Amendment to, 274
  tie to abolitionist concerns, 2
Ninth Amendment, 9, 148, **220–21**
Nix v. Williams (1984), 143
Nixon, Richard M., 51, 241, 242, 277–78, 266, 286, 317

Nixon, Walter L., 162
Nixon v. United States (1993), 162, 235
"No confidence" vote. *See* Presidency, vote of no confidence.
Noell, John, 243
Norris, George, 111, 314
North American Free Trade Agreement (NAFTA), 101, 297, 309
North Carolina, ratification of Twenty-fourth Amendment, 321
Northwest Ordinance of 1787, 19, 190, 282, 304
Notes on the State of Virginia (Jefferson), 127
Nullification, 42
Nullification Crisis of 1828–1832, 297
Number of proposed amendments, ix, 17, **221–22**
Nunn, Sam, 176
Nye, Gerald P., 116, 341

O'Brien, William, 36
Obscenity and pornography, 96, 134, **223**
O'Connor, Sandra Day, 145, 273, 285, 320
O'Conor, Charles, **223–24**, 263
O'Daniel, Wilbert, 261
Offices, forfeiture of or ineligibility to, **224–25**
Ogden v. Saunders (1827), 26
Old Age and Survivors Insurance Program of 1972, 84
Oliver, Frank, 60
Olmstead v. United States (1928), 143
Ombudsmen, 29, 196, 311
Open fields, 143
Open shop, 261
Oregon v. Mitchell (1970), 34, **225–26,** 325, 337
Orfield, Lester B., 286
Organized crime, 107, 319
Original intent, 81
Original jurisdiction, 175
Osborn v. Bank of the United States (1924), 113–14
Ottinger, Richard, 118
Owen, Robert Dale, 139
Owens, Major, 116–17, 270

Pace, James O., **227**
Packwood, Bob, 224

Palko v. Connecticut (1937), 4, 102, 126, 163, **227–28**
Palmer, Mitchell, 274
Pardon power. *See* Presidency, pardon power.
Parental rights amendment, 202
Parenting. *See* Marriage, divorce, and parenting.
Parental Rights and Responsibility Act, 202
Parliamentary sovereignty, 135, 200, **228**
Parliamentary system, **228–29**
  advocates of, 6, 25, 96–97, 114, 186, 196, 205, 258
  advocates' critique of divided government, 99–100
  cabinet officers in legislature, 41
  elections in, 73
Parochial schools, aid to, **229–30**
Parris, Stanford, 326
Patents and copyrights, **230**
Patterson, Elizabeth, 307
Paul, Alice, 119, 219, **230–31**
Paul v. Virginia (1869), 166
Paulsen, Michael S., ix
Payne-Aldrich Tariff Bill, 275, 297
Payne v. Tennessee (1991), 336
Peace Convention, 83, 90, **231**
Peace movements, 164
Peckham, Rufus, 191
Peffer, William, 73, 164
Pei, Mario, **231–32**
Pell, Claiborne, 326
Pendleton, George H., 41
Pendleton Act (1883), 54
Penn, William, 16, 58, **232**
Pennsylvania Council of Censors, 85
Penny, Timothy, 325
Pensions, **232**
Pentagon Papers, 67
Perez v. Brownell (1958), 53
Permanent Commission for Constitutional Review, 96
Perot, Ross, 43
Personal liberty laws, 281
Phantom amendment. *See* Titles of nobility.
Philadelphia Female Anti-Slavery Society, 211
Philippine independence, **233**
Physical intimidation, 129
Piburn, John, **233–34**
Pinckney, Charles, 105

Pizzigati, Sam, 189–90
Plain view, 143
Plan To Stop the Present and Prevent Future Wars, A (Beasley), 27
Planned Parenthood of Southeastern Pennsylvania v. Casey (1992), 254, 259, 262–63
Planning, governmental, 310–11, 339–40
Phelan, James, 141
Plessy v. Ferguson (1896), 5, 20, 38, 54, 141, **234–35**, 267, 271, 292
Plumley, Charles, 70
Plyler v. Doe (1982), 33
Pocket veto, 246
Political parties
  critiqued, 249, 292
  eliminated, 146
  limited, 28
  multiparty system favored, 101
  prohibited from nominating members of Congress, 183
  recognized, 25
  role and status defined, 976
  strengthened, 59, 66
Political questions, 10, **235–36.** *See also Baker v. Carr; Luther v. Borden.*
Poll taxes. *See* Twenty-fourth Amendment.
Pollock v. Farmers' Loan & Trust Co. I & II (1895), **236,** 275, 285, 297, 300
Polygamy, 28, 201–2, 225
Pomerene, Atlee, 162
Populist movement, 164–65
Populist Party, 15
Porter, Luke, 201
Post office, **236–37**
Postal Reorganization Act of 1970, 237
Postmasters, 55, 237
Potter, Charles, 73
Potter, Clarkson, 82
Powell, Adam Clayton, 44, 63
Powell, Lazarus, 84
Powell, Lewis, 145
Powell v. Alabama (1932), 277
Powell v. McCormack (1969), 63, 103, 224, 235, 333, 342
Prayer in public schools, 51, 81, 122, **237–39,** 253
Preamble of U.S. Constitution, 9, **239**
Presentment clause, 246

Presidency
   age limits for, **239–40**
   appointment and removal
      powers of, **240**
   compensation for, 172,
      240–41, 346
   creation of a separate chief of
      state, 156, **241**
   line-item veto, 13, 61, 82,
      108, 114, 295
   membership in Senate for ex-
      presidents, **241–42**
   oath of, **242**
   pardon power, 28, **242–43**
   plural executive, 42, 131, **243**
   qualifications for, 13, 52,
      243–44
   in the amending process,
      244–45
   powers of, **245**
   selection. *See* Electoral college.
   term, 25, 55, 61, 88
   veto power of, **245–46**
   vote of no confidence, 230,
      247–48
Presidency of the United States,
   The (Woodward), 348
President John Smith (Adams), 4
President pro tempore of Senate,
   316
Presidential election tournament
   (PET), 29
Presidential initiatives, 18
Presidential Power and Account-
   ability (Hardin), 153
Press, freedom of. *See* First
   Amendment.
Price fixing, **248**
Prigg v. Pennsylvania (1842),
   281
Prior state rejection of amend-
   ments, 47, 57, **248**
Privacy, right to, 13, 217. *See*
   Griswold v. Connecticut; Roe
   v. Wade.
Progress and Poverty (George),
   185
Progressive Democracy (Croly), 91
Progressive era, 4, 9, 10, 12, 89,
   174, 179, **248–49.** *See also*
   Eighteenth Amendment;
   Nineteenth Amendment;
   Seventeenth Amendment;
   Sixteenth Amendment.
Progressive Party, 158
Promise of American Life,The
   (Croly), 91
Promulgation of amendments,

249–50
Proportional plan for electoral
   college reform, 111
Proportional representation, 65,
   101
Proposal of amendments, **250**
Proposed Constitution for the
   United States of America
   (Gardiner), 146
Proposition 13 (CA), 166
Puerto Rico, representation in
   electoral college, **250**

Question hour, 132, 192, 229
Quilici v. Village of Morton Grove
   (1983), 270

Race rider, 273
Railroad regulation, 7
Rainbow Coalition, 112
Randall, William, 286
Randolph, Jennings, 325
Randolph, John, 178
Rangel, Charles, 160
Rantoul, Robert, 2
Rarick, John, 142, 174, 178,
   242, 308
Raskob, John J., 319
Ratification of amendments, 10,
   16, 161–62, **251–52**
Ray, George Washington, 209
Reagan, Ronald, 24, 238, 239,
   246, 318
Recall, **252**
   of members of Congress, 14,
      70–71, 74
   of judges, 55
   of president, 4
Reconstruction of the Government
   of the United States of Amer-
   ica (Wedgwood), 343
"Red rose" brigade, 219
Reed, Philip, 307
Reed, Stanley, 4, 163
Reed, Thomas B., 211
Reed amendment, 125, 307
Reed v. Reed (1971), 120
Rees, Grover III, 80
Referendums, 3, 4, 9, 18, 29,
   71, 101, 108, 272. *See also*
   Initiative and referendum.
Reformed Presbyterian Church,
   49–50
Reframing the Constitution: An
   Imperative for Modern
   America (Baldwin), 25
Rehnquist, William, 62, 64, 145,
   183, 325

Reid v. Covert (1957), 204, 209,
   252
Religious equality amendment,
   36, 51, 82, 230, 239,
   252–54
Religious Freedom Restoration
   Act, 134, 252–54
Republican Party, 2, 283
Reproductive rights, **254**
Rescission of ratification of pend-
   ing amendments, 10, 128,
   169, 188, **254–55**
Responsibilities, of citizens, 206,
   310
Retrocession, 99
Reuss, Henry, 242, 247
Reuss Resolution, 97, 241
Revenue Act of 1919, 48
Revenue Reconciliation Act of
   1993, 299
Revenue sharing, **255**
Revolution, 16, 89, 170, 190,
   255–56
Revolution, The (Anthony), 13
Reynolds, Eustace, **256–57**
Reynolds v. Sims (1964), 59, 98,
   141, **257,** 342
Reynolds v. United States (1879),
   201
Rhode Island v. Palmer (1920).
   See National Prohibition
   cases.
Rhodes, John, 244
Rice, Isaac L., **258**
Rice v. Sioux City Memorial Park
   (1955), 37
Right to life, 13, **258–60**
Right to work, **261**
Rigid constitution, 10, 228, **261**
Roane, Spencer, 195
Robert, Ernest, 41
Roberts, Owen, 87, 175, 331,
   350
Robinson, Donald L., **262–63**
Robinson, Joe, 87
Rockefeller, Nelson, 318
Roddenbery, Seaborn, 167
Roe v. Wade (1973), 52, 121,
   141, 149, 202, 254,
   258–60, **262–63,** 294
Rogers, Walter, 290
Romer v. Evans (1996), 166
Romney, George, 243
Roosevelt, Franklin D.
   admired by Cram, 88
   appointment of Black, 34
   broke two-term precedent, xiv,
      322

Roosevelt, Franklin D. *(cont.)*
Court-packing plan, 69, **86–87**
favored amending expanding general welfare clause, 147
New Deal programs, 7, 64, 116
opposed Ludlow amendment, 165
Roosevelt, Theodore, 165, 249, 322
Rosen, Jeffrey, 77
Rosenberger v. Rector and Visitors of the University of Virginia (1994), 253
Ros-Lehtinen, Ileana, 336
Roth, William, 285
Roth v. United States (1957), 223
Rousseau, Jean-Jacques, 70
Rush, Benjamin, 105
Rutledge, John, 76, 78
Rutledge, Wiley, 5, 163

Safety-valve analogy, 89, 135, 169, 256, **265**, 294
Safroth, John, 350
St. Lawrence Seaway, 309
Salary Grab Act (1873), 324
Saloon, 106–7
San Mateo Co. v. Southern Pacific R.R. (1883), 83
Saulsburg, Willard, 205
Schechter Poultry Corporation v. United States (1935), 7, 48, 86
Schenck v. United States (1919), 134
Schinck v. Reed (1974), 242
Schlafly, Phyllis, 120, 255–56
Schlesinger, Arthur M., Jr., 318
School busing, 39, **266–67**
Schools, public, **267**
Scientific capitalism, 339
Scott v. Sandford, xv, 5, 28, 33, 51, 69, 83, 139, 190, **267–68**, 283, 294, 304
Searches and seizures. *See* Fourth Amendment.
Secession of states, 38, 42, 57
Secessionists, Limiting the right of, **268**. *See also* Fourteenth Amendment.
Second Amendment, 25, 164, 205, 206, **269–70**
Second Employers' Liability Case (1912), 350
Secretary of state, 4, 5, 15, **270–71**

Securities Act of 1933, 83
Securities Exchange Act of 1934, 83
Security Council (UN), 330
Sedition Acts. *See* Alien and Sedition Acts.
Segregation, **271**
Selective exclusiveness, 64
Selective incorporation, 4–5, 31, 163. *See also Palko v. Connecticut.*
Selective incorporation plus, 163
Self-incrimination, **271**
Seminole Tribe v. Florida (1996), 114
Senate, U.S.
elimination proposed, 4, 45, 192, 273
proposed changes, 25, 153, 156
representation in, 16–17, 55
terms, 25, 57, 59, 152, 153, 231
Seneca Falls Convention (1848), 211, 217–18, 230, 286
Seneca Falls Declaration of Rights and Sentiments, 219
Seniority, 75, 132
Sentinels of the Republic, 48
Separate but equal. *See Plessy v. Ferguson.*
Separation of powers, 30, 41, 59, 68, 114, 186, 229, 258
Seventeenth Amendment, 16, 55, 76, 88, 92, 249, **271–74**
Seventh Amendment, 13, 164, 181, **274**
Seward, William, 84
Shadow cabinet, 59, 153
Shafroth, John F., 274
Shafroth-Palmer Amendment of 1914, 218, 230, **274**
Shapiro v. Thompson (1969), 345
Share the Wealth Program, 189
Shaw v. Reno (1993), 292
Shays's Rebellion, 78
Sheppard, Morris, 7, 106, 298, 319
Sherman, Roger, **274–75**
Connecticut Compromise, 76
Declaration of Independence, 95
proposed adding amendments to end of text, 30
Senate representation, 78
Tenth Amendment, 21
Sherman Antitrust Act, 166, 210

Sikes, Robert, 175
Simon, Paul, 23
Simple resolutions, 171
Single-member district representation, 65
Sixteenth Amendment, 23, 55, 144, 189, 232, 249, **275–76**, 297–98
Sixth Amendment, 181, 271, **276–77**
Slaughterhouse cases (1973), 5, 31, 141, 163, 268, **277–78**, 294
Slavery, 5, 28, 90
and colonization, 190, **278–79**
compensation for, **279**, 282
in District of Columbia, 90, **279**
foreign commerce, **279–80**
insurrections, **280**
interstate commerce, 90, **280–81**
protection for, **281**
return of fugitives, 181, **281–82**
right to travel with slaves, **282**
the territories and, 28, 90, **282–83**
Slaves, importation of, 16–17, 76, 90
Slayton, William H., 319
Smith, Al, 319
Smith, Goldwin, 129, **283–84**
Smith, Margaret Chase, 63
Smith, Munroe, 91
Smith v. Allwright (1944), 109, 129
Smith v. Goguen (1974), 137
Smith, William, 107
Smith v. Union Bank of Georgetown (1831), **284**
Social and economic rights, 13, 35, 160
Social Security system, 232–33, 339
Social services, right to, 13
Socialism, 339–40
Socialist Party of America, 143, **284**
Souter, David, 263
South Carolina Seaman Act of 1822, 280
South Carolina v. Baker (1988), 86, **285**, 300
South Carolina v. Dole (1987), 56, 320

South Carolina v. Katzenbach (1966), 337
Southard, Milton, 243
Southern Textile Bulletin (Clark), 48
Sovereign immunity, 54
Sovereignty, **285**
Spanish-American War of 1898, 233, 289, 309
Speaker of the House of Representatives, 316
Special prosecutor, **286**
Speech and debate clause, 67
Speech, freedom of. *See* First Amendment.
Speed limits, 56
Spence v. Washington (1969), 137
Spoils system, 54
Sprague v. United States (1931), 107
Springer v. United States (1881), 236, 275
Standing army, 269
Stanton, Edwin M., 240
Stanton, Elizabeth Cady, 12, 140, 211, 218, **286–87**
Start, Pete, 203–4
State constitutions
  as protections for individual rights, 32
  as source of Bill of Rights, 31
  convention mechanisms, 80
  proposed changes in, 25, 115, 146, 344
State-federal relations, **287–88**
States
  admission of new, **288–89**
  boundaries of, 25, 35, 89, 114, 151, 192, 206, 212 **289**
  constitutional revision, **290**
  control over natural resources, **290–91**
  legislative apportionment, **291–92**. *See also Baker v. Carr; Reynolds v. Sims.*
  police powers, 292. *See also* Tenth Amendment.
Statutory interpretation, 70
Stevens, John Paul, 121, 161, 251, 333
Stevens, Lillian M., 347
Stevens, Thaddeus, 32, 139
Steward Machine Co. v. Davis (1937), 232
Stewart, Potter, 1, 117, 149, 154
Stewart, William, 128
Stickney, Albert, **292–93**

Stone, Harlan Fiske, 69, 301
Stone, Lucy, 218
Stone v. Powell (1976), 62
Stop and frisk, 143
Story, Joseph, 41, 135, 265, **293–94**
Stowe, Harriet Beecher, 2
Straight-ticket voting, 59
Street v. New York (1969), 137
Stromberg v. California (1931), 136
Strong, William, 50
Sturges v. Crowinshield (1819), 26
Submerged Lands Act (1953), 290
Substantive due process, **294**
Subversion, **294–95**
Sumner, Charles, 149
Sunday rest, 38, 50
Sundquist, James, 97, **295**
Susan B. Anthony amendment. *See* Nineteenth Amendment.
Supremacy clause, 37
Supreme Court, U.S. *See under* Judiciary.
Supreme Court decisions, reversed by amendments, 18, 70. *See also individual case names.*
Suspect categories, 121
Sutherland, George, 207–8
Swann v. Charlotte-Mecklenburg Board of Education (1971), 266
Swayne, Noah, 278
Sweating system, 207
Swindler, William, 86
Swiss parliamentary model, 183
Synder, John, 189

Taft, Henry, 21
Taft, William Howard, 41, 48, 177, 240, 275, 308–9
Taft-Hartley Act of 1947, 245, 267, 341
Taney, Roger, 5, 33, 51, 267–68, 281, 283
Tariffs, 284, **297**
Tax Equity and Fiscal Responsibility Act of 1985, 285
Taxation, church property, 192
Taxation
  direct, **297–98**
  export, **298**
  inheritance, **298**
  land, **298**

  majorities needed to increase, **298–99**
  retroactive, **299**
  state and federal employees, **299**
  state income tax of nonresidents, **299**
  state securities, **299–300**
Taxing and spending power, 56
Taylor, John of Caroline, 195
Teague, Olin (Tiger), 237, 240
Telschow, Roger, 165
Temperance Education Foundation, 15
Ten times rule, 189, 332
Tennessee Valley Authority, 143
Tenth Amendment, **300–301**
  as possible limit on Article V, 21, 331
  interpreted in *McCulloch v. Maryland*, 195
  proposals to add "expressly" to, 142, 227
  renewed attention to, 288, 301
  state police powers, 8, 56, 204, 209, 225, 292
  tax immunities, 285
Term limits. *See* Congress, term limits.
Territories, **301–2**
Texas, 289
Texas v. Johnson (1989), 16, 134, 136, **302–3**, 330
Texas v. Mitchell (1970), 225
Texas v. White (1869), 288
Thayer, John Randolph, 186
Theft, punishment for, 28
Theocracy, 344
Third Amendment, 164, **303**
Thirteenth Amendment, **303–4**
  and *Scott* decision, 268
  as model for alcoholic prohibition, 15
  Mott's role in, 211
  prohibits slavery, 2, 71, 84, 115, 138, 190
  signed by Lincoln, 244
Thomas, Clarence, 180, 333
Thomas, Norman, 284
Thompson, Standish, 255
Three-fifths clause, 5, 71, 154, 297, **304–5**
Thurmond, Strom, 63, 102, 130, 173, 285, 323
Tiedeman, Christopher, **305–6**
Time limits on amendments, 10, **306–7**
Tinker v. Des Moines (1969), 34

Titles of nobility, 52, **307**
Total incorporation. 5, 163. *See also* Black, Hugo.
Total incorporation plus, 5
Trade Act of 1974, 309
Trade Mark cases (1879), 307
Trademark Counterfeiting Act of 1984, 308
Trademarks, **307–8**
Treason, **308**
Treasury, Department of, 240, **308–9**
Treaties, ratification of, 4, 37, 57, 108, 204, 295, **309–10**
Treaty of Versailles, 309
Trial of the Constitution, The (Fisher), 135
Tribe, Laurence, x, 137
Trinsley v. Pennsylvania (1991), 273
Trono v. United States (1905), 102
Trop v. Dulles (1958), 53
Truman, Harry S, 111, 242, 245, 246, 316, 322, 341, 350
Tucker amendment, 201
Tugwell, Rexford, 97, 310–12, 330
Tuller, Walter, **312**
Twelfth Amendment, 89, 109, **312–14**
Twentieth Amendment, 20, 55, **314–16**, 335
Twenty-fifth Amendment, 234, 244, 246, 315, **316–18,** 335
Twenty-first Amendment, 15, 16, 56, **318–20**
21st Century Constitution, The (Krusch), 29
Twenty-fourth Amendment, 8, **320–21**
Twenty-second Amendment, xiv, 74, 92, 131, 153, **321–23**
Twenty-seventh Amendment, x, 10, 15, 18, 31, 58, 73, 75, 125, 169, 173, 252, 270, 306, **323–24,** 343
Twenty-sixth Amendment, 8, 34, 63, 225, **324–25**
Twenty-third Amendment, 98–99, 109, 250, **325–26**
Twining v. New Jersey (1908), 4
Two-thirds majority necessary to propose amendments, 250, **326–27**
Tydings-McDuffie Act of 1934, 233

Tyler, John, 71, 149, 194, 231, 245, 317, 335

Udall, Morris, 118, 241
Uncle Tom's Cabin (Stowe), 2
Understanding clauses, 129
Underwood, John, 309
Underwood, Joseph, 41
Unfunded federal mandates, 145, **329–30**
Unfunded Mandate Reform Act (1995), 329
Union Signal, 347
Unitary form of government, 287
United Nations, 37, **330,** 350
United Nations Genocide Convention, 37
U.S. Claims Court, 54
U.S. Conference of Mayors, 329
U.S. Court of Claims, 54
United States Department of Commerce v. Montana (1972), 72
United States of America, proposed name changes, **330**
United States of the World, 348
U.S. Term Limits v. Thornton (1995), 75, **332–33**
U.S. Trademark Act of 1946, 306
United States v. Anthony (1872), 13
United States v. Arizona (1970), 225
United States v. Brewster (1972), 67
United States v. Butler (1936), 7, 56, 147
United States v. California (1947), 290
United States v. Classic (1941), 109, 204
United States v. Darby (1941), 49, 64, 209, 301
United States v. E.C. Knight Company (1895), 64, 210
United States v. Eichmann (1990), 16, 134, 137, 303, **330–31**
United States v. Guest (1966), 280
United States v. Leon (1984), 143
United States v. Lopez (1995), 64, 301
United States v. McCullagh (1915), 204
United States v. Miller (1939), 269–70

United States v. Nixon (1974), 286
United States v. Pink (1942), 37
United States v. Price (1966), 280
United States v. Robel (1967), 295
United States v. Shauver (1914), 204
United States v. South-Eastern Underwriters Association (1944), 166
United States v. Sprague (1931), 21, 77, 215, 251, **331**
United States v. Wong Kim Ark (1898), 51–52
Universal suffrage, 88
Unwritten constitution. *See* Customs and usages.
Upham, Thomas Carlyle, **331–32**
Utah, 288

Vallandigham, Clement, 42
Van Alstyne, William, 79
Van Buren, Martin, 167
Van Devanter, Willis, 97, 215
Vanderberg, Arthur, 325
Varnum, Joseph, 288
Veto. *See* Presidency, veto power of.
Viability, 262
Vice-presidency, 4, 25, 153, 186, 293, 318, **335–36**
Victimless crimes, 29
Victims' rights, 336
Vietnam War, 35, 325
Vile, John, xii, xiv–xv, 261
Virginia Declaration of Rights, 107
Virginia and Kentucky Resolutions, 154
Virginia Plan, 16, 71, 78, 123, 147, 198, 321
Vocation as basis for representation, 72, 151
Volstead Act, 60, 97, 107, 215, 319
Voorhis, Horace, 51, 298
Vose, Clement, xiii
Vote of no confidence, 29
Voting Rights Act of 1965, 118, 337
Voting Rights Act Amendments of 1970, 34, 225, 325
Voting rights
literacy tests, 129, **336–37**
residency requirements, **337**

Voucher system, 229, 254

Wadsworth, James W., 10, 319
Waiting for the Signal (Morris), 210
Walker, Robert, 82
Wallace v. Jaffree (1985), 2, 117, 239
Wallace, William Kay, 330–40
War, 154
  declaration of, **340**
  opposition to government during, **340**
  power during, **340–41**
  prohibition of, 332, **341**
War of 1812, 22, 49, 53, 116, 205
War Powers Resolution of 1973, 295, 340
War Time Prohibition Act (1919), 7
Warren, Earl, 38, 177, 257
Warren Court, **341–42**
  criminal justice, 122
  Dirksen and, 98
  incorporation of Bill of Rights, 31–32
  judicial activism, 81
  legislation against subversion, 295
  legislative apportionment, 291
  See also individual judicial decisions.
Washington, George, **342–43**
  as chair of convention, 78
  oath of office, 242
  on national bank, 26
  president during ratification of Bill of Rights, 343
  two-term precedent, 322
Washington Peace Convention. *See* Peace Convention.
Watkins v. United States (1957), 60
Watson, Gregory, 324, **343**
Wayne, James, 100
Webb-Kenyon Act of 1913, 106
Webster, Daniel, 42, 193, 256, 324

Webster v. Reproductive Health Services (1989), 254, 259, 262
Wedgwood, William B., **343–44**
Weed, Helen Hill, 119
Weeks v. United States (1914), 143
Welfare payments, right to, **344**
Welfare reform, 46
Wesberry v. Sanders (1964), 66, 72, 291
West, James C., **345–46**
West Coast Hotel v. Parrish (1937), 69, 87, 147, 185, 208
West Point, 105
West Virginia Board of Education v. Barnett (1943), 136
Wheeler, Joseph, 70
White, Byron, 148, 176
White, Edward, 213
Whitman, Alden, xii
Wickard v. Filburn (1942), 8
Wickersham, Victor, 325
Wiener v. United States (1958), 240
Wiggins, Charles, 148
Willard, Frances, 347
Williams, John Bell, 271
Williams v. Florida (1970), 181, 276
Wilmot Proviso, 283
Wilson, Don, 15, 324
Wilson, James, 105, 243
Wilson, Pete, 33
Wilson, Thomas, 9
Wilson, Thomas Woodrow, **346–47**
  cabinet seats in Congress, 41, 160
  child labor amendment, 47
  cites Stickney, 293
  considered third term, 322
  criticized filibuster, 66
  Nineteenth Amendment, 219
  plans for no-confidence vote, 247
  progressive, 249
  State of Union address, 92
  stroke, 316

  support for referendum, 163
  veto of Volstead Act, 197
Wilson Act, 106
Winner-take-all, 110–11
Wiretapping, 143
Wirt, William, 281
Wittmyer, Annie, 347
Wolff, Joseph, 308
Woman Patriot, 48
Woman's Bible (Stanton), 287
Woman's Centennial Congress of 1940, 46
Woman's Party (WP), 219
Women's Christian Temperance Union, 105, 218, 319, **347**
Women's Organization for National Prohibition Reform (WONPR), 319
Women's Trade Union League, 207
Woodhull, Victoria Chaflin, 330, **348**
Woodhull and Chaflin's Weekly, 348
Woodson v. North Carolina (1976), 44
Woodward, Augustus B., 98, **348–49**
Worcester v. Georgia (1832), 216
Workers' Compensation Laws, **349–50**
Workingwoman's Association, 387
World government, **350**
World War II, 324, 340
Writs of assistance, 142
Written constitution, 228, 305
Written Constitution and the Unwritten Attitude, The (Merriam), 204
Wyoming Territory, 218

Yakus v. United States (1944), 248
Young, Horace, 273
Younger, Jesse, 174–75
Youngstown Sheet & Tube Co. v. Sawyer (1952), 245, 341

Zablocki v. Redhail (1978), 202